AFTER THE NEW TESTAMENT
100–300 CE

AFTER THE NEW TESTAMENT

100–300 CE

A Reader in Early Christianity

Second Edition

Bart D. Ehrman

New York   Oxford

Oxford University Press

Oxford University Press is a department of the University of Oxford.
It furthers the University's objective of excellence in research,
scholarship, and education by publishing worldwide.

Oxford   New York
Auckland   Cape Town   Dar es Salaam   Hong Kong   Karachi
Kuala Lumpur   Madrid   Melbourne   Mexico City   Nairobi
New Delhi   Shanghai   Taipei   Toronto

With offices in
Argentina   Austria   Brazil   Chile   Czech Republic   France   Greece
Guatemala   Hungary   Italy   Japan   Poland   Portugal   Singapore
South Korea   Switzerland   Thailand   Turkey   Ukraine   Vietnam

For titles covered by Section 112 of the US Higher Education
Opportunity Act, please visit www.oup.com/us/he for the
latest information about pricing and alternate formats.

Published in the United States of America by
Oxford University Press
198 Madison Avenue, New York, NY 10016
http://www.oup.com

Library of Congress Cataloging-in-Publication Data
After the New Testament.
   After the New Testament, 100–300 C.E. : a reader in early Christianity / [compiled by] Bart D.
Ehrman. -- [Second edition].
      pages cm
   ISBN 978-0-19-539892-2
 1. Christian literature, Early--Textbooks. I. Ehrman, Bart D. II. Title.
   BR63.E37 2015
   270.1--dc23

                                                                        2014014139

To Mom

Contents

15 Leading the Upright Life:
The Role of Ethics in Early Christianity   505

16 The Emergence of Orthodoxy:
Theological Writings of Proto-orthodox Christians   529

Preface

Iproduced the first edition of *After the New Testament* fifteen years ago and have thought for a long while that it needs to be seriously revised. There are several texts that I (and every other thinking person I know) cannot believe I left out of the first edition. And there are others that can very profitably be added to that collection. Altogether there are nearly twenty new selections in this revised edition.

Moreover, a good number of the texts that I included in the first edition are now available in newer English translations. Some of these are my own (for example, the Apostolic Fathers and some of the Apocryphal Gospels), and others—principally writings from Nag Hammadi and other Gnostic texts—are available in translations that I now prefer, produced by such stalwarts as Marvin Meyer and my colleague Zlatko Pleše. Some twenty-five of the selections in the new edition are represented in new translations.

In thinking carefully through the fourteen main rubrics that I employed for the first edition, there were two rather obvious lacunae that needed to be filled this time around. And so I have added a section, with appropriate texts, on Women in the Early Church and another on Early Christian Biblical Interpretation. Each of these has its own introduction, of course. In some instances I have shifted previously used selections under these rubrics, but for the most part the additions are new.

Over the past fifteen years my views have shifted in some areas, especially with regard to the messy world of early Christian "Gnosticism." I continue to think that the term can be used (contra some outstanding scholars, such as Michael Williams), and I do not think that it should be restricted only to the Sethians (contra others, such as David Brakke). But I do think it is useful to speak of different *kinds* of Gnosticism and to leave open the question of whether it is appropriate to consider Thomasine texts as Gnostic in any meaningful way. And so, instead of having one undifferentiated grouping of Gnostic writings that evidence a variety of ideological and literary perspectives, I have grouped the texts of Chapter 6 ("Writings Later Deemed Heretical") as Jewish-Christian, Sethian, Valentinian, Thomasine, and "Other Gnostic."

Finally, I have taken the occasion of this second edition to update all the bibliographies found at the end of my discussion of each of the now-sixteen rubrics.

Acknowledgments

I would like to thank those who have helped make this new edition both possible and better. Many thanks go to two of my graduate student research assistants at the University of North Carolina at Chapel Hill: Shaily Patel and Travis Proctor. They have been hard-working, clear-sighted, and unafraid to force an advisor to realize that he is wrong. Well, on occasion. My gratitude extends as well to Nicola Denzy Lewis of Brown University, for her generous help and comments on portions of the book. In addition, deep and heartfelt thanks go to a range of scholars who graciously worked through the first edition of the book for Oxford University Press and made numerous helpful and insightful suggestions about how it could be modified in the second edition. These are David Brakke of the Ohio State University, Bruce Chilton of Bard College, Rebecca Denova of the University of Pittsburgh, Susan Ashbrook Harvey of Brown University, Dan Machiela of McMaster University, Shelly Matthews of Brite Divinity School, Charlotte Radler of Loyola Marymount University, Christine Shepardson of the University of Tennessee-Knoxville, and James VanderKam of the University of Notre Dame. May all authors have such generous and perspicacious readers! This second edition is much better for their suggestions, and probably much worse for not implementing all of them.

1

General Introduction

Over the past century and a half, archaeological discoveries have played a significant role in our understanding of early Christianity. These include *(a)* the serendipitous discovery of entire libraries of ancient texts, such as the Dead Sea Scrolls found in the wilderness of Judea and the library of Gnostic writings uncovered near Nag Hammadi, Egypt; *(b)* the equally fortuitous unearthing of individual documents, such as a non-canonical Gospel and an Apocalypse, attributed to the apostle Peter, the newly discovered Gospel of Judas, and an early church manual called the *Didache* (the latter of which was "found," actually, in a monastic library); and *(c)* the uncovering and excavation of buried sites such as Dura Europas in Syria on the Euphrates, a city that housed the earliest surviving structure known to have served as a Christian church. These findings have enriched our understanding of early Christianity; but more than that, they have forced scholars to reconceptualize major aspects of the religion, leading to what is perhaps the most significant "discovery" of them all, made not in the sands of Egypt or the dirt of Mesopotamia but in the private libraries of historians—the discovery that Christianity during the first three centuries of the Common Era was remarkably diverse.

Most of our evidence for these early years of Christianity consists of literary texts produced by the Christians themselves. This surviving literature is by no means complete or even completely representative, even with our newly discovered texts. It is nonetheless a rich testimony to the social history of early Christianity and to the wide-ranging concerns, values, beliefs, and practices of its adherents. But readers who are interested in earliest Christianity are, as a rule, poorly informed concerning this literature; as a result, very few people outside the ranks of the professional scholar realize the diverse character of the religion in its earliest period. Even among church people, it is scarcely realized that early Christians engaged in heated and often acrimonious debates over completely fundamental issues, such as whether there was only one God or two or twelve or thirty, whether the Jews were the chosen people of God or the evil children of the Devil, whether women could serve as ministers of the church or were to remain silent and subservient to men, whether a Christian should seek to be martyred for the faith or avoid persecution at all costs, whether the Scriptures included the Gospels allegedly written by Matthew and John or those in the names of Mary Magdalene and Jesus' own twin brother Thomas. Each of these positions—and many others on many other issues—had strong and vocal advocates among the Christian faithful of the second and third centuries.

The present book is concerned with such issues and others like them; its purpose is to make more widely available to the general reader the primary materials that are relevant for discussing them.

Probably the one ancient book that most students of the period are already familiar with, or at least have heard of, is the famous *Ecclesiastical History* of Eusebius, commonly known as the "Father of Church History." Eusebius was the first Christian author to provide a full sketch of the history of the church, from the days of Jesus down to his own time (his first edition was published in 311 CE). Scholars of early Christianity have naturally turned to this volume for their information. And quite valuable information it is, too, for Eusebius not only narrates what happened over the course of the first three Christian centuries, but he also cites primary texts written in the period, many of which no longer survive. Still, as researchers have come to realize, Eusebius cannot be blindly trusted to provide a disinterested account of earliest Christianity. For he, like everyone else, had his own particular "slant," his own beliefs and perspectives that affected his retelling of the early days of Christianity, determining both how he told the story and which sources he decided to cite.

In Eusebius's view, Jesus taught his disciples the truth about God and the world, and they passed these views along, after his death, to their own followers. From the outset, Christianity grew by miraculous leaps and bounds as God's hand guided and directed the mission to nonbelievers. Any setbacks that the Christians experienced at the hands of their opponents—for example, in persecutions and martyrdoms—were turned to the good, leading to further growth and strength. Moreover, according to Eusebius, the Christian communities enjoyed internal peace and unity. There were, to be sure, false teachers who occasionally disrupted the tranquility of the church, "heretics" inspired by the Devil to pervert the truth of God. But these stood merely on the margins of the Great Church and were easily overpowered by the truth affirmed by the genuine followers of Christ, the representatives of Christian "orthodoxy" (literally: right doctrine or correct belief). For Eusebius, the vast majority of believers have always subscribed to the orthodox views promulgated by Jesus' disciples, passed along through the powerful bishops of the major churches throughout the known world and embodied in the Christian Scriptures, books penned by the apostles themselves. These "orthodox" views, needless to say, were the ones that Eusebius himself happened to embrace.

Historians are no longer able to accept Eusebius's account uncritically. A careful analysis of his text, along with other documents that survive from the period, shows that Christianity before his time was in fact widely diverse and that many of the issues he discusses could be, and were, understood differently by other Christians of the time. Whether or not this scholarly opinion is right, it should at least be clear that for those who want to understand the history of the early Christian church, restricting oneself to Eusebius's *Ecclesiastical History* would not be the best way to proceed. It is far better, and now more widely possible, to supplement Eusebius's accounts with the primary texts.

That is where the present collection can serve a useful purpose. For in it is presented a broad range of primary texts from the early years of Christianity, roughly between the last book of the "New Testament" (say, 100 or 120 CE) and the time Eusebius began writing his church history. For the sake of convenience, we may speak of the second and third Christian centuries, 100–300 CE. My objective in making the collection has been to provide readers with as full a set of texts as possible, within the restrictions naturally imposed by a work of a single volume.

Other collections of Christian texts already exist, of course, and here I should say a word about how this one is distinct. Among the other anthologies, some present scattered quotations from the writings of early authors such as Irenaeus, Tertullian, and Origen, arranged according to the categories of systematic theology (i.e., brief quotations that illustrate "the" early Christian views of God, Christ, the Holy Spirit, the church, and so on); others are fuller assemblages of proto-orthodox authors artificially grouped together, such as those labeled the "apostolic fathers" or simply the "early Church fathers" (by which are meant, again, the early "orthodox" fathers; i.e., those who stand within the tradition embraced by Eusebius). Yet others are translations of important "heterodox" works, such as those of the Gnostics (for example, the "Nag Hammadi library") or of documents forged in the name of the apostles, collectively known as the early Christian Apocrypha. Each of these collections is important and valuable in its own right. But none is like the one presented here, which attempts to provide as broad a spectrum as possible of the surviving early Christian texts, dealing with a range of significant issues such as the conversion of nonbelievers, persecution and martyrdom, apologetics, antagonism toward Jews and "heretics," the development of church offices, women in the church, liturgical practices, ethics, doctrines, and so on.

Moreover, rather than presenting little snippets of texts I have decided to provide large chunks—complete texts when possible, lengthy excerpts when not. Readers can thus get a feel for the literary quality of these works, rather than settle for brief extracts designed to illustrate a simple point. It did not make sense to organize these texts according to the categories of systematic theology, since many of them are unrelated to such matters. Nor could I give them in simple chronological sequence, since many of them cannot be dated with any degree of confidence except to say that they certainly, or very probably, fall within the chronological parameters I have envisaged. It seemed best, then, to group these texts according to the topics that they themselves address and to arrange these topical rubrics in accordance with how one might want to think through various aspects of early Christianity—for example, in a college or seminary course devoted to the subject.

It might be useful then, by way of introduction, to say a word about the nature of these rubrics and the logic of their sequencing. This need not entail a lengthy discussion: each chapter begins with a sketch of the important historical aspects of the topic, and each individual text is introduced with brief comments concerning its historical context and significance.

One of the first things to consider about early Christianity is how it spread so far and wide in its early years. Starting out as a Jewish sect—a handful of followers of Jesus of Nazareth located in the Jewish homeland of Judea—it somehow managed to convert masses of people, so that in less than three centuries it could number nearly three million adherents. But how did this happen? What did the Christians say, and how did they make their message convincing—especially to audiences that were overwhelmingly non-Jewish, who were gentiles following the various polytheistic religions scattered throughout the empire? No complete answers can be found in our surviving texts, but it may be at least worth seeing what Christians themselves said about their message and the reasons for its success. Several texts that narrate conversions to Christianity—representative of the few such texts that survive—are given in Chapter 2.

Most non-Christians, of course, completely rejected the Christian message; many scorned it as ludicrous, some found it to be socially and religiously dangerous. As a result, from the earliest of times Christianity met hostile opposition, sometimes resulting in mob violence or official actions ending in martyrdom. We have numerous accounts of the social and political antipathy expressed toward Christians from the pens of second-century and third-century Christians themselves, including several firsthand reports of actual legal proceedings and executions. Several such accounts of persecutions and martyrdoms, some of them graphic in their detail, are given in Chapter 3.

Sometimes opposition to Christians came not in mob violence or official proceedings against them but in literary attacks made on them and their religion by educated pagans who found their religious claims to be wrong-headed and foolish. Examples of these attacks can be seen in the writings of such philosophers as Celsus and Porphyry, portions of whose writings are provided in the first part of Chapter 4. In the face of such widespread opposition, Christians had a natural tendency to defend themselves. These defenses became a literary art form in the hands of some of the more highly educated Christians who converted to the religion beginning in the middle of the second century, authors who produced literary defenses, or "apologies" for the faith, arguing that Christians were completely innocent of all slanders and charges against them and that their faith was in fact morally and theologically superior to every other religion. Selections from some of the most important and best known Greek and Latin apologists—including Justin Martyr, Tertullian, and Origen—are provided in the second part of Chapter 4.

Early Christians had to defend themselves not only against angry mobs, powerful state officials, and educated opponents, but also against Jews who found Christian claims objectionable or even ludicrous—especially the claims that Jesus, a crucified criminal, was the Messiah and that his gentile believers, who did not follow the Jewish Law, were the true people of the God of Israel. The Christian response to this kind of rejection turned aggressive, as Christians claimed for themselves the Scriptures and traditions of the Jews, insisting that the Jewish God had in fact rejected the people of Israel to bestow his favor upon the Christians. Some of the harsh polemic against the Jews and their religion can be found in the anti-Judaic texts excerpted in Chapter 5.

Early Christians were engaged in polemics not only against those on the outside, gentile and Jewish nonbelievers, but also within, among believers in Christ who took radically different views on matters of practical and theological importance. Fundamental issues were at stake, including such matters as the nature of God (is there only one?), the person of Christ (is he human? divine? both?), the status of the Jewish Scriptures (are they inspired by the true God? by a malevolent deity?), the world (is it good, created by God? evil, created by cruel demons?), and just about everything else. Few writings have survived from Christians who took views *other* than the ones that came to dominate Christianity by the time of Eusebius, although in the second and third centuries the questions were harshly debated and the answers were not at all obvious. But some alternative views have turned up, especially from Christians who remained true to their Jewish heritage and from those who accepted various forms of Christian Gnosticism (for example, the writings from the Nag Hammadi library). A range of texts from such groups is introduced and presented in Chapter 6.

Given the importance early Christians ascribed to what a person believes (a unique aspect of the religion, oddly enough, in the ancient world), it is no surprise that the "heterodox" groups whose writings are excerpted in Chapter 6 came under attack by

Christians who took opposing points of view. What is somewhat more surprising, perhaps, is that even Christians who embraced "proto-orthodox" positions—namely, the views that eventually came to be dominant as embodied in such fourth-century productions as the Apostles' and the Nicene Creeds—were condemned by their opponents (for example, some of the Gnostics) for propagating false religion. Chapter 7 presents selections from two of the most famous proto-orthodox heresiologists (describers of heresy) of the second and early third centuries, Irenaeus and Tertullian, along with two Gnostic treatises, including a book allegedly written by the apostle Peter, attacking views later declared to be orthodox.

Christians of every theological persuasion appear to have supported their views by appealing to books that claimed to be written by Jesus' own apostles. The second and third centuries saw a host of Christian documents forged to provide just such support—as well as other forgeries meant, evidently, simply to exhort or entertain their audiences. Many of these "pseudepigrapha" ("writings under a false name") were at one time or another accepted as Scripture by various Christian groups. Not surprisingly, they represent the same genres of writing attested in the books that eventually came to be called the New Testament (i.e., Gospels, Acts, Epistles, and Apocalypses)—books that were also allegedly written by Jesus' apostles, even though modern scholars have sometimes called their traditional ascriptions into question. Chapter 8 presents a range of early noncanonical pseudepigrapha, some of them "orthodox," that have come down to us today.

Given the wide dissemination of forgeries in the names of the apostles, different groups eventually had to decide which "apostolic" books were to be ascribed authority and which were not. The New Testament as we have it today comprises 27 books that were collected and deemed Scripture by the group that won the early struggles for theological dominance. Other groups had other sets of books; and even within proto-orthodox circles there was no complete agreement as to which books should be included and which rejected. This much can be seen from the various "canon" lists that survive from second-century and third-century authors, Christians living many years before any final decisions were reached (the first "canon list" that gives exactly our own set of 27 books was written in 367 CE—nearly 300 years after most of the books of the New Testament were actually written!). The most important surviving lists are presented in Chapter 9.

Christians of all theological persuasions in the second and third centuries realized that having a set of books deemed authoritative or "scriptural" could not, in itself, provide guidance over what to believe or how to behave. Books needed to be *interpreted* in order to be understood, and to be understood *correctly*. And so the early centuries of the church witnessed numerous debates over just how books were to be read and used. Among the debates was the question of whether a "literal" interpretation of a sacred text was the only legitimate approach, or "figurative" understandings (in which the text was taken to mean something other than what it literally said) were acceptable as well. These debates over biblical interpretation can be found in the selections excerpted from various writers in Chapter 10.

The public exposition of Scripture was one of the chief methods of exhortation and teaching throughout this period. Some early preachers produced written copies of their homilies for a broader audience. Few of these sermons happen now to survive, but those that do can show how various Christian leaders approached their texts of Scripture and used them to guide their congregations in how to live and what to believe. Several representative examples from the second and third centuries are presented in Chapter 11.

Just as the canon of Scripture came to be discussed and, eventually, settled in order to help define and shape the nature of "orthodox" Christianity, so too there was a movement to solidify and structure the organization of the church, in part to prevent "heretics" from acquiring any kind of foothold within it. Early on in the second century there were calls for a rigid church structure that could bring order out of chaos in the early Christian communities and thereby guarantee the preservation and perpetuation of the true religion. By the middle of the third century, the leaders of the Christian church could exercise considerable power over their congregations. Developments throughout the period in the matter of church government can be seen in the range of texts provided in Chapter 12.

From the earliest of times, Christians gathered together as worshiping communities, to worship the true God who had called the followers of Jesus to be his people. Already in the first century, important liturgical practices had developed throughout the Christian church, with two in particular holding a special prominence: the ritual of baptism for converts (an initiatory rite), and the periodic celebration of the Eucharist for those already among the elect (a sacred meal commemorating Jesus' death). Both aspects of Christian liturgy developed dramatically over the second and third centuries, as can be seen in the descriptions of the services of worship and ritual given by the Christians themselves, excerpted in the selections found in Chapter 13.

A perennial question in early Christianity—and still, of course, today—involves the role of women in the church. Are women to be treated differently from men? Are they to be allowed to exercise the same kind of authority and to occupy the same kinds of ecclesiastical offices? Are men to dictate to women how to behave? Are wives to be subject to their husbands? Or does the Christian faith promote a sense of equality between the sexes? These are the issues that are addressed in the texts gathered together in Chapter 14.

Christian leaders regularly exhorted their fellow believers to ethical behavior, not only in their public addresses and sermons but also in literary tractates explicitly devoted to the purpose. This entails another distinctive aspect of the religion in its Greco-Roman milieu: although personal ethical behavior, as a rule, was as important to pagans then as it is to most people now, ethics did not normally play any part in sacred cult; it was instead a matter of social norm and expectation (and of philosophy, for the more highly educated). Christians, however, like Jews before them, tied ethical behavior to religious belief and practice. And so Christian leaders became particularly assiduous in demanding that their readers (or hearers) behave in certain ways, as will be seen in the selection of moral tractates included in Chapter 15.

Finally, while Christian doctrines did not encompass the entire concern of the early Christians—even though some historians of Christianity continue to think so, portraying Christianity as an intellectual rather than a social movement—theology *was*, nonetheless, a matter of particular importance for Christians, especially those who have left us the texts. Proto-orthodox Christians insisted that the content of what one believed mattered for one's standing before God. As a result, early Christian intellectuals felt compelled to work out the correct system of Christian doctrine. This doctrinal emphasis can be seen in a number of the selections throughout this volume, but it is the sole concern of the final chapter. Here are presented some of the more sophisticated attempts at theological reflection among Christian scholars who became important forerunners for the doctrinal positions that later came to define fourth-century orthodoxy.

Many more selections of Christian texts from the second and third centuries could have been provided in this collection, and much more could have been said about each one of them. Some scholars would no doubt substitute other texts for the ones I have chosen to include; others would construe the background or significance of this or that text in a different way or provide an entirely different understanding of the early Christian movement. But choices have had to be made, and I have tried to make them judiciously. For all of the chapters, in addition to the introductory remarks, I have provided a brief bibliography to guide the reader to further discussions.

In any event, the best way to become familiar with the history of early Christianity is not simply to read *about* it in the works of modern-day scholars, but to become inundated in the primary sources themselves. The present collection should, at the very least, provide a useful entrée into this venture for anyone choosing to undertake it.

For Further Reading

Chadwick, Henry. *The Early Church*. New York: Penguin, 1967.

Döpp, Siegmar and Wilhelm Geerlings. *Dictionary of Early Christian Literature*, trans. Matthew O'Connell. New York: Crossroad, 2000.

Ferguson, Everett, ed. *The Encyclopedia of Early Christianity*. 2nd edition. New York: Garland, 1997.

Frend, W. H. C. *The Rise of Christianity*. Philadelphia: Fortress, 1984.

Harvey, Susan Ashbrook and David G. Hunter. *The Oxford Handbook of Early Christian Studies*. Oxford: Oxford University Press, 2008.

Livingstone, E. A. and F. L. Cross, eds. *The Oxford Dictionary of the Christian Church*. 3rd revised edition. Oxford: Oxford University Press, 2005.

Rousseau, Philip. *The Early Christian Centuries*. New York: Longman, 2002.

Vermes, Geza. *Christian Beginnings: From Nazareth to Nicaea*. London: Allen Lane, 2012.

2

The Spread of Christianity
Early Christians and Their Converts

Christianity started out as a small band of Jews who had followed Jesus during his ministry and remained faithful to him after his death. According to New Testament sources, the original group consisted of the eleven disciples (after Judas had killed himself), a handful of women, and several other men, all of whom had evidently accompanied Jesus from Galilee to Jerusalem the last week of his life (Acts 1). Having become convinced of Jesus' resurrection, these earliest believers immediately set out to persuade others that Jesus was the Jewish Messiah sent from God to die for the sins of others.

Their success was limited at first, especially among their Jewish compatriots. But with the conversion of one of their earliest opponents, Paul, the mission was taken beyond the world of Judaism; gentiles, who, as participants in various so-called "pagan" religions, were polytheists rather than followers of the God of Israel, became the chief target of evangelism. The church soon spread throughout much of the Roman empire, with major urban areas the chief foci of the mission.

By the end of the third century, the new religion had become numerically significant. Most experts think that the Roman empire comprised some 60 million persons at this time, nearly 5% of them Christian. Soon thereafter, due largely to the conversion of the emperor Constantine in the early part of the fourth century, their numbers rose dramatically; by the end of the century, nearly half the empire called itself Christian.

A range of questions could be asked about the early spread of Christianity. Prior to the conversion mania of the fourth century, what led to the Christians' success? How did a small group of illiterate, lower-class Jewish peasants transform themselves into a significant world religion, claiming some three million adherents, in less than three centuries? What did Christians tell potential converts to convince them to abandon their worship of the gods and to believe in the one God of Israel and in his Son Jesus, to spurn the socially acceptable and often joyous and festive cultic practices of their families and friends in order to join a relatively secretive, frequently maligned, and sometimes persecuted group?

Unfortunately, the paucity of our sources restricts what we can know about such things. To be sure, modern scholars who examine these problems have developed some interesting and compelling theories, especially through cross-cultural studies of modern religious movements that accumulate converts through their cultivation of close personal contacts with outsiders. (The Mormons, for example, have grown at a comparable rate to the early Christians—about 40% each decade; see Stark). The ancient Christians who tell the stories of conversions, however, were obviously not trained sociologists. They ascribe the success of the mission, ultimately, to the miraculous working of God.

Our earliest source is the apostle Paul, who informed his gentile listeners that their idols were dead and lifeless and that there was only one true and living God, whose Son had died and been raised and was soon to return from heaven in judgment (1 Thessalonians 1:9–10). It is difficult to say why some of his hearers found this message persuasive, but Paul intimates that it may have been because of the "powerful deeds" (miracles?) that he accomplished in their midst as corroborating proof (2 Corinthians 12:12). Much clearer on this matter is the book of Acts, which actually narrates the miraculous deeds (and their later retellings) that provided all the evidence people needed (for example, Acts 2–3).

Accounts of conversions from the second and third centuries continue to emphasize the miraculous. Very few descriptions of large-scale conversions have survived from antiquity, but those that do stress the importance of such spectacular events as the supernatural destruction of idol temples and miraculous public healings, exorcisms, and revivifications.

Other factors appear to have played a role as well. Christians, for example, were highly distinctive in claiming to have an exclusive corner on the "truth." Other religions of antiquity were widely tolerant of one another, with none of them claiming that it alone was "right" and that the others, therefore, were "wrong." That is to say, as polytheistic religions, Greco-Roman cults recognized each other's validity: all the gods deserved to be worshipped, and so a person could (and should) participate in a variety of cultic practices. Christians, however, maintained that there was only one true God, that this God was the only one to be worshipped, and that this true worship could come only through God's Son, Jesus. Anyone who rejected this true religion would pay the penalty, if not in this life then in the next. Those who converted to Christianity, therefore, necessarily gave up their pagan ways—so that unlike the other religions of the empire (which did not insist on exclusive devotion), Christians automatically destroyed other religions while promoting their own (see Macmullen).

This exclusivity in early Christianity helps explain the willingness of some Christians to suffer persecution and even martyrdom for their faith (see Chapter 3). Christians who wrote about these martyrdoms claimed that in them God's miraculous hand was again at work, that the supernatural courage Christians displayed in the face of torment and death convinced numerous bystanders of the supreme power of the Christian God. Possibly this is what Tertullian means when he claims that the persecution of Christians, rather than devastating their spirit, only swelled their ranks, since "the blood of Christians is seed" (see Chapter 4, *Apology*, 50).

Moreover, the Christian accounts of martyrdoms invariably stress that God's miraculous power extends beyond this life to the life to come. Martyrs are said to be eager to endure the torments of an hour in exchange for the bliss of eternity. Possibly this was a factor in conversion as well, as Christians proclaimed the rewards of those who worshipped their God but the eternal torments of those who resisted.

Eventually, highly educated persons such as Justin in Rome and Tertullian in Carthage came to be converted to the faith. These literary persons—from whom a good deal of our evidence survives—tended to emphasize the more intellectual aspects of the religion as positive forces of conversion, including the philosophical superiority of Christian views and the convincing evidence of its truth claims in Jesus' own fulfillment of ancient prophecies from the Hebrew Scriptures. It is difficult to know, though, how far these more cerebral aspects of the religion played a role in the conversions of the thousands and thousands of persons who joined the religion in the second and third centuries.

The following texts provide a cross-sample of ancient narrations of conversion to Christianity as understood and presented, of course, by Christians themselves.

For Further Reading

Dodds, E. R. *Pagan and Christian in an Age of Anxiety: Some Aspects of Religious Experience from Marcus Aurelius to Constantine.* New York: W. W. Norton, 1965.

Grant, Robert M. *Augustus to Constantine: The Rise and Triumph of Christianity in the Roman World.* Louisville: Westminster John Knox Press, 2004.

Lane Fox, Robin. *Pagans and Christians.* New York: Alfred A. Knopf, 1987.

Macmullen, Ramsey. *Christianizing the Roman Empire A.D. 100–400.* New Haven: Yale University Press, 1984.

Stark, Rodney. *The Rise of Christianity.* Princeton: Princeton University, 1996.

von Harnack, Adolph. *The Mission and Expansion of Early Christianity,* trans. J. Moffat, 2 vols. New York: G. P. Putnam's Sons, 1908.

THE TEXTS

1. The Acts of John

The "Acts of John" is one of the Apocryphal Acts (see Chapter 8), early legendary accounts of the exploits of Jesus' disciples after his death. Throughout these narratives, the apostles do miraculous deeds that convince the crowds of the superior power of their God, leading, then, to massive conversions. In the first excerpt that follows, John is said to heal a paralyzed woman named Cleopatra, leading the entire city of Ephesus to marvel; in the second, he engages in a kind of battle of the gods, overthrowing the pagan idols in Ephesus, killing their priest, and destroying their temple—all by a word of prayer. The crowds who are present are completely convinced and terrified; they convert to worship the God John proclaims and to beg his forgiveness. Such entertaining narratives may not present "history as it actually happened," but they do indicate how Christians from the period understood the process of conversion to belief in the God of Jesus.

The Acts of John is preserved only in fragmentary manuscripts and probably dates to the late second century. Additional excerpts can be found in Chapter 8.

19 When we came near the city Lycomedes, the commander-in-chief of the Ephesians, a wealthy man, met us, fell down before John and asked him for help, with these words, "Your name is John; the God whom you preach has sent you to help my wife, who has been paralyzed for seven days and lies past recovery. But glorify your God and treat her out of compassion for us. Whilst I was reflecting what to do, a man came to me and said, 'Desist, Lycomedes, from the evil thought which militates against you. Do not submit. For out of compassion for my servant Cleopatra I have sent you a man from Miletus, named John, who will comfort her and restore her to you cured.' Delay not, therefore, servant of the God who announced you to me, but hasten to the ailing woman." And John went at once from the gate with the brethren who were with him, and followed Lycomedes into his house. And Cleobius said to his servants, "Go to my relative Callippus and make yourselves comfortable in his house—for I am coming there with his son—that we may find everything prepared!"

20 When Lycomedes and John had come into the house in which the woman was lying, he grasped his feet again, and said, "See, Lord, the lost beauty, see the youth, see the much talked of bloom of my unhappy wife, the admiration of all Ephesus! Woe to me, unhappy man! I was envied, humbled, the enemy's eye was fixed on me. I never wronged anyone, although I could harm many. I envisaged this situation and I was always anxious to experience no sorrow or anything like it! Of what use is my care now, Cleopatra? What good was it to me, that I was called godly to this day? I suffer more than a heathen, seeing you, Cleopatra,

---

suffering so. The sun in his circuit shall not see me, if you are no more with me. Cleopatra, I will die before you. I will not spare my life though I am still youthful. I will justify myself before the goddess of right, whom I served in righteousness, though I might indict her for her unrighteous sentence. I will avenge myself on her by coming as a shade. I will say to her, 'You have forced me to leave the light of life, because you tore away Cleopatra. You are the cause of my death, by having prepared for me this fate. You have forced me to blaspheme Providence by destroying my joy.'"

21 And Lycomedes spoke more to Cleopatra, went to her couch, and cried bitterly. But John drew him away and said, "Abandon these tears and unbecoming words! It is not proper for you, who saw the vision, to be disbelieving. Know that your partner for life will be restored to you. Therefore join us, who have come for her sake, and pray to the God whom you saw, when he showed me to you in a vision! What is the matter, Lycomedes? Wake up and open also your soul! Cast from you heavy sleep! Call on the Lord, beseech him for your wife, and he will support her." But he fell to the ground and wept dejectedly. And John said with tears, "Woe to the treachery of the vision, woe to the new temptation prepared for me, woe to the new craft of him who devises cunnings against me! Did the voice from heaven, which came to be the way, intend this for me, predicting to me what should here take place? Will it deliver me up to such a great multitude of citizens, for the sake of Lycomedes? The man lies here lifeless, and I know that I shall not leave this house alive. Why do you delay, Lord? Why have you deprived us of your gracious promise? I beseech you, Lord, let him not rejoice who delights in the sorrow of others. Let him not dance who always laughs at us! But let your holy name and your compassion come quickly! Waken the bodies of the two, who are against me!"

22 While John was crying, the city of Ephesus ran to the house of Lycomedes, supposing him dead. And when John saw the great multitude,

he prayed to the Lord, "Now the time of refreshing and confidence has come with you, O Christ; now is the time for us weary ones to have help from you, physician, who heal freely. Keep my entrance here free from derision! I beseech you, Jesus, help such a great multitude to come to the Lord of the universe. Behold the affliction, behold those who lie here! Even those who came here, make holy instruments for your service, after they have seen your gift. For you have said yourself, O Christ, 'Ask and it shall be given you.'[1] We therefore beseech you, O King, not for gold, not for silver, not for riches, not for possession, nor for any transient, earthly goods, but for two souls through whom you will convert those present to your way, to your knowledge, to your confidence, and to your infallible promise. For many of them shall be saved, after they have known your power through the resurrection of the departed. Give us, therefore, hope in you! I will go to Cleopatra and say, 'Arise, in the name of Jesus Christ.'"

23 And he went, touched her face, and said, "Cleopatra, he whom every ruler fears, and every creature, power, abyss, and darkness and unsmiling death and the heights of heaven and the caverns of the lower world and the resurrection of the dead and the sight of the blind and the whole power of the ruler of the world, and the pride of its prince, says, 'Rise and become not a pretext for many who will not believe, and an affliction for souls who hope and could be saved.'" And Cleopatra cried out at once, "I will rise, master, save your handmaiden!" When she had risen after the seven days, the whole city of Ephesus was stirred by the miraculous sight. . . .

38 After two days the birthday of the idol's temple was celebrated. While everybody was dressed in white garments, John wore black and went to the temple. They laid hold of him and tried to kill him. But John said, "Men, you are mad

---

1 Matt 7:7.

to lay hold of me, the servant of the only God." And climbing on to the platform he spoke to them:

39 "Men of Ephesus, you are in danger of behaving like the sea. Every discharging river and every precipitating spring, downpours and incessant waves and torrents rushing from the rock, are permeated by the bitter salt which is in the sea. Thus to this day you are unchangeably hostile to true piety, and you perish in your old idolatry. How many miraculous deeds did you see me perform, how many cures! And still you are hardened in the heart and cannot see clearly. What now, men of Ephesus? I have ventured now to come up to this idol's temple, to convince you that you are wholly without God and dead to human reasoning. Behold, here I stand. You all assert that Artemis is powerful. Pray to her, that I alone die! Or if you cannot accomplish this, I alone will call upon my God to kill you all because of your unbelief."

40 Since they already knew him and had seen the dead raised, they cried aloud, "Do not treat us so and kill us, we beseech you, John; we know indeed that you can do it." And John answered them, "If you do not wish to die, let me convince you of your idolatry. Any why? So that you may desist from your old error. Be now converted by my God or I will die at the hands of your goddess. For I will pray in your presence to my God, and ask him to have mercy upon you."

41 After these words he prayed, "God, who are God above all so-called gods, who to this day have been despised at Ephesus, you induced me to come to this place, which I never had in view. You have abrogated every form of worship through conversion to you. In your name every idol, every demon, and every unclean spirit is banished. May the deity of this place, which has deceived so many, now also give way to your name, and thus show your mercy on this place! For they walk in error."

42 And with these words of John the altar of Artemis suddenly split into many parts, and the oblations put up in the temple suddenly fell

to the ground, and its glory broke, and so did more than seven of the idols. And half of the temple fell down, so that when the roof came down, the priest also was killed at one stroke. And the people of the Ephesians cried, "There is only one God, that of John, only one God who has compassion for us; for you alone are God; now we have become converted, since we saw your miraculous deeds. Have mercy upon us, God, according to your will, and deliver us from our great error." And some of them lay on their faces and cried; others bent their knees and prayed; others rent their garments and lamented; still others tried to escape.

43 And John stretched out his hands and prayed with uplifted soul to the Lord, "Glory be to you, my Jesus, the only God of truth, who procure your servants in manifold ways!" And after these words he said to the people, "Rise up from the ground, people of Ephesus, pray to my God, and know how his invisible power was made manifest and his miraculous deeds took place before your eyes! Artemis herself should have helped. Her servant should have received help from her and not have died. Where is the power of the deity? Where are the sacrifices? Where the birthday? Where the festivals? Where the garlands? Where the great enchantment and the poison allied to it?"

44 And the people rose up from the ground and made haste to destroy the remainder of the temple, crying, "We know that the God of John is the only one, and henceforth we worship him, since we have obtained mercy from him." And as John came down, many of the people touched him, saying, "Help us, John, help us who die in vain! You see our intention; you see how the multitude following you cleaves to hope in your God. We have seen the way in which we have gone astray when we were lost. We have seen that our gods were erected in vain. We have seen their great and disgraceful derision. But give us, we beseech you, help without hindrance, when we have come to your house! Receive us, who are desperate!"

2. The Acts of Thomas

The Acts of Thomas recounts the missionary trip to India made by the apostle Jude (Judas), also called Thomas (Aramaic for "twin"). According to legends circulated in Syria, Judas Thomas was allegedly Jesus' own twin brother. Among the legendary accounts of these Acts are two fascinating episodes that show how belief in the afterlife played a central role in the Christian evangelization of pagans. The first story, about the heavenly palace of King Gundaphorus, emphasizes the otherworldly rewards for those who renounce pleasure in this life for the sake of doing good to others. The second, a description of the terrors of hell by a woman raised from the dead, stresses the horrific punishments reserved for those who continue in lives of sin. Both the prospect of heavenly reward and the fear of hellish torments are said to lead unbelievers to repent in this life, while there is still time.

The Acts of Thomas was probably written sometime in the early third century. For additional excerpts, see Chapter 8.

17 When the apostle came into the cities of India with Abban the merchant, Abban went away to greet King Gundaphorus and told him about the carpenter whom he had brought with him. And the king was glad and ordered him to appear before him. When he had come in the king said to him, "What trade do you know?" The apostle said to him, "That of the carpenter and the house-builder." The king said to him, "What work in wood do you know and what in stone?" The apostle said, "In wood, plows, yokes, balances, pulleys, and ships and oars and masts; in stone, monuments, temples, and royal palace." And the king said, "Will you build me a palace?" And he answered, "Yes, I shall build it and finish it; for because of this I have come, to build and to do carpenter's work."

18 And the king, having accepted him, took him out of the gates of the city, and on the way began to discuss with him the building of the palace, and how the foundations should be laid, till they came to the place where the work was to be carried out. And he said, "Here is where I wish the building to be!" And the apostle said, "Yes, this place is suitable for the building." For the place was wooded and there was water there. And the king said, "Begin at once!" And he answered, "I cannot commence now." The king said, "When can you?" He said, "I shall begin in November and finish in April." And the king was surprised, and said, "Every building is built in the summer, but can you build and finish a palace in the winter?" And the apostle replied "Thus it must be done; it is impossible any other way." And the king said, "If you have resolved upon this, draw a plan for me how the work is to be done, since I shall come here after some time." And the apostle took a reed, measured the place, and marked it out: the doors to be set towards the rising of the sun, to face the light; the windows toward the west, to the winds; the bakehouse he made toward the

The Acts of Thomas, from *The Apocryphal New Testament*, ed. J. K. Elliott. © Oxford University Press, 1993. Reprinted by permission of Oxford University Press.

south; and the water-pipes necessary for the supply toward the north. When the king saw this, he said to the apostle, "You are truly a craftsman, and it is fitting that you should serve kings." And having left a lot of money with him, he went away.

19 And at the appointed times the king sent coined silver and the necessities for his and the workmen's living. And the apostle took everything and divided it, going about in the cities and surrounding villages, distributing to the poor and needy, and bestowing alms, and gave them relief, saying, "The king knows that he will receive royal recompense, but the poor must be refreshed, as their condition requires it." After this the king sent a messenger to the apostle, having written the following: "Let me know what you have done or what I should send to you or what you need." The apostle sent word to him saying, "The palace is built, and only the roof remains to be done." Upon hearing this the king sent him again gold and uncoined silver and wrote, "If the palace is built, let it be roofed." And the apostle said to the Lord, "I thank you, Lord, in every respect, that you died for a short time, that I may live in you for ever, and that you have sold me, to deliver many through me." And he did not cease to teach and refresh the afflicted, saying, "The Lord has dispensed this to you and he gives to each his food. For he is the support of the orphans and the nourisher of the widows, and rest and repose to all who are afflicted."

20 When the king came to the city he inquired of his friends concerning the palace which Judas, surnamed Thomas, had built for him. And they said to him, "He has neither built a palace, nor did he do anything of that which he promised to do, but he goes about in the cities and villages, and if he has anything he gives it to the poor, and teaches a new God, heals the sick, drives out demons, and performs many miracles. And we believe that he is a magician. But his acts of compassion and the cures done by him as a free gift, still more his simplicity and gentleness and fidelity, show that he is a just man, or an apostle of the new God, whom he preaches. For he continually fasts and prays and eats only bread with salt, and his drink is water, and he wears one coat, whether in warm weather or in cold, and he takes nothing from anyone but gives to others what he has." Upon hearing this the king hit his face with his hands, shaking his head for a long time.

21 And he sent for the merchant who had brought him, and for the apostle, and said to him, "Have you built the palace?" And he said, "Yes, I have built it." The king said, "When shall we go to inspect it?" And he answered and said, "Now you cannot see it, but you shall see it when you depart this life." And the king was very angry and ordered both the merchant and Judas Thomas to be bound and cast into prison, until he should find out to whom the property of the king had been given, and so destroy him and the merchant. And the apostle went to prison rejoicing and said to the merchant, "Fear nothing, believe only in the God who is preached by me, and you shall be freed from this world, and obtain life in the world to come."

And the king considered by what death he should kill them. He decided to flog them and burn them with fire. On that very night Gad, the king's brother, fell ill; and through the grief and disappointment which the king had suffered he was grievously depressed. And having sent for the king he said to him, "Brother and king, I commend to you my house and my children. For I have been grieved on account of the insult that has befallen you, and lo, I am dying, and if you do not proceed against the life of that magician you will give my soul no rest in Hades." And the king said to his brother, "I considered the whole night by what death I should kill him, and I have decided to flog him and burn him with fire, together with the merchant who brought him."

22 While they were talking, the soul of Gad, his brother, departed, and the king mourned for Gad exceedingly, because he loved him, and ordered him to be prepared for burial in a royal and costly robe. While this was going on, angels received the soul of Gad, the king's brother, and took it up into heaven, showing him the palaces and mansions there, asking him, "In what place do you wish to dwell?" And when they came near the edifice of the apostle Thomas, which he had erected for the king, Gad, upon beholding it, said to the angels, "I entreat you, my lords, let me dwell in one of these lower chambers." But they said to him, "In this building you cannot dwell." And he said, "Why not?" They answered, "This palace is the one which that Christian has built for your brother." But he said, "I entreat you, my lords, allow me to go to my brother to buy this palace from him. For my brother does not know what it is like, and he will sell it to me."

23 And the angels let the soul of Gad go. And as they were putting on him the burial robe his soul came into him. And he said to those standing round him, "Call my brother to me, that I may beg of him a request." Straightway they sent the good news to their king, saying, "Your brother has become alive again!" And the king arose and with a great multitude went to his brother. And coming in he went to the bed as if stupefied, unable to speak to him. And his brother said, "I know and I am convinced, brother, that if anyone had asked of you the half of your kingdom, you would give it for my sake. Wherefore I entreat you to grant one favor, which I beg of you to do: that you sell to me that which I ask from you." And the king answered and said, "And what is it that you wish me to sell to you?" And he said, "Assure me by an oath that you will grant it to me." And the king swore to him, "Whatever of my possession you ask I will give you." And he said to him, "Sell me the palace which you have in heaven." And the king said, "A palace in heaven— where does this come to me from?" And he said, "It is the one that Christian built for you, the man who is now in prison, whom the merchant brought, having bought him from a certain Jesus. I mean that Hebrew slave whom you wished to punish, having suffered some deception from him,

on account of whom I also was grieved and died, and now have come alive again."

24 Then the king heard and understood his words about the eternal benefits that were conferred upon him and destined for him, and said, "That palace I cannot sell you, but I pray to be permitted to enter into it and to dwell there, being deemed worthy to belong to its inhabitants. And if you really wish to buy such a palace, behold, the man is alive, and will build you a better one than that." And immediately he sent and brought the apostle out of prison, and the merchant who had been shut up along with him, saying, "I entreat you, as a man entreating the servant of God, pray for me, and ask him, whose servant you are, to pardon me and to overlook what I have done to you or intended to do, and that I may become worthy to be an inhabitant of that house for which indeed I have done nothing, but which you, laboring alone, have built for me with the help of the grace of your God, and that I may also become a servant and serve this God, whom you preach." His brother also fell down before the apostle and said, "I entreat you and supplicate before your God that I may become worthy of this service and become partaker of that which was shown to me by his angels. . . ."

51 Now there was a certain young man, who had committed a nefarious deed. He came and partook of the eucharist. And his two hands withered, so that he could no longer put them to his mouth. When those present saw him, they told the apostle what had happened. And the apostle called him and said, "Tell me, my son, and be not afraid of what you have done before you came here. For the eucharist of the Lord has convicted you. For this gift, by entering many, brings healing, especially to those who come in faith and love; but you it has withered away, and what has happened has happened not without some justification." And the young man convicted by the eucharist of the Lord came up, fell at the apostle's feet, and besought him and said, "An evil deed has been done

by me, whilst I thought to do something good. I loved a woman who lived in an inn outside the city, and she loved me also. And when I heard about you, believing that you proclaim the living God, I came and received the seal from you along with the others. And you said, 'Whoever shall indulge in impure intercourse, especially in adultery, shall not have life with the God whom I preach.' As I loved her very much, I entreated her and tried to persuade her to live with me in chaste and pure conduct, as you teach. And she would not. Since she would not, I took a sword and killed her. For I could not see her commit adultery with another."

52 When the apostle heard this he said, "O insane intercourse, how you lead to shamelessness! O unrestrained lust, how have you excited this man to do this! O work of the serpent, how you rage in your own!" And the apostle ordered some water to be brought in a dish. And when the water had been brought he said, "Come, waters from the living waters; everlasting, sent to us from the everlasting; rest, sent to us from the one who gives rest; power of salvation, proceeding from that power which overcomes all and subjects it to its will—come and dwell in these waters, that the gift of the Holy Spirit may be completely fulfilled in them!" And to the young man he said, "Go, wash your hands in these waters." And when he had washed them they were restored. And the apostle said to him, "Do you believe in our Lord Jesus Christ, that he can do all things?" And he said, "Though I am the least, yet I believe. But I did this in the hope of doing something good. For I entreated her, as I told you already, but she would not be persuaded by me to keep herself chaste."

53 And the apostle said to him, "Come, let us go to the inn where you committed the deed, and let us see what happened." And the young man went before the apostle on the road. When they had come to the inn they found her lying there. And when the apostle saw her he was sad, for she was a beautiful girl. And he ordered her to be brought into the middle of the inn. And putting her on a couch they carried it out and set it in the midst of the courtyard of the inn. And the apostle laid his hand on her and began to say, "Jesus, who appear to us at all times—for this is your will, that we should always seek you, and you have given us the right to ask and to receive, and have not only permitted us this, but have also taught us how to pray—who are not seen by us with the bodily eyes, but who are never hidden from those of our soul, and who are hidden in form, but manifested to us by your works; by your many deeds we have recognized you as much as we are able, and you have given us your gifts without measure saying, 'Ask, and it shall be given you; seek, and you shall find; knock, and it shall be opened unto you.'[1] We pray, therefore, being afraid of our sins. And we ask you not for riches or gold or silver or possessions or any of those things that come from earth and go into the earth again; but we beg of you and entreat that in your holy name you raise this woman lying here by your power, to your glory and to an awakening of faith in those who stand by."

54 And he said to the young man, after sealing him, "Go and take her hand and say to her, 'With iron I killed you with my hands, and with my hands I raise you because of faith in Jesus.'" And the young man went and stood by her, saying, "I have believed in you, O Christ Jesus." And looking upon Judas Thomas the apostle, he said to him, "Pray for me, that my Lord, upon whom I call, may come to my help." And laying his hand on her hand he said, "Come, Lord Jesus Christ, give her life and me the reality of your faith." And he drew her by the hand, and she sprang up and sat looking at the great multitude standing around. And she also saw the apostle standing opposite her, and leaving her couch she sprang up and fell at his feet and took hold of his garments, saying, "I pray, Lord, where is your

---

1 Matt 7:7.

companion who has not left me to remain in that fearful and grievous place, but has given me up to you, saying, 'Take this one, that she may be made perfect, and thereafter be brought into her own place'?"

55 And the apostle said to her, "Tell us where you have been." And she answered, "Do you, who were with me, to whom also I was entrusted, wish to hear?" And she commenced thus: "An ugly-looking man, entirely black, received me; and his clothing was exceedingly filthy. And he took me to a place where there were many chasms, and a great stench and most hateful vapor were given forth thence. And he made me look into each chasm, and in the first I saw blazing fire, and fiery wheels running, and souls were hung upon these wheels, dashing against each other. And there was crying and great lamentation and no Savior was there. And that man said to me, 'These souls are akin to you, and in the days of reckoning they were delivered to punishment and destruction. And then others are brought in their stead; in like manner all these are again succeeded by others. These are they who perverted the intercourse of man and wife.' And again I looked down, and saw infants heaped upon each other, struggling and lying upon each other. And he said to me, 'These are their children, and for this they are placed here for a testimony against them.'

56 "And he brought me to another chasm, and as I looked into it I saw mud and worms spouting forth, and souls swallowing there; and I heard a great gnashing of teeth come from them. And that man said to me, 'These are the souls of women who left their husbands and committed adultery with others, and they have been brought to this torment.' And he showed me another chasm, and looking into it I saw souls hung up, some by the tongue, some by the hair, some by the hands, others by the feet, head downward, and reeking with smoke and sulphur. Concerning these the man who accompanied me said

the following: 'The souls hung up by the tongue are slanderers and such as have spoken false and disgraceful words and are not ashamed. Those hung up by their hair are the shameless, who are not ashamed at all and go about with uncovered heads in the world. Those hung up by the hands are they who took that which did not belong to them and have stolen, and who never gave anything to the poor, nor helped the afflicted; but they did so because they wished to get everything, and cared neither for law nor right. And these hung up by the feet are those who lightly and eagerly walked in wicked ways and disorderly paths, not visiting the sick nor escorting those who depart this life. On this account each soul receives what it has done.'

57 "And again he led me forth and showed me a very dark cavern, exhaling a very bad stench. Many souls were peeping out thence, wishing to get some share of the air. And their keepers would not let them look out. And my companion said to me, 'This is the prison of those souls which you saw. For when they have fully received their punishment for that which each has done, others succeed them. Some are fully consumed, others are given up to other punishments.' And the keepers of the souls in the dark cavern said to the man that had charge of me, 'Give her to us, that we may bring her to the others till the time comes when she is handed over to punishment.' But he said to them, 'I will not give her to you, because I am afraid of him who delivered her to me. For I was not told to leave her here; I shall take her back with me, till I get an injunction about her.' And he took me and brought me to another place, where there were men who were cruelly tortured. He who is like you took me and gave me up to you, saying to you, 'Take her, for she is one of the sheep which have wandered away.' And received by you, I now stand before you. I beg, therefore, and supplicate you that I may not come to those places of punishment which I have seen."

58 And the apostle said, "You have heard what this woman has recounted. And these are not the only punishments, but there are others worse than these. And you too, unless you turn to the God whom I preach, and abstain from your former works and from the deeds which you did in ignorance, shall find your end in these punishments. Believe, therefore, in Christ Jesus, and he will forgive you the former sins and will cleanse you from all your bodily desires that remain on the earth, and will heal you from the faults that follow after you and go along with you and are found before you. Let every one of you put off the old man and put on the new, and leave your former course of conduct and behavior. Those who steal, let them steal no more, but let them live, laboring and working. The adulterers are no more to commit adultery, lest they give themselves up to everlasting punishment. For with God adultery is an evil exceedingly wicked above all other evils. Put away also covetousness and lying and drunkenness and slandering, and do not return evil for evil! For all these are alien and strange to the God whom I preach. But walk rather in faith and meekness and holiness and hope, in which God rejoices, that you may become this kin, expecting from him those gifts which only a few receive."

59 The whole people therefore believed and presented obedient souls to the living God and Christ Jesus, rejoicing in the blessed works of the Most High and in his holy service. And they brought money for the service of the widows. For he had them gathered together in the cities, and he sent to all of them by his deacons what was necessary, both clothing as well as food. He himself did not cease to preach and to speak to them and to show that this Jesus is the Messiah of whom the Scriptures have spoken that he should be crucified and be raised after three days from the dead. He also showed to them and explained, beginning from the prophets, what was said concerning the Messiah, that it was necessary for him to come, and that everything had to be accomplished which had been prophesied of him. And the fame of him spread over all the cities and villages, and all who had sick persons or such as were troubled by unclean spirits brought them to him; and some they laid on the road by which he was to pass, and he healed all by the power of the Lord. And those who were healed by him said with one accord and one voice, "Glory to you, Jesus, who in like manner has given healing to all through your servant and apostle Thomas! And being in good health and rejoicing, we pray that we may become members of your flock and be counted among your sheep. Receive us, therefore, O Lord, and consider not our trespasses and our former transgressions, which we did while we were in ignorance!"

3. Justin's Dialogue with Trypho

Justin was a Christian philosopher who lived in Rome in the mid–second century. One of the first intellectuals to convert to Christianity, he authored three major works that still survive: two apologies (intellectual defenses of Christianity; see Chapter 4 below) and the "Dialogue with Trypho," an account of a two-day debate with a non-Christian Jewish scholar, Trypho, over whether Jesus could be the Jewish

Justin: Dialogue with Trypho, from *Saint Justin Martyr*, ed. Thomas Falls. *Fathers of the Church*, 6. Washington, DC: Catholic University Press of America, 1977. Used with permission.

Messiah predicted in the Jewish Scriptures. The debate allegedly took place around 135 CE in the city of Ephesus; Justin's account of the event, written perhaps 20 years later, strives to show the superiority of Christianity to Judaism. He begins by narrating his initial encounter with Trypho and explaining how as a young man he experimented with a range of Greek philosophical schools before becoming convinced, largely on the basis of the prophecies of the Hebrew prophets, that Jesus was the savior of the world who alone could teach the true meaning of life.

For further excerpts from the Dialogue with Trypho, see Chapter 5.

Chapter 1

One morning as I was walking along a broad avenue, a man, accompanied by some friends, came up to me and said: "Good morning, Philosopher." Whereupon, he and his friends walked along beside me.

After returning his greeting, I asked: "What is the matter? Is there anything special you wish of me?"

He answered: "Corinthus the Socratic taught me in Argos never to slight or ignore those who wear your garb, but to show them every consideration and to converse with them, since from such a conversation some good might be derived by them or myself. It would be to the advantage of both if either should benefit from this meeting. Accordingly, whenever I see anyone wearing such a robe, I gladly accost him. So, for this same reason, it has been a pleasure to greet you. These friends of mine share my hope of hearing something profitable from you."

"Who, indeed, are you, most excellent sir?" I asked with a smile.

He did not hesitate to tell me his name and background. "Trypho," he said, "is my name. I am a Hebrew of the circumcision, a refugee from the recent war, and at present a resident of Greece, especially of Corinth."

"How," I asked, "can you gain as much from philosophy as from your own lawgiver and prophets?"

"Why not," he replied, "for do not the philosophers speak always about God? Do they not constantly propose questions about his unity and providence? Is this not the task of philosophy, to inquire about the Divine?"

"Yes, indeed," I said, "we, too, are of the same opinion. But the majority of the philosophers have simply neglected to inquire whether there is one or even several gods, and whether or not a divine providence takes care of us, as if this knowledge were unnecessary to our happiness. Moreover, they try to convince us that God takes care of the universe with its genera and species, but not of me and you and of each individual, for otherwise there would be no need of our praying to him night and day. It is not difficult to see where such reasoning leads them. It imparts a certain immunity and freedom of speech to those who hold these opinions, permitting them to do and to say whatever they please, without any fear of punishment or hope of reward from God. How could it be otherwise, when they claim that things will always be as they are now, and that you and I shall live in the next life just as we are now, neither better nor worse. But there are others who think that the soul is immortal and incorporeal, and therefore conclude that they will not be punished even if they are guilty of sin; for, if the soul is incorporeal, it cannot suffer; if it is immortal, it needs nothing further from God."

Then, smiling politely, he said, "Explain to us just what is your opinion of these matters, and what is your idea of God, and what is your philosophy."

Chapter 2

"I will explain to you," I replied, "my views on this subject. Philosophy is indeed one's greatest possession, and is most precious in the sight of God, to whom it alone leads us and to whom it unites us, and they in truth are holy who have applied themselves to philosophy. But, many have failed to discover the nature of philosophy, and the reason why it was sent down to men; otherwise, there would not be Platonists, or Stoics, or Peripatetics, or Theoretics, or Pythagoreans, since this science of philosophy is always one and the same. Now, let me tell you why it has at length become so diversified. They who first turned to philosophy, and, as a result, were deemed illustrious, were succeeded by others who gave no time to the investigation of truth, but, amazed at the courage and self-control of their teachers as well as with the novelty of their teachings, held that to be the truth which each had learned from his own teacher. And they in turn transmitted to their successors such opinions, and others like them, and so they became known by the name of him who was considered the father of the doctrine. When I first desired to contact one of these philosophers, I placed myself under the tutelage of a certain Stoic. After spending some time with him and learning nothing new about God (for my instructor had no knowledge of God, nor did he consider such knowledge necessary), I left him and turned to a Peripatetic who considered himself an astute teacher. After a few days with him, he demanded that we settle the matter of my tuition fee in such a way that our association would not be unprofitable to him. Accordingly, I left him, because I did not consider him a real philosopher. Since my spirit still yearned to hear the specific and excellent meaning of philosophy, I approached a very famous Pythagorean, who took great pride in his own wisdom. In my interview with him, when I expressed a desire to become his pupil, he asked me, 'What? Do you know music, astronomy, and geometry? How do you expect to comprehend any of those things that are conducive to happiness, if you are not first well acquainted with those studies which draw your mind away from objects of the senses and render it fit for the intellectual, in order that it may contemplate what is good and beautiful?' He continued to speak at great length in praise of those sciences,

and of the necessity of knowing them, until I admitted that I knew nothing about them; then he dismissed me. As was to be expected, I was downcast to see my hopes shattered, especially since I respected him as a man of considerable knowledge. But, when I reflected on the length of time that I would have to spend on those sciences, I could not make up my mind to wait such a long time. In this troubled state of mind the thought occurred to me to consult the Platonists, whose reputation was great. Thus it happened that I spent as much time as possible in the company of a wise man who was highly esteemed by the Platonists and who had but recently arrived in our city. Under him I forged ahead in philosophy and day by day I improved. The perception of incorporeal things quite overwhelmed me and the Platonic theory of ideas added wings to my mind, so that in a short time I imagined myself a wise man. So great was my folly that I fully expected immediately to gaze upon God, for this is the goal of Plato's philosophy."

Chapter 3

"As I was in this frame of mind and desired absolute solitude devoid of human distractions, I used to take myself to a certain spot not far from the sea. One day, as I approached that place with the intention of being alone, a respectable old man, of meek and venerable mien, followed me at a short distance. I stopped, turned quickly, and stared sharply at him."

"'Do you know me?' he asked.

"I replied that I did not.

"'Why, therefore,' he continued, 'do you stare at me so?'

"'Because,' I answered, 'I am surprised to find you here. I didn't expect to see anyone here.'

"'I am worried,' he said, 'about some missing members of my household, and I am therefore looking around with the hope that they may show up somewhere in the vicinity. But what brings you here?'

"'I take great delight,' I answered, 'in such walks, where I can converse with myself without hindrance because there is nothing to distract my attention. Places like this are most suitable for philology.'

"'Are you, then, a philologian,' he asked, 'rather than a lover of deeds and of truth? Do you not strive to be a practical man rather than a sophist?'

"'But what greater deed,' I replied, 'could one perform than to prove that reason rules all, and that one who rules reason and is sustained by it can look down upon the errors and undertakings of others, and see that they do nothing reasonable or pleasing to God. People cannot have prudence without philosophy and straight thinking. Thus, everyone should be devoted to philosophy and should consider it the greatest and most noble pursuit; all other pursuits are only of second- or third-rate value, unless they are connected with philosophy. Then they are of some value and should be approved; if they are devoid of philosophy and are not connected with it in any way, they then become base and coarse pursuits to those who practise them.'

"Interrupting, he asked, 'Does philosophy therefore produce happiness?'

"'Absolutely,' I replied, 'and it alone.'

"'Tell me,' he asked, 'what is philosophy and what is the happiness it engenders, if there is nothing which prevents your speaking.'

"'Philosophy,' I answered, 'is the knowledge of that which exists, and a clear understanding of the truth; and happiness is the reward of such knowledge and understanding.'

"'But how do you define God?' he asked.

"'God is the Being who always has the same nature in the same manner, and is the cause of existence to all else,' I replied.

"Pleased with my words, he once again asked, 'Is not knowledge a word applied commonly to different matters? For, whoever is skilled in any of the arts, for example, in the art of military strategy or of navigation or of medicine, is called skillful. But this is not true in divine and human matters. Is there a science which furnishes us with an understanding of human and divine things, and, besides, a higher science of the divinity and virtue in them?'

"'Certainly,' I replied.

"'Well, now,' he asked, 'is the knowledge of humanity and God similar to that of music, arithmetic, astronomy, and the like?'

"'Not at all,' I answered.

"'Your answer has not been correct, then,' he continued, 'for we acquire the knowledge of some things by study or practice, and of other things by sight. Now, if anyone were to say to you that in India there exists an animal different from all others, of such and such a species, assuming many shapes and colors, you would have no definite knowledge of it unless you saw it, nor could you attempt to give any description of it, unless you had heard of it from one who had seen it.'

"'Absolutely not,' I agreed.

"'Then, how,' he reasoned, 'can the philosophers speculate correctly or speak truly of God, when they have no knowledge of him, since they have never seen nor heard him?'

"'But the Deity, father,' I rejoined, 'cannot be seen by the same eyes as other living beings are. He is to be perceived by the mind alone, as Plato affirms, and I agree with him.'

Chapter 4

"'Does our mind, then,' he inquired, 'possess such and so great a power? Or does it not perceive that which exists through the senses? Or will the human mind be capable of seeing God, if not aided by the Holy Ghost?'

"'Plato truly states,' I retorted, 'that the eye of the mind has this special power, which has been given to us in order that we may see with it, when it is pure, the very Being who is the cause of everything the mind perceives, who has neither color, nor form, nor size, nor anything the eye can see, but who is beyond all essence, who is ineffable and indescribable, who alone is beautiful and good, and who comes at once into those souls which are well disposed because of their affinity to and desire of seeing him.'

"'What affinity, then,' he asked, 'have we with God? Is the soul also divine and immortal and a part of the Supreme Mind itself? And as this Supreme Mind sees God, are we, in like manner, able to perceive the Deity in our mind, and thus be happy even now?'

"'Absolutely,' I replied.

"'Do all the souls," he asked, 'of all the animals perceive Him? Or is a human's soul different from that of a horse or an ass?'

"'No,' I answered, 'the souls of all creatures are the same.'

"'Then,' he continued, 'shall horses and asses see God, or have they ever seen God at any time?'

"'No,' I replied, 'for not even most people see him; only those who are honest in their life, and who have been purified through their justice and every other virtue.'

"'Then you would say,' he persisted, 'that one does not see God because of an affinity with him, nor because one possesses an intellect, but because one is temperate and just?'

"'Certainly,' I answered, 'and also because one has the faculty of thinking of God.'

"'Would you say,' he asked, 'that goats or sheep do an injustice to anyone?'

"'They do not in any way do an injustice to anyone,' I replied.

"'So, according to your reasoning,' he said, 'these animals will see God?'

"'No, they won't,' I answered, 'because they are hindered from doing so by the form of their bodies.'

"'If these animals had the power of speech,' he retorted, 'you can be sure that they would have more right to revile our bodies. But, for the present let us ignore this topic and I'll concede that what you say is true. Tell me this: Does the soul see God while it is in the body, or after it has been released from it?'

"'Even while it is in the human body,' I replied, 'it can see God by means of the intellect, but especially after it has been released from the body, and exists of itself, does it perceive God whom it always loved.'

"'Does it remember,' he asked, 'this vision of God when it is again united to a human body?'

"'I don't think so,' I answered.

"'What, then,' he continued, 'is the advantage of having seen God? What advantage has one who has seen God over one who has not, unless one at least remembers the fact that one has seen Him?'

"'That I cannot answer,' I admitted.

"'And what,' asked he, 'will be the punishment for those deemed unworthy to see God?'

"'As a punishment,' I answered, 'they will be imprisoned in the bodies of certain wild beasts.'

"'Will they be conscious that for this reason they are imprisoned in such bodies and that they have committed some sin?'

"'I don't think so.'

"'Then, it would seem that they benefit in no way from such punishment; in fact, I would say that they suffer no punishment at all, unless they are conscious that it is a punishment.'

"'No, indeed,' I conceded.

"'Therefore,' he concluded, 'souls do not see God, nor do they transmigrate into other bodies, for they would know that they were being thus punished, and they would be afraid thereafter to commit even the slightest sin. But I do concede that souls can perceive that there is a God, and that justice and piety are admirable.'

"'You speak the truth,' I agreed.

Chapter 5

"'Those philosophers, then, know nothing,' he went on, 'about such matters, for they can't even explain the nature of the soul.'

"'It seems not,' I consented.

"'Nor should we call the soul immortal, for, if it were, we would certainly have to call it unbegotten.'

"'Some Platonists,' I answered, 'consider the soul both unbegotten and immortal.'

"'Do you affirm,' he asked, 'that the universe also is unbegotten?'

"'There are some who hold that opinion,' I replied, 'but I don't agree with them.'

"'Right you are,' he continued. 'Why would one think that a body that is so solid, firm, composite, and mutable, a body that deteriorates and is renewed each day, has not originated from some first cause? Now, if the universe has been begotten, souls, too, of necessity, are begotten. Perhaps there is a time when they do not exist, for they were created for the sake of humans and other living creatures, even if you claim that they have been begotten separately by themselves, and not together with their own bodies.'

"'I think you are right. The souls, then, are not immortal?'

"'No,' he said, 'since it appears that the world itself was generated.'

"'On the other hand,' he continued, 'I do not claim that any soul ever perishes, for this would certainly be a benefit to sinners. What happens to them? The souls of the devout dwell in a better place, whereas the souls of the unjust and the evil abide in a worse place, and there they await the judgment day. Those, therefore, who are deemed worthy to see God will never perish, but the others will be subjected to punishment as long as God allows them to exist and as long as he wants them to be punished.'

"'Does not your assertion agree with what Plato taught in his *Timaeus* concerning the world, namely, that it can be destroyed since it is a created thing, but that it will not be destroyed or be destined for destruction since such is the will of God? Don't you think that the same thing could be said of the soul and, in short, of all other creatures? For, whatever exists or shall exist after God has a nature subject to corruption, and therefore capable of complete annihilation, for only God is unbegotten and incorruptible. For this reason he is God, and all other things after him are created and corruptible. This is also the reason why souls die and are punished, for, if they were unbegotten, they would not have sinned nor have become so foolish; they would not have been so timid at one time, and so daring at another; nor would they, of their own account, ever have entered into swine, serpents, and dogs. Furthermore, if they were unbegotten it would not be right to coerce them, for one who is unbegotten is similar and equal to

another unbegotten, nor can he be preferred to the other either in power or in honor. We must conclude, therefore, that there are not many beings that are unbegotten, for, if there were some difference between them, you could not, no matter how you searched, find the cause of such difference; but, after sending your thought always to infinity, you would finally become tired and have to stop before the one Unbegotten and declare that he is the cause of all things. Do you think that these things escaped the notice of Plato and Pythagoras, those wise men who became, so to say, a wall and bulwark of our philosophy?'

Chapter 6

"'I don't care,' he answered, 'if Plato or Pythagoras or anyone else held such views. What I say is the truth, and here is how you may learn it. The soul itself either is life or it possesses life. If it is life, it would cause something else to exist, not itself, just as motion causes something other than itself to move. Now, no one would deny that the soul lives; and if it lives, it does not live as life itself, but as a partaker of life. But, that which partakes of anything is different from that of which it partakes. Now, the soul partakes of life because God wishes it to live; it will no longer partake of life whenever God doesn't wish it to live. For the power to live is not an attribute of the soul as it is of God. As one does not live forever, and one's body is not forever united to one's soul, since, whenever this union must be discontinued, the soul leaves the body and one no longer exists, so also, whenever the soul must cease to live, the spirit of life is taken from it and it is no more, but it likewise returns to the place of its origin.'

Chapter 7

"'If these philosophers,' I asked, 'do not know the truth, what teacher or method shall one follow?'

"'A long time ago,' he replied, 'long before the time of those reputed philosophers, there lived blessed men who were just and loved by God, men who spoke through the inspiration of the Holy Spirit and predicted events that would take place in the future, which events are now taking place. We call these men the Prophets. They alone knew the truth and communicated it to people, whom they neither deferred to nor feared. With no desire for personal glory, they reiterated only what they heard and saw when inspired by the Holy Spirit. Their writings are still extant, and whoever reads them with the proper faith will profit greatly in his knowledge of the origin and end of things, and of any other matter that a philosopher should know. In their writings they gave no proof at that time of their statements, for, as reliable witnesses of the truth, they were beyond proof; but the happenings that have taken place and are now taking place force you to believe their words. They also are worthy of belief because of the miracles which they performed, for they exalted God, the Father and Creator of all things, and made known Christ, his Son, who was sent by him. This the false prophets, who are filled with an erring and unclear spirit, have never done nor even do now, but they undertake to perform certain wonders to astound people and they glorify the demons and spirits of error. Above all, beseech God to open to you the gates of light, for no one can perceive or understand these truths unless he has been enlightened by God and his Christ.'

Chapter 8

"When he said these and many other things which it is not now the fitting time to tell, he went his way, after admonishing me to mediate on what he had told me, and I never saw him again. But my spirit was immediately set on fire, and an affection for the prophets, and for those who are friends of Christ, took hold of me; while pondering on his words, I discovered that his was the only sure and useful philosophy. Thus it is that I am now a philosopher. Furthermore, it is my wish that everyone would be of the same sentiments as I, and never spurn the Savior's words; for they have in themselves such tremendous majesty that they can instil fear into those who have wandered from the path of righteousness, whereas they ever remain a great solace to those who heed them. Thus, if you have any regard for your own welfare and for the salvation of your soul, and if you believe in God, you may have the chance, since I know you are no stranger to this matter, of attaining a knowledge of the Christ of God, and, after becoming a Christian, of enjoying a happy life."

3

The Attack on Christianity

Persecution and Martyrdom in the Early Church

Since Christianity began as a group of Jews who saw in Jesus the Jewish Messiah sent from the Jewish God in fulfillment of the Jewish Scriptures, they naturally began to propagate their views by trying to convert other Jews (see Chapter 2). The early Jewish mission was not an overwhelming success, however, as most Jews found the Christian claims about Jesus unbelievable and ludicrous, or even blasphemous. First-century Jews who were expecting a Messiah anticipated a person of power and grandeur, for example, a great warrior-king who would overthrow Israel's political enemies or a cosmic deliverer who would destroy the evils of this world. Jesus, on the other hand, was a relatively unknown teacher from a remote rural area who had been executed for sedition against the state. The Christian claim that he was the Messiah seemed nonsensical to most Jews; the corollary claim by some that gentiles who did not keep the Jewish Law were the true heirs of the promises made to the Jewish ancestors simply served to exacerbate the tensions.

Understandably, then, the earliest persecution of Christians was by Jews. This is clear from the oldest historical account of the incipient Christian movement, the book of Acts, and from the writings of Paul, who indicates that as a Jewish Pharisee he had persecuted Christians (Galatians 1:13) and that later, as a Christian, he himself was punished by Jewish authorities (2 Corinthians 11:24).

Even bigger problems were in store for Christians, however, when the movement transcended its original Jewish matrix and entered more broadly into the larger Greco-Roman world. To be sure, it is not true, as is sometimes believed, that Christianity was immediately outlawed in the Roman Empire and that Christians had to go into hiding. But there was considerable and widespread social antipathy toward Christians in the first three centuries, regular threats of mob violence, and occasional instances of governmental persecution.

New Testament sources indicate that early on, Christians were seen as antisocial and that their refusal to participate in normal cultic and social activities in their communities led to hatred and opposition (for example, 1 Peter 4:3–5). Throughout non-Christian sources of the second and third centuries the Christians are written off as ignorant, lower-class, obstinate, superstitious, and antisocial (see Wilken). Early in the period, the Roman historian Tacitus indicates that they were widely known for their "hatred of the human race." Sometimes specific charges were leveled against them. As we will see in Chapter 4, since they did not worship any of the state or local gods they were called "atheists" (literally, "without the gods"); and since they held secret meetings at night, in which they exchanged a "kiss" of peace and ate the body of the Son of God and drank his blood, they were accused of holding nocturnal orgies that included cannibalistic rites.

Widespread suspicion against the Christians may have led to the occasional acts of mob violence against them. Firmly held religious convictions among the non-Christian populace at large may have played a role as well: pagans who believed that their own gods were to be worshipped and that a community that failed to do so could evoke divine wrath were increasingly prone to blame Christian "nonworshippers" when any disaster arose. In the words of Tertullian: "They consider that the Christians are the cause of every public calamity and every misfortune of the people. If the Tiber rises as high as the city walls, if the Nile does not rise to the fields, if the weather will not change, if there is an earthquake, a famine, a plague—straightway the cry is heard: 'Toss the Christians to the lion!'" (*Apology* 40; see Chapter 4).

In some scattered instances, local governmental officials stepped in both to prevent uncontrolled riot and to provide a legal outlet for the will of the people. There is some ambiguity in our sources concerning the legal charges against the Christians in such cases, since there were no Roman laws that proscribed the new religion (until the emperor Decius, ca. 250 CE). But it should be emphasized that throughout the Roman provinces, criminal law in general was lax by our modern standards. There were no mandated criminal codes or proceedings; instead, the Romans appointed governors and other administrators to rule the provinces, and these appointed officials were responsible for maintaining the peace and administering justice as the situation demanded. Troublemakers could be tried and punished on the spot, with no possibility of trial by jury or legal appeals (see selection 4, below, from Pliny, governor of a Roman province).

Why, then, if there were no explicit laws against Christianity, were Christians occasionally put on trial, punished, and even executed? Any ruling official who suspected that Christians engaged in crimes against nature as part of their religion (incestuous orgies, cannibalism) would certainly have grounds to act; in such a case, simply being a Christian would be a guilty offense. Moreover, since Christians were known not to worship the Roman gods—who were widely acknowledged as providing the peace and prosperity of the state—and since failing to worship the gods could bring divine retribution on the state itself, the existence of the Christians may have been seen as dangerous to the state, at least by the masses if not by the more highly educated governors (whose job it was to keep peace among the masses and who may have been willing to sacrifice some Christians in order to do so). In particular, the Roman emperor was widely understood in the provinces to represent the gods and so to be worthy of divine honors.

Only on rare occasions did emperors themselves actually engage in active opposition to Christians. The first to do so was Nero in 64 CE. According to Tacitus, when a large portion of Rome was burned and the populace began to suspect the emperor's involvement (since the destruction of the city would have allowed him to implement his new building plans) he found a ready scapegoat in the Christians, many of whom he rounded up and subjected to public tortures and executions. It is important to realize that Nero persecuted Christians only in Rome (not throughout the empire) and that he did so not for their religion per se, but for arson (even though the charge was false). Nonetheless, his actions may have set a precedent for future generations. The next recorded imperial involvement occurred some 50 years later, when Trajan approved the actions of his governor of Bythinia-Pontus, Pliny the Younger, for executing Christians when they refused to recant and perform an act of worship toward his own cultic image (see below). Some 60 years after that, the emperor Marcus Aurelius sanctioned the terrible persecution of the Christians in Lyons and Vienne (see below). But it was not until the emperor Decius saw the church as a threat and tried (unevenly and unsuccessfully) to wipe it out by an empire-wide persecution (ca. 250 CE) that being a Christian was actually deemed "illegal."

Included among our ancient sources of early Christianity are several eyewitness accounts of the trial proceedings against Christians and of their martyrdoms. These are all written by Christians and portray a decidedly Christian perspective on the proceedings. According to these accounts, many Christians found a way to hide or to escape during times of persecution; others could afford to bribe their way out of punishment, and yet others found no problem in recanting their beliefs for a time until the persecution had passed. But there were some who refused to budge and so paid the full price of their convictions. We do not know how many Christians were martyred in the first three centuries; judging from the details provided in the early Christian historian Eusebius, however, they probably numbered in the hundreds (rather than many thousands).

For Further Reading

Bowersock, G. W. *Martyrdom and Rome*. Cambridge: Cambridge University Press, 1995.

Boyarin, Daniel. *Dying for God: Martyrdom and the Making of Christianity and Judaism*. Stanford: Stanford University Press, 1999.

Castelli, Elizabeth. *Martyrdom and Memory: Early Christian Culture Marking*. New York: Columbia University Press, 2004.

Cobb, L. Stephanie. *Dying to Be Men: Gender and Language in Early Christian Martyr Texts*. New York: Columbia University Press, 2008.

Ferguson, Everett, ed. *Church and State in the Early Church*. New York: Garland, 1993. (A collection of classic essays; see especially G. E. M. de Ste. Croix, "Why Were the Early Christians Persecuted?" and the subsequent exchange with A. N. Sherwin-White.)

Frend, W. H. C. *Martyrdom and Persecution in the Early Church*. Oxford: Blackwell, 1965.

Moss, Candida. *Early Christian Martyrdom: Diverse Practices, Theologies, and Traditions*. New Haven: Yale University, 2012.

Moss, Candida. *The Myth of Persecution: How Early Christians Invented a Story of Martyrdom*. San Francisco: HarperOne, 2013.

Musurillo, H., ed. *The Acts of the Christian Martyrs*. Oxford: Clarendon, 1972.

Perkins, Judith. *The Suffering Self*. New York: Routledge, 1995.

Wilken, Robert. *The Christians as the Romans Saw Them*. New Haven: Yale University, 1984.

THE TEXTS

4. Pliny's Letter to Trajan

Pliny the Younger was a Roman aristocrat appointed by the emperor Trajan to be the governor of the province of Bythinia-Pontus (in Asia Minor, modern Turkey) in 109 or 110 CE. A number of the letters that he wrote back to the emperor during his administration, as well as the replies he received from Trajan, can be found in Book 10 of his collected letters. Of greatest interest to students of early Christianity are letters 96 and 97, in which we find, for the first time, a reference to the early Christian movement by a pagan source. As one might expect, the reference is antagonistic.

Pliny indicates that he had placed anyone identified as a Christian on trial. Those who denied that they were Christian he subjected to a test: if they would offer incense and wine to an image of the emperor and curse Christ, they were released. Those who refused to do so after several urgings were executed for showing an obstinacy in not worshiping the gods of the state.

Pliny's procedure is interesting, in part, because it shows that having been a Christian previously was not a crime (unlike, say, having been a murderer); only *being* one was. Pliny writes Trajan to see if he is acting properly. Trajan replies that the procedure is sound: Christians are indeed to be punished; those who demonstrate that they are not Christians are to be released; but anonymous accusations are not to be accepted.

96. Gaius Pliny to the Emperor Trajan

It is my regular custom, my lord, to refer to you all questions which cause me doubt, for who can better guide my hesitant steps or instruct my ignorance? I have never attended hearings concerning Christians, so I am unaware what is usually punished or investigated, and to what extent. I am more than a little in doubt whether there is to be a distinction between ages, and to what extent the young should be treated no differently from the more hardened; whether pardon should be granted to repentance; whether the person who has been a Christian in some sense should not benefit by having renounced it; whether it is the name Christian, itself untainted with crimes, or the crimes which cling to the name which should be punished.

In the meantime, this is the procedure I have followed, in the cases of those brought before me as Christians. I asked them whether they were Christians. If they admitted it, I asked them a second and a third time, threatening them with execution. Those who remained obdurate I ordered to be executed, for I was in no doubt, whatever it was which they were confessing, that their obstinacy and their inflexible stubbornness should at any rate be punished. Others similarly lunatic were Roman citizens, so I registered them as due to be sent back to Rome.

Later in the course of the hearings, as usually happens, the charge rippled outwards, and more examples appeared. An anonymous document was published containing the names of many. Those who denied that they were or had been Christians and called upon the gods after me, and with incense and wine made obeisance to your statue, which I had ordered to be brought in together with images of the gods for this very purpose, and who moreover cursed Christ (those who are truly Christian cannot, it is said, be forced to do any of these things), I ordered to be acquitted.

Others who were named by an informer stated that they were Christians and then denied it. They said that in fact they had been, but had abandoned their allegiance, some three years previously, some more years earlier, and one or two as many as twenty years before. All these as well worshipped your statue and images of the gods, and blasphemed Christ. They maintained, however, that all that their guilt or error involved was that they were accustomed to assemble at dawn on a fixed day, to sing a hymn antiphonally to Christ as God, and to bind themselves by an oath, not for the commission of some crime, but to avoid acts of theft, brigandage, and adultery, not to break their word, and not to withhold money deposited with them when asked for it. When these rites were completed, it was their custom to depart, and then to assemble again to take food, which was however common and harmless. They had ceased, they said, to do this following my edict, by which in accordance with your instructions I had outlawed the existence of secret brotherhoods. So I thought it all the more necessary to ascertain the truth from two maidservants, who were called deaconesses, even by employing torture. I found nothing other than a debased and boundless superstition.

I therefore postponed the inquiry, and hastened to consult you, since this issue seemed to me to merit consultation, especially because of the number indicted, for there are many of all ages, every rank, and both sexes who are summoned and will be summoned to confront danger. The infection of this superstition has extended not merely through the cities, but also through the villages and country areas, but it seems likely that it can be halted and corrected. It is at any rate certain that temples which were almost abandoned have begun to be crowded, and the solemn rites which for long had been suspended are being restored. The flesh of the victims, for which up to now only a very occasional buyer was found, is now on sale in many places, This leads me readily to believe that if opportunity for repentance is offered, a large crowd of people can be set right.

97. Trajan to Pliny

You have followed the appropriate procedure, my Secundus, in examining the cases of those brought before you as Christians, for no general rule can be laid down which would establish a definite routine. Christians are not to be sought out. If brought before you and found guilty, they must be punished, but in such a way that a person who denies that he is a Christian and demonstrates this by his action, that is, by worshipping our gods, may obtain pardon for repentance, even if his previous record is suspect. Documents published anonymously must play no role in any accusation, for they give the worst example, and are foreign to our age.

5. The Letter of Ignatius to the Romans

Ignatius, the bishop of Antioch in Syria, was arrested around 110 CE, evidently for Christian activities. Rather than being tried on the spot, he was sent to Rome under armed guard to face trial and execution. Along the way he was greeted by representatives of various local churches, to which he then wrote letters sending his greetings and warning against false teachers, church dissension, and, especially, lack of reverence for the ruling bishops. Seven of Ignatius's letters survive. The one given here is perhaps the most distinctive of all. It is written to the Christians of Rome, pleading with them not to interfere with the proceedings against him. Ignatius wants to be thrown to the wild beasts and so become a martyr for Christ, a true Christian. He urges the Roman Christians to grant him his wish and allow him to imitate the passion of his Lord.

Unfortunately, we do not have a historically reliable account of what happened to Ignatius once he arrived in Rome.

To the Romans

Ignatius, who is also called God-bearer, to the church that has obtained mercy by the greatness of the Father Most High and Jesus Christ his only Son; the church that is loved and enlightened by the will of the one who has willed everything that is, according to the faith and love of Jesus Christ, our God; the church that is presiding in the land of the Romans, worthy of God, worthy of honor, worthy of blessing, worthy of praise, worthy of success, worthy of holiness, and preeminent in love, a church that keeps the law of Christ and bears the name of the Father; this is the church that I greet in the name of Jesus Christ, the Son of the Father. And I extend warmest greetings blamelessly in Jesus Christ, our God, to those who are united in both flesh and spirit in his every commandment, filled with the gracious gift of God without wavering, and filtered from every unsuitable taint.

1 Since by my prayer to God I have managed to see your faces, which are worthy of God—as indeed I have asked to receive even more, for I hope to greet you while in chains in Christ Jesus, if indeed it be the will of the one who has made me worthy to endure until the end.

2 For the beginning is auspicious, if I can indeed obtain the gracious gift I need to receive my lot without any impediment. For I am afraid of your love, that it may do me harm. For it is easy for you to do what you want, but it is difficult for me to attain to God, if you do not spare me.

2 For I do not want you to please people but to please God,[17] as indeed you are doing. For I will have no other such opportunity to attain to God, nor can you be enlisted for a better work—if,

---

17 Cf. 2 Thess. 2:4.

---

that is, you keep silent. For if you keep silent about me, I will be a word of God; but if you desire my flesh, I will once again be a mere noise.

2 But grant me nothing more than to be poured out as a libation to God while there is still an altar at hand, that by becoming a chorus in love, you may sing forth to the Father in Jesus Christ, saying that God has deemed the bishop of Syria worthy to be found at the setting of the sun, after sending him from where it rises. For it is good for me to set from the world to God, that I may rise up to him.

3 At no time have you been envious of anyone; instead you have taught others. But my wish is that the instructions you enjoin on others be firm, when you make them disciples.

2 For me, ask only that I have power both inside and out, that I not only speak but also have the desire, that I not only be called a Christian but also be found one. For if I be found a Christian, I can also be called one and then be faithful—when I am no longer visible in the world.

3 Nothing that is visible is good. For our God Jesus Christ, since he is in the Father, is all the more visible. The work is not a matter of persuasion, but Christianity is a matter of greatness, when it is hated by the world.

4 I am writing all the churches and giving instruction to all, that I am willingly dying for God, unless you hinder me. I urge you, do not become an untimely kindness to me. Allow me to be bread for the wild beasts; through them I am able to attain to God. I am the wheat of God and am ground by the teeth of the wild beasts, that I may be found to be the pure bread of Christ.

2 Rather, coax the wild beasts, that they may become a tomb for me and leave no part of my body behind, that I may burden no one once I have died. Then I will truly be a disciple of Jesus Christ, when the world does not see even my body. Petition Christ on my behalf, that I may be found a sacrifice through these instruments of God.

3 I am not enjoining you as Peter and Paul did. They were apostles, I am condemned; they were

free, until now I have been a slave. But if I suffer, I will become a freed person who belongs to Jesus Christ, and I will rise up, free, in him. In the meantime I am learning to desire nothing while in chains.

5 From Syria to Rome I have been fighting the wild beasts, through land and sea, night and day, bound to ten leopards, which is a company of soldiers, who become worse when treated well. But I am becoming more of a disciple by their mistreatment. Still, it is not because of this that I have been made upright.[18]

2 May I have the full pleasure of the wild beasts prepared for me; I pray they will be found ready for me. Indeed, I will coax them to devour me quickly—not as happens with some, whom they are afraid to touch. And even if they do not wish to do so willingly, I will force them to it.

3 Grant this to me; I know what benefits me. Now I am beginning to be a disciple. May nothing visible or invisible show any envy toward me, that I may attain to Jesus Christ. Fire and cross and packs of wild beasts, cuttings and being torn apart, the scattering of bones, the mangling of limbs, the grinding of the whole body, the evil torments of the devil—let them come upon me, only that I may attain to Jesus Christ.

6 Neither the ends of the world nor the kingdoms of this age will benefit me in the least. It is better for me to die in Jesus Christ than to rule the ends of the earth. That is the one I seek, who died on our behalf; that is the one I desire, who arose for us. But pains of birth have come upon me.

2 Grant this to me, brothers: do not keep me from living; do not wish me to die; do not hand over to the world the one who wants to belong to God or deceive him by what is material. Allow me to receive the pure light; when I have arrived there, I will be a human.

3 Allow me to be an imitator of the suffering of my God. If anyone has him within himself, let him

---

18 1 Cor 4:4.

both understand what I want and sympathize with me, realizing the things that constrain me.

7 The ruler of this age wishes to snatch me away and corrupt my mind, which is directed toward God. And so let none of you who are present assist him; rather be on my side—that is, on God's. Do not speak about Jesus Christ but long for the world.

2 Let no envy dwell among you. Even if I urge you otherwise when I arrive, do not be persuaded; instead be persuaded by what I am writing you now. For I write to you while living, desiring to die. My passion has been crucified[19] and there is no burning love within me for material things; instead there is living water,[20] which also is speaking in me, saying to me from within: "Come to the Father."

3 I have no pleasure in the food that perishes nor in the pleasures of this life. I desire the bread of God, which is the flesh of Jesus Christ, from the seed of David; and for drink I desire his blood, which is imperishable love.

8 I no longer desire to live like a human; and I will succeed, if you also desire it. Desire it, that you may also be desired.

2 Through just a few words I ask you: trust me! Jesus Christ will show you that I speak the truth. He is the mouth that does not lie, by whom the Father spoke the truth.

3 Pray for me, that I may attain to God. I have not written you according to the flesh but according to the mind of God. If I suffer, you have desired it; if I am rejected, you have hated me.

9 In your prayer remember the church of Syria, which has God as its shepherd in my place. Jesus Christ alone will oversee it *[Or: be its bishop]*, along with your love.

2 But I am ashamed to be called one of them; for I am not at all worthy, as the least of them and a miscarriage.[21] But I have found mercy to be someone, if I attain to God.

3 My spirit greets you, as does the love of the churches that received me in the name of Jesus Christ, and not just as one passing by. For even those that did not lie on my actual route went ahead of me from city to city.

10 I am writing this to you from Smyrna, through the Ephesians, who are worthy to be blessed. Along with many others, Crocus is with me, a name that is dear to me.

2 I believe you know about those who have preceded me from Syria to Rome for the glory of God. Tell them I am near. For they are all worthy of God and of you. It is fitting for you to refresh them in every way.

3 I am writing this to you on August 24. Farewell until the end, in the endurance of Jesus Christ.

---

19 Cf. Gal 6:14.

20 Cf. John 4:10, 14.

21 1 Cor 15:8–9.

6. The Martyrdom of Polycarp

One of the persons to whom Ignatius addressed a letter was Polycarp, the bishop of Smyrna in Asia Minor. Some 45 years later, around 155 CE, Polycarp himself was arrested, tried, and executed for being a Christian. The surviving account is the earliest "martyrology" (description of a martyrdom) to have survived from early Christianity outside of the New Testament (see Acts 7:56–60). It claims to be based on an eyewitness report and is embedded in a letter written soon thereafter by the church of Smyrna to the church in Philomelium, also in Asia Minor. Scholars have debated whether the account is authentic or, instead, was later written in such a way so as to appear to be based on an eyewitness report.

The author indicates that Polycarp's death was "conformable to the Gospel," and he has modeled his description on familiar traditions of Christ's own death (for example, the betrayal, the officer named Herod, Polycarp's prayer for God's will to be done, his entry into the city on a donkey, etc.). In addition to such legendary accretions as the fragrant aroma arising from Polycarp's body on the pyre, the story is important for showing that a Christian could be condemned simply for refusing to worship the state gods and could escape punishment by reverencing the divine spirit (genius) of the Emperor. As typically happens in the martyrologies, Polycarp steadfastly refuses, insisting that the tortures of the moment are far to be preferred to the eternal torments that await those who deny Christ.

Martyrdom of Saint Polycarp, Bishop of Smyrna

The church of God that temporarily resides in Smyrna to the church of God that temporarily resides in Philomelium, and to all congregations of temporary residents everywhere, who belong to the holy and universal church. May the mercy, peace, and love of God the Father and of our Lord Jesus Christ be multiplied.

1 We are writing you, brothers, about those who were martyred, along with the blessed Polycarp, who put an end to the persecution by, as it were, setting a seal on it through his death as a martyr. For nearly everything leading up to his death occurred so that the Lord might show us from above a martyrdom in conformity with the gospel.

2 For Polycarp waited to be betrayed, as also did the Lord, that we in turn might imitate him, thinking not only of ourselves, but also of our neighbors.[1] For anyone with true and certain love wants not only himself but also all the brothers to be saved.

2 Blessed and noble, therefore, are all the martyrdoms that have occurred according to the

---

1 Phil 2:4.

The Martyrdom of Polycarp, reproduced from *The Apostolic Fathers,* ed. Bart D. Ehrman; Loeb Classical Library, vol. 1. Cambridge, MA: Harvard University, 2003. Used with permission of Harvard University Press.

will of God. For we must be reverent and attribute the ultimate authority to God.

2 For who would not be astounded by their nobility, endurance, and love of the Master? For they endured even when their skin was ripped to shreds by whips, revealing the very anatomy of their flesh, down to the inner veins and arteries, while bystanders felt pity and wailed. But they displayed such nobility that none of them either grumbled or moaned, clearly showing us all that in that hour, while under torture, the martyrs of Christ had journeyed far away from the flesh, or rather, that the Lord was standing by, speaking to them.

3 And clinging to the gracious gift of Christ, they despised the torments of the world, in one hour purchasing for themselves eternal life. And the fire of their inhuman torturers was cold to them, because they kept their eyes on the goal of escaping the fire that is eternal and never extinguished. And with the eyes of their hearts they looked above to the good things preserved for those who endure, which no ear has heard nor eye seen, which have never entered into the human heart,[2] but which the Lord revealed to them, who were no long humans but already angels.

4 In a similar way, those who were condemned to the wild beasts endured horrible torments, stretched out on sharp shells and punished with various other kinds of tortures, that, if possible, he[3] might force them to make a denial through continuous torment.

3 For the devil devised many torments against them. But thanks be to God: he had no power over any of them. For the most noble Germanicus strengthened their cowardice through his endurance, and he fought the wild beasts impressively. For when the proconsul wanted to persuade him, saying "Take pity on your age," he forcefully dragged the wild beast onto himself, wanting to leave their unjust and lawless life without delay.

2 Because of this, the entire multitude, astounded by the great nobility of the godly and reverent race of the Christians, cried out, "Away with the atheists! Find Polycarp!"

4 But there was a person named Quintus, a Phrygian who had recently come from Phrygia, who was overcome with cowardice once he saw the wild beasts. This is the one who compelled both himself and several others to turn themselves in. But the insistent pleas of the proconsul convinced him to take the oath and offer a sacrifice. Because of this, brothers, we do not praise those who hand themselves over, since this is not what the gospel teaches.

5 Now when the most marvelous Polycarp first heard, he was not disturbed, but wanted to remain in the city. But most of the others were persuading him to leave. And so he left for a small country house not far from the city and stayed there with a few others, night and day doing nothing but pray for everyone and for the churches throughout the world, as was his custom.

2 Three days before he was arrested, while praying, he had a vision and saw his pillow being consumed by fire. Then he turned to those with him and said, "I must be burned alive."

6 While they continued searching for him, he moved to a different country house—just as those who were seeking him arrived at the other. Since they could not find him, they arrested two young slaves, one of whom made a confession under torture.

2 For it was impossible for him to keep in hiding, since the ones who betrayed him were members of his household. And the chief of police, who was called by the same name—for his name was Herod—was eager to lead him into the stadium, that he might fulfill his special destiny as a partner with Christ, while those who betrayed him might suffer the punishment of Judas himself.

7 And so, taking the young slave, on the Day of Preparation around the dinner hour, the

---

2 1 Cor 2:9.

3 I.e., the devil; see 3.1.

mounted police and horsemen went out with their usual weapons, as if running down a thief.[4] And when the hour was late, they converged and found Polycarp lying down in a small room upstairs. He could have fled elsewhere even from there, but he chose not to, saying, "God's will be done."[5]

2 And so, when he heard them come in, he came downstairs and talked with them; and those who were there were astonished at how old and composed he was, and they wondered why there was so much haste to arrest an old man like him. Straight away he ordered them to be given everything they wanted to eat and drink, then and there. And he asked them for an hour to pray without being disturbed.

3 When they gave their permission, he stood and prayed, being so filled with God's grace that for two hours he could not be silent. Those who heard him were amazed, and many of them regretted coming out for such a godly old man.

8 Then he finished his prayer, having remembered everyone he had ever met, both small and great, reputable and disreputable, as well as the entire universal church throughout the world; and when it came time for him to leave, they seated him on a donkey and led him into the city. It was a great Sabbath.[6]

2 The chief of police Herod, along with his father Nicetas, met him and transferred him to their carriage. Sitting on either side, they were trying to persuade him, saying, "Why is it so wrong to save yourself by saying 'Caesar is Lord,' making a sacrifice, and so on?" He did not answer them at first; but when they persisted, he said, "I am not about to do what you advise."

3 Having failed to persuade him, they began speaking horrible words and hastily shoved him out, so that when he came down out of the carriage he scraped his shin. But he did not turn around, but quickly walked on in haste as if he had not been hurt. And he was led into the stadium, where there was such an uproar that no one could be heard.

9 But as he entered the stadium a voice came to Polycarp from heaven: "Be strong, Polycarp, and be a man *[Or: be courageous]*."[7] No one saw who had spoken, but those among our people who were there heard the voice. Finally, when he was brought forward, there was a great uproar among those who heard that Polycarp had been arrested. When he was brought forward the proconsul asked if he was Polycarp. When he said he was, the proconsul began trying to persuade him to make a denial, saying, "Have respect for your age," along with other related things they customarily say: "Swear by the Fortune of Caesar, repent, and say 'Away with the atheists.'" But Polycarp looked with a stern face at the entire crowd of lawless Gentiles in the stadium; and gesturing to them with his hand, he sighed, looked up to heaven, and said, "Away with the atheists."

3 The proconsul became more insistent and said, "Take the oath and I will release you. Revile Christ." But Polycarp responded, "For eighty-six years I have served him, and he has done me no wrong. How can I blaspheme my king who has saved me?"

10 When the proconsul persisted and said, "Swear by the Fortune of Caesar," Polycarp answered, "If you are so foolish as to think that I will swear by the Fortune of Caesar, as you say, and if you pretend not to know who I am, listen closely: I am a Christian. But if you wish to learn an account of Christianity, appoint a day and listen."

2 The proconsul replied, "Persuade the people." Polycarp said, "I think you deserve an account, for we are taught to render all due honor to rulers and authorities appointed by God,[8] in so far as it does us no harm. But as to those, I do not consider them worthy to hear a reasoned defense."

---

4 Matt 26:55. The Day of Preparation is Friday.

5 Acts 21:14; cf. Luke 22:42, Matt 6:10.

6 Cf. John 19:31.

7 Josh 1.6.

8 Rom 13:1; 1 Pet 2:13.

11 The proconsul said, "I have wild beasts, and I will cast you to them if you do not repent." He replied, "Call them! For it is impossible for us to repent from better to worse; it is good, though, to change from what is wicked to what is right."

2 Again the proconsul said to him, "If you despise the wild beasts, I will have you consumed by fire, if you do not repent." Polycarp replied, "You threaten with a fire that burns for an hour and after a short while is extinguished; for you do not know about the fire of the coming judgment and eternal torment, reserved for the ungodly. But why are you waiting? Bring on what you wish."

12 While he was saying these and many other things, he was filled with courage and joy, and his face was full of grace, so that not only did he not collapse to the ground from being unnerved at what he heard, but on the contrary, the proconsul was amazed and sent his herald into the center of the stadium to proclaim three times, "Polycarp has confessed himself to be a Christian."

2 When the herald said this, the entire multitude of both Gentiles and Jews who lived in Smyrna cried out with uncontrollable rage and a great voice, "This is the teacher of impiety, the father of the Christians, the destroyer of our own gods, the one who teaches many not to sacrifice or worship the gods." Saying these things, they began calling out to Philip, the Asiarch, asking him to release a lion on Polycarp. But he said that he could not do so, since he had already concluded the animal hunts.

3 Then they decided to call out in unison for him to burn Polycarp alive. For the vision that had been revealed about the pillow had to be fulfilled; for he had seen it burning while he prayed. And when he turned he said prophetically to the faithful who were with him, "I must be burned alive."

13 These things then happened with incredible speed, quicker than can be described. The crowds immediately gathered together wood and kindling from the workplaces and the baths, with the Jews proving especially eager to assist, as is their custom.

2 When the pyre was prepared, Polycarp laid aside all his garments and loosened his belt. He was also trying to undo his sandals, even though he was not accustomed to do so, since each of the faithful was always eager to do it, to see who could touch his skin most quickly. For he was adorned with every good thing because of his exemplary way of life, even before he bore his testimony unto death.

3 Immediately the instruments prepared for the pyre were placed around him. When they were about to nail him, he said, "Leave me as I am; for the one who enables me to endure the fire will also enable me to remain in the pyre without moving, even without the security of your nails."

14 So they did not nail him, but they tied him. And when he placed his hands behind his back and was tied, he was like an exceptional ram taken from a great flock for a sacrifice, prepared as a whole burnt offering that is acceptable to God. Looking up into heaven he said, "Lord God Almighty, Father of your beloved and blessed child Jesus Christ, through whom we have received knowledge of you, the God of angels, of powers, and of all creation, and of every race of the upright who live before you,

2 I bless you for making me worthy of this day and hour, that I may receive a share among the number of the martyrs in the cup of your Christ, unto the resurrection of eternal life in both soul and body in the immortality of the Holy Spirit. Among them may I be received before you today as a sacrifice that is rich and acceptable, just as you prepared and revealed in advance and now fulfilled—the true God who does not lie.

3 For this reason and for all things I praise you, I bless you, I glorify you through the eternal and heavenly high priest Jesus Christ, your beloved child, through whom be glory to you, with him and the Holy Spirit, both now and for the ages to come. Amen."

15 When he sent up the "Amen" and finished the prayer, the men in charge of the fire touched it off. And as a great flame blazoned forth we beheld a marvel—we to whom it was granted to see, who have also been preserved to report the events to the others.

2 For the fire, taking on the appearance of a vaulted room, like a boat's sail filled with the wind, formed a wall around the martyr's body. And he was in the center, not like burning flesh but like baking bread or like gold and silver being refined in a furnace. And we perceived a particularly sweet aroma, like wafting incense or some other precious perfume.

16 Finally, when the lawless ones saw that his body could not be consumed by the fire, they ordered an executioner to go up and stab him with a dagger. When he did so, a dove came forth, along with such a quantity of blood that it extinguished the fire, striking the entire crowd with amazement that there could be so much difference between the unbelievers and the elect.

2 One of the latter was this most astounding Polycarp, who in our time was an apostolic and prophetic teacher and bishop of the universal church in Smyrna. For every word that came forth from his mouth was fulfilled and will be fulfilled.

17 But the jealous and envious Evil One, the enemy of the race of the upright, having seen the greatness of Polycarp's death as a martyr and the irreproachable way of life that he had from the beginning—and that he had received the crown of immortality and was awarded with the incontestable prize—made certain that his poor body was not taken away by us, even though many were desiring to do so and to have a share in [Or: to commune with; or: to have fellowship with] his holy flesh.

2 So he incited Nicetas, the father of Herod and brother of Alce, to petition the magistrate not to hand over his body, "Lest," he said, "they desert the one who was crucified and begin to worship this one." The Jews instigated and strongly urged these things, and kept watch when we were about to take him from the fire. For they did not realize that we are never able to abandon Christ, who suffered for the salvation of the entire world of those who are being saved, the one who was blameless for sinners; nor are we able to worship any other.

3 For we worship this one who is the Son of God, but we love the martyrs as disciples and imitators of the Lord. And they are worthy, because of their unsurpassable affection for their own king and teacher. May we also become partners and fellow disciples with them!

18 When the centurion saw the contentiousness caused by the Jews, he placed Polycarp's body in the center and burned it, as is their custom.

2 And so, afterwards, we removed his bones, which were more valuable than expensive gems and more precious than gold, and put them in a suitable place.

3 There, whenever we can gather together in joy and happiness, the Lord will allow us to commemorate the birthday of his martyrdom, both in memory of those who have already engaged in the struggle and as a training and preparation for those who are about to do so.

19 Such are the matters pertaining to the blessed Polycarp, who along with those from Philadelphia was the twelfth martyr in Smyrna; but he alone is remembered by all, discussed even by the outsiders in every place. For he was not only an exceptional teacher but also a superb martyr. Everyone longs to imitate his martyrdom, since it occurred in conformity with the gospel of Christ.

2 Through endurance he overcame the unjust ruler and thus received the crown of immortality. And now he rejoices together with the apostles and all those who are upright, and he glorifies God the Father and blesses our Lord Jesus Christ, the savior of our souls, pilot of our bodies, and shepherd of the universal church throughout the world.

20 You had asked for a lengthier explanation of what took place, but for the present we have mentioned only the principal points through our brother Marcion. When you have learned these things, send our letter to the brothers who are further afield, that they may also glorify the Lord who selects his chosen ones from among his own slaves.

2 And now to the one who is able to lead us all by his grace and gift into his eternal kingdom, through his child, the unique one, Jesus Christ, be the glory, honor, power, and greatness forever. Greet all the saints. Those who are with us greet you, as does Evaristus, the one who is writing the letter, with his entire household.

21 But the blessed Polycarp bore his witness unto death on the second day of the new month of Xanthikos, February 23, on a great Sabbath, at 2:00 in the afternoon. But he was arrested by Herod while Philip of Tralles was high priest, Statius Quadratus was proconsul, and Jesus Christ was ruling as king forever. To him be the glory, honor, greatness, and eternal throne, from one generation to the next. Amen.

22 We bid you farewell, brothers, you who conduct yourselves in the word of Jesus Christ according to the gospel; with him be glory to God, both Father and Holy Spirit *[Or: God, and the Father, and the Holy Spirit]*, for the salvation of his holy chosen ones, just as the blessed Polycarp bore witness unto death. May we be found to have followed in his footsteps in the kingdom of Jesus Christ!

2 Gaius transcribed these things from the papers of Irenaeus, a disciple of Polycarp; he also lived in the same city as Irenaeus. And I, Socrates, have written these things in Corinth from the copies made by Gaius. May grace be with everyone.

3 And I, Pionius, then sought out these things and produced a copy from the one mentioned above, in accordance with a revelation of the blessed Polycarp, who showed it to me, as I will explain in what follows. And I gathered these papers together when they were nearly worn out by age, so that the Lord Jesus Christ may gather

me together with his chosen ones into his heavenly kingdom. To him be the glory with the Father and Holy Spirit forever and ever. Amen.

Another Epilogue, From the Moscow Manuscript

Gaius transcribed these things from the writings of Irenaeus; he also lived in the same city with Irenaeus, a disciple of the holy Polycarp.

2 For this Irenaeus was in Rome when the bishop Polycarp was martyred, and he taught many people. And many of his writings—which are excellent and supremely true—are in circulation; in them he remembers Polycarp, because he studied under him. He powerfully refuted every heresy and passed on the ecclesiastical and universal rule of faith, as he received it from the holy one.

3 He also says that Marcion, from whom come those who are called Marcionites, once met the holy Polycarp and said, "You need to recognize us, Polycarp." But he then replied to Marcion, "I do recognize you—I recognize the firstborn of Satan!"

4 This also its found in the writings of Irenaeus that on the day and hour that Polycarp was martyred in Smyrna, Irenaeus, who was in the city of the Romans, heard a voice like a trumpet saying, "Polycarp has been martyred."

5 And so, as was indicated before, Gaius made a transcription from the writings of Irenaeus, as Isocrates did, in Corinth, from the copies of Gaius. And then I, Pionius, wrote a copy from those of Isocrates, in accordance with a revelation of the holy Polycarp, after seeking out these writings and gathering them together when they were nearly worn out by age, so that the Lord Jesus Christ may gather me together with his chosen ones into his heavenly kingdom. To him be the glory, with the Father and the Son and Holy Spirit, forever and ever. Amen.

7. The Letter of the Churches of Lyons and Vienne

A major persecution erupted in 177 CE in the towns of Lyons and Vienne (in Gaul; modern France) during the reign of the emperor Marcus Aurelius, who sanctioned the proceedings. The surviving account was written by Christians who managed to escape, who saw the hand of the Devil behind the brutalities. The persecution started with widespread social antagonism against the Christians (as they were banned from public places), erupted into mob violence, and ended in governmental intervention and official prosecution. Those confessing to be Christian were imprisoned and subjected to horrific tortures, explicitly designed to make them apostatize. Those who did so were then released. Most of those arrested, however, remained true to their convictions, displaying remarkable zeal in their loyalty to one another and to their God, claiming that despite the rumors of wrongdoing they had done nothing to deserve punishment and insisting that the torments of the present were not at all to be compared with the fire that burns forever.

The servants of Christ at Vienne and Lyons in Gaul to our brothers in Asia and Phrygia who have the same faith and hope of redemption as we: peace, grace, and glory from God the Father and Christ Jesus our Lord.

The severity of our trials here, the unbridled fury of the heathen against God's people, the untold sufferings of the blessed martyrs, we are incapable of describing in detail: indeed no pen could do them justice. The adversary swooped on us with all his might, giving us now a foretaste of his advent, which undoubtedly is imminent. He left no stone unturned in his efforts to train his adherents and equip them to attack the servants of God, so that not only were we debarred from houses, baths, and the forum: they actually forbade any of us to be seen in any place whatever. But against them the grace of God put itself at our head, rescuing the weak and deploying against our enemies unshakeable pillars, able by their endurance to draw upon themselves the whole onslaught of the evil one. These charged into the fight, standing up to every kind of abuse and punishment, and made light of their heavy load as they hastened to Christ, proving beyond a doubt that the sufferings of the present time are not to be compared with the glory that is in store for us.

To begin with, they heroically endured whatever the surging crowd heaped on them, noisy abuse, blows, dragging along the ground, plundering, stoning, imprisonment, and everything that an infuriated mob normally does to hated enemies. Then they were marched into the forum and interrogated by the tribune and the city authorities before the whole population. When they confessed Christ, they were locked up in jail to await the governor's arrival. Later, when they were taken before him and he treated them with all the cruelty he reserves for Christians, Vettius Epagathus, one of our number, full of love towards God and towards

The Letter of the Churches of Vienne and Lyons, from *Eusebius: The History of the Church from Christ to Constantine,* trans. G. A. Williamson, rev. Andrew Louth (Penguin Classic 965, rev. ed. 1989) copyright © G. A. Williamson, 1965. Revisions copyright © Andrew Louth, 1989. Used with permission.

his neighbor, came forward. His life conformed so closely to the Christian ideal that, young as he was, the same tribute might be paid to him as to old Zacharias: he had scrupulously observed all the commandments and ordinances of the Lord, and was untiring in service to his neighbor, utterly devoted to God and fervent in spirit. As such he found the judgment so unreasonably given against us more than he could bear: boiling with indignation, he applied for permission to speak in defence of the Christians, and to prove that there was nothing godless or irreligious in our society. The crowd round the tribunal howled him down, as he was a man of influence, and the governor dismissed his perfectly reasonable application with the curt question: "Are *you* a Christian?" In the clearest possible tones Vettius replied: "I am." And he, too, was admitted to the ranks of the martyrs. He was called the Christians' advocate, but he had in himself the Advocate, the Spirit that filled Zacharias, as he showed by the fullness of his love when he gladly laid down his own life in defence of his brother Christians. For he was and is a true disciple of Christ, following the Lamb wherever he goes.

Then the rest fell into two groups. It was clear that some were ready to be the first Gallic martyrs: they made a full confession of their testimony with the greatest eagerness. It was equally clear that others were not ready, that they had not trained and were still flabby, in no fit condition to face the strain of a struggle to the death. Of these some ten proved stillborn, causing us great distress and inexpressible grief, and damping the enthusiasm of those not yet arrested. However, in spite of the agonies they were suffering, these people stayed with the martyrs and did not desert them. But at the time we were all tormented by the doubts about their confessing Christ: we were not afraid of the punishments inflicted, but looking to the outcome and dreading lest anyone might fall away. But the arrests went on, and day after day those who were worthy filled up the number of the martyrs, so that from the two dioceses were collected all the active members who had done most to build up our church life. Among those arrested were some of our heathen domestics, as the governor had publicly announced that we were to be hunted out. These were ensnared by Satan, so that fearing the tortures which they saw inflicted on God's people, at the soldiers' instigation they falsely accused us of Thyestean banquets and Oedipean incest, and things we ought never to speak or think about, or even believe that such things ever happened among human beings. When these rumors spread, people all raged like wild beasts against us, so that even those who because of blood-relationship had previously exercised restraint now turned on us, grinding their teeth with fury. So was proved true the saying of our Lord: "The time will come when whoever kills you will think he is doing a service to God."[1] From then on the holy martyrs endured punishments beyond all description, while Satan strove to wring even from them some of the slanders.

The whole fury of crowd, governor, and soldiers fell with crushing force on Sanctus, the deacon from Vienne; on Maturus, very recently baptized but heroic in facing his ordeal; on Attalus, who had always been a pillar and support of the church in his native Pergamum; and on Blandina, through whom Christ proved that things which men regard as mean, unlovely, and contemptible are by God deemed worthy of great glory, because of her love for him shown in power and not vaunted in appearance. When we were all afraid, and her earthly mistress (who was herself facing the ordeal of martyrdom) was in agony lest she should be unable even to make a bold confession of Christ because of bodily weakness, Blandina was filled with such power that those who took it in turns to subject her to every kind of torture from morning to night were exhausted by their efforts and confessed themselves beaten—they could think of nothing else to do to her. They were amazed that she was still breathing, for her whole body was mangled and her wounds

---

1 John 16:2.

gaped; they declared that torment of any one kind was enough to part soul and body, let alone a succession of torments of such extreme severity. But the blessed woman, wrestling magnificently, grew in strength as she proclaimed her faith, and found refreshment, rest, and insensibility to her sufferings in uttering the words: "I am a Christian: we do nothing to be ashamed of."

Sanctus was another who with magnificent, superhuman courage nobly withstood the entire range of human cruelty. Wicked people hoped that the persistence and severity of his tortures would force him to utter something improper, but with such determination did he stand up to their onslaughts that he would not tell them his own name, race, and birthplace, or whether he was a slave or free; to every question he replied in Latin: "I am a Christian." This he proclaimed over and over again, instead of name, birthplace, nationality, and everything else, and not another word did the heathen hear from him. Consequently, the governor and his torturers strained every nerve against him, so that when they could think of nothing else to do to him they ended by pressing red-hot copper plates against the most sensitive parts of his body. These were burning, but Sanctus remained unbending and unyielding, firm in his confession of faith, bedewed and fortified by the heavenly fountain of the water of life that flows from the depths of Christ's being. But his poor body was a witness to what he had suffered—it was all one wound and bruise, bent up and robbed of outward human shape, but, suffering in that body, Christ accomplished most glorious things, utterly defeating the adversary and proving as an example to the rest that where the Father's love is nothing can frighten us, where Christ's glory is nothing can hurt us. A few days later wicked people again put the martyr on the rack, thinking that now that his whole body was swollen and inflamed a further application of the same instruments would defeat him, unable as he was to bear even the touch of a hand; or that by dying under torture he would put fear into the rest. However, nothing of the sort happened: to their amazement

his body became erect and straight as a result of these new torments, and recovered its former appearance and the use of the limbs; thus through the grace of Christ his second spell on the rack proved to be not punishment but cure.

Biblis again, one of those who had denied Christ, was handed over to punishment by the devil, who imagined that he had already devoured her and hoped to damn her as a slanderer by forcing her to say wicked things about us, being— so he thought—a feeble creature, easily broken. But on the rack she came to her senses, and, so to speak, awoke out of deep sleep, reminded by the brief chastisement of the eternal punishment in hell. She flatly contradicted the slanderers: "How could children be eaten by people who are not even allowed to eat the blood of brute beasts?" From then on she insisted that she was a Christian, and so she joined the ranks of the martyrs.

When the tyrant's instruments of torture had been utterly defeated by Christ through the endurance of the blessed saints, the devil resorted to other devices—confinement in the darkness of a filthy prison; clamping the feet in the stocks, stretched apart to the fifth hole; and other agonies which warders when angry and full of the devil are apt to inflict on helpless prisoners. Thus the majority were suffocated in prison—those whom the Lord wished to depart in this way, so revealing His glory. Some, though tortured so cruelly that even if they received every care it seemed impossible for them to survive, lived on in the prison, deprived of all human attention but strengthened by the Lord and fortified in body and soul, stimulating and encouraging the rest. But the young ones who had been recently arrested and had not previously undergone physical torture could not bear the burden of confinement and died in prison.

Blessed Pothinus, who had been entrusted with the care of the Lyons diocese, was over ninety years of age and physically very weak. He could scarcely breathe because of his chronic physical weakness, but was strengthened by spiritual enthusiasm because of his pressing desire for martyrdom. Even he was dragged before the tribunal, and though his body was feeble from age and disease, his life was preserved in him, that thereby Christ might triumph. He was conveyed to the tribunal by the soldiers, accompanied by the civil authorities and the whole populace, who shouted and jeered at him as though he were Christ himself. But he bore the noble witness. When the governor asked him "Who is the Christians' god?", he replied: "If you are a fit person, you shall know." Thereupon he was mercilessly dragged along beneath a rain of blows, those close by assailing him viciously with hands and feet and showing no respect for his age, and those at a distance hurling at him whatever came to hand, and all thinking it a shocking neglect of their duty to be behind-hand in savagery towards him, for they imagined that in this way they would avenge their gods. Scarcely breathing, he was flung into prison, and two days later he passed away.

Then occurred a great dispensation of God, and the infinite mercy of Jesus was revealed to a degree rarely known in the brotherhood of Christians, but not beyond the skill of Christ. Those who when the first arrests took place had denied him were jailed with the others and shared their sufferings: on this occasion they gained nothing by their denial, for whereas those who declared what they were were jailed as Christians, no other charge being brought against them, the others were further detained as foul murderers and punished twice as much as the rest. For the faithful were relieved of half their burden by the joy of martyrdom and hope of the promises, and by love towards Christ and the Spirit of the Father, but the unfaithful were tormented by their conscience, so that as they passed they could easily be picked out from the rest by the look on their faces. The faithful stepped out with a happy smile, wondrous glory and grace blended on their faces, so that even their fetters hung like beautiful ornaments around them and they resembled a bride adorned with golden lace elaborately wrought; they were perfumed also with the sweet savour of Christ, so that some people thought they had smeared themselves with worldly cosmetics. The unfaithful were

dejected, downcast, ill-favoured, and devoid of charm; in addition they were gibed at by the heathen as contemptible cowards; they were accused of homicide, and had lost the honorable, glorious, life-giving name. The sight of this stiffened the resistance of the rest: those who were arrested unhesitatingly declared their faith without one thought for the devil's promptings. . . .

From that time on, their martyrdoms embraced death in all its forms. From flowers of every shape and color they wove a crown to offer to the Father; and so it was fitting that the valiant champions should endure an everchanging conflict, and having triumphed gloriously should win the mighty crown of immortality. Maturus, Sanctus, Blandina, and Attalus were taken into the amphitheater to face the wild beasts, and to furnish open proof of the inhumanity of the heathen, the day of fighting wild beasts being purposely arranged for our people. There, before the eyes of all, Maturus and Sanctus were again taken through the whole series of punishments, as if they had suffered nothing at all before, or rather as if they had already defeated their opponents in bout after bout and were now battling for the victor's crown. Again they ran the gauntlet of whips, in accordance with local custom; they were mauled by the beasts, and endured every torment that the frenzied mob on one side or the other demanded and howled for, culminating in the iron chair which roasted their flesh and suffocated them with the reek. Not even then were their tormentors satisfied: they grew more and more frenzied in their desire to overwhelm the resistance of the martyrs, but do what they might they heard nothing from Sanctus beyond the words he had repeated from the beginning—the declaration of his faith.

In these two, despite their prolonged and terrible ordeal, life still lingered; but in the end they were sacrificed, after being made all day long a spectacle to the world in place of the gladiatorial contest in its many forms. But Blandina was hung on a post and exposed as food for the wild beasts let loose in the arena. She looked as if she were hanging in the form of a cross, and through her ardent prayers she stimulated great enthusiasm in those undergoing their ordeal, who in their agony saw with their outward eyes in the person of their sister the One who was crucified for them, that he might convince those who believe in him that any man who has suffered for the glory of Christ has fellowship forever with the living God. As none of the beasts had yet touched her she was taken down from the post and returned to the jail, to be kept for a second ordeal, that by victory in further contests she might make irrevocable the sentence passed on the crooked serpent, and spur on her brother Christians—a small, weak, despised woman who had put on Christ, the great invincible champion, and in bout after bout had defeated her adversary and through conflict had won the crown of immortality.

Attalus too was loudly demanded by the mob, as he was a man of note. He strode in, ready for the fray, in the strength of a clear conscience, for he had trained hard in the school of Christ and had been one of our constant witnesses to the truth. He was led round the amphitheater preceded by a placard on which was written in Latin "This is Attalus the Christian," while the people were bursting with fury against him. But when the governor was informed that he was a Roman, he ordered him to be put back in jail with the others, about whom he had written to Caesar and was awaiting instructions.

Their time of respite was not idle or unfruitful: through their endurance the infinite mercy of Christ was revealed; for through the living the dead were being brought back to life; and martyrs were bestowing grace on those who had failed to be martyrs, and there was great joy in the heart of the Virgin Mother, who was receiving her stillborn children back alive; for by their means most of those who had denied their Master travelled once more the same road, conceived and quickened a second time, and learned to confess Christ. Alive now and braced up, their ordeal sweetened by God, who does not desire the death of the sinner but is gracious towards repentance, they

advanced to the tribunal to be again interrogated by the governor. For Caesar had issued a command that they should be tortured to death, but any who still denied Christ should be released; so at the inauguration of the local festival, at which all the heathen congregate in vast numbers, the governor summoned them to his tribunal, making a theatrical show of the blessed ones and displaying them to the crowds. After re-examination, all who seemed to possess Roman citizenship were beheaded and the rest sent to the beasts. Christ was greatly glorified in those who had previously denied him but now confounded heathen expectation by confessing him. They were individually examined with the intention that they should be released, but they confessed him and so joined the ranks of the martyrs. Left outside were those who had never had any vestige of faith or notion of the wedding-garment or thought of the fear of God, but by their very conduct brought the Way into disrepute—truly the sons of perdition. But the rest were all added to the Church. . . .

To crown all this, on the last day of the sports Blandina was again brought in, and with her Ponticus, a lad of about fifteen. Day after day they had been taken in to watch the rest being punished, and attempts were made to make them swear by the heathen idols. When they stood firm and treated these efforts with contempt, the mob was infuriated with them, so that the boy's tender age called forth no pity and the woman no respect. They subjected them to every horror and inflicted every punishment in turn, attempting again and again to make them swear, but to no purpose. Ponticus was encouraged by his sister in Christ, so that the heathen saw that she was urging him on and stiffening his resistance, and he bravely endured every punishment till he gave back his spirit to God. Last of all, like a noble mother who had encouraged her children and sent them before her in triumph to the King, blessed Blandina herself passed through all the ordeals of her children and hastened to rejoin them, rejoicing and exulting at her departure as if invited to a wedding supper, not thrown to the beasts. After the whips, after the beasts, after the griddle, she was finally dropped into a basket and thrown to a bull. Time after time the animal tossed her, but she was indifferent now to all that happened to her, because of her hope and sure hold on all that her faith meant, and of her communing with Christ. Then she, too, was sacrificed, while the heathen themselves admitted that never yet had they known a woman suffer so much or so long.

Not even this was enough to satisfy their insane cruelty to God's people. Goaded by a wild beast, wild and barbarous tribes were incapable of stopping, and the dead bodies became the next object of their vindictiveness. Their defeat did not humble them, because they were without human understanding; rather it inflamed their bestial fury, and governor and people vented on us the same inexcusable hatred, so fulfilling the scripture. "Let the wicked man be wicked still, the righteous man righteous still."[2] Those who had been suffocated in jail they threw to the dogs, watching carefully night and day to see that no one received the last offices at our hands. Then they threw out the remains left by the beasts and the fire, some torn to ribbons, some burnt to cinders, and set a military guard to watch for days on end the trunks and severed heads of the rest,

denying burial to them also. Some raged and ground their teeth at them, longing to take some further revenge on them; others laughed and jeered, magnifying their idols and giving them credit for the punishment of their enemies; while those who were more reasonable, and seemed to have a little human feeling, exclaimed with the utmost scorn: "Where is their god? and what did they get for their religion, which they preferred to their own lives?" Such were their varied reactions, while we were greatly distressed by our inability to give the bodies burial. Darkness did not make it possible, and they refused all offers of payment and were deaf to entreaty; but they guarded the remains with the greatest care, regarding it as a triumph if they could prevent burial . . .

Thus the martyrs' bodies, after six days' exposure to every kind of insult and to the open sky, were finally burnt to ashes and swept by these wicked men into the Rhône which flows near by, that not even a trace of them might be seen on the earth again. And this they did as if they could defeat God and rob the dead of their rebirth, "in order," they said, "that they may have no hope of resurrection—the belief that has led them to bring into this country a new foreign cult and treat torture with contempt, going willingly and cheerfully to their death. Now let's see if they'll rise again, and if their god can help them and save them from our hands."

---

2 Rev 22:11.

8. The Acts of the Scillitan Martyrs

The oldest Christian document to survive from North Africa, the Latin account of the Scillitan Martyrs provides an actual trial narrative of twelve Christians in Carthage under the proconsul Saturninus in the year 180 CE. The account is remarkable for showing both the firm resolve of the prisoners, who refuse to countenance any form of compromise, and the sincere attempts of the magistrate to convince them of the folly of their ways and to make a simple act of worship of the divine spirit (genius) of the emperor. Refusing to bow under pressure, the twelve are condemned to death and immediately taken out and beheaded.

In the consulship of Praesens (for the second time) and Claudian, on the seventeenth day of July there were arraigned at Carthage in the governor's chambers Speratus, Nartzalus, Cittinus, [Veturius, Felix, Aquilinus, Laetantius, Januaria, Generosa,][1] Donata, Secunda, and Vestia.

The proconsul Saturninus said: "If you return to your senses, you can obtain the pardon of our lord the emperor."

Speratus said: "We have never done wrong; we have never lent ourselves to wickedness. Never have we uttered a curse; but when abused, we have given thanks, for we hold our own emperor in honor."

Saturninus the proconsul said: "We too are a religious people, and our religion is a simple one: we swear by the genius of our lord the emperor and we offer prayers for his health—as you also ought to do."

Speratus said: "If you will give me a calm hearing, I shall tell you the mystery of simplicity."

"If you begin to malign our sacred rites," said Saturninus, "I shall not listen to you. But swear rather by the genius of our lord the emperor."

Speratus said: "I do not recognize the empire of this world. Rather, I serve that God whom no one has seen, nor can see, with these eyes. I have not stolen; and on any purchase I pay the tax, for I acknowledge my lord who is the emperor of kings and of all nations."

The proconsul Saturninus said to the others: "Cease to be of this persuasion."

Speratus said: "It is an evil persuasion to commit murder, to bear false witness."

Saturninus the proconsul said: "Have no part in this folly of his!"

Cittinus said: "We have no one else to fear but our Lord God who is in heaven."

Donata said: "Pay honor to Caesar as Caesar: but it is God we fear."

Vestia said: "I am a Christian."

Secunda said: "I wish to be what I am."

---

1 The list here, which gives only six of the martyrs instead of the twelve who are executed (in § 16), seems to have been accidentally shortened in the manuscripts.

The Acts of the Scillitan Martyrs, from *The Acts of the Christian Martyrs,* trans. Herbert Musurillo. © Oxford University Press, 1972. Reprinted by permission of Oxford University Press.

The proconsul Saturninus said to Speratus: "Do you persist in remaining a Christian?"

Speratus said: "I am a Christian." And all agreed with him.

Saturninus the proconsul said: "You wish no time for consideration?"

Speratus said: "In so just a matter there is no need for consideration."

The proconsul Saturninus said: "What have you in your case?"

Speratus said: "Books and letters of a just man named Paul."

The proconsul Saturninus said: "You are granted a reprieve of thirty days: think it over."

Once again Speratus said, "I am a Christian!" And with him all the others agreed.

Saturninus the proconsul read his decision from a tablet: "Whereas Speratus, Nartzalus, Cittinus, Donata, Vestia, Secunda, and the others have confessed that they have been living in accordance with the rites of the Christians, and whereas though given the opportunity to return to the usage of the Romans they have persevered in their obstinacy, they are hereby condemned to be executed by the sword."

Speratus said: "We thank God!"

Nartzalus said: "Today we are martyrs in heaven. Thanks be to God!"

The proconsul Saturninus had the following proclaimed by a herald: "Sperata, Nartzalus, Cittinus, Veturius, Felix, Aquilinus, Laetantius, Januaria, Generosa, Vestia, Donata, Secunda, are to be led forth to execution."

They all said: "Thanks be to God!" And straightway they were beheaded for the name of Christ.

9. The Martyrdom of Perpetua and Felicitas

An account filled with gripping pathos, "The Martyrdom of Perpetua and Felicitas" records the arrest, imprisonment, trials, and execution of a young Roman matron, Perpetua, and her female slave, Felicitas. Remarkably, the first part of the account claims to be based on Perpetua's own diary, kept while she was in prison and edited by the anonymous author who provided the concluding story of the martyrdom itself. The action takes place in Carthage in 202–203 CE, during the reign of the emperor Septimius Severus. Among the notable features of the report are (a) Perpetua's familial relations, especially with her infant child whom she must relinquish, her anguished (non-Christian) father who begs her to relent, and her dead brother whom she sees twice in dreams; (b) her vivid night visions, which she narrates as divine predictions of her fate but which also reveal a good deal about her understanding of the world and her own internal struggles; and (c) the explicit details of her prison life and, especially, of the martyrdom she endures along with her slave, Felicitas, who herself has just recently given birth.

The Martyrdom of Perpetua and Felicitas, from *The Acts of the Christian Martyrs*, trans. Herbert Musurillo. © Oxford University Press, 1972. Reprinted by permission of Oxford University Press.

1 The deeds recounted about the faith in ancient times were a proof of God's favor and achieved the spiritual strengthening of people as well; and they were set forth in writing precisely that honor might be rendered to God and comfort to people by the recollection of the past through the written word. Should not then more recent examples be set down that contribute equally to both ends? For indeed these too will one day become ancient and needful for the ages to come, even though in our own day they may enjoy less prestige because of the prior claim of antiquity.

Let those then who would restrict the power of the one Spirit to times and seasons look to this: the more recent events should be considered the greater, being later than those of old, and this is a consequence of the extraordinary graces promised for the last stage of time. For "in the last days, God declares, I will pour out my Spirit upon all flesh and their sons and daughters shall prophesy and on my manservants and my maidservants I will pour my Spirit and the young men shall see visions and the old men shall dream dreams."[1] So too we hold in honor and acknowledge not only new prophecies but new visions as well, according to the promise. And we consider all the other functions of the Holy Spirit as intended for the good of the Church; for the same Spirit has been sent to distribute all his gifts to all, as the Lord apportions to everyone. For this reason we deem it imperative to set them forth and to make them known through the word for the glory of God. Thus no one of weak or despairing faith may think that supernatural grace was present only among men of ancient times, either in the grace of martyrdom or of visions, for God always achieves what he promises, as a witness to the nonbeliever and a blessing to the faithful.

And so, my brethren and little children, that which we have heard and have touched with our hands we proclaim also to you, so that those of you that were witnesses may recall the glory of the Lord and those that now learn of it through hearing may

have fellowship with the holy martyrs and, through them, with the Lord Christ Jesus, to whom belong splendor and honor for all ages. Amen.

2 A number of young catechumens were arrested, Revocatus and his fellow slave Felicitas, Saturninus and Secundulus, and with them Vibia Perpetua, a newly married woman of good family and upbringing. Her mother and father were still alive and one of her two brothers was a catechumen like herself. She was about twenty-two years old and had an infant son at the breast. (Now from this point on the entire account of her ordeal is her own, according to her own ideas and in the way that she herself wrote it down.)

3 While we were still under arrest (she said) my father out of love for me was trying to persuade me and shake my resolution. "Father," said I, "do you see this vase here, for example, or waterpot or whatever?"

"Yes, I do," said he.

And I told him: "Could it be called by any other name than what it is?"

And he said: "No."

"Well, so too I cannot be called anything other than what I am, a Christian."

At this my father was so angered by the word "Christian" that he moved towards me as though he would pluck my eyes out. But he left it at that and departed, vanquished along with his diabolical arguments.

For a few days afterwards I gave thanks to the Lord that I was separated from my father, and I was comforted by his absence. During these few days I was baptized, and I was inspired by the Spirit not to ask for any other favor after the water but simply the perseverance of the flesh. A few days later we were lodged in the prison; and I was terrified, as I had never before been in such a dark hole. What a difficult time it was! With the crowd the heat was stifling; then there was the extortion of the soldiers; and to crown all, I was tortured with worry for my baby there.

---

1 Acts 2:17–18.

Then Tertius and Pomponius, those blessed deacons who tried to take care of us, bribed the soldiers to allow us to go to a better part of the prison to refresh ourselves for a few hours. Everyone then left that dungeon and shifted for himself. I nursed my baby, who was faint from hunger. In my anxiety I spoke to my mother about the child, I tried to comfort my brother, and I gave the child in their charge. I was in pain because I saw them suffering out of pity for me. These were the trials I had to endure for many days. Then I got permission for my baby to stay with me in prison. At once I recovered my health, relieved as I was of my worry and anxiety over the child. My prison had suddenly become a palace, so that I wanted to be there rather than anywhere else.

4 Then my brother said to me: "Dear sister, you are greatly privileged; surely you might ask for a vision to discover whether you are to be condemned or freed."

Faithfully I promised that I would, for I knew that I could speak with the Lord, whose great blessings I had come to experience. And so I said: "I shall tell you tomorrow." Then I made my request and this was the vision I had.

I saw a ladder of tremendous height made of bronze, reaching all the way to the heavens, but it was so narrow that only one person could climb up at a time. To the sides of the ladder were attached all sorts of metal weapons: there were swords, spears, hooks, daggers, and spikes; so that if anyone tried to climb up carelessly or without paying attention, he would be mangled and his flesh would adhere to the weapons.

At the foot of the ladder lay a dragon of enormous size, and it would attack those who tried to climb up and try to terrify them from doing so. And Saturus was the first to go up, he who was later to give himself up of his own accord. He had been the builder of our strength, although he was not present when we were arrested. And he arrived at the top of the staircase and he looked back and said to me: "Perpetua, I am waiting for you. But take care; do not let the dragon bite you."

"He will not harm me," I said, "in the name of Christ Jesus."

Slowly, as though he were afraid of me, the dragon stuck his head out from underneath the ladder. Then, using it as my first step, I trod on his head and went up.

Then I saw an immense garden, and in it a grey-haired man sat in shepherd's garb; tall he was, and milking sheep. And standing around him were many thousands of people clad in white garments. He raised his head, looked at me, and said: "I am glad you have come, my child."

He called me over to him and gave me, as it were, a mouthful of the milk he was drawing; and I took it into my cupped hands and consumed it. And all those who stood around said: "Amen!" At the sound of this word I came to, with the taste of something sweet still in my mouth. I at once told this to my brother, and we realized that we would have to suffer, and that from now on we would no longer have any hope in this life.

5 A few days later there was a rumor that we were going to be given a hearing. My father also arrived from the city, worn with worry, and he came to see me with the idea of persuading me.

"Daughter," he said, "have pity on my grey head—have pity on me your father, if I deserve to be called your father, if I have favored you above all your brothers, if I have raised you to reach this prime of your life. Do not abandon me to be the reproach of others. Think of your brothers, think of your mother and your aunt, think of your child, who will not be able to live once you are gone. Give up your pride! You will destroy all of us! None of us will ever be able to speak freely again if anything happens to you."

This was the way my father spoke out of love for me, kissing my hands and throwing himself down before me. With tears in his eyes he no longer addressed me as his daughter but as a woman. I was sorry for my father's sake, because he alone of all my kin would be unhappy to see me suffer.

I tried to comfort him saying: "It will all happen in the prisoner's dock as God wills; for you may be sure that we are not left to ourselves but are all in his power."

And he left me in great sorrow.

6 One day while we were eating breakfast we were suddenly hurried off for a hearing. We arrived at the forum, and straight away the story went about the neighborhood near the forum and a huge crowd gathered. We walked up to the prisoner's dock. All the others when questioned admitted their guilt. Then, when it came my turn, my father appeared with my son, dragged me from the step, and said: "Perform the sacrifice—have pity on your baby!"

Hilarianus the governor, who had received his judicial powers as the successor of the late proconsul Minucius Timinianus, said to me: "Have pity on your father's grey head; have pity on your infant son. Offer the sacrifice for the welfare of the emperors."

"I will not," I retorted.

"Are you a Christian?" said Hilarianus.

And I said: "Yes, I am."

When my father persisted in trying to dissuade me, Hilarianus ordered him to be thrown to the ground and beaten with a rod. I felt sorry for father, just as if I myself had been beaten. I felt sorry for his pathetic old age.

Then Hilarianus passed sentence on all of us: we were condemned to the beasts, and we returned to prison in high spirits. But my baby had got used to being nursed at the breast and to staying with me in prison. So I sent the deacon Pomponius straight away to my father to ask for the baby. But father refused to give him over. But as God willed, the baby had no further desire for the breast, nor did I suffer any inflammation; and so I was relieved of any anxiety for my child and of any discomfort in my breasts.

7 Some days later when we were all at prayer, suddenly while praying I spoke out and uttered the name Dinocrates. I was surprised; for the name had never entered my mind until that moment. And I was pained when I recalled what had happened to him. At once I realized that I was privileged to pray for him. I began to pray for him and to sigh deeply for him before the Lord. That very night I had the following vision. I saw Dinocrates come out of a dark hole, where there were many others with him, very hot and thirsty, pale and dirty. On his face was the wound he had when he died.

Now Dinocrates had been my brother according to the flesh; but he had died horribly of cancer of the face when he was seven years old, and his death was a source of loathing to everyone. Thus it was for him that I made my prayer. There was a great abyss between us: neither could approach the other. Where Dinocrates stood there was a pool full of water; and its rim was higher than the child's height, so that Dinocrates had to stretch himself up to drink. I was sorry that, though the pool had water in it, Dinocrates could not drink because of the height of the rim. Then I woke up, realizing that my brother was suffering. But I was confident that I could help him in his trouble; and I prayed for him every day until we were transferred to the military prison. For we were supposed to fight with the beasts at the military games to be held on the occasion of the emperor Geta's birthday. And I prayed for my brother day and night with tears and sighs that this favor might be granted me.

8 On the day we were kept in chains, I had this vision shown to me. I saw the same spot that I had seen before, but there was Dinocrates all clean, well dressed, and refreshed. I saw a scar where the wound had been; and the pool I had seen before now had its rim lowered to the level of the child's waist. And Dinocrates kept drinking water from it, and there above the rim was a golden bowl full of water. And Dinocrates drew close and began to drink from it, and yet the bowl

remained full. And when he had drunk enough of the water, he began to play as children do. Then I awoke, and I realized that he had been delivered from his suffering.

9 Some days later, an adjutant named Pudens, who was in charge of the prison, began to show us great honor, realizing that we possessed some great power within us. And he began to allow many visitors to see us for our mutual comfort.

Now the day of the contest was approaching, and my father came to see me overwhelmed with sorrow. He started tearing the hairs from his beard and threw them on the ground; he then threw himself on the ground and began to curse his old age and to say such words as would move all creation. I felt sorry for his unhappy old age.

10 The day before we were to fight with the beasts I saw the following vision. Pomponius the deacon came to the prison gates and began to knock violently. I went out and opened the gate for him. He was dressed in an unbelted white tunic, wearing elaborate sandals. And he said to me: "Perpetua, come; we are waiting for you."

Then he took my hand and we began to walk through rough and broken country. At last we came to the amphitheater out of breath, and he led me into the center of the arena.

Then he told me: "Do not be afraid. I am here, struggling with you." Then he left.

I looked at the enormous crowd who watched in astonishment. I was surprised that no beasts were let loose on me; for I knew that I was condemned to die by the beasts. Then out came an Egyptian against me, of vicious appearance, together with his seconds, to fight with me. There also came up to me some handsome young men to be my seconds and assistants.

My clothes were stripped off, and suddenly I was a man. My seconds began to rub me down with oil (as they are wont to do before a contest). Then I saw the Egyptian on the other side rolling in the dust. Next there came forth a man of

marvellous stature, such that he rose above the top of the amphitheater. He was clad in a beltless purple tunic with two stripes (one on either side) running down the middle of his chest. He wore sandals that were wondrously made of gold and silver, and he carried a wand like an athletic trainer and a green branch on which there were golden apples.

And he asked for silence and said: "If this Egyptian defeats her he will slay her with the sword. But if she defeats him, she will receive this branch." Then he withdrew.

We drew close to one another and began to let our fists fly. My opponent tried to get hold of my feet, but I kept striking him in the face with the heels of my feet. Then I was raised up into the air and I began to pummel him without as it were touching the ground. Then when I noticed there was a lull, I put my two hands together linking the fingers of one hand with those of the other and thus I got hold of his head. He fell flat on his face and I stepped on his head.

The crowd began to shout and my assistants started to sing psalms. Then I walked up to the trainer and took the branch. He kissed me and said to me: "Peace be with you, my daughter!" I began to walk in triumph towards the Gate of Life. Then I awoke. I realized that it was not with wild animals that I would fight but with the Devil, but I knew that I would win the victory. So much for what I did up until the eve of the contest. About what happened at the contest itself, let him write of it who will.

11 But the blessed Saturus has also made known his own vision and he has written it out with his own hand. We had died, he said, and had put off the flesh, and we began to be carried towards the east by four angels who did not touch us with their hands. But we moved along not on our backs facing upwards but as though we were climbing up a gentle hill. And when we were free of the world, we first saw an intense light. And I said to Perpetua (for she was at my

side): "This is what the Lord promised us. We have received his promise."

While we were being carried by these four angels, a great open space appeared, which seemed to be a garden, with rose bushes and all manner of flowers. The trees were as tall as cypresses, and their leaves were constantly falling. In the garden there were four other angels more splendid than the others. When they saw us they paid us homage and said to the other angels in admiration: "Why, they are here! They are here!"

Then the four angels that were carrying us grew fearful and set us down. Then we walked across to an open area by way of a broad road, and there we met Jucundus, Saturninus, and Artaxius, who were burnt alive in the same persecution, together with Quintus who had actually died as a martyr in prison. We asked them where they had been. And the other angels said to us: "First come and enter and greet the Lord."

12 Then we came to a place whose walls seemed to be constructed of light. And in front of the gate stood four angels, who entered in and put on white robes. We also entered and we heard the sound of voices in unison chanting endlessly: "Holy, holy, holy!" In the same place we seemed to see an aged man with white hair and a youthful face, though we did not see his feet. On his right and left were four elders, and behind them stood other aged men. Surprised, we entered and stood before a throne: four angels lifted us up and we kissed the aged man and he touched our faces with his hand. And the elders said to us: "Let us rise." And we rose and gave the kiss of peace. Then the elders said to us: "Go and play."

To Perpetua I said: "Your wish is granted."

She said to me: "Thanks be to God that I am happier here now than I was in the flesh."

13 Then we went out and before the gates we saw the bishop Optatus on the right and Aspasius the presbyter and teacher on the left, each of them far apart and in sorrow. They threw themselves at our feet and said: "Make peace

between us. For you have gone away and left us thus."

And we said to them: "Are you not our bishop, and are you not our presbyter? How can you fall at our feet?"

We were very moved and embraced them. Perpetua then began to speak with them in Greek, and we drew them apart into the garden under a rose arbor.

While we were talking with them, the angels said to them: "Allow them to rest. Settle whatever quarrels you have among yourselves." And they were put to confusion.

Then they said to Optatus: "You must scold your flock. They approach you as though they had come from the games, quarreling about the different teams."

And it seemed as though they wanted to close the gates. And there we began to recognize many of our brethren, martyrs among them. All of us were sustained by a most delicious odor that seemed to satisfy us. And then I woke up happy.

14 Such were the remarkable visions of these martyrs, Saturus and Perpetua, written by themselves. As for Secundulus, God called him from this world earlier than the others while he was still in prison, by a special grace that he might not have to face the animals. Yet his flesh, if not his spirit, knew the sword.

15 As for Felicitas, she too enjoyed the Lord's favor in this wise. She had been pregnant when she was arrested, and was now in her eighth month. As the day of the spectacle drew near she was very distressed that her martyrdom would be postponed because of her pregnancy; for it is against the law for women with child to be executed. Thus she might have to shed her holy, innocent blood afterwards along with others who were common criminals. Her comrades in martyrdom were also saddened; for they were afraid that they would have to leave behind so fine a companion to travel alone on the same road to hope. And so, two days before the contest, they poured forth a prayer to the Lord in one torrent of common grief. And immediately after their prayer the birth pains came upon her. She suffered a good deal in her labor because of the natural difficulty of an eight months' delivery.

Hence one of the assistants of the prison guards said to her: "You suffer so much now—what will you do when you are tossed to the beasts? Little did you think of them when you refused to sacrifice."

"What I am suffering now," she replied, "I suffer by myself. But then another will be inside me who will suffer for me, just as I shall be suffering for him."

And she gave birth to a girl; and one of the sisters brought her up as her own daughter.

16 Therefore, since the Holy Spirit has permitted the story of this contest to be written down and by so permitting has willed it, we shall carry out the command or, indeed, the commission of the most saintly Perpetua, however unworthy I might be to add anything to this glorious story. At the same time I shall add one example of her perseverance and nobility of soul.

The military tribune had treated them with extraordinary severity because on the information of certain very foolish people he became afraid that they would be spirited out of the prison by magical spells.

Perpetua spoke to him directly. "Why can you not even allow us to refresh ourselves properly? For we are the most distinguished of the condemned prisoners, seeing that we belong to the emperor; we are to fight on his very birthday. Would it not be to your credit if we were brought forth on the day in a healthier condition?"

The officer became disturbed and grew red. So it was that he gave the order that they were to be more humanely treated; and he allowed her brothers and other persons to visit, so that the prisoners could dine in their company. By this time the adjutant who was head of the jail was himself a Christian.

17 On the day before, when they had their last meal, which is called the free banquet, they celebrated not a banquet but rather a love feast. They spoke to the mob with the same steadfastness, warned them of God's judgment, stressing the joy they would have in their suffering, and ridiculing the curiosity of those that came to see them. Saturus said: "Will not tomorrow be enough for you? Why are you so eager to see something that you dislike? Our friends today will be our enemies on the morrow. But take careful note of what we look like so that you will recognize us on the day." Thus everyone would depart from the prison in amazement, and many of them began to believe.

18 The day of their victory dawned, and they marched from the prison to the amphitheater joyfully as though they were going to heaven with calm faces, trembling, if at all, with joy rather than fear. Perpetua went along with shining countenance and calm step, as the beloved of God, as a wife of Christ, putting down everyone's stare by her own intense gaze. With them also was Felicitas, glad that she had safely given birth so that now she could fight the beasts, going from one blood bath to another, from the midwife to the gladiator, ready to wash after childbirth in a second baptism.

They were then led up to the gates and the men were forced to put on the robes of priests of Saturn, the women the dress of the priestesses of Ceres. But the noble Perpetua strenuously resisted this to the end.

"We came to this of our own free will, that our freedom should not be violated. We agreed to pledge our lives provided that we would do no such thing. You agreed with us to do this."

Even injustice recognized justice. The military tribune agreed. They were to be brought into the arena just as they were. Perpetua then began to sing a psalm: she was already treading on the head of the Egyptian. Revocatus, Saturninus, and Saturus began to warn the onlooking mob. Then when they came within sight of Hilarianus, they suggested by their notions and gestures: "You have condemned us, but God will condemn you" was what they were saying.

At this the crowds became enraged and demanded that they be scourged before a line of gladiators. And they rejoiced at this that they had obtained a share in the Lord's sufferings.

19 But he who said, "Ask and you shall receive,"[2] answered their prayer by giving each one the death he had asked for. For whenever they would discuss among themselves their desire for martyrdom, Saturninus indeed insisted that he wanted to be exposed to all the different beasts, that his crown might be all the more glorious. And so at the outset of the contest he and Revocatus were matched with a leopard, and then while in the stocks they were attacked by a bear.

As for Saturus, he dreaded nothing more than a bear, and he counted on being killed by one bite of a leopard. Then he was matched with a wild boar; but the gladiator who had tied him to the animal was gored by the boar and died a few days after the contest, whereas Saturus was only dragged along. Then when he was bound in the stocks awaiting the bear, the animal refused to come out of the cages, so that Saturus was called back once more unhurt.

20 For the young women, however, the Devil had prepared a mad heifer. This was an unusual animal, but it was chosen that their sex might be matched with that of the beast. So they were stripped naked, placed in nets, and thus brought out into the arena. Even the crowd was horrified when they saw that one was a delicate young girl and the other was a woman fresh from childbirth with the milk still dripping from her breasts. And so they were brought back again and dressed in unbelted tunics.

First the heifer tossed Perpetua and she fell on her back. Then sitting up she pulled down the tunic that was ripped along the side so that it covered her thighs, thinking more of her modesty

than of her pain. Next she asked for a pin to fasten her untidy hair: for it was not right that a martyr should die with her hair in disorder, lest she might seem to be mourning in her hour of triumph.

Then she got up. And seeing that Felicitas had been crushed to the ground, she went over to her, gave her her hand, and lifted her up. Then the two stood side by side. But the cruelty of the mob was by now appeased, and so they were called back through the Gate of Life.

There Perpetua was held up by a man named Rusticus who was at the time a catechumen and kept close to her. She awoke from a kind of sleep (so absorbed had she been in ecstasy in the Spirit) and she began to look about her. Then to the amazement of all she said: "When are we going to be thrown to that heifer or whatever it is?"

When told that this had already happened, she refused to believe it until she noticed the marks of her rough experience on her person and her dress. Then she called for her brother and spoke to him together with the catechumens and said: "You must all stand fast in the faith and love one another, and do not be weakened by what we have gone through."

21 At another gate Saturus was earnestly addressing the soldier Pudens. "It is exactly," he said, "as I foretold and predicted. So far not one animal has touched me. So now you may believe me with all your heart: I am going in there and I shall be finished off with one bite of the leopard." And immediately as the contest was coming to a close a leopard was let loose, and after one bite Saturus was so drenched with blood that as he came away the mob roared in witness to his second baptism: "Well washed! Well washed!" For well washed indeed was one who had been bathed in this manner.

Then he said to the soldier Pudens: "Goodbye. Remember me, and remember the faith. These things should not disturb you but rather strengthen you."

And with this he asked Pudens for a ring from his finger, and dipping it into his wound he gave it back to him again as a pledge and as a record of his bloodshed.

2 John 16:24.

Shortly after he was thrown unconscious with the rest in the usual spot to have his throat cut. But the mob asked that their bodies be brought out into the open that their eyes might be the guilty witnesses of the sword that pierced their flesh. And so the martyrs got up and went to the spot of their own accord as the people wanted them to, and kissing one another they sealed their martyrdom with the ritual kiss of peace. The others took the sword in silence and without moving, especially Saturus, who being the first to climb the stairway was the first to die. For once again he was waiting for Perpetua. Perpetua, however, had yet to taste more pain. She screamed as she was struck on the bone; then she took the trembling hand of the young gladiator and guided it to her throat. It was as though so great a woman, feared as she was by the unclean spirit, could not be dispatched unless she herself were willing.

Ah, most valiant and blessed martyrs! Truly are you called and chosen for the glory of Christ Jesus our Lord! And any one who exalts, honors, and worships his glory should read for the consolation of the Church these new deeds of heroism which are no less significant than the tales of old. For these new manifestations of virtue will bear witness to one and the same Spirit who still operates, and to God the Father almighty, to his Son Jesus Christ our Lord, to whom is splendor and immeasurable power for all the ages. Amen.

4

The Defense of Christianity

Pagan Antagonists and Christian Apologists

When Christians came under attack by their opponents—whether non-Christian Jews or pagans, whether families, friends, mobs, or governmental officials—they naturally had to defend themselves. In the Greek language spoken throughout the Roman empire, the term for "defense" is *apologia*. An "apology," in this context, does not mean saying "I'm sorry"; it means mounting a reasoned defense. An apologist is therefore a defender of a religious or philosophical point of view.

From the earliest times, Christians were involved in apologetics: within the New Testament, the book of 1 Peter urges its readers to "be prepared always to make a defense (literally: an apology) to anyone who asks you a reason for the hope in you" (3:15), and in the last part of the book of Acts, the apostle Paul is repeatedly put on trial and made to defend his beliefs and actions. Many scholars have suspected that the book of Acts itself is a kind of literary apology, written to a Roman administrator named Theophilus (1:1) precisely to show that Christians are socially innocuous and should therefore not be persecuted.

By the middle of the second century, attacks began to be leveled against the Christians by highly educated pagan authors who had studied the religion and its sacred texts. These attacks were smart and incisive. These authors attacked the ethical behavior of the Christians, found numerous problems with their sacred writings, mocked the life and person of Jesus, and generally leveled an assault on all that Christians held to be near and dear. A selection of these learned pagan attacks is included here (Celsus and Porphyry).

At about the same time, well-trained and educated apologists began to appear among the ranks of the Christians, intellectuals such as Justin in Rome, Athenagoras in Athens, Tertullian in Carthage, and Origen in Alexandria. These individuals were themselves fine scholars who were able to mount intellectual arguments to establish the innocence of Christians and, even more, to assert the superiority of the Christian religion over other Greco-Roman cults, including Judaism. It is difficult to know how much these scholarly defenses represent the views of the common Christian, from whom we have no surviving testimony (except in quotations preserved by the literary elite among them); most Christians, like most other people in the ancient world, could neither read nor write. But these surviving works do give us a sense of how intellectuals beginning to join the Christian movement understood and argued for its religious superiority.

In their defense of Christianity against the standard charges brought against it, the early apologists replayed several themes time and again. Against the charge that Christians were "atheists," they insisted that Christians alone worshipped the true creator God who is superior to every other divine being (including the pagan deities, who were alleged to be wicked demons); against the charge that Christians were wildly promiscuous, the apologists pointed to Jesus' teachings in the Sermon on the Mount, where believers are instructed not only to behave morally but to remain pure even in their thoughts; to the charge of ritual cannibalism, they argued that Christians did not even allow abortions or the exposure of infants (common practices throughout the empire); to the charge that they were withdrawn from the social and civic life of their communities, they replied that the Christians' high morality improved society and preserved it from the wrath of God; to the charge that they refused to worship the emperor and to embrace the cause of the empire, they noted that they prayed for the well-being of the state and its ruler.

The apologists were never content, however, simply to mount a defense against charges. They were also determined to prove the absolute superiority of their Christian views. To do so, they sometimes went on the attack, maligning other religions for worshipping gods that were portrayed in the pagan myths themselves as wild, capricious, and sexually immoral, and mocking the wide varieties and (in their Christian eyes) mutually exclusive views of the pagan cults.

In addition, they were quick to adduce proofs for the Christian message. For the most part, these proofs were built on assumptions that were widely held in the ancient world, for example, that for a religion or philosophy to be "true" it had to be ancient (how could something be "true" if no one believed it before?). On the one hand, this assumption created a problem for Christian apologists since they (and everyone else) knew that Jesus had lived relatively recently. But the apologists claimed that the religion founded on Jesus was much, much older, that in fact Jesus fulfilled the promises made to Moses and the Jewish prophets centuries before, as evident in everything from Jesus' virgin birth in Bethlehem to his death, resurrection, and ascension. Thus, for them, Christianity was not a new thing; it was quite ancient—older even than the oldest Greek philosophies and cults, since Moses lived 800 years before Plato (the great philosopher) and 400 years before Homer and Hesiod (sources for the Greek stories about the gods). In addition, the apologists claimed, the greater antiquity of Christianity explains why so many of the things Jesus did and experienced (his supernatural birth, miracles, ascent to heaven, etc.) were similarly attributed to figures in Greek and Roman myths: ancient pagan writers gleaned stories from Moses and applied them to their own heroes!

The constant insistence that Jesus fulfilled ancient prophecy relates to another weapon in the apologists' arsenal, the claim that divine miracles vindicate the truthfulness of the Christian religion. No mere human could have performed the supernatural acts of Jesus, faithfully recorded by his followers; Jesus was clearly the Son of God. And the miracles did not cease with his departure; his apostles also performed wonders in his name. According to some of the apologists, miracles continued to occur down to their own time. On occasion, the apologists challenged their readers to bring forth anyone who was demon-possessed and watch the person be healed in the name of Jesus.

Finally, the Christian apologists appealed on humanitarian grounds to the rulers of the empire to put a halt to their senseless suffering. They maintained that since Christians harm no one, they should be allowed to worship in any way they see fit—in effect, that there should be a separation between the powers of a government and the religious observances of its people. This notion of the separation of church and state never did catch on in the ancient world, where most people believed that matters of the gods were concerns of public policy. Eventually Christians too came to share this view, especially after the emperors themselves converted to the faith and became more than willing to use their political, economic, and military power to promote the Christian cause.

Even though the apologists addressed their writings to their opponents (especially to the Roman emperors), it is generally thought that their books were principally designed for internal consumption among the Christians as a way to buttress their faith and strengthen their resolve, and possibly to provide them with the ammunition they needed to fight off the attacks of their public adversaries.

For Further Reading

Chadwick, Henry. *Early Christian Thought and the Classical Tradition: Studies in Justin, Clement and Origen*. New York: Oxford University Press, 1965.

Droge, Arthur J. *Moses or Homer: Early Christian Interpretations of the History of Culture*. Tübingen Mohr/Siebeck, 1989.

Edwards, Mark, Martin Goodman, and Simon Price, eds. *Apologetics in the Roman Empire: Pagans, Jews, and Christians*. Oxford: Oxford University Press, 1999.

Fiorenza, Elizabeth Schüssler. *Aspects of Religious Propaganda in Judaism and Early Christianity*. Notre Dame: Notre Dame University Press, 1976.

Gallagher, Eugene. *Divine Man or Magician? Celsus and Origen on Jesus*. Chico, CA: Scholars Press, 1982.

Grant, Robert, M. *Greek Apologists of the Second Century*. Philadelphia: Westminster Press, 1988.

Nasrallah, Laura. *Christian Responses to Roman Art and Architecture: The Second Century Church Amid the Spaces of Empire*. Cambridge: Cambridge University Press, 2012.

Parvis, Sarah and Paul Foster, eds. *Justin Martyr and His Worlds*. Minneapolis: Fortress Press, 2007.

Wilken, Robert. *The Christians as the Romans Saw Them*. New Haven: Yale University, 1984.

The Texts

Pagan Assaults on Christianity

10. Minucius Felix: Octavius

Even though the "Octavius" is a Christian text, it preserves a vivid account of the accusations made against Christians by their pagan opponents throughout the second and third centuries. The author of the book is Minucius Felix, a Christian intellectual originally from North Africa, who appears to have practiced law in Rome during the early part of the third century. This is his only surviving work.

It is allegedly a firsthand account, in Latin, of a day-long discussion beside the sea in which one of the author's friends, the Christian Octavius, addresses the hostile arguments of another, the pagan Caecilius, and finally convinces him of the superiority of the Christian religion. The portion excerpted here comes from Caecilius's opening statement, in which he (a) praises the Romans for their serious devotion to religion and their respect for ancient sacred practices, and (b) levels the charges commonly made against Christians for their repudiation of the Roman gods, their flagrant immorality, and their senseless adherence to an ineffectual religion.

Chapter 6

1 "Thus [claimed Caecilius] we have either Fortune, whose character we know, or Nature, whose character we do not know. In that case, you [Christians], hierophants of truth, would surely show greater reverence—and hence be better advised—if you embraced the system taught by your ancestors, if you worshipped according to traditional practice, if the gods you adored were those whom your parents trained you as children first to fear—only later might you get to know them more intimately. You would be better advised if you did not pronounce any opinion of your own on deities; you should, rather, trust your forbears who in a still uncultured age at the very infancy of the world were blessed with gods who were propitious—or their kings.

"And this is precisely the explanation why right throughout all empires, provinces, and towns, we observe that individual groups have their native rites and rituals and worship their local gods. For example, the Eleusinians have Ceres, the Phrygians the Great Mother Goddess, the Epidaurians Aesculapius, the Chaldaeans Baal, the Syrians Astarte, the Taurians Diana, the Gauls Mercury, and the Romans have them all.

2 "As a result, the power and sway of the Romans has encompassed the entire circuit of the globe, it has spread its domain beyond the paths of the sun, the very bounds of Ocean. And this is so because they have been plying arms with religious

The Octavius of Minucius Felix, from *The Octavius of Marcus Minucius Felix,* ed. G. W. Clarke. Mahwah, NJ: Paulist Press, 1974. Used by permission of Paulist Press.

valor, fortifying their city with religious rituals, with the chastity of their virgins, and with the many dignities and titles they grant their priests. When, for example, they had been taken by siege and captured all but for the Capitol, they still worshiped their gods—and gods whom anyone else would by that time have rejected as angered with them; the Romans astounded the Gauls with their intrepid piety—they moved through their battle ranks unprotected by weapons save for the arms of their religious observances.

"Even though the Romans have stood on the enemies' ramparts which they have captured, still flushed with victory, they have persisted in respecting the divinities they conquered; from every quarter they have continued to seek gods to be their guests, to make them their own, to erect altars even to unknown deities and to the shades of the dead.

3 "By adopting the rites of all nations in this way, they have won their empires as well. And to this day there has been no pause in the unending reverence they show; indeed, it has been strengthened rather than impaired with the long passage of time; for, as a general rule, the greater the age that ceremonies and shrines accumulate, the more hallowed these institutions become with their accruing years.

Chapter 7

1 "At this stage I might venture myself to concede a point—and to err in better company. It was not, I would claim, without sound reasons that our forebears zealously strove to watch auguries, consult entrails, establish rituals, and dedicate sanctuaries.

2 "Consider what you read in our chronicles. You readily discover why they introduced every manner of religious ritual; it was to repay divine favor, to avert impending wrath, or to placate the actual rage and fury of the gods.

Chapter 8

1 "And so the conclusion I draw is that while the origin and nature of the immortal gods may still remain obscure, there nevertheless continues to be unhesitating agreement from all nations about their existence. This religious belief is so venerable, so beneficial, and so salutary; and I cannot therefore tolerate that anyone in the arrogance of his irreligious 'enlightenment' should have the effrontery to try to weaken or destroy it. . . .

"In view of this, is it not an absolute scandal—you will allow me, I hope, to be rather forthright about the strong feelings I have for my case—is it not scandalous that the gods should be mobbed by a gang of outlawed and reckless desperadoes?

4 "They have collected from the lowest possible dregs of society the more ignorant fools together with gullible women (readily persuaded, as is their weak sex); they have thus formed a rabble of blasphemous conspirators, who with nocturnal assemblies, periodic fasts, and inhuman feasts seal their pact not with some religious ritual but with desecrating profanation; they are a crowd that furtively lurks in hiding places, shunning the light; they are speechless in public but gabble away in corners.

"They despise our temples as being no more than sepulchres, they spit after our gods, they sneer at our rites, and, fantastic though it is, our priests they pity—pitiable themselves; they scorn the purple robes of public office, though they go about in rags themselves.

5 "How amazingly stupid, unbelievably insolent they are. Tortures of the present they scoff at, but they live in dread of the uncertain tortures of the future; they are afraid to die after they are dead, but meantime they have no fear of death. So effectively are they beguiled of alarm by the comforting expectation of a renewal of life hereafter.

Chapter 9

1 "Evil weeds grow apace and so, day by day, this depraved way of life now creeps further over all the face of the globe and the foul religious shrines of this abominable congregation are getting a stronger hold. This confederacy must be torn out, it must be sworn to perdition.

2 "They recognize each other by secret marks and signs; hardly have they met when they love each other, throughout the world uniting in the practice of a veritable religion of lusts. Indiscriminately they call each other brother and sister, thus turning even ordinary fornication into incest by the intervention of these hallowed names. Such a pride does this foolish, deranged superstition take in its wickedness.

3 "Unless there were some underlying truth, such a wide variety of charges, and very serious ones, would not be made about them; they can hardly be repeated in polite company. Rumor is a shrewd informant. I hear, for example, that they do reverence to the head of that most degraded of beasts, an ass; I cannot imagine what absurdity has persuaded them to consecrate it, but it is indeed a cult born of such morals and well suited for them.

4 "It is also reported that they worship the genitals of their pontiff and priest, adoring, it appears, the sex of their 'father.' Perhaps this is incorrect but it certainly is a suspicion that befits their clandestine and nocturnal ceremonies. There are also stories about the objects of their veneration: they are said to be a man who was punished with death as a criminal and the fell wood of his cross, thus providing suitable liturgy for the depraved fiends: they worship what they deserve.

5 "To turn to another point. The notoriety of the stories told of the initiation of new recruits is matched by their ghastly horror. A young baby is covered over with flour, the object being to deceive the unwary. It is then served before the person to be admitted into their rites. The recruit is urged to inflict blows onto it—they appear to be harmless because of the covering of flour. Thus the baby is killed with wounds that remain unseen and concealed. It is the blood of this infant—I shudder to mention it—it is this blood that they lick with thirsty lips; these are the limbs they distribute eagerly; this is the victim by which they seal their covenant; it is by complicity in this crime that they are pledged to mutual silence; these are their rites, more foul than all sacrileges combined.

6 "We all know, too, about their banquets; they are on everyone's lips, everywhere as the speech of our Cirtensian testifies. On a special day they gather for a feast with all their children, sisters, mothers—all sexes and all ages. There, flushed with the banquet after such feasting and drinking, they begin to burn with incestuous passions. They provoke a dog tied to the lampstand to leap and bound towards a scrap of food which they have tossed outside the reach of his chain.

7 "By this means the light is overturned and extinguished, and with it common knowledge of their actions; in the shameless dark with unspeakable lust they copulate in random unions, all equally being guilty of incest, some by deed, but everyone by complicity. For whatever may happen in individual cases is the general aspiration and desire of them all.

Chapter 10

1 "I am deliberately passing over a number of points—those that I have already given are more than enough; and that all of them, or practically all, are true is revealed by the very obscurity which shrouds this perverted religion.

2 "Why else should they go to such pains to hide and conceal whatever it is they worship? One is always happy for honorable actions to be made public; crimes are kept secret. Why do they have no altars, no temples, no publicly-known images? Why do they never speak in the open, why do they always assemble in stealth? It must be that whatever it is they worship—and suppress—is deserving either of punishment or of shame.

3 "Furthermore, who is this unique god of theirs, what is his origin, where does he live, so solitary, so totally forlorn that no free nation has knowledge of him, nor any empire—not even the religious fanatics of Rome?

4 "The only other group to have worshipped one god is the wretched tribe of the Jews, but they did so in the open, with temples and altars, with sacrifice and ceremonial. But you can see that this god has neither power nor strength; he and his very own people are captives of the Romans, who are but humans. . . .

Chapter 12

2 "Look: some of you, the greater half (the better half, you say), go in need, suffer from cold, from hunger and toil. And yet your god allows it, he connives at it; he will not or he cannot assist his own followers. This proves how weak he is—or wicked.

3 "You have dreams of posthumous immortality, but when you quake in the face of danger, when you burn with fever or are racked by pain, are you still unaware of your real condition? Do you still not recognize your human frailty? Poor wretch, whether you like it or not, you have proof of your own infirmity, and still you will not admit it!

4 "But these evils, common to us all, I omit. Look: you Christians are menaced with threats, torments and tortures, with crosses—meant not this time to be adored but endured—and with fire

as well, just as you foretell and fear. And where is that god of yours who can help those who come to life again, but cannot help those who are alive?

5 "Is it not true that without the help of your god Rome has her dominions and empire, she has the whole world to enjoy, and she has you as well beneath her sway?

"But in the meantime, in your anxious state of expectation, you refrain from honest pleasures: you do not go to our shows, you take no part in our processions, you are not present at our public banquets, you shrink in horror from our sacred games, from food ritually dedicated by our priests, from drink hallowed by libation poured upon our altars. Such is your dread of the very gods you deny.

6 "You do not bind your head with flowers, you do not honor your body with perfumes; ointments you reserve for funerals, but even to your tombs you deny garlands; you anemic, neurotic creatures, you indeed deserve to be pitied—but by our gods. The result is, you pitiable fools, that you have no enjoyment of life while you wait for the new life which you will never have."

11. Celsus

The pagan philosopher Celsus was one of the most vociferous adversaries of Christianity. Unfortunately, his writing *The True Word*—like the writings of all the early intellectual opponents of the new faith—has not survived intact from antiquity. In this case, however, we are fortunate that lengthy and reliable quotations from it are preserved in the writings of a third-century Christian apologist, Origen (see selection 17), who cited Celsus's attacks in order to refute them.

Celsus was a conservative supporter of the pagan religious status quo, who believed that traditional pagan religions were both true and beneficial for society and the state. Christianity was not only dangerous, however; it was also inherently implausible, wrong-headed, and foolish. Among other things, Christians worshiped a low-life crucified criminal as a God. The absurdity of the religion was matched only by the

The True Word, reproduced from Celsus, in *On the True Doctrine: A Discourse Against the Christians*, tr. R. Joseph Hoffmann. New York: Oxford University Press, 1987. Used with permission of Oxford University Press.

ignorance of its followers—illiterate riff-raff from among the peasants, for the most part, who were opposed to intelligence, learning, and philosophy.

Origen, who is our only source of knowledge of Celsus, thought that he was an Epicurean philosopher. Modern analysis has shown that instead he was an adherent of Platonic thinking (with some influence from Stoicism). It is usually thought that *The True Word* was written in the final quarter of the second century, possibly around the time of the persecution against Christians in Gaul, as recorded in the Letter of Vienne and Lyons in 177 CE (see selection 7).

The True Word

The cult of Christ is a secret society whose members huddle together in corners for fear of being brought to trial and punishment. Their persistence is the persistence of a group threatened by a common danger, and danger is a more powerful incentive to fraternal feeling than is any oath. As to their doctrine, it was originally barbarian, and while even barbarians are capable of discovering truth, it happens to be the case that Greeks are best equipped to judge the merit of what passes for truth these days. They also practice their rites in secret in order to avoid the sentence of death that looms over them. There is nothing new or impressive about their ethical teaching; indeed, when one compares it to other philosophies, their simple-mindedness becomes apparent. Take their aversion to what they term idolatry. As Herodotus shows, the Persians long before our time held the view that things made with human hands cannot be regarded as gods. Indeed, it is preposterous that the work of a craftsman (often the worst sort of person!) should be considered a god. The wise Heracleitus says that "those who worship images as gods are as foolish as men who talk to the walls."

The Christians claim to get some sort of power from pronouncing the names of demons or saying certain incantations, always incorporating the name Jesus and a short story about him in the formula. Even this practice is old stuff: Jesus himself was thought to work wonders by the use of magic and incantations. He knew that others would follow him in these practices, yet he seems to have expelled those who did from his society. Perhaps this is the origin of the hypocrisy for which the Christians are so well known: Was he right to drive them away for copying him? Being guilty of magic himself he had no reason to accuse others, nor could they be accounted bad men for following their leader.

More and more the myths put about by these Christians are better known than the doctrines of the philosophers. Who has not heard the fable of Jesus' birth from a virgin or the stories of his crucifixion and resurrection? And for these fables the Christians are ready to die—indeed do die. Now I would not want to say that a man who got into trouble because of some eccentric belief should have to renounce his belief or pretend that he has renounced it. But the point is this, and the Christians would do well to heed it: One ought first to follow reason as a guide before accepting any belief, since anyone who believes without testing a doctrine is certain to be deceived. We have plenty of examples in our own time: the snivelling beggars of Cybele, the soothsayers, the worshippers of Mithras and Sabazius; those gullible believers in the apparitions of Hecate, and assorted other gods. Just as the charlatans of the cults take advantage of a simpleton's lack of education to lead him around by the nose, so too with the Christian teachers: they do not want to give or to receive reasons for what they believe. Their favorite expressions are "Do not ask questions, just believe!" and: "Your faith will save you!" "The wisdom of this world," they say, "is evil; to be simple is to be good." If only they would undertake to answer my question—which I do not ask as one who is trying to understand their beliefs (there being little to understand!). But they refuse to answer, and indeed discourage asking questions of any sort. For this reason I have undertaken to compose a treatise for their edification, so that they can see for themselves the true character of the doctrines they have chosen to embrace and the true sources of their opinions.

I shall take up the matter of the Jewish doctrines in due course. First, however, I must deal with the matter of Jesus, the so-called savior, who not long ago taught new doctrines and was thought to be a son of God. This savior, I shall attempt to show, deceived many and caused them to accept a form of belief harmful to the wellbeing of mankind. Taking its root in the lower classes, the religion continues to spread among the vulgar: nay, one can even say it spreads because of its vulgarity and the illiteracy of its adherents. And while there are a few moderate, reasonable, and intelligent people who are inclined to interpret its beliefs allegorically, yet it thrives in its purer form among the ignorant.

Let us imagine what a Jew—let alone a philosopher—might put to Jesus: "Is it not true, good sir, that you fabricated the story of your birth from a virgin to quiet rumours about the true and unsavory circumstances of your origins? Is it not the case that far from being born in royal David's city of Bethlehem, you were born in a poor country town, and of a woman who earned her living by spinning? Is it not the case that when her deceit was discovered, to wit, that she was pregnant by a Roman soldier named Panthera she was driven away by her husband—the carpenter—and convicted of adultery? Indeed, is it not so that in her disgrace, wandering far from home, she gave birth to a male child in silence and humiliation? What more? Is it not so that you hired yourself out as a workman in Egypt, learned magical crafts, and gained something of a name for yourself which now you flaunt among your kinsmen?"

What absurdity! Clearly the Christians have used the myths of the Danae and the Melanippe, or of the Auge and the Antiope in fabricating the story of Jesus' virgin birth. A beautiful woman must his mother have been, that this Most High God should want to have intercourse with her! An interesting point in itself, since if, as their philosophers (copying ours) say, God by nature does not love corruptible bodies, he cannot love a woman. Are we to think that this high God would have fallen in love with a woman of no breeding—one unknown and unregarded even by her neighbors? Odd that the kingdom of God, the core of their teaching, is made to hang on the disgrace of a rejected woman, whose husband turned her aside. Let us pursue further the questions put to this Jesus by the Jew: "When you were bathing in the Jordan near John, I understand you saw what looked like a bird fly towards you out of the air. Now let me understand what witnesses saw this wondrous event. And I should be most eager to know who heard the voice attesting that you are the Son of God? For I have so far heard only your voice, and have but your word for it. Now perhaps you will want to argue that we have the words of the holy prophets—that they bore witness concerning you. With due respect, I must ask why you are to be taken as the subject of these prophecies rather than the thousands of others who lived after the prophecy was uttered? What can be applied to you surely can be applied to others; you are not the only one who goes about begging and claiming to be the Son of God. And would it not seem reasonable that if you are, as you say, God's son, God would have helped you out of your calamity, or that you would have been able to help yourself? You say as well that divine grace makes everyone a son of God. This being so, what is the difference between you and anyone else?

"But let us review a story about your birth: You say that Chaldeans came to worship you as God while you were still an infant, and that they told Herod the Tetrarch of this, and that he sent men to kill those born just at that time, hoping to destroy you along with them. This was done, so it is said, in order to ensure that you would not reign as king when you were grown up. Now this is very puzzling: if Herod did this in order to prevent you from becoming king when you were grown instead of him, why then have you not become a king? Why—though a son of God—do you go about begging for food, cowering before the threats of the people, and wandering about homeless?"

According to the Jews, Jesus collected around him ten or eleven unsavory characters—tax collectors, sailors, and the like, and these scurried about making a living as best they were able, usually through double dealing and in otherwise questionable ways. But (the Jew will want to say): "Is it not wonderful that you survived at all! I mean, what when you were an infant you had to be taken away to Egypt lest you should be murdered. I am disturbed by the news that you, though a god, should have been afraid of death. An angel from heaven persuaded your family of the danger that you were doomed lest they escape with you. This is the second angel, if I hear rightly, who had been sent to provide a warning. One wonders why many more could not have been sent by the great God above— you being his beloved son! After all, the old myths of the Greeks that attribute a divine birth to Perseus, Amphion, Aeacus and Minos are equally good evidence of their wondrous works on behalf of mankind—and are certainly no less lacking in plausibility than the stories of your followers. What have you done by word or deed that is quite so wonderful as those heroes of old? Challenged in the Temple to produce some sign that you were the son of God you showed us nothing.

"Perhaps you will point to those tricks about which your disciples boast: those cures and resurrections, or feeding the crowds with but a few loaves (and having some left over to boot!). Monstrous tales, to be sure. But let us say for the sake of argument that such things were actually done by you. Are they then so different from the sort of things done by sorcerers—who also claim to do wonderful miracles, having been taught their tricks by the Egyptians. The sorcerers at least, for a few pence, make their magic available to everyone in the marketplace. They drive away demons, conquer diseases of all kinds, and make the dead heroes of the past appear—indeed sitting at long tables and eating imaginary cakes and dishes. They make things move about, as if they were alive—all illusion to be sure, but quite appealing to the average imagination. Now I ask you: As these men are able to do such wonderful things, ought we not regard them also as sons of God? Or ought we rather to say that they are the contrivances of evil men who are themselves possessed by demons? I think, Jesus, that the High God would not have chosen a body such as yours; nor would the body of a god have been born as you were born. We even hear of your eating habits. What! Does the body of a god need such nourishment? And we hear often of your unsuccessful attempts to win over others to your cause—the tricks evidently not being enough to hold their attention. One wonders why a god should need to resort to your kind of persuasion— even eating a fish after your resurrection. I should rather think that your actions are those of one hated by God, the actions of a sorcerer." So says our Jew to Jesus.

Let our Jew continue his sally against the Christians, now with a view to the prophets who, so say the Christians, foretold the story of Jesus beforehand: "These same prophecies could easily be applied to a thousand others besides Jesus, for our prophets say that the one who is to come (the Messiah) will be a great prince; he will be the lord of this world, and the leader of nations and armies. From this it is obvious that the prophets do not anticipate a low-grade character like this Jesus—a man who is able to make himself the son of a god by trickery, deceit and the most incredible stories. A true son of God, like the sun that illuminated the world by first illuminating itself, ought first to have been revealed as a true god. The Christians put forth this Jesus not only as the son of God but as the very Logos—not the pure and holy Logos known to the philosophers, mind you, but a new kind of Logos: a man who managed to get himself arrested and executed in the most humiliating of circumstances.

"This boaster and sorcerer whom you designate the Logos is unique in having a human genealogy. The men who fabricated this genealogy were insistent on the point that Jesus was descended from the first man and from the king of the Jews. The poor carpenter's wife seems not to have known she had such a distinguished bunch of ancestors; they were all kept in the closet until such time as they could be of some use. A fine god indeed, this boaster and sorcerer who performed not one godly action, who could not counter even the opposition of men, or avoid the disaster that ended his life in disgrace. According to your tales, the man who sentenced him did not suffer the fate of a Pentheus by going mad or being torn to pieces; rather, Jesus permitted himself to be mocked and bedecked with a purple robe and crowned with thorns. Why did this son of a god not show one glimmer of his divinity under these conditions? Why did he refuse to deliver himself from shame—at least play the man and stand up for his own or for his father's honor? But what does he say when his body is stretched out on the cross? 'Is this blood not ichor such as flows in the veins of the blessed?' When thirsty, he drinks greedily from a sponge full of vinegar and gall, not bearing his thirst with godly patience. Yet you who call yourselves true believers dare to criticize us Jews because we refuse to acknowledge this man as a god or admit that he underwent these sufferings for the good of mankind so that we all may avoid punishment? Have you forgotten that while he lived this Jesus convinced nobody—not even his own disciples—of his divinity, and was punished shamefully for his blasphemies? Were he a god he should not have died, if only in order to convince others for good and all that he was no liar; but die he did—not only that, but died a death that can hardly be accounted an example to men. Nor was he free from blame, as you imagine. Not only was he poor, he was also a coward and a liar as well. Perhaps you Christians will say that having failed to convince men on earth of his divinity, he descended into hell to convince them there. In all of these beliefs you have been deceived; yet you persist doggedly to seek justification for the absurdities you have made doctrines. If the central doctrine of Christianity bears testing, why should

we not wonder whether every condemned man is an angel even greater than your divine Jesus? I mean, why not be completely shameless and confess that every robber, every convicted murderer, is neither robber nor murderer but a god? And why? Because he had told his robber band beforehand that he would come to no good end and wind up a dead man. Your case is made the harder because not even his disciples believed in him at the time of his humiliation: those who had heard him preach and were taught by him, when they saw he was heading for trouble, did not stick with him. They were neither willing to die for his sake nor to become martyrs for his cause—they even denied they had known him! Yet on the example of those original traitors, you stake your faith and profess your willingness to die.

"When I ask what arguments you would cite to show that this man was a son of God, you offer that his death was meant to destroy the father of evil. But then, others have been punished by means just as disgraceful. Why did their deaths not bring about an end of evil? Or will you say that he was a son of God because he healed the lame and the blind and (as you declare) raised the dead?"

But—leaving our Jew to ponder for a moment—is this sort of thing not the very essence of sorcery and deception? As the Christians themselves have said, Jesus himself spoke of rivals entering the contest with his followers, wicked men and magicians, who would perform just the same sort of wonders, only under the supervision of Satan. Even Jesus admitted there was nothing exclusively "divine" about working these signs—that they could just as easily be done by wicked men. Nonetheless, in acknowledging this capacity in others, he unwittingly proves his own performances to be a lie. Good Lord! Is it not a silly sort of argument to reckon by the same works that one man is a god whilst his rivals are mere "sorcerers"? Why should we conclude from your argument that the sorcerers are worse than your god—that is if we take the testimony of Jesus about their powers seriously? He himself has said that such works were not produced by any divine nature but were instead the works of cheats and imposters. But to return to our quizzical Jew: Let him ask a question of his countrymen newly converted to the religion of this Jesus:

"Is your belief based on the 'fact' that this Jesus told in advance that he would rise again after his death? That your story includes his predictions of triumphing over the grave? Well, let it be so. Let's assume for the present that he foretold his resurrection. Are you ignorant of the multitudes who have invented similar tales to lead simpleminded hearers astray? It is said that Zamolxis, Pythagoras' servant, convinced the Scythians that he had risen from the dead, having hidden himself away in a cave for several years; and what about Pythagoras himself in Italy!—or Rhampsinitus in Egypt. The last of these, by the way, is said to have played dice with Demeter in Hades and to have received a golden napkin as a present from her. Now then, who else: What about Orpheus among the Odrysians, Protesilaus in Thessaly and above all Herakles and Theseus. But quite apart from all these risings from the dead, we must look carefully at the question of the resurrection of the body as a possibility given to mortals. Doubtless you will freely admit that these other stories are legends, even as they appear to me; but you will go on to say that your resurrection story, this climax to your tragedy, is believable and noble. (This, of course, notwithstanding his cry from the cross.) I suppose you will say that the earthquake and the darkness that covered the earth at the time of his death prove him a god, and that even though he did not accept the challenge to remove himself from the cross or to escape his persecutors when he was alive, yet he overcame them all by rising from the dead and showing the marks of his punishment, pierced hands and all, to others. But who really saw this? A hysterical woman, as you admit and perhaps one other person—both deluded by his sorcery or else so wrenched with grief at his failure that they hallucinated him risen from the dead by a sort of wishful thinking. This mistaking a fantasy for reality is not at all uncommon; indeed, it has happened to thousands. Just as possible, these deluded women wanted to impress the others—who had already the good sense to have abandoned him—by spreading their hallucinations about as "visions." After getting some few to believe them, it was a small matter for the fire of superstition to spread. If this Jesus were trying to convince anyone of his powers, then surely he ought to have appeared first to the Jews who treated him so badly—and to his accusers—indeed to everyone, everywhere. Or better, he might have saved himself the trouble of getting buried and simply have disappeared from the cross. Has there ever been such an incompetent planner: When he was in the body, he was disbelieved but preached to everyone; after his resurrection, apparently wanting to establish a strong faith, he chooses to show himself to one woman and a few comrades only. When he was punished, everyone saw; yet risen from the tomb, almost no one. The Christians are fond of saying that Jesus wanted to be unnoticed, and point to places in their sacred books where Jesus enjoins silence on the demons and those he has healed. But again, they contradict themselves, condemning the Jews for failing to recognize the Christ. If he wanted to be unnoticed, why was the voice from heaven heard, declaring him the Son of God? If he did not want to be unnoticed, then why was he punished and executed? At the very least it would seem that he would want his followers to know why he had come to earth. But your Jesus does not let his followers in on his secret, and thus occasions their disbelief. This is not my own guessing: I base what I say on your own writings, which are self-refuting. What god has ever lived among men who offers disbelief as the proof of his divinity? What god appears in turn only to those who already look for his reappearance, and is not even recognized by them? The sort of god, you should answer, who piles empty abuses on his hearers by threatening them with woes for misunderstanding things which were never made plain to them. What is plain is that this Jesus was a mere man, and rather more a reason to disbelieve in resurrection than to hold fast to the doctrine of our fathers, which says that it is within God's power to raise men from the dead." So our Jew would say to his deceived countrymen.

Even the more intelligent Christians preach these absurdities. Their injunctions are like this: "Let no one educated, no one wise, no one sensible draw near. For these abilities are thought by us to be evils. But as for anyone ignorant, anyone stupid, anyone uneducated, anyone childish, let him come boldly." By the fact that they themselves admit that these people are worthy of their god, they show that they want and are able to convince only the foolish, dishonorable and stupid, and only slaves, women and little children.

Further, we see that these Christians display their trickery in the marketplace and go around begging. They would not dare to enter into conversation with intelligent men, or to voice their sophisticated beliefs in the presence of the wise. On the other hand, wherever one finds a crowd of adolescent boys, or a bunch of slaves, or a company of fools, there will the Christian teachers be also—showing off their fine new philosophy. In private houses one can see wool workers, cobblers, laundry workers, and the most illiterate country bumpkins, who would not venture to voice their opinions in front of their intellectual betters. But let them get hold of children in private houses— let them find some gullible wives—and you will hear some preposterous statements: You will hear them say, for instance, that they should not pay any attention to their fathers or teachers, but must obey them. They say that their elders and teachers are fools, and are in reality very bad men who like to voice their silly opinions. These Christians claim that they alone know the right way to live, and that if only the children will believe them, they will be happy and their homes will be happy as well. Now if, as they are speaking thus to the children, they happen to see a schoolteacher coming along, some intelligent person, or even the father of one of the children, these Christians flee in all directions, or at least the more cautious of them. The more reckless encourage the children to rebel. They tell the children that they remain silent in the presence of the parents and the schoolteachers only because they do not want to have

anything to do with men as corrupt as these pagans, who, did they know what the children had been hearing, would likely punish them for hearing it. These Christians also tell the children that they should leave their fathers and teachers and follow the women and their little chums to the wooldresser's shop, or to the cobbler's or to the washerwoman's shop, so that they might learn how to be perfect. And by this logic they have persuaded many to join them.

Please do not think I criticize the Christians any more bitterly than they deserve. I think anyone may see that the summons to join the other mysteries is rather different, however. It runs: Come forward, whoever has a pure heart and wise tongue, or else, whoever is free of sin and whose soul is pure—you who are righteous and good— come forward. In the mystery religions, such talk is typical, as is the promise that membership brings about a sort of purification from sins. But the call to membership in the cult of Christ is this: Whoever is a sinner, whoever is unwise, whoever is childish—yea, whoever is a wretch—his is the kingdom of God. And so they invite into membership those who by their own account are sinners: the dishonest, thieves, burglars, poisoners, blasphemers of all descriptions, grave robbers. I mean—what other cult actually invites robbers to become members! Their excuse for all of it is that their god was sent to call sinners: well, fair enough. But what about the righteous? How do they account for the fact that their appeal is to the lowest sort of person? Why was their Christ not sent to those who had not sinned—Is it any disgrace not to have sinned? Are they saying that a god who will receive an unrighteous man who repents of his unrighteousness, provided he humbles himself, will *not* receive a righteous man, even if he has remained steadfast in his righteousness and honored God from the beginning of his days?

But of course, the Christians postulate that everyone is a sinner, so that they are able to extend their appeal to the public at large. Now, it is perhaps the case that everyone is inclined to sin—though not everyone does sin. But if it is the case that everyone sins, why did their god not merely call mankind in general to salvation rather than the wicked? I mean, why on earth this preference for sinners?

I suspect I know why the Christians pitch their message as they do: because they are unable to convert anyone truly virtuous and good. This can be the only explanation for their clear preference of the wicked and sinful.

12. Porphyry

Arguably the most learned opponent of early Christianity was the philosopher Porphyry (232–310 CE), whose 15-volume work *Against the Christians* was considered so potentially damaging to the faith that all copies were ordered burned in 448 CE. All that remains of it are scattered references in church fathers who occasionally responded to its claims.

As a young man, Porphyry had heard the Christian Origen preach and found his scholarship dubious. Porphyry himself was trained under the great philosopher Plotinus. Once he saw that Christianity was a serious threat to the well-being of pagan religiosity, which he considered central to the social fabric of the empire, he undertook a rigorous study of the Christian scriptures to allow him to attack them as full of contradictions, historical discrepancies, and implausibilities. Porphyry's ultimate goal was not only to show the inferiority of the scriptural basis of Christianity but also, by implication, to embrace the moral and religious superiority of established pagan religion.

The first excerpt below shows Porphyry claiming that the gods no longer benefit the human race now that it is turning to worship Christ; the others set forth his historical analysis of the book of Daniel, in which he demonstrates that—contrary to the standard Christian view—it was not a prediction of the coming of the Messiah Jesus, but in fact was written about past events that transpired during the reign of Antiochus Epiphanes of Syria, at the time of the Maccabean revolt—a view that critical scholars now accept today.

15 *Eusebius Preparation for the Gospel, 5.1.9*

. . . it is again the same author, who in our time is the advocate of demons, who in his work, which he wrote against us, bears witness as follows: "That these bad demons are no longer powerful after the arrival of our saviour to mankind. And now today they wonder why this sickness has overtaken the city. While Asclepius and the other gods were worshipped there was no sickness. But since Jesus alone is worshipped, who is aware of any public utility coming from these gods?" These then are the words of Porphyry.

Porphyry Against the Christians, reproduced from Robert Berchman, *Porphyry Against the Christians*. Leiden Brill, 2005, used with permission of E. J. Brill.

70 *Jerome Commentary on Daniel, Prologue*

Porphyry wrote his twelfth book against Daniel's prophecy, denying that it was written by the person to whom it is referred in its title, but rather by some person residing in Judea at the time of that Antiochus, who was surnamed Epiphanes. Furthermore he alleged that "Daniel" did not foretell the future as much has he narrated the past, and finally whatever he said until the time of Antiochus contained true history, while anything he may have opined beyond that point was false, inasmuch as he could not have foreknown the future.

71 *Jerome Commentary on Daniel, Prologue*

But we should recognize among other things that Porphyry raises this objection to us about the Book of Daniel, that it is an obvious forgery, not to be thought of as belonging to the Hebrew Scriptures, but is an invention composed in Greek. He deduces this from the fact that in the story of Susanna, where Daniel speaks to the elders, we discover the expressions "to split from the mastic tree," and "to cut from the evergreen oak"—a play on words convenient to Greek rather than Hebrew.

79 *Jerome Commentary on Daniel, 7:7*

Porphyry placed the last two beasts, the Macedonian and the Roman, in the realm of the Macedonians, and divided them up in the following manner. He claimed that the leopard was Alexander himself, and the beast, which was unlike the other ones, represented Alexander's four successors. And then he counts ten kings up until the time of Antiochus, surnamed Epiphanes, and who were quite cruel. He did not associate the kings themselves with separate kingdoms, for example—Macedon, Syria, Asia, or Egypt. Rather he ordered the diverse kingdoms into a single kingdom making up a series. He did this clearly in order that the words which were written: "a mouth speaking boasts" would be thought of as spoken about Antiochus rather than the Antichrist.

80 *Jerome Commentary on Daniel, 7: 8, 14*

(7:8): Porphyry vainly surmises the little horn that rose after ten horns is Antiochus Epiphanes, and that the three uprooted horns from the ten are Ptolemy VI, surnamed Philometer, Ptolemy VII, surnamed Euergetes, and the Armenian king Artarxias. The first of these kings died long before Antiochus was born . . . (7:14). Let Porphyry answer the question from all mankind to whom this language refers to, or who this person might be who was so strong as to break and crush to pieces the little horn, whom he contrives to be Antiochus? If he answers the princes of Antiochus were defeated by Judas Maccabaeus, then he must explain how Judas could be said to arrive with the heavenly clouds as the Son of Man.

83 *Jerome Commentary on Daniel, 11:20*

Porphyry, however, asserts that it was not this Seleucus who is alluded to, but Ptolemy Epiphanes, who plotted a conspiracy against Seleucus with the consequence that Seleucus was poisoned by his own generals. They did this because when somebody asked Seleucus where he was to get the funds for the great undertakings he was planning, he replied that his monetary resources were his friends. When this statement was publicly revealed, the generals became worried that he might take their resources from them, and on that basis by malicious means they put him to death.

84 *Jerome Commentary on Daniel, 11:21f*

Until this point the historical order has been followed, and there has been no point of contention between Porphyry and us. But the remainder of the document, from here to the end of the volume, he interprets as referring to the person of Antiochus, who was surnamed Epiphanes, brother of Seleu-cus, and Antiochus the Great's son. He ruled Syria for eleven years after Seleucus, and he seized Judea. God's law was persecuted under him, and the Maccabaean War occurred.

Our adversaries say that the one who was to "stand up in the place" of Seleucus was his brother Antiochus Epiphanes. At first the faction in Syria that favored Ptolemy would not give him the regal honor. But later he gained control of Syria through the pretence of clemency . . . and not only does the document state he defeated Ptolemy by cheating, but that he overcame through treachery the prince of the covenant, that is Judas Maccabaeus. Or else this is what is referred to: That after he (Judas) had offered peace with Ptolemy, and became prince of the covenant, later he (Seleucus) set up a plot against him (Judas). Now Ptolemy understood here was not Epiphanes, the fifth Ptolemy to reign in Egypt, but it was Ptolemy Philometer, the son of Antiochus' sister Cleopatra. Thus Antiochus was his maternal uncle. And after Cleopatra's death Egypt was ruled by Eulaeus—Philometer's eunuch teacher, and by Leneus. And they strove to retake Syria, which Antiochus took wrongly. War erupted between the young boy Ptolemy and his uncle. And they fought a battle between Pelusium and Mount Casium. Ptolemy's generals were defeated. Antio-chus exhibited leniency to the young boy, and making a pretence of friendship, he went up to Memphis, and according to the Egyptian custom he received the crown there. Stating that he way look-ing out for the boy's interests, he conquered all Egypt for himself (with only a tiny force). And he entered into rich and prosperous cities; and thus he accomplished things his father had never done, nor even his father's fathers. For none of the Syrian kings had ever desolated Egypt in this manner, and scattered all its wealth. Furthermore he was so clever that by deceit he vanquished the well-formulated plans of those who were the generals of the boy-king. This is the line of interpretation Porphyry followed, pursuing with much repetition the se-quence of Suctorius, speaking of events, which we related in a brief compendium.

85 *Jerome Commentary on Daniel, 11:25ff*

Porphyry interprets this as referring to Antiochus, who with a large army went out on a campaign against his sister's son. But the king of the south, that is Ptolemy's generals, also will be roused to war with many and rather powerful auxiliary forces; but they will not be able to resist Antio-chus' false schemes. For he will feign peace with his sister's son, and will eat bread with him, and afterwards he will conquer Egypt.

88 *Jerome Commentary on Daniel, 11:3ff*

Those of another perspective claim that the per-sons spoken about are those who were sent by An-tiochus two years after he had looted the temple to exact tribute from the Jews—and also to erase rev-erence for God, he set up an image of Jupiter Olympius in the Temple at Jersalem, and also stat-ues of Antiochus. Now this is called the abomina-tion of desolation, having been set up when the holocaust and continual sacrifice were abolished . . . (11:34ff.). Porphyry thinks that the little aux-iliary was Mattathias from the village of Modin because he rebelled against Antiochus' generals, and tried to preserve the worship of the true God. He says he was called "little auxiliary" because Mattathias was killed in battle, and later his son Judas, who was called Maccabaeus, also fell in combat. And in similar fashion the remainder of his brothers were deceived by the falseness of their enemies. . . . Porphyry, and others who follow him, certify the reference to be Antiochus Epiph-anes, noting that he rose against the reverence of God. And his arrogance reached so far as to demand that his own statue be set up in the Jeru-salem Temple. And concerning the subsequent saying: "and he shall successfully maintain until the anger be consummated for the consummation shall be within him"—they understand it to mean that his power will continue until such time as God becomes angry with him, and orders him to be killed. Now indeed, Polybius and Diodorus, who wrote the histories of the Bibliothecae, tell that Antiochus acted not only against the God of Judea, but was compelled as well by a consuming greed to plunder Diana's temple in Elymias because it was exceedingly rich. But he was resisted powerfully by the temple guard and by the neighboring people, and was afflicted by terrible phantasies, became insane, and eventually died of illness. And they say that this happened to him because he tried to plunder Diana's Temple . . . (11:37ff.). Porphyry has a ridiculous interpretation for the God Moazim, claiming that Antiochus' generals placed a statue of Jupiter in the town of Modin from which came Mattathias and his sons. Furthermore they compelled the Jews to offer blood-sacrifices to it, that is to the God of Modin . . . "Garrisons ect." Porphyry explains this as meaning the man is to fortify the Acra at Jerusalem and will station garrisons in the remaining cities, and will compel the Jews to worship an alien God, which without doubt refers to Jupiter. And showing the God to them, he will persuade them that they shall worship it. Then to those deceived he will give both honor and great glory; and he will make them rule over the remainder in Judea, and for their falsehood parcel out states to them, and will distribute gifts . . . (11:40f.). This is also ascribed to Antiochus by Porphyry on the grounds that in the eleventh year of his reign he battled for a second time against his nephew—Ptolemy Philometer. For when the latter heard Antiochus had arrived, he gathered many thousands of people together. But as a tempest with his chariots, cavalry, and large navy Antiochus invaded many lands. And as he proceeded he laid everything to waste; and he came to the wondrous land Judea . . . and Antiochus used the city's ruined walls to strengthen the Acra, and then he continued to Egypt. . . . They say that in his haste to battle Ptolemy, the king of the south, Antiochus ignored the Idumaeans, Moabites, and Ammonites, who lived on the periphery of Judea, least he make Ptolemy stronger by engaging in some other campaign.

90 *Jerome Commentary on Daniel, 12: 1 ff*

Up to this point, somehow, Porphyry managed to maintain his position and impose upon the credulity of the naive among our followers and the poorly informed among his own. But what can he say of this chapter in which is described the resurrection of the dead? . . . But what will not stubborn obduracy not resort to? . . . This also, he declares, was written in reference to Antiochus, for after he had invaded Persia, he left his army with Lysias, who was in command of Antioch and Phoenicia, for the purpose of warring against the Jews and destroying their city of Jerusalem. All these details are narrated by Josephus, the author of the Jewish Histories. Porphyry claims that the difficulty was such as never occurred previously, and that a time occurred that had never been, from the time that races began to exist even to that time. But when victory was given to them, and Antiochus' generals were killed, and Antiochus himself had died in Persia, the people of Israel experienced salvation, even all those written down in the book of God, namely, those who defended the law with utmost bravery. In contrast to them were those who proved to be transgressors of the law and allied with the party of Antiochus. It was then, he claims, that these guardians of the law, who had been, sleeping in the dust of the earth and were burdened with a load of afflictions, and hidden away, as it were, in the tombs of wretchedness, rose up again from the dust of the earth to a triumph unhoped for, and lifted up their heads, rising up to eternal life, just as the transgressors rose to eternal disgrace. But those masters and teachers who had a knowledge of the law shall shine as the heaven, and those who have exhorted the simple people to observe the rites of God shall blaze forth like stars for all eternity. Also he adduces the historical account concerning the Maccabees, in which it is said many Jews under the leadership of Mattathias and Judas Maccabaeus fled to the desert and hid away in caves and holes in the rocks, and re-emerged after the victory.

These things, thus, were foretold in metaphorical speech as if it concerned a resurrection of the dead.

91 *Jerome Commentary on Daniel, 12:7, 11, 12*

(12:7) Porphyry interprets "a time and times and half a time" to mean three and a half years; and we do not deny on our part that this agrees with the idiom of sacred scripture. . . . If therefore the previous references about the Antichrist, which were clearly written, are given by Porphyry to Antiochus and to the three and a half years duration, which he claims the Temple was deserted, then he is under an obligation to prove the next statement: "His kingdom is eternal, and all kings shall serve and obey him" also refers to Antiochus, or else (as he himself proposes) to the Jewish people. But it is abundantly clear that such an argument will never stand. . . . When it is said that "God's people shall have been scattered," under Antiochus' persecution, as Porphyry claims . . . "at that time shall all things be fulfilled" . . . (12:11). Porphry asserts that these one thousand two hundred and ninety days to have been completed in Antiochus' time and in the desolation of the Temple (12:12). Porphyry explains this passage in this manner—that the forty-five days after the one thousand two hundred and ninety-five signifies the interval of victory over Antiochus' generals, of the period when Judas Maccabaeus fought with courage, and cleaned the Temple, and shattered the idol into pieces, offering blood-sacrifices in the Temple of God.

CHRISTIAN APOLOGIES

13. Justin's First Apology

Justin Martyr was the first major Christian apologist. Born and raised in Samaria, he moved to Rome after his conversion (see Chapter 2) and opened a Christian school there. His *First Apology* was composed around 155 CE. As became customary for Christian apologists, Justin wrote the book as a kind of open letter to the Roman authorities, in this case to the emperor Antoninus Pius and his two sons, Marcus Aurelius and Lucius Verus. Many scholars think, though, that the book was actually meant not for the imperial court but for internal consumption among the Christians.

The book sets the tone for many of the subsequent Christian apologists. In the excerpts that follow, Justin demands a fair hearing for Christians rather than summary condemnation, he attacks pagan idolatry and defends Christians against charges of atheism and immorality, and he warns his readers about punishment in the afterlife for those who refuse to believe. Perhaps most important, Justin argues that pagan philosophers who spoke the truth were inspired by the divine "logos" (translated as either "reason" or "word"), and that since Christ is himself the Logos (Word) become flesh, he embodies what is truest of all religion and philosophy, foreshadowed in the pagan myths and predicted in Moses and the ancient Jewish prophets.

For other extracts from the *First Apology*, see Chapter 13.

1 To the Emperor Titus Aelius Hadrianus Antoninus Pius Augustus Caesar, and to his philosopher son Verissimus, and to Lucius the philosopher, Caesar's natural son and Pius's adopted son, a lover of culture, and to the Sacred Senate and all the Roman people—on behalf of people of every nation who are unjustly hated and grossly abused, I, Justin, son of Priscus and grandson of Bacchius, from Flavia Neapolis in Syria-Palestine, myself being one of them, have drawn up this address and petition.

2 Reason dictates that those who are truly pious and philosophers should honor and love only the truth, declining to follow the opinions of the ancients, if they are worthless. For not only does sound reason dictate that one should not follow those who do or teach unjust things, but the lover of truth should choose by all means, and even before his own life, even though death should remove him, to speak and do righteous things. So you, then, since you are called pious and philosophers and guardians of justice and lovers of culture, listen in every way; and it will be shown if you are such. For we have come into your company not to flatter you by this writing, nor please you by our address, but to ask that you give judgment, after an exact and searching enquiry, not moved by

Justin: "First Apology," from *St. Justin Martyr: The First and Second Apologies*, ed. Leslie William Barnard. Mahwah, NJ: Paulist Press, 1997. Used by permission of Paulist Press.

prejudice or by a wish to please superstitious people, nor by irrational impulse or long prevalent rumors, so as to give a decision which will prove to be against yourselves. For we indeed reckon that no evil can be done to us, unless we are proved to be evildoers, or shown to be wicked. You are able to kill us, but not to hurt us.

3 But that nobody should think that this is an unreasonable and daring utterance, we ask that the charges against us be investigated, and that, if they are substantiated let us be punished as is fitting. But if nobody can prove anything against us, true reason forbids you, because of an evil rumor, to wrong innocent people, and indeed rather [to wrong] yourselves, who think fit to instigate action, not by judgment, but by passion. Every honorable person will recognize this as the only fair and righteous challenge, namely, that the subjects should give a straightforward account of their own life and teaching; and likewise that the rulers should give their decision as having followed, not violence and tyranny, but piety and philosophy. For thus both rulers and subjects would reap benefit. For even one of the ancients said somewhere, "Unless both rulers and ruled love wisdom it is impossible to make cities prosper." It is then our task to offer to all an opportunity of inspecting our life and teachings, lest, on account of those who do not really know of our affairs, we should incur the penalty due to them for mental blindness. But it is for you, as reason demands, to listen [to us] and to be found good judges. For if, having learned the truth, you fail to do what is righteous, you have no defense before God.

4 By the mere statement of a name, nothing is decided, either good or evil, apart from the actions associated with the name; indeed, as far as the name with which we are accused goes, we are most gentle people. But we do not think it just to ask to be acquitted on account of the name, if we are convicted as evildoers, so, on the other hand, if we are found to have committed no wrong, either in the appellation of the name, or in

our citizenship, you must be exceedingly anxious against incurring righteous judgment by unjustly punishing those who are not convicted. For from a name neither approval nor punishment could fairly come, unless something excellent or evil in action could be shown about it. For you do not punish the accused among yourselves before they are convicted; but in our case you take the name as proof against us, and this although, as far as the name goes, you ought rather to punish our accusers. For we are accused of being Christians, and to hate what is favorable is unjust. Again if one of the accused deny the name, saying that he is not [a Christian], you acquit him, as having no proof that he is an evildoer; but if any one acknowledges that he is one, you punish him on account of this acknowledgement. You ought also to enquire into the life both of the confessor and the denier, that by his deeds it would appear what kind of person each is. For as some who have been taught by the Teacher, Christ, not to deny him encourage others when they are put to the test, so similarly do those who lead evil lives give some excuse to those who, without consideration, like to accuse all the Christians of impiety and wickedness. And this also is improper. For in philosophy, too, some assume the name and the dress who do nothing worthy of their profession; and as you are aware those among the ancients whose opinions and teachings were quite different are yet called by the one name of philosopher. And some of these taught atheism; and those who became poets get a laugh out of the impurity of Zeus with his own children. And those who follow such teaching are unrestrained by you; but, on the contrary, you offer prizes and honors to those who euphoniously insult them.

5 Why, then, should this be? In our case, who pledge ourselves to do nothing wicked, nor to hold these godless opinions, you do not investigate the charges made against us; but, giving in to unreasoning passion, and the instigation of evil demons, you punish us without trial or consideration. For the truth shall be told; since of old these evil demons manifested themselves, both defiled

women and corrupted boys, and showed terrifying sights to people, that those who did not use their reason in judging the acts that were done, were filled with terror; and being taken captive by fear, and not knowing that these were demons, they called them gods, and gave to each the name which each of the demons had chosen for himself. And when Socrates tried, by true reasoning and definite evidence, to bring these things to light, and deliver people from the demons, then the demons themselves, by means of people who rejoiced in wickedness, compassed his death, as an atheist and impious person, on the charge of introducing new divinities, and in our case they show a similar activity. For not only among the Greeks through Socrates were these things revealed by reason [logos], but also among the Barbarians were they revealed by logos personally, when he had taken shape, and become man, and was called Jesus Christ; and in obedience to him, we not only deny that they who did such things as these are gods, but state that they are wicked and impious demons, whose actions will not bear comparison with those even of people who long after virtue.

6 Hence we are called atheists. And we confess that we are atheists with reference to gods such as these, but not with reference to the most true God, the Father of righteousness and temperance and the other virtues, who is unmixed with evil. But we worship and adore both him and the Son who came from him, and taught us these things, and the army of the other good angels, who follow him and are made like him, and the prophetic Spirit, giving honor [to him] in reason and truth, and to everyone who wishes to learn handing over without grudging, what we have been taught. . . .

8 Consider that we have said these things for your sakes, for it is in our power when we are examined to deny [our Christianity]; but we would not live by telling a lie. For, impelled by the desire for the eternal and pure life, we seek to dwell with God, the Father and Demiurge of all things, and hasten to confess [our faith], being persuaded and

convinced that those who have shown to God by their works that they follow him, and long to dwell with him where there is no evil to cause disturbance, are able to obtain these things. This, then, to speak briefly, is what we look for and have learned from Christ, and teach. Likewise Plato said that Rhadamanthus and Minos would punish the wicked who came before them; and we say that this is what will happen, but at the hand of Christ, and to the same bodies, reunited with their souls and destined for eternal punishment, and not for a thousand-year period only, as he said. And if anyone says that this is incredible or impossible, this mistake of ours is one which concerns us only, and no one else, as long as we are not convicted of doing any evil.

9 But neither do we honor with many sacrifices and garlands of flowers the objects that people have formed and set in temples and named gods; since we know that they are lifeless and dead and have not the form of God [for we do not think that God has such a form as some say is fashioned to his honor], but have the names and shapes of those evil demons which have appeared. For why must we tell you who already know, what the craftsmen fashion their material into, by planing and cutting, casting and hammering? And often out of vessels used for dishonorable purposes, by merely changing the form, and making an image of the appropriate shape, they make what they call gods. We consider this not only irrational, but to be even insulting to God, who, though of ineffable glory and form, yet has his name set upon things which are corruptible and need to be cared for. And that the craftsmen of these are impure and, not to enter into details, are given to all kinds of vice, you very well know; they even corrupt their own slave girls who work alongside them. What stupidity, that dissolute people should be said to fashion and make gods for public worship, and that you should appoint such people the guardians of temples where they are set up, not recognizing that it is unlawful even to think or say that people are the guardians of gods. . . .

13 What sober-minded person then will not admit that we are not atheists, since we worship the Maker of this Universe, and declare, as we have been taught, that he has no need of blood and libations and incense, whom we praise to the utmost of our power through the word of prayer and thanksgiving for all things that we receive. We have been taught that the only honor that is worthy of him is not to consume by fire the things he has brought into being for our sustenance, but contribute them for ourselves and those in need, and with thanksgiving to him celebrating our solemnities in hymns and speech, for our creation, and for all the means of health, and for the qualities of the different kinds of things, and for the changes of the seasons, and presenting before him petitions that we may live again in incorruption through faith in him. Our teacher of these things is Jesus Christ, who was also born for this purpose, and was crucified under Pontius Pilate, procurator of Judaea in the time of Tiberius Caesar; and we will show that we worship Him rationally, having learned that he is the Son of the true God himself, and holding him in the second place, and the prophetic Spirit in the third rank. For they charge our madness to consist in this, that we give to a crucified man second place after the unchangeable and eternal God, begetter of all things, for they do not know the mystery involved in this, to which we ask you to give heed as we expound it to you.

14 For we warn you in advance to be on your guard, lest the demons whom we have previously accused should deceive you and divert you from reading and understanding what we say. For they strive to have you as their slaves and servants, and sometimes by appearances in dreams, sometimes by magical tricks, they subdue all who do not struggle to the utmost for their own salvation, as we do also who, after being persuaded by the Word, renounced them, and follow the only unbegotten God through his Son. Those who formerly delighted in fornication now embrace chastity alone, those who formerly made use of magical arts have

dedicated themselves to the good and unbegotten God, we who once valued above everything the gaining of wealth and possessions now bring what we have into a common stock, and share with everyone in need; we who hated and destroyed one another, and would not share the same hearth with people of a different tribe on account of their different customs, now since the coming of Christ, live familiarly with them, and pray for our enemies, and try to persuade those who unjustly hate us to live according to the good advice of Christ, to the end that they may share with us the same joyful hope of a reward from God the Master of all. But lest we should seem to deceive, we consider it right, before embarking on our promised demonstration, to cite a few of the precepts given by Christ himself. It is for you then, as powerful rulers, to find out whether we have been taught and do teach these things truly. Short and concise utterances come from Him, for he was no sophist, but his word was the power of God.

15 Concerning chastity he said this. "Whosoever looks upon a woman to lust after her has already committed adultery with her in his heart before God."[1] And: "If your right eye offends you, cut it out; for it is better for you to enter into the Kingdom of Heaven with one eye, than with two eyes to be cast into eternal fire."[2] And: "Whosoever shall marry her that is divorced from another husband, commits adultery."[3] And: "There are some who have been made eunuchs by men, and some who were born eunuchs, and some who have made themselves eunuchs for the Kingdom of Heaven's sake; but not all can receive this saying."[4] So that all who according to human law make second marriages are sinners in the sight of our Master, as are those who look on a woman to lust after her. For not only the man who in act

---

1 Matt 5:28.

2 Matt 5:29.

3 Matt 5:32.

4 Matt 19:12.

commits adultery is condemned by him, but also the man who desires to commit adultery; since not only our deeds but also our thoughts are open before God. And many, both men and women, who have been Christ's disciples from childhood, have preserved their purity at the age of sixty or seventy years; and I am proud that I could produce such from every race of men and women. . . .

18 Since consciousness remains for all who have lived, and eternal punishment awaits [the wicked], do not neglect to be convinced and believe that these things are true. For necromancy, and the divinations you practice through innocent children, and the invoking of departed human souls, and those who are called among the magi dream-senders and familiars, and all that is done by those who are skilled in such things—let these persuade you that even after death souls are still conscious; and those who are seized and torn by the spirits of the dead, whom all call demoniacs or madmen; and what you call oracles, both of Amphilochus, Dodona, Pytho, and many others such as exist; and the teachings of the authors, Empedocles and Pythagoras, Plato and Socrates, and the pit in Homer and the descent of Odysseus to visit the dead, and all that has been spoken of a like kind. Receive us, even if you receive us only on an equality with them, who believe in God not less but more firmly than they do, since we expect to receive again our own bodies, though they be dead and buried in the earth, saying that nothing is impossible with God.

19 And to any thoughtful person what would seem more incredible, than if we were not in the body, and someone should say it was possible that from a small drop of human seed, bones and sinews and flesh were formed into a shape such as we see? For let this now be said by way of supposition: If you were not such as you now are, born of such parents, and one were to show you the human seed and a picture of a man or woman, and were to say confidently that from such a substance such a being could grow, would you believe before

you saw it happening? No one would dare to contradict [and to say that you would disbelieve]. In the same way, then, you are now incredulous because you have never seen a dead person rise again. But as at first you would not have believed it possible that from a small drop such persons could be produced, yet now you see them thus produced, so also consider that it is not impossible for the bodies of men and women, dissolved and like seeds resolved into earth, to rise again in God's appointed time and put on incorruption. . . .

21 And when we say also that the Word, who is the First-begotten of God, was born for us without sexual union, Jesus Christ our teacher, and that he was crucified and died and rose again and ascended into heaven, we propound nothing new beyond [what you believe] concerning those whom you call sons of Zeus. For you know of how many sons of Zeus your esteemed writers speak:

Hermes, the interpreting Word and teacher of all; Asclepius, who, though he was a great healer, after being struck by a thunderbolt ascended into heaven; and Dionysus too who was torn in pieces; and Heracles, when he had committed himself to the flames to escape his pains; and the Dioscuri, the sons of Leda; and Perseus, son of Danae; and Bellerophon, who, though of mortal origin, rose to heaven on the horse Pegasus. For what shall I say of Ariadne, and those who, like her, have been said to have been placed among the stars? And what of your deceased emperors, whom you think it right to deify, and on whose behalf you produce someone who swears that he has seen the burning Caesar ascend to heaven from the funeral pyre? And what kind of deeds are related of each of these reputed sons of Zeus, it is needless to tell those who already know. This only shall be said, that they are written for the benefit and instruction of students, for all consider it an honorable thing to imitate the gods. But far be it from every sound mind to entertain such a thought concerning the deities as to believe that Zeus himself, the governor and begetter of all things, was both a parricide and the son of a parricide, and that being overcome by the love of evil and shameful pleasures he came into Ganymede and to those many women whom he seduced, and that his sons did like actions. But, as we have said above, wicked devils perpetrated these things. And we have been taught that only those are deified who have lived near to God in holiness and virtue; and we believe that those who live unjustly and do not change their ways are punished in eternal fire.

22 Now the Son of God, called Jesus, even if only an ordinary man, is on account of his wisdom worthy to be called Son of God; for all writers call God Father of humans and gods. For if we say that the Word of God was begotten of God in a peculiar manner, different from the ordinary method of birth, let this, as said before, be not a strange thing to you, who say that Hermes is the announcing word from God. But if anyone objects that he was crucified, this is in common with those whom you call sons of Zeus, who suffered as we have now enumerated. For their sufferings at death are recorded as not all alike, but different; so that not even by the strangeness of his passion does he seem to be inferior to them; but, as we promised in the preceding part of this discourse, we will now prove him better—or rather have already proved him to be so—for the better is revealed by his deeds. And even if we say that he was born of a virgin, let this be to you in common with Perseus. And when we say that he healed the lame, the paralytic, and those born blind, and raised the dead, we appear to say things similar to those said to have been done by Asclepius.

23 And that this may now be clear to you [firstly], that whatever things we say as having been learned from Christ, and the prophets who came before him, are alone true, and older than all the writers who have lived, and we ask to be accepted, not because we say the same things as they do, but because we speak the truth; and [secondly] that Jesus Christ alone was really begotten as Son by God, being his Word and First-begotten and Power, and becoming man by his will he taught us these things for the conversion and restoration of the

human race; and [thirdly] that before he became a human among humans some, under the influence of the wicked demons already mentioned, related as real occurrences the myths which the demons had devised through the poets, in the same manner as they have caused to be fabricated the scandalous reports against us and impious deeds, of which there is neither witness nor proof—we shall bring forward this proof. . . .

30 But lest anyone should argue against us, what excludes [the reasoning] that he who is called by us Christ, a human born of humans, performed what we call his might works by magical art, and by this appeared to be Son of God?—we will now offer proof, not trusting in mere assertions, but being of necessity persuaded by those who prophesied [these things] before they happened, for with our own eyes we see things that have happened and are happening just as they were predicted; and this will, we think, appear to you the strongest and surest evidence.

31 Then there were certain persons among the Jews, who were prophets of God, through whom the prophetic Spirit announced beforehand things that were to come to pass before they happened. And the successive rulers of the Jews carefully preserved in their possession their prophecies, as they were spoken and when they were uttered, in their own Hebrew language when they had been arranged in books by the prophets themselves. But when Ptolemy, the King of Egypt, formed a library and set out to collect the writings of all people, he heard also about these prophecies, and sent to Herod, who was at that time King of the Jews, asking that the prophetic books be sent to him. And King Herod indeed sent them, writing in the already mentioned Hebrew language. Since their contents were found to be unintelligible to the Egyptians, he again sent and asked that people be sent to translate them into the Greek language. And when this was done the books remained with the Egyptians where they are until now; and they are everywhere with all the Jews; but though they read them they do not understand what is said, but consider us enemies and opponents; and like yourselves they kill and punish us whenever they can, as you can well realize. For in the Jewish war which lately happened, Bar-Cochba, the leader of the revolt of the Jews, gave orders that Christians alone should be led to terrible punishments, unless they would deny Jesus the Christ and blaspheme. In these books, then, of the prophets we have found it predicted that Jesus our Christ would come, born of a virgin, growing up to manhood, and healing every disease and every sickness and raising the dead, and hated and unrecognized and crucified, and dying and rising again and ascending into heaven, and both being and being called Son of God. [We find it also predicted] that certain people should be sent by him into every nation to proclaim these things, and that rather among the Gentiles people should believe on him. And he was predicted before he appeared, first five thousand years before, and again three thousand, and then two thousand, and again one thousand, and yet again eight hundred, for in the succession of generations other prophets again and again arose.

But lest some, reasoning absurdly, with a view to refuting what we teach, should maintain that we say that Christ was born a hundred and fifty years ago under Cyrenius, and somewhat later, under Pontius Pilate, taught what we say he taught, and should object as though all people who were born before him were not accountable—let us anticipate and solve the difficulty. We have been taught that Christ is the First-born of God, and we have suggested above that he is the logos of whom every race of men and women were partakers. And they who lived with the logos are Christians, even though they have been thought atheists; as, among the Greeks, Socrates and Heraclitus, and people like them; and among the barbarians, Abraham, and Ananias, and Asarias, and Misael, and Elias, and many others whose actions and names we now decline to recount, because we know it would be tedious. So that even they who lived before Christ, and lived without logos, were wicked and hostile to Christ, and slew those who lived with the logos. . . .

52 Since then we show that all things that have already happened had been proclaimed through the prophets before they came to pass, it must necessarily be believed also that those things that were similarly predicted, but are yet to come to pass, will certainly take place. For as the things that have already happened came to pass when proclaimed before, and even unrecognized, so will the things that remain, even though unknown and disbelieved, come to pass. For the prophets have proclaimed before two comings of his: one, which has already happened, as that of a dishonored and suffering man; and the second, when, as has been proclaimed, he will come from heaven with glory with his angelic host; when also he will raise the bodies of all the people who have lived, and will cloth the worthy with incorruption, but will send those of the wicked eternally conscious, into eternal fire with the wicked demons. . . .

54 But those who deliver the myths invented by the poets offer no proof to the youths who learn them—and we proceed to prove that they have been told by the power of the wicked demons to deceive and lead astray the human race. For when they heard it proclaimed through the prophets that the Christ was to come, and that the ungodly among men and women would be punished by fire, they caused many to be called sons of Zeus, thinking that they would be able to cause people to believe that the statements about Christ were marvelous tales, like the assertions of poets. And these things were said both among the Greeks and among all nations where they [the demons] heard the prophets proclaiming that Christ would be especially believed in. But that in hearing what was said through the prophets they did not understand it accurately, but imitated, like people in error, what was said concerning our Christ, we will make plain. The prophet Moses, then, was, as we have said before, older than all writers, and through him, as we have also said before, it was thus predicted: "A ruler will not depart from Judah nor the leader from his thighs, until he comes for whom it is reserved; and he will be the expectation of the nations, binding his foal to the vine, washing his robe in the blood of the grape."[5] Therefore when the demons heard these prophetic words they said that Dionysus had been the son of Zeus, and handed down that he was the discoverer of the vine, and they ascribe wine among his mysteries, and taught that, having been torn in pieces, he ascended into heaven. And since through the prophecy of Moses it had not been expressly signified whether he who was to come would be the Son of God, and whether, mounted on a foal, he would remain on earth or ascend into heaven, and because the name "foal" could signify either the foal of an ass or a horse, they, not knowing whether the predicted one would bring the foal of an ass or of a horse as the sign of his coming, nor whether he was the Son of God or of a man, as we said before, said that Bellerophon, a human born of humans, had himself gone up to heaven on the horse Pegasus. And when they heard it said through the other prophet Isaiah, that he would be born of a virgin, and would ascend into heaven by his own [power], they caused Perseus to be spoken of. And when they knew what was said, as has been cited before, in the ancient prophecies, "Strong as a giant to run his course,"[6] they said that Heracles was strong, and had traveled over the whole earth. And, again, when they learned that it had been predicted that he would heal every disease and raise the dead, they brought forwarded Asclepius.

---

5 Gen 49:10–11.

6 Ps 19:5.

55 But in no instance, not even in the case of those called sons of Zeus, did they imitate the crucifixion; for they did not understand, as had been explained, that all the things said about it were put symbolically. Yet, as the prophet predicted, [this] is the greatest symbol of his power and rule, as also is shown from the things which fall under view. For consider all the things in the cosmos, whether without this form they could be governed or be interrelated. For the sea is not traversed except this token of victory, which is called a sail, remains safe in the ship; and the land is not ploughed without it; likewise diggers and craftsmen do not do their work except with tools which have this form. And the human form differs from that of the irrational animals in nothing else than in its being erect and having the hands stretched out, and having on the face extending from the forehead what is called the nose, through which there is breath for the living creature—and this shows no other form than that of the Cross. And so it was said throughout the prophet, "The breath before our face is Christ the Lord." And the power of this form is shown by your own symbols on what are called standards and trophies to the accompaniment of which all your state processions are made, using these as the signs of your rule and power, even though you do so without knowing. And with this form you set up the images of your deceased emperors, and you name them gods by inscriptions. Since, then, we have urged you both by reason and by the visible form, as far as we can, we know that now we are blameless even though you disbelieve; for our part is done and finished.

14. Athenagoras: Plea Regarding the Christians

Although arguably the most eloquent of the Greek apologists, Athenagoras is scarcely mentioned in our ancient sources. Possibly from Athens, he composed his apology in 177 CE, addressing it to the emperor Marcus Aurelius and his son Commodus. In it he makes an impassioned plea that Christians should not be condemned merely for their name but for criminal activities. He devotes the bulk of his defense to showing that the charges often leveled against Christians— atheism, cannibalism, and incest—are completely unfounded.

Athenagoras maintains that far from being atheists (without the gods), Christians worship the one true God, along with his Son, the embodiment of God's Logos, and the divine Spirit (three beings, he claims, who are unified in power but distinguished in rank). This true worship, he insists, stands in sharp contrast to the senseless idolatry of the pagans. Moreover, the high moral standards of the Christians, who ban even the thought of evildoing, shows the absurdity of the charges of incest and cannibalism— charges better leveled, Athenagoras wryly observes, against the gods that pagans describe in their own myths. Athenagoras concludes by arguing that the surest incentive for upright behavior is the uniquely Christian belief in the resurrection of the dead to everlasting reward or punishment.

To the Emperors Marcus Aurelius Antoninus and Lucius Aurelius Commodus, conquerors of Armenia and Sarmatia, and—what is more important—philosophers:

1 In your Empire, Your Most Excellent Majesties, different peoples observe different laws and customs; and no one is hindered by law or fear of punishment from devotion to his ancestral ways, even if they are ridiculous. A citizen of Troy calls Hector a god, and worships Helen, taking her for Adrasteia. The Lacedaemonian venerates Agamemnon as Zeus, and Phylonoë, the daughter of Tyndareus, under the name of Enodia.

The Athenian sacrifices to Erechtheus as Poseidon. The Athenians also perform religious rites and celebrate mysteries in honor of Agraulus and Pandrosus, whom they imagine guilty of impiety for opening the box. In brief, among every nation and people, people perform whatever sacrifices and mysteries they wish. The Egyptians reckon among their gods even cats, crocodiles, serpents, asps, and dogs. And to all these cults both you and the laws grant toleration. For you think it impious and wicked to believe in no god at all; and you hold it necessary for everyone to worship the gods he pleases, so that they may be kept from wrongdoing by fear of the divine. [With us, on the contrary, although you yourselves are not, like the crowd, led astray by rumors, our name is the object of hatred. But names do not deserve to be hated. It is wrongdoing which merits penalty and punishment.]

Accordingly, while everyone admires your mildness and gentleness and your peaceful and kindly attitude toward all, they enjoy equal rights

Athenagoras: Plea Regarding Christians, reproduced from *Early Christian Fathers*, ed. Cyril C. Richardson (Library of Christian Classics Series), 1970. Used by permission of Westminster John Knox Press.

under the law. The cities, according to their rank, share in equal honor, and the whole Empire through your wisdom enjoys profound peace.

But you have not cared for us who are called Christians in this way. Although we do no wrong, but, as we shall show, are of all people most religiously and rightly disposed toward God and your Empire, you allow us to be harassed, plundered, and persecuted, the mob making war on us only because of our name. We venture, therefore, to state our case before you. From what we have to say you will gather that we suffer unjustly and contrary to all law and reason. Hence we ask you to devise some measures to prevent our being the victims of false accusers.

The injury we suffer from our persecutors does not concern our property or our civil rights or anything of less importance. For we hold these things in contempt, although they appear weighty to the crowd. We have learned not only not to return blow for blow, nor to sue those who plunder and rob us, but to those who smite us on one cheek to offer the other also, and to those who take away our coat to give our overcoat as well. But when we have given up our property, they plot against our bodies and souls, pouring upon us a multitude of accusations which have not the slightest foundation, but which are the stock in trade of gossips and the like.

2 If, indeed, anyone can convict us of wrongdoing, be it trifling or more serious, we do not beg off punishment, but are prepared to pay the penalty however cruel and unpitying. But if the accusation goes no farther than a name—and it is clear that up to today the tales about us rest only on popular and uncritical rumor, and not a single Christian has been convicted of wrongdoing—it is your duty, illustrious, kind, and most learned Emperors, to relieve us of these calumnies by law. Thus, as the whole world, both individuals and cities, shares your kindness, we too may be grateful to you, rejoicing that we have ceased to be defamed.

It does not befit your sense of justice that others, accused of wrongdoing, are not punished before they have been convicted, while with us the mere name is of more weight than legal proof. Our judges, moreover, do not inquire if the accused has committed any wrong, but let loose against the name as if *it* were a crime. But no name in and of itself is good or bad. It is by reason of the wicked or good actions associated with names that they are bad or good. You know all that better than anyone, seeing you are versed in philosophy and thoroughly cultured.

That is why those who are tried before you, though arraigned on the most serious charges, take courage. For they know that you will examine their life and not be influenced by names if they mean nothing, or by accusations if they are false. Hence they receive a sentence of condemnation on a par with one of acquittal. We claim for ourselves, therefore, the same treatment as others. We should not be hated and punished because we are called Christians, for what has a name to do with our being criminals? Rather should we be tried on charges brought against us, and either acquitted on our disproving them or punished on our being convicted as wicked people, not because of a name (for no Christian is wicked unless he is a hypocrite), but because of a crime.

It is in this way, we know, that philosophers are judged. None of them before the trial is viewed by the judge as good or bad because of his system or profession, but he is punished if he is found guilty. (No stigma attaches to philosophy on that account, for he is a bad person for not being a philosopher lawfully, and philosophy is not responsible.) On the other hand, he is acquitted if he disproves the charges. Let the same procedure be used in our case. Let the life of those who are accused be examined, and let the name be free from all reproach.

I must at the outset of my defense beg you, illustrious Emperors, to hear me impartially. Do not prejudge the case through being influenced by popular and unfounded rumor, but apply your love of learning and of truth to our cause. Thus you will not be led astray through ignorance, and we, disproving the uncritical rumors of the crowd, shall cease to be persecuted.

3 Three charges are brought against us: atheism, Thyestean feasts, and Oedipean intercourse. If these are true, spare no class; proceed against our crimes; destroy us utterly with our wives and children, if anyone lives like a beast. Beasts, indeed, do not attack their own kind. Nor for mere wantonness do they have intercourse, but by nature's law and only at the season of procreation. They recognize, too, those who come to their aid. If, then, anyone is more savage than brutes, what punishment shall we not think it fitting for him to suffer for such crimes?

But if these charges are inventions and unfounded slanders, they arise from the fact that it is natural for vice to oppose virtue and it is in accord with God's law for contraries to war against each other. You yourselves, moreover, are witness to the fact that we are guilty of none of these things, since it is only the confession of a name that you forbid. It remains for you, then, to examine our lives and teachings, our loyalty and obedience to you, to your house, and to the Empire. By doing so you will concede to us no more than you grant to our persecutors. And we shall triumph over them, giving up our very lives for the truth without any hesitation.

4 We are of course not atheists (I will meet the charges one by one)—and I hope it does not sound too silly to answer such an allegation. Rightly, indeed, did the Athenians accuse Diagoras of atheism, since he not only divulged the Orphic doctrine as well as the mysteries of Eleusis and of the Cabiri and chopped up a statue of Heracles to boil his turnips, but he proclaimed outrightly that God simply did not exist. In our case, however, is it not mad to charge us with atheism, when we distinguish God from matter, and show that matter is one thing and God another, and that there is a vast difference between them? For the divine is uncreated and eternal, grasped only by pure mind and intelligence, while matter is created and perishable.

If we shared the views of Diagoras when we have so many good reasons to adore God—the order, harmony, greatness, color, form, and arrangement of the world—we should rightly be charged with impiety and there would be due cause to persecute us. But since our teaching affirms one God who made the universe, being himself uncreated (for what exists does not come into being, only what does not exist), and who made all things through his Word, on two scores, then, we are treated unreasonably—by being slandered and by being persecuted. . . .

10 I have sufficiently shown that we are not atheists since we acknowledge one God, who is uncreated, eternal, invisible, impassible, incomprehensible, illimitable. He is grasped only by mind and intelligence, and surrounded by light, beauty, spirit, and indescribable power. By him the universe was created through his Word, was set in order, and is held together. [I say "his Word"], for we also think that God has a Son.

Let no one think it stupid for me to say that God has a Son. For we do not think of God the Father or of the Son in the way of the poets, who weave their myths by showing that gods are no better than humans. But the Son of God is his Word in idea and in actuality; for by him and through him all things were made, the Father and the Son being one. And since the Son is in the Father and the Father in the Son by the unity and power of the Spirit, the Son of God is the mind and Word of the Father.

But if, owing to your sharp intelligence, it occurs to you to inquire further what is meant by the Son, I shall briefly explain. He is the first offspring of the Father. I do not mean that he was created, for, since God is eternal mind, he had his Word within himself the beginning, being eternally wise. Rather did the Son come forth from God to give form and actuality to all material things, which essentially have a sort of formless nature and inert quality, the heavier particles being mixed up with the lighter. The prophetic Spirit agrees with this opinion when he says, "The Lord created me as the first of his ways, for his works."[1]

---

1 Prov 8:22.

Indeed we say that the Holy Spirit himself, who inspires those who utter prophecies, is an effluence from God, flowing from him and returning like a ray of the sun. Who, then, would not be astonished to hear those called atheists who admit God the Father, God the Son, and the Holy Spirit, and who teach their unity in power and their distinction in rank? Nor is our theology confined to these points. We affirm, too, a crowd of angels and ministers, whom God, the maker and creator of the world, appointed to their several tasks through his Word. He gave them charge over the good order of the universe, over the elements, the heavens, the world, and all it contains.

11 Do not be surprised that I go into detail about our teaching. I give a full report to prevent your being carried away by popular and irrational opinion, and so that you may know the truth. Moreover, by showing that the teachings themselves, to which we are attached, are not human, but were declared and taught by God, we can persuade you not to hold us for atheists. What, then, are these teachings in which we are reared? "I say to you, love your enemies, bless those who curse you, pray for those who persecute you, that you may be sons of your Father in heaven, who makes his sun to shine on the evil and on the good, and sends his rain on the just and on the unjust.". . .[2]

13 Since many of those who charge us with atheism do not have the vaguest idea of God, being unversed in, and ignorant of, physics and theology, they measure religion by the observance of sacrifices, and charge us with not having the same gods as the cities. Heed what I have to say, Your Majesties, on both these counts. And first about our not sacrificing.

The creator and Father of the universe does not need blood or the smell of burnt offerings or the fragrance of flowers or incense. He himself is perfect fragrance. He lacks nothing and has need of nothing. But the greatest sacrifice in his eyes is for us to realize who stretched out the heavens in a sphere, who set the earth in the center, who gathered the water into seas and separated the light from darkness, who adorned the sky with the stars and made the earth bring forth all kinds of seed, who made the animals and fashioned humans. When, therefore, we recognize God the creator of the universe, who preserves it and watches over it with the wisdom and skill he does, and lift up holy hands to him, what need has he then of a hecatomb?

"It is with sacrifices and humble prayer,
With libation and burnt offering that people implore [the gods]
And turn [their wrath], when any has offended or sinned."[3]

What need have I of burnt offerings, when God does not need them? Rather is it needful to present a bloodless sacrifice, to offer a spiritual worship.

14 Regarding their other charge, that we neither accept nor venerate the same gods as the cities, it is quite senseless. The very ones who accuse us of atheism for not acknowledging the same gods that they believe in are not agreed among themselves about the gods. The Athenians have set up Celeus and Metanira as gods; the Lacedaemonians, Menelaus—they sacrifice to him and keep his festival; the Trojans cannot bear his name, and worship Hector; the Ceans adore Aristaeus, imagining he is identical with Zeus and Apollo; the Thasians worship Theagenes, who committed a murder at the Olympian games; the Samians, Lysander for all his slaughter and wickedness! . . . The Cilicians worship Niobe; the Sicilians, Philip the son of Boutacides; the Amathusians, Onesilus; the Carthaginians, Hamilcar. The day is too short to enumerate the rest.

When, then, they fail to agree among themselves about their gods, why do they charge us with disagreeing with them?

15 But grant that they worship the same gods. What then? Since the populace cannot distinguish between matter and God or appreciate

---

2 Matt 5:44, 45; Luke 6:27, 28.

3 *Iliad* 9:499–501.

the chasm that separates them, they have recourse to idols made of matter. Shall we, then, who can distinguish and differentiate between uncreated and created, between being and nonbeing, between the intelligible and the sensible, and who call these things by their proper names—shall we, just because of the populace, come and worship statues? If matter and God are identical, two names for the same thing, we are surely irreligious for not thinking that stones, wood, gold, and silver are gods. But if there is a vast difference between them, as great as separates the craftsman and his materials, why are we called to account?

It is like the potter and the clay. The clay is matter, the potter is an artist. So is God the creator an artist, while matter is subject to him for the sake of his art. But as clay cannot by itself become pottery without art, so matter, which is altogether pliable, cannot receive distinction, form, or beauty apart from God the creator. We do not, moreover, reckon pottery of more value than the potter, or bowls or vessels of gold than the artisan. If they have artistic merit, we praise the artist. It is he who reaps the renown for making them. So it is with matter and God. It is not matter which justly receives praise and honor for the arrangement and beauty of the world, but its creator, God. If, then, we were to worship material forms as gods, we should seem to be insensitive to the true God, identifying what is eternal with what is subject to dissolution and corruption.

For when your subjects come to you, they do not fail to pay their homage to you, their lords and masters, from whom they may obtain what they need. They do not have recourse to the magnificence of your palace. . . .

That, therefore, we are not atheists, since we worship God the creator of this universe, and his Word, I have proved as best I can, even if I have not done the subject justice.

31 Our accusers have made up the further charges against us of impious feasts and intercourse. They do this to convince themselves that they have grounds for hating us. They imagine, moreover, that by fear they will either draw us away

from our present mode of life or else, by the enormity of the accusations, render our princes harsh and implacable. But this a foolish approach toward those who realize that of old, and not merely in our time, wickedness has a habit of warring against virtue, in obedience to some divine law and principle. Thus, for instance, Pythagoras with three hundred companions was put to the flames. Heraclitus and Democritus were banished, the one from the city of Ephesus, the other, charged with insanity, from Abdera. Finally, the Athenians condemned Socrates to death. And just as the virtue of these men suffered no whit from the opinions of the mob, so our uprightness of life is in no way obscured by the reckless calumnies of some persons. For we are in good standing with God.

Nonetheless, I will meet these charges too, although I am very confident that I have made my case by what I have already said. You, who are more intelligent than others, know that those who faithfully regulate their lives by reference to God, so that each of us stands before him blameless and irreproachable, will not entertain even the thought of the slightest sin. Were we convinced that this life is the only one, then we might be suspected of sinning, by being enslaved to flesh and blood and by becoming subject to gain and lust. But since we realize that God is a witness day and night of our thoughts and our speech, and that by being pure light he can see into our very hearts, we are convinced that when we depart this present life we shall live another. It will be better than this one, heavenly, not earthly. We shall live close to God and with God, our souls steadfast and free from passion. Even if we have flesh, it will not seem so: we shall be heavenly spirits. Or else, if we fall along with the rest, we shall enter on a worse life and one in flames. For God did not make us like sheep and oxen, a bywork to perish and be done away with. In the light of this it is not likely that we would be purposely wicked, and deliver ourselves up to the great Judge to be punished.

32 It is nothing surprising that our accusers should invent the same tales about us that they tell of their gods. They present their sufferings as mysteries; and, had they wanted to judge shameless and indiscriminate intercourse as a frightful thing, they should have hated Zeus. For he had children from his mother, Rhea, and his daughter Kore, and married his own sister. Or else, they should have detested Orpheus, who invented these tales, because he made Zeus even more unholy and wicked than Thyestes. For the latter had intercourse with his daughter in pursuance of an oracle, and because he wanted to gain a throne and avenge himself.

But we, on the contrary, are so far from viewing such crimes with indifference that we are not even allowed to indulge a lustful glance. For, says the Scripture, "He who looks at a woman lustfully, has already committed adultery in his heart."[4]

We feel it is a matter of great importance that those, whom we thus think of as brothers and sisters and so on, should keep their bodies undefiled and uncorrupted. For the Scripture says again, "If anyone kisses a second time because he found it enjoyable . . ." Thus the kiss, or rather the religious salutation, should be very carefully guarded. For if it is defiled by the slightest evil thought, it excludes us from eternal life.

33 Having, therefore, the hope of eternal life, we despise the enjoyments of the present, even the pleasures of the soul. According to our laws, each of thinks of the woman he has married as his wife only for the purpose of bearing children. For as the farmer casts his seed on the soil and awaits the harvest without sowing over it, so we limit the pleasure of intercourse to bearing children.

You would, indeed, find many among us, both men and women, who have grown to old age unmarried, in the hope of being closer to God. If, then, to remain virgins and eunuchs brings us closer to God, while to indulge in wrong thoughts and passions drives us from him, we have all the more reason to avoid those acts, the very thought of which we flee from. For we center our attention not on the skill of making speeches but on the proof

and lessons of actions. We hold that a man should either remain as he is born or else marry only once. For a second marriage is a veiled adultery. The Scripture says, "Whoever puts away his wife and marries another, commits adultery."[5]

34 Since we are such (and why should I speak of such degrading things?), our situation resembles that of the proverb, "The harlot reproves the chaste." It is these people who revile us with the very things they are conscious of in themselves and which they attribute to their gods. They boast of them indeed, as noble acts and worthy of gods. Adulterers and corrupters of boys, they insult eunuchs and those once married.

35 Since this is our character, what person of sound judgment would say that we are murderers? For you cannot eat human flesh until you have killed someone. If their first charge against us is a fiction, so is the second. For if anyone were to ask them if they had seen what they affirm, none of them would be so shameless as to say he had.

Moreover, we have slaves: some of us more, some fewer. We cannot hide anything from them; yet not one of them has made up such tall stories against us. Since they know that we cannot endure to see any one being put to death even justly, who of them would charge us with murder or cannibalism? Who among our accusers is not eager to witness contests of gladiators and wild beasts, especially those organized by you? But we see little difference between watching a man being put to death and killing him. So we have given up such spectacles. How can we commit murder when we will not look at it, lest we should contract the stain of guilt? What reason would we have to commit murder when we say that women who induce abortions are murderers, and will have to give account of it to God? For the same person would not regard the fetus in the womb as a living thing and therefore an object of God's care, and at the same time slay it, once it had come to life. Nor would he refuse to

4 Matt 5:28.

5 Mark 10:11.

expose infants, on the ground that those who expose them are murderers of children, and at the same time do away with the child he has reared. But we are altogether consistent in our conduct. We obey reason and do not override it.

36 What person, moreover, who is convinced of the resurrection would make himself into a tomb for bodies that will rise again? The same persons would surely not believe that our bodies will rise again and then eat them as if there were no resurrection. They would not think that

the earth will give back its dead and then imagine that it will fail to demand those entombed in them.

On the contrary, those who deny they will have to give account of the present life, be it wicked or good, who reject the resurrection and who count on the soul's perishing along with the body and, so to say, flickering out, are likely to stop at no outrage. But those who are convinced that God will look into everything and that the body which has aided the soul in its unreasonable lusts and passions will be punished along with it, they have no good reason to commit even the slightest sin.

15. *The Letter to Diognetus*

We know very little about the origin of the Letter to Diognetus. It was written anonymously and was addressed to someone who cannot otherwise be identified. It is never mentioned in other ancient sources. Scholars generally date the book to the end of the second century or the beginning of the third.

Like other apologists, the author attacks the folly of both pagan idolatry and Jewish superstition (as seen, he contends, in such customs as kosher food laws and circumcision). Christians are portrayed as good citizens who have done nothing to harm the social order; on the contrary, since their full allegiance is to heaven, they are to the world as the soul is to the body. For this author, Christ was sent from God to convince the world of the error of its ways and to bring all people to God. But in striking contrast to other apologists, this author explicitly denies that pagan philosophy and myth reflect the divine logos as precursors to Christ; before the coming of the Maker of the universe into the world, all people stood in complete error and darkness.

Letter to Diognetus

1 Since I see, most excellent Diognetus, that you are extremely eager to learn about the religion of the Christians and are making such an exacting and careful inquiry about them, wishing to discover which God they obey and how they worship him, so that they all despise the world and

disdain death, neither giving credence to those thought to be gods by the Greeks nor keeping the superstition of the Jews, and what deep affection they have for one another, and just why this new race or way of life came into being now and not before, I welcome this eagerness of yours and ask

The Letter to Diognetus, reproduced from *The Apostolic Fathers*, ed. Bart D. Ehrman; Loeb Classical Library, vol. 2. Cambridge MA: Harvard University, 2003. Used with permission of Harvard University Press.

God—who enables us both to speak and to hear—that I may be allowed to speak in such a way that you derive special benefit by hearing, and that you hear in such a way that the speaker not be put to grief.

2 And so come, purge yourself of all the notions that previously constrained your understanding, leave behind your misguided habit of thought, and become as it were a person made new at the beginning, one who is about to hear a new teaching, just as you yourself have admitted. Consider the true nature and form of those you call and consider to be gods, not only with your eyes but also with your mind.

2 Is not one of them a stone, like that which we walk on? And another copper, no better than utensils forged for our use? And another wood, already rotted? And another silver, needing someone to guard it, to keep it from being stolen? And another iron, being eaten away by rust? And another pottery, no more attractive than that which is fashioned for the most disreputable purposes?

3 Are not all of these formed of destructible matter? Are they not forged with iron and fire? Were they each not made by the sculptor, coppersmith, silversmith, and potter? Before they were shaped by these crafts into the form that each of them now has, could they not have been made into other forms—indeed, could they not be remade even now? And the utensils that we have now, which come from the same material: could they not be made like them, if they came into the hands of the same artisans?

4 Or again, these things that are now worshiped by you: could they not be formed by human hands into utensils similar to the rest? Are they not all deaf? And blind? And lifeless? And unable to perceive? And unable to move? Are they not all rotting? Are they not all decaying?

5 These are what you call gods. These are what you serve. These are what you worship. And in the end, these are what you become like.

6 Is this why you hate the Christians, because they do not consider these to be gods?

7. But do you yourselves not show disdain for these gods, even while supposing and imagining that you praise them? Do you not much more ridicule and abuse them—worshiping the ones made of stone and clay without keeping close watch on them, but locking up those made of silver and gold, putting guards over them night and day to keep them from being stolen?

8 If these had any powers of perception, you would be punishing them by the honors you imagine you are bestowing on them. And if they lack perception, you offer proof against them by worshiping them with the blood and fat of your sacrifices.

9 See if one of you could put up with this kind of treatment or bear such things if they happened to you. But no one would endure this kind of punishment willingly, because he has sense perception and reason. But the stone endures it because it has no perception. And so do you not prove that it cannot perceive?

10 I could say many other things about why Christians do not serve such gods, but if someone supposes that these comments are not enough, I imagine saying anything more would be superfluous.

3 And next I suppose you especially long to hear about why the Christians do not worship like the Jews.

2 Now by abstaining from the kind of divine worship just mentioned, the Jews rightly claim to worship the one God who is over all and to consider him Master. But when they worship him like those already mentioned, they go astray.

3 For just as the Greeks give evidence of their foolishness by making offerings to those that are without perception and deaf, so too these should realize that they manifest their own foolishness, rather than the worship of God, when they regard him as needing anything.

4 For the one who made heaven and earth and all that is in them,[1] and who supplies all of us with what we need, is himself in need of none of the

---

1 Ps 146:6; cf. Acts 14:15.

things that he himself provides to those who suppose that they are giving them.

5 But those who suppose they are performing sacrifices of blood and fat and whole burnt offerings, and thereby to be bestowing honor on him by these displays of reverence, seem no different to me from those who show the same honor to the gods who are deaf—one group giving to gods who cannot receive the honor, the other thinking that it can provide something to the one who needs nothing.

4 But I do not think you need to learn from me about their anxiety over food, their superstition about the sabbath, their arrogance over circumcision, and the pretense they make of fasting and of their celebration of the new moon—ridiculous matters and unworthy of argument.

2 For how is it not completely unwarranted to accept some of the things created by God for human use as made well, but to reject others as useless and superfluous?

3 And how is it not impious to lie against God by saying that he does not allow anything good to be done on the sabbath?

4 And how is it not worthy of scorn to boast in the mutilation of the flesh as a testimony to their election, as if they were especially loved by God because of it?

5 And who would consider as proofs of their divine worship, rather than of their utter foolishness, their constant observation of the stars and moon to keep track of months and days, and the distinctions they make in the divine orderings of the world and in the alternations of the seasons for their own impulses—setting aside some times for feasts and others for mourning?

6 I suppose you have learned enough about how the Christians are right to abstain from the vulgar silliness, deceit, and meddling ways of the Jews, along with their arrogance. But do not expect to be able to learn from any human the mystery of the Christians' own way of worship.

5 For Christians are no different from other people in terms of their country, language, or customs.

2 Nowhere do they inhabit cities of their own, use a strange dialect, or live life out of the ordinary.

3 They have not discovered this teaching of theirs through reflection or through the thought of meddlesome people, nor do they set forth any human doctrine, as do some.

4 They inhabit both Greek and barbarian cities, according to the lot assigned to each. And they show forth the character of their own citizenship in a marvelous and admittedly paradoxical way by following local customs in what they wear and what they eat and in the rest of their lives.

5 They live in their respective countries, but only as resident aliens; they participate in all things as citizens, and they endure all things as foreigners. Every foreign territory is a homeland for them, every homeland foreign territory.

6 They marry like everyone else and have children, but they do not expose them once they are born.

7 They share their meals but not their sexual partners.

8 They are found in the flesh but do not live according to the flesh.

9 They live on earth but participate in the life of heaven.

10 They are obedient to the laws that have been made, and by their own lives they supersede the laws.

11 They love everyone and are persecuted by all.

12 They are not understood and they are condemned. They are put to death and made alive.

13 They are impoverished and make many rich. They lack all things and abound in everything.

14 They are dishonored and they are exalted in their dishonors. They are slandered and they are acquitted.

15 They are reviled and they bless, mistreated and they bestow honor.

16 They do good and are punished as evil; when they are punished they rejoice as those who have been made alive.

17 They are attacked by Jews as foreigners and persecuted by Greeks. And those who hate them cannot explain the cause of their enmity.

6 To put the matter simply, what the soul is in the body, this is what Christians are in the world.

2 The soul is spread throughout all the limbs of the body; Christians are spread throughout the cities of the world.

3 The soul lives in the body, but it does not belong to the body; Christians live in the world but do not belong to the world.

4 The soul, which is invisible, is put under guard in the visible body; Christians are known to be in the world, but their worship of God remains invisible.

5 The flesh hates the soul and attacks it, even though it has suffered no harm, because it is hindered from indulging in its pleasures. And the world hates the Christians, even though it has suffered no harm, because they are opposed to its pleasures.

6 The soul loves the flesh that hates it, along with its limbs; Christians love those who hate them.

7 The soul is imprisoned in the body, but it sustains [Or: constrains] the body; Christians are detained in the prison of the world, but they sustain [Or: constrain] the world.

8 The soul, which is immortal, dwells in a mortal tent; Christians temporarily dwell in perishable surroundings but await that which is imperishable in the heavens.

9 The soul grows stronger even when mistreated by what the body eats and drinks; Christians increase daily even when punished.

10 God has appointed them to such a position, and it would not be right for them to abandon it.

7 For, as I have said, this is no earthly discovery that has been handed over to them, nor is it a mortal idea that, in their judgment, merits such diligent oversight. Nor have they been entrusted with the administration of merely human mysteries.

2 But the truly all-powerful God himself, creator of all and invisible, set up and established in their hearts the truth and the holy word from heaven, which cannot be comprehended by humans. To do so, he did not, as one might suppose, send them one of his servants or an angel or a ruler or any of those who administer earthly activities or who are entrusted with heavenly affairs, but he sent the craftsman and maker of all things himself, by whom he created the heavens, by whom he enclosed the sea within its own boundaries, whose mysteries all the elements of creation guard faithfully, from whom the sun was appointed to guard the courses that it runs during the day, whom the moon obeys when he commands it to shine at night, whom the stars obey by following the course of the moon, by whom all things are set in order and arranged and put into subjection, the heavens and the things in the heavens, the earth and the things in the earth, the sea and the things in the sea, fire, air, the abyss, creatures in the heights, creatures in the depths, and creatures in between—this is the one he sent to them.

3 So then, did he, as one might suppose, send him to rule in tyranny, fear, and terror?

4 Not at all. But with gentleness and meekness, as a king sending his own son, he sent him as a king; he sent him as a god; he sent him as a human to humans. So that he might bring salvation and persuasion he sent him, not to coerce—for God does not work through coercion.

5 He sent him to issue his call, not to persecute. He sent him to show forth his love, not to judge.

6 For later he will send him in judgment—and who will withstand his coming? . . .

7 Do you not see[2] how they are cast to the wild beasts that they might deny the Lord, and yet they are not overcome?

8 Do you not see that the more the multitude is punished, the more others increase their numbers?

9 These things do not appear to be human works. These are the power of God; these are proofs of his coming.

8 For what person formerly had any idea what God was like, before he came?

2 Or do you accept the vain and ridiculous teachings of those specious philosophers, some of whom asserted that God was fire (where they themselves are about to go, this is what they call

---

2 The text has been emended to restore the sense.

God!), and others water, and others one of the other elements created by God?

3 And if any of these teachings was acceptable, then every one of the other things created by God could also appear to be God.

4 But these ideas are illusions and the deception of tricksters.

5 For no one either saw him or made him known, but he revealed himself.

6 And he revealed himself through faith, through which alone is one permitted to see God.

7 For God, the Master and Creator of all, the one who created all things and set them in order, was not only benevolent but also patient.

8 Indeed, he was always this way, and is and will be: kind and good and without anger and true. He alone is good.

9 And when he had a great and inexpressible thought, he communicated it to his child alone.

10 And so, as long as he enshrouded it in a mystery and kept his wise plan to himself, he seemed not to care for us or give us any heed.

11 But when he revealed it through his beloved child and showed the things prepared from the beginning, he shared all things with us at once, that we might participate in and see and understand his kindly acts. Who among us would have ever expected these things?

16. Tertullian: Apology

Tertullian was a prolific and enormously influential Christian author from Carthage. Raised as a pagan and thoroughly trained in secular schools of rhetoric, Tertullian converted to Christianity near the end of the second century. He then focused his keen rhetorical sense and acerbic wit on a range of critical issues facing the Christian church, especially in the areas of apologetics, heresy, and ethics. The breadth of his interests can be seen throughout this anthology (see Chapters 5, 7, 15, and 16). In particular, his doctrinal writings became foundational for later thinkers, especially in Western Christendom; he is widely known as the father of Latin theology.

As an apologist, Tertullian dealt with many of the same issues as his Greek predecessors, especially the standard charges against the Christians and the injustice of their condemnation. What makes his work particularly interesting is not so much his perspective as the way he phrases it. His rhetoric is brilliant and biting, and he bars no holds. Using keen (and sometimes dubious) logic and rapier-like (and often sarcastic) wit he dismantles and ridicules both the serious accusations and the popular sentiment against the Christians.

The following excerpts come from Tertullian's earliest and best known apologetic treatise, the "Apology," written, probably, around 197 CE.

Apology, from *Tertullian: Apologetical Works and Minucius Felix: Octavius,* ed. Rudolph Arbesmann. Fathers of the Church, 10; 2nd ed. Washington, DC: Catholic University Press of America, 1977. Used with permission.

Chapter 2

1 If, then, it is decided that we are the most wicked of people, why do you treat us so differently from those who are on a par with us, that is, from all other criminals? The same treatment ought to be meted out for the same crime.

2 When others are charged with the same crimes as we, they use their own lips and the hired eloquence of others to prove their innocence. There is full liberty given to answer the charge and to cross-question, since it is unlawful for people to be condemned without defense or without a hearing.

3 Christians alone are permitted to say nothing that would clear their name, vindicate the truth, and aid the judge to come to a fair decision. One thing only is what they wait for; this is the only thing necessary to arouse public hatred: the confession of the name of Christian, not an investigation of the charge.

4 Yet, suppose you are trying any other criminal. If he confesses to the crime of murder, sacrilege, incest, or treason—to particularize the indictments hurled against us—you are not satisfied to pass sentence immediately; you weigh the attendant circumstances, the character of the deed, the number of times it was committed, the time, the place, the witnesses, and the partners-in-crime.

5 In our case there is nothing of this sort. No matter what false charge is made against us, we must be made to confess it; for example, how many murdered babies one has devoured, how many deeds of incest one has committed under cover of darkness, what cooks and what dogs were on hand. Oh, what glory for that governor who should have discovered someone who had already consumed a hundred infants! . . .

Chapter 7

1 We are spoken of as utter reprobates and are accused of having sworn to murder babies and to eat them and of committing adulterous acts after the repast. Dogs, you say, the pimps of darkness, overturn candles and procure license for our impious lusts.

2 We are always spoken of in this way, yet you take no pains to bring into the light the charges which for so long a time have been made against us. Now, either bring them into the light, if you believe them, or stop believing them, inasmuch as you have not brought them to light! Because of your hypocrisy, the objection is made against you that the evil does not exist which you yourselves dare not bring to light. Far different is the duty you enjoin upon the executioner against the Christians, not to make them state what they do, but to make them deny what they are.

3 The origin of this religion, as we have already said, dates from the time of Tiberius. Truth and hatred came into existence simultaneously. As soon as the former appeared, the latter began its enmity. It has as many foes as there are outsiders, particularly among Jews because of their jealousy, among soldiers because of their blackmailing, and even among the very members of our own household because of corrupt human nature.

4 Day by day we are besieged; day by day we are betrayed; oftentimes, in the very midst of our meetings and gatherings, we are surprised by an assault.

5 Who has ever come upon a baby wailing, as the accusation has it? Who has ever kept for the judge's inspection the jaws of Cyclopes and Sirens, bloodstained as he had found them? Who has ever found any traces of impurity upon [Christian] wives? Who has discovered such crimes, yet concealed them or been bribed to keep them secret when dragging these people off to court? If we always keep under cover, whence the betrayal of our crimes?

6 Rather, who could have been the traitors? Certainly not the accused themselves, since the obligation of pledged silence is binding upon all mysteries by their very nature. The mysteries of Samothrace and of Eleusis are shrouded in silence; how much more such rites as these which, if they were made public, would provoke at once the hatred of all humankind—while God's wrath is reserved for the future?

7 If, then, Christians themselves are not the betrayers, it follows that outsiders are. Whence do outsiders get their knowledge, since even holy initiation rites always ban the uninitiated and are wary of witnesses? Unless you mean that the wicked are less afraid.

8 The nature of rumor is well known to all. It was your own poet who said: "Rumor, an evil surpassing all evils in speed."[1] . . .

Chapter 10

1 "You do not worship the gods," you say, "and you do not offer sacrifice for the emperors." It follows that we do not offer sacrifices for others for the same reason that we do not do it even for ourselves— it follows immediately from our not worshipping the gods. Consequently, we are considered guilty of sacrilege and treason. This is the chief accusation against us—in fact, it is the whole case—and it certainly deserves investigation, unless presumption and injustice dictate that decision, the one despairing of the truth, the other refusing it.

2 We cease worshipping your gods when we find out that they are non-existent. This, then, is what you ought to demand, that we prove that those gods are non-existent and for that reason should not be worshipped, because they ought to be worshipped only if they were actually gods. Then, too, the Christians ought to be punished if the fact were established that those gods do exist whom they will not worship because they consider them non-existent.

3 "But, for us," you say, "the gods do exist." We object and appeal from you to your conscience. Let this pass judgment on us, let this condemn us, if it can deny that all those gods of yours have been mere men.

4 But, if it should deny this, it will be refuted by its own documents of ancient times from which it has learned of the gods. Testimony is furnished to this very day by the cities in which they were born, and the regions in which they left traces of something they had done and in which it is pointed out that they were buried. . . .

---

1 Virgil, *Aeneid* 4.174.

Chapter 17

1 The object of our worship is the one God, who, out of nothing, simply for the glory of his majesty, fashioned this enormous universe with its whole supply of elements, bodies, and spirits, and did so simply by the Word wherewith he bade it, the Reason whereby he ordered it, the Power wherewith he was powerful. Hence it is that even the Greeks apply the appropriate word "cosmos" to the universe.

2 He is invisible, although he may be seen; intangible, although manifested by grace; immeasurable, although he may be measured by human senses. Therefore, he is so true and so great. However, what can be generally seen, touched, and measured is less than the eyes by which it is seen, the hands by which it is touched, and the senses by which it is discovered. But, what is infinite is known only to itself.

3 Thus it is that God can be measured, although he is beyond all measure; thus, the force of his magnitude makes him known to people and yet unknown. And this is the gravest part of the sin of those who are unwilling to recognize him of whom they cannot remain in ignorance. . . .

Chapter 18

1 But, in order that we might more fully and more energetically approach God himself as well as his designs and desires, he has added the assistance of books, in case one wishes to search for God; and after searching, discover him; and after discovering him, believe in him; and after believing in him, serve him.

2 From the beginning he sent into the world people who, because of their innocence and righteousness, were worthy to know God and to make him known to others. These people he filled with the Holy Spirit that they might teach that there is but one God who made the universe and formed man from the earth. He is the true Prometheus, who has regulated the world with a fixed order and fixed endings for the ages.

3 Furthermore, what signs of his sovereign power to judge has he manifested by means of rain and fire! What regulations has he prescribed for placing people under obligation to himself! What recompense has he determined for those who are ignorant of them, those who neglect them, and those who observe them; for, after the present life is ended, he will direct his faithful followers to the reward of eternal life, but the wicked to everlasting and unending fire. Then, all those who have died from the beginning of time will be revived. Their bodies will be reformed. There will be a general review, and everyone will be examined according to his own merits.

4 These are points at which we, too, laughed in times past. We are from your own ranks: Christians are made, not born!

5 These teachers whom we mentioned are called prophets, because it is their function to foretell the future. Their words, as well as the miracles which they performed to win faith in their divine mission, are preserved in the treasures of literature and these are accessible. . . .

Chapter 19

1 Their great antiquity claims prime authority for these records. Among you, too, it is in accord with your superstitious ideas to make faith depend on times past. . . .

Moses was the first of the Prophets; he wove from the past the account of the foundation of the world and the formation of the human race and afterwards the mighty deluge which took vengeance upon the godlessness of that age; he prophesied events right up to his own day. Then, by means of conditions of his own time, he showed forth an image of times to come; according to him, too, the order of events, arranged from the beginning, supplied the reckoning of the age of the world: Moses is found to be alive about 300 years before Danaus, your most ancient of men, came over to Argos.

2 He is 1,000 years earlier than the Trojan War and, therefore, the time of Saturn himself. For, according to the history of Thallus, where it is related

that Belus, King of the Assyrians, and Saturn, King of the Titans, fought with Jupiter, it is shown that Belus antedated the fall of Troy by 322 years. It was by this same Moses, too, that their own true law was given to the Jews by God. . . .

Chapter 24

1 This whole confession of [the devils], whereby they deny that they are gods and declare that there is no other god but the One whose subjects we are, is quite sufficient to repel the charge of treason to the Roman religion. For, if the existence of the gods is uncertain, then surely the existence of your religion is uncertain, too. If there is no religion, since you have no gods for certain, then it is certain we are not guilty of violating religion.

2 On the contrary, your charge will act as a boomerang upon yourselves. In worshipping falsehood you not only neglect—or, I should say (even more than this), do violence to—the true religion of the true God, you actually commit the crime of positive irreligion.

3 Now, suppose the fact were established that gods exist: do you not acquiesce in the common opinion that some god is more sublime and more powerful, and, as it were, the ruler of this universe, a god of perfect majesty? That is the way most people apportion divine power; they would have the power of supreme command in the hands of one, but its exercise in the hands of many. Thus, Plato describes the mighty Jupiter in heaven attended by a host of both gods and demons; so (they say) the procurators, prefects, and governors ought to be held in equal esteem.

4 Yet, what crime does one commit who, in order to render better service to Caesar, transfers his attention and his hope and declares that the title of God, like that of emperor, belongs to none other than the one sovereign, since it is considered a capital offense to call anyone Caesar but Caesar and to listen to such talk?

5 Let one worship God, and another Jupiter; let one extend his hands in supplication to heaven, and another to the altar of Fides; let one (if you so suppose), count the clouds as he prays, and another the squares of the panelled ceiling; let one offer to his God his own soul, and another the soul of a goat.

6 See to it, rather, that this, too, does not tend to confirm the reproach of irreligion; namely, for you to take away one's freedom of religion and put a ban on one's free choice of a god, with the result that it is not lawful for me to worship whom I will, but I am compelled to worship contrary to my will. No one, not even a human, will be willing to receive the worship of an unwilling client.

7 Even the Egyptians were allowed the right— vain superstition that it was—to deify birds and beasts and to condemn to death anyone who killed a god of this sort.

8 Then, too, every province and city has its own god; for example, there is Atargatis in Syria, Dusares in Arabia, Belenus in Noricum, Caelestis in Africa, and the petty kings in Mauretania. The provinces which I have mentioned are, I believe, Roman, but the gods are not, because they are not worshipped at Rome any more than those gods who are listed on the roster of local deities all through Italy itself: Delventinus of Casinum, Visidianus of Narnia, Ancharia of Asculum, Nortia of Volsinii, Valentia of Ocriculum, and Hostia of Sutrium; Juno, among the Faliscans, even received a surname in honor of Father Curis.

9 We are the only ones kept from having our own religion. We offend the Romans and are not considered Romans because we do not worship the god of the Romans.

10 It is well that there is one God of all, to whom we all belong whether we will or not. But among you it is lawful to worship anything you choose except the true God, as if he were not the God of all to whom we all belong.

Chapter 25

1 It seems to me that I certainly have given sufficient proof of [the difference between] false and true divinity, now that I have pointed out how the proof depends not merely on discussion and argument, but also on the spoken testimony of those very ones whom you believe to be gods; so that there is no necessity of adding anything further to this topic.

2 However, since we made particular mention of the name of Rome, I will not avoid the issue which is provoked by that presumption on the part of those who say that the Romans, as a result of their painstaking, scrupulous, religious observance, have been exalted to such sublime heights that they have become masters of the world; and that, in consequence, their gods have brought it about that those surpass all others in prosperity who surpass all others in devotion to their deity.

3 You may be sure that the price was paid by the Roman gods to the name of Rome for the favor. . . .

12 But, how senseless it is to attribute the dignity of the Roman name to their scrupulous religious observances, for it was after the institution of imperial, or, call it, still kingly power, that religion made advances. Although it was Numa who begot the superstitious punctiliousness, nevertheless divine service, with statues and temples, was not established among the Romans at that time.

13 Religious services were shabby, the rituals were unpretentious, and there was no Capitol struggling skyward; altars were improvised and built of sod, vessels were still made of clay from Samos, the odor from sacrifice was slight; the god himself had nowhere put in his appearance. At that time the genius of the Greeks and Tuscans for fashioning statues had not deluged the city. Consequently, the Romans' religious attitude did not precede their greatness, and, therefore, it was not for the fact that they were religious that they are great. . . .

14 On the contrary, how could their greatness be attributed to their religious attitude, since their greatness resulted from their indifference to religion? For, unless I am mistaken, every kingdom or empire is acquired by wars and extended by victories. Yet, wars and victories generally consist in the capture and destruction of cities. This business is not without its violence to the gods; there is indiscriminate destruction of city walls and temples, slaughter of citizens and priests without distinction, pillaging of treasures sacred and profane alike.

15 The sacrileges of the Romans are as numerous as their trophies; their triumphs over the gods as many as those over nations; there is as much plunder as there are statues of the captured gods still on hand.

16 The gods, therefore, endure being adored by their enemies and decree "empire without end" to those whose offences they should have requited, rather than their servile fawning. However, the injury of those who are devoid of feeling is as free from punishment as the worship of them is devoid of significance.

17 Certainly, the assumption cannot harmonize with truth that those people seem to have attained greatness on the merits of their religious service who, as we have pointed out, have either grown by giving offence to religion or have given offence by their growth. Even those whose realms were melted into the sum total of the Roman Empire were not devoid of religious attitudes when they lost their power. . . .

Chapter 37

1 If, as I have said above, we are commanded to love our enemies, who is there for us to hate? Likewise, if we are forbidden to return an injury, lest, through our action, we become wrong-doers like them, who is there for us to injure?

2 Examine yourselves on this point! How often do you rage furiously against the Christians, partly in response to your own feelings, partly out of respect for the laws? How often, too, has a hostile mob, without consulting you, attacked us on their own initiative, with stones and torches in their hands? Why, with the very fury of Bacchanals, they spare not even the corpses of Christians, but drag them from the repose of the grave, from that resting place, as it were, of death; although they are already changed and by now rotting in corruption, they cut them into bits and tear them limb from limb.

3 Yet, what fault do you ever find with people who are bound together by such intimate ties, what retaliation for injury do you ever experience from those who are so disposed even to death, though

even a single night, with a few little torches, could produce such rich vengeance, if it were permitted us to requite evil with evil? But, far be it from us that our God-given religion avenge itself with human fire or that it grieve to endure the suffering whereby it is put to the test.

4 If we wanted to act as open enemies and not merely as secret avengers, would we lack the strength of numbers and troops? Take the Moors and Marcomani and the Parthians themselves or any tribes at all who, even if they are numerous, still live in one place and inhabit their own territories— are they really more numerous than the Christians who are scattered over the whole world? We are but of yesterday, yet we have filled every place among you—cities, islands, fortresses, towns, marketplaces, camp, tribes, town councils, the palace, the senate, the forum; we have left nothing to you but the temples of your gods.

5 For what war would we not have been fit and ready, even though unequally matched in military strength, we who are so ready to be slain, were it not that, according to our rule of life, it is granted us to be killed rather than to kill?

6 Even unarmed and without any uprising, merely as malcontents, simply through hatred and withdrawal, we could have fought against you. For, if such a multitude of people as we are had broken loose from you and had gone into some remote corner of the earth, the loss of so many citizens, of whatever kind they might be, would certainly have made your power blush for shame; in fact, it would even have punished you by this very desertion.

7 Without a doubt, you would have been exceedingly frightened at your loneliness, at the silence of your surroundings, and the stupor, as it were, of a dead world. You would have had to look around for people to rule; there would have been more enemies than citizens left to you.

8 For, now, the enemies whom you have are fewer because of the number of Christians, inasmuch as nearly all the citizens you have in nearly all the cities are Christians. But, you have preferred to call them the enemies of the human race rather than of human error.

9 But, who would snatch you away from those secret enemies that are constantly destroying your spiritual and bodily health—I mean, from the attacks of demons which we ward off from you without any reward and without pay? This alone would have been sufficient revenge for us, if from then on you were left open and exposed to the possession of the impure spirits.

10 Furthermore, instead of thinking of any compensation for so great a protection, you have preferred to consider as enemies a class of people, who, far from being a troublesome burden to you, are actually indispensable. To tell the truth, we are enemies, not, however, of the human race, but rather of human error.

Chapter 40

1 On the other hand, those people deserve the name of a secret society who band together in hatred of good and virtuous people, who cry out for the blood of the innocent, at the same time offering as a justification of their hatred the idle plea that they consider that the Christians are the cause of every public calamity and every misfortune of the people.

2 If the Tiber rises as high as the city walls, if the Nile does not rise to the fields, if the weather will not change, if there is an earthquake, a famine, a plague—straightway the cry is heard: "Toss the Christians to the lion!" So many of them for just one beast?

3 I ask you, before the reign of Tiberius, that is, before the coming of Christ, what great misfortunes befell the world and its cities? We read that the islands of Hiera, Anaphe, Delos, Rhodes, and Cos were swallowed up with many thousands of people.

4 Plato, too, relates that a land larger than Asia or Africa was washed away by the Atlantic Ocean. An earthquake emptied the Corinthian Sea, and the might of the waves wrested Lucania away [from Italy] and left it separate under the name of Sicily. Naturally, these happenings could not fail to be attended by injury to the inhabitants.

5 In those days, when the great flood poured its waters over the whole world, or, as Plato thought, merely over the plains, where then were—I shall not say the Christians who scorn your gods—but your gods themselves? . . .

9 It is to be noted, in connection with such misfortune, that if any disaster befell the cities, the same destruction was visited upon temples as upon city walls; hence, I can clearly demonstrate that the gods were not the cause of the misfortunes, inasmuch as similar misfortunes befell them, too.

10 At all times the human race has deserved ill at God's hands. . . .

12 So, the race now must experience the anger of this same God just as [it did] also in times past, before the name of Christian was even mentioned. His were the blessings people enjoyed, bestowed before they fashioned any of their own deities; why do they not realize that the misfortunes as well come from him whose blessings they have failed to recognize? They are guilty before him toward whom they have been ungrateful. . . .

Chapter 47

11 Everything against truth has been constructed from truth itself. The spirits of error effect this rivalry. By them has this kind of corruption of our life-giving doctrine been instigated; by them, too, have certain tales been started, which, by virtue of their resemblance to the truth, would weaken faith in the latter, or rather, would win it over for themselves, so that anyone may consider that Christians must not be believed because poets and philosophers must not be—or he may think that poets and philosophers should be believed all the more because they are not Christians.

12 Hence, we are ridiculed when we proclaim that God will hold a final judgment. Yet, in like manner the poets and philosophers establish a tribunal in the underworld. And, if we threaten hell, which is a subterranean storehouse of punishment consisting of a mysterious fire, we are laughed to scorn for it. Yet, Pyriphlegethon is also called a river among the dead.

13 If we mention paradise, a place of supernatural beauty destined to receive the souls of the blessed, separated from knowledge of the ordinary world by the wall, as it were, of that fiery zone, the Elysian Fields have already won belief.

14 Whence, I ask you, comes such close resemblance with the philosophers and poets? From no place else but from our own doctrines. If from our doctrines as their primary source, then our doctrines are more reliable and more worthy of belief than the copies of them which also find belief. But, if from their own ideas, then our doctrines will be considered copies of things subsequent to themselves—something which the nature of things precludes. For, no shadow ever exists before the body nor does a copy precede the original. . . .

Chapter 50

12 But, carry on, good officials; you will become much better in the eyes of the people if you sacrifice the Christians for them. Crucify us—torture us—condemn us—destroy us! Your iniquity is the proof of our innocence. For this reason God permits us to suffer these things. In fact, by recently condemning a Christian maid to the *pander* rather than to the *panther* [in the arena], you confessed that among us a stain on our virtue is considered worse than any punishment or any form of death.

13 Yet, your tortures accomplish nothing, though each is more refined than the last; rather, they are an enticement to our religion. We become more numerous every time we are hewn down by you: the blood of Christians is seed.

14 Many among you urge people to endure suffering and death, as Cicero does in his *Tusculans*, Seneca in his essay on chance, Diogenes, Pyrrho, and Callinicus; yet, their words do not discover such disciples as do the Christians who teach by deeds.

15 That very obstinacy which you rebuke is the teacher. For, who is not stirred by the contemplation of it to inquire what is really beneath the surface? And who, when he has inquired, does not approach us? Who, when he has approached, does not desire to suffer so that he may procure the full grace of God, that he may purchase from him full pardon by paying with his own blood?

16 For, by this means, all sins are forgiven. That is why we thank you immediately for your sentences of condemnation. Such is the difference between things divine and human. When we are condemned by you, we are acquitted by God.

17. Origen: Against Celsus

Origen was the most brilliant, prolific, and influential author of the early church. Born in 185 CE and raised by Christian parents, he was something of a child prodigy among the Christians of Alexandria, Egypt. While still in his late teens, he was, according to Eusebius, appointed head of the famed Catechetical School, a kind of school of Christian higher education for converts. Origen soon became the leading proto-orthodox spokesperson of his day. Unfortunately, his sophisticated exegetical

Origen: Against Celsus, from *Origen: Contra Celsum*, ed. H. Chadwick. 2nd ed. Cambridge: Cambridge University Press, 1965. Reprinted with the permission of Cambridge University Press.

and theological works survive only in part, largely because some of his views were pronounced heretical three centuries after his death (see Chapter 16).

Unlike the other apologies given here, Origen's *Against Celsus* is directed against a specific opponent, Celsus, whom we have seen already (see selection 11). Celsus's knowledge of Christianity was based on first-hand knowledge of the Gospels and other Christian writings. Origen's detailed refutation, in which he quotes Celsus's work at length, ran to a full eight books. The following are excerpts drawn from Book I, including Origen's dismissal of the arguments of an imaginary character that Celsus had introduced, a Jewish intellectual who attacked the rational basis of Christianity.

1 Celsus' first main point in his desire to attack Christianity is that the Christians secretly make associations with one another contrary to the laws, because *societies which are public are allowed by the laws, but secret societies are illegal.*[1] And wishing to slander the so-called *love (agape) which Christians have for one another*, he says that *it exists because of the common danger and is more powerful than any oath.* As he talks much of *the common law* saying that *the associations of the Christians violate this*, I have to make this reply. Suppose that a person were living among the Scythians whose laws are contrary to the divine law, who had no opportunity to go elsewhere and was compelled to live among them; such a person for the sake of the true law, though illegal among the Scythians, would rightly form associations with like-minded people contrary to the laws of the Scythians. So, at the bar of truth, the laws of the nations such as those about images and the godless polytheism are laws of the Scythians or, if possible, more impious than theirs. Therefore it is not wrong to form associations against the laws for the sake of truth. For just as it would be right for people to form associations secretly to kill a tyrant who had seized control of their city, so too, since the devil, as Christians call him, and falsehood reign as tyrants, Christians form associations against the devil contrary to his laws, in order to save others whom they might be able to persuade to abandon the law which is like that of the Scythians and of a tyrant.

2 Next he says that *the doctrine* (obviously meaning Judaism with which Christianity is connected) *was originally barbarian.* Having an open mind he does not reproach the gospel for its barbarian origin, but praises *the barbarians* for being *capable of discovering doctrines*; but he adds to this that *the Greeks are better able to judge the value of what the barbarians have discovered, and to establish the doctrines and put them into practice by virtue.* Taking up the words he has used this is our reply in respect of the fundamental truths of Christianity. A person coming to the gospel from Greek conceptions and training would not only *judge* that it was true, but would also *put* it *into practice* and so prove it to be correct; and he would complete what seemed to be lacking judged by the criterion of a Greek proof, thus establishing the truth of Christianity. Moreover, we have to say this, that the gospel has a proof which is peculiar to itself, and which is more divine than a Greek proof based on dialectical argument. This more divine demonstration the apostle calls a "demonstration of the Spirit and of power"—of spirit because of the prophecies and especially those which refer to Christ, which are capable of convincing anyone who reads them; of power because of the prodigious miracles which may be proved to have happened by this argument among many others, that traces of them still remain among those who live according to the will of the Logos.

---

1 Italics in this document indicate statements that Origen has evidently drawn directly from Celsus' book, *The True Word.*

3 After this he says that *Christians perform their rites and teach their doctrines in secret,* and *they do this with good reason to escape the death penalty that hangs over them.* He compares the *danger* to *the risks encountered for the sake of philosophy as by Socrates.* He could also have added "as by Pythagoras and other philosophers." I reply to this that in Socrates' case the Athenians at once regretted what they had done, and cherished no grievance against him or against Pythagoras; at any rate, the Pythagoreans have for a long time established their schools in the part of Italy which has been called Magna Graecia. But in the case of the Christians the Roman Senate, the contemporary emperors, the army, the people, and the relatives of believers fought against the gospel and would have hindered it; and it would have been defeated by the combined force of so many unless it had overcome and risen above the opposition by divine power, so that it has conquered the whole world that was conspiring against it. . . .

9 After this he urges us to *follow reason and a rational guide in accepting doctrines* on the ground that *anyone who believes people without so doing is certain to be deceived.* And he compares those who believe without rational thought to the *begging priests of Cybele and soothsayers, and to worshippers of Mithras and Sabazius, and whatever else one might meet, apparitions of Hecate or of some daemon or daemons. For just as among them scoundrels frequently take advantage of the lack of education of gullible people and lead them wherever they wish, so also,* he says, *this happens among the Christians.* He says that *some do not even want to give or to receive a reason for what they believe, and use such expressions as "Do not ask questions; just believe," and "Your faith will save you."* And he affirms that they say: *"The wisdom in the world is an evil, and foolishness a good thing."* My answer to this is that if every one could abandon the business of life and devote his time to philosophy, no other course ought to be followed but this alone. For in Christianity, if I make no vulgar boasting, there will be found to be no less profound study of the writings that are believed;

we explain the obscure utterances of the prophets, and the parables in the gospels, and innumerable other events or laws which have a symbolical meaning. However, if this is impossible, since, partly owing to the necessities of life and partly owing to human weakness, very few people are enthusiastic about rational thought, what better way of helping the multitude could be found other than that given to the nations by Jesus?

Moreover, concerning the multitude of believers who have renounced the great flood of evil in which they formerly used to wallow, we ask this question—is it better that those who believe without thought should somehow have been made reformed characters and be helped by the belief that they are punished for sin and rewarded for good works, or that we should not allow them to be converted with simple faith until they might devote themselves to the study of rational arguments? For obviously all but a very few would fail to obtain the help which they have derived from simple belief, but would remain living a very evil life. Therefore whatever other proof there may be that a doctrine so beneficial to mankind could not have come to human life apart from divine providence this consideration must also be enumerated with the rest. A religious person will not suppose that even a physician concerned with bodies, who restores many people to health, comes to live among cities and nations without divine providence, for no benefit comes to humankind without God's action. If a person who has healed the bodies of many or improved their condition does not cure people without divine providence, how much more must that be true of him who cured, converted, and improved the souls of many, and attached them to the supreme God, and taught them to refer every action to the standard of his pleasure, and to avoid anything that is displeasing to him, down to the most insignificant of words or deeds or even of casual thoughts? . . .

27 Anyone who examines the facts will see that Jesus ventured to do things beyond the power of human nature and that what he ventured to do he accomplished. From the beginning every one opposed the spread of his doctrine over the whole world, the emperors in each period, the chief generals under them, and all governors, so to speak, who had been entrusted with any power at all, and furthermore, the rulers in each city, the soldiers, and the people. Yet it conquered, since as the word of God it could not be prevented; and as it was stronger than all those adversaries it overcame all Greece and the most part of the barbarian countries, and converted innumerable souls to follow its worship of God. However, it was inevitable that in the great number of people overcome by the word, because there are many more *vulgar and illiterate* people than those who have been trained in rational thinking, the former class should far outnumber the more intelligent. But as Celsus did not want to recognize this fact, he thinks that the love to humankind shown by the word, which even extends to every soul from the rising of the sun, is *vulgar* and that *it is successful only among the uneducated because of its vulgarity and utter illiteracy.* Yet not even Celsus asserts that only vulgar people have been converted by the gospel to follow the religion of Jesus; for he admits that *among them there are some moderate, reasonable, and intelligent people who readily interpret allegorically.*

28 He also introduces an imaginary character, somehow imitating a child having his first lessons with an orator, and brings in a Jew who addresses childish remarks to Jesus and says nothing worthy of a philosopher's grey hairs. This too let us examine to the best of our ability and prove that he has failed to keep the character entirely consistent with that of a Jew in his remarks. After this he represents the Jew as having a conversation with Jesus himself and refuting him on many charges, as he thinks: first, because *he fabricated the story of his birth from a virgin*; and he reproaches him because *he came from a Jewish village and from a poor country woman who earned her living by spinning. He says that she was driven out by her husband, who was a carpenter by trade, as she was convicted of adultery.* Then he says that *after*

she had been driven out by her husband and while she was wandering about in a disgraceful way she secretly gave birth to Jesus. And he says that *because he was poor he hired himself out as a workman in Egypt, and there tried his hand at certain magical powers on which the Egyptians pride themselves; he returned full of conceit because of these powers, and on account of them gave himself the title of God.* In my judgment, however, (and I cannot allow anything said by unbelievers to pass unexamined, but study the fundamental principles), all these things are in harmony with the fact that Jesus was worthy of the proclamation that he is son of God.

29 Among people noble birth, honorable and distinguished parents, an upbringing at the hands of wealthy people who are able to spend money on the education of their child, and a great and famous native country, are things which help to make a person famous and distinguished and get his name well known. But when a man whose circumstances are entirely contrary to this is able to rise above the hindrances to him and to become well known, and to impress those who hear him so that he becomes eminent and famous throughout the whole world so that people alter their tone about him, should we not admire at once such a nature for being noble, for tackling great difficulties, and for possessing remarkable boldness?

If one were also to inquire further into the circumstances of such a man, how could one help trying to find out how a man, brought up in meanness and poverty, who had no general education and had learnt no arguments and doctrines by which he could have become a persuasive speaker to crowds and a popular leader and have won over many hearers, could devote himself to teaching new doctrines and introduce to mankind a doctrine which did away with the customs of the Jews while reverencing their prophets, and which abolished the laws of the Greeks particularly in respect of the worship of God? How could such a man, brought up in this way, who had received no serious instruction from humans (as even those who speak evil of him admit), say such noble utterances about the judgment of God, about the punishment for wickedness, and rewards for goodness, that not only rustic and illiterate people were converted by his words, but also a considerable number of the more intelligent, whose vision could penetrate the veil of apparently quite simple expressions, which conceals within itself, as one might say, a more mysterious interpretation?

The Seriphian in Plato reproached Themistocles after he had become famous for his generalship, saying that he had not won his fame by his own character, but from the good luck to have had the most famous city in all Greece as his home. From Themistocles, who was open-minded and saw that his home had also contributed to his fame, he received the answer: "I would never have been so famous if I had been a Seriphian, nor would you have been a Themistocles if you had had the good luck to be an Athenian." But our Jesus, who is reproached for having *come from a village,* and that not a Greek one, who did not belong to any nation prominent in public opinion, and who is maligned as the son of *a poor woman who earned her living by spinning* and as having left his home country *on account of poverty* and *hired himself out as a workman in Egypt,* was not just a Seriphian, to take the illustration I have quoted, who came from the least and most insignificant island, but was a Seriphian of the very lowest class, if I may say so. Yet he has been able to shake the whole human world, not only more than Themistocles the Athenian, but even more than Pythagoras and Plato and any other wise men or emperors or generals in any part of the world.

30 Who, therefore, that does not give merely a cursory study to the nature of the facts, would not be amazed at a man who overcame and was able to rise above all the factors that tended to discredit him, and in his reputation to surpass all the distinguished men that have ever lived? It is uncommon for people who are eminent among others to have the ability to acquire fame for several things at once. One has been admired and become famous for wisdom, another

for generalship, and some barbarians for miraculous powers in incantations, and some for one talent, some for another; they have not been admired and become eminent for several abilities at the same time. Yet Jesus, in addition to his other abilities, is admired for his wisdom, for his miracles, and for his leadership. For he persuaded some to join him in abandoning the laws, not like a tyrant, nor like a robber who incites his followers against others, nor like a rich person who provides support for those who come over to his side, nor like any who by common consent are regarded as blameworthy. He did this as a teacher of the doctrine about the God of the universe, of the worship offered to him and of every moral action which is able to bring the person whose life follows his teaching into relationship with the supreme God. To Themistocles or any of the other eminent men nothing happened to militate against their fame; but in the case of Jesus, besides the points I have mentioned which have sufficient influence to hide a man's character in ignominy even if he were a most noble person, his death by crucifixion which seems to be disgraceful was enough to take away even such reputation as he had already gained, and to make those who had been deluded (as people who do not agree with his teaching think) abandon their delusion and condemn the man who had deceived them.

31 In addition to this, if, as people who malign Jesus say, his disciples did not see him after he rose from the dead and were not convinced that there was something divine about him, one might wonder how it came about that they were not afraid to suffer the same fate as their master and met danger boldly, and that they left their homes to obey Jesus' will by teaching the doctrines which he gave to them. I think that a person who examines the facts with an open mind would say that these men would not have given themselves up to a precarious existence for the sake of Jesus' teaching unless they had some deep conviction which he implanted in them when he taught them that they should not only live according to his precepts but should also influence others—and should do so in spite of the fact that destruction, as far as human life is concerned, clearly awaited anyone who ventured to introduce new opinions in all places and to all people, and who would not keep up friendship with any one who continued to hold his former opinions and habits. Did the disciples of Jesus fail to see this? They dared not only to show to the Jews from the sayings of the prophets that he was the one to whom the prophets referred, but also showed to the other nations that he who was crucified quite recently accepted this death willingly for the human race, like those who have died for their country to check epidemics of plague, or famines, or stormy seas. For it is probable that in the nature of things there are certain mysterious causes which are hard for the multitude to understand, which are responsible for the fact that one righteous man dying voluntarily for the community may avert the activities of evil daemons by expiation, since it is they who bring about plagues, or famines, or stormy seas, or anything similar.

Let people therefore who do not want to believe that Jesus died on a cross for others, tell us whether they would not accept the many Greek and barbarian stories about some who have died for the community to destroy evils that had taken hold of cities and nations. Or do they think that, while these stories are historically true, yet there is nothing plausible about this man (as people suppose him to be) to suggest that he died to destroy a great daemon, in fact the ruler of daemons, who held in subjection all the souls of humans that have come to earth? As the disciples of Jesus saw this and much more besides, which they probably learnt from Jesus in secret, and as they were also filled with a certain power, since it was not just a virgin imagined by a poet who gave them "strength and courage" but the true understanding and wisdom of God, they sought eagerly that they might become "well-known among all people," not only among all the Argives, but even among all the Greeks and barbarians also, and that "they might carry away a good report."

32 Let us return, however, to the words put into the mouth of the Jew, where *the mother of Jesus* is described as having been *turned out by the carpenter who was betrothed to her, as she had been convicted of adultery and had a child by a certain soldier named Panthera.* Let us consider whether those who fabricated the myth that the virgin and Panthera committed adultery and that the carpenter turned her out, were not blind when they concocted all this to get rid of the miraculous conception by the Holy Spirit. For on account of its highly miraculous character they could have falsified the story in other ways without, as it were, unintentionally admitting that Jesus was not born of an ordinary marriage. It was inevitable that those who did not accept the miraculous birth of Jesus would have invented some lie. But the fact that they did not do this convincingly, but kept as part of the story that the virgin did not conceive Jesus by Joseph, makes the lie obvious to people who can see through fictitious stories and show them up. Is it reasonable that a man who ventured to do such great things for humankind in order that, so far as in him lay, all Greeks and barbarians in expectation of the divine judgment might turn from evil and act in every respect acceptably to the Creator of the universe, should have had, not a miraculous birth, but a birth more illegitimate and disgraceful than any? As addressing Greeks and Celsus in particular who, whether he holds Plato's doctrines or not, nevertheless quotes them, I would ask this question. Would he who sends souls down into human bodies compel a man to undergo a birth more shameful than any, and not even have brought him into human life by legitimate marriage, when he was to do such great deeds and to teach so many people and to convert many from the flood of evil? Or is it more reasonable (and I say this now following Pythagoras, Plato, and Empedocles, whom Celsus often mentions) that there are certain secret principles by which each soul that enters a body does so in accordance with its merits and former character? It is therefore probable that this soul, which lived a more useful life on earth than many others (to avoid appearing to beg the question by saying "all" others), needed a body which was not only distinguished among human bodies, but was also superior to all others.

33 Suppose it is true that a certain soul which in accordance with certain mysterious principles does not deserve to be in the body of a completely irrational being, yet is not worthy to be in that of a purely rational being, puts on a monstrous body so that reason cannot be fully developed in one born in this way, whose head is out of proportion to the rest of the body and is far too small; and suppose that another soul receives a body of such a kind that it is slightly more rational than the former instance, and another still more so, the nature of the body being more or less opposed to the apprehension of reason. Why then should there not be a certain soul that takes a body which is entirely miraculous, which has something in common with others in order to be able to live with them, but which also has something out of the ordinary, in order that the soul may remain uncontaminated by sin? Suppose that the views of the physiognomists are granted, of Zopyrus, Loxus, or Polemon, or anyone else who wrote about these matters and professed to possess some remarkable knowledge, that all bodies conform to the habits of their souls; then for the soul that was to live a miraculous life on earth and to do great things, a body was necessary, not, as Celsus thinks, produced by the adultery of Panthera and a virgin (for the offspring of such impure intercourse must rather have been some stupid man who would harm people by teaching licentiousness, unrighteousness, and other evils, and not a teacher of self-control, righteousness and the other virtues), but, as the prophets foretold, the offspring of a virgin who according to the promised sign should give birth to a child whose name was significant of his work, showing that at his birth God would be with people.

34 It appears to me that it would have been appropriate to the words he has put into the mouth of the Jew to have quoted the prophecy of Isaiah which says that Emmanuel shall be born of a virgin. Celsus, however, did not quote this, either because he did not know it, though he professes to know everything, or if he had read it, because he wilfully said nothing of it to avoid appearing unintentionally to support the doctrine which is opposed to his purpose. The passage reads as follows: "And the Lord spoke again to Ahaz saying, Ask a sign of the Lord your God, either in the depth or in the height. And Ahaz said, I will not ask, neither will I tempt the Lord. And he said, Hear now, oh house of David, is it a small thing to you to strive with people? How also do you strive with the Lord? Therefore shall the Lord give you a sign. Behold a virgin shall conceive in her womb and bring forth a son, and you shall call his name Emmanuel," which is interpreted "God with us."[2] That it was out of wickedness that Celsus did not quote the prophecy is made clear to me from the fact that although he has quoted several things from the gospel according to Matthew, such as *the star that arose at the birth of Jesus* and other miracles, yet he has not even mentioned this at all. But if a Jew should ingeniously explain it away by saying that it is not written "Behold a virgin" but, instead of that, "behold a young woman," we should say to him that the word Alma, which the Septuagint translated by "parthenos" (virgin) and others by "neanis" (young woman), also occurs, so they say, in Deuteronomy applied to a virgin. The passage reads as follows: "If a girl that is a virgin is betrothed to a man, and a man finds her in a city and lie with her, you shall bring both out to the gate of the city and stone them with stones that they die, the young woman because she did not cry out in the city, and the man because he disgraced his neighbor's wife." And after that: "If a man finds a girl that is betrothed in the country and the man force her and lie with her, you shall kill only the man that lay with her, and you shall do nothing to the young woman; there is no sin worthy of death in the young woman."[3]

---

2 Isa 7:10–14; cf Matt 1:23.

3 Deut 22:23–26.

35 However, lest we appear to depend on a Hebrew word to explain to people, who do not understand whether to accept it or not, that the prophet said that this man would be born of a virgin (concerning whose birth it was said "God with us"), let us explain the affirmation from the passage itself. The Lord, according to the scripture, said to Ahaz: "Ask a sign from the Lord your God, either in the depth or in the height." And then the sign that is given in this: "Behold a virgin shall conceive and bear a son." What sort of a sign would it be if a young woman not a virgin bore a son? And which would be more appropriate as the mother of Emmanuel, that is "God with us," a woman who had had intercourse with a man and conceived by female passion, or a woman who was still chaste and pure and a virgin? It is surely fitting that the latter should give birth to a child at whose birth it is said "God with us." If, however, he explains this away by saying that Ahaz was addressed in the words "ask a sign of the Lord your God," we will say: Who was born in Ahaz's time whose birth is referred to in the words "Emmanuel, which is God with us"? For if no one is to be found, obviously the words to Ahaz were addressed to the house of David, because according to the scripture our Saviour was "of the seed of David according to the flesh."[4] Furthermore, this sign is said to be "in the depth or in the height," since "this is he who descended and who ascended far above all heavens that he might fill all things."[5] I say these things as speaking to a Jew who believes the prophecy. But perhaps Celsus or any who agree with him will tell us with what kind of mental apprehension the prophet speaks about the future, whether in this instance or in the others recorded in the prophecies. Has he foreknowledge of the future or not? If he has, then the prophets possessed divine inspiration. If he has not, let Celsus account for the mind of a man who ventures to speak about the future and is admired for his prophecy among the Jews. . . .

37 I think that it has been fairly substantiated not only that our Saviour was to be born of a virgin, but also that there were prophets among the Jews who did not merely make general pronouncements about the future, such as those about Christ and about the kingdoms of the world, and the future destiny of Israel, and that the Gentiles would believe in the Saviour, and many other utterances about him. They also made particular predictions, as for instance of the way in which the lost asses of Kish were to be found, and of the illness which the son of the king of Israel suffered, or any other story of this sort.

To Greeks, however, who disbelieve in the virgin birth of Jesus I have to say that the Creator showed in the birth of various animals that what he did in the case of one animal, he could do, if he wished, also with others and even with people themselves. Among the animals there are certain females that have no intercourse with the male, as writers on animals say of vultures; this creature preserves the continuation of the species without any copulation. Why, therefore, is it incredible that if God wished to send some divine teacher to humankind he should have made the organism of him that was to be born come into being in a different way instead of using a generative principle derived from the sexual intercourse of men and women? Moreover, according to the Greeks themselves not all people were born from a man and a woman. For if the world was created as even many Greeks think, the first people must have had come into existence without sexual intercourse, but from the earth instead, generative principles having existed in the earth. But I think this more incredible than that Jesus should have been born half like other people. And in addressing Greeks it is not out of place to quote Greek stories, lest we should appear to be the only people to have related this incredible story. For some have thought fit (not in respect of any ancient stories and heroic tales but of people born quite recently) to record as though it were possible that when Plato was born of Amphictione Ariston was prevented from having sexual intercourse with her

---

4 Rom 1:3.

5 Eph 4:10.

until she had brought forth the child which she had by Apollo. But these stories are really myths, which have led people to invent such a tale about a man because they regarded him as having superior wisdom and power to the multitude, and as having received the original composition of his body from better and more divine seed, thinking that this was appropriate for people with superhuman powers. But when Celsus has introduced the Jew as disputing with Jesus and pouring ridicule on the pretence, as he thinks, of his birth from a virgin, and as quoting the Greek myths about *Danae* and *Melanippe* and *Auge* and *Antiope*, I have to reply that these words would be appropriate to a vulgar buffoon and not to a person who takes his professed task seriously.

38 Moreover, although he took the story of Jesus' departure to Egypt from the narrative in the gospel according to Matthew, he did not believe all the miracles connected with it, nor that an angel directed this, nor that Jesus' departure from Judaea and sojourn in Egypt had some hidden meaning. He made up another tale. For although he somehow accepts the incredible miracles which Jesus did, by which he persuaded the multitude to follow him as Christ, yet he wants to attack them as though they were done by magic and not by divine power. He says: *He was brought up in secret and hired himself out as a workman in Egypt, and after having tried his hand at certain magical powers he returned from there, and on account of those powers gave himself the title of God.* I do not know why a magician should have taken the trouble to teach a doctrine which persuades everyone to do every action as before God who judges each one for all his works, and to instill this conviction in his disciples whom he intended to use as the ministers of his teaching. Did they persuade their hearers because they had been taught to do miracles in this way, or did they not do any miracles? It is quite irrational to maintain that they did no miracles at all, but that, although they had believed without any adequate reasons comparable to the dialectical wisdom of the Greeks, they devoted themselves to teaching a new doctrine to any whom they might visit. What inspired them with confidence to teach the doctrine and to put forward new ideas? On the other hand, if they did perform miracles, is it plausible to suggest that they were magicians, when they risked their lives in great dangers for a teaching which forbids magic?

39 I do not think it worthwhile to combat an argument which he does not put forward seriously, but only as mockery: *Then was the mother of Jesus beautiful? And because she was beautiful did God have sexual intercourse with her, although by nature He cannot love a corruptible body? It is not likely that God would have fallen in love with her since she was neither wealthy nor of royal birth; for nobody knew her, not even her neighbors.* It is just ridicule also when he says: *When she was hated by the carpenter and turned out, neither divine power nor the gift of persuasion saved her. Therefore,* he says, *these things have nothing to do with the kingdom of God.* What is the difference between this and vulgar abuse at street corners, and the talk of people who say nothing worth serious attention?

40 After this he takes the story from the gospel according to Matthew and perhaps also from the other gospels, about the descent of the dove upon the Saviour when he was baptized by John, and wants to attack the story as a fiction. But after he has pulled to pieces, as he thought, the story of our Saviour's birth from a virgin, he does not quote the next events in order. For passion and hatred have no orderly method, and people who are in a rage and have some personal hostility say whatever comes into their heads when they attack those whom they hate, since they are prevented by their passion from stating their accusations carefully and in order. If he had been careful about the order, he would have taken the gospel and, having set out to criticise it, would have brought his objections against the first story first, and then the second, and so on with the rest. But in fact after the birth from the virgin Celsus, who professed to know everything, goes on to criticize our story about the appearance of the Holy Spirit in the form of a dove at the Baptism; then after this he attacks the prophecy about our Saviour's advent, and after that runs back to what is recorded after the birth of Jesus, the story about the star and the magi who came from the east to worship the child. And if you were to look yourself, you would find many muddled statements of Celsus throughout his book; so by this those who know how to preserve and to look for order may prove that he was very arrogant and boastful when he entitled his book *The True Doctrine,* a title used by none of the distinguished philosophers. Plato says that a sensible person will not be confident about such obscure questions. And Chrysippus, who always gave an account of the reasons which influenced him, refers us to people whom we might find to give a better explanation than himself. Celsus, therefore, is wiser than both these men and the other Greeks; it was consistent with his assertion that he knows everything when he entitled his book *The True Doctrine.*

41 Lest we should appear to pass over his points intentionally for lack of an answer, we decided to refute each of his objections to the best of our ability, with a view not to the natural order and sequence of subjects but to the order of the objections written in his book. Let us, then, see what he says when attacking the story of the physical appearance, as it were, of the Holy Spirit seen by the Saviour in the form of a dove. His Jew continues by saying this to him whom we confess to be our Lord Jesus: *When,* he says, *you were bathing near John, you say that you saw what appeared to be a bird fly towards you out of the air.* His Jew then asks: *What trustworthy witness saw this apparition, or who heard a voice from heaven adopting you as son of God? There is no proof except for your word and the evidence which you may produce of one of the men who were punished with you.*

42 Before we begin the defence, we must say that an attempt to substantiate almost any story as historical fact, even if it is true, and to produce complete certainty about it, is one of the most difficult tasks and in some cases is impossible. Suppose, for example, that someone says the Trojan war never happened, in particular because it is bound up with the impossible story about a certain Achilles having had Thetis, a sea-goddess, as his mother, and Peleus, a man, as his father, or that Sarpedon was son of Zeus, or Ascalaphus and Ialmenus of Ares, or Aeneas of Aphrodite. How could we substantiate this, especially as we are embarrassed by the fictitious stories which for some unknown reason are bound up with the opinion, which everyone believes, that there really was a war in Troy between the Greeks and the Trojans? Suppose also that someone does not believe the story about Oedipus and Jocasta, and Eteocles and Polyneices, the sons of them both, because the half-maiden Sphinx has been mixed up with it. How could we prove the historicity of a story like this? So also in the case of the Epigoni, even if there is nothing incredible involved in the story, or in that of the return of the Heraclidae, or innumerable other instances. Anyone who reads the stories with a fair mind, who wants to keep himself from being deceived by them, will decide what he will accept and what he will interpret allegorically, searching out the meaning of the authors who wrote such fictitious stories, and what he will disbelieve as having been written to gratify certain people. We have said this by way of introduction to the whole question of the narrative about Jesus in the gospels, not in order to invite people with intelligence to mere irrational faith, but with a desire to show that readers need an open mind and considerable study, and, if I may say so, need to enter into the mind of the writers to find out with what spiritual meaning each event was recorded. . . .

46 The law and the prophets are filled with accounts as miraculous as that recorded of Jesus at the baptism about the dove and the voice from heaven. But I think that the miracles performed by Jesus are evidence that the Holy Spirit was seen then in the form of a dove, although

Celsus attacks them by saying that he learnt how to do them among the Egyptians. And I will not mention these only, but also, as is reasonable, those which were done by Jesus' apostles. For without miracles and wonders they would not have persuaded those who heard new doctrines and new teachings to leave their traditional religion and to accept the apostles' teachings at the risk of their lives. Traces of that Holy Spirit who appeared in the form of a dove are still preserved among Christians. They charm daemons away and perform many cures and perceive certain things about the future according to the will of the Logos. Even if Celsus, or the Jew that he introduced, ridicule what I am about to say, nevertheless it shall be said that many have come to Christianity as it were in spite of themselves, some spirit having turned their mind suddenly from hating the gospel to dying for it by means of a vision by day or by night. We have known many instances like this. But if we were to commit them to writing, although we were eyewitnesses at the time, we would bring upon ourselves downright mockery from the unbelievers, who would think that we were inventing the stories ourselves like those whom they suspect of having invented such tales. But as God is witness of our good conscience, we want to lend support to the divine teaching not by any false reports, but by definite facts of various kinds.

Since, however, it is a Jew who raises difficulties in the story of the Holy Spirit's descent in the form of a dove to Jesus, I would say to him: My good man, who is the speaker in Isaiah that says "And now the Lord sent me and his spirit"? In this text although it is doubtful whether it means that the Father and the Holy Spirit sent Jesus or that the Father sent Christ and the Holy Spirit, it is the second interpretation which is right. After the Saviour had been sent, then the Holy Spirit was sent, in order that the prophet's saying might be fulfilled; and, as it was necessary that the fulfillment of the prophecy should also be made known to posterity, for this reason the disciples of Jesus recorded what had happened.

47 I would like to have told Celsus, when he represented the Jew as in some way accepting John as a baptist in baptizing Jesus, that a man who lived not long after John and Jesus recorded that John was a baptist who baptized for the remission of sins. For Josephus in the eighteenth book of the Jewish antiquities bears witness that John was a baptist and promised purification to people who were baptized.[6] The same author, although he did not believe in Jesus as Christ, sought for the cause of the fall of Jerusalem and the destruction of the temple. He ought to have said that the plot against Jesus was the reason why these catastrophes came upon the people, because they had killed the prophesied Christ; however, although unconscious of it, he is not far from the truth when he says that these disasters befell the Jews to avenge James the Just, who was a brother of "Jesus the so-called Christ," since they had killed him who was a very righteous man. This is the James whom Paul, the true disciple of Jesus, says that he saw, describing him as the Lord's brother, not referring so much to their blood-relationship or common upbringing as to his moral life and understanding. If therefore he says that the destruction of Jerusalem happened because of James, would it not be more reasonable to say that this happened on account of Jesus the Christ? His divinity is testified by great numbers of churches, which consist of people converted from the flood of sins and who are dependent on the Creator and refer every decision to his pleasure. . . .

68 After this, suspecting that the great works done by Jesus would be pointed out, of which, although there is much to say, we have only said a little, Celsus pretends to grant that the scriptures may be true when they speak of *cures or resurrection or a few loaves feeding many people, from which many fragments were left over, or any other monstrous tales,* as he thinks, *related by the disciples.* And he goes on to say: *Come, let us believe that these miracles really were done by you.* Then he at

---

6 *Antiquities* 18.5.2.

once puts them on a level with *the works of sorcerers who profess to do wonderful miracles, and the accomplishments of those who are taught by the Egyptians, who for a few obols make known their sacred lore in the middle of the market-place and drive daemons out of people and blow away diseases and invoke the souls of heroes, displaying expensive banquets and dining-tables and cakes and dishes which are nonexistent, and who make things move as though they were alive although they are not really so, but only appear as such in the imagination.* And he says: *Since these men do these wonders, ought we to think them sons of God? Or ought we to say that they are the practices of wicked men possessed by an evil daemon?*

You see how by these words he gives his assent, as it were, to the reality of magic. I do not know whether he is the same as the man who wrote several books against magic. But because it happens to be to his advantage for his purpose he compares the stories about Jesus with tales of magic. They might have been comparable if Jesus had done his miracles, like magicians, merely to show his own powers. But in fact no sorcerer uses his tricks to call the spectators to moral reformation; nor does he educate by the fear of God

people who were astounded by what they saw, nor does he attempt to persuade the onlookers to live as people who will be judged by God. Sorcerers do none of these things, since they have neither the ability nor even the will to do so. Nor do they even want to have anything to do with reforming people, seeing that they themselves are filled with the most shameful and infamous sins. Is it not likely that one who used the miracles that he performed to call those who saw the happenings to moral reformation, would have shown himself as an example of the best life, not only to his genuine disciples but also to the rest? Jesus did this in order that his disciples might give themselves up to teaching people according to the will of God, and that the others, who have been taught as much by his doctrine as by his moral life and miracles the right way to live, might do every action by referring to the pleasure of the supreme God. If the life of Jesus was of this character, how could anyone reasonably compare him with the behavior of sorcerers and fail to believe that according to God's promise he was God who had appeared in a human body for the benefit of our race?

5

Anti-Judaic Polemic

The Opposition to Jews in Early Christianity

Jesus and his followers were Jews who worshipped the Jewish God, followed the Jewish Law, interpreted the Jewish Scriptures, and kept Jewish customs. And yet, within a century of Jesus' death, the Christian church had become widely and actively anti-Jewish. How did that happen?

Many scholars locate the roots of the problem, ultimately, in the failure of the Christian mission to the Jews (see Chapter 2). When Jews by and large rejected the Christian message about Jesus, Christians naturally sought to defend this message by appealing to the Jewish Bible itself. Their interpretations of Scripture, however, were not widely accepted outside of Christian circles; a rift resulted, each side arguing that the other was blind both to the obvious sense of the text and to the will of God who inspired it. Battle lines were drawn, and the resultant polemic and counter-polemic grew harsh. Eventually there emerged two separate religions: one maintaining that Jesus was the Messiah who brought salvation for all people, Jews and gentiles, apart from the Jewish Law, and the other denying Jesus' messiahship and insisting that Jews alone were God's chosen people, whose special standing before God was shown precisely by the practice of Judaism as set forth in the Law.

This situation naturally presented the followers of Jesus with a range of sociopolitical and theological difficulties. On the sociopolitical level were the questions already mentioned in Chapter 4: how could Christians claim to represent an ancient religion (and thereby justify their existence in a world that respected antiquity but not innovation), when communities that originally embraced that religion were still thriving—especially when the Christians themselves did not observe the religion's best-known practices and customs such as circumcision, kosher foods, and Sabbath?

Theologically the problems were no less acute: if the God of the Old Testament had called the people of Israel and given them his Law, how could Christians who did not follow that Law claim to be his people? And if there was only one God, how could they both—Jews and Christians—uniquely be his special people? Moreover, how were Jews who accepted Jesus as Messiah to be treated in the church? Should they be required to give up their Jewishness? Ultimately the questions involved the relationship of the New to the Old, of Christ to Moses, of salvation through Jesus' death and resurrection to the election of the children of Israel.

As with most aspects of early Christianity, an almost endless range of answers emerged. Some Christians who had converted from Judaism maintained that Christianity needed to remain true to its Jewish roots, that contrary to the more general opinion (which was indebted to the persuasive influence of the apostle Paul), anyone who believed in Jesus needed to become Jewish to be a full heir of the promises made to Israel. For these believers the New fulfilled the Old; but the Old, as rightly interpreted by Jesus, was still true and valid. This was the view advanced by Paul's Christian opponents in Galatia, possibly by the community behind the Gospel of Matthew, and by such second-century Jewish-Christian groups as the Ebionites.

Other Christians maintained that the New was foreshadowed by the Old and that when Jesus came in fulfillment of the Old, the earlier foreshadowings were no longer needed. In this view, the Old Testament was a useful pointer to Christ, but Christ alone embodied the reality that it foreshadowed, so that the Old necessarily was to pass away. This was the view advanced by the author of the New Testament book of Hebrews and later, in a more extreme form, by the second-century Melito of Sardis.

Other Christians maintained that the Old had been given by God, but the Jews had never understood its true meaning because of the hardness of their hearts. In this view, the Jews had broken God's covenant as soon as it was made with them; as a result, they misunderstood their own Law. Jews had always, therefore, propagated a false religion—for in fact, the Old Testament was a Christian, not a Jewish book. This is the view advanced by the Epistle of Barnabas.

Yet other Christians went so far as to say that Judaism and its Scriptures were and always had been completely false, because the God of Israel is not the true God, the God of Jesus. In this view, the God who created this world, chose Israel, and gave it his Law is a secondary and inferior deity; Jesus came to save all people from this God of wrath and justice. Christians therefore are to reject all things Jewish, including the Old Testament. This was a view advanced by the followers of a prominent second-century Christian named Marcion.

From among these views, most of the anti-Judaic writings that happen to survive portray Christianity as superior to but in basic continuity with Judaism. The authors of these works attack Jews for their rejection of the Christian message and maintain that the hardness of their hearts has blinded them to the workings of God. A good deal of emphasis is placed on the Jewish rejection of Jesus himself. During this period Jews came to be maligned as "Christ-killers." Moreover, as Christians became increasingly convinced that Christ was himself divine, the charges escalated: Jews came to be implicated with the murder of God.

As a result of the Jews' rejection of God, these Christian authors maintain, God has in turn rejected them. This opinion was thought to be borne out by the course of historical events—in particular the destruction of Jerusalem by Roman armies in 70 CE and the brutal suppression of the second Jewish revolt in 135 CE. To support these claims, Christians turned to the Hebrew prophets, who had predicted that God would make a "new covenant" since the Jews had broken the old one (Jeremiah 31:31–34) and who indicated that God had declared that "those who were not my people I will call my people" (Romans 9:25–26; see Hosea 1:10; 2:23). Some Christian authors maintained, in fact, that God gave his Law to the Jews as a punishment for their rejection of him; in particular, he gave Jews the rite of circumcision to mark them off from all other peoples for persecution. Christians, circumcised spiritually in their hearts rather than physically on their penises, were the true heirs of the tradition.

This kind of harsh polemic did not have serious political implications early on, during the second and third centuries when Christianity was an insignificant and powerless minority in the empire. But when Christians acquired political, economic, and military clout after the conversion of Constantine, Christian leaders took the rhetorical claims of their forebears seriously and implemented them socially, leading to the widespread acts of hatred and violence against Jews known to us from the horrific history of Christian anti-Semitism.

For Further Reading

Becker, Adam H. and A.Y. Reed, eds. *The Ways That Never Parted*. Philadelphia: Fortress, 2007.

Boyarin, Daniel. *Border Lines: The Partition of Judaeo-Christianity*. Philadelphia: University of Pennsylvania, 2004.

Gager, John. *The Origins of Anti-Semitism: Attitudes toward Judaism in Pagan and Christian Antiquity*. New York: Oxford University Press, 1983.

Isaac, Jules. *Jesus and Israel*, trans. Sally Gran. New York: Holt, Rinehart & Winston, 1971.

Paget, James Carleton. *Jews, Christians and Jewish Christians in Antiquity*. Tübingen: Mohr Siebeck, 2010.

Ruether, Rosemary. *Faith and Fratricide: The Theological Roots of Anti-Semitism*. New York: Seabury, 1974.

Setzer, Claudia. *Jewish Responses to Early Christians: History and Polemics 30–150 CE*. Minneapolis: Fortress, 1994.

Simon, Marcel. *Verus Israel: A Study of the Relations between Christians and Jews in the Roman Empire (135–425)*, trans. H. McKeating. Oxford: Oxford University Press, 1986.

Skarsaune, Oskar, and Reidar Hvalvik, eds. *Jewish Believers in Jesus: The Early Centuries*. Peabody, MA: Hendrickson, 2007.

Wilson, Stephen. *Related Strangers: Jews and Christians 70–170 C.E.* Minneapolis: Fortress, 1995.

The Texts

18. The Epistle of Barnabas

The Epistle of Barnabas was widely read in churches of the second and third centuries; some Christians thought that it should be included among the books of the New Testament. Although it came to be attributed to Barnabas, the companion of the apostle Paul, the book itself is anonymous. Most scholars think it was written around 130 CE, possibly in Alexandria, Egypt, where it was especially popular.

The purpose of the book is to show that Christianity is superior to Judaism—that Judaism, in fact, is and always has been a false religion. In this author's opinion, Jews have misunderstood the Law given to them by God: because they hardened their hearts and broke God's covenant, they mistakenly assumed that he meant his Law to be taken literally. Instead, according to this author, it was all along intended symbolically as a pointer to Christ. Using an allegorical method of interpretation popular among other Alexandrian thinkers—Jew, pagan, and Christian alike—the author thus interprets key passages of the Old Testament as mysterious witnesses to Christ, whose meaning completely escaped the Jews to whom it was originally given. For this author the Old Testament is a Christian, not a Jewish book; and it is Christians, not Jews, who are the people of God.

1 Greetings, sons and daughters, in the name of the Lord who loved us, in peace.

2 Since, then, the days are evil and the one who is at work holds sway,[1] we should commit ourselves to seeking out the righteous acts of the Lord.

2 Reverential awe and endurance assist our faith, and patience and self-restraint do battle on our side.

3 And so while these things remain in a holy state before the Lord, wisdom, understanding, perception, and knowledge rejoice together with them.

4 For through all the prophets he has shown us that he has no need of sacrifices, whole burnt offerings, or regular offerings. For he says in one place,

5 "What is the multitude of your sacrifices to me? says the Lord. I am sated with whole burnt offerings, and have no desire for the fat of lambs, the blood of bulls and goats—not even if you should come to appear before me. For who sought these things from your hands? Trample my court no longer. If you bring fine flour, it is futile; incense is loathsome to me. I cannot stand your new moons and sabbaths."[2]

---

1 I.e. The Devil

2 Isa 1:11–13.

Epistle of Barnabas, reproduced from *The Apostolic Fathers*, ed. Bart D. Ehrman; Loeb Classical Library, vol. 2. Cambridge: Harvard University, 2003. Used with permission of Harvard University Press.

6 And so he nullified these things that the new law of our Lord Jesus Christ, which is without the yoke of compulsion, should provide an offering not made by humans.

7. And again he says to them, "Did I command your fathers who came out from the land of Egypt to offer whole burnt offerings and sacrifices to me?"[3]

8 "No, this is what I commanded them: Let none of you bear a grudge against your neighbor in your heart, and do not love a false oath."[4]

9 And so, since we are not ignorant, we should perceive the good intention of our Father. For he is speaking to us, wanting us to seek how to make an offering to him without being deceived like them.

10 And so he says to us: "A sacrifice to the Lord is a crushed heart; a sweet fragrance to the Lord is a heart that glorifies the one who made it."[5] And so, brothers, we ought to learn clearly about our salvation, to keep the Evil One from hurling us away from our life after bringing error in through the backdoor.

3 And so he speaks to them again concerning these things, "Why do you fast for me, says the Lord, so that your voice is heard crying out today? This is not the fast I have chosen, says the Lord—not a person humbling his soul.

2 Not even if you bend your neck into a circle and put on sackcloth and make for yourself a bed of ashes—not even so should you call this a proper fast."[6]

3 But he says to us, "See, this is the fast I have chosen, says the Lord. Loosen every bond of injustice; unravel the strangle hold of coercive agreements; send forth in forgiveness those who are downtrodden; tear up every unfair contract. Break your bread for the hungry, and provide clothing for anyone you see naked. Bring the homeless under your roof. And if you see anyone who has been humbled, do not despise him—neither you nor anyone from your children's household.

4 Then your light will burst forth at dawn, your garments will quickly rise up, your righteousness will go forth before you, and the glory of God will clothe you.

5 Then you will cry out and God will hear you. While you are still speaking he will say, 'See! Here I am!'—if, that is, you remove from yourself bondage, the threatening gesture, and the word of complaint, and from your heart you give your bread to the poor and show mercy to the person who has been humbled."[7]

6 The one who is patient anticipated, brothers, that the people he prepared in his beloved would believe, in a state of innocence. And so he revealed all things to us in advance, that we not be dashed against their law as newcomers *[Or: proselytes]*.

4 And so by carefully investigating what is here and now, we must seek for the things that can save us. We should flee, entirely, all the works of lawlessness; otherwise, they may overwhelm us. And we should hate the error of the present age, that we may be loved in the age to come.

2 We should not allow our souls to relax, thinking they can consort with sinners and the wicked; otherwise we may become like them.

3 The final stumbling block is at hand, about which it has been written, just as Enoch says. For this reason the Master shortened the seasons and the days, that his beloved may hurry and arrive at his inheritance.

4 For also the prophet says, "Ten kingdoms will rule the earth and a small king will rise up afterwards; he will humble three of the kings at one time."[8]

5 So too Daniel speaks about the same thing: "I saw the fourth beast, wicked and strong, and

---

3 Jer 7:22.

4 Zech 8:17.

5 Ps 51:17.

6 Isa 58:3–5.

7 Isa 58:6–10.

8 Dan 7:24.

worse than all the beasts of the sea, and I saw how ten horns rose up from him, and from them a small horn as an offshoot; and I saw how he humbled three of the great horns at one time."[9]

6 And so you should understand. And yet again, I am asking you this as one who is from among you and who loves each and every one of you more than my own soul: watch yourselves now and do not become like some people by piling up your sins, saying that the covenant is both theirs and ours.

7 For it is ours. But they permanently lost it, in this way, when Moses had just received it. For the Scripture says, "Moses was on the mountain fasting for forty days and forty nights, and he received the covenant from the Lord, stone tablets written with the finger of the Lord's own hand."[10]

8 But when they turned back to idols they lost it. For the Lord says this: "Moses, Moses, go down quickly, because your people, whom you led from the land of Egypt, has broken the law."[11] Moses understood and cast the two tablets from his hands. And their covenant was smashed—that the covenant of his beloved, Jesus, might be sealed in our hearts, in the hope brought by faith in him.

9 Since I want to write many things, not as a teacher, but as is fitting for one who is eager to abandon none of the things we have, I hasten to write, as your lowly scapegoat. Therefore, we should pay close attention here in the final days. For the entire time of our faith will be of no use to us if we do not stand in resistance, as is fitting for the children of God, both against this present lawless age and against the stumbling blocks that are yet to come,

10 that the Black One not sneak in among us. We should flee from all that is futile and completely hate the works of the evil path. Do not sink into yourselves and live alone, as if you were already made upright; instead, gathering together for the same purpose, seek out what is profitable for the common good.

11 For the Scripture says, "Woe to those who have understanding in themselves and are knowledgeable before their own eyes."[12] We should be spiritual; we should be a perfect temple to God. As much as we can, we should concern ourselves with the reverential awe of God and struggle to guard his commandments, that we may be glad in his righteous acts.

12 The Lord will judge the world, playing no favorites. Each will receive according to what he has done. If he is good, his righteousness will precede him; if evil, the reward for his wickedness will be before him.

13 As those who are called we must never lie down and lose consciousness of our sins, allowing the evil ruler to receive the authority against us and force us out of the Lord's kingdom.

14 And still, my brothers, consider when you observe that Israel was abandoned even after such signs and wonders had occurred in it, we too should pay close attention, lest, as it is written, "many of us were found called, but few chosen."[13]

5 This is why the Lord allowed his flesh to be given over to corruption, that we might be made holy through the forgiveness of sins, which comes in the sprinkling of his blood.

2 For some of the things written about him concern Israel; others concern us. And so it says: "He was wounded because of our lawless acts and weakened because of our sins. By his bruising we were healed. He was led like a sheep going to slaughter; and like a lamb, silent before the one who shears it."[14]

3. Therefore we ought to give thanks to the Lord even more abundantly, because he revealed to us the things that have taken place and made us wise in the things that are now; and we are not ignorant of the things that are yet to happen.

---

9 Dan 7:7–8.

10 Exod 31:18, 34:28.

11 Exod 32:7.

12 Isa 5:21.

13 Matt 22:14.

14 Isa 53:5, 7.

4 And the Scripture says, "Not unjustly are the nets spread out for the birds."[15] It says this because the person who knows the path of righteousness but keeps himself in the path of darkness deserves to perish.

5 Consider this, my brothers: if the Lord allowed himself to suffer for our sake, even though he was the Lord of the entire world, the one to whom God said at the foundation of the world, "Let us make a human according to our image and likeness,"[16] how then did he allow himself to suffer by the hand of humans? Learn this!

6 Because the prophets received his gracious gift, they prophesied looking ahead to him. He allowed himself to suffer in order to destroy death and to show that there is a resurrection of the dead. For he had to be manifest in the flesh.

7 And he allowed himself to suffer in order to redeem the promise given to the fathers and to show, while he was on earth preparing a new people for himself, that he is to execute judgment after raising the dead.

8 Moreover, while teaching Israel and doing such wonders and signs, he preached to them and loved them deeply.

9 And when he selected his own apostles who were about to preach his gospel, they were altogether lawless beyond all sin. This was to show that he did not come to call the upright but sinners. Then he revealed that he was the Son of God.

10 For if he had not come in the flesh, how would people have been able to look upon him and survive? For they cannot even look intently at the sun, gazing directly into its rays, even though it is the work of his hands and will eventually cease to exist.

11 Therefore, the Son of God came in the flesh for this reason, that he might total up all the sins of those who persecuted his prophets to death.

12 And so this is why he allowed himself to suffer. For God speaks of the blow they delivered against his flesh: "When they smite their own shepherd, then the sheep of the flock will perish."[17]

13 But he wished to suffer in this way, for he had to suffer on a tree. For the one who prophesied about him said, "Spare my life from the sword," and "Nail my flesh, because an assembly *[Or: synagogue]* of evildoers has risen up against me."[18]

14 Again he says, "See! I have set my back to whips and my cheeks to blows; and I have set my face as a hard rock."[19] . . .

7 And so you should understand, children of gladness, that the good Lord has revealed everything to us in advance, that we may know whom to praise when we give thanks for everything.

2 And so, if the Son of God suffered, that by being beaten he might give us life (even though he is the Lord and is about to judge the living and the dead), we should believe that the Son of God could not suffer unless it was for our sakes.

3 But also when he was crucified he was given vinegar and gall to drink. Listen how the priests in the Temple made a revelation about this. For the Lord gave the written commandment that "Whoever does not keep the fast must surely die,"[20] because he himself was about to offer the vessel of the Spirit as a sacrifice for our own sins, that the type might also be fulfilled that was set forth in Isaac, when he was offered on the altar.

4 What then does he say in the prophet? "Let them eat some of the goat offered for all sins on the day of fasting." Now pay careful attention: "And let all the priests alone eat the intestines, unwashed, with vinegar."[21]

---

15 Prov 1:17.

16 Gen 1:26.

17 Cf. Zech 13:7; Matt 26:31.

18 Ps 22:20, 16.

19 Isa 50:6–7.

20 Lev 23:29.

21 Source unknown. Cf. Lev 16.

5 Why is this? Since you are about to give me gall mixed with vinegar to drink—when I am about to offer my flesh on behalf of the sins of my new people—you alone are to eat, while the people fast and mourn in sackcloth and ashes. He says this to show that he had to suffer at their hands.

6 Pay attention to what he commands: "Take two fine goats who are alike and offer them as a sacrifice; and let the priest take one of them as a whole burnt offering for sins."[22]

7 But what will they do with the other? "The other," he says, "is cursed."[23] Pay attention to how the type of Jesus is revealed.

8 "And all of you shall spit on it and pierce it and wrap a piece of scarlet wool around its head, and so let it be cast into the wilderness."[24] When this happens, the one who takes the goat leads it into the wilderness and removes the wool, and places it on a blackberry bush, whose buds we are accustomed to eat when we find it in the countryside. (Thus the fruit of the blackberry bush alone is sweet.)

9 And so, what does this mean? Pay attention: "The one they take to the altar, but the other is cursed," and the one that is cursed is crowned. For then they will see him in that day wearing a long scarlet robe around his flesh, and they will say, "Is this not the one we once crucified, despising, piercing, and spitting on him? Truly this is the one who was saying at the time that he was himself the Son of God."

10 For how is he like that one? This is why "the goats are alike, fine, and equal," that when they see him coming at that time, they may be amazed at how much he is like the goat. See then the type of Jesus who was about to suffer.

11 But why do they place the wool in the midst of the thorns? This is a type of Jesus established for the church, because whoever wishes to remove the scarlet wool must suffer greatly, since the thorn is a fearful thing, and a person can retrieve the wool

only by experiencing pain. And so he says: those who wish to see me and touch my kingdom must take hold of me through pain and suffering.

8 And what do you suppose is the type found in his command to Israel, that men who are full of sin should offer up a heifer, and after slaughtering it burn it, and that children should then take the ashes and cast them into vessels, and then tie scarlet wool around a piece of wood (see again the type of the cross and the scarlet wool!), along with the hyssop, and that the children should thus sprinkle the people one by one, that they might be purified from their sins?

2 Understand how he speaks to you simply. The calf is Jesus; the sinful men who make the offering are those who offered him up for slaughter. Then they are no longer men and the glory of sinners is no more.

3 The children who sprinkle are those who proclaimed to us the forgiveness of sins and the purification of our hearts. To them he has given the authority to preach the gospel. There are twelve of them as a witness to the tribes, for there were twelve tribes in Israel.

4 But why are there three children who sprinkle? As a witness to Abraham, Isaac, and Jacob, because these were great before God.

5 And why is the wool placed on a piece of wood? Because the kingdom of Jesus is on the tree, and because those who hope in him will live forever.

6 But why are the wool and hyssop together? Because in his kingdom there will be evil and foul days, in which we will be saved. And because the one who is sick in the flesh is healed by the foul juice of the hyssop.

7 And thus the things that have happened in this way are clear to us, but they are obscure to them, because they have not heard the voice of the Lord.

9 For he speaks again about the ears, indicating how he has circumcised our hearts. The Lord says in the prophet, "They obeyed me because of

---

22 Lev 16:7, 9.

23 Cf. Lev 16:8.

24 Cf. Lev 16:10, 20–22.

what they heard with their ears."[25] Again he says, "Those who are far off will clearly hear; they will know what I have done."[26] And, "Circumcise your hearts,"[27] says the Lord.

2 Again he says, "Hear O Israel, for thus says the Lord your God."[28] And again the Spirit of the Lord prophesies, "Who is the one who wants to live forever? Let him clearly hear the voice of my servant."[29]

3 Again he says, "Hear, O heaven, and give ear, O earth, for the Lord has said these things as a witness."[30] And again he says, "Hear the word of the Lord, you rulers of this people."[31] And again he says, "Hear, O children, the voice of one crying in the wilderness."[32] Thus he circumcised our hearing, that once we heard the word we might believe.

4 But even the circumcision in which they trusted has been nullified. For he has said that circumcision is not a matter of the flesh. But they violated his law, because an evil angel instructed them.

5 He says to them, "Thus says the Lord your God" (here is where I find a commandment) "Do not sow among the thorns; be circumcised to your Lord."[33] And what does he say? "Circumcise your hardened hearts and do not harden your necks."[34] Or consider again, "See, says the Lord, all the nations are uncircumcised in their foreskins, but this people is uncircumcised in their hearts."[35]

6 But you will say, "Yet surely the people have been circumcised as a seal [of the covenant]." But every Syrian and Arab and all the priests of the idols are circumcised as well. So then, do those belong to their covenant? Even the people of Egypt are circumcised!

7 Thus learn about the whole matter fully, children of love. For Abraham, the first to perform circumcision, was looking ahead in the Spirit to Jesus when he circumcised. For he received the firm teachings of the three letters.

8 For it says, "Abraham circumcised eighteen and three hundred men from his household."[36] What knowledge, then, was given to him? Notice that first he mentions the eighteen and then, after a pause, the three hundred. The number eighteen [in Greek] consists of an Iota [J], 10, and an Eta [E], 8. There you have Jesus.[37] And because the cross was about to have grace in the letter Tau [T], he next gives the three hundred, Tau. And so he shows the name Jesus by the first two letters, and the cross by the other.

9 For the one who has placed the implanted gift of his covenant in us knew these things. No one has learned a more reliable lesson from me. But I know that you are worthy.

10 And when Moses said, "Do not eat the pig, or the eagle, or the hawk, or the crow, or any fish without scales,"[38] he received three firm teachings in his understanding.

2 Moreover, he said to them in the book of Deuteronomy, "I will establish a covenant with this people in my righteous demands."[39] So, then, the commandment of God is not a matter of avoiding food; but Moses spoke in the Spirit.

3 This is why he spoke about the pig: "Do not cling," he says, "to such people, who are like pigs."

25 Ps 18:44.
26 Cf. Isa 33:13.
27 Isa 33:13; Jer 4:4.
28 Cf. Jer 7:2–3; Ps 34:12–13.
29 Cf. Ps 34:12–13; Isa 50:10; Exod 15:26.
30 Cf. Isa 1:2.
31 Cf. Isa 1:10; 28:14.
32 Cf. Isa 40:3.
33 Jer 4:3–4.
34 Cf. Deut 10:16.
35 Jer 9:26.

36 Cf. Gen 14:14; 17:23.
37 I.e., the number eighteen in Greek is JE, taken here as an abbreviation for the name "Jesus."
38 Cf. Lev 11:7–15; Deut 14:8–14.
39 Cf. Deut 4:10, 13.

That is to say, when they live in luxury, they forget the Lord, but when they are in need, they remember the Lord. This is just like the pig: when it is eating, it does not know its master, but when hungry, it cries out—until it gets its food, and then is silent again.

4 "And do not eat the eagle, the hawk, the kite, or the crow."[40] "You must not," he says, "cling to such people or be like them, people who do not know how to procure food for themselves through toil and sweat, but by their lawless behavior seize food that belongs to others. And they are always on the watch, strolling about with ostensible innocence, but looking to see what they can plunder because of their greed." For these are the only birds that do not procure their own food, but sit by idly, waiting to see how they might devour the flesh procured by others, being pestilent in their evil.

5 "And do not," he says, "eat the lamprey-eel, the octopus, or the cuttlefish."[41] "You must not," he says, "be like such people, who are completely impious and condemned already to death." For these fish alone are cursed and hover in the depths, not swimming like the others but dwelling in the mud beneath the depths.

6 But also "do not eat the hare."[42] For what reason? "You must not," he says, "be one who corrupts children or be like such people." For the rabbit adds an orifice every year; it has as many holes as years it has lived.

7 "Nor shall you eat the hyena."[43] "You must not," he says, "be an adulterer or a pervert nor be like such people." For what reason? Because this animal changes its nature every year, at one time it is male, the next time female.

8 And he has fully hated the weasel. "You must not," he says, "be like those who are reputed to perform a lawless deed in their mouth because of

their uncleanness, nor cling to unclean women who perform the lawless deed in their mouth." For this animal conceives with its mouth.

9 And so, Moses received the three firm teachings about food and spoke in the Spirit. But they received his words according to the desires of their own flesh, as if he were actually speaking about food.

10 And David received the knowledge of the same three firm teachings and spoke in a similar way: "How fortunate is the man who does not proceed in the counsel of the impious" (like the fish who proceed in darkness in the depths) "and does not stand in the path of sinners" (like those who appear to fear God but sin like the pig) "and does not sit in the seat of the pestilent"[44] (like the birds who sit waiting for something to seize). Here you have a perfect lesson about food.

11 Again Moses said, "Eat every animal with a split hoof and that chews the cud."[45] What does he mean? He means that the one who receives food knows who has provided it and appears to be glad, having relied on him. He spoke well, looking to the commandment. What does he mean then? Cling to those who fear the Lord, to those who meditate on the special meaning of the teaching they have received in their heart, to those who discuss and keep the upright demands of the Lord, to those who know that meditation is a work that produces gladness, and to those who carefully chew over the word of the Lord. But why does he mention the split hoof? Because the one who is upright both walks in this world and waits for the holy age. Do you see how well Moses has given the Law?

12 But how could they know or understand these things? We, however, speak as those who know the commandments in an upright way, as the Lord wished. For this reason he circumcised our hearing and our hearts, that we may understand these things.

---

40 Cf. Lev 11:13–16.

41 Source unknown.

42 Cf. Lev 11:6.

43 Source unknown.

44 Ps 1:1.

45 Cf. Lev 11:3; Deut 14:6.

14 Yes indeed. But we should see if he has given the covenant that he swore to the fathers he would give the people. Let us pursue the question. He has given it, but they were not worthy to receive it because of their sins.

2 For the prophet says, "Moses was fasting on Mount Sinai for forty days and forty nights, that he might receive the covenant of the Lord for the people. And Moses received from the Lord the two tablets written with the finger of the Lord's hand in the Spirit."[46] When Moses received them he brought them down to give to the people.

3 And the Lord said to Moses, "Moses, Moses, go down at once, because your people, whom you brought out of the land of Egypt, has broken the Law." Moses understood that they had again made molten images for themselves, and he hurled the tablets from his hands. And the tablets of the Lord's covenant were smashed.[47]

4 So Moses received the covenant, but they were not worthy. Now learn how we have received it. Moses received it as a servant, but the Lord himself gave it to us, as a people of the inheritance, by enduring suffering for us.

5 He was made manifest so that those people might be completely filled with sins, and that we might receive the covenant through the Lord Jesus, who inherited it. He was prepared for this end, that when he became manifest he might make a covenant with us by his word, after redeeming our hearts from darkness, hearts that were already paid out to death and given over to the lawlessness of deceit.

6 For it is written how the Father commanded him to prepare for himself a holy people after he redeemed us from darkness.

7 And so the prophet says, "I the Lord your God called you in righteousness; and I will grasp your hand and strengthen you. I have given you as a covenant of the people, as a light to the nations, to open the eyes of the blind, to bring out of their bondage those in shackles and out of prison those who sit in darkness."[48] And so we know the place from which we have been redeemed.

8 Again the prophet says, "See, I have set you as a light to the nations that you may bring salvation to the end of the earth; so says the Lord God who redeems you."[49]

9 Again the prophet says, "The Spirit of the Lord is upon me, because he anointed me to preach the good news of grace to the humble; he sent me to heal those whose hearts are crushed, to proclaim a release to the captives and renewed sight to the blind, to call out the acceptable year of the Lord and the day of recompense, to comfort all those who mourn."[50]

15 Something is also written about the Sabbath in the ten commandments, which God spoke to Moses face to face on Mount Sinai: "Make the Sabbath of the Lord holy, with pure hands and a pure heart."[51]

2 In another place it says, "If my children keep the Sabbath, I will bestow my mercy on them."[52]

3 This refers to the Sabbath at the beginning of creation: "God made the works of his hands in six days, and he finished on the seventh day; and he rested on it and made it holy."[53]

4 Pay attention, children, to what it means that "he finished in six days." This means that in six thousand years the Lord will complete all things. For with him a day represents a thousand years. He himself testifies that I am right, when he says, "See, a day of the Lord will be like a thousand years."[54] And so, children, all things will be completed in six days—that is to say, in six thousand years.

---

46 Cf. Exod 24:18; 31:18.

47 Cf. Exod 32:7–19.

48 Isa 42:6–7.

49 Cf. Isa 49:6–7.

50 Isa 61:1–2.

51 Cf. Exod 20:8; Deut 5:12.

52 Cf. Jer 17:24–25.

53 Gen 2:2–3.

54 Cf. Ps 90:4; 2 Pet 3:8.

5 "And he rested on the seventh day." This means that when his Son comes he will put an end to the age of the lawless one, judge the impious, and alter the sun, moon, and stars; then he will indeed rest on the seventh day.

6 Moreover, it says, "Make it holy with pure hands and a pure heart." We are very much mistaken if we think that at the present time anyone, by having a pure heart, can make holy the day that the Lord has made holy.

7 And so you see that at that time, when we are given a good rest, we will make it holy—being able to do so because we ourselves have been made upright and have received the promise, when lawlessness is no more and all things have been made new by the Lord. Then we will be able to make the day holy, after we ourselves have been made holy.

8 Moreover he says to them, "I cannot stand your new moons and Sabbaths."[55] You see what he means: It is not the Sabbaths of the present time that are acceptable to me, but the one I have made, in which I will give rest to all things and make a beginning of an eighth day, which is the beginning of another world.

9 Therefore also we celebrate the eighth day with gladness, for on it Jesus arose from the dead, and appeared, and ascended into heaven.

16 I will also speak to you about the Temple, since those wretches were misguided in hoping in the building rather than in their God who made them, as if the Temple were actually the house of God.

2 For they consecrated him in the Temple almost like the Gentiles do. But consider what the Lord says in order to invalidate it: "Who has measured the sky with the span of his hand or the earth with his outstretched fingers? Is it not I, says the Lord? The sky is my throne and the earth is the footstool for my feet. What sort of house will you build me, or where is the place I

can rest?"[56] You knew that their hope was in vain!

3 Moreover he says again, "See, those who have destroyed this temple will themselves build it."[57]

4 This is happening. For because of their war, it was destroyed by their enemies. And now the servants of the enemies will themselves rebuild it.

5 Again it was revealed how the city, the Temple, and the people of Israel were about to be handed over. For the Scripture says, "It will be in the last days that the Lord will hand over to destruction the sheep of the pasture along with their enclosure and tower."[58] And it has happened just as the Lord said.

6 But let us inquire if a temple of God still exists. It does exist, where he says that he is making and completing it. For it is written, "It will come about that when the seventh day is finished, a temple of God will be gloriously built in the name of the Lord."[59]

7 And so I conclude that a temple exists. But learn how it will be built in the name of the Lord. Before we believed in God, the dwelling place of our heart was corrupt and feeble, since it really was a temple built by hand; for it was full of idolatry and was a house of demons, because we did everything that was opposed to God.

8 "But it will be built in the name of the Lord." Now pay attention, so that the temple of the Lord may be gloriously built. And learn how: we have become new, created again from the beginning, because we have received the forgiveness of sins and have hoped in the name. Therefore God truly resides within our place of dwelling—within us.

9 How so? His word of faith, his call to us through his promise, the wisdom of his upright demands, the commandments of the teaching, he himself prophesying in us and dwelling in us who had served death, opening up to us the door of the temple,

---

55 Isa 1:13.

56 Cf. Isa 40:12; 66:1.

57 Cf. Isa 49:17.

58 Cf. 1 Enoch 89:56.

59 Cf. Dan 9:24; 1 Enoch 91:13.

which is the mouth, and giving repentance to us—thus he brings us into his imperishable temple.

10 For the one who longs to be saved looks not merely to a person but to the one who dwells and speaks in him. For he is amazed at him since he has never heard him speak these words from his mouth nor even ever desired to hear them. This is a spiritual temple built for the Lord.

17 Insofar as I have been able to set forth these matters to you simply, I hope to have fulfilled my desire not to have omitted anything that pertains to salvation.

2 For if I should write to you about things present or things to come, you would not understand, because they are set forth in parables. And so these things will suffice.

19. Justin: Dialogue with Trypho

We have already encountered Justin's "Dialogue with Trypho" in Chapter 2 (see the Introduction there). The excerpts given below begin with the opening discussion between Justin and his Jewish interlocutor.

In his attempt to convince Trypho of the superiority of his Christian philosophy, Justin appeals to the Old Testament to show that God had planned from the very beginning for Judaism to be superseded by Christianity. In his view, God gave the Jews his laws (for example, of circumcision and Sabbath observance) not because they were special in his eyes but because he wanted to punish them. For Justin, therefore, since Jews have always violated God's will, as they continue to do (as is evident in their violent and slanderous opposition to the Christians), they are not God's chosen people. Instead, it is the followers of Christ who are the true heirs of the promises made to the Jewish ancestors. Thus the Jewish Scriptures actually belong to Christians, not Jews, and when properly understood, Justin repeatedly argues, they point directly to Christ.

It is difficult to know whether this discussion really took place, and, if so, how Trypho reacted to Justin's opinions. As with all such dialogues (for example, those of Plato), we hear only the arguments of the author and the responses he himself placed in the mouth of his opponent. Still, it is hard to imagine a Jew finding Justin's arguments convincing—which makes it all the more interesting that at the end, Trypho is not said to convert.

Chapter 10

When they had finished their conversation, I once again addressed them in this fashion: "My friends, is there any other accusation you have against us than this, that we do not observe the Law, nor circumcise the flesh as your forefathers, nor keep the sabbaths as you do? Or do you also condemn

---

Justin: Dialogue with Trypho, from *Saint Justin Martyr*, ed. Thomas Falls. Fathers of the Church, 6. Washington, DC: Catholic University Press of America, 1977. Used with permission.

our customs and morals? This is what I say, lest you, too, believe that we eat human flesh and that after our banquets we extinguish the lights and indulge in unbridled sensuality. Or do you only condemn us for believing in such doctrines and holding opinions which you consider false?"

"This last charge is what surprises us," replied Trypho. "Those other charges which the rabble lodge against you are not worthy of belief, for they are too repulsive to human nature. But the precepts in what you call your Gospel are so marvelous and great that I don't think that anyone could possibly keep them. For I took the trouble to read them. But this is what surprises us most, that you who claim to be pious and believe yourselves to be different from the others do not segregate yourselves from them, nor do you observe a manner of life different from that of the Gentiles, for you do no keep the feasts or sabbaths, nor do you practice the rite of circumcision. You place your hope in a crucified man, and still expect to receive favors from God when you disregard his commandments. Have you not read that the male who is not circumcised on the eighth day shall be cut off from his people?[1] This precept was for stranger and purchased slave alike. But you, forthwith, scorn this covenant, spurn the commands that come afterwards, and then you try to convince us that you know God, when you fail to do those things that every God-fearing person would do. If, therefore, you can give a satisfactory reply to these charges and can show us on what you place your hopes, even though you refuse to observe the Law, we will listen to you most willingly, and then we can go on and examine in the same manner our other differences."

Chapter 11

"Trypho," I began, "there never will be, nor has there ever been from eternity, any other God except him who created and formed this universe. Furthermore, we do not claim that our God is different from yours, for he is the God who, with a strong hand and outstretched arm, led your ancestors out of the land of Egypt. Nor have we placed our trust in any other (for, indeed, there is no other), but only in him whom you also have trusted, the God of Abraham and of Isaac and of Jacob. But, our hope is not through Moses or through the Law, otherwise our customs would be the same as yours. Now, indeed, for I have read, Trypho, that there should be a definitive law and a covenant, more binding than all others, which now must be respected by all those who aspire to the heritage of God. The law promulgated at Horeb is already obsolete, and was intended for you Jews only, whereas the law of which I speak is simply for all people. Now, a later law in opposition to an older law abrogates the older; so, too, does a later covenant void an earlier one. An everlasting and final law, Christ himself, and a trustworthy covenant has been given to us, after which there shall be no law, or commandment, or precept. Have you not read these words of Isaiah: 'Give ear to me, and listen to me, my people; and you kings, give ear unto me: for a law shall go forth from me, and my judgment shall be a light to the nations. My Just One approaches swiftly, and my Savior shall go forth, and nations shall trust in my arm'?[2] Concerning this new covenant, God thus spoke through Jeremiah: 'Behold the days shall come, says the Lord, and I will make a new covenant with the house of Israel, and with the house of Judah: not according to the covenant which I made with their fathers, in the day that I took them by the hand to bring them out of the land of Egypt.'[3] If, therefore, God predicted that he would make a new covenant, and this for a light to the nations, and we see and are convinced that, through the name of the crucified Jesus Christ, people have turned to God, leaving behind them idolatry and other sinful practices, and have kept the faith and have practiced piety even unto death, then everyone can clearly see from these

---

1 Gen 17:14.

2 Isa 51:4–5.

3 Jer 31:31–32.

deeds and the accompanying powerful miracles that he is indeed the new law, the new covenant, and the expectation of those who, from every nation, have awaited the blessings of God. We have been led to God through this crucified Christ, and we are the true spiritual Israel, and the descendants of Judah, Jacob, Isaac, and Abraham, who, though uncircumcised, was approved and blessed by God because of his faith and was called the father of many nations. . . .

Chapter 16

"God himself, through Moses, exclaimed: 'Circumcise therefore the hardness of your hearts, and stiffen your neck no more. For the Lord is your God, and the Lord of lords, a great God and mighty and terrible, who regards not persons nor takes bribes.'[4] And in Leviticus it is written: 'Because they have transgressed against me and despised me, and because they have walked contrary to me, I also will walk contrary to them, and I will destroy them in the land of their enemies. Then shall their uncircumcised heart be ashamed.'[5] Indeed the custom of circumcising the flesh, handed down from Abraham, was given to you as a distinguishing mark, to set you off from other nations and from us Christians. The purpose of this was that you and only you might suffer the afflictions that are now justly yours; that only your land be desolate, and your cities ruined by fire; that the fruits of your land be eaten by strangers before your very eyes; that not one of you be permitted to enter your city of Jerusalem. Your circumcision of the flesh is the only mark by which you can certainly be distinguished from other people. Nor do I believe that any of you will attempt to deny that God either had or has foreknowledge of future events, and that he does not prepare beforehand what everyone deserves. Therefore, the above-mentioned tribulations were justly imposed upon you, for you have murdered

the Just One, and his prophets before him; now you spurn those who hope in him, and in him who sent him, namely, Almighty God, the Creator of all things; to the utmost of your power you dishonor and curse in your synagogues all those who believe in Christ. Now, indeed, you cannot use violence against us Christians, because of those who are in power, but as often as you could, you did employ force against us. For this reason, God cries out to you through Isaiah, saying: 'Behold how the just perish, and no one lays it to heart. For the just one is taken away from before the face of evil. His burial shall be in peace, he is taken away from among us. But draw near hither, you wicked ones, seed of the adulterers and children of the harlot. Upon whom have you jested, and upon whom have you opened your mouth wide, and put out your tongue?'"[6]

Chapter 17

"The other nations have not treated Christ and us, his followers, as unjustly as have you Jews, who, indeed, are the very instigators of that evil opinion they have of the Just One and of us, his disciples. After you had crucified the only sinless and just man (through whose sufferings are healed all those who approach the Father through him), and after you realized that he had risen from the dead and had ascended into heaven (as had been predicted by the prophets), you not only failed to feel remorse for your evil deed, but you even dispatched certain picked men from Jerusalem to every land, to report the outbreak of the godless heresy of the Christians and to spread those ugly rumors against us which are repeated by those who do not know us. As a result, you are to blame not only for your own wickedness, but also for that of all others. With good reason, therefore, does Isaiah cry out: 'Because of you My name is blasphemed among the Gentiles.' And: 'Woe unto their soul, for they have taken evil counsel against themselves, saying, Let us bind the Just One, for

---

4 Deut 10:16–17.

5 Lev 26:40–41.

6 Isa 57:1–4.

he is useless to us. Therefore they eat the fruit of their deeds. Woe unto the wicked: evil shall be rendered to him, in accordance with the works of his hands.'[7] And again, in another passage: 'Woe unto them that draw iniquity as with a long cord, and their injustices as it were with the rope of a cart. That say: Let his speed come near, and let the counsel of the Holy One of Israel come, that we may know it. Woe unto them that call evil good, and good evil; that put light for darkness, and darkness for light; that put bitter for sweet, and sweet for bitter.'[8] Thus have you spared no effort in disseminating in every land bitter, dark, and unjust accusations against the only guiltless and just Light sent to people by God. For he seemed to be inconvenient to you, when he cried out, 'It is written. My house shall be called a house of prayer, but you have made it a den of thieves.'[9] Then he even overturned the money-changers' tables in the temple, and exclaimed, 'Woe to you, Scribes and Pharisees, hypocrites! because you pay tithes on mint and rue, and never think of the love of God and justice. You are whited sepulchres, which outwardly appear beautiful, but within are full of dead people's bones.'[10] And to the scribes he said, 'Woe unto you, scribes, for you have the keys, and you do not enter in yourselves, and you hinder them that are entering; you blind guides!'"[11]

Chapter 18

"Since you, Trypho, admit that you have read the teachings of him who is our Savior, I do not consider it out of place to have added those few short sayings of his to the quotations from the prophets: 'Wash yourselves, be clean, and take away evil from your souls.'[12] Thus does God order you to be washed in this laver, and to be circumcised with the true circumcision. We, too, would observe your circumcision of the flesh, your sabbath days, and, in a word, all your festivals, if we were not aware of the reason why they were imposed upon you, namely, because of your sins and your hardness of heart. If we patiently bear all the evils thrust upon us by vicious persons and demons, and still, amid indescribable tortures and death, ask mercy even for our persecutors and do not wish that anybody be requited with even a little of them, as our new Lawgiver decreed, why is it, Trypho, that we should not observe those rites which cannot harm us, such as the circumcision of the flesh, the sabbaths, and the festivals?"

Chapter 19

"That," interposed Trypho, "is precisely what we are puzzled about—why you endure all sorts of tortures, yet refuse to follow the [Jewish] customs now under discussion."

"As I already explained," I answered, "it is because circumcision is not essential for all people, but only for you Jews, to mark you off for the suffering you now so deservedly endure. Nor do we approve of your useless baptism of the wells, which has no connection at all with our baptism of life. Thus has God protested that you have forsaken him, 'the fountain of living water, and have digged for yourselves broken cisterns which can hold no water,'[13] You Jews, who have the circumcision of the flesh, are in great need of our circumcision, whereas we, since we have our circumcision, do not need yours. For if, as you claim, circumcision had been necessary for salvation, God would not have created Adam uncircumcised; nor would he have looked with favor upon the sacrifice of the uncircumcised Abel, nor would He have been pleased with the uncircumcised Enoch, who 'was seen no more, because God took him.'[14] The Lord and his

---

7 Isa 3:9–11.

8 Isa 5:18–20.

9 Matt 21:13.

10 Matt 23:23, 27; Luke 11:43.

11 Luke 11:52.

12 Isa 1:16.

---

13 Jer 2:13.

14 Gen 5:24.

angels led Lot out of Sodom; thus was he saved without circumcision. Noah, the uncircumcised father of our race, was safe with his children in the ark. Melchisedech, the priest of the Most High, was not circumcised, yet Abraham, the first to accept circumcision of the flesh, paid tithes to him and was blessed by him; indeed, God, through David, announced that he would make him a priest forever according to the order of Melchisedech. Circumcision, therefore, is necessary only for you Jews, in order that, as Hosea, one of the twelve prophets, says, 'your people should not be a people, and your nation not a nation.'[15] Furthermore, all these men were just and pleasing in the sight of God, yet they kept no sabbaths. The same can be said of Abraham and his descendants down to the time of Moses, when your people showed itself wicked and ungrateful to God by molding a golden calf as an idol in the desert. Wherefore, God, adapting his laws to that weak people, ordered you to offer sacrifices to his name in order to save you from idolatry, but you did not obey even then, for you did not hesitate to sacrifice your children to the demons. Moreover, the observance of the sabbaths was imposed upon you by God so that you would be forced to remember him, as he himself said, 'That you may know that I am God your Savior.'"[16]

Chapter 20

"You were likewise forbidden to eat certain kinds of meat, so that when you ate and drank you would keep God before your eyes, for you have always been disposed to forget him, as Moses himself testifies: 'The people ate and drank, and rose up to play.'[17] And in another passage: 'Jacob ate and was filled, and grew fat; my beloved kicked, he grew fat and thick and broad, and forsook God who made him.'"[18] . . .

---

15 Hos 1:9.

16 Ezek 20:20.

17 Exod 32:6.

18 Deut 32:15.

Chapter 23

. . . "Is it not evident to you that the elements are not idle, and that they do not observe the sabbaths? Stay as you were at birth. For if circumcision was not required before the time of Abraham, and before Moses there was no need of sabbaths, festivals, and sacrifices, they are not needed now, when in accordance with the will of God, Jesus Christ, his Son, has been born of the Virgin Mary, a descendant of Abraham. Indeed, when Abraham himself was still uncircumcised, he was justified and blessed by God because of his faith in him, as the Scriptures tell us. Furthermore, the Scriptures and the facts of the case force us to admit that Abraham received circumcision for a sign, not for justification itself. Thus was it justly said of your people: 'That soul which shall not be circumcised on the eighth day shall be destroyed out of his people.'[19] Moreover, the fact that females cannot receive circumcision of the flesh shows that circumcision was given as a sign, not as an act of justification. For God also bestowed upon women the capability of performing every good and virtuous act. We see that the physical formation of male and female is different, but it is equally evident that the bodily form is not what makes either of them good or evil. Their righteousness is determined by their acts of piety and justice." . . .

Chapter 25

. . . "Do I understand you to say," interposed Trypho, "that none of us Jews will inherit anything on the holy mountain of God?"

Chapter 26

"I didn't say that," I replied, "but I do say that those who have persecuted Christ in the past and still do, and do not repent, shall not inherit anything on the holy mountain, unless they repent.

---

19 Gen 17:14.

Whereas the Gentiles, who believe in Christ and are sorry for their sins, shall receive the inheritance, along with the Patriarchs, the Prophets, and every just descendant of Jacob, even though they neither practise circumcision nor observe the sabbaths and feasts. . . ."

Chapter 27

. . . "Thus, as your sinfulness was the reason why God first issued those precepts, so now because of your enslavement to sin, or rather your greater inclination to it, by means of the same precepts, he calls you to remember and know him. But you Jews are a ruthless, stupid, blind, and lame people, children in whom there is no faith. As God himself says: 'Honoring him only with your lips, but your hearts are far from him, teaching your own doctrines and not his.'"[20] . . .

Chapter 29

. . . "I am positive that I can persuade by these words even those of weak intellectual faculties, for the words which I use are not my own, nor are they embellished by human rhetoric, but they are the words as David sang them, as Isaiah announced them as good news, as Zachariah proclaimed them, and as Moses wrote them. Aren't you acquainted with them, Trypho? You should be, for they are contained in your Scriptures, or rather not yours, but ours. For we believe and obey them, whereas you, though you read them, do not grasp their spirit. You should not be angry with us, therefore, nor blame us for the uncircumcision of our body; indeed, God created us that way. Nor should you consider it dreadful if we drink hot water on the Sabbath, for God doesn't stop controlling the movement of the universe on that day, but he continues directing it then as he does on all other days. Besides, your chief priests were commanded by God to offer sacrifices on the Sabbath, as well as on other days. Then, too, there are so many just people

who are approved by God himself, yet they never performed any of your legal ceremonies."

Chapter 30

"The fact that God can be falsely accused by the foolish of not having always taught the same truthful doctrines to all, you can blame on your own sinfulness. Indeed, many deemed such doctrines senseless and unworthy of God, for they were not illuminated by grace to understand that these same doctrines have called your people, mired in sin and sick of a spiritual disease, to conversion and spiritual repentance; nor did they understand that prophecy, which was given to mankind after the death of Moses, is eternal. This, my friends, is indeed mentioned in the Psalm. That we, who have been enlightened by these doctrines, consider them to be sweeter than honey and the honey-comb, is evident from the fact that even under the threat of death we do not deny his name. Furthermore, it is equally clear (as the word of the prophecy, speaking in the name of one of his followers, metaphorically affirms) that we believers beseech him to safeguard us from strange, that is, evil and deceitful, spirits. We constantly ask God through Jesus Christ to keep us safe from those demons who, while they are strangers to the worship of God, were once adored by us; we pray, too, that, after our conversion to God through Christ, we may be without blame. We call him our helper and redeemer, by the power of whose name even the demons shudder; even to this day they are overcome by us when we exorcise them in the name of Jesus Christ, who was crucified under Pontius Pilate, the Governor of Judaea. Thus, it is clear to all that his Father bestowed upon him such a great power that even the demons are subject both to his name and to his preordained manner of suffering.". . .

Chapter 40

"The mystery of the lamb which God ordered you to sacrifice as the Passover was truly a type of Christ, with whose blood the believers, in proportion to

20 Isa 29:13.

the strength of their faith, anoint their homes, that is, themselves. You are all aware that Adam, the result of God's creative act, was the abode of his inspiration. In the following fashion I can show that God's precept concerning the paschal lamb was only temporary. God does not allow the paschal lamb to be sacrificed in any other place than where his name is invoked (that is, in the Temple at Jerusalem), for he knew that there would come a time, after Christ's Passion, when the place in Jerusalem (where you sacrificed the paschal lamb) would be taken from you by your enemies, and then all sacrifices would be stopped. Moreover, that lamb which you were ordered to roast whole was a symbol of Christ's Passion on the Cross. Indeed, the lamb, while being roasted, resembles the figure of the cross, for one spit transfixes it horizontally from the lower parts up to the head, and another pierces it across the back, and holds up its forelegs. Likewise, the two identical goats which had to be offered during the fast (one of which was to be the scapegoat and the other the sacrificial goat) were an announcement of the two advents of Christ: of the first advent, in which your priests and elders sent him away as a scapegoat, seizing him and putting him to death; of the second advent, because in that same place of Jerusalem you shall recognize him whom you had subjected to shame, and who was a sacrificial offering for all sinners who are willing to repent and to comply with that fast which Isaiah prescribed when he said 'loosing the knot of violent contracts,'[21] and to observe likewise all the other precepts laid down by him (precepts which I have already mentioned and which all Christian believers fulfill). You also know very well that the offering of the two goats, which had to take place during the fast, could not take place anywhere else outside of Jerusalem."

Chapter 41

"Likewise," I continued, "the offering of flour, my friends, which was ordered to be presented

for those cleansed from leprosy, was a prototype of the eucharistic bread, which our Lord Jesus Christ commanded us to offer in remembrance of the Passion he endured for all those souls who are cleansed from sin, and that at the same time we should thank God for having created the world, and everything in it, for the sake of mankind, and for having saved us from the sin in which we were born, and for the total destruction of the powers and principalities of evil through him who suffered in accordance with his will.". . .

Chapter 44

"I will be absolutely without blame in my obligations to you, if I endeavor to convince you with every possible proof. But, if you persist in your obstinacy of heart and feebleness of mind, or if you refuse to agree to the truth through fear of the death which awaits every Christian, you will have only yourselves to blame. And you are sadly mistaken if you think that, just because you are descendants of Abraham according to the flesh, you will share in the legacy of benefits which God promised would be distributed by Christ. No one can by any means participate in any of these gifts, except those who have the same ardent faith as Abraham, and who approve of all the mysteries. For I say that some precepts were given for the worship of God and the practice of virtue, whereas other commandments and customs were arranged either in respect to the mystery of Christ [or] the hardness of your people's hearts.". . .

Chapter 47

"But," Trypho again objected, "if a person knows that what you say is true, and, professing Jesus to be the Christ, believes in and obeys him, yet desires also to observe the commandments of the Mosaic Law, shall he be saved?"

"In my opinion," I replied, "I say such a person will be saved, unless he exerts every effort

21 Isa 58:6.

to influence other people (I have in mind the Gentiles whom Christ circumcised from all error) to practice the same rites as himself, informing them that they cannot be saved unless they do so. You yourself did this at the opening of our discussion, when you said that I would not be saved unless I kept the Mosaic precepts."

"But why," pressed Trypho, "did you say, 'In my opinion such a person will be saved?' There must, therefore, be other Christians who hold a different opinion."

"Yes, Trypho," I conceded, "there are some Christians who boldly refuse to have conversation or meals with such persons. I don't agree with such Christians. But if some [Jewish converts], due to their instability of will, desire to observe as many of the Mosaic precepts as possible—precepts which we think were instituted because of your hardness of heart—while at the same time they place their hope in Christ, and if they desire to perform the eternal and natural acts of justice and piety, yet wish to live with us Christians and believers, as I already stated, not persuading them to be circumcised like themselves, or to keep the Sabbath, or to perform any other similar acts, then it is my opinion that we Christians should receive them and associate with them in every way as kinfolk and brethren. But if any of your people, Trypho, profess their belief in Christ, and at the same time force the Christian Gentiles to follow the Law instituted through Moses, or refuse to share in communion with them this same common life, I certainly will also not approve of them. But I think that those Gentiles who have been induced to follow the practices of the Jewish Law, and at the same time profess their faith in the Christ of God, will probably be saved. Those persons, however, who had once believed and publicly acknowledged Jesus to be the Christ, and then later, for one reason or another, turned to the observance of the Mosaic Law, and denied that Jesus is the Christ, cannot be saved unless they repent before their death. The same can be said of those descendants of Abraham, who follow the Law and

refuse to believe in Christ to their very last breath. Especially excluded from eternal salvation are they who in their synagogues have cursed and still do curse those who believe in that very Christ in order that they may attain salvation and escape the avenging fires of hell. God in his goodness, kindness, and infinite richness considers the repentant sinner to be just and innocent, as he declared through the prophet Ezechiel, and the one who turns from the path of piety and justice to follow that of injustice and impiety God judges to be an impious and unjust sinner. Thus has our Lord Jesus Christ warned us: 'In whatsoever things I shall apprehend you, in them also I shall judge you.'"...

Chapter 59

Then I continued, "Allow me now to show you from the words of the book of Exodus how this very person who was at the same time Angel and God and Lord and Man, and who was seen by Abraham and Jacob, also appeared and talked to Moses from the flame of the fiery bush." And when I was assured by my audience that they would listen gladly, patiently, and eagerly, I went on, . . .

"Trypho," I said, "I now wish to prove to you that in the apparition under discussion, He who is termed an angel and is God was the only One who talked to and was seen by Moses. Here is the Scriptural proof: 'The angel of the Lord appeared to him in a flame of fire out of the midst of a bush; and he saw that the bush was on fire and was not burnt. And Moses said: I will go and see this great sight, why the bush is not burnt. And when the Lord saw that he went forward to see, he called to him out of the midst of the bush.'[22] Now, as the Scripture refers to him who appeared to Jacob in a dream as an angel, and then states that the same angel said to Jacob in his sleep, 'I am the God who appeared to you

---

22 Exod 3:2–4.

when you did flee from the face of your brother Esau,'[23] and as Scripture also affirms that, in the judgment of Sodom in the days of Abraham, the Lord executed the will of the Lord who is in heaven; so when the Scripture here states that an angel of the Lord appeared to Moses, and then announces that he is Lord and God, it refers to the same person who is identified in many of our earlier quotations as the minister to God, who is above the world, and above whom there is no other God."

Chapter 61

"So, my friends," I said, "I shall now show from the Scriptures that God has begotten of himself a certain rational power as a beginning before all other creatures. The Holy Spirit indicates this power by various titles, sometimes the Glory of the Lord, at other times Son, or Wisdom, or Angel, or God, or Lord, or Word. He even called himself Commander-in-chief when he appeared in human guise to Joshua, the son of Nun. Indeed, he can justly lay claim to all these titles from the fact both that he performs the Father's will and that he was begotten by an act of the Father's will. But, does not something similar happen also with us humans? When we utter a word, it can be said that we beget the word, but not by cutting it off, in the sense that our power of uttering words would thereby be diminished. We can observe a similar example in nature when one fire kindles another, without losing anything, but remaining the same; yet the enkindled fire seems to exist of itself and to shine without lessening the brilliancy of the first fire.". . .

Chapter 96

"The words of the Law, 'Cursed is every one who hangs on a tree,'[24] strengthen our hope which is

sustained by the crucified Christ, not because the crucified one is cursed by God, but because God predicted what would be done by all of you Jews, and others like you, who are not aware that this is he who was before all things, the eternal priest of God, the King, and Christ. Now, you can clearly see that this has actually happened. For, in your synagogues you curse all those who through him have become Christians, and the Gentiles put into effect your curse by killing all those who merely admit that they are Christians. To all our persecutors we say: 'You are our brothers; apprehend, rather, the truth of God.' But when neither they nor you will listen to us, but you do all in your power to force us to deny Christ, we resist you and prefer to endure death, confident that God will give us all the blessings which he promised us through Christ. Furthermore, we pray for you that you might experience the mercy of Christ; for he instructed us to pray even for our enemies, when he said: 'Be kind and merciful, even as your heavenly Father is merciful.'[25] We can observe that almighty God is kind and merciful, causing his sun to shine on the ungrateful and on the just, and sending rain to both the holy and the evil; but all of them, he has told us, he will judge."

Chapter 97

"Besides, the fact that the prophet Moses remained until evening in the form of the cross, when his hands were held up by Aaron and Hur, happened in the likeness of this sign. For the Lord also remained upon the cross almost until evening when he was buried. Then he arose from the dead on the third day, as David foretold when he said: 'I have cried to the Lord with my voice, and he has heard me from his holy hill. I have slept and have taken my rest; and I have risen up, because the Lord has sustained me.'[26] Isaiah likewise foretold

---

23 Gen 35:7.
24 Deut 21:23.

25 Luke 6:36.
26 Ps 3:4–5.

the manner of his death in these words: 'I have spread forth my hands to an unbelieving and contradicting people, who walk in a way that is not good.'[27] And the same Isaiah also predicted his resurrection: 'His burial has been taken out of the midst,'[28] and: 'I will give the rich for his death.'[29] And again, David, in his twenty-first Psalm, refers to his passion on the cross in mystical parable: 'They have pierced my hands and feet. They have numbered all my bones. And they have looked and stared upon me. They parted my garments amongst them, and upon my vesture they cast lots.'[30] For, when they nailed him to the cross they did indeed pierce his hands and feet, and they who crucified him divided his garments among themselves, each casting lots for the garment he chose. You are indeed blind when you deny that the above-quoted Psalm was spoken of Christ, for you fail to see that no one among your people who was ever called King ever had his hands and feet pierced while alive, and died by this mystery (that is, of the cross), except this Jesus only."...

Chapter 108

"Now, you Jews were well acquainted with these facts in the life of Jonah and though Christ proclaimed to you that he would give you the sign of Jonah, and he pleaded with you to repent of your sins at least after His resurrection from the dead, and to lament before God as did the Ninevites that your nation and city might not be seized and destroyed, as it has been; yet you not only refused to repent after you learned that he arose from the dead, but, as I stated, you chose certain men and commissioned them to travel throughout the whole civilized world and announce: 'A godless and lawless sect has been started by an impostor, a certain Jesus of Galilee, whom we nailed to the cross, but whose body, after it was taken from the cross, was stolen at night from the tomb by his disciples, who now try to deceive people by affirming that he has arisen from the dead and has ascended into heaven.' And you accuse him of having taught those irreverent, riotous, and wicked things, of which you everywhere accuse all those who look up to and acknowledge him as their Christ, their teacher, and the Son of God. And, to top your folly, even now, after your city has been seized and your whole country ravaged, you not only refuse to repent, but you defiantly curse him and his followers. But, as far as we Christians are concerned, we do not hate you, nor those who believed the wicked rumors you have spread against us; on the contrary, we pray that even now you may mend your ways and find mercy from God the Father of all, who is most benign and compassionate."

---

27 Isa 65:2.

28 Isa 57:2.

29 Isa 53:9.

30 Ps 22:16–18.

20. Melito of Sardis: "On the Passover"

One of the most eloquent homilies from the early church (see Chapter 11) comes from the pen of Melito, an otherwise little-known bishop of the city of Sardis in Asia Minor. Entitled "On the Passover," the sermon provides a rhetorically powerful and religiously polemical exposition of the Old Testament account of the Passover meal instituted under Moses. For Melito, Jesus himself was the true Passover lamb whose shed blood brings salvation. As the reality to which the Old Testament pointed, Christ is far superior to the religion of Judaism, which therefore no longer has any independent value (just as a model of a building can be destroyed once construction is completed). Moreover, Jesus' death, for Melito, is not only a message of salvation but also of judgment, especially for the Jews who were responsible for it. In executing Jesus, the Jews killed their own Messiah. Indeed, since Melito sees Jesus as divine ("by nature, both God and man"), Jews are guilty of murdering their own God, the God who created the world and called Israel to be his people.

This is the first known instance of a Christian charging Jews with deicide in the death of Jesus. The emotional impact of the charge is significantly heightened by the powerful and gripping rhetoric that Melito uses to put it forth.

Melito is known to have died around 190 CE; this sermon therefore would have been preached sometime in the second half of the second century.

1 First of all, the Scripture about the Hebrew
    Exodus has been read
and the words of the mystery have been
    explained
as to how the sheep was sacrificed
and the people were saved.
2 Therefore, understand this, O beloved:
The mystery of the passover is
new and old,
eternal and temporal,
corruptible and incorruptible,
mortal and immortal
in this fashion:
3 It is old insofar as it concerns the law,
but new insofar as it concerns the gospel;

temporal insofar as it concerns the type,
eternal because of grace;
corruptible because of the sacrifice of the
    sheep,
incorruptible because of the life of the Lord;
mortal because of his burial in the earth,
immortal because of his resurrection from the
    dead.
4 The law is old,
but the gospel is new;
the type was for a time,
but grace is forever.
The sheep was corruptible,
but the Lord is incorruptible,
who was crushed as a lamb,

Melito of Sardis: On the Passover, from "A New English Translation of Melito's Paschal Homily," by Gerald F. Hawthorne. *Current Issues in Biblical and Patristic Interpretation*, ed. Gerald F. Hawthorne. Grand Rapids: Eerdmans, 1975. Used with permission.

but who was resurrected as God.
For although he was led to sacrifice as a sheep,
yet he was not a sheep;
and although he was as a lamb without voice,
yet indeed he was not a lamb.
The one was the model;
the other was found to be the finished product.

5 For God replaced the lamb,
and a man the sheep;
but in the man was Christ,
who contains all things.

6 Hence, the sacrifice of the sheep,
and the sending of the lamb to slaughter,
and the writing of the law—
each led to and issued in Christ,
for whose sake everything happened in the ancient law,
and even more so in the new gospel.

7 For indeed the law issued in the gospel—
the old in the new,
both coming forth together from Zion and Jerusalem;
and the commandment issued in grace,
and the type in the finished product,
and the lamb in the Son,
and the sheep in a man,
and the man in God.

8 For the one who was born as Son,
and led to slaughter as a lamb,
and sacrificed as a sheep,
and buried as a man,
rose up from the dead as God,
since he is by nature both God and man.

9 He is everything:
in that he judges he is law,
in that he teaches he is gospel,
in that he saves he is grace,
in that he begets he is Father,
in that he is begotten he is Son,
in that he suffers he is sheep,
in that he is buried he is man,
in that he comes to life again he is God.

10 Such is Jesus Christ,
to whom be the glory forever. Amen.

11 Now comes the mystery of the passover,

even as it stands written in the law,
just as it has been read aloud only moments ago.[1]
But I will clearly set forth the significance of the words of this Scripture,
showing how God commanded Moses in Egypt,
when he had made his decision,
to bind Pharaoh under the lash,
but to release Israel from the lash
through the hand of Moses.

12 For see to it, he says,
that you take a flawless and perfect lamb,
and that you sacrifice it in the evening
with the sons of Israel,
and that you eat it at night, and in haste.
You are not to break any of its bones.

13 You will do it like this, he says:
In a single night
you will eat it by families and by tribes,
your loins girded,
and your staves in your hands.
For this is the Lord's passover,
an eternal reminder for the sons of Israel.

14 Then take the blood of the sheep,
and anoint the front door of your houses
by placing upon the posts of your entrance-way
the sign of the blood, in order to ward off the angel.
For behold I will strike Egypt,
and in a single night
she will be made childless from beast to man.

15 Then, when Moses sacrificed the sheep
and completed the mystery at night
together with the sons of Israel,
he sealed the doors of their houses
in order to protect the people
and to ward off the angel.

16 But when the sheep was sacrificed,
and the passover consumed,
and the mystery completed,
and the people made glad,
and Israel sealed,

---

1 Exod 12:11–30.

then the angel arrived to strike Egypt,
who was neither
initiated into the mystery,
participant of the passover,
sealed by the blood,
nor protected by the Spirit,
but who was the enemy and the unbeliever.

17 In a single night the angel struck and made
        Egypt childless.
    For when the angel had encompassed Israel,
    and had seen her sealed with the blood of the
        sheep,
    he advanced against Egypt,
    and by means of grief subdued the stubborn
        Pharaoh,
    clothing him,
    not with a cloak of mourning,
    nor with a torn mantle,
    but with all of Egypt, torn,
    and mourning for her firstborn.

18 For all Egypt,
    plunged in troubles and calamities,
    in tears and lamentations,
    came to Pharaoh in utter sadness,
    not in appearance only,
    but also in soul,
    having torn not only her garments
    but her tender breasts as well.

19 Indeed it was possible to observe an extraor-
        dinary sight:
    in one place people beating their breasts,
    in another those wailing,
    and in the middle of them Pharaoh,
    mourning, sitting in sackcloth and cinders,
    shrouded in thick darkness
    as in a funeral garment,
    girded with all Egypt,
    as with a tunic of grief.

20 For Egypt clothed Pharaoh
    as a cloak of wailing.
    Such was the mantle that had been woven for
        his royal body.
    With just such a cloak did the angel of righ-
        teousness clothe
    the self-willed Pharaoh:

with bitter mournfulness,
and with thick darkness,
and with childlessness.
For that angel warred against the firstborn of
    Egypt.
Indeed, swift and insatiate
was the death of the firstborn.

21 And an unusual monument of defeat,
    set up over those who had fallen dead in a
        moment,
    could be seen.
    For the defeat of those who lay dead
    became the provisions of death.

22 If you listen
    to the narration of this extraordinary event
    you will be astonished.
    For these things befell the Egyptians:
    a long night,
    and darkness which was touchable,
    and death which touched,
    and an angel who oppressed,
    and Hades which devoured
    their firstborn.

23 But you must listen to
    something still more extraordinary and
        terrifying:
    in the darkness which could be touched
    was hidden death which could not be touched.
    And the ill-starred Egyptians touched the
        darkness,
    while death, on the watch,
    touched the firstborn of the Egyptians
    as the angel had commanded.

24 Therefore, if anyone touched the darkness
    he was led out by death.
    Indeed one firstborn,
    touching a dark body with his hand,
    and utterly frightened in his soul,
    cried aloud in misery and in terror:
    What has my right hand laid hold of?
    At what does my soul tremble?
    Who cloaks my whole body with darkness?
    If you are my father, help me;
    if my mother, feel sympathy for me;
    if my brother, speak to me;

if my friend, sit with me;
if my enemy, go away from me
since I am a firstborn son!

25 And before the firstborn was silent,
the long silence held him in its power, saying:
You are mine, O firstborn!
I, the silence of death, am your destiny.

26 And another firstborn,
taking note of the capture of the firstborn,
denied his identity,
so that he might not die a bitter death:
I am not a firstborn son;
I was born like a third child.
But he who could not be deceived
touched that firstborn,
and he fell forward in silence.
In a single moment
the firstborn fruit of the Egyptians was
    destroyed.
The one first conceived,
the one first born,
the one sought after,
the one chosen
was dashed to the ground;
not only that of men
but that of irrational animals as well.

27 A lowing was heard in the fields of the earth,
of cattle bellowing for their nurslings,
a cow standing over her calf,
and a mare over her colt.
And the rest of the cattle,
having just given birth to their offspring
and swollen with milk,
were lamenting bitterly and piteously
for their firstborn.

28 And there was a wailing and lamentation
because of the destruction of the people,
because of the destruction of the firstborn
    who were dead.
And all Egypt stank,
because of the unburied bodies.

29 Indeed one could see a frightful spectacle:
of the Egyptians
there were mothers with dishevelled hair,
and fathers who had lost their minds,

wailing aloud in terrifying fashion in the
    Egyptian tongue:
O wretched persons that we are!
We have lost our firstborn
in a single moment!
And they were striking their breasts with
    their hands,
beating time in hammerlike fashion to the
    dance for their dead.

30 Such was the misfortune which encompassed
    Egypt.
In an instant it made her childless.
But Israel, all the while, was being protected
by the sacrifices of the sheep
and truly was being illumined
by its blood which was shed;
for the death of the sheep
was found to be a rampart for the people.

31 O inexpressible mystery!
the sacrifice of the sheep
was found to be the salvation of the people,
and the death of the sheep
became the life of the people.
For its blood warded off the angel.

32 Tell me, O angel,
At what were you turned away?
At the sacrifice of the sheep,
or the life of the Lord?
At the death of the sheep,
or the type of the Lord?
At the blood of the sheep,
or the Spirit of the Lord?
Clearly you were turned away

33 because you saw the mystery of the Lord
taking place in the sheep,
the life of the Lord
in the sacrifice of the sheep,
the type of the Lord
in the death of the sheep.
For this reason you did not strike Israel,
but it was Egypt alone that you made
    childless.

34 What was this extraordinary mystery?
It was Egypt struck to destruction
but Israel kept for salvation.

Listen to the meaning of this mystery:

35 Beloved, no speech or event takes place
without a pattern or design;
every event and speech
involves a pattern—
that which is spoken, a pattern,
and that which happens, a prefiguration—
in order that as the event
is disclosed through the prefiguration,
so also the speech
may be brought to expression through its
outline.

36 Without the model,
no work of art arises.
Is not that which is to come into existence
seen through the model which typifies it?
For this reason a pattern of that which is to be
is made
either out of wax,
or out of clay,
or out of wood,
in order that by the smallness of the model,
destined to be destroyed,
might be seen that thing which is to arise
from it—
higher than it in size,
and mightier than it in power,
and more beautiful than it in appearance,
and more elaborate than it in ornamentation.

37 So, whenever the thing arises
for which the model was made,
then that which carried the image of the
future thing
is destroyed as no longer of use,
since it has transmitted its resemblance to
that which is
by nature true.
Therefore, that which once was valuable, is
now without value
because that which is truly valuable has
appeared.

38 For each thing has its own time:
there is a distinct time for the type,
there is a distinct time for the material,
and there is a distinct time for the truth.

You construct the model.
You want this,
because you see in it the image of the future
work.
You procure the material for the model.
You want this,
on account of that which is going to arise because of it.
You complete the work
and cherish it alone,
for only in it do you see both the type and the
truth.

39 Therefore, if it was like this with models of
perishable objects,
so indeed will it also be with those of imperishable objects.
If it was like this with earthly things,
so indeed also will it be with heavenly things.
For even the Lord's salvation and his truth
were prefigured in the people,
and the teaching of the gospel
was proclaimed in advance by the law.

40 The people, therefore, became the model for
the church,
and the law a parabolic sketch.
But the gospel became the explanation of the
law
and its fulfilment,
while the church became the storehouse of
truth.

41 Therefore, the type had value
prior to its realization,
and the parable was wonderful
prior to its interpretation.
This is to say that
the people had value
before the church came on the scene,
and the law was wonderful
before the gospel was brought to light.

42 But when the church came on the scene,
and the gospel was set forth,
the type lost its value
by surrendering its significance to the truth,
and the law was fulfilled
by surrendering its significance to the gospel.

Just as the type lost its significance
by surrendering its image to that which is
    true by nature,
and as the parable lost its significance
by being illumined through the interpretation,
43 so indeed also the law was fulfilled
when the gospel was brought to light,
and the people lost their significance
when the church came on the scene,
and the type was destroyed
when the Lord appeared.
Therefore, those things which once had value
are today without value,
because the things which have true value have
    appeared.
44 For at one time the sacrifice of the sheep was
    valuable,
but now it is without value because of the life
    of the Lord.
The death of the sheep once was valuable,
but now it is without value because of the sal-
    vation of the Lord.
The blood of the sheep once was valuable,
but now it is without value because of the
    Spirit of the Lord.
The silent lamb once was valuable,
but now it has no value because of the blame-
    less Son.
The temple here below once was valuable,
but now it is without value because of the
    Christ from above.
45 The Jerusalem here below once had value,
but now it is without value because of the
    Jerusalem from
above.
The meager inheritance once had value;
now it is without value because of the abun-
    dant grace.
For not in one place alone,
nor yet in narrow confines,
has the glory of God been established,
but his grace has been poured out
upon the uttermost parts of the inhabited
    world,

and there the almighty God
has taken up his dwelling place
through Jesus Christ,
to whom be the glory for ever. Amen.
46 Now that you have heard the explanation of
the type and of that which corresponds to it,
hear also what goes into making up the
    mystery.
What is the passover?
Indeed its name is derived
from that event—
"to celebrate the passover" (*to paschein*) is de-
    rived from
"to suffer" (*tou pathein*).
Therefore, learn
who the sufferer is
and who he is who suffers along with the
    sufferer.
47 Why indeed was the Lord present upon the
    earth?
In order that having clothed himself with the
    one who suffers,
he might lift him up to the heights of heaven.
In the beginning, when God made heaven
    and earth,
and everything in them through his word,
he himself formed man from the earth
and shared with that form his own breath,
and himself placed him in paradise,
which was eastward in Eden,
and there they lived most luxuriously.[2]
Then by way of command God gave them this
    law:
For your food you may eat from any tree,
but you are not to eat
from the tree of the one who knows good and
    evil.
For on the day you eat from it,
you most certainly will die.
48 But man,
who is by nature capable of receiving good
    and evil

---

2 Gen 2–3.

as soil of the earth is capable of receiving seeds from
both sides,
welcomed the hostile and greedy counsellor,
and by having touched that tree
transgressed the command,
and disobeyed God.
As a consequence, he was cast out into this world
as a condemned man is cast into prison.

49 And when he had fathered many children,
and had grown very old,
and had returned to the earth
through having tasted of the tree,
an inheritance was left behind by him for his children.
Indeed, he left his children an inheritance—
not of chastity but of unchastity,
not of immortality but of corruptibility,
not of honor but of dishonor,
not of freedom but of slavery,
not of sovereignty but of tyranny,
not of life but of death,
not of salvation but of destruction.

50 Extraordinary and terrifying indeed
was the destruction of people upon the earth.
For the following things happened to them:
They were carried off as slaves by sin, the tyrant,
and were led away into the regions of desire
where they were totally engulfed
by insatiable sensual pleasures—
by adultery,
by unchastity,
by debauchery,
by inordinate desires,
by avarice,
by murders,
by bloodshed,
by the tyranny of wickedness,
by the tyranny of lawlessness.

51 For even a father of his own accord lifted up a dagger against his son;
and a son used his hands against his father;

and the impious person smote the breasts that nourished him;
and brother murdered brother;
and host wronged his guest;
and friend assassinated friend;
and one man cut the throat of another
with his tyrannous right hand.

52 Therefore all people on the earth
became either murderers,
or parricides,
or killers of their children.
And yet a thing still more dreadful and extraordinary was
to be found:
A mother attacked the flesh which she gave birth to,
a mother attacked those whom her breasts had nourished;
and she buried in her belly
the fruit of her belly.
Indeed, the ill-starred mother became a dreadful tomb,
when she devoured the child which she bore in her womb.

53 But in addition to this
there were to be found among people
many things still more monstrous and terrifying and brutal:
father cohabits with his child,
and son with his mother,
and brother with sister,
and male with male,
and each man lusting after the wife of his neighbor.

54 Because of these things sin exulted,
which, because it was death's collaborator,
entered first into the souls of people,
and prepared as food for him the bodies of the dead.
In every soul sin left its mark,
and those in whom it placed its mark
were destined to die.

55 Therefore, all flesh fell under the power of sin,
and every body under the dominion of death,

for every soul was driven out from its house of flesh.

Indeed, that which had been taken from the earth

was dissolved again into earth,

and that which had been given from God

was locked up in Hades.

And that beautiful ordered arrangement was dissolved,

when the beautiful body was separated (from the soul).

56 Yes, the human was divided up into parts by death.

Yes, an extraordinary misfortune and captivity enveloped him:

he was dragged away captive under the shadow of death,

and the image of the Father remained there desolate.

For this reason, therefore,

the mystery of the passover has been completed

in the body of the Lord.

57 Indeed, the Lord

prearranged his own sufferings

in the patriarchs,

and in the prophets,

and in the whole people of God,

giving his sanction to them through the law and the prophets.

For that which was to exist in a new and grandiose fashion

was pre-planned long in advance,

in order that when it should come into existence

one might attain to faith,

just because it had been predicted long in advance.

58 So indeed also the suffering of the Lord,

predicted long in advance by means of types,

but seen today,

has brought about faith, just because it has taken place

as predicted.

And yet people have taken it as something completely new.

Well, the truth of the matter is

the mystery of the Lord

is both old and new—

old insofar as it involved the type,

but new insofar as it concerns grace.

And what is more, if you pay close attention to this type

you will see the real thing through its fulfillment.

59 Accordingly, if you desire to see the mystery of the Lord,

pay close attention to Abel who likewise was put to death,

to Isaac who likewise was bound hand and foot,

to Joseph who likewise was sold,

to Moses who likewise was exposed,

to David who likewise was hunted down,

to the prophets who likewise suffered

because they were the Lord's anointed.

60 Pay close attention also

to the one who was sacrificed as a sheep in the land of Egypt,

to the one who smote Egypt

and who saved Israel

by his blood.

61 For it was through the voice of prophecy

that the mystery of the Lord was proclaimed.

Moses, indeed, said to his people:

"Surely you will see your life suspended before your eyes night and day,

but you surely will not believe on your Life."[3]

62 And David said:

"Why were the nations haughty

and the people concerned about nothing?

The kings of the earth presented themselves

and the princess assembled themselves together

against the Lord and against his anointed."[4]

---

3 Deut 28:66.

4 Ps 2:1–2.

63 And Jeremiah:
"I am as an innocent lamb
being led away to be sacrificed.
They plotted evil against me and said:
Come! let us throw him a tree for his food,
and let us exterminate him from the land of
    the living,
so that his name will never be recalled."[5]

64 And Isaiah:
"He was led as a sheep to slaughter,
and, as a lamb is silent
in the presence of the one who shears it,
he did not open his mouth.
Therefore who will tell his offspring?"[6]

65 And indeed there were many other things
proclaimed by numerous prophets
concerning the mystery of the passover,
which is Christ,
to whom be the glory forever. Amen.

66 When this one came from heaven to earth
for the sake of the one who suffers,
and had clothed himself with that very one
through the womb of a virgin,
and having come forth as a man,
he accepted the sufferings of the sufferer
through his body which was capable of
    suffering.
And he destroyed those human sufferings
by his spirit which was incapable of dying.
He killed death which had put humans to
    death.

67 For this one,
who was led away as a lamb,
and who was sacrificed as a sheep
by himself delivered us from servitude to the
    world
as from the land of Egypt,
and released us from bondage to the devil
as from the hand of Pharaoh,
and sealed our souls by his own spirit
and the members of our bodies by his own
    blood.

---

5 Jer 11:19.

6 Isa 53:7.

68 This is
the one who covered death with shame
and who plunged the devil into mourning
as Moses did Pharaoh.
This is the one who smote lawlessness
and deprived injustice of its offspring,
as Moses deprived Egypt.
This is the one who delivered us
from slavery into freedom,
from darkness into light,
from death into life,
from tyranny into an eternal kingdom,
and who made us a new priesthood,
and a special people forever.

69 This one is the passover of our salvation.
This is the one who patiently endured many
    things in many people:
This is the one who was murdered in Abel,
and bound as a sacrifice in Isaac,
and exiled in Jacob,
and sold in Joseph,
and exposed in Moses,
and sacrificed in the lamb,
and hunted down in David,
and dishonored in the prophets.

70 This is the one who became human in a
    virgin,
who was hanged on the tree,
who was buried in the earth,
who was resurrected from among the dead,
and who raised humankind up
out of the grave below
to the heights of heaven.

71 This is the lamb that was slain.
This is the lamb that was silent.
This is the one who was born of Mary, that
    beautiful ewe-lamb.
This is the one who was taken from the flock,
and was dragged to sacrifice,
and was killed in the evening,
and was buried at night,
the one who was not broken while on the tree,
who did not see dissolution while in the earth,
who rose up from the dead,
and who raised up humankind

from the grave below.
72 This one was murdered.
And where was he murdered?
In the very center of Jerusalem!
Why?
Because he had healed their lame,
and had cleansed their lepers,
and had guided their blind with light,
and had raised up their dead.
For this reason he suffered.
Somewhere it has been written in the law and
    prophets,
"They paid me back evil for good,
and my soul with barrenness,
plotting evil against me,
saying, Let us bind this just man
because he is troublesome to us."[7]
73 Why, O Israel, did you do this strange injustice?
You dishonored the one who had honored
    you.
You held in contempt the one who held you in
    esteem.
You denied the one who publicly acknowl-
    edged you.
You renounced the one who proclaimed you
    his own,
You killed the one who made you to live,
Why did you do this, O Israel?
74 Has it not been written for your benefit:
"Do not shed innocent blood
lest you die a terrible death"?
Nevertheless, Israel admits, I killed the Lord!
Why?
Because it was necessary for him to die.
You have deceived yourself, O Israel,
rationalizing thus about the death of the
    Lord.
75 It was necessary for him to suffer, yes,
but not by you;
it was necessary for him to be dishonored,
but not by you;
it was necessary for him to be judged,

but not by you;
it was necessary for him to be crucified,
but not by you,
nor by your right hand.
76 O Israel!
You ought to have cried aloud to God with
    this voice:
"O Lord,
if it was necessary for your Son to suffer,
and if this was your will,
let him suffer indeed,
but not at my hands.
Let him suffer at the hands of strangers.
Let him be judged by the uncircumcised.
Let him be crucified by the tyrannical right
    hand,
but not by mine."
77 But you, O Israel,
did not cry out to God with this voice,
nor did you absolve yourself of guilt before
    the Lord,
nor were you persuaded by his works.
78 The withered hand which was restored whole
    to its body
did not persuade you;
nor did the eyes of the blind which were
    opened by his hand;
nor did the paralyzed bodies
restored to health again through his voice;
nor did that most extraordinary miracle per-
    suade you,
namely, the dead man raised to life from the
    tomb
where already he had been lying for four days.
Indeed, dismissing these things,
you, to your detriment, prepared the following
for the sacrifice of the Lord at eventide;
sharp nails,
and false witnesses,
and fetters,
and scourges,
79 and vinegar,
and gall,
and a sword,
and affliction,

and all as though it were for a blood-stained
    robber.
For you brought to him
scourges for his body,
and the thorns for his head.
And you bound those beautiful hands of his,
which had formed you from the earth.
And that beautiful mouth of his,
which had nourished you with life,
you filled with gall.
And you killed your Lord
at the time of the great feast.

80 Surely you were filled with gaiety,
    but he was filled with hunger;
you drank wine and ate bread,
but he vinegar and gall;
you wore a happy smile,
but he had a sad countenance;
you were full of joy,
but he was full of trouble;
you sang songs,
but he was judged;
you issued the command,
he was crucified;
you danced,
he was buried;
you lay down on a soft bed,
but he in a tomb and coffin.

81 O lawless Israel,
    why did you commit this extraordinary crime
of casting your Lord into new sufferings—
your master,
the one who formed you,
the one who made you,
the one who honored you,
the one who called you Israel?

82 But you were found not really to be Israel,
    for you did not see God,
you did not recognize the Lord,
you did not know, O Israel.
that this one was the firstborn of God.
the one who was begotten before the morning
    star,
the one who caused the light to shine forth,
the one who made bright the day,

the one who parted the darkness,
the one who established the primordial start-
    ing point,
the one who suspended the earth,
the one who quenched the abyss,
the one who stretched out the firmament,
the one who formed the universe,

83 the one who set in motion the stars of heaven,
    the one who caused those luminaries to shine,
the one who made the angels in heaven,
the one who established their thrones in that
    place,
the one who by himself fashioned humans
    upon the earth.
This was the one who chose you,
the one who guided you,
from Adam to Noah,
from Noah to Abraham,
from Abraham to Isaac and Jacob and the
    Twelve Patriarchs.

84 This was the one who guided you into Egypt,
    and guarded you,
and himself kept you well supplied there.
This was the one who lighted your route with
    a column of fire,
and provided shade for you by means of a
    cloud,
the one who divided the Red Sea,
and led you across it,
and scattered your enemy abroad.

85 This is the one who provided you with manna
    from heaven,
the one who gave you water to drink from a
    rock,
the one who established your laws in Horeb,
the one who gave you an inheritance in the
    land,
the one who sent out his prophets to you,
the one who raised up your kings.

86 This is the one who came to you,
    the one who healed your suffering ones
and who resurrected your dead.
This is the one whom you sinned against.
This is the one whom you wronged.
This is the one whom you killed

This is the one whom you sold for silver,
although you asked him for the didrachma.

87 O ungrateful Israel, come here
and be judged before me for your ingratitude.
How high a price did you place on being created by him?
How high a price did you place on the discovery of your fathers?
How high a price did you place on the descent
  into Egypt,
and the provision made for you there
through the noble Joseph?

88 How high a price did you place on the ten
  plagues?
How high a price did you place on the nightly
  column of fire,
and the daily cloud,
and the crossing of the Red Sea?
How high a price did you place on the gift of
  manna from heaven,
and the gift of water from the rock,
and the gift of law in Horeb,
and the land as an inheritance,
and the benefits accorded you there?

89 How high a price did you place on your suffering people
whom he healed when he was present?
Set me a price on the withered hand,
which he restored whole to its body.

90 Put me a price on the people born blind,
whom he led into light by his voice.
Put me a price on those who lay dead,
whom he raised up alive from the tomb.
Inestimable are the benefits that come to you
  from him.
But you, shamefully,
have paid him back with ingratitude,
returning to him
evil for good,
and affliction for favor
and death for life—

91 a person for whom you should have died.
Furthermore, if the king of some nation is
  captured by an enemy,
a war is started because of him,
fortifications are shattered because of him,

cities are plundered because of him,
ransom is sent because of him,
ambassadors are commissioned because of him
in order that he might be surrendered,
so that either he might be returned if living,
or that he might be buried if dead.

92 But you, quite to the contrary,
voted against your Lord,
whom indeed the nations worshipped,
and the uncircumcised admired,
and the foreigners glorified,
over whom Pilate washed his hands.
But as for you—
you killed this one at the time of the great
  feast.

93 Therefore, the feast of unleavened bread
has become bitter to you
just as it was written:
"You will eat unleavened bread with bitter
  herbs."
Bitter to you are the nails which you made
  pointed.
Bitter to you is the tongue which you sharpened.
Bitter to you are the false witnesses whom
  you brought forward.
Bitter to you are the fetters which you
  prepared.
Bitter to you are the scourges which you
  wove.
Bitter to you is Judas whom you furnished
  with pay.
Bitter to you is Herod whom who followed.
Bitter to you is Caiaphas whom you obeyed.
Bitter to you is the gall which you made
  ready.
Bitter to you is the vinegar which you
  produced.
Bitter to you are the thorns which you plucked.
Bitter to you are your hands which you
  bloodied,
when you killed your Lord
in the midst of Jerusalem.

94 Pay attention, all families of the nations, and
  observe!
An extraordinary murder has taken place
in the center of Jerusalem,

in the city devoted to God's law,
in the city of the Hebrews,
in the city of the prophets,
in the city thought of as just.
And who has been murdered?
And who is the murderer?
I am ashamed to give the answer,
but give it I must.
For if this murder had taken place at night,
or if he had been slain in a desert place,
it would be well to keep silent;
but it was in the middle of the main street,
even in the center of the city,
while all were looking on,
that the unjust murder of this just person took
    place.

95 And thus he was lifted upon the tree,
and an inscription was affixed
identifying the one who had been murdered.
Who was he?
It is painful to tell,
but it is more dreadful not to tell.
Therefore, hear and tremble
because of him for whom the earth trembled.

96 The one who hung the earth in space, is him-
    self hanged;
the one who fixed the heavens in place, is
    himself impaled;
the one who firmly fixed all things, is himself
    firmly fixed to the tree.
The Lord is insulted,
God has been murdered,
the King of Israel has been destroyed
by the right hand of Israel.

97 O frightful murder!
O unheard of injustice!
The Lord is disfigured
and he is not deemed worthy of a cloak for his
    naked body,
so that he might not be seen exposed.
For this reason the stars turned and fled,
and the day grew quite dark,
in order to hide that naked person hanging on
    the tree,
darkening not the body of the Lord,
but the eyes of humans.

98 Yes, even though the people did not tremble,
the earth trembled instead;
although the people were not afraid,
the heavens grew frightened;
although the people did not tear their garments,
the angels tore theirs;
although the people did not lament,
the Lord thundered from heaven,
and the most high uttered his voice.

99 Why was it like this, O Israel?
You did not tremble for the Lord.
You did not fear for the Lord.
You did not lament for the Lord,
yet you lamented for your firstborn.
You did not tear your garments at the cruci-
    fixion of the Lord,
yet you tore your garments for your own who
    were murdered.
You forsook the Lord;
you were not found by him.
You dashed the Lord to the ground;
you, too, were dashed to the ground,
and lie quite dead.

100 But he arose from the dead
and mounted up to the heights of heaven.
When the Lord had clothed himself with
    humanity,
and had suffered for the sake of the sufferer,
and had been bound for the sake of the
    imprisoned,
and had been judged for the sake of the
    condemned,
and buried for the sake of the one who was
    buried,

101 he rose up from the dead,
and cried aloud with this voice:
Who is he who contends with me?
Let him stand in opposition to me.
I set the condemned one free;
I gave the dead one life;
I raised up the one who had been entombed.

102 Who is my opponent?
I, he says, am the Christ.
I am the one who destroyed death,
and triumphed over the enemy,
and trampled Hades under foot,

and bound the strong one,
and carried off humanity
to the heights of heaven,
I, he says, am the Christ.

103 Therefore, come, all human families,
you who have been befouled with sins,
and receive forgiveness for your sins.
I am your forgiveness,
I am the passover of your salvation,
I am the lamb which was sacrificed for you,
I am your ransom,
I am your light,
I am your savior,
I am your resurrection,
I am your king,
I am leading you up to the heights of heaven,
I will show you the eternal Father,
I will raise you up by my right hand.

104 This is the one who made the heaven and the
         earth,
and who in the beginning created humans,
who was proclaimed through the law and
         prophets,
who became human via the virgin,
who was hanged upon a tree,

who was buried in the earth,
who was resurrected from the dead,
and who ascended to the heights of heaven,
who sits at the right hand of the Father,
who has authority to judge and to save
         everything,
through whom the Father created everything
from the beginning of the world to the end of
         the age.

105 This is the alpha and the omega.
This is the beginning and the end—
an indescribable beginning
and an incomprehensible end.
This is the Christ.
This is the king.
This is Jesus.
This is the general.
This is the Lord.
This is the one who rose up from the dead.
This is the one who sits at the right hand of
         the Father.
He bears the Father
and is borne by the Father,
to whom be the glory
and the power forever. Amen.

21. Tertullian: Answer to the Jews

Among Tertullian's writings (see Chapter 4) is a lengthy treatise against the Jews. Only the first chapter has been excerpted here, in which Tertullian states that following a public debate between a Jew and a Christian (Tertullian himself?), he decided to clarify matters at greater length in writing. Possibly his public performance was not overly persuasive.

Tertullian's short discussion of Genesis 25 and Exodus 32 provides a nice, brief example of how Christians worked to turn the Scriptures of the Jews against them, claiming that God planned from the beginning to reject the Jews in favor of his new people, the Christians.

Tertullian: Answers to the Jews, from *The Ante-Nicene Fathers*; vol. 3. *Latin Christianity: Its Founder, Tertullian,* ed. A. Cleveland. Reprinted; 2nd ed. Grand Rapids: Eerdmans, 1989.

It happened very recently that a dispute was held between a Christian and a Jewish proselyte. Alternately with contentious cable they each spun out the day until evening. By the opposing din, moreover, of some partisans of the individuals, truth began to be overcast by a sort of cloud. It was therefore our pleasure that that which, owing to the confused noise of disputation, could be less fully elucidated point by point, should be more carefully looked into, and that the pen should determine, for reading purposes, the questions handled.

For the occasion, indeed, of claiming Divine grace even for the Gentiles derived a preeminent fitness from this fact, that the man who set up to vindicate God's Law as his own was of the Gentiles, and not a Jew of the stock of the Israelites. For this fact—that Gentiles are admissible to God's Law—is enough to prevent Israel from priding himself on the notion that the Gentiles are accounted as a little drop of a bucket, or else as dust out of a threshing-floor: although we have God himself as an adequate engager and faithful promiser, in that he promised to Abraham that "in his seed should be blest all nations of the earth";[1] and that out of the womb of Rebecca "two peoples and two nations were about to proceed,"[2]—of course those of the Jews, that is, of Israel; and of the Gentiles, that is ours. Each, then, was called a *people* and a *nation*; lest, from the nuncupative appellation, any should dare to claim for himself the privilege of grace. For God ordained "two peoples and two nations" as about to proceed out of the womb of one woman: nor did grace make distinction in the nuncupative appellation, but in the order of birth; to the effect that, which ever was to be prior in proceeding from the womb, should be subjected to "the less," that is, the posterior. For thus unto Rebecca did God speak: "Two nations are in thy womb, and two peoples shall be divided from thy bowels; and people shall overcome people, and the greater shall serve the less."[3] Accordingly, since the *people* or *nation* of the Jews is anterior in time, and "greater" through the grace of primary favor in the Law, whereas ours is understood to be "less" in the age of times, as having in the last era of the world attained the knowledge of divine mercy: beyond doubt, through the edict of the divine utterance, the *prior* and "greater" people—that is, the Jewish—must necessarily serve the "less"; and the "less" people—that is, the Christian—overcome the "greater." For, withal, according to the memorial records of the divine Scriptures, the *people* of the Jews—that is, the more ancient—quite forsook God, and did degrading service to idols, and, abandoning the Divinity, was surrendered to images; while "the people" said to Aaron, "Make us gods to go before us."[4] And when the gold out of the necklaces of the women and the rings of the men had been wholly smelted by fire, and there had come forth a calf-like head, to this figment Israel with one consent (abandoning God) gave honor, saying, "These are the gods who brought us from the land of Egypt."[5] For thus, in the later times in which kings were governing them, did they again, in conjunction with Jeroboam, worship golden kine, and groves, and enslave themselves to Baal. Whence is proved that they have ever been depicted, out of the volume of the divine Scriptures, as guilty of the crime of idolatry; whereas our "less"—that is, posterior—*people,* quitting the idols which formerly it used slavishly to serve, has been converted to the same God from whom Israel, as we have above related, had departed. For thus has the "less"—that is, posterior—*people* overcome the "greater people," while it attains the grace of divine favor, from which Israel has been divorced.

---

1 Gen 22:18.
2 Gen 25:23.

3 Gen 25:23.
4 Exod 32:1, 23.
5 Exod 32:4.

6

The Diversity of Early Christianity
Writings Later Deemed Heretical

Arguably the most significant breakthrough in the modern understanding of early Christianity is the realization that, contrary to what had earlier been thought, this religion was exceptionally diverse. The older, traditional view, which prevailed till the mid–twentieth century, had been that Christianity was basically monolithic: that there was one dominant form of Christianity reflected in the beliefs, practices, and ethics of most Christians everywhere throughout the first three centuries, a form of Christianity that was then ratified by the great church councils of the fourth century, which were organized principally to work out some of the more complicated details. To be sure, it was recognized that there were other "non-orthodox" views represented by scattered groups of "heretics"; but these were seen as fringe groups with little historical significance.

In this traditional understanding of early Christianity, the term *orthodoxy* (from two Greek words meaning "correct belief" or "right doctrine") referred to the views promoted by Jesus and his apostles and subscribed to by a solid and pervasive core of the Christian church from the earliest of times; *heresies* (from a Greek word meaning "choice") comprised marginal groups that had willfully chosen to corrupt and depart from the true faith.

As already pointed out in Chapter 1, many scholars now recognize that this traditional understanding does not conform to historical realities. There were, in fact, numerous Christian groups in the second and third centuries with a wide range of beliefs and practices. Each of these groups claimed to represent the original teachings of Jesus and his apostles; most of them had books allegedly written by the apostles to sustain their claims. But in the struggle to acquire the greatest number of adherents, only one of these groups "won out." It was this group that then deemed itself orthodox and marginalized all the other groups as heretical—insisting that it had held the majority position all along, maintaining that its views, and only its views, went back to the teachings of Jesus' apostles and writing the history of its own movement as if it had been the only significant form of Christianity from the beginning (thus the *Ecclesiastical History* of Eusebius, who stood within this "orthodox" line).

Why did the "non-orthodox" Christians not simply read their New Testaments and realize that the "orthodox" views were right? In addressing this question, we need always to remember that the final collection of books that we call the "New Testament"—books also attributed to Jesus' apostles—was not yet in existence during this period. In fact, the decision concerning which books to include in the collection was largely made as a result of the struggles to determine which form of Christianity was "true" (orthodox) and which ones were "false" (heretical) (see Chapter 9). Before these books were collected into a canon that was to be authoritative for all Christians everywhere, there was a diversity of belief and practice that makes the varieties of Christianity today look altogether tame by comparison.

Throughout the second and third centuries, for example, there were Christians who believed that there was not just one God but two; others believed in as many as twelve, or thirty. Whereas many Christians believed that the true God had created the world, others claimed that God was not the Creator and that he had never had any dealings with the world; for them, it had been created by an inferior, ignorant deity or group of deities. While many Christians accepted the Jewish Scriptures as the true word of God to be interpreted and followed literally, others insisted they were to be read allegorically, and yet others argued that they were not to be read at all, since they had been inspired by the Jewish God, who was not the one true God. Throughout this period we know of Christians who believed that Jesus was divine but not human, others who believed he was human but not divine, others who believed that he was two different creatures, one divine and one human, and yet others who believed he was one being, simultaneously both divine and human. There were some Christians who believed that Jesus had died for the sins of the world, other Christians who said that Jesus' death had nothing to do with the sins of the world, and yet others who said that he never died. In the second and third centuries, Christianity was diverse in the extreme.

As already pointed out, all of the early Christian groups that maintained these various points of view had writings that authorized, explicated, or simply assumed them; many of these writings claimed to be written by apostles. Unfortunately, the vast majority of these "non-orthodox" writings have disappeared from memory; many of them were destroyed after one form of Christianity assumed such overwhelming dominance in the fourth century; many others simply passed out of use and were lost. During modern times, however, a number of these writings have been accidentally discovered. Far and away the most dramatic discovery was in 1945, when farmhands digging for fertilizer near the village of Nag Hammadi, Egypt, uncovered a large earthenware jar containing 13 leather-bound volumes. As scholars soon discovered, the papyrus leaves of these books contained some 52 documents, almost all of them produced by "non-orthodox" Gnostic Christians (on what such Christians believed, see below). The texts were written in Coptic, an ancient form of Egyptian; but they were clearly translations of works that had originally been composed in Greek. And even though the volumes themselves were manufactured in the fourth century, the treatises they contained were composed much earlier. Some of them were already known, but by name only, from the writings of the anti-heretical church writers of the second and third centuries. In other words, this cache included texts used by early Gnostic Christian groups that were later deemed heretical.

There continue to be debates over how these texts, now commonly called the "Nag Hammadi library," came to be hidden in an earthenware jar in the wilderness. Since an ancient Christian monastery was located nearby, many scholars have assumed that when the writings were proscribed in the late fourth century (i.e., when the contours of the New Testament canon were becoming fixed; see Chapter 9), resident monks who revered these books, or at least wanted to keep them intact, decided to hide rather than destroy them, possibly for later use.

A selection of these texts is provided below, along with several other writings used widely among other, non-Gnostic forms of Christianity. It should be emphasized, however, that even with the new additions to our collections of "non-orthodox" texts, our knowledge of various early forms of Christianity is lamentably incomplete; this is particularly to be regretted, since many scholars now recognize that in the second and third centuries, some regions of the Mediterranean were more or less dominated by these forms of Christianity rather than the form that came to hold almost universal sway by the fourth century. A case in point involves the churches that followed the teachings of the second-century thinker and evangelist, Marcion. According to his opponents, Marcion's churches were nearly ubiquitous throughout large portions of Asia Minor. Unfortunately, all of the writings of Marcion and his followers are completely lost except as they are quoted to by his opponents among the "orthodox" (for some of Marcion's views, see Chapter 7).

The non-orthodox texts that have survived, however, do make for very interesting reading and provide a glimpse, at least, into the wide-ranging and rich diversity of the early Christian movement. The following selection organizes and introduces the surviving works into two major groups, Jewish-Christian and Gnostic-Christian, the latter of which is subdivided into four categories.

For Further Reading

Bauer, Walter. *Orthodoxy and Heresy in Earliest Christianity*, trans. Robert Kraft et al., eds. Robert Kraft and Gerhard Krodel. Philadelphia: Fortress, 1971.

Brakke, David. *The Gnostics: Myth, Ritual, and Diversity in Early Christianity*. Cambridge: Harvard University, 2010.

Dunderberg, Ismo. *Beyond Gnosticism: Myth, Lifestyle, and Society in the School of Valentinus*. New York: Columbia University Press, 2008.

Ehrman, Bart. *Lost Christianities: The Battles for Scripture and the Faiths We Never Knew*. New York: Oxford University Press, 2003.

Ehrman, Bart. *Lost Scriptures: Books That Did Not Make It Into the New Testament*. New York: Oxford University Press, 2003.

Elliott, J. K., ed. *The Apocryphal New Testament*. Oxford: Clarendon, 1993.

King, Karen. *What is Gnosticism?* Cambridge, MA: Harvard University Press, 2003.

Klijn, A. F. J. *Jewish–Christian Gospel Tradition*. Leiden: E. J. Brill, 1992.

Layton, Bentley. *The Gnostic Scriptures*. Garden City: Doubleday, 1987.

Lewis, Nicola Denzy. *Introduction to "Gnosticism": Ancient Voices, Christian Worlds*. New York: Oxford University Press, 2013.

Marjanen, Antti and Petri Luomanen. *A Companion to Second-Century "Heretics"*. Leiden: E. J. Brill, 2005.

Meyer, Marvin, ed. *The Nag Hammadi Scriptures*. San Francisco: HarperOne, 2007.

Pagels, Elaine. *The Gnostic Gospels*. New York: Random House, 1976.

Williams, Michael. *Rethinking Gnosticism: An Argument for Dismantling a Dubious Category*. Princeton: Princeton University Press, 1996.

Jewish Christian Texts
Introduction

Since Jesus and his followers were all Jews, it is no surprise that some form of Jewish-Christianity was dominant throughout much of the first century. The earliest Christians kept the Jewish Law as interpreted by Jesus and insisted that their converts do so as well (cf. Matthew 5:17–20). Soon, though, the religion became predominantly gentile—largely the result of the work of such missionaries as Paul, who was himself a Jew but who was dedicated to evangelizing pagans. Paul insisted that pagan converts did not need to become Jewish in order to be full-fledged members of the Christian church. The nature of the religion shifted as a result of such views, most Christians understanding themselves to be a separate religion from Judaism, which was itself seen, then, as misguided at best and demonic at worst (see Chapter 5).

But there were Jews who continued to convert to Christianity even after the end of the first century. Many of these retained their Jewishness and believed that in doing so they were following the teachings of Jesus and the examples set by his apostles, especially the disciple Peter and Jesus' own brother James, the leader of the Christian church in Jerusalem. Jewish-Christian groups were found in various parts of the Mediterranean, though we know of them best in the area in and around Palestine. Many of them did not look favorably upon Paul and his teachings; most of them revered Moses and kept the laws of circumcision, kosher foods, and Sabbath observance that he gave; some were known to pray toward the holy city Jerusalem three times a day and to follow other Jewish customs.

At least one of these groups was said to appeal to a Hebrew Gospel, allegedly written by Matthew, as the chief authority for their views. This Gospel was different from the Matthew that was eventually included in the New Testament, in that it lacked what are now the first two chapters. For these Jewish-Christians did not think that Jesus was miraculously born of a virgin; he was a flesh-and-blood human being with a nature and birth like all other humans. Even so, Jesus was special before God: as the most righteous person on earth, he had been adopted by God, at his baptism, to be his son, the Messiah who would save his people by dying for their sins.

Other Jewish-Christian groups revered yet other Gospels, as seen below; some of these groups came to be influenced by still other forms of Christianity over a period of time. Some Jewish-Christians, for example, evidently adopted perspectives found more widely among Gnostics. Our sources for all these groups are quite sparse. The following are among the most important ones that survive.

THE TEXTS

22. *The Gospel of the Ebionites*

The Gospel of the Ebionites does not survive intact but only in quotations by an opponent of the Jewish-Christians, the fourth-century heresy hunter Epiphanius of Salamis. These quotations, however, give us some idea of what the entire Gospel must have looked like. It was written in Greek and represented a kind of harmony of the Gospels of Matthew, Mark, and Luke. This can be seen most clearly in the account of the voice at Jesus' baptism. In the three canonical versions, the voice says slightly different things. These differences are harmonized, however, in the Gospel according to the Ebionites, where the voice comes from heaven three times, saying something slightly different on each occasion, corresponding to the words found in each of the Synoptics.

Some of the Ebionites' distinctive concerns were embodied in their Gospel. For example, possibly because they believed that Jesus' sacrifice on the cross had put an end to all animal sacrifices in fulfillment of the Mosaic Law, they appear to have abstained from meat. Their convictions on this score are evident in their Gospel's account of the diet of John the Baptist, where the canonical statement that John ate locusts and wild honey is modified by the change of one letter so that now the Baptist, in anticipation of the Ebionites themselves, maintains a strictly vegetarian cuisine, eating pancakes and wild honey.

It is difficult to assign a date to this Gospel, but since it betrays a knowledge of Matthew, Mark, and Luke, and presupposes a thriving community of Jewish Christians, it is perhaps best to locate it sometime in the early or mid–second century. The following extracts are all that remain of the Gospel and are drawn from Epiphanius's work, *The Medicine Chest*, Book 30.

The Gospel of the Ebionites

1 The beginning of the Gospel they use reads as follows: "And so in the days of Herod, King of Judea, John came baptizing a baptism of repentance in the Jordan River. He was said to have come from the tribe of Aaron, the priest, and was the child of Zacharias and Elizabeth. And everyone went out to him."[1] (Epiphanius, *Panarion* 30.13.6)

2 For by chopping off the genealogies of Matthew they make their Gospel begin as we indicated before, with the words: "And so in the days of Herod, King of Judea, when Caiaphas was high priest, a certain one named John came baptizing a baptism of repentance in the Jordan River." (Epiphanius, *Panarion* 30.14.3)

---

1 Cf. Matt 3:1–12; Mark 1:4–8; Luke 3:1–20.

The Gospel of the Ebionites, reproduced from Bart D. Ehrman and Zlatko Pleše, *The Apocryphal Gospels: Texts and Translations*. New York: Oxford University Press, 2011. Used with permission of Oxford University Press.

3 And so John was baptizing, and Pharisees came out to him and were baptized, as was all of Jerusalem. John wore a garment of camel hair and a leather belt around his waist; and his food was wild honey that tasted like manna, like a cake cooked in olive oil.[2] (Epiphanius, *Panarion* 30.13.4–5)

4 And after a good deal more, it goes on: "When the people were baptized, Jesus also came and was baptized by John. When he came up out of the water, the heavens opened and he saw the Holy Spirit in the form of a dove, descending and entering him. And a voice came from heaven, 'You are my beloved Son, in you I am well pleased.' Then it said, 'Today I have given you birth.' Immediately a great light enlightened the place. When John saw this," it says, "he said to him, 'Who are you, Lord?' Yet again a voice came from heaven to him, 'This is my beloved Son, with whom I am well pleased.'[3] And then," it says, "John fell before him and said, 'I beg you, Lord—you baptize me!' But Jesus restrained him by saying, 'Let it be, for it is fitting that all things be fulfilled in this way.' "[4] (Epiphanius, *Panarion* 30.13.3–4)

5 In the Gospel that they call "according to Matthew"—which is not at all complete, but is falsified and mutilated—which they refer to as the Hebrew Gospel, the following is found:

"There was a certain man named Jesus, who was about thirty years old. He is the one who chose us. When he came to Capernaum he entered the house of Simon, also called Peter, and he opened his mouth to say, 'As I was passing by the lake of Tiberias I chose John and James, the sons of Zebedee, and Simon, Andrew, Thaddaeus, Simon the Zealot, and Judas Iscariot; and I called you, Matthew, while you were sitting at the tax collector's booth, and you followed me.[5] I want you, therefore, to be the twelve apostles as a witness to Israel." (Epiphanius, *Panarion* 30.13.2–3)

6 Again they deny that he was a man, apparently based on the word the Savior spoke when it was reported to him, "See, your mother and brothers are standing outside." "Who," (he asked) "are my mother and brothers?" Stretching out his hand over his disciples he said, "These are my brothers and mother and sisters—those who do the will of my Father."[6] (Epiphanius, *Panarion* 30.14.5)

7 They do not allege that he was born from God the Father, but that he was created as one of the archangels, yet was made greater than they, since he rules over the angels and all things made by the Almighty. And, as found in their Gospel, they say that when he came he taught, "I have come to destroy the sacrifices. And if you do not stop making sacrifice, God's wrath will not stop afflicting you." (Epiphanius, *Panarion* 30.16.4–5)

8 They have changed the saying by abandoning its true sequence, as is clear to everyone who considers the combination of the words. For they had the disciples say, "Where do you want us to make preparations for you to eat the Passover lamb?"[7] And they made him respond, "I have no desire to eat the meat of this Passover lamb with you." (Epiphanius, *Panarion* 30.22.4)

---

2 Cf. Matt 3:4–5; Mark 1:5–6.

3 See Matt 3:17; Mark 1:11; and Luke 3:22 (in MS D and several Old Latin witnesses).

4 Matt 3:14–15.

---

5 Cf. Matt 4:18–22; 9:9–13; Mark 1:16–20; 2:13–14; Luke 5:1–11, 27–32.

6 See Matt 12:47–50; Mark 3:32–35; and Luke 8:20–21.

7 See Matt 26:17; Mark 14:12; and especially Luke 22:15.

23. The "Letter of Peter to James" and its "Reception"

The "Letter of Peter to James" is one of a number of early Christian writings produced pseudonymously in the name of Jesus' disciple, Simon Peter (cf. the Gospel of Peter and the two Apocalypses of Peter, Chapters 7 and 8). It does not survive as an independently transmitted letter but only as the preface to the "Homilies of Clement," a collection of legendary stories and sermons of Clement of Rome (see below). The account of its "Reception" by James, the brother of Jesus and leader of the church in Jerusalem, is also part of this preface. The date of the composition of these works is difficult to determine, but they are probably to be situated in the early third century.

The Letter of Peter urges James to pass along the accompanying sermons carefully, and only to those who are worthy to receive them. The clear concern is that Peter's teachings not be corrupted by those who have a different understanding of the truth. Both the Letter and the Reception are Jewish-Christian in their orientation, as seen in their emphasis on emulating the actions of Moses, on keeping the Law, and on opposing the person Peter calls "the man who is my enemy," commonly understood to be none other than the apostle Paul (cf. Galatians 2:11–14), who taught that salvation comes to all people, Jew and gentile, apart from following the Law of Moses, and who urged gentiles not to be circumcised (see Galatians). This Pauline notion stood in sharp contrast to the views of Jewish Christians like the Ebionites, as seen here, for example, in the insistence by James (allegedly the brother of Jesus himself) that only "one who has been circumcised is a believing Christian."

Letter of Peter to James

1 Peter to James, the lord and bishop of the holy church: Peace be with you always from the Father of all through Jesus Christ.

2 Knowing well that you, my brother, eagerly take pains about what is for the mutual benefit of us all, I earnestly beseech you not to pass on to any one of the Gentiles the books of my preachings which I (here) forward to you, nor to any one of our own tribe before probation. But if some one of them has been examined and found to be worthy, then you may hand them over to him in the same way as Moses handed over his office of a teacher to the seventy.

3 Wherefore also the fruit of his caution is to be seen up to this day. For those who belong to his people preserve everywhere the same rule in their belief in the one God and in their line of conduct, the Scriptures with their many senses being unable to incline them to assume another attitude.

4 Rather they attempt, on the basis of the rule that has been handed down to them, to harmonise the contradictions of the Scriptures, if haply some

The Letter of Peter to James, from *New Testament Apocrypha*, vol. 2; ed. Wilhelm Schneemelcher, 2nd ed. Cambridge/Louisville: Lutterworth Press/Westminster John Knox Press, 1991. Used with permission of Lutterworth Press and Westminster John Knox Press.

one who does not know the traditions is perplexed by the ambiguous utterances of the prophets.

5 On this account they permit no one to teach unless he first learn how the Scriptures should be used. Wherefore there obtain amongst them one God, one law, and one hope.

2 In order now that the same may also take place among us, hand over the books of my preachings in the same mysterious way to our seventy brethren that they may prepare those who are candidates for positions as teachers.

2 For if we do not proceed in this way, our word of truth will be split into many options. This I do not know as a prophet, but I have already the beginning of the evil before me.

3 For some from among the Gentiles have rejected my lawful preaching and have preferred a lawless and absurd doctrine of the man who is my enemy.

4 And indeed some have attempted, whilst I am still alive, to distort my words by interpretations of many sorts, as if I taught the dissolution of the law and, although I was of this opinion, did not express it openly. But that may God forbid!

5 For to do such a thing means to act contrary to the law of God which was made known by Moses and was confirmed by our Lord in its everlasting continuance. For he said: "The heaven and the earth will pass away, but one jot or one title shall not pass away from the law."[1]

6 This he said that everything might come to pass. But those persons who, I know not how, allege that they are at home in my thoughts wish to expound the words which they have heard of me better than I myself who spoke them. To those whom they instruct they say that this is my opinion, to which indeed I never gave a thought.

7 But if they falsely assert such a thing while I am still alive, how much more after my death will those who come later venture to do so?

3 In order now that such a thing may not happen I earnestly beseech you not to pass on the books of my preachings which I send you to any one of our own tribe or to any foreigner before probation, but if some one is examined and found to be worthy, let them then be handed over in the way.

2 In which Moses handed over his office of a teacher to the seventy, in order that they may preserve the dogmas and extend farther the rule of the truth, interpreting everything in accordance with our tradition and not being dragged into error through ignorance and uncertainty in their minds to bring others into the like pit of destruction.

3 What seems to me to be necessary I have now indicated to you. And what you, my lord, deem to be right, do you carry fittingly into effect. Farewell.

The Reception of the Letter

1 Now when James had read the epistle he called the elders together, read it to them and said: "As is necessary and proper, our Peter has called our attention to the fact that we must be cautious in the matter of the truth, that we should pass on the books of his preachings that have been forwarded to us not indiscriminately, but only to a good and religious candidate for the position of a teacher, a man who as one who has been circumcised is a believing Christian, and indeed that we should not pass on all the books to him at once, so that, if he shows indiscretion in handling the first, he may not be entrusted with the others.

2 He ought therefore to be proved for not less than six years. Thereafter, according to the way of Moses, let him be brought to a river or a fountain where there is living water and the regeneration of the righteous takes place; not that he may swear, for that is not permitted, but he should be enjoined to stand by the water and to vow, as we also ourselves were made to do at the time of our regeneration, to the end that we might sin no more.

2 And let him say: 'As witness I invoke heaven, earth, and water, in which everything is comprehended, and also in addition the all-pervading

---

1 Matt 24:35; 5:18.

air, without which I am unable to breathe, that I shall always be obedient to him who hands over to me the books of the preachings and shall not pass on to any one in any way the books which he may give to me, that I shall neither copy them nor give a copy of them nor allow them to come into the hands of a copyist, neither shall I myself do this nor shall I do it through another, and not in any other way, through cunning or tricks, through keeping them carelessly, through depositing them with another or through underhand agreement, nor in any other manner or by means of any other artifice will I pass them on to a third party.

2 Only if I have proved someone to be worthy—proving him as I myself have been proved, or even more, in no case for less than six years—if he is a religious and good candidate for the position of a teacher, I will hand them over to him as I have received them and certainly in agreement with my bishop.

3 Otherwise, though he be either my son or a brother or a friend or any other relation, if he is unworthy, I shall keep information away from him since it does not befit him.

2 I shall allow myself neither to be frightened by persecutions nor to be deceived by gifts. And even if I should ever come to the conviction that the books of the preachings which have been handed to me do not contain the truth, then also I shall not pass them on but shall hand them back.

3 When I am on a journey, I shall carry with me all the books that are in my possession. And if I purpose not to take them with me, I shall not leave them behind in my house, but shall consign them to the care of my bishop, who is of the same faith and of like extraction.

4 If I am sick and see death before me, I shall, if I am childless, proceed in the same way. I shall do the like if at the time of my death my son is not worthy or is not yet of age. I shall deposit the books with my bishop that if, when my son has come of age, he should prove to be worthy of the trust that he may hand them over to him as a father's legacy according to the terms of the vow.

4 And that I shall proceed in this way, I again invoke as witnesses heaven, earth, and water, in which everything is comprehended, and also in addition the all-pervading air without which I am unable to breathe: I shall be obedient to him who hands over to me the books of the preachings, I shall keep them in every respect as I have vowed and even beyond that.

2 If now I observe the agreements, then will my portion be with the saints; but if I act against my vow, then may the universe and the all-pervading ether and God, who is over all and is mightier and more exalted than any other, be hostile to me.

3 And if even I should come to believe in another god, then I swear also by him, whether he now is or is not, that I shall not proceed otherwise. In addition to all that, if I am false to my word, I shall be accursed living and dead and suffer eternal punishment.' And thereupon let him partake of bread and salt with him who hands over the books to him."

5 When James had said this, the elders were pale with fright. Accordingly, observing that they feared greatly, James said, "Hear me, brethren and fellow-servants.

2 If we pass on the books to all without discrimination and if they are falsified by audacious people and are spoiled by interpretations—as indeed you have heard that some have already done—then it will come to pass that even those who earnestly seek the truth will always be led into error.

3 On this account it is better that we keep the books and, as we have said, hand them with all caution only to those who wish to live and to save others. But if any one, after that he has made such a vow, does not adhere to it, then will he rightly suffer eternal punishment.

4 For why should he not go to ruin who has been guilty of the corruption of others?" Then were the elders pleased with James's conclusion and said, "Praised be he who has foreseen all things and destined you to be our bishop." And when they had said this, we rose up and prayed to God the Father of all, to whom be glory for ever. Amen.

24. The Homilies of Clement

The "Homilies of Clement" is an example of a pseudonymous Christian writing produced in the name of a famous person living after the apostles: Clement, thought to be the fourth bishop of Rome at the end of the first century. The Homilies comprise 20 legendary discourses allegedly delivered by Clement in Rome and sent to James of Jerusalem. In them Clement narrates his family background, his search for truth, and, principally, his travels to the East, where he meets Simon Peter, whom he then accompanies, observing his words, deeds, and controversies (especially with the magician Simon Magus).

As the following excerpts show, the Homilies embrace a Jewish-Christian perspective. Peter is shown to be the chief apostle, bearer of Christ's power and leader of Christ's church. He claims ascendancy over his archrival, the magician Simon Magus, who is portrayed as the principal missionary to the gentiles (and is sometimes, therefore, thought to be a cipher for the apostle Paul). Particularly striking are Peter's views of the relation of Jesus and Moses, the acceptance of either one of whom, he claims, can bring salvation.

The Homilies are closely related to another surviving work of the third century attributed to Clement, the *Recognitions*; both were evidently based on an earlier legendary account of Clement's travels that is now lost.

The following excerpts follow the sequence of the chapters determined by scholars to be more likely original.

Book 1

18 (Peter says to Clement:) The will of God has fallen into oblivion for many sorts of reasons,

2 above all in consequence of inadequate instruction, careless upbringing, bad company, unseemly conversation and erroneous statements.

3 Thence there comes ignorance, and there come also dissoluteness, unbelief, unchastity, avarice, vanity, and innumerable vices of this kind, which have occupied the world as it were a house which, like a cloud of smoke, they have filled; they have thus made muddy the eyes of those who dwell in the house and have prevented them from looking up and recognising the Creator God from his works and inferring his will.

4 Therefore the friends of truth who are in the house must cry from the depth of their heart for help for their truth-seeking souls, that if someone is outside the smoke-filled house, he may come and open the door, so that the sunlight from outside may invade the house and that the smoke within may be dissipated.

19 Now the man who can help here, I call the true prophet; he alone can enlighten the souls of people that with their own eyes they may be able to see the way to eternal salvation.

The Homilies of Clement, from *New Testament Apocrypha*, vol. 2; ed. Wilhelm Schneemelcher, 2nd ed. Cambridge/Louisville: Lutterworth Press/Westminster John Knox Press, 1991. Used with permission of Lutterworth Press and Westminster John Knox Press.

2 That is not possible in any other way, as indeed you yourself know; only just now you said

3 that every view has its friends and opponents and counts as true or false according to the qualification of its advocate, and in consequence different opinions do not come to light as what they are, but receive the semblance of worth or worthlessness from their advocates.

4 Wherefore the world needs the godly efforts of the true prophet that he may describe things to us as they actually are and tell us what we have to believe regarding everything.

5 First of all then we must examine the prophet with all seriousness and arrive at the certainty that he is a true prophet,

6 and then we should believe him in all matters and ought not to quibble at the least small particular in his teaching, but should accept all his words as valid, as it may appear in faith, yet actually on the ground of the sound examination that we have made. . . .

15 (Peter:) Now that he might bring people to the true knowledge of all things, God, who himself is a single person, made a clear separation by way of pairs of opposites, in that he, who from the beginning was the one and only God, made heaven and earth, day and night, life and death.

2 Among these he has gifted free-will to humans alone so that they may be just or unjust. For them he has also permuted the appearing of the pairs of opposites, in that he has set before their eyes first the small and then the great, first the world and then eternity, this world being transitory, but the one to come eternal; so also ignorance precedes knowledge.

3 In the same way he has ordered the bearers of the prophetic spirit. For since the present is womanly and like a mother gives birth to children, but the future, manly time on the other hand takes up its children in the manner of a father,

4 therefore there come first the prophets of this world (who prophesy falsely, and) those who have the knowledge of eternal things follow them because they are sons of the coming age.

5 Had the God-fearing known this secret, then they would never have been able to go wrong, and also they would even now have known that Simon, who now confounds all, is merely a helpmate of the feeble left hand (of God, i.e., the evil one).

16 As regards the disposition of the prophetic mission the case is as follows. As God, who is one person, in the beginning made first the heaven and then the earth, as it were on the right hand and on the left, he has also in the course of time established all the pairs of opposites. But with humans it is no longer so—rather does he invert the pairs.

2 For as with him the first is the stronger and the second the weaker, so with humans we find the opposite, first the weaker and then the stronger.

3 Thus directly from Adam, who was made in the image of God, there issued as the first son the unrighteous Cain and as the second the righteous Abel.

4 And in the same way from the man who amongst you is called Deucalion two symbols of the Spirit, the unclean and the clean, were sent out, the black raven and after it the white dove.

5 And also from Abraham, the progenitor of our people, there issued two sons, the older Ishmael and then Isaac, who was blessed by God.

6 Again from this same Isaac there sprang two sons, the godless Esau and the godly Jacob.

7 Likewise there came first, as first-born into the world, the high priest (Aaron) and then the lawgiver (Moses).

17 The syzygy associated with Elijah, which ought to have come, willingly held off to another time, being resolved to take its place when the occasion arises.

2 Then in the same way there came first he who was among them that are born of women and only after that did he who belongs to the sons of men appear as the second.

3 Following up this disposition it would be possible to recognise where Simon belongs, who as first and before me went to the Gentiles, and where I belong, I who came after him and followed him as the light follows darkness, knowledge ignorance, and healing sickness.

4 Thus then, as the true prophet has said, a false gospel must first come from an impostor and only then, after the destruction of the holy place, can a true gospel be sent forth for the correction of the sects that are to come.

5 And thereafter in the end Antichrist must first come again and only afterwards must Jesus, our actual Christ, appear and then, with the rising of eternal light, everything that belongs to darkness must disappear.

18 Since now, as has been said, many do not know this conformity of the syzygies with law, they do not know who this Simon, my forerunner, is. For were it known, no one would believe him. But now, as he remains unknown, confidence is wrongly placed in him.

2 Thus he who does what haters do finds love; the enemy is received as a friend; people long for him who is death as a bringer of salvation; although he is fire, he is regarded as light; although he is a cheat, he obtains a hearing as a proclaimer of truth. . . .

Book 7

1 In Tyre not a few people from the neighbourhood and numerous inhabitants of the city came to Peter and cried to him: "May God have mercy upon us through you, and may he through you bring us healing!" And Peter, having mounted a high rock that he might be seen of all, greeted them in a godly way and began as follows:

2 "God, who has made heaven and the universe, is not wanting in power to save those who desire to be saved. . . .

4 "And what is pleasing to God is this, that we pray to him and ask from him as the one who dispenses everything according to a righteous law, that we keep away from the table of devils, that we do not eat dead flesh, that we do not touch blood, that we wash ourselves clean from all defilement.

3 "Let the rest be said to you also in one word, as the God-fearing Jews heard it, while you show yourselves, many as you are, of one mind: 'What good a person wishes for himself, let him confer the same also on his neighbor!'. . ."

5 After they had thus been instructed for some days by Peter and had been healed, they were baptized. At the time of his other miraculous deeds the rest sat beside one another in the middle of the market-place in sackcloth and ashes and did penance for their former sins.

2 When the Sidonians heard this, they did likewise; and because they themselves were not able on account of their diseases to come to Peter, they sent a petition to him.

3 After he had stayed for some days in Tyre and had instructed all the inhabitants and freed them from numerous sufferings, Peter founded a church and appointed a bishop for them from the number of the elders who were accompanying him; then he set out for Sidon.

6 When Peter entered Sidon, the people brought many sick folk in beds and set them down before him.

2 And he said to them: "Do not on any account believe that I, a mortal man, myself subject to many sufferings, can do anything to heal you! But I greatly desire to tell you in what way you can be delivered. . . .

7 "For I mention to you two ways, showing you in the first place in what way people fall into misfortune and in the second place in what way under God's guidance they are delivered.

2 "The way of those who perish is broad and very easy, but it leads straight away to misfortune; the way of those who are delivered is narrow and rough, but in the end it leads to salvation those who have taken its burdens upon themselves. Before these two ways there stand belief and unbelief. . . ."

8 Such were the addresses that Peter gave in Sidon. There also within a few days many were converted and believed and were healed. So Peter founded a church there and enthroned as bishop one of the elders who were accompanying him. He then left Sidon.

9 Immediately after the arrival of Peter in Berytus an earthquake took place; and people came to Peter saying: "Help, for we greatly fear that we shall all together perish!"

2 Then Simon dared, along with Appion, Annubion, Athenodorous and his other comrades, to turn against Peter in the presence of all the people: "Flee, people from this man;

3 "for he is a magician—you may believe me—and has himself occasioned this earthquake and has caused these diseases to frighten you, as if he himself was a god!"

4 And many other false charges of this sort did Simon and his followers bring against Peter, suggesting that he possessed superhuman power.

5 As soon as the multitude gave him a hearing, Peter with a smile and an impressive directness spoke the words: "Oh people, I admit that, God willing, I am capable of doing what these men here say and in addition am ready, if you will not hear my words, to turn your whole city upside down."

10 Now when the multitude took alarm and readily promised to carry out his commands, Peter said: "Let no one of you associate with these magicians or in any way have intercourse with them."

2 Scarcely had the people heard this summons when without delay they laid hold of cudgels and pursued these fellows till they had driven them completely out of the city. . . .

12 After he had stayed for several days with the inhabitants of Berytus, had made many conversant with the worship of the one God, and had baptized them, Peter enthroned as bishop one of the elders who were accompanying him and then journeyed to Byblus.

3 On coming there he learned that Simon had not waited for him even for a single day, but had started at once for Tripolis. Accordingly Peter remained a few days with the people of Byblus, effected not a few healings, and gave instruction in the Holy Scriptures. He then journeyed in the track of Simon to Tripolis, being resolved to pursue him rather than to make room for him.

Book 8

1 Along with Peter there entered into Tripolis people from Tyre, Sidon, Berytus, Byblus and neighboring places, who were eager to learn, and in numbers that were not smaller, people from the city itself crowded about him desiring to get to know him. . . .

4 Astonished at this eagerness of the multitudes, Peter answered: "You see, beloved brethren, how the words of our Lord are manifestly fulfilled. For I remember how he said: 'Many will come from east and west, from north and south, and repose in the bosom of Abraham, Isaac and Jacob.'[1] Nevertheless 'many are called, but few are chosen.'[2]

2 "In their coming in response to the call so much is fulfilled.

3 "But since it rests not with them but with God who has called them and permitted them to come, on this account alone they have no reward. . . .

4 "But if after being called they do what is good, and that rests with them themselves, for that they will receive their reward.

5 "For even the Hebrews who believe in Moses . . . are not saved unless they abide by what has been said to them.

2 "For their believing in Moses lies not with a decision of their own will but with God, who said to Moses. 'Behold, I come to you in a pillar of cloud that the people may hear me speaking to

---

1 Matt 8:11.
2 Matt 22:14.

you and believe for ever!'[3] Since then it is granted to the Hebrews and to them that are called from the Gentiles to believe the teachers of truth, while it is left to the personal decision of each individual whether he will perform good deeds, the reward rightly falls to those who do well.

4 "For neither Moses nor Jesus would have needed to come if of themselves people had been willing to perceive the way of discretion. And there is no salvation in believing in teachers and calling them lords.

6 "Therefore is Jesus concealed from the Hebrews who have received Moses as their teacher, and Moses hidden from those who believe Jesus.

2 "For since through both one and the same teaching becomes known, God accepts those who believe in one of them.

3 "But belief in a teacher has as its aim the doing of what God has ordered.

4 "That this is the case our Lord himself declares, saying: 'I confess to you, Father of heaven and earth, that you have hidden this from the wise and elder, but have revealed it to simpletons and infants.[4] Thus has God himself hidden the teacher

from some since they know beforehand what they ought to do, and has revealed him to others since they know not what they have to do.

7 "Thus the Hebrews are not condemned because they did not know Jesus . . . provided only they act according to the instructions of Moses and do not injure him whom they did not know.

2 "And again the offspring of the Gentiles are not judged, who . . . have not known Moses, provided only they act according to the words of Jesus and thus do not injure him whom they did not know.

3 "Also it profits nothing if many describe their teachers as their lords, but do not do what it befits servants to do.

4 "Therefore our Lord Jesus said to one who again and again called him Lord, but at the same time did not abide by any of his commands. 'Why call me Lord and not do what I say?'[5] For it is not speaking that can profit any one, but doing.

5 "In all circumstances goods works are needed; but if a person has been considered worthy to know both teachers as heralds of a single doctrine, then that one is counted rich in God. . . ."

3 Exod 19:9.
4 Matt 11:25; Luke 10:21.

5 Matt 7:21; Luke 6:46.

GNOSTIC CHRISTIAN TEXTS
INTRODUCTION

(See also the Apocalypse of Peter and the Second Treatise of the Great Seth in Chapter 7; the Gospel of Thomas, the Gospel of Mary, and the Gospel of Judas in Chapter 8; and Ptolemy's Letter to Flora in Chapter 10)

Prior to the discovery of the Nag Hammadi library, we were ill-informed concerning the beliefs and practices of early Christian Gnostics, since virtually all of our information came from attacks leveled against them by their proto-orthodox opponents. An enemy can scarcely be trusted to provide a fair or accurate portrayal of one's views.

The discovery of the Nag Hammadi texts did not completely remedy the problem, however. For one thing, these texts do not themselves present a unified view of what Gnosticism was, but represent a remarkable range of perspective and belief. Even more problematic, these documents do not as a rule lay out what the Gnostics believed and practiced but presuppose such matters as the backdrop for what they do want to discuss. That is to say, these books were written by Gnostics for Gnostics, and so do not go to any great lengths to explain what the authors and readers together assume to be true (any more than an article on the sports page about the first game of the World Series explains the rules and history of baseball). Modern readers who want to know what Gnosticism was about, then, are compelled to read between the lines to try to reconstruct the underlying assumptions about the divine realm, the world, and the place of humanity in it, as well as to see what ritual practices and ethical systems were found among such groups.

As a result, scholars devoted to uncovering such matters continue to dispute rather basic issues. These include the most fundamental question of all: whether it makes sense even to use the term *Gnosticism*, given the circumstance that it has been used to describe so many different ancient religious groups and phenomena. Most scholars continue to utilize the term, either to refer to only one such group (the Sethians, who will be discussed below) or as an umbrella term to cover a number of groups with many similarities among themselves. Those who use the term in this latter sense have heated debates over such matters as where Gnosticism came from, whether it was originally connected with Christianity, and what its various permutations were. It is often thought, in any event, that (a) a wide range of Gnostic groups, many of them Christian, thrived in the second century of the common era; (b) these groups agreed that this material world is not the creation of the one true God but of lower divinities, often thought to be ignorant or inferior, and that the world is a place of imprisonment for elements of the divine who are trapped here in human bodies; (c) these groups stressed "knowledge" (= gnosis, hence the term *gnostic*) as a way of salvation from this awful world; and (d) this saving knowledge was brought from above by

Christ, and it is this revelation of truth rather than his death and resurrection that ultimately matters for salvation.

Several of the texts from Nag Hammadi represent explications of the Gnostic myths that convey these views; these are probably to be allowed poetic license rather than taken as propositional truths or historical sketches of what "really" happened in the mythic past. Many of these are interpretations of the Jewish Scriptures, especially the opening chapters of Genesis, which provided fuel for the mythological imagination. Other texts are poetical reflections on the divine realm, the need for liberating knowledge, and the nature of the world or of the human place in it; yet others contain attacks on literal-minded Christians who failed to recognize the truth (see Chapter 7). The few Gnostic texts that have survived in other places (i.e., outside of Nag Hammadi), also seem to share many of these basic perspectives.

We know of three major religious groups that subscribed to such views to one degree or another: the Sethians, the Valentinians, and (possibly) the Thomasines. I will explain the characteristics of each of these groups and introduce an undifferentiated set of fourth texts (different from the three, but not cohesive as a separate group) below.

SETHIAN GNOSTICS

The group of Gnostics that scholars have labeled the "Sethians" are known from the writings of proto-orthodox heresiologists beginning with Irenaeus (around 180 CE) and from some of the significant writings of the Nag Hammadi library. They were a thriving sect already by the middle of the second century.

Members of the group may not have called themselves Sethians. Scholars call them this because among their distinctive features they understood themselves to be the spiritual descendants of Seth, the third son of Adam and Eve. Many of the books associated with the Sethians present detailed and complex myths that explain the origins of the divine realm, the material world, and the humans who inhabit it. These mind-stretching myths, best seen in the Apocryphon of John (the first selection included here), were not simply intellectual flights of fancy meant to mystify outsiders. They were understood as explanations of the very real, but inordinate, complexities of the world—especially of the divine, spiritual world above, which was separated from the material realm we inhabit. By understanding the world one could be united with the mind of God and separated from the concerns of the body. As was true of other systems of thought influenced by the writings of Plato, the Sethian exercise of coming to understand the true nature of things was a means of ascending to the spiritual realm above, away from the crass material existence of our daily lives.

The Sethian myths begin by describing the original, single, perfect divine being called the Invisible Spirit. This one is both unknown and unknowable—so distinct from anything we can imagine that it cannot be described. This Spirit is said to evolve into an entire Pleroma (fullness) of other divine beings called *aeons*. The first of these is the Mother of all, named Barbelo, who is often accompanied by a being called Son (or Christ, or "Self-Originate")—making, then, a kind of original Trinity. The Pleroma within which the ensuing aeons emerge and exist is encompassed by four realms of light, each assigned to a different being: Harmozel, Oroiael, Daueithai, and Eleleth. There are numerous other beings who occupy these realms, including the first Human, named Adamas, who is the divine version of the first material human, Adam.

In a number of these myths, the various aeons that make up the Pleroma come into existence in gendered pairs, male and female. One of the female figures, far down the chain of divinity, is named Sophia (wisdom), who for one reason or another conceives progeny without her male consort. Among the resulting offspring of Sophia is a divinity named Yaldabaoth (sometimes called Sakla and sometimes accompanied by one named Nebruel). Since this one is born outside the realm of the divine Pleroma—or was cast out from there—it is portrayed as haughty, ignorant, and sometimes even malevolent. Ialdabaoth, in his ignorance, boasts that he alone is God. For the Sethians he is, in fact, considered to be the Creator God of the Old Testament.

Based on what little they know or recall of the spiritual realm of the Pleroma, this outcast deity and his divine minions that come into being create the material world, a place of imperfection, injustice, and suffering. There is, therefore, a strong dualistic element in these Sethian myths: the imperfect and awful material world stands in stark contrast with the perfection of the spiritual realm above. Humans themselves are created as purely material beings; but the spiritual power from on high is breathed into them by Sophia herself (or by another divine being, such as Barbelo).

The goal of the Sethian religion is to return this divine power, resident in humans, to its heavenly home. For that to happen, this imperfect creation in which we live needs to be corrected. The "seed of Seth"—those among humans who have the power of Sophia resident within them—can restore lost humanity to the spiritual realm. This happens when one learns the truth of one's divine origin.

But how can one learn this truth? It happens when the divine Seth himself comes to be incarnate in the man Jesus, who is the human form of the savior above. He then provides the means for perfection and a return to the divine realm. In this understanding of things, Jesus has a real body, but he is an incarnation of an aeon from the Pleroma come to bring salvation for the souls that are trapped in the prisons of their material bodies, who need to return to their heavenly home. This return comes not only by learning the truth of the world and our place in it but also by receiving a baptism that involves being sealed with five mystical seals. This baptism allows one to transcend this limited material existence and to experience a mystical ascent to the realm above, so as to contemplate its greatness, becoming one with the divine. In addition to learning the truth and undergoing baptism, the Sethian Gnostic is to live an ascetic life, avoiding the pleasures of the flesh that tie one to this material existence and preparing the soul for its ascent to the divine world of the Pleroma.

THE TEXTS

25. The Secret Book of John

The Secret Book (sometimes called *Apocryphon*) of John was one of the most remarkable discoveries of the Nag Hammadi library. Cast as a post-resurrection discussion of Jesus with his disciple, John the son of Zebedee, the book contains one of the clearest expositions of a Gnostic myth of creation and redemption—an exposition designed, ultimately, to explain the existence of evil in the world and the path of escape for those who recognize their plight.

In intricate detail the account discusses the propagation of the divine realm from the one invisible, imperishable, incomprehensible God prior to creation and the tragic mistake of the aeon Sophia, who produced an offspring apart from her divine consort.

The result was the monster Creator God Yaldabaoth (the God of the Hebrew Bible), ultimately responsible for the creation of the world and humans in the image of God (much of this part of the myth represents an exposition of Genesis 1–4). The tale continues with the appearance of Christ from above to provide the knowledge necessary for escape to the divine souls entrapped within mortal bodies.

Since this particular version of the Gnostic myth was known, in a slightly different form, to the late second-century church father Irenaeus, most scholars date the Secret Book of John sometime prior to 180 CE. (NB: the brackets [] used in this text and in the ones that follow indicate places where the original words have been lost because of holes in the manuscript but have been reconstructed by modern editors.)

The Secret Book of John

The teaching of the Savior, and [the revelation] of the mysteries [and the things] hidden in silence, things he taught his disciple John.

One day when John the brother of James, who are the sons of Zebedee, went up to the temple, it happened that a Pharisee named Arimanios came up to him and said to him, "Where is your teacher, whom you followed?"

I said to him, "He has returned to the place he came from."

The Pharisee said to me, "This Nazarene really has deceived you, filled your ears with lies, closed [your minds], and turned you from the traditions of your ancestors."

When I, John, heard this, I turned away from the temple and went to a mountainous and barren place. I was distressed within, and I asked how the Savior was chosen:

Why was he sent into the world by his Father?
Who is his Father who sent him?
To what kind of eternal realm shall we go?
And why did he tell us, when he spoke,
that this eternal realm [to which we shall go]
is modeled after the incorruptible realm,
but he did not teach us what kind of aeon that
    one is?

At the moment I was thinking about this, look, the heavens opened, all creation under heaven lit up, and the world shook. [2] I was afraid, and look, I saw within the light [someone standing] by me.

As I was looking, it seemed to be an elderly person. Again it changed its appearance to be a youth. Not that there were several figures before me. Rather, there was a figure with several forms within the light. These forms were visible through each other, and the figure had three forms.

The figure said to me, "John, John, why are you doubting? Why are you afraid? Aren't you familiar with this figure? Then do not be fainthearted. I am with you always. I am [the Father], I am the Mother, I am the Child. I am the incorruptible and the undefiled one. [Now I have come] to teach you what is, what [was], and what is going to come, that you may [understand] what is invisible and what is visible; and to teach you about the [unshakable generation of] the perfect [human]. So now, lift up your [head] that you may [hear] the things I shall tell you today, and that you may relate them to your spiritual friends who are from the unshakable generation of the perfect human."

I asked if I might understand this, and it said to me, The One is a sovereign that has nothing over it. It is God and Parent, Father of the All, the invisible one that is over the All, that is incorruptible, that is pure light at which no eye can gaze.

The One is the Invisible Spirit. We should not think of it as a god or like a god. For it is greater than a god, because it has nothing over it and no [3] lord above it. It does not [exist] within anything inferior [to it, since everything] exists within it, [for it established] itself. It is eternal, since it does not need anything. For it is absolutely complete. It has never lacked anything in order to be completed by it. Rather, it is always absolutely complete in light.

The One is

illimitable, since there is nothing before it to limit it,
unfathomable, since there is nothing before it to fathom it,
immeasurable, since there was nothing before it to measure it,
invisible, since nothing has seen it,
eternal, since it exists eternally,
unutterable, since nothing could comprehend it to utter it,
unnamable, since there is nothing before it to give it a name.

The One is the immeasurable light, pure, holy, immaculate. It is unutterable, and is perfect in incorruptibility. Not that it is just perfection, or blessedness, or divinity: it is much greater.

The One is not corporeal and it is not incorporeal.
The One is not large and it is not small.
It is impossible to say,
How much is it?
What [kind is it]?
For no one can understand it.

The One is not among the things that exist, but it is much greater. Not that it is greater. Rather, as it is in itself, it is not a part of the aeons or time. For whatever is part of a realm was once prepared by another. Time was not allotted to it, since it receives nothing from anyone: what would be received would be on loan. The one who is first does not need to receive anything from another. It beholds itself in [4] its light.

The One is majestic and has an immeasurable purity.

The One is a realm that gives a realm,
life that gives life,

a blessed one that gives blessedness,
knowledge that gives knowledge,
a good one that gives goodness,
mercy that gives mercy and redemption,
grace that gives grace.

Not that the One possesses this. Rather, the One gives immeasurable and incomprehensible light.

What shall I tell you about it? Its eternal realm is incorruptible, at peace, dwelling in silence, at rest, before everything.

It is the head of all realms, and it is the one who sustains them through its goodness.

We would not know [what is ineffable], we would not understand what is immeasurable, were it not for the one who has come from the Father. This is the one who has told these things to us [alone].

This Father is the one who beholds himself in the light surrounding him, which is the spring of living water and provides all the realms. He reflects on his image everywhere, sees it in the spring of the Spirit, and becomes enamored of his luminous water, [for his image is in] the spring of pure luminous water surrounding him.

His thought became a reality, and she who appeared in his presence in shining light came forth. She is the first power who preceded everything and came forth from his mind as the Forethought of the All. Her light shines like the Father's light; she, the perfect power, is the image of the Perfect and Invisible Virgin Spirit.

She, [the first] power, the glory of Barbelo, the perfect [5] glory among the aeons, the glory of revelation, she glorified and praised the Virgin Spirit, for because of the Spirit she had come forth.

She is the first Thought, the image of the Spirit. She became the universal womb, for she precedes everything,

the Mother-Father,
the first Human,
the holy Spirit,
the triple male,
the triple power,

the androgynous one with three names,
the aeon among the invisible beings,
the first to come forth.

Barbelo asked the Invisible Virgin Spirit to
give her Foreknowledge, and the Spirit consented. When the Spirit consented, Foreknowledge appeared and stood by Forethought. This is
the one who came from the Thought of the Invisible Virgin Spirit. Foreknowledge glorified the
Spirit and the Spirit's perfect power, Barbelo, for
because of her Foreknowledge had come into
being.

She asked again to be given Incorruptibility,
and the Spirit consented. When the Spirit consented, Incorruptibility appeared and stood by
Thought and Foreknowledge. Incorruptibility
glorified the invisible one and Barbelo. Because
of her they had come into being.

Barbelo asked to be given Life Eternal, and the
Invisible Spirit consented. When the Spirit consented, Life Eternal appeared, and they stood together and glorified the Invisible Spirit and Barbelo.
Because of her they had come into being.

She asked again to be given Truth, and the Invisible Spirit consented. Truth appeared, and they
stood together and glorified the good Invisible [6]
Spirit and its Barbelo. Because of her they had
come into being.

These are the five aeons of the Father. They are:

the first human, the image of the Invisible
    Spirit, that is, Forethought, which is Bar-
    belo, and Thought,
along with Foreknowledge,
Incorruptibility,
Life Eternal
and Truth.

These are the five androgynous aeons, which
are the ten aeons, which is the Father.

The Father gazed into Barbelo, with the pure
light surrounding the Invisible Spirit, and his ra-
diance. Barbelo conceived from him, and he produced a spark of light similar to the blessed light

but not as great. This was the only Child of the
Mother-Father that had come forth, the only offspring, the only Child of the Father, the pure
light. The Invisible Virgin Spirit rejoiced over the
light that was produced, that came forth from the
first power of the Spirit's Forethought, who is
Barbelo. The Spirit anointed it with his own
goodness until it was perfect, with no lack of
goodness, since it was anointed with the goodness of the Invisible Spirit. The Child stood in the
presence of the Spirit as the Spirit anointed the
Child. As soon as the Child received this from
the Spirit, it glorified the holy Spirit and perfect
Forethought. Because of her it had come forth.

The Child asked to be given Mind as a companion to work with, and the Spirit consented.
When the Invisible Spirit consented, [7] Mind appeared and stood by the anointed, and glorified the
Spirit and Barbelo.

All these beings came into existence in silence.

Mind wished to create something by means of
the word of the Invisible Spirit. Its Will became a
reality and appeared, with Mind and the light, glorifying it. Word followed Will. For the anointed,
the divine Self-Generated, created everything by
the Word. Life Eternal, Will, Mind, and Foreknowledge stood together and glorified the Invisible Spirit and Barbelo, for because of her they had
come into being.

The holy Spirit brought the divine Self-
Generated Child of himself and Barbelo to perfection, so that the Child might stand before the
great Invisible Virgin Spirit as the divine Self-
Generated, the anointed, who honored the Spirit
with loud acclaim. The Child came forth through
Forethought. The Invisible Virgin Spirit set the
true, divine Self-Generated over everything and
caused all authority and the truth within to be
subject to it, so that the Child might understand
everything, the one called by a name greater than
every name, for that name will be told to those
who are worthy of it.

Now from the light, which is the anointed,
and from Incorruptibility, by the grace of the
Spirit, the Four Luminaries that derive from the

divine Self-Generated gazed out in order to stand [8] before it. The three beings are:

will,
thought,
life.

The four powers are:

understanding,
grace,
perception,
thoughtfulness.

Grace dwells in the eternal realm of the luminary Harmozel, who is the first angel. There are three other aeons with this eternal realm:

grace,
truth,
form.

The second luminary is Oroiael, who has been appointed over the second eternal realm. There are three other aeons with it:

Insight,
perception,
memory.

The third luminary is Daveithai, who has been appointed over the third eternal realm. There are three other aeons with it:

understanding,
love,
idea.

The fourth eternal realm has been set up for the fourth luminary, Eleleth. There are three other aeons with it:

perfection,
peace,
Sophia.

These are the Four Luminaries that stand before the divine Self-Generated; these are the twelve aeons that stand before the Child of the Great One, the Self-Generated, the anointed, by the will and grace of the Invisible Spirit. The twelve aeons belong to the Child, the Self-Generated, and everything was established by the will of the holy Spirit through the Self-Generated.

From the Foreknowledge of the perfect Mind, through the expressed will of the Invisible Spirit and the will of the Self-Generated, came the perfect human, the first revelation, the truth. The Virgin Spirit named the human Pigeradamas, and appointed him to [9] the first eternal realm with the great Self-Generated, the anointed, by the first luminary, Harmozel. Its powers dwell with it. The invisible one gave him an invincible power of mind.

Pigeradamas spoke and glorified and praised the Invisible Spirit by saying,

Because of you everything has come into
    being,
and to you everything will return.
I shall praise and glorify you,
the Self-Generated,
the eternal realms,
the three, Father, Mother, Child,
perfect power.

He appointed his son Seth to the second eternal realm, before the second luminary, Oroiael.

In the third eternal realm were stationed the offspring of Seth, with the third luminary, Daveithai. The souls of the saints were stationed there.

In the fourth eternal realm were stationed the souls of those who were ignorant of the Fullness. They did not repent immediately, but held out for a while and repented later. They came to be with the fourth luminary, Eleleth.

These are creatures that glorify the Invisible Spirit.

Now, Sophia, who is the Wisdom of Insight and who constitutes an aeon, conceived of a thought from herself, with the conception of the Invisible Spirit and Foreknowledge. She wanted to bring forth something like herself, without the consent of the Spirit, who had not given approval, without her partner and without his consideration. The male did not give approval. She did not find her partner, and she considered this without the Spirit's consent and without the knowledge of her partner. Nonetheless, she gave birth. [10] And because of the invincible power within her, her thought was not an idle thought. Something came out of her that was imperfect and different in appearance from her, for she had produced it without her partner. It did not resemble its mother and was misshapen.

When Sophia saw what her desire had produced, it changed into the figure of a snake with the face of a lion. Its eyes were like flashing bolts of lightning. She cast it away from her, outside that realm so that none of the immortals would see it. She had produced it ignorantly.

She surrounded it with a bright cloud and put a throne in the middle of the cloud so that no one would see it except the holy Spirit, who is called the Mother of the living. She named her offspring Yaldabaoth.

This is the first ruler, the archon who took great power from his mother. Then he left her and moved away from the place where he was born. He took control and created for himself other aeons with luminous fire, which still exists. He mated with the mindlessness in him and produced authorities for himself:

The name of the first is Athoth, whom generations call the [reaper].
The second is Harmas, who is the jealous eye.
The third is Kalila-Oumbri.
The fourth is Yabel.
The fifth is Adonaios, who is called Sabaoth.
The sixth is Cain, whom generations of people call the sun.
The seventh is Abel.

The eighth is Abrisene.
The ninth is Yobel. [11]
The tenth is Armoupieel.
The eleventh is Melcheir-Adonein.
The twelfth is Belias, who is over the depth of the underworld.

Yaldabaoth stationed seven kings, one for each sphere of heaven, to reign over the seven heavens, and five to reign over the depth of the abyss. He shared his fire with them, but he did not give away any of the power of the light he had taken from his mother. For he is ignorant darkness.

When light mixed with darkness, it made the darkness shine. When darkness mixed with light, it dimmed the light, and it became neither light nor darkness, but rather gloom.

This gloomy archon has three names: the first name is Yaldabaoth, the second is Sakla, the third is Samael.

He is wicked in the mindlessness within him. He said, "I am God and there is no other god beside me," since he did not know from where his own strength had come.

The rulers each created seven powers for themselves, and the powers each created six angels, until there were 365 angels. These are the names and the corresponding physiques:

The first is Athoth, and has the face of a sheep.
The second is Eloaios, and has the face of a donkey.
The third is Astaphaios, and has the face of a hyena.
The fourth is Yao, and has the face of a snake with seven heads.
The fifth is Sabaoth, and has the face of a snake.
The sixth is Adonin, and has the face of an ape.
The seventh is Sabbataios, and has a face of flaming fire.
This is the sevenfold nature of the week.

Yaldabaoth has many [12] faces, more than all of these, so that he could show whatever face he wanted when he was among the seraphim. He shared his fire with them, and lorded it over them because of the glorious power he had from his mother's light. That is why he called himself God and defied the place from which he came.

In his thought he united the seven powers with the authorities that were with him. When he spoke, it was done. He named each of the powers, beginning with the highest:

First is goodness, with the first power, Athoth.
Second is forethought, with the second power, Eloaios.
Third is divinity, with the third power, Astaphaios.
Fourth is lordship, with the fourth power, Yao.
Fifth is kingdom, with the fifth power, Sabaoth.
Sixth is jealousy, with the sixth power, Adonin.
Seventh is understanding, with the seventh power, Sabbataios.

Each has a sphere in its own realm.

They were named after the glory above for the destruction of the powers. Although the names given them by their maker were powerful, the names given them after the glory above would bring about their destruction and loss of power. That is why they have two names.

Yaldabaoth organized everything after the pattern of the first aeons that had come into being, so that he might [13] create everything in an incorruptible form. Not that he had seen the incorruptible ones. Rather, the power that is in him, that he had taken from his mother, produced in him the pattern for the world order.

When he saw creation surrounding him, and the throng of angels around him that had come forth from him, he said to them, "I am a jealous god and there is no other god beside me."

But by announcing this, he suggested to the angels with him that there is another god. For if there were no other god, of whom would he be jealous?

Then the Mother began to move around. She realized that she was lacking something when the brightness of her light diminished. She grew dim because her partner had not collaborated with her.

I said, "Lord, what does it mean that she moved around?"

The Lord laughed and said, Do not suppose that it is as Moses said, above the waters. No, when she recognized the wickedness that had taken place and the robbery her son had committed, she repented. When she became forgetful in the darkness of ignorance, she began to be ashamed. She did not dare to return, but she was agitated. This agitation is the moving around.

The arrogant one took power from his mother. He was ignorant, for he thought no one existed except his mother alone. When he saw the throng of angels he had created, he exalted himself over them.

When the Mother realized that the trappings of darkness had come into being imperfectly, she understood that her partner had not collaborated with her. She repented [14] with many tears. The whole realm of Fullness heard her prayer of repentance and offered praise on her behalf to the Invisible Virgin Spirit, and the Spirit consented. When the Invisible Spirit consented, the holy Spirit poured upon her some of the fullness of all. For her partner did not come to her on his own, but he came to her through the realm of Fullness, so that he might restore what she lacked. She was taken up not to her own eternal realm, but instead to a position above her son. She was to remain in the ninth heaven until she restored what was lacking in herself.

A voice called from the exalted heavenly realm,

Humanity exists
and the Child of Humanity.

The first ruler, Yaldabaoth, heard the voice and thought it had come from his mother. He did not realize its source.

The holy perfect Mother-Father,
the complete Forethought,
the image of the invisible one,

being the Father of the All,
through whom everything came into being,
the first human—

this is the one who showed them and appeared in human shape.

The entire realm of the first ruler quaked, and the foundations of the abyss shook. The bottom side of the waters above the material world was lit up by this image that had appeared. When all the authorities and the first ruler stared at this appearance, they saw the whole bottom side as it was lit up. And through the light they saw the shape of the image in the water. [15] Yaldabaoth said to the authorities with him, "Come, let's create a human being after the image of God and with a likeness to ourselves, so that this human image may give us light."

They created through their respective powers, according to the features that were given. Each of the authorities contributed a psychical feature corresponding to the figure of the image they had seen. They created a being like the perfect first human, and said, "Let's call it Adam, that its name may give us power of light."

All the angels and demons worked together until they fashioned the psychical body. But for a long time their creation did not stir or move at all.

. . .

When the Mother wanted to take back the power she had relinquished to the first ruler, she prayed to the most merciful Mother-Father of the All. With a sacred command the Mother-Father sent five luminaries down upon the place of the angels of the first ruler. They advised him so that they might recover the mother's power.

They said to Yaldabaoth, "Breathe some of your spirit into the face of Adam, and the body will arise."

He breathed his spirit into Adam. The spirit is the power of his mother, but he did not realize this, because he lives in ignorance. The Mother's power went out of Yaldabaoth and into the psychical body that had been made to be like the one who is from the beginning.

The body moved and became powerful. And it was enlightened.

At once the rest of [20] the powers became jealous. Although Adam came into being through all of them, and they gave their power to this human, Adam was more intelligent than the creators and the first ruler. When they realized that Adam was enlightened and could think more clearly than they and was stripped of evil, they took and threw Adam into the lowest part of the whole material realm.

The blessed, benevolent, merciful Mother-Father had compassion for the Mother's power that had been removed from the first ruler. The archons might be able to overpower the psychical, perceptible body once again. So with its benevolent and most merciful Spirit, the Mother-Father sent a helper to Adam—enlightened Insight, who is from the Mother-Father and who was called Life. She helped the whole creature, laboring with it, restoring it to its fullness, teaching it about the descent of the seed, teaching it about the way of ascent, which is the way of descent.

Enlightened Insight was hidden within Adam so that the archons might not recognize her, but that Insight might be able to restore what the Mother lacked.

The archons took Adam and put Adam in paradise. They said, "Eat," meaning, Do so in a leisurely manner. But in fact their pleasure is bitter and their beauty is perverse. Their pleasure is a trap, their trees are a sacrilege, their fruit is deadly poison, and their promise is death.

They put their tree of life in the middle of paradise.

I shall teach you what the secret of their life is—the plan they devised together, the nature of their spirit. The root of their tree is bitter, its branches are death, its shadow is hatred, a trap is in its leaves, its blossom is bad ointment, its fruit is death, desire is its seed, and it blossoms in darkness. The dwelling place of those who taste [22] of it is the underworld, and darkness is their resting place.

But the archons lingered in front of what they call the tree of the knowledge of good and evil, which is enlightened Insight, so that Adam might not behold its fullness and recognize his shameful nakedness.

But I was the one who induced them to eat.

I said to the Savior, "Lord, was it not the serpent that instructed Adam to eat?"

The Savior laughed and said, The serpent instructed them to eat of the wickedness of sexual desire and destruction so that Adam might be of use to the serpent.

The first ruler knew Adam was disobedient to him because of enlightened Insight within Adam, which made Adam stronger of mind than he. He wanted to recover the power that he himself had passed on to Adam. So he brought deep sleep upon Adam.

Enlightened Insight hid herself within Adam. The first ruler wanted to take her from Adam's side, but enlightened Insight cannot be apprehended. Although darkness pursued her, it did not apprehend her. The first ruler removed part of Adam's power and created another figure in the form of a female, like the image of Insight that had appeared to him. He put [23] the part he had taken from the power of the human being into the female creature. It did not happen, however, the way Moses said: "Adam's rib."

Adam saw the woman beside him. At once enlightened Insight appeared and removed the veil that covered his mind. He sobered up from the drunkenness of darkness. He recognized his counterpart and said, "This is now bone from my bones and flesh from my flesh."

For this reason a man will leave his father and his mother and will join himself to his wife, and the two of them will become one flesh. For his partner will be sent to him, and he will leave his father and his mother.

Our sister Sophia is the one who descended in an innocent manner to restore what she lacked. For this reason she was called Life—that is, the Mother of the living—by the Forethought of the sovereignty of heaven and by [the Insight that appeared] to Adam. Through her have the living tasted perfect knowledge.

As for me, I appeared in the form of an eagle upon the tree of knowledge, which is the Insight of the pure enlightened Forethought, that I might teach the human beings and awaken them from the depth of sleep. For the two of them were fallen and realized that they were naked. Insight appeared to them as light and awakened their minds.

When Yaldabaoth realized that the humans had withdrawn from him, he cursed his earth. He found the woman as she was [24] preparing herself for her husband. He was master over her. And he did not know the mystery that had come into being through the sacred plan. The two of them were afraid to denounce Yaldabaoth. He displayed to his angels the ignorance within him, and he threw the humans out of paradise and cloaked them in thick darkness.

The first ruler saw the young woman standing next to Adam and noticed that enlightened Insight of Life had appeared in her. Yet Yaldabaoth was full of ignorance. So when the Forethought of the All realized this, she dispatched emissaries, and they stole Life out of Eve.

He called them by the names Cain and Abel, with a view to deceive.

He placed these two rulers over the elements so that they might rule over the cave.

When Adam came to know the counterpart of his own foreknowledge, he produced a son like [25] the child of humanity. He called him Seth, after the manner of the generation in the eternal realms. Similarly, the mother sent down her spirit, which is like her and is a copy of what is in the realm of Fullness, for she was going to prepare a dwelling place for the eternal realms that would come down.

The human beings were made to drink water of forgetfulness by the first ruler, so that they might not know where they had come from. For a time the seed remained and helped so that when the spirit descends from the holy realms, it may raise up the seed and heal what it lacks, that the entire realm of Fullness may be holy and lack nothing.

I said to the Savior, "Lord, will all the souls then be led safely into pure light?"

He answered and said to me, These are great matters that have arisen in your mind, and it is difficult to explain them to anyone except those of the unshakable generation.

Those upon whom the spirit of life will descend and whom the spirit will empower will be saved, and will become perfect and worthy of greatness, and will be cleansed there of all evil and the anxieties of wickedness, since they are no longer anxious for anything except the incorruptible alone, and concerned with that from this moment on, without anger, jealousy, envy, desire, or greed for anything.

They are affected by nothing but being in the flesh alone, and they wear the flesh as they look forward to a time when they will be met [26] by those who receive them. Such people are worthy of the incorruptible, eternal life and calling. They endure everything and bear everything so as to finish the contest and receive eternal life.

I said to him, "Lord, will the souls of people be [rejected] who have not done these things, but upon whom the power and the spirit of life have descended?"

He answered and said to me, If the spirit descends upon them, by all means they will be saved and transformed. Power will descend upon every person, for without it no one could stand. After birth, if the spirit of life grows and power comes and strengthens that soul, no one will be able to lead it astray with evil actions. But people upon whom the false spirit descends are misled by it and go astray.

I said, "Lord, where will their souls go when they leave their flesh?"

He laughed and said to me, The soul in which there is more power than the contemptible spirit is strong. She escapes from evil, and through the intervention of the incorruptible one, she is saved and is taken up to eternal rest.

I said, "Lord, where will the souls go of people who have not known to whom they belong?"

He said to me, The contemptible spirit has [27] grown stronger in such people while they were going astray. This spirit lays a heavy burden on the soul, leads her into evil deeds, and hurls her down into forgetfulness. After the soul leaves the body, she is handed over to the authorities who have come into being through the archon. They bind her with chains and throw her into prison. They go around with her until she awakens from forgetfulness and acquires knowledge. This is how she attains perfection and is saved.

I said, "Lord, where will the souls go of people who had knowledge but turned away?"

He said to me, They will be taken to the place where the angels of misery go, where there is no repentance. They will be kept there until the day when those who have blasphemed against the spirit will be tortured and punished eternally.

Look, now I shall ascend to the perfect realm. I have finished everything for you in your hearing. I have told you everything for you to record and communicate secretly to your spiritual friends. This is the mystery of the unshakable generation.

The Savior communicated this to John for him to record and safeguard. He said to him, "Cursed be anyone who will trade these things for a gift, for food, drink, clothes, or anything [32] like this."

These things were communicated to him in a mystery, and at once the Savior disappeared. Then John went to the other disciples and reported what the Savior had told him.

Jesus Christ
Amen

The Secret Book According to John

26. The First Thought in Three Forms

Discovered at Nag Hammadi, the First Thought in Three Forms (sometimes called the *Trimorphic Protennoia*) contains a series of three mystical discourses on the world, humans, and salvation through knowledge, placed on the lips of a female aeon. Comparable in many ways to the Secret Book of John, the discourses contain several of the key elements of the Gnostic myth. Particularly emphasized in this account are the revelations of divine knowledge from on high, culminating in the incarnation of the Word (cf. John 1:1–18).

The "First Thought" (Protennoia), is the first emanation from the one true inscrutable God, and is also known, along with other names, as Barbelo. She begins her discourse by revealing her own mysterious and ineffable greatness and then describes the three descents that she made from the heavenly realm in order to bring to humans the heavenly knowledge that can illuminate their souls, delivering them from darkness into light. Each of these descents is associated with one of Barbelo's three forms, since she is the Thought of the Father (or Voice), the Mother (or Sound), and the Son (or Word, i.e., the Logos). It is her final descent in the appearance of human flesh that brings the ultimate illumination to those who dwell in ignorance and darkness, leading to their ascent into the world of Light.

It is difficult to date this work, but many scholars think it was written around 200 CE.

Three Forms of First Thought

[I] am First [Thought, the] thought that is in [light].
[I] am movement that is in the [All],
[she in whom the] All takes its stand,
the firstborn among those who [came to be],
[she who] exists before the All.
[She] is called by three names, though she dwells alone,
[since she is complete].

I am invisible within the thought of the invisible one,
although I am revealed in the immeasurable and the ineffable.

I am incomprehensible, dwelling in the incomprehensible,
although I move in every creature.

I am the life of my Epinoia
that is within every power and every eternal movement,
and in invisible lights,
and within the rulers and angels and demons
and every soul in Tartaros,
and in every material soul.
I dwell in those who came to be.
I move in everyone and probe them all.
I walk upright, and those who sleep I awaken.

The First Thought in Three Forms, reproduced from Marvin Meyer, *The Nag Hammadi Scriptures*. San Francisco: HarperOne, 2007. Used with permission of HarperOne.

And I am the sight of those who are asleep.
I am the invisible one within the All.
I counsel those who are hidden,
since I know everything that exists in the All.
I am numberless beyond everyone.
I am immeasurable, ineffable, yet whenever I [wish],
[I] shall reveal myself through myself.
I [am the movement of] the All.
I am before [all, and] I am all, since I [am in] everyone.

I am a [softly resounding] voice.
I exist from [the first].
[I am] in the silence [that surrounds] every [one] of them. [36]
[It is] the hidden [voice] that [is in] me,
[in] the incomprehensible, immeasurable [thought],
[in] the immeasurable silence.
I [descended to the] midst of the underworld
and I shone [down on the] darkness.
I made the [water] surge.
I am hidden in [radiant] waters.
I gradually made the All radiant by my thought.
I am laden with the voice.
Through me comes knowledge.
I inhabit the ineffable and the unknowable.
I am perception and knowledge,
uttering voice by means of thought.

I am the real voice.
I resonate in everyone,
and they know it, since a seed is in [them].
I am the thought of the Father,
and through me came the voice,
the knowledge of everlasting things.
I exist as thought for all,
being joined to the unknowable and incomprehensible thought.
I, I revealed myself among all who recognize me,
for I am joined with everyone
through hidden thought and exalted <voice>,
a voice from invisible thought.

The voice is immeasurable, since it is in the immeasurable one.
It is a mystery, it is an [unknowable] deriving from [the incomprehensible one].
It is invisible [to all who are] visible in the All.
[It is light] in light.

We too [have ourselves left the] visible [world], since we [are saved by] hidden [wisdom through the] [37] ineffable, immeasurable [voice]. And what is hidden within us confers the product of its fruit upon the water of life.

The Son is perfect in every respect. He is the word originating through that voice, who came from on high, who has within him the name, who is light. He revealed everlasting things, and all that was unknown became known. Those things difficult to interpret and secret he revealed, and to those who are in silence with the first thought he preached. He revealed himself to those in darkness, and he showed himself to those in the abyss. To those in the hidden treasuries he told ineffable mysteries, and he taught unrepeatable doctrines to all who became children of light.

Now the voice that came from my thought—it exists as three abiding entities: the Father, the Mother, and the Child—exists as perceptible speech, and it has within it a word endowed with every <glory>. It has three masculine aspects, three powers, and three names. Thus they exist as the three n n n, three quadrangles, secretly in ineffable silence.

[The anointed one, the Christ], alone came to be. I anointed him with [goodness] as the glory [of the] invisible [spirit. The three] I established [alone in] eternal [glory] over [the eternal realms in] living [water]. This [is the glory surrounding the one] [38] who made the light of those exalted aeons radiate gloriously and in everlasting stability. And [he] stood in his own light surrounding him, the eye of light shining gloriously on me. He provided aeons for the father of all the aeons.

This is I myself, the thought of the Father,
First Thought,

Barbelo, the [perfect] glory,
the [immeasurable] invisible one who is hidden.
I am the image of the Invisible Spirit.
Through me all took shape.
I am the Mother,
and the light that she appointed as virgin,
she who is called Meirothea,
the incomprehensible womb,
the unrestrainable and immeasurable voice.

Then the perfect Son revealed himself to his aeons that originated through him. He revealed and glorified them and gave them thrones, and he stood in the glory with which he glorified himself. They blessed the perfect Son, the Christ, the only god!

And they gave glory and said,

He is. He is.
Son of God!
Son of God!
It is he who is!
The aeon of aeons beholding the eternal realms
    that he generated!
For you generated by your own desire.
Therefore [we] glorify you:
MA MŌ
ŌŌŌ EI
A EI
ON EI!
The [aeon] of [aeons]!
The aeon that he <honored>!

Then the [god who was generated] gave the aeons the power of [life on which they might rely], and [he] established [them].

The first aeon he established [over the first],
Armedon, Nousanios, [Armozel];
the second he established [over the second
    aeon], [39]
Phaionios, Ainios, Oroiael;
the third over the third aeon,
Mellephaneus, Loios, Daveithai;
the fourth over the fourth,
Mousanios, Amethes, Eleleth.

Now these aeons were conceived by the god who was generated, the Christ, and they received and gave glory. They came forth, exalted in their thought, and each aeon gave myriads of glories in great untraceable lights, and all together they blessed the perfect Son, the god who was generated.

Then came a word from the great luminary Eleleth, and said, "I am king. Who is king of chaos and who is king of the underworld?"

At that moment his light appeared radiant, endowed with Epinoia. The powers of the powers did not entreat him. And immediately there appeared the great demon who rules over the lowest part of the underworld and chaos. He has neither form nor perfection, but rather he has the form of the splendor of those conceived in darkness. He is called Sakla, Samael, Yaldabaoth, who took power, who snatched it from the innocent one, who overpowered her beforehand. She is the Epinoia of light who came down, from whom Yaldabaoth originally came into being.

The Epinoia of the [luminary Eleleth] realized that [Yaldabaoth] had begged him for another [order, even though he was lower] than she, and she said to Eleleth, "Give [me another order], so that you may become for me [a dwelling place and I may not] dwell in disorder [forever." The order of the] whole house of [40] glory agreed with her request. A blessing was brought for her, and the higher order yielded to her.

And the great demon began to produce aeons in the likeness of the real aeons, except that he produced them out of his own power.

Then I too revealed my voice secretly and said, "Stop, stop, you who tread on matter. Look, I am coming down to the world of mortals for my portion that was there from the time when innocent Sophia was conquered. She descended so that I might thwart their plot, which was devised by the one who came from her."

All were disturbed, and everyone in the house of the unknowable light and the abyss trembled. And the chief creator of ignorance reigned over chaos and the underworld and produced a human being in my likeness. But he did not know that

this creature would be a death sentence for him,
nor did he recognize the power in the creature.

But now I have descended and reached chaos.
I was [with] my own who were there.
I am hidden in them, empowering [them],
    giving them shape.
From [the first day] until the day [I shall
    grant] mighty [power]
to those who are mine,
[I shall reveal myself to] those who have heard
    [my mysteries], [41]
the children of light.

I am their father, and I shall tell you a mystery,
ineffable and unspeakable by [any] mouth.
Every bond I loosed from you,
and the chains of the demons of the under-
    world I broke,
the very chains that bound and restrained my
    members.
The high walls of darkness I overthrew,
and the secure gates of those pitiless ones I
    broke,
and I smashed their bars.
And the evil force and the one who beats and
    hinders you,
and the tyrant, the adversary, the king, and
    the present enemy,
all these I explained to those who are mine,
who are the children of light,
so that they might nullify them all,
be liberated from all bonds,
and return to the place where they were in the
    beginning.

I am the first one who descended
for my portion that remains,
the spirit in the soul,
which came from the water of life.

And out of the immersion of the mysteries
    I spoke,
I with the rulers and authorities,
for I went below their language.
I spoke my mysteries to my own,

a hidden mystery,
and the bonds and eternal oblivion were
    nullified.
I bore fruit in them,
the thought of the unchanging aeon,
and my house, and their father.
And I went down [to those who were] mine
    from the first,
and I reached [them and broke] the first
    strands that [enslaved them].
[Then] everyone in me shone, [42]
and I prepared [a pattern] for those ineffable
    lights in me.
Amen.

I am the voice that appeared through my thought.
I am he who is in union
since I am called the thought of the invisible one.
Since I am called the unchanging speech,
I am called she who is in union.

I am alone and undefiled.
I am the mother [of] the voice, speaking in
    many ways, completing the All.
In me is knowledge, knowledge of things
    everlasting.
I speak in every creature, and I was known by
    everyone.
I lift up the speech of the voice to the ears of
    those who have known me, the children
    of light.

Now I have come the second time in the likeness of a female, and have spoken with them.
I shall tell them of the coming end of this age, and
teach them about the beginning of the age to
come, the one without change, wherein our appearance will be changed.

We shall be purified in those aeons from
which I revealed myself in the thought of the likeness of my masculinity.

I settled among those who are worthy in the
thought of my changeless aeon.

For I shall tell you a mystery of this age and
tell you about the forces in it. Birth beckons
[birth], hour gives birth to hour, day [gives birth

to] day. Months inform the month, [time goes around] following [time]. This age [43] was completed in [this] fashion, and it turned out to be short, as a finger releases a finger and a joint separates from a joint.

When the great authorities knew that the time of fulfillment had appeared—just as the time of birth pains came, so also the time of destruction approached—all the elements trembled, and the foundations of the underworld and the ceilings of chaos shook, and a great fire shone in their midst, and the rocks and the earth were shaken like a reed shaken by the wind. And the allotments of fate and those who apportion the celestial houses were greatly disturbed by loud thunder. The thrones of the powers were disturbed because they were overturned, and their king was afraid.

And those who follow fate paid their allotment of visits to the path, and they said to the powers, "What is this disturbance and shaking that has come over us through the voice of exalted speech? Our entire world has been shaken, and the entire circuit of our path of ascent has been destroyed, and the path upon which we go, which takes us up to the chief creator of our birth, is no longer steady for us."

Then the powers answered and said, "We too are at a loss about it, because we did not know what caused it, But arise, let's go to the chief creator and ask him."

The powers all gathered and went up to the chief creator. They [said to] him, "Where is your boasting by which you boast? Didn't we [hear you say], 'I am God, [and I am] your father, [44] and it is I who engendered you, and there is no other but me'? Now look, we have heard a voice of the invisible speech of [the aeon] that we do not know. And we ourselves have not recognized to whom we belong, for the voice we heard is foreign to us, and we do not recognize it, we do not know where it came from. It came and terrified us and left us weak in our knees. So let us weep and mourn most bitterly. So let us take flight before we are forcibly imprisoned and taken down to the bowels of the underworld. For already the slackening of our bondage is at hand, and the time is short, and the

days are brief, and our age is fulfilled, and the weeping of our destruction is near, so that we may be taken we know <not> where. For the tree from which we grew has fruit of ignorance. Death is in its leaves, and darkness is under the shadow of its boughs. In deceit and lust we harvested the tree, and through it ignorant chaos became our dwelling place. For look, even the chief creator of our birth, about whom we boast, did not know this speech."

So now, children of thought, listen to me, listen to the speech of your merciful mother. You have become worthy of the mystery hidden from the beginning of the ages, so that you [might receive] it. And the end of this age and of the evil life [is near, and there dawns [45] the] beginning of the [age to come], which [will never change].

I am androgynous.
[I am mother and I am] father, since I [mate] with myself.
I [mate] with myself [since it is] myself that [I] love.
Through me alone the All [stands firm].
I am the womb [that puts forth] the All
by giving birth to light [shining] in splendor.
I am the age to [come].
[I] am the fulfillment of all, Meirothea, the glory of the Mother.
I cast voiced speech into the ears of those who know me.

And I invite you into the exalted, perfect light.
When you enter the light,
you will be glorified by those who give glory,
and those who enthrone will enthrone you.
You will receive robes from those who give robes,
and the baptizers will baptize you,
and you will become exceedingly glorious,
as you were in the beginning, when you were light.

And I hid myself in everyone
and revealed [myself] in them,
and every mind seeking me longed for me,
for I gave shape to everything when it had no form.
I transformed their forms into other forms

until the time when form will be given to everything.

Through me came the voice,

and I put breath in my own.

And I cast the eternally holy spirit into them,

and I ascended and entered my light.

I [went] up on my branch

and sat [there among the] children of [holy] light.

And [I withdrew] to their dwelling place [46] . . . become [glorious] . . . .

[Amen].

I am the [Word in the] ineffable [voice].

I am in undefiled [light].

A thought [was expressed] perceptibly through [the great] speech of the Mother, although a male offspring [supports me] as my foundation. The speech exists from the beginning in the foundations of the All.

But light is hidden in silence, and it was first to appear. While the Mother alone exists as silence, I alone am the word, ineffable, incorruptible, immeasurable, inconceivable.

The word is hidden light, bearing fruit of life, pouring living water from the invisible, incorruptible, immeasurable spring. This is the inimitable voice of the glory of the Mother, the glory of the offspring of god, a male virgin from hidden intellect, silence hidden from the All, inimitable, immeasurable light, the source of everything, the root of the entire aeon.

It is the foundation that supports every movement of the aeons of the mighty glory.

It is the foundation of every foundation.

It is the breath of the powers.

It is the eye of the three abiding entities, which exists as voice from thought.

And it is word from speech.

It was sent to illumine those in darkness.

Now look, I [shall] reveal to you [my mysteries], since you are my [brethren, and you will] know them all [47] . . . .

I told [all of them about my mysteries]

that exist in [the incomprehensible], inexpressible [aeons].

I taught [them the mysteries] through the [voice] [that exists] in perfect intellect,

[and I] became a foundation for all,

and [I] empowered them.

The second time I came as the [speech] of my voice.

I gave shape to those who [took] shape, until their consummation.

The third time I revealed myself to them in their tents as the word,

and I revealed myself in the likeness of their shape.

I wore everyone's garment.

I hid in them,

and [they] did not know who empowers me.

For I am in all sovereignties and powers

and in angels and every movement in all matter.

I hid in them

until I revealed myself to my brethren.

None of the powers knew me, [though] I work in them.

[They] thought they created everything, because they are ignorant.

They did not know the root and place of their growth.

[I] am the light illumining all.

I am the light rejoicing [in my] brothers and sisters.

I came down to the world [of] mortals

on account of the spirit left behind in what [descended]

and came from innocent Sophia.

I [came] and delivered . . . and [went] [48] . . . that which he [originally] had.

[I gave him] some of the water [of life],

[that strips] him of the chaos

[in the] uttermost darkness [in] the whole [abyss],

which is [corporeal] and psychical thought.

All these I put on.
I stripped him of that thought,
and I clothed him in shining light,
the knowledge of the thought of the fatherhood.

I delivered him to those who give robes,
Yammon, Elasso, Amenai,
and they clothed him with a robe from the robes of light.
I delivered him to the baptizers, and they baptized him,
Micheus, Michar, Mnesinous,
and they immersed him in the spring of the [water] of life.
I delivered him to those who enthrone,
Bariel, Nouthan, Sabenai,
and they enthroned him from the throne of glory.
I delivered him to those who glorify,
Ariom, Elien, Phariel,
and they glorified him with the glory of the fatherhood.
Those who rapture raptured,
Kamaliel, . . .anen, Samblo,
the servants of <the> great holy luminaries,
and they took him into the place of the light of his fatherhood.
And he received the Five Seals from the light of the Mother Protennoia, First Thought,
and it was [granted] him to partake of the mystery of knowledge,
and [he became light] in light.
So, now, [49] . . .
[I] was in them, [inhabiting each one's form].
[The rulers] thought [I] was their Christ.
In fact, I [dwell in] everyone.
Indeed, within those in whom [I revealed myself] as light,
[I eluded] the rulers.
I am their beloved, for in that place
I clothed myself [as] the son of the chief creator,
and I was like him until the end of his regime,
which is the ignorance of chaos.
And among the angels I revealed myself in their likeness,
and among the powers as if I were one of them,
but among the children of humanity as if I were a son of humanity,
even though I am father of everyone.
I hid in them all
until I revealed myself among my members, who are mine.

I taught them about the ineffable ordinances and the brethren, but the ordinances of the Father are inexpressible to every sovereignty and every ruling power, and expressible only to the children of light.

These are the glories that are higher than every glory, the Five Seals, complete by virtue of intellect. One who possesses the Five Seals with these names has stripped off garments of ignorance and put on shining light. And nothing will appear to one who belongs to the powers of the rulers. In them darkness will dissolve and [ignorance] will die. And the thought of the creature that [is scattered] will have a single appearance, and [dark chaos] will dissolve [50] and . . . .

. . . incomprehensible . . . within the . . . until I reveal myself [to all my brothers and sisters] and gather all [my] brothers and sisters in my [eternal kingdom].

I proclaimed the ineffable [Five] Seals to them
so that [I might] abide in them
and they also might abide in me.

And I put on Jesus.
I bore him from the cursed wood
and established him in the dwelling places of his father.
And those who guard their places did not recognize me.

For my seed and I cannot be restrained.
My seed is mine,
and I shall [place] it in holy light
within incomprehensible silence.
Amen.

27. The Revelation of Adam

Unlike the Secret Book of John, the Nag Hammadi treatise known as the Revelation of Adam does not provide a detailed exposition of the Sethian myth to explain the origin of the divine realm, the creation of the world, or the entrapment of elements of the divine in human bodies. But some such myth clearly underlies the discussion, and there is no doubt that this is a Sethian document: Adam, the first human, reveals the truth about the world, and the humans' place in it, precisely to Seth, the only one of his three sons capable of receiving the truth and obtaining salvation by returning to the realm above. The descendants of Seth—these Gnostics themselves—are the heirs of this salvation.

In his revelation, Adam explains how he and Eve came to recognize that they ultimately belonged to a God far superior to the creator and explains how the creator God had oppressed the human race throughout history. He then describes a dream in which three figures from the heavenly realm came to him to reveal the conflict between the God of this world and the greater divinities from above. He also describes a revealer yet to come, and then launches into a poetic account of thirteen (false) explanations of where this "illuminator of knowledge" derived from. The book ends by indicating that the offspring of Seth—his spiritual descendants—will be saved by acquiring the necessary eternal knowledge and receiving the sacred rite of baptism.

As with most Gnostic treatises this one is difficult to date; it likely was composed sometime in the mid-second century.

The Revelation of Adam

The revelation that Adam taught his son Seth in the seven hundredth year. And he said, Listen to my words, my son Seth.

After God created me out of earth, along with your mother Eve, I went about with her in a glory that she had beheld in the eternal realm we had come from. She instructed me in the knowledge of the eternal God. We resembled the great eternal angels, for we were superior to the god who had created us and the powers with him, whom we did not know.

God, the ruler of the realms and the powers, angrily divided us. Then we became two beings, and the glory in our hearts departed from your mother Eve and me, as did the previous knowledge that breathed in us. The glory fled from us and entered another great [aeon] and another great [generation]. [65] It was not from this present aeon, from which your mother Eve and I derive, that knowledge [came]. Rather, knowledge entered the seed of great eternal beings. For this reason I myself have called you by the name of that human who is the seed of the great generation, or from whom it comes. After those days, the eternal knowledge of the God of truth left your mother Eve and me, and from then on we learned about mortal things, like human beings.

Then we came to recognize the god who had created us, for his powers were not foreign to us. We served him in fear and subservience. And after that we grew dim in our minds.

I was asleep in the thought of my mind, and I saw in front of me three persons whose appearance I could not recognize, since they were not from the powers of the god who had [created us]. They surpassed . . . glory . . . , [66] saying to me, "Adam, arise from the sleep of death, and hear about the eternal realm and the seed of that human to whom life has come, who came from your partner Eve and you."

When I had heard these words from the great persons standing before me, Eve and I sighed in our hearts. The Lord, the God who had created us, stood before us and said to us, "Adam, why were you both sighing in your hearts? Don't you know that I am the god who created you? And that I breathed into you a spirit of life, so you might be a living soul?"

Our eyes became dim. Then the god who created us created a son from himself and [your] mother Eve . . . . . . in . . . [67] the thought [of procreation]. I felt a sweet desire for your mother. The power of our eternal knowledge was gone and weakness overtook us, and the days of our life became few. I realized I had come under the authority of death.

So now, my son Seth, I shall reveal to you what those people whom I once saw before me revealed to me. After I have completed the times of this present generation and the years of [the generation] have come to an end, then [Noah will come, a] servant [of the Lord God who created us]. [69]

In order that [God], the ruler of the universe, might destroy [all] flesh from the earth because of what they seek, his rainstorms will pour down on those who are from the offspring of people to whom has passed the life of knowledge, which came from your mother Eve and me. For those people were strangers to him. After that great angels will come on high clouds, and they will bring those people into the place where the spirit of life dwells . . . . . . [70] come from heaven to [earth]. The whole population of fleshly beings will be lost in the [waters].

Then God will rest from his wrath. He will cast his power on the waters and endow his sons and [their wives] with power, by means of the ark, along with the animals that pleased him and the birds of heaven that he called and released on the earth.

God will say to Noah, whom generations will call Deucalion, "Look, I have protected <you> in the ark, along with your wife, your sons, their wives, their animals, and the birds [of heaven] that you called [and released on the earth] . . . . [71] Therefore I shall give you and your sons the [earth]. You and your sons will rule over it as kings, and you will refrain from producing offspring of people who will stand in some other glory instead of in my presence."

Then people will come to be like a cloud of great light.

Those people who have been expelled from the knowledge of the great eternal realms and the angels will come forward and stand before Noah and the realms.

God will say to Noah, "Why have you ignored what I told you? You have created another generation so that you might bring contempt upon my power."

Noah will say, "I testify before the might of your arm that the generation of these people did not come from me or [my] sons . . . ." [72]

. . . knowledge . . . . Those people will be brought into the land they deserve, and a holy dwelling place will be built for them. And they will be called by that name and live there six hundred years in knowledge of incorruptibility, and angels of the great light will be with them. They will have no improper thought in their hearts, but only the knowledge of God.

Then Noah will divide the entire earth among his sons, Ham, Japheth, and Shem. He will say to them, "My sons, listen to my words. Look, I have divided the earth among you. But serve God in fear and subservience all the days of your life, and do not let your offspring turn away from the face of God, the ruler of the universe, . . . your . . . and I . . . ." [73]

[Then Shem] the son of Noah [will say, "My] offspring will be pleasing before you and your power. Seal it with your strong hand by fear and commandment. None of the offspring that have come from me will turn away from you and God, the ruler of the universe, but they will serve in humility and fear within the limits of their perception."

Then others from the offspring of Ham and Japheth, four hundred thousand in number, will go out and enter another land and sojourn there with those people who came from the great eternal knowledge. The shadow of their power will protect those who sojourn with them from all evil and all unclean desires.

Then the offspring of Ham and Japheth will form twelve kingdoms, and their other offspring will enter the kingdom of another group of people.

[Then] . . . will take counsel . . . aeons . . . [74] mortal . . . the great realms of incorruptibility. They will approach their god Sakla, and they will go in to the powers and accuse the great people who are in their glory.

They will say to Sakla, "What is the power of these people who have stood in your presence, who have separated from the offspring of Ham and Japheth and are <four hundred thousand> in number? They have been received into another realm, one from which they have come, and they have overturned all the glory of your power and the dominion of your hand. The offspring of Noah through his son has fully accomplished your will and the will of all the powers in the realms where your mighty power reigns supreme. But those people and the people who sojourn in their glory have not done your will, and they have turned aside your entire throng."

Then the god of the aeons will hand over to them some who serve [him] . . . . They will come to that land [75] where the great people will be, who have not been defiled and will not be defiled

by any desire. For their souls came not from a defiled hand, but from a great commandment of an eternal angel.

Then fire, sulfur, and asphalt will be cast upon those people, and fire and smoke will cover those realms. The eyes of the powers of the heavenly luminaries will be darkened, and the inhabitants of the realms will not be able to see in those days.

But great clouds of light will descend, and more clouds of light will come down on them from the great eternal realms. Abrasax, Sablo, and Gamaliel will descend and rescue those people from the fire and wrath, and take them above the realms and domains of the powers, and [take] them away . . . living . . . and take them [away] . . . the realms . . . [76] dwelling place of the great . . . there with the holy angels and the eternal realms. The people will become like those angels, for they are not foreign to them. Rather, they labor with the incorruptible seed.

Once again, for a third time, the illuminator of knowledge will pass by in great glory, in order to leave behind some of the offspring of Noah and the sons of Ham and Japheth, to leave behind for himself trees that bear fruit. The illuminator will redeem their souls from the day of death. For all creation that came from mortal earth will be under the authority of death, but those who reflect in their hearts on the knowledge of the eternal God will not perish. They have received spirit not from this kingdom, but from something eternal, angelic . . . illuminator . . . will come . . . mortal . . . [77] Seth. And he will perform signs and wonders in order to bring contempt upon the powers and their ruler.

The god of the powers will be troubled and say, "What is the power of this human who is superior to us?"

He will arouse great wrath against that human, and the glory will depart and dwell in holy houses it has chosen for itself. The powers will not see it with their own eyes, and they will not see the illuminator either.

Then they will punish the flesh of the human on whom the holy Spirit has come.

The angels and all the generations of the powers will use the name erroneously and ask, "Where did this come from?" Or again, "Where did the words of falsehood, which all the powers have failed to understand, come from?"

Now the first kingdom [says of him],
He came [from] . . . . [78]
A spirit . . . up.
He was nourished in the heavens.
He received its glory and power.
He came to the bosom of his mother,
and in this way he came to the water.

The second kingdom says of him,
He came from a great prophet.
A bird came, took the child who was born,
and brought him onto a high mountain.
He was nourished by the bird of heaven.
An angel came from there and said to him,
"Arise, God has given you glory."
He received glory and strength,
and in this way he came to the water.

The third kingdom says of him,
He came from a virgin womb.
He was banished from his city, with his mother,
and was brought to a desert place.
He nourished himself there.
He came and received glory and power,
and in this way he came to the water.

The fourth kingdom says of him,
He came [from a virgin] . . . .
[Solomon] [79] sought her,
along with Phersalo and Sauel
and his armies that had been sent out.
Solomon himself sent his army of demons
to search for the virgin.
They did not find the one they sought,
but rather the virgin who was given to them.

They brought her, Solomon took her,
and the virgin became pregnant
and gave birth to the child there.
She nourished him on a border of the desert.
When he was nourished,
he received glory and power
from the seed from which he had been conceived,
and in this way he came to the water.

The fifth kingdom says of him,
He came from a heavenly droplet
and was cast into the sea.
The abyss received him, gave birth to him,
and bore him up.
He received glory and power,
and in this way he came to the water.

The sixth kingdom [says],
A . . . [went] down to the realm [80] below
to gather flowers.
She became pregnant from desire for the flowers,
and gave birth to him in that place.
The angels of the flower garden nourished him.
He received glory and power there,
and in this way he came to the water.

The seventh kingdom says of him,
He is a droplet and came from heaven to earth.
Dragons brought him down to their caves,
and he became a child.
A spirit came over him
and brought him on high
to where the droplet had come from.
He received glory and power there,
and in this way he came to the water.

The eighth kingdom says of him,
A cloud came over the earth
and enveloped a rock, and he came from it.
The angels over the cloud nourished him.
He [received] glory and power there,

and [in this way he] came to [the water]. [81]

The ninth kingdom says of him,
One of the nine muses went away by herself.
She came to a high mountain and relaxed
    there,
so that she desired herself alone
to become androgynous.
She fulfilled her desire
and became pregnant from it.
He was born.
The angels over desire nourished him.
He received glory and power there,
and in this way he came to the water.

The tenth kingdom says of him,
His god loved a cloud of desire.
He produced him by his hand
and ejaculated some of the droplet
upon the cloud near him,
and he was born.
He received glory and power there,
and in this way he came to the water.

The eleventh kingdom says of him,
The father desired his [own] daughter,
and she became pregnant from her father.
She cast . . . tomb out in the desert. [82]
The angel nourished him there,
and in this way he came to the water.

The twelfth kingdom says of him,
He came from two luminaries.
They nourished him there,
He received glory and power,
and in this way he came to the water.

And the thirteenth kingdom says of him,
Every offspring of their ruler is a word,
and this word received a mandate there.
He received glory and power,
and in this way he came to the water,
so that the desire of those powers might
    be satisfied.

But the generation without a king says,
God chose him from all the eternal realms.
He made knowledge of the undefiled one
    of truth
to come to be [in] him.
He said, "The [great] illuminator has come
[from] foreign air, [from a] great eternal realm."
And [he] [83] illumined the generation
    of those people,
whom he had chosen for himself,
so that they might illumine the whole eternal
    realm.

Then the offspring, who will receive his name
in the water, and that of them all, will oppose the
power, and a dark cloud will overshadow them.
    The people will cry out with a loud voice and
say, "Blessed are the souls of those people, because
they have known God with knowledge of truth.
They will live for ever and ever, because they have
not been corrupted by their desires, as the angels
have, and they have not accomplished the deeds of
the powers. Rather, they have stood before him in
knowledge of God, like light that has come from
fire and blood.
    "But we have done everything through the
foolishness of the powers. We have boasted
about the transgression of [all] our deeds. We
have cried out against [the God] of [truth], because all of his work . . . [84] is eternal. Take
pity on our spirits. For now we know our souls
will surely die."
    Then a voice came to them <from> Micheus,
Michar, and Mnesinous, who are over holy baptism and living water, saying, "Why were you
crying out against the living God with lawless
voices and unlawful tongues and souls full of blood
and foulness? You are filled with deeds far from
truth, yet your ways are full of fun and laughter.
You have defiled the water of life and have drawn
it to the will of the powers, into whose hands you
have been given, to serve them.
    "Your thought is not like that of those people
whom you persecute . . . desire . . . . [85] Their

fruit does not wither. Rather, they will be known up to the great eternal realms."

The preserved words of the God of the eternal realms were not copied in a book or put in writing. Angelic beings, whom none of the human generations know, will convey them, and they will be placed on a high mountain, on a rock of truth. They will be called words of incorruptibility and truth for those who know the eternal God, through wisdom of knowledge and teaching of the eternal angels, because the eternal God knows all things.

These are the revelations Adam disclosed to his son Seth, and his son taught them to his offspring. This is the hidden knowledge of Adam that he gave to Seth, and this is holy baptism for people who have eternal knowledge, through those born of the word and the incorruptible illuminators, who have come from the holy seed,

Yesseus Mazareus Yessedekeus,
the living water.

The Revelation of Adam

VALENTINIANS

Unlike the Sethian Gnostics, the Valentinians were named after an actual person, Valentinus, the founder and original leader of the group. We know about the Valentinians from the writings of proto-orthodox heresiologists beginning with Irenaeus and by some of the writings discovered among the Nag Hammadi library that almost certainly derive from Valentinian authors, including one book that may actually have been written by Valentinus himself (The Gospel of Truth).

Valentinus was born around 100 CE and was raised in Alexandria Egypt. He allegedly was a student of the Christian teacher Theudas, who was in turn a disciple of the apostle Paul. Valentinus moved to Rome in the late 130s and there became an influential speaker and teacher. According to some of our early reports, he very nearly was elected to be the bishop of Rome. Despite his distinctive views—which for the proto-orthodox seemed completely aberrant—he and his followers continued on in the Roman church. There is nothing to suggest that he or his followers started their own churches; they worshiped with proto-orthodox Christians and were in outer appearance very difficult to tell apart from them.

Valentinus nonetheless had been heavily influenced by the Sethian Gnostic myth and adopted it into a kind of proto-orthodox framework. His understanding of the divine and material realms were somewhat less complex than the Sethian; his views of the creator God were not as harsh, he was not as condemning of the material world, and he had a more developed understanding of the human race. According to Irenaeus, Valentinus and his followers taught that just as a person has a body, soul, and spirit, so too the race itself is divided up into people who are purely animal (bodies that ceased to exist when they died), or psychic (i.e., "soulish"—these are regular Christians who can be saved and given a decent afterlife if they have faith and do good works), or pneumatic (i.e., "spiritual—these are the Valentinians who understand the deeper truths that are necessary for a full salvation in a return to the Pleroma above).

None of the surviving Valentinian writings lays out their understanding of how the divine and human realms came into being in a way comparable to the Sethians (for example, the Secret Book of John). But it is clear that the Valentinians not only worshiped in the proto-orthodox churches, they also accepted proto-orthodox Scriptural texts (books that were coming to be seen as canonical) and adhered to proto-orthodox doctrinal teachings—at least on the surface. What made the Valentinians distinctive is that they interpreted both these writings and these doctrines in their own, decidedly non-orthodox, ways, to teach the fuller truths of the nature of the divine Pleroma, the inferiority of this material world, the entrapment of elements of the divine here in human bodies, and the need for them to be set free by recognizing the truths that could be brought from above by Christ and by undergoing the rituals necessary for redemption.

Because they remained in the proto-orthodox churches, confessed the proto-orthodox doctrines, and read the proto-orthodox writings—all the while interpreting them in a vastly different way from the non-Valentinians among them—they were seen by the proto-orthodox heresiologists to be a particularly nefarious group, hard to detect and difficult to root out. And they were thought to be dangerous to the communities in which they resided, as they taught their views as a kind of elitist understanding of the faith for those who wanted to advance to a higher level of spiritual knowledge.

The lure of the Valentinian view can be seen in the beautiful reflection known as the Gospel of Truth which, as indicated, may actually derive from the pen of Valentinus himself. Others of their writings show how close to the proto-orthodox views of Scripture the Valentinians stood (in contrast to the Sethians), as in the Letter of Ptolemy to Flora (see Chapter 10) and the Treatise on the Resurrection. Yet other writings show how mystical, deep, and esoteric Valentinian reflections on the nature of the world and our place in it can be, as in the powerful, but difficult, Gospel of Philip.

THE TEXTS

28. *The Gospel of Truth*

A moving expression of Gnostic joy in experiencing enlightenment, the "Gospel of Truth" is one of the real treasures of the Nag Hammadi library. The book is not a Gospel in the traditional sense—there is no account of the life or teachings of Jesus here; it is called a gospel because it presents the "good news" of God's gracious revelation of saving knowledge, gnosis, which comes through Jesus Christ. Some scholars believe that it was originally a sermon preached to a Gnostic or possibly a more broadly Christian congregation; many are convinced that it was authored by the most famous Gnostic Christian of the second century, Valentinus himself.

The Gospel of Truth presupposes important aspects of Gnostic myth, but it does not explicate them; there are only scattered hints about how the divine realm, the material world, and human beings came into existence. Instead, the book focuses on the truth that brings redemption to an anguished humanity languishing in darkness and ignorance, and especially on the one who brought this revealed truth, Jesus Christ, the Word who comes forth from the Father as his Son. Through Christ's revelation, the fog of error has been dissipated and the illusions of falsehood have been exposed, opening those who receive the truth to understand who they are, allowing them to be reunited with the incomprehensible and inconceivable Father of all.

Whether or not the work actually came from the pen of Valentinus, it was known to the church father Irenaeus, and so must date to before 180 CE.

The Gospel of Truth, reproduced from Marvin Meyer, *The Nag Hammadi Scriptures*. San Francisco: HarperOne, 2007. Used with permission of HarperOne.

The Gospel of Truth

The gospel of truth is joy for people who have received grace from the Father of truth, that they might know him through the power of the Word. The Word has come from the fullness in the Father's thought and mind. The Word is called "Savior," a term that refers to the work he is to do to redeem those who had not known [17] the Father. And the term "gospel" refers to the revelation of hope, since it is the means of discovery for those who seek him.

All have sought for the one from whom they have come forth. All have been within him, the illimitable, the inconceivable, who is beyond all thought. But ignorance of the Father brought terror and fear, and terror grew dense like a fog, so that no one could see. Thus Error grew powerful. She worked on her material substance in vain. Since she did not know the truth, she assumed a fashioned figure and prepared, with power and in beauty, a substitute for truth.

This was not humiliating for the illimitable, inconceivable one. For this terror and forgetfulness and this deceptive figure were as nothing, whereas established truth is unchanging, unperturbed, and beyond beauty.

For this reason despise Error.

Error had no root; she was in a fog regarding the Father. She was there preparing works and deeds of forgetfulness and fear in order, by them, to attract those of the middle and take them captive.

The forgetfulness of Error was not apparent. It is not [18] . . . from the Father. Forgetfulness did not come into being from the Father, but if it did come into being, it is because of him. What comes into being within him is knowledge, which appeared so that forgetfulness might be destroyed and the Father might be known. Forgetfulness came into being because the Father was not known, so as soon as the Father comes to be known, forgetfulness will cease to be.

This is the gospel of him whom they seek, revealed to the perfect through the Father's mercy. Through the hidden mystery Jesus Christ enlightened those who were in darkness because of forgetfulness. He enlightened them and showed the way, and that way is the truth he taught them.

For this reason Error was angry with him and persecuted him, but she was restrained by him and made powerless. He was nailed to a tree, and he became fruit of the knowledge of the Father. This fruit of the tree, however, did not bring destruction when it was eaten, but rather it caused those who ate of it to come into being. They were joyful in this discovery, and he found them within himself and they found him within themselves.

And as for the illimitable, inconceivable perfect Father who made all, the All is within him and needs him. Although he kept within himself their perfection, which he had not given to all, the Father was not jealous. What jealousy could there be between himself and his own members? For even if [19] the members of the eternal realm had [received] their [perfection], they could not have approached . . . the Father. He kept their perfection within himself, giving it to them as a means to return to him with complete, single-minded knowledge. He is the one who set the All in order, and the All is within him. The All was in need of him, just as a person who is not known to other people wants them to know him and love him. For what did the All need if not the knowledge of the Father?

He became a guide, a person of rest who was busy in places of instruction. He came forward and spoke the word as a teacher. Those wise in their own eyes came to test him, but he refuted them, for they were foolish, and they hated him because they were not really wise.

After them came the little children, who have knowledge of the Father. When they gained strength and learned about the expressions of the Father, they knew, they were known, they were glorified, they gave glory.

In their hearts the living book of the living was revealed, the book that was written in the

Father's thought and mind and was, [20] since the foundation of the All, in his incomprehensible nature. No one had been able to take up this book, since it was ordained that the one who would take it up would be slain. And nothing could appear among those who believed in salvation unless that book had come out.

For this reason the merciful, faithful Jesus was patient and accepted his sufferings to the point of taking up that book, since he knew that his death would be life for many.

As in the case of a will that has not been opened, the fortune of the deceased owner of the house is hidden, so also in the case of all that had been hidden while the Father of the All was invisible but that issues from him from whom every realm comes.

Jesus appeared,
put on that book,
was nailed to a tree,
and published the Father's edict on the cross.
Oh, what a great teaching!
He humbled himself even unto death,
though clothed in eternal life.
He stripped off the perishable rags
and clothed himself in incorruptibility,
which no one can take from him.

When he entered the empty ways of fear, he passed by those stripped by forgetfulness. For he encompasses knowledge and perfection, and he proclaims what is in the heart [21]. . . . [He] teaches those who will learn. And those who will learn are the living who are inscribed in the book of the living. They learn about themselves, receiving instruction from the Father, returning to him.

Since the perfection of the All is in the Father, all must go up to him. When all have received knowledge, they receive what is theirs and draw it to themselves. For those who are ignorant are in need, and their need is great, because they need what would make them perfect. Since the perfection of the All is in the Father, all must go up to him and receive what is theirs. He inscribed these things first, having prepared them to be given to those who came from him.

Those whose names he knew at the beginning were called at the end, as it is with every person who has knowledge. Such names the Father has uttered. One whose name has not been spoken is ignorant, for how could a person hear if that person's name had not been pronounced? Whoever remains ignorant until the end is a creature of forgetfulness and will perish with it. Otherwise why do these wretches have no [22] name, why no voice?

So whoever has knowledge is from above. If called, that person hears, replies, turns to the one who is calling, and goes up to him. He knows how he is called. That person has knowledge and does the will of him who called. That person wishes to please him, finds rest, and has the appropriate name. Those who have knowledge in this way know where they come from and where they are going. They know as one who, having become intoxicated, has turned from his drunkenness and, having come to his senses, has gotten control of himself.

He has brought many back from Error. He went before them to the places from which they had turned when they followed Error, because of the depth of him who surrounds every place, though nothing surrounds him. Indeed, it is amazing that they were in the Father without knowing him and that they could leave on their own, since they were not able to contemplate or know the one in whom they were.

For if his will had not come from him . . . he revealed it as knowledge that is in harmony with the expressions of his will—that is, knowledge of the living book, which he revealed to the eternal realms at the end [23] as his [letters]. He showed that they are not merely vowels or consonants, so that one may read them and think them devoid of meaning. Rather, they are letters of truth; they speak and know themselves. Each letter is a perfect truth like a perfect book, for they are letters written in unity, written by the Father for the eternal realms, so that by means of his letters they might come to know the Father.

As for the Word,
his wisdom meditates on it,
his teaching utters it,
his knowledge has revealed it,
his patience is a crown upon it,
his joy is in harmony with it,

A great disturbance occurred among the jars, for some were empty and others were filled, some were ample and others were depleted, some were purified and others were broken.

All the realms were shaken and disturbed, for they had no order or stability. Error was agitated, and she did not know what to do. She was troubled, she lamented, she attacked herself, because she knew nothing. For knowledge, which leads to the destruction of Error and all her expressions, approached. Error is empty; there is nothing within her.

Truth appeared, and all its expressions recognized it. They greeted the Father in truth and power that is complete and joins them with the Father.

Whoever loves truth, whoever touches [27] truth, touches the Father's mouth, because truth is the Father's mouth. His tongue is the Holy Spirit, and from his tongue one will receive the Holy Spirit. This is the manifestation of the Father and his revelation to his eternal realms. He revealed his hidden self and explained it. For who has anything within if not the Father alone?

All the realms are from him. They know that they have come from him as children who were within a mature person but who knew that they had not yet received form or been given a name. The Father brings forth each of them when they receive the essence of his knowledge. Otherwise, though they were in him, they could not know him. The Father is perfect, and he knows every realm within himself. If he wishes, what he wishes appears when he gives it form and a name—and he does give it a name. He brings into being those who before coming into being were ignorant of the one who made them.

I am not saying that those who have not yet come to be are nothing. They are [28] within one

who may wish that they come into being if at some future point he so wishes. On the one hand, he knows, before anything appears, what he will produce. On the other hand, the fruit that has not yet appeared knows nothing and does nothing. Thus each realm in the Father comes from what is, but what has set itself up is from what is not. For whatever has no root has no fruit, and although thinking, "I have come into being," it will perish by itself. So whatever does not exist will never exist.

What, then, does he want such a one to think? It is this: "I have come into being like shadows and phantoms of the night." When the light shines, the person knows the terror that had been experienced was nothing.

Thus they were ignorant of the Father, for they did not see him. [29] Since there had been terror and confusion and uncertainty and doubt and division, there were many illusions among them, and inane ignorance—as if they were fast asleep and found themselves a prey to nightmares. In these dreams they are fleeing somewhere, or they cannot get away when chased, or they are in a fight, or they themselves are beaten, or they are falling from on high, or they fly through the air with no wings. Or it seems people are trying to kill them, though there is no one chasing them, or they are killing their neighbors and are covered with their blood. This continues until those experiencing all these dreams wake up. Those caught in the middle of all these confusing things see nothing because the dreams are nothing.

So it is with those who cast off ignorance from themselves like sleep. They do not consider it to be anything, nor do they regard its [30] features as real, but they put them aside like a dream in the night and understand the knowledge of the Father to be the dawn. This is how each person acts while in ignorance, as if asleep, and this is how a person comes to knowledge, as if awakened. Good for one who comes to himself and awakens. And blessed is one who has opened the eyes of the blind.

The spirit came to this person in haste when the person awakened. Having given its hand to the one lying prone on the ground, the spirit placed him firmly on his feet, for he had not yet risen.

Knowledge of the Father and the revelation of his Son gave them the means of knowing. For when they saw and heard him, he let them taste him and smell him and touch the beloved Son. He appeared, informing them of the Father, the illimitable, and he inspired them with what is in the thought, doing his will. Many received the light and turned [31] to him. But material people were strangers to him and did not discern his appearance or recognize him. For he came in the likeness of flesh, and nothing blocked his way, for incorruptibility cannot be grasped. Moreover, while saying new things and speaking about what is in the Father's heart, he produced the faultless Word. Light spoke through his mouth and his voice brought forth life. He gave them thought and understanding and mercy and salvation and the spirit of strength from the Father's infinity and sweetness. He made punishments and afflictions cease, for they caused those in need of mercy to stray from him in error and bondage. He destroyed them with might and confounded them with knowledge.

He became a way for those who strayed,
knowledge for those who were ignorant,
discovery for those who sought,
support for those who tremble,
purity for those who were defiled.

He is the shepherd who left behind the ninety-nine [32] sheep that had not strayed and went in search of the one that was lost. He rejoiced when he found it. For ninety-nine is a number expressed with the left hand, but when another one is found, the numerical sum is transferred to the right hand. In this way what needs one more—that is, the whole right hand—attracts what it needs, takes it from the left and brings it to the right, and so the number becomes one hundred. This is the meaning of the pronunciation of these numbers.

The Father is like that. He labored even on the Sabbath for the sheep that he found fallen into the pit. He saved the life of the sheep and brought it up from the pit.

Understand the inner meaning, for you are children of inner meaning. What is the Sabbath? It is a day on which salvation should not be idle. Speak of the heavenly day that has no night and of the light that does not set because it is perfect. Speak from the heart, for you are the perfect day and within you dwells the light that does not fail. Speak of truth with those who seek it and of knowledge with those who have sinned in their error. [33]

Steady the feet of those who stumble and extend your hands to the sick. Feed the hungry and give rest to the weary. Awaken those who wish to arise and rouse those who sleep, for you embody vigorous understanding. If what is strong acts like this, it becomes even stronger.

Focus your attention upon yourselves. Do not focus your attention upon other things—that is, what you have cast away from yourselves. Do not return to eat what you have vomited. Do not be moth-eaten, do not be worm-eaten, for you have already gotten rid of that. Do not be a place for the devil, for you have already destroyed him. Do not strengthen what stands in your way, what is collapsing, to support it. One who is lawless is nothing. Treat the lawless one more harshly than the just one, for the lawless does what he does because he is lawless, but the just does what he does with people because he is righteous. Do the Father's will, then, for you are from him.

For the Father is sweet, and goodness is in his will. He knows what is yours, in which you find rest. By the fruit one knows what is yours. For the Father's children [34] are his fragrance; they are from the beauty of his face. The Father loves his fragrance and disperses it everywhere, and when it mixes with matter, it gives his fragrance to the light. Through his quietness he makes his fragrance superior in every way to every sound. For it is not ears that smell the fragrance, but it is the spirit that possesses the sense of smell, draws the fragrance to itself, and immerses itself in the Father's fragrance. Thus it cares for it and takes it to where it came from, the original fragrance, which has grown cold in psychical form. It is like cold water that has sunk into soft soil, and those who see it think there is only soil. Later the water evaporates when the wind draws it up, and it becomes warm. So cold fragrances are from division.

For this reason faith came, did away with division, and brought the warm fullness of love, so that what is cold may not return, but the unity of perfect thought may prevail.

29. The Treatise on the Resurrection

Discovered at Nag Hammadi, the provocative philosophical discourse known as the "Treatise on the Resurrection" is a letter addressed by an unknown Valentinian teacher to an inquirer, possibly a non-Gnostic Christian, named Rheginus. In response to Rheginus's questions, the treatise provides basic instruction about the nature of death and resurrection—both of Jesus and, more important, of humans.

The author assures Rheginus that the resurrection is by no means an illusion; it will certainly take place. But it will not involve some kind of crass revivification of the material body (which, he claims, is itself more illusory than real). After death, even though the body passes away, a person's spirit will ascend to the heavenly realm, drawn up by Jesus himself. The flesh, in other words, is completely transitory, but the spirit is eternal. Those who live in such a way as to deny their flesh have begun to escape this bodily existence and started along the path to their heavenly home; for people like this, the resurrection has already occurred.

This teaching stands in sharp contrast with proto-orthodox notions of the future bodily resurrection (cf. 2 Timothy 2:18). Although it is impossible to say when this intriguing treatise was written, many scholars date it to the late second century.

The Treatise on Resurrection

Rheginus my son, some people want to become intellectuals. That is their goal when they try to explain unsolved problems, and if they are successful, they have an exalted opinion of themselves. I do not think they are established on the word of truth. Rather, they seek their own rest, which we have received from Christ our Savior and Lord. [44] We received rest when we came to know the truth and rested on it.

Since you ask about the main issues on resurrection in such a pleasant way, I am writing to you. Resurrection is essential. Many do not believe in it and few find it, so let us discuss it in our treatise.

The Treatise on the Resurrection, reproduced from Marvin Meyer, *The Nag Hammadi Scriptures*. San Francisco: HarperOne, 2007. Used with permission of HarperOne.

How did the Lord live his life? While he was in flesh and after he revealed himself as Son of God, he went about in this world where you live and spoke about the law of nature, which I call death. Rheginus, the Son of God was a son of humanity. He embraced both aspects, humanity and divinity, so that by being a son of God he might conquer death, and by being a son of humanity fullness might be restored. For originally he was from above, a seed of truth, before the structure of the world, with all its dominions and deities, came into being.

I know I am presenting [45] this explanation in difficult terms, but there is nothing in the word of truth that is difficult. Christ came to provide the explanation, to leave nothing hidden, but to reveal everything clearly about coming into being, the destruction of evil, and the revelation of the chosen. This means the emergence of truth and spirit, and grace belongs to truth.

The Savior swallowed death. You must know this. When he laid aside the perishable world, he exchanged it for an incorruptible eternal realm. He arose and swallowed the visible through the invisible, and thus he granted us the way to our immortality.

As the apostle said of him, we suffered with him, we arose with him, we ascended with him.

Since we are visibly present in this world, we wear the garment of the world. From the Savior we radiate like beams of light, and we are sustained by him until our sunset, our death in this life. We are drawn upward by him, like rays by the sun, and nothing holds us down. This is the resurrection of the spirit, [46] which swallows the resurrection of the soul and the resurrection of the flesh.

If some do not believe, they cannot be persuaded. My son, the affirmation that the dead will arise belongs to the realm of faith, not of argument.

Among the world's philosophers is there one who believes? Certainly that philosopher will arise. But that philosopher should not trust anyone who turns to himself alone, even for our faith.

We know the Son of Humanity, and we believe that he arose from the dead. We say of him, "He became death's destroyer."

The object of belief is great and the believers are also great. The thought of believers will not perish and the mind of those who know will not perish. We are chosen for salvation and redemption, since from the beginning it was determined that we would not fall into the folly of the ignorant, but we would enter into the understanding of those who know the truth.

The truth they guard cannot be lost. Nor will it be. The system of the Fullness is strong; what broke loose and became the world is insignificant. What is held fast is the All. It did not [47] come into being. It was.

So never doubt the resurrection, Rheginus my son. Although once you did not exist in flesh, you took on flesh when you entered this world. Why is it, then, that you will not take your flesh with you when you ascend into the eternal realm? What is better than flesh is what animates the flesh. What came into being because of you, isn't it yours? If it is yours, doesn't it exist with you?

But while you are in the world, what are you missing? Is that what you have attempted to learn about: the outflow of the body, which is old age? Are you nothing but corruption?

Leaving this behind will profit you, for you will not give up the better part when you leave. The inferior part will suffer loss, but there is grace for it. Nothing redeems us from this world, but we are of the All, and we are saved. We have been saved from start to finish. Let us think about it in this way; let us accept it in this way.

Some inquire further and want to know whether one will be saved immediately, if the body is left behind. Let there be no doubt about this. Surely the visible parts of the body are dead [48] and will not be saved. Only the living parts that are within will arise.

What is the resurrection? It is always the disclosure of those who have arisen. If you remember reading in the gospel that Elijah and Moses appeared with Jesus, do not think that the resurrection is an illusion. It is no illusion. It is truth. It is more appropriate to say that the world is illusion rather than the resurrection that came into being through our Lord and Savior Jesus Christ.

What am I telling you?
All at once the living die.
How do they live in illusion?
The rich become poor,
kings are overthrown,
everything changes.
The world is illusion.
Let me not speak so negatively.
The resurrection is different.
It is real,
it stands firm.
It is revelation of what is,
a transformation of things,
a transition into newness.
Incorruptibility [49] [flows] over corruption,
light flows over darkness, swallowing it,
Fullness fills what it lacks.
These are symbols and images of resurrection.
This brings goodness.

Rheginus, do not get lost in details, nor live according to the flesh for the sake of harmony. Flee from divisions and bonds, and then you already have resurrection. If the mortal part knows itself, knows that it will die even though it has lived many years in this life, why not look at yourself and see that you already have arisen and have been received in?

You have the resurrection but go on as if you are to die when it is that mortal part that knows it is dead. Why am I so patient? Only because of your lack of training. Everyone needs to practice ways to be released from this element so as not to wander in error, but rather to recover what one was at the beginning.

What I received through the generosity of my [50] Lord Jesus Christ I have taught you and your brothers and sisters, who are my children, about them, and I have left out nothing that may strengthen you. If anything in the explanation of the treatise is too deep, ask and I shall clarify it.

Do not be worried about sharing this treatise with anyone among you, for it can be helpful. Many are awaiting what I have written to you. I say, peace and grace be with them.

I greet you and those who love you with the love of family.

The Treatise on Resurrection

30. The Gospel of Philip

Even though the Gospel of Philip, also discovered at Nag Hammadi, is easily recognized as Valentinian, the book is notoriously difficult to understand in its details. In part this is due to the form of its composition. It is not a narrative Gospel of the type found in the New Testament or a group of self-contained sayings like the Gospel of Thomas (see Chapter 8). It is instead a collection of mystical reflections that have evidently been excerpted from previously existing sermons, treatises, and theological meditations, brought together here under the name of Philip—presumably Jesus' own disciple. Since they are given in relative isolation, without any real narrative context,

The Gospel of Philip, reproduced from Marvin Meyer, *The Nag Hammadi Scriptures*. San Francisco: HarperOne, 2007. Used with permission of HarperOne.

the reflections are difficult to interpret. There are, at any rate, extensive uses of catch-words to organize some of the material, and several principal themes emerge upon a careful reading.

Among the clearest emphases is precisely the contrast between those who can understand and those who cannot, between knowledge that is exoteric (available to all) and that which is esoteric (available only to insiders), between the immature outsiders (regular Christians, called "Hebrews") and the mature insiders (Valentinians, called "gentiles"). Those who do not understand—that is, the outsiders with only exoteric knowledge—err in many of their judgments; for example, in taking such notions as the virgin birth or the resurrection of Jesus as literal statements of historical fact, rather than symbolic expressions of deeper truths.

Throughout much of the work the Christian sacraments figure prominently. Five are explicitly named: baptism, anointing, eucharist, salvation, and bridal chamber. It is hard to know what deeper meaning these rituals had for the author (especially the "bridal chamber," which has stirred considerable debate among scholars), or even what he imagined them to entail when practiced literally.

It is difficult to assign a date to this work, but it was probably compiled during the third century, although it draws on earlier sources.

The Gospel of Philip

A Hebrew makes a Hebrew, and such a person is called a convert. A convert does not make a convert. [Some people] are as they [are] and make others [like them], while others [52] simply are.

A slave seeks only to be free and does not seek the master's estate.

For a child it is not enough to be a child, but a child claims the father's inheritance.

Heirs to the dead are dead, and what they inherit is dead. Heirs to the living are alive, and they inherit both the living and the dead. The dead inherit nothing, for how could a dead person inherit? If a dead person inherits the living, the living will not die and the dead will come to life.

A gentile does not die, never having been alive so as to die. One who has believed in truth is alive, but this person is at risk of dying just by being alive.

Since Christ came, the world has been created, cities have been beautified, and the dead have been buried.

When we were Hebrews we were orphans, with only a mother, but when we became Christians we had a father and a mother.

Whoever sows in winter reaps in summer. Winter is the world, summer is the other aeon, the eternal realm. Let's sow in the world to reap in summer. And for this reason we should not pray in winter.

From winter comes summer. If someone reaps in winter, the person will not really reap but will pull out the young plants, and such do not produce a crop. [That person's field] is barren not only [now] but also on the Sabbath.

Christ came [53] to purchase some, to save some, to redeem some. He purchased strangers and made them his own, and he brought back his own whom he had laid down of his own will as a deposit. Not only when he appeared did he lay the soul of his own will as a deposit, but from the beginning of the world he laid down the soul, for the proper moment, according to his will. Then he came forth to take it back, since it had been laid down as a deposit. It had fallen into the hands of robbers and had been stolen, but he saved it. And he redeemed the good in the world and the bad.

Light and darkness, life and death, and right and left are siblings of one another, and inseparable.

For this reason the good are not good, the bad are not bad, life is not life, and death is not death. Each will dissolve into its original nature, but what is superior to the world cannot be dissolved, for it is eternal.

The names of worldly things are utterly deceptive, for they turn the heart from what is real to what is unreal. Whoever hears the word "god" thinks not of what is real but rather of what is unreal. So also with the words "father," "son," "holy spirit," "life," "light," "resurrection," "church," and all the rest, people do not think of what is real but of what is unreal, [though] the words refer to what is real. The words [that are] heard belong to this world. [Do not be] [54] deceived. If words belonged to the eternal realm, they would never be pronounced in this world, nor would they designate worldly things. They would refer to what is in the eternal realm.

Only one name is not pronounced in the world, the name the Father gave the Son. It is the name above all; it is the Father's name. For the Son would not have become Father if he had not put on the Father's name. Those who have this name understand it but do not speak it. Those who do not have it cannot even understand it.

Truth brought forth names in the world for us, and no one can refer to truth without names. Truth is one and many, for our sakes, to teach us about the one, in love, through the many.

The rulers wanted to fool people, since they saw that people have a kinship with what is truly good. They took the names of the good and assigned them to what is not good, to fool people with names and link the names to what is not good. So, as if they are doing people a favor, they take names from what is not good and transfer them to the good, in their own way of thinking. For they wished to take free people and enslave them forever.

Before Christ came there was no bread in the world, just as paradise, where Adam lived, had many trees for animal food but no wheat for human food; and people ate like animals. But when Christ, the perfect human, came, he brought bread from heaven, that humans might be fed with human food.

The rulers thought they did all they did by their own power and will, but the Holy Spirit was secretly accomplishing all through them by the Spirit's will.

Truth, which has existed from the beginning, is sown everywhere, and many see it being sown, but few see it being reaped.

Some said Mary became pregnant by the Holy Spirit. They are wrong and do not know what they are saying. When did a woman ever get pregnant by a woman?

Mary is the virgin whom none of the powers defiled. This is greatly repugnant to the Hebrews, who are the apostles and apostolic persons. This virgin whom none of the powers defiled [wishes that] the powers would defile themselves.

The master [would] not have said, "My [Father who is] in heaven," if [he] did not also have another father. He would simply have said, "[My Father]."

The master said to the disciples, "[Take something] [56] from every house and bring it to the Father's house, but do not steal while in the Father's house and take something away."

Jesus is a hidden name, Christ is a revealed name. The name Jesus does not exist in any other language, but he is called by the name Jesus. The word for Christ in Syriac is *messias* and in Greek is *christos,* and likewise all other people have a word for it in their own language. Nazarene is the revealed form of the hidden name.

Christ has everything within himself, whether human or angel or mystery, and the Father.

Those who say that the master first died and then arose are wrong, for he first arose and then died. If someone is not first resurrected, wouldn't that person die? As God lives, that one would <die>.

No one would hide something valuable and precious in a valuable container, but countless sums are commonly kept in a container worth only a cent. So it is with the soul. It is something precious, and it has come to be in a worthless body.

Some people are afraid that they may arise from the dead naked, and so they want to arise in flesh. They do not know that it is those who wear the [flesh] who are naked. Those who are [able] to take it off are not naked.

"Flesh [and blood will] not inherit God's kingdom." What is this flesh that will not [57] inherit? It is what we are wearing. And what is this flesh that will inherit? It is the flesh and blood of Jesus.

For this reason he said, "One who does not eat my flesh and drink my blood does not have life within." What does this mean? His flesh is the word and his blood is the Holy Spirit. Whoever has received these has food, drink, and clothing.

And I also disagree with others who say that the flesh will not arise. Both views are wrong. You say that the flesh will not arise? Then tell me what will arise, so we may salute you. You say it is the spirit in the flesh, and also the light in the flesh? But what is in the flesh is the word, and what you are talking about is nothing other than flesh. It is necessary to arise in this sort of flesh, since everything exists in it.

In this world those who wear clothes are superior to the clothes. In heaven's kingdom the clothes are superior to those who wear them.

By water and fire this whole realm is purified, the visible by the visible; the hidden by the hidden. Some things are hidden by the visible. There is water within water, there is fire within the oil of anointing.

Jesus tricked everyone, for he did not appear as he was, but he appeared so that he could be seen. He appeared to everyone. He [appeared] to the great as great, he [appeared] to the small as small, he [appeared [58] to the] angels as an angel and to humans as a human. For this reason his word was hidden from everyone. Some looked at him and thought they saw themselves. But when he appeared to his disciples in glory upon the mountain, he was not small. He became great. Or rather, he made the disciples great, so they could see him in his greatness.

He said on that day in the prayer of thanksgiving,

You who have united perfect light with Holy
   Spirit,
unite the angels also with us, as images.

Do not despise the lamb, for without it no one could see the <king>.

No one can meet the king while naked.

The heavenly person has more children than the earthly person. If the children of Adam are numerous but die, how much more numerous are the children of the perfect human, who do not die but are continually being born.

Three women always walked with the master: Mary his mother, <his> sister, and Mary of Magdala, who is called his companion. For "Mary" is the name of his sister, his mother, and his companion.

"Father" and "son" are simple names, "holy spirit" is a double name. They are everywhere, above and below, in the hidden and in the visible. The Holy Spirit is in the visible, and then it is below, and the Holy Spirit is in the hidden, and then it is above.

Evil forces serve the saints, for they have been blinded by the Holy Spirit into thinking they are helping their own people when they really are helping the saints.

So a disciple once asked the master for something from the world and he said, "Ask your mother, and she will give you something from another realm."

God is a man-eater, [63] and so humans are [sacrificed] to him. Before humans were sacrificed, animals were sacrificed, because those to whom they were sacrificed were not gods.

Glass and ceramic vessels are both made with fire. If glass vessels break, they are redone, since they have been made through breath. But if ceramic vessels break, they are destroyed, since they have been made without breath.

A donkey turning a millstone walked a hundred miles. When it was set loose, it found itself in the same place. Some people travel long distances but get nowhere. By nightfall they have seen no cities or villages, nothing man-made or natural, no powers or angels. These miserable people have labored in vain.

The eucharist is Jesus. In Syriac it is called *pharisatha*, which means "that which is spread out." For Jesus came to crucify the world.

The master went into the dye works of Levi, took seventy-two colored cloths, and threw them into a vat. He drew them out and they all were white. He said, "So the son of humanity has come as a dyer."

Wisdom, who is called barren, is the Mother of the angels.

The companion of the [Savior] is Mary of Magdala. The [Savior loved] her more than [all] the disciples, [and he] kissed her often on her [mouth].

The other [disciples] [64] . . . said to him, "Why do you love her more than all of us?"

The Savior answered and said to them, "Why don't I love you like her? If a blind person and one who can see are both in darkness, they are the same. When the light comes, one who can see will see the light, and the blind person will stay in darkness."

The master said, "Blessed is one who is before coming into being. For whoever is, was and will be."

The superiority of human beings is not apparent to the eye, but lies in what is hidden. Consequently, they are dominant over animals that are stronger than they are and greater in ways apparent and hidden. So animals survive. But when human beings leave them, animals kill and devour each other. Animals have eaten each other because they have found no other food. Now, however, they have food, because humans till the ground.

Anyone who goes down into the water and comes up without receiving anything and says, "I am a Christian," has borrowed the name. But one who receives the Holy Spirit has the name as a gift. A gift does not have to be paid back, but what is borrowed must be paid. This is how it is with us, when one of us experiences a mystery.

Do not fear the flesh and do not love it. If you fear the flesh, it will dominate you. If you love the flesh, it will swallow you up and strangle you.

A person is either in this world or in the resurrection—or in the middle place. May I not be found there! In this world there is good and evil, but the good of the world is not really good and

the evil of the world is not really evil. After this world there is evil that is really evil: this is called the middle. The middle is death. As long as we are in this world, we should acquire resurrection, so that when we take off the flesh we may be found in rest and not wander in the middle. For many go astray on the way.

Truth did not come into the world naked, but in symbols and images. The world cannot receive truth in any other way. There is rebirth and an image of rebirth, and it is by means of this image that one must be reborn. What image is this? It is resurrection. Image must arise through image. By means of this image the bridal chamber and the image must approach the truth. This is restoration.

Those who receive the name of the Father, Son, and Holy Spirit and have accepted them must do this. If someone does not accept them, the name will also be taken from that person. A person receives them in the chrism with the oil of the power of the cross. The apostles called this power the right and the left. This person is no longer a Christian but is Christ.

The master [did] everything in a mystery: baptism, chrism, eucharist, redemption, and bridal chamber.

It is necessary to utter a mystery. The Father of the All united with the virgin who came down, and fire shone on him.

On that day that one revealed the great bridal chamber, and in this way his body came into being.

On that day he came forth from the bridal chamber as one born of a bridegroom and a bride.

So Jesus established all within it, and it is fitting for each of the disciples to enter into his rest.

Adam came from two virgins, the Spirit and the virgin earth. Christ was born of a virgin to correct the fall that occurred in the beginning.

There are two trees growing in paradise. One produces [animals] and the other produces people. Adam [ate] of the tree that produces animals, and [he] became an animal and brought forth animals. As a result Adam's children worship animals. The tree [whose] fruit [he ate] is the [tree of knowledge, and because of this, sins] increased. [If he had] eaten the [fruit of the other tree], the fruit of [the tree of life, which] produces people, [gods would] worship people. As [in paradise] God created people [that people] [72] might create God, so also in this world people make gods and worship what they have created. It would be more fitting for gods to worship people.

The world came into being through a mistake. The creator wanted to make it incorruptible and immortal, but he failed and did not get what he hoped for. For the world is not incorruptible and the creator of the world is not incorruptible. Things are not incorruptible, but offspring are. Nothing can receive incorruptibility unless it is an offspring. And whatever cannot receive certainly cannot give.

The cup of prayer contains wine and water, for it represents the blood for which thanksgiving is offered. It is full of the Holy Spirit, and it belongs to the completely perfect human. When we drink it, we take to ourselves the perfect human.

The living water is a body, and we must put on the living human. Thus, when one is about to go down into the water, one strips in order to put on the living human.

As long as the seed of the Holy Spirit is hidden, wickedness is ineffective, though it is not yet removed from the midst of the seed, and they are still enslaved to evil. But when the seed is revealed, then perfect light will shine on everyone, and all who are in the light will [receive the] chrism. Then slaves will be freed and captives ransomed. "Every plant that my Father in heaven has not planted [will be] pulled out." What is separated will be united, [what is empty] will be filled.

Everyone who [enters] the bedchamber will kindle the [light. This is] like marriages that occur [in secret and] take place at night. The light of the fire [shines] [86] during the night and then goes out. The mysteries of that marriage, however, are performed in the day and the light, and neither that day nor its light ever sets.

If someone becomes an attendant of the bridal chamber, that person will receive the light. If one does not receive it while here in this place, one cannot receive it in the other place.

Those who receive the light cannot be seen or grasped. Nothing can trouble such people even while they are living in this world. And when they leave this world, they have already received truth through images, and the world has become the eternal realm. To these people the eternal realm is Fullness.

This is the way it is. It is revealed to such a person alone, hidden not in darkness and night but hidden in perfect day and holy light.

The Gospel According to Philip

THOMASINES

A number of books from the early Christian tradition are connected with a figure known as Didymus Judas Thomas. The word *didymus* means "twin" in Greek; so too the name "Thomas" means "twin" in Aramaic. And so this person is Judas, or Jude, the twin. But the twin of whom? In our earliest surviving Gospel, Jesus himself is said to have a brother who is named Jude (for example, Mark 6). And in later traditions, especially from Syria, this Jude was thought to have been a twin of Jesus himself. In fact, in some traditions—including the Acts of Thomas that we have already seen (Chapter 2)—Thomas is Jesus' identical twin. How Jesus could have a (mortal) twin if he was born of a virgin is something these traditions never explain.

There appears to have been a range of Christians who especially revered Didymus Judas Thomas. And who better to acclaim the truth among Jesus' earthly associates than his own identical twin brother? Several of these books share important views and concerns, making it appear that these Thomasine Christians may have been their own Christian group, sharing key theological views and accepting various literary texts associated with Thomas.

Among these texts would be the Gospel of Thomas, given elsewhere here (see selection 43); the Acts of Thomas, also given elsewhere (see selection 48); a beautiful poem called the "Hymn of the Pearl," embedded in these Acts of Thomas; and a book discovered among the Nag Hammadi library called the Book of Thomas the Contender, or sometimes simply the Book of Thomas.

It is debated whether any or all of these books should be considered "Gnostic." Many scholars today think that the answer is no, but it must be admitted that there is at least a Gnostic-like quality about these writings. They certainly do not narrate any of the complex Gnostic myths, as can be found among Sethian writings such as the Secret Book of John. If the narration of these myths is what makes a book Gnostic, then obviously the Thomasine literature does not qualify. On the other hand, these Thomasine writings do seem to presuppose a mythological understanding of the world which, without all the complexities of the developed Gnostic systems that we read elsewhere, has in broad outline many fundamental parallels with and similarities to the Gnostic myths.

These books, for example, understand that the real human is a being that has come from another realm into this world, and that it has been trapped here in the realm of matter. Being here, in the human body, is like being drunk or forgetful—out of touch with reality. The real person needs to escape this entrapment in the body by becoming sober again, wakeful, and alert. This can happen when the person comes to the gnosis—the knowledge—of the truth, as revealed, for example, by Christ. And part of this salvation by gnosis comes through the practice of rigorous asceticism, the rejection of the pleasures of the flesh. These are all themes that would have resonated with Gnostic Christians, and so it may be that even if this Thomasine literature was not generated by Gnostics and for Gnostics, it would have easily been amenable to Gnostic understandings of the world. This may be why two of these Thomasine writings were included among the treatises of the Nag Hammadi library, most of which are more clearly Gnostic in their orientation.

THE TEXTS

31. The Hymn of the Pearl

One of the most elegant compositions of early Christianity, the "Hymn of the Pearl" is embedded in the third-century Acts of Thomas (see Chapter 2). Most scholars agree, however, that the hymn was composed by a different hand and at an earlier date. On the surface, it appears to be a simple folktale of a prince sent by his royal parents on a mission to snatch a pearl from the lair of a ravenous dragon in Egypt, only to arrive at his destination and forget his task and his identity, needing a message from the royal court to be saved from his torpor. When he then remembers who he is, he seizes the pearl and returns to the glories of his father's realm.

The hymn may be something far more than a simple folktale, however. Hints within the text itself—such as the "knowledge" (literally "gnosis") intrinsic to the prince's heavenly garment (I. 88)—along with parallels to other literature suggest, in fact, that the story represents a Gnostic allegory of the incarnation of the soul, which enjoys a glorious heavenly existence ("my father's palace") from which it descends (to "Egypt") to become entrapped in matter ("clothed myself in garments like theirs"). Forgetting whence it came, the soul eventually relearns its true nature from a divine emissary. When it awakens to its true identity ("son of kings"), it returns to its heavenly home where it receives the full knowledge of itself.

108 1 When I was a little child, in my father's palace,

2 And enjoyed the wealth and luxury of those who nurtured me,

3 My parents equipped me with provisions and sent me out from the East, our homeland.

4 From the wealth of our treasury they gave me a great burden,

5 Which was light so that I could carry it by myself:

6 Gold from the land above, silver from great treasuries,

7 And stones, chalcedonies of India and agates from Kushan.

8 And they girded me with steel,

9 And they took away from me the garment set with gems and spangled with gold

Which they had made out of love for me

10 And the yellow robe which was made for my size,

11 And they made a covenant with me

And wrote it in my mind that I might not forget:

12 "If you go down to Egypt and bring the one pearl

13 Which is in the land of the devouring serpent,

14 You shall put on again that garment set with stones and the robe which lies over it,

The Hymn of the Pearl, from *The Apocryphal New Testament*, ed. J. K. Elliott. © Oxford University Press, 1993. Reprinted by permission of Oxford University Press.

15 And with your brother, our next in command, you shall be a herald for our kingdom."

16 So I departed from the East on a difficult and frightening road led by two guides,

17 And I was very young to travel on it.

18 I passed over the borders of the Mosani, where there is the meeting-place of the merchants of the East,

19 And reached the land of the Babylonians.

20 I went down to Egypt, and my companions parted from me.

21 I went straight to the serpent and stayed near his den

22 Until he should slumber and sleep, so that I might take the pearl from him.

23 Being alone I altered my appearance and seemed an alien even to my own people,

24 But I saw one of my kinsmen there, a freeborn man from the East,

25 A youth fair and beautiful, the son of courtiers.

26 He came and kept me company.

27 And I made him my intimate friend, a comrade with whom I communicated my business.

28 Being exhorted to guard against the Egyptians and against partaking of unclean things,

29 I clothed myself in garments like theirs, so that I would not be seen as a stranger

30 And as one who had come from abroad to take the pearl,
Lest the Egyptians might arouse the serpent against me.

31 But somehow they learned that I was not their countryman.

32 They dealt with me treacherously, and I tasted their food.

33 I no longer recognized that I was a king's son, and I served their king.

34 I forgot the pearl for which my parents had sent me.

35 And I fell into a deep sleep because of the heaviness of their food.

110 **36** While I was suffering these things my parents were aware of it and grieved over me.

37 And a proclamation was heralded in our kingdom that all should present themselves at our doors.

38 The kings of Parthia and those in office, and the great men of the East

39 Resolved that I should not be left in Egypt.

40 So the courtiers wrote me a letter:

41 "From your father the king of kings and your mother, the mistress of the East

42 And their brothers, who are second to us, To our son in Egypt, greetings!

43 Awake, and rise from your sleep.

44 Listen to the words in this letter,
Remember you are the son of kings,
You have fallen beneath the yoke of slavery.

45 Remember your gold-spangled garment,

46 Recall the pearl for which you were sent to Egypt,

47 Your name has been called to the book of life,

48 Together with that of your brother whom you have received in our kingdom."

111 **49** And the king sealed it to make it an ambassador,

50 Because of the wicked Babylonian children and the tyrannical demons of the Labyrinth.

53 I rose from sleep when I recognized its voice,

54 I took it up and kissed it and I read.

55 And what was written concerned that which was engraved on my heart.

56 And I immediately remembered that I was a son of kings and that my freedom demanded my people.

57 I remembered the pearl for which I had been sent to Egypt,

58 And the fact that I had come to snatch it from the terrifying serpent.

59 I subdued it by calling out my father's name,

61 And I snatched the pearl and turned about to go to my parents.

62 And I took off the dirty clothing and left it behind in their land.

63 And directed my way forthwith to the light of our Eastern home.

64 And on the road I found a female who lifted me up.

65 She awakened me, giving me an oracle with her voice, and guided me to the light.

66 The Royal silken garment shone before my eyes.

68 And with familial love leading me and drawing me on

69 I passed by the Labyrinth,
And leaving Babylon behind on the left,

70 I reached Meson which is a great coast.

112

75 But I could not recall my splendor, For it had been when I was still a child and quite young that I had left it behind in my father's palace.

76 But, when suddenly I saw my garment reflected as in a mirror,

77 I perceived in it my whole self as well
And through it I knew and saw myself.

78 For though we originated from the one and the same we were partially divided,
Then again we were one, with a single form.

79 The treasurers too who had brought the garment

80 I saw as two beings, but there existed a single form in both,
One royal symbol consisting of two halves.

81 And they had my money and wealth in their hands and gave me my reward:

82 The fine garment of glorious colors,

83 Which was embroidered with gold, precious stones, and pearls to give a good appearance.

84 It was fastened at the collar.

86 And the image of the King of Kings was all over it.

87 Stones of lapis lazuli had been skillfully fixed to the collar,

88 And I saw in turn that motions of knowledge were stirring throughout it,

89 And that it was prepared to speak.

90 Then I heard it speak:

91 "It is I who belong to the one who is stronger than all people and for whose sake I was written about by the father himself."

92 And I took note of my stature,

93 And all the royal feelings rested on me as its energy increased.

94 Thrust out by his hand the garment hastened to me as I went to receive it,

95 And a longing aroused me to rush and meet it and to receive it.

96 And I stretched out and took it and adorned myself with the beauty of its colors.

97 And I covered myself completely with my royal robe over it.

98 When I had put it on I ascended to the land of peace and homage.

99 And I lowered my head and prostrated myself before the splendor of the father who had sent it to me.

100 For it was I who had obeyed his commands
And it was I who had also kept the promise,

101 And I mingled at the doors of his ancient royal building.

102 He took delight in me and received me in his palace.

103 All his subjects were singing hymns with harmonious voices.

104 He allowed me also to be admitted to the doors of the king himself,

105 So that with my gifts and the pearl I might appear before the king himself.

32. The Book of Thomas

The Book of Thomas, a tractate discovered among the Nag Hammadi library, is difficult to date, with some scholars placing it at the of the second century and others as late as the fourth. There is no question that it stands firmly within the Thomasine tradition. The book begins with words reminiscent of the Gospel of Thomas (see Chapter 8), speaking of "the secret words that the savior spoke to Judas Thomas." Even more than the Gospel, though, Thomas's relationship with Jesus is spelled out. Jesus calls him his "brother" as well as his "twin and true friend."

The first two-fifths of the text are a dialogue between Jesus and Thomas; the final portion is a monologue delivered by Jesus. The overarching emphasis of the book is the need to lead an ascetic life, not controlled by the passions of the flesh that can ruin the soul. This anti-fleshly message fits well within some kind of Gnostic context, and there are other clear Gnostic connections here, as, for example, it refers to the Pleroma and archon (ruler) in charge of this world. The book is even more obviously connected with Platonic thinking, with its emphasis on the need to set the soul free from bodily appetites.

One of the overarching images of the text involves "fire"—specifically the fire that burns within human bodies and makes them deranged in the soul. This fire is the bodily passions. Those who do not come to the truth—presumably those outside the author's community of like-minded, ascetically-driven Christians—will be forever burned by this fire and blinded to the true nature of reality.

The Book of Thomas

The hidden sayings that the Savior spoke to Judas Thomas, which I, Mathaias, in turn recorded. I was walking, listening to them speak with each other.

The Savior said, "Brother Thomas, while you are still in the world, listen to me and I shall reveal to you what you have thought about in your heart.

"Since it is said that you are my twin and true friend, examine yourself and understand who you are, how you exist, and how you will come to be. Since you are to be called my brother, it is not fitting for you to be ignorant of yourself. And I know that you have understood, for already you have understood that I am the knowledge of truth. So while you are walking with me, though you do lack understanding, already you have obtained knowledge and you will be called one who knows himself. For those who have not known themselves have known nothing, but those who have known themselves already have acquired knowledge about the depth of the All. So then, my brother Thomas, you have seen what is hidden from people, what they stumble against in their ignorance."

Thomas said to the master, "That is why I beg you to tell me what I ask before your ascension. When I hear from you about what is hidden, I can speak of it. And it is clear to me that the truth is difficult to accomplish before people."

The Book of Thomas, reproduced from Marvin Meyer, *The Nag Hammadi Scriptures*. San Francisco: HarperOne, 2007. Used with permission of HarperOne.

The Savior answered and said, "If what is visible to you is obscure to you, how can you comprehend what is invisible? If deeds of truth visible in the world are difficult for you to accomplish, how will you accomplish things of the exalted majesty and fullness, which are invisible? How will you be called workers? You are beginners and have not attained the greatness of perfection."

Thomas answered and said to the Savior, "Tell us about these things that you say are invisible and hidden from us."

The Savior said, "[All] bodies [have come into being in the same irrational way] that animals are produced, and so they are visible, as [creatures lusting after creatures]. Those that are above, however, [do not exist like] those that are visible. Rather, [they] live [139] from their own root, and their crops nourish them. But the visible bodies feed on creatures that are like them, and so the bodies are subject to change. Whatever is subject to change will perish and be lost, and henceforth has no hope of life, because this body is an animal body. Just as an animal body perishes, these modeled forms also will perish. Are they not from sexual intercourse like that of the animals? If the body too is from intercourse, how will it give birth to anything different from them? So, then, you are children until you become perfect."

Thomas answered, "This is why I say to you, master, those who speak about what is invisible and difficult to explain are like people who shoot their arrows at a target during the night. Of course, they shoot their arrows as any people do, since they are shooting at the target, but it is not visible. When light comes, however, and banishes darkness, then the accomplishment of each person will be clear. And you, our light, bring enlightenment, master."

Jesus said, "It is through light that light exists."

Thomas spoke and said, "Master, why does this visible light that shines for people rise and set?"

The Savior said, "Blessed Thomas, surely this visible light has shone for you not to keep you here, but that you might leave. And when all the chosen ones lay down their animal nature, this light will withdraw up to its being, and its being will welcome it to itself, because the light is a good helper."

The Savior continued and said, "Oh, unsearchable love of light! Oh, bitterness of the fire! You blaze in the bodies of people and in the marrow of their bones, blazing in them night and day, burning their limbs and [making] their minds drunk and their souls deranged. [You dominate] males and females day and night; you move [and arouse] them secretly and visibly. When the males are [aroused, they are attracted to the] females and the females to the males. That is why it is said [140] that everyone who seeks truth from true wisdom will fashion wings to fly, fleeing from the passion that burns human spirits. And one will fashion wings to flee from every visible spirit."

Thomas answered and said, "Master, this is precisely what I ask you, since I understand that you are beneficial to us through what you say."

Again the Savior answered and said, "This is why we must speak to you, because this is the teaching for the perfect. If you wish to become perfect, keep these sayings. If not, the name for you is 'ignorant,' since an intelligent person cannot associate with a fool. The intelligent person is perfect in all wisdom, but to the fool good and evil are the same. The wise person will be nourished by truth, and will be like a tree growing by the stream of water. Some people have wings but rush toward visible things that are far from truth. The fire that guides them gives them an illusion of truth. It will shine on them with a perishable beauty, and it will imprison them in dark delight and capture them in sweet-smelling pleasure. And it will make them blind with insatiable desire, inflame their souls, and be like a stake that is jammed into their heart and can never be removed. Like a bit in the mouth, it leads them according to its own wish.

"It has bound them with its chains, and tied all their limbs with the bitterness of the bondage of desire for those visible things that perish and change and fluctuate impulsively. They have always been drawn downward. When they are slain, they are drawn to all the animals of corruption."

Thomas answered and said, "It is clear and has been said that [many are] . . . those who do not know . . . soul."

[The Savior] answered and said, "[Blessed] is the wise person who has [sought truth, and] when it has been found, has rested [141] upon it forever, and has not been afraid of those who wish to trouble him."

Thomas answered and said, "Master, is it beneficial for us to rest among our own?"

The Savior said, "Yes, it is useful, and it is good for you, since the things visible among people will pass away. For the vessel of their flesh will pass away, and when it disintegrates, it will come to be among visible things, among things that can be seen. The visible fire gives them pain, because of the love of faith they once had. They will be gathered back to the visible realm. Moreover, among the invisible things, those who can see will perish, without the first love, in their concern for this life and the burning of the fire. There is only a little time before what is visible will pass away. Then shapeless phantoms will come and dwell forever in the midst of the tombs on corpses, in pain and destruction of soul."

Thomas answered and said, "What can we say in the face of these things? What shall we say to those who are blind? What teaching shall we give those miserable mortals who say, 'We have come to [do] good and not to curse,' and will [say] further, 'If we had not been born in the flesh, we would not have known iniquity'?"

The Savior said, "To tell the truth, do not think of these as human beings, but regard them [as] animals. As animals devour each other, so people like this devour each other. They are deprived of the kingdom, since they love the delight of fire and are slaves of death and rush to deeds of corruption. They fulfill the desire of their parents. They will be cast down into the abyss and be afflicted by the compulsion of the bitterness of

their evil nature. They will be whipped to drive them down to a place they do not know, and they will leave their limbs behind, not with fortitude but with despair. And they rejoice in [the fire, they love] madness and derangement, because they are [fools]. They pursue derangement, not realizing their madness but thinking they are wise. They . . . the love of their body . . . , [142] their hearts turning to themselves and their thoughts being on their affairs. But fire will consume them."

Thomas answered and said, "Master, what can one cast down to them do? I am very concerned about them, for many oppose them."

The Savior answered and said, "What is evident to you?"

Judas, called Thomas, said, "Master, you should speak and I should listen."

The Savior answered, "Listen to what I tell you and believe the truth. What sows and what is sown will pass away in their fire, in fire and water, and will be hidden in tombs of darkness. And after a long time the fruit of evil trees will appear and be punished and slain in the mouths of animals and people through the agency of the rains, the winds, the air, and the light shining above."

Thomas answered, "You certainly have convinced us, master. We realize in our hearts it is clearly so, and your word is not meager. But these sayings that you tell us are laughable and ridiculous to the world, since they are not understood. How can we go forth and preach them when we are [not] respected in the world?"

The Savior answered and said, "I tell you the truth, whoever listens to [your] word and turns away or sneers at it or smirks at these things, I tell you the truth, that person will be handed over to the ruler who is on high, who rules as king over all the powers, and the ruler will turn him away and cast him down from on high into the abyss, and he will be imprisoned in a cramped, dark place. So he cannot turn or move because of the great depth of Tartaros and the [burdensome bitterness] of

Hades. Whoever relies on what [is brought] to him . . . will not be forgiven [his] madness, but will [be judged. Whoever has] persecuted you will be handed over to the angel Tartarouchos, [who has flaming] fire that pursues them, [143] and fiery whips that spew forth sparks into the face of one pursued. If he flees to the west, he finds fire. If he turns south, he finds it there as well. If he turns north, the threat of erupting fire meets him again. Nor can he find the way to the east, to flee there and be saved, for he did not find it while embodied so as to find it on the day of judgment."

Then the Savior continued and said, "Woe to you, godless people, who have no hope, who are secure in things that do not last.

"Woe to you who hope in the flesh and in the prison that will perish. How long will you sleep and think that what is imperishable will also perish? Your hope is based upon the world, and your god is this present life. You are destroying your souls.

"Woe to you with the fire that burns within you. It is insatiable.

"Woe to you because of the wheel that turns in your minds.

"Woe to you because of the smoldering within you. It will devour your flesh visibly, tear your souls secretly, and prepare you for each other.

"Woe to you, prisoners, for you are bound in caves. You laugh, you rejoice in mad laughter. You do not perceive your destruction. Neither do you perceive your plight, nor have you understood that you dwell in darkness and death. Rather, you are drunk with fire and [full] of bitterness. Your hearts are deranged because of the smoldering within you, and the poison and blows of your enemies are a delight to you. Darkness has risen in you like the light, for you have surrendered your freedom to slavery. You have darkened your hearts and surrendered your minds to foolishness. You have filled your minds with the smoke of the fire within you, and your light has been hidden in the [dark] cloud. You [love] the garment you wear, [although it is filthy], and you have been gripped

[by] non-existent hope. [You have] believed in what you do [not] know. You all live in [bondage] but pride yourselves [in your freedom]. [144] You have baptized your souls in the water of darkness. You have pursued your own wishes.

"Woe to you who dwell in error, not seeing that the light of the sun, which judges the universe and looks down on the universe, will encircle everything to make slaves of the enemies. Nor do you perceive how the moon looks down night and day, seeing the bodies of your slaughters.

"Woe to you who love intercourse and filthy association with the female.

"And woe to you because of the powers of your bodies, for they will mistreat you.

"Woe to you because of the actions of the evil demons.

"Woe to you who entice your limbs with fire. Who will sprinkle a restful dew on you, to extinguish the many fires within you, and your burning? Who will make the sun shine on you, to dispel the darkness within you and hide the darkness and filthy water?

"The sun and the moon will give a fragrant aroma to you, as will the air, the spirit, the earth, and the water. If the sun does not shine on these bodies, they will rot and perish just like weeds or grass. If the sun shines on them, they grow strong and choke the grapevine. But if the grapevine becomes strong and casts its shadow over the weeds and all the rest of the brush growing with it, and [spreads] and fills out, it alone inherits the land where it grows, and dominates wherever it has cast its shadow. So when it grows, it dominates the whole land, and it is productive for its master and pleases him greatly. He would have gone to great pains because of the weeds before pulling them out, but the grapevine by itself disposed of them and choked them, and they died and became like earth."

Then Jesus continued and said to them, "Woe to you, for you have not accepted the teaching, and those who [wish to accept it] will suffer when they preach. [You will persecute them], but you will rush into [your own traps]. You will cast them down [to the lions] and put them to death, daily, [145] and they will rise from death.

"Blessed are you who understand beforehand the temptations and flee from things that are alien.

"Blessed are you who are mocked and are not respected because of the love your master has for you.

"Blessed are you who weep and are oppressed by those who have no hope, for you will be released from all bondage.

"Watch and pray that you may not remain in the flesh, but that you may leave the bondage of the bitterness of this life. And when you pray, you will find rest, for you have left pain and reproach behind. When you leave the pains and the passions of the body, you will receive rest from the Good One. You will reign with the King, you united with him and he with you, from now on and forever. Amen."

The Book of Thomas

The Contender Writing to the Perfect

Remember me also, my brothers, in your prayers. Peace be with the holy and the spiritual.

OTHER GNOSTIC TEXTS

As we have seen, scholars over the past two decades have come to realize that Gnosticism was an inordinately complex and messy set of religious traditions and practices. In some ways it is very convenient, but completely misleading, to categorize all Gnostics as Sethians, Valentinians, and Thomasines. Just as Christianity itself has a mind-boggling range of variant groups supporting divergent beliefs and practices—yet all of them in some way or another cohering enough to warrant labeling them "Christian"—so too with Gnosticism.

Some of the texts discovered at Nag Hammadi library do not fit neatly into the narrow confines of Sethian, Valentinian, or Thomasine texts, yet they share many of the same concerns. In particular, there are texts that recount myths about the rise of the divine realm, the creation of the material world, and the beginning of the human race that do not contain many of the most salient features of the specifically Sethian myths. They may talk about divine Sophia or the creator God Yaldabaoth, for example, but they make no reference to the distinctively Sethian concept of the four luminaries: Harmozel, Oroiael, Daueithai, and Eleleth. And so these texts are not Sethian (and certainly not Valentinian or Thomasine), and yet they are very much aligned with Sethian understandings of the world and the human's place in it.

These various texts do not cohere particularly well with one another either, so that they do not represent yet another Gnostic school of thought. And so it is perhaps better simply to say that they represent "Other Gnostic" views or that they are "Gnostic-like" in their concerns, views, and myths. Here we will see two such documents that can give a sense of what non-Sethian Gnostic myth can look like.

THE TEXTS

33. On the Origin of the World

This Nag Hammadi tractate is not provided with a title in its manuscript; modern scholars have called it "On the Origin of the World" simply as a precise summation of its contents. Evidently speaking to outsiders, its unknown author explains in involved and intricate detail a Gnostic view of how the world came into being. The account is largely based on an imaginative exposition of the opening chapters of Genesis, in which

On the Origin of the World, reproduced from Marvin Meyer, *The Nag Hammadi Scriptures*. San Francisco: HarperOne, 2007. Used with permission of HarperOne.

a number of the gaps of the narrative (including the events that transpired before Genesis 1:1) are filled in. Many important aspects of Gnostic mythology are covered here: the existence of the divine Pleroma before all things, the emergence of Yaldabaoth the creator God, his generation of other divine beings, the creation of the material world, and the formation of the human race. The following excerpt gives approximately two-thirds of the treatise, from its beginning through the creation of Adam.

Scholars debate the dating of the work; possibly it was written near the end of the third century.

On the Origin of the World

Since everyone, both the gods of the world and people, says that nothing existed before chaos, I shall prove they all are wrong, because they do not know the [origin] of chaos or its root. Here [is the] proof.

Although certainly [98] people in general are [inclined] to say that chaos is darkness, in actuality chaos comes from a shadow, and it is the shadow that has been called darkness. The shadow comes from something that has existed from the beginning, and so it is obvious that something in the beginning existed before chaos came into being, and chaos came after what was in the beginning.

Let us consider the facts of the matter, and particularly what was in the beginning, from which chaos came. In this way will the truth be clearly demonstrated.

After the world of the immortals was brought to completion out of the infinite, a being with this likeness, called Sophia, flowed from Pistis. This being expressed its wish that it come to resemble the first light, and at once its wish appeared as a heavenly likeness with an incomprehensible greatness. This being came to be between the immortals and what came after them, like what is above, and Sophia served as a veil separating humanity from the things above.

The aeon of truth has no shadow <within> it because infinite light shines everywhere within it. There is a shadow, however, outside it, and the shadow has been called darkness. From the shadow appeared a power set over the darkness, and the powers that came afterward called the shadow limitless chaos. From it [every] sort of deity

emerged, [one after] another, along with the whole world. So [the shadow] came after [99] something that existed in the beginning, and then it became visible. The abyss also came from Pistis, whom we have mentioned.

The shadow sensed that there was one stronger than it. It was jealous, and when it became pregnant by itself, all of a sudden it gave birth to envy. Since then the principle of envy has appeared in all the aeons and their worlds. But envy turned out to be an aborted fetus, without any spirit in it, and it came into being as a shadow in an expanse of watery substance. Bitter wrath came into being from the shadow and was cast into a region of chaos.

Since that day watery substance has been visible. What lurked in the shadow flowed out and appeared in chaos. Just as all the afterbirth of a woman who gives birth to a baby flows out, so also the matter that came into being from the shadow was cast out. Matter did not come out of chaos; it was in chaos, in a region of chaos.

After these things happened, Pistis came and appeared over chaotic matter, which had been expelled like an aborted fetus, without any spirit in it. For chaos is all limitless darkness and unfathomable water. When Pistis saw what came into being from her deficiency, she was disturbed. And her disturbance appeared as something frightful, and it fled to her in the chaos. She turned to it and [blew] into its face in the abyss, [100] below all of the heavens.

When Pistis Sophia wanted to cause this thing with no spirit to be made into a likeness of the divine and rule over matter and all its powers, for the first time an archon appeared, out of the waters, lionlike in appearance, androgynous, with great authority in himself but ignorant of where he came from.

When Pistis Sophia saw him moving in the depth of the waters, she said to him, "Young man, move over here," which is the meaning of Yaldabaoth.

Since then the faculty of speech has come to expression, and the faculty of speech pertains to the gods, angels, and people. The gods, angels, and people have brought to completion what has come into being by means of the word.

The ruler Yaldabaoth is ignorant of the power of Pistis. He did not see her face, but in the water he saw the likeness that spoke to him, and from that voice he called himself Yaldabaoth. Those who are perfect call him Ariael, because he is like a lion.

After Yaldabaoth assumed authority over matter, Pistis Sophia withdrew up to her light.

When the ruler saw his greatness, he saw only himself and nothing else except water and darkness. He thought that only he existed. His [thought] was completed by means of the word, and it [101] appeared as a Spirit moving to and fro over the waters. When the Spirit appeared, the ruler separated the watery substance to one region and the dry substance to another region. From matter the ruler created for himself a dwelling place and called it heaven, and from matter he created a footstool and called it earth.

After this the ruler had a thought in accordance with his nature, and he created an androgynous being by means of the word. He opened his mouth and cooed to him. The child opened his eyes and saw his father, and he said to him, "EE," so his father called him Yao.

The ruler created a second son and cooed to him. The child opened his eyes and said to his father, "EH," so his father called him Eloai.

The ruler created a third son and cooed to him. The child opened his eyes and said to his father, "AS," so his father called him Astaphaios.

These are the three sons of their father.

Seven androgynous beings appeared in chaos, and they have masculine names and feminine names.

Yaldabaoth's feminine name is forethought, Sambathas, which designates the week.
His son is called Yao, and his feminine name is mastery.
Sabaoth's feminine name is divinity.
Adonaios's feminine name is kingship.
Eloaios's feminine name is envy.
Oraios's feminine name is wealth.
Astaphaios's feminine name [102] is Sophia.

These are the [seven] powers of the seven heavens of [chaos].

The powers were androgynous in accordance with the immortal pattern that existed before them and the will of Pistis, so that the likeness of what was from the beginning might have power to the end.

You will find the function of the masculine names and powers in the *Archangelic Book of Moses the Prophet*. The feminine names are in the *First Book of Noraia*.

Since the chief creator Yaldabaoth had great authorities at his disposal, he created beautiful heavens, by means of the word, as dwelling places for each of his sons, and in each heaven he created great glories, seven times glorious. Each son has within his heaven thrones, mansions, temples, chariots, virgin spirits, and their glories, extending up to an invisible realm, as well as armies of divine, lordly, angelic, and archangelic powers, myriads without number, so they might serve.

You will find a precise account of this in the *First Discourse of Oraia*.

Everything was completed in this <way> up to the sixth heaven, the heaven of Sophia.

This heaven and earth were disrupted by the troublemaker who was beneath them all. The six heavens shook, for the powers of chaos did not know who had disturbed the heaven beneath them. When Pistis found out about the harm caused by the troublemaker, she blew her breath, and she [bound him] and cast him down to Tartaros.

[Since then] heaven and [103] earth have established themselves through Sophia, who is the daughter of Yaldabaoth and is beneath them all.

After the heavens, their powers, and their entire government were established, the chief creator exalted himself, and he was glorified by the whole army of angels. All the gods and their angels praised and glorified him.

He was delighted. He boasted over and over again and said to them, "I don't need anything."

He said, "I am God, and there is no other but me."

When he said this, he sinned against all the immortals who speak forth, and they watched him carefully.

When Pistis saw the impiety of the supreme ruler, she became angry. Without being seen, she said, "You are wrong, Samael"—which means "blind god." "An enlightened, immortal human exists before you and will appear within the forms you have shaped. The human will trample upon you as potter's clay is trampled, and you will descend with those who are yours to your mother the abyss. And when your work comes to an end, all the deficiency that appeared from truth will be dissolved. It will cease to be, and it will be like what never was."

After Pistis said this, she revealed the likeness of her greatness in the waters, and then she withdrew up to her light.

When Sabaoth son of Yaldabaoth heard the voice of Pistis, he sang songs of praise to her, but he condemned his father [and mother] [104] on account of the word of Pistis. He glorified her because she told them about the immortal human and the light of the human. Pistis Sophia pointed her finger and poured over him light from her light, as condemnation of his father. When Sabaoth was enlightened, he received great authority over all of the powers of chaos, and since then he has been called "lord of the powers."

He hated his father, who is darkness, and his mother, who is the abyss. He loathed his sister, who is the thought of the chief creator and who moves to and fro over the waters.

All of the authorities of chaos were jealous of Sabaoth because of his light. They were upset, and they waged a great war in the seven heavens.

When Pistis Sophia saw the war, she sent seven archangels to Sabaoth from her light. The archangels carried him up to the seventh heaven and stood in his presence as his attendants. Then she sent three more archangels to him and established his kingdom above everyone, so that he might dwell above the twelve gods of chaos.

When Sabaoth occupied the place of rest because of his repentance, Pistis also gave him her daughter Zoe, with great authority, so that she might tell him about everything in the eighth heaven. And since he had authority, he first made himself a mansion. It is immense, magnificent, seven times as great as all the mansions in the seven heavens.

In front of [105] his mansion he created a large throne on a chariot with four faces, called cherubim. The cherubim throne has eight figures on each side of the four corners, figures of lions, bulls, humans, and eagles, and there are a total of sixty-four figures. Seven archangels stand before the throne. Sabaoth is the eighth, and he has authority, and so there are seventy-two figures in all. From this chariot the seventy-two gods took shape, so that they might rule over the languages of the seventy-two nations. Beside that throne he created other, serpentlike angels called seraphim, who glorify him unceasingly.

Then he created a congregation of angels, thousands, myriads without number, which was like the congregation in the eighth heaven. He also created a firstborn called Israel—that is, "the person who sees God"—and he created another being called Jesus Christ, who is like the Savior above in the eighth heaven and who sits at the right of Sabaoth on a remarkable throne. At his left the virgin of the holy Spirit sits upon a throne and glorifies him. Seven virgins stand before her, with thirty harps and lyres and [106] trumpets in their hands, and they glorify him. All the armies of angels glorify and praise him.

Sabaoth sits on a throne covered by a great light cloud. No one was with him in the cloud except Sophia daughter of Pistis, and she taught him about all the things in the eighth heaven, so that what resembles these things might be created and his reign might last until the end of the heavens of chaos and their powers.

Pistis Sophia moved him away from the darkness and summoned him to her right, and she put the chief creator at her left. Since then right has been called justice and left has been called injustice. They all received a realm in the congregation of justice, and injustice is set over all their creations.

When the chief creator of chaos saw his son Sabaoth amid the glory in which he dwells, and recognized that he was the greatest of all the authorities of chaos, he was jealous of him. He was angry, and he engendered death from his own death. Death was established over the sixth heaven, for Sabaoth had been carried away from there. So the complete number of the six authorities of chaos was realized.

Since death was androgynous, he had sex with himself and produced seven androgynous children. These are the names of the males: envy, wrath, tears, sighs, grief, lament, tearful groans. These are the names of the females: anger, pain, lust, sighs, curses, bitterness, strife. They had sex with each other, and each one conceived seven children, so that the children total [107] forty-nine androgynous demons.

You will find their names and functions in the *Book of Solomon*.

In the presence of these, Zoe, who dwells with Sabaoth, created seven good androgynous powers. These are the names of the males: the one not jealous, the blessed, the joyful, the true, the one not envious, the beloved, the faithful. These are the names of the females: peace, gladness, joyfulness, blessedness, truth, love, faith. Many good and pure spirits come from these powers.

You will find their accomplishments and functions in the *Configurations of the Fate of Heaven Beneath the Twelve*.

When the chief creator saw the reflection of Pistis in the waters, he was deeply distressed, especially when he heard her voice, which was like the first voice that called to him out of the waters.

When he knew that she was the one who gave him his name, he groaned. He was ashamed because of his transgression. And when he knew for certain that an enlightened, immortal human existed before him, he was greatly disturbed, because earlier he had said to all the gods and their angels, "I am God; there is no other but me." For he feared that they might know another existed before him and condemn him.

But the chief creator was a fool. He had contempt for condemnation and acted rashly, and he said, "If [108] anything existed before me, let it appear so that we may see its light."

And at once, look, light shone out of the eighth heaven above and passed through all the heavens of the earth.

When the chief creator saw that the light was beautiful as it shone forth, he was amazed and very much ashamed. The light appeared and a human likeness was visible within it, and it was marvelous. No one saw it except the chief creator and Forethought, who was with him. But its light was visible to all the powers of the heavens, and so they all were disturbed by it.

When Forethought saw this messenger of light, she fell in love with him, but he hated her because she was in darkness. She desired to mate with him, but she was not able. When she was unable to satisfy her desire, she poured out her light upon the earth.

Since then this messenger has been called Adam of light, which means "the enlightened person of blood." The earth upon <which the light of Forethought> spread was called holy Adamas, which means "the holy adamantine earth."

From that time on all the authorities have honored the blood of the virgin, and the earth was purified because of the blood of the virgin.

Further, the water was purified by the reflection of Pistis Sophia, who had appeared to the chief creator in the waters. Rightly has it been said, "through the waters." Since the holy water gives life to all, [109] it purifies all.

Out of this first blood Eros appeared. Eros is androgynous. His masculine side is Himeros, because he is fire from the light, and his feminine side is a soul of blood from the substance of Fore-thought. He is extremely handsome in appearance, and more attractive than all the creatures of chaos.

When all the gods and their angels saw Eros, they fell in love with him. He appeared within them all and made them burn with desire. Just as many lamps are lit from a single lamp and all the light is the same but the light of the single lamp is not diminished, so also Eros was dispersed in all the creatures of chaos but was not diminished. Just as Eros appeared in the middle of light and darkness, and the sexual intercourse of Eros was accomplished in the middle of angels and people, so too the first sexual desire sprouted on the earth.

> Woman followed the earth,
> marriage followed woman,
> birth followed marriage,
> decay followed birth.

After Eros, a grapevine sprouted up from the blood that was shed upon the earth, and so those who drink of the fruit of the vine are filled with sexual desire.

After the grapevine, a fig tree and a pome-granate tree sprouted up from the earth, along with the rest of the trees, of every kind, and the seed of the trees came from the [110] semen of the authorities and their angels.

Then justice created paradise. Paradise is beautiful, and is outside the circuit of the moon and the circuit of the sun in the land of pleasure, which is in the east in the rocky region. Desire dwells in the middle of the beautiful, stately trees. The tree of life eternal; as it appeared by the will of God, is in the north of paradise to give immor-tality to the souls of holy people, who will leave their poor modeled bodies at the end of the age. The tree of life looks like the sun, and its branches are lovely. Its leaves are like the leaves of the cy-press, its fruit is like a cluster of white grapes, and its height reaches the sky.

Next to it is the tree of knowledge, which is endowed with the power of God. It is glorious as the moon shining brightly, and its branches are lovely. Its leaves are like fig leaves and its fruit is like a bunch of good, delicious dates. The tree of knowledge is in the north of paradise to arouse the souls from demonic stupor, so that they might come to the tree of life, eat its fruit, and condemn the authorities and their angels.

The impact of this tree is described in the *Holy Book:*

> You are the tree of knowledge,
> which is in paradise,
> from which the first man ate.
> You opened his mind,
> and he loved his female partner
> and condemned [111] other strange figures,
> and he loathed them.

After this the olive tree sprouted, and it was to purify kings and high priests of justice who were to come in the last days. The olive tree ap-peared through the light of the first Adam for the sake of the oil of anointing that kings and high priests would receive.

The first soul, Psyche, loved Eros, who was with her, and she poured her blood upon him and upon the earth. From that blood the first rose sprouted upon the earth, out of a thorn bush, to give joy to the light that would appear in the bramble.

Next beautiful, fragrant flowers of every kind sprouted upon the earth from the blood of each of the virgin daughters of Forethought. They fell in love with Eros and poured their blood upon him and upon the earth.

Next, plants of every kind sprouted upon the earth, and they had the seed of the authorities and their angels within them.

Then the authorities created animals, reptiles, and birds of every kind from the waters, and they had the seed of the authorities and their angels within them.

But before all this, when Adam of light ap-peared on the first day, he remained upon the earth about two days. He left the lower Forethought in heaven and ascended toward his light, and at once darkness covered the whole world. [112]

When she wished, Sophia, who is in the lower heaven, received authority from Pistis and created great heavenly lights and all the stars, and she placed them in the sky to shine upon the earth and designate chronological signs, seasons, years, months, days, nights, moments, and so on. Thus the whole region of the sky was organized.

When Adam of light wished to enter his light, which is the eighth heaven, he could not do so because of the poverty mingled with his light. So he created a great aeon for himself, and in that eternal realm he created six more realms and their worlds, which are six in number and seven times better than the heavens of chaos and their worlds.

All these realms and their worlds are within the boundless region between the eighth heaven and chaos below it, and they are considered part of the world of poverty.

If you want to understand the organization of all these, you will find it described in the *Seventh Cosmos of Hieralias the Prophet*.

Before Adam of light made his return, the authorities saw him in chaos. They laughed at the chief creator because he lied when he said, "I am God; no one exists before me."

When they came to the chief creator, they said, "Is this being not the God who ruined our work?"

He answered and said, "Yes. If you do not want him to be able to ruin our work, come, let's create a human being out of earth in the image of our body and with a likeness [113] to this being, to serve us, so that when this being sees his likeness, he may fall in love with it. Then he will no longer ruin our work, and we shall make the children of the light our slaves for this entire age."

All this happened in accordance with Pistis's forethought, so that humanity might appear in this likeness and condemn the authorities because of their modeled bodies. For their modeled bodies contained the light.

The authorities received knowledge they needed to create humanity. Sophia Zoe, who is with Sabaoth, anticipated them. She laughed at their decision, because they are blind, and they created humanity in ignorance and against their own interests. They did not know what they were doing.

So she anticipated them. She created her own human being first, so that he might tell the modeled bodies of the authorities how to despise them and how to escape them.

The birth of the instructor happened like this. When Sophia let a drop of light fall, it landed on the water, and at once there appeared an androgynous human being. Sophia first made the drop into the form of a female body, and then she took the body and gave it a shape like the Mother who had appeared. She finished it in twelve months.

An androgynous human being was born, whom the Greeks call Hermaphrodite. The Hebrews call the child's mother Eve of life, which means the female instructor of life, and the child born to her is lord. Later the authorities [114] called the child the beast so that it might lead their modeled bodies astray. The meaning of the beast is the instructor, for it turned out to be the wisest of all creatures.

Eve is the first virgin, and she gave birth to her first child without a man. She was her own physician. For this reason she is said to have declared:

I am part of my mother, and I am the mother.
I am the wife, I am the virgin.
I am pregnant, I am the physician,
I am the comforter of birth pains.
My husband produced me, and I am his mother,
and he is my father and lord.
He is my strength,
he speaks of what he wants reasonably.
I am becoming,
but I have given birth to a lordly person.

This was revealed by the will of Sabaoth and his Christ to the souls who were going to enter the modeled bodies of the authorities, about whom the holy voice said, "Flourish and multiply, rule over all creatures." These souls were taken captive, in accordance with their destinies, by the chief creator, and they were locked up in the prisons of the modeled bodies <. . . until> the end of the age.

Then the chief creator voiced his opinion about humankind to those who were with him. Then each of them ejaculated his semen into the middle of the navel of the earth.

Since then the seven archons have formed humanity with a body resembling their own body, but the likeness of humankind reflects the human being who appeared to them. The modeled body came into being, part by part, from each of the rulers, and the leader of the rulers created the brain and marrow.

Afterward the person appeared like the one before him. He became [115] a person with soul, and he was called Adam, which means father, after the name of the one who was before him.

34. The Wisdom of Jesus Christ

The "Wisdom (or Sophia) of Jesus Christ" recounts a discussion between Jesus and his disciples after his resurrection. In it, Jesus responds to the eager questions of his followers about the ultimate nature of reality. This kind of post-resurrection dialogue was a popular form of Gnostic writing; by placing the ultimate revelation of truth to the period after Jesus' life, the author was able to show its hidden, esoteric quality (see the Secret Book of John).

Here Jesus is shown to be a divine aeon, come to reveal the true nature of the Perfect God and Father; of the divine, celestial realm above; of the constitution of humans and of the way of ultimate salvation through perfect knowledge, a salvation that involves a return to the one God in whom the enlightened will repose forever.

This tractate is closely related to another one discovered at Nag Hammadi, usually called "Eugnostos the Blessed." Since Eugnostos does not contain explicitly Christian elements, but is cast as a philosophical letter sent by a teacher to his followers, many scholars think that the "Wisdom of Jesus Christ" represents a later Christianized version of the account, which evidently originated sometime in the second century. (NB: the sequence of the chapter numbers have become confused near the end of this text because it is drawn from two different manuscripts, neither one of which is complete.)

The Wisdom of Jesus Christ

After he rose from the dead, his twelve disciples and seven women continued to be his followers. They went to Galilee, up on the mountain [91] called "Prophecy and Joy." As they gathered together, they were confused about the true nature of the universe, and the plan of salvation, and divine forethought, and the strength of the authorities, and everything the Savior was doing with them in the secret plan of salvation. Then the Savior appeared, not in his previous form but in invisible spirit. He looked like a great angel of light, but I must not describe his appearance. Mortal flesh could not bear it, but only pure and perfect flesh, like what he taught us about, in Galilee, on the mountain called Olivet.

The Wisdom of Jesus Christ, reproduced from Marvin Meyer, *The Nag Hammadi Scriptures*. San Francisco: HarperOne, 2007. Used with permission of HarperOne.

He said, "Peace be with you. My peace I give to you." They all marveled, and they were afraid.

The Savior [92] laughed and said to them, "What are you thinking about? Are you confused? What do you want to find out about?"

Philip said, "About the nature of the universe and the plan of salvation."

The Savior said to them, "I want you to know that all people born on earth from the foundation of the world until now are of dust, and though they have inquired about God, who he is and what he is like, they have not found him. The wisest of people have speculated on the basis of the order and movement of the universe, yet their speculation has missed the truth. It is said that philosophers voice three distinct opinions about the order of the universe, and they disagree with each other. Some of them say that the world governs itself, [93] others say that divine forethought governs it, still others that fate is in charge. All these opinions are wrong. Of the three opinions I have just mentioned, none of them comes close to the truth. They are mere human opinions.

"I have come from infinite light; I am here, and I can tell you exactly what the truth is. For any life that comes from itself is defiled, made by itself. Forethought lacks wisdom. Fate remains senseless.

"It is given to you, however, to know the truth. Whoever deserves knowledge will receive it, whoever has not been conceived by the semen of unclean sexual rubbing but by the first one who was sent, for that person is immortal among mortal people."

Matthew said [94] to him, "Master, no one can find truth except through you. Teach us the truth."

The Savior said, "The One Who Is is ineffable. From the foundation of the world until now, no power, no authority, no creature, no nature has known the One Who Is. Only the One Who Is, and anyone to whom this One wishes to give revelation through the emissary from the first light, knows the One Who Is. Henceforth, I am the great Savior.

The One Who Is is
immortal and eternal, and being eternal, is
    without birth,

for whoever is born will die;
unconceived, without a beginning,
for whoever has a beginning has an end;
undominated, without a name,
for whoever has a name has been made by
    another; [84]
unnamable, with no human form,
for whoever has a human form has been made
    by another.
The One Who Is has an appearance of its
    own, [95]
not like anything you have seen and received,
but an alien appearance that surpasses
    everything
and is superior to the universe.
It looks everywhere and beholds itself in itself.

The One is infinite,
incomprehensible,
and constantly imperishable.
The One is unequalled,
immutably good,
without fault,
eternal,
blessed,
unknown,
yet it knows itself.
The One is immeasurable,
untraceable,
perfect,
without defect,
The One is blessed,
imperishably,
and is called the Father of all."

Philip said, "Master, then how did the One Who Is appear to those who are perfect?"

The perfect Savior said, "Before anything becomes visible of visible things, the majesty and the authority are [96] in him, since he grasps everything while nothing grasps him. He is all mind; he is thought, consideration, reflection, reason, and power, and all are equally powerful. These are the sources of all that is, and the entire generation, from first to last, was in the foreknowledge of the infinite unconceived Father."

Thomas said to him, "Master, Savior, why did these come to be, and why were they revealed?"

The perfect Savior said to him, "I have come from the infinite to tell you everything. The Spirit who is was the one who conceives, the one who has the power of conception [97] and can [give] form, so that the abundant wealth within might be revealed. In mercy and love the Spirit wished to produce fruit independently, that the Spirit might not enjoy goodness alone but that other spirits of the unshakable generation might produce bodies and fruit, glory and honor, in imperishability and the infinite grace of the Spirit. In this way the goodness of the Spirit could be revealed by the self-conceived God, the Father of all imperishability and those who were to come later. But nothing had become visible yet.

"There are many differences among the imperishable beings."

He spoke out and said, "Whoever has ears to hear about infinite things should hear. It is to those who are awake that I speak."

He went on [98] and said, "Everything from the perishable will perish, since it is from the perishable. But everything from the imperishable does not perish but becomes imperishable, since it is from the imperishable. Many people have gone astray because they did not know about this distinction, and they have died."

Mary said to him, "Master, then how can we know this?"

The perfect Savior said, "Bring yourselves from what is invisible to the end of those who are visible, and the emanation of thought itself will reveal to you how faith in what is invisible can be found in those who are visible, who belong to the unconceived Father. Whoever has ears to hear should hear.

"The Lord of the universe is addressed not as Father but as Forefather. <The Father is> the beginning of those who will appear, but the Lord [99] is the Forefather without a beginning. When the Forefather saw himself within himself in a mirror, his resemblance appeared there, but his image appeared as the divine Father by himself and the reflection above reflections and the first-existing unconceived Father. He is as old as the light before him but not as powerful. Afterward there was revealed a multitude of beings, just as old and powerful, who are self-conceived and reflective. Glorious and without number, their generation is designated the generation over whom there is no kingdom. You yourselves have appeared from the people of this generation. And the whole multitude of beings with no kingdom over them is designated [100] the children of the unconceived Father, God, Savior, Son of God, whose likeness is among you. This is the unknowable one who is full of imperishable glory and ineffable joy, and all these beings are at rest in him, constantly rejoicing in ineffable joy in the Father's unfading glory and unending praise that was never heard or known among the aeons and their worlds until now."

Matthew said to him, "Master, Savior, how was Humanity revealed?"

The perfect Savior said, "I want you to know that the being who appeared before the universe in infinity is the one who grows by himself, [101] the self-made Father. He is full of bright light and ineffable. In the beginning, when he decided to turn his likeness into a great power, at once the strength of that light appeared as an immortal androgynous Human, so that through that immortal Human, people might come to salvation and wake up from forgetfulness, through the interpreter who was sent, who is with you until the end of the time of poverty of those who are robbers.

"The companion of the immortal Human is great Sophia, who from the beginning was destined to be united with him, by the self-conceived Father, through the immortal Human who appeared as the first one and as divinity and kingdom. The Father, [102] called the Human, Father by himself, revealed this. He created an exalted aeon, named the Eight, for his own majesty, and he was given great authority. He rules over the impoverished creation, and he created gods and angels and archangels, myriads without number, to serve him, through that light, and the triple-male Spirit, which is of his companion Sophia:

"Through this God came divinity and kingdom. For that reason this God was called God of gods and King of kings. The first Human has a mind of his own within, and thought, appropriate to him, and consideration, reflection, reason, [103] and power.

"All these attributes are perfect and immortal. They are equally imperishable but not equally powerful. They are different, like the difference between father and son, <and son> and thought, and thought and the rest.

"As I said before, about what was produced, the One is first. After everything, all that was revealed came from his power. From what was created came what was fashioned. From what was fashioned came what was formed. From what was formed came what was named. This is how differences came to be among what was unconceived, from beginning to end."

Then Bartholomew said to him, "How is it that this being was called [104] a human being and the Son of Humanity in the gospel? To which of these figures is the Son related?"

The Holy One said to him, "I want you to know that the first Human is referred to as the one who conceives, the self-perfected mind. He reflected with his companion great Sophia and disclosed his first-begotten androgynous child. Its male name is first-begetting Son of God, its female name first-begetting Sophia, Mother of the universe. Some call her love, and the first-begotten is called Christ. With authority from his Father, he created a host of angels [105] without number to serve him, from spirit and light."

His disciples said to him, "Master, tell us about the one called the Human, so that we also might have a precise understanding of his glory."

The perfect Savior said, "Whoever has ears to hear should hear. The first-conceiving father is called Adam, eye of light, because he came from shining light, and his holy angels, ineffable and with no shadow, constantly rejoice in their reflections, received from their father. The entire kingdom of the Child of Humanity, who is called the Son of God, is full of ineffable joy, with no shadow, and eternal praise. They rejoice over his imperishable [106] glory, which until now has never been heard and never been revealed in the aeons that came later and their worlds.

"I have come from the self-conceived one and the first infinite light, to reveal everything to you."

His disciples said again, "Tell us exactly how they have come down from what is invisible, from the immortal realm to the world of mortality."

The perfect Savior said, "The Child, the Son of Humanity, came together with his companion Sophia and disclosed a bright androgynous light. The male name of the light is Savior, the one who conceives all, and the female name is all-conceiving Sophia. Some call her Pistis, Faith.

"All who come into the world, like [107] a droplet from the light, are sent by him into the world of the ruler of the universe, to be guarded by him. The fetter of his forgetfulness has kept the light bound, by the will of Sophia, so that the reality of the circumstance might be <revealed> through the light to the whole impoverished world, on account of the arrogance and blindness of the ruler of the universe and the name of ignorance he was given.

"I have come from the places above by the will of the bright light, and I have escaped from that fetter. I have smashed the work of those who are robbers. I have awakened the droplet sent from Sophia, that it might produce an abundance of fruit through me, and be made perfect and never again be defective. Then the droplet from the light may be <made whole> through me, the great Savior, and its glory may be revealed, and Sophia also may be vindicated of what was defective, and her [108] children may never again be defective, but may attain glory and honor and go up to their Father and know the words of the light of maleness.

"You in turn were sent by the Son, who was sent that you might receive light and escape the forgetfulness of the authorities. In this way the unclean sexual rubbing from the ferocious fire of the flesh of the authorities may never again come to expression through you. Trample on their evil intentions."

Then Thomas said to [him], "Master, Savior, how many realms are there of those who surpass the heavens?"

The perfect Savior said, "I congratulate you for asking about the exalted realms, for your roots are in infinite places. [107] When those whom I have already discussed were revealed, the self-conceiving Father moved to create twelve eternal realms to serve twelve angels. They all are perfect and good. This is the way in which the defect of femaleness became apparent."

They said to him, "How many realms are there for the immortals, starting with those that are infinite?"

The perfect Savior said, "Whoever has ears to hear should [108] hear. The first eternal realm is that of the Child of Humanity, who is called the first to conceive, and the Savior, who has appeared. The second eternal realm is that of the Human called Adam, eye of light. What holds these is the realm over which there is no kingdom, the realm of the eternal infinite God, the self-conceived aeon of the aeons in it, the eternal aeon of the immortals, whom I have already described. [109] This is the aeon above the seventh realm that appeared from Sophia, which is the first realm.

"The immortal Human has revealed realms, powers, and kingdoms, and has given authority to all who come through him, that they might do what they want until the last things above chaos. They came together with each other and disclosed every majesty, even from spirit, and a multitude of lights, glorious and without number. The first, the second, and the third eternal realms [110] were named in the beginning. The first is called unity and rest. Each has its own name, and the third realm was called assembly, after the great multitude that appeared. A multitude of beings revealed themselves in One. Because the many [111] gather and experience unity, <they> are called the assembly, from the assembly that surpasses heaven. [111] We call them the assembly of the eighth realm. It appeared in an androgynous form and was given male and female names. The male part was called the assembly and the female part life, to indicate that from a female came life for all the realms.

"All the names came from the original source. That is the one who united with thought, and at once powers appeared, called gods. From their wisdom the gods of gods revealed gods, and from their wisdom <the gods> revealed lords, and from their thoughts the lords of lords revealed lords, and from their power the lords revealed archangels, and from their words the archangels revealed angels, [112] and from them came ideas, with structure and form and names for all the aeons and their worlds.

"The immortals whom I have described, all of them, have authority from the immortal Human, who is called silence, because by reflecting without speaking the entire majesty of silence was perfected. For the imperishable beings had authority, and each created a great kingdom in the eighth realm, and thrones and temples and firmaments for their own majesties. All these came to be by the will of the Mother of all."

Then the holy apostles said to him, "Master, Savior, tell us about those who are in the eternal realms, for we must ask about them."

The perfect [113] Savior said, "Whatever you ask about I shall tell you. These beings created hosts of angels, myriads without number, to serve and glorify them. They created virgin spirits, ineffable and unchangeable lights, and they are free of sickness and weakness. There is will, and they come to be at once.

"Thus the eternal realms were completed, quickly, with the heavens and firmaments, in the glory of the immortal Human and his companion Sophia. This is where every realm and the world and those that were to follow got their ideas for their creation of patterns in the heavens of chaos and their worlds. All natures, beginning with the revelation of chaos, are in the light that shines with no shadow but with indescribable joy and unspeakable praise. They continue to rejoice over their unfading glory [114] and immeasurable rest, which cannot be described among all the realms that came to be later and all their powers. I have said all this to you so that you might shine in light even more brightly than these."

Mary said to him, "Holy master, where did your disciples come from, where are they going, and what should they do here?"

The perfect Savior said to them, "I want you to know that Sophia, the Mother of all and the companion, desired all by herself to bring these creatures into being without her male companion. By the will of the Father of all, that his unimaginable goodness might be released, he created a curtain between the immortals and those who were to come later, so that this might follow [118] every realm and chaos, that what is defective from the female might appear, and error might contend with her. These constituted [119] the curtain of the spirit.

"From the eternal realms above the emanations of light, as I said before, a droplet from light and spirit came down to the lower regions of the ruler of the universe, in chaos, so that the forms they shaped might appear from that droplet. This is judgment against the chief creator, called Yaldabaoth.

"That droplet revealed the forms they shaped, through breath, as a [120] living soul. This was withered and asleep in the ignorance of the soul. When this being was warmed by the breath of the bright light of the male, he formulated a thought, and names were given to everything in the world of chaos, through the immortal one, when breath blew into him. This happened by the will of Mother Sophia, so that the immortal Human might reassemble [121] the garments there as judgment against those who are robbers. Then <he> welcomed the breath that was blown, but he was like soul and could not assume that power until the number of chaos and the time set by the great angel could be complete.

"I have taught you about the immortal Human, and I have freed him from the fetters of the robbers. I have broken the gates of [122] those without pity, right in front of them. I have humiliated their evil intentions, and they all have been put to shame and have emerged from their ignorance.

"For this reason I have come here, that these may he united with spirit and breath, [117] and two may become one, as in the beginning. Then you may produce an abundance of fruit and go up to the one who is from the beginning, in ineffable joy and glory and [honor and] grace of [the Father of all].

"Whoever knows [the Father in pure] knowledge [will depart] to the Father [and be at rest in] the unconceived [Father. Whoever knows him in a defective way] will depart [to what is defective] and experience the rest [that the eighth realm provides]. Let whoever knows the immortal [spirit] of light in silence, through reflection and agreement in truth, bring me signs of the invisible one, and such a person will become a light in the spirit of silence. Let whoever knows the Child of Humanity in knowledge and love bring me a sign [118] of the Child of Humanity, so that such a person may depart to the dwelling places with those in the eighth realm.

"Look, I have revealed to you the name of the perfect one, all the will of the mother of the holy angels, in order that the male [multitude] may be made complete here. Then there [may appear, in the realms, the infinite beings and] those who [have come to be in the] untraceable [wealth of the great] invisible [Spirit, and] all may receive from his goodness, even the wealth [of their rest] with no [kingdom over it].

"I have come [from the first] who was sent to reveal to you the one who is from the beginning, because of the arrogance of the chief creator and his angels, for they claim to be gods. I have come to eradicate their blindness, that I might tell everyone about the God who is above all. [119]

"So trample on their graves, humiliate their wicked intentions, break their yoke, and raise up those who are mine. I have given you authority over everything as children of light, to trample on their power with your feet."

This is what the blessed Savior [said, and then he disappeared] from them. [All the disciples] remained in [great, ineffable joy] in [the spirit from] that day on. [And his disciples] began to preach the gospel of God, the eternal, imperishable Spirit Amen.

The Wisdom of Jesus

7

The Internal Conflicts of Christianity
Writings against the "Heretics"

As odd as it might seem to modern persons, religions in the ancient world were not, as a rule, concerned with what people believed. Greco-Roman religions were principally concerned with appropriate behavior toward the gods, especially in the regular and proper observance of the sacrificial practices that had been handed down from antiquity. What one happened to believe about the gods was of very little importance. As a consequence, there was no such thing as orthodoxy or heresy in these religions, no written Scriptures to guide one's relationship to the divine (except, of course, in Judaism), and no creeds to be confessed. Perhaps this is why none of these religions was exclusivistic, why none of them insisted on a person's exclusive devotion (except, again, Judaism). People were free to participate in as many religions as they liked.

Christianity emerged as a major exception. From the earliest times, Christians insisted that what a person believed was absolutely essential to true religion, that a person's beliefs were either true or false—that true beliefs helped put a person in a proper standing before God, and false beliefs permanently endangered a person's standing. As a result, Christianity from the outset had a strongly exclusivistic strain.

The emphasis on right and wrong belief is already evident in the earliest Christian author whose works have survived, the apostle Paul, who insisted that his opponents, for example, in Galatia or Corinth, advocated false notions about such matters as the importance of the Jewish Law for salvation or the future reality of the resurrection. For Paul, failing to understand the gospel of Christ properly could lead to serious consequences in both this life and the life to come.

As time progressed, Christians developed certain doctrinal perspectives that they imposed on all persons coming into the religion. The irony, of course, is that different Christians had different understandings about what these correct beliefs were (see Chapter 6); strikingly, most advocates of one or another view insisted that their perspectives had been taught by Jesus and his apostles. And to prove it, they usually could appeal to books that claimed to be written by the apostles.

Thus, along with the development of various kinds of doctrine—about God, Christ, salvation, the Spirit, creation, and so forth—came heated disputes over which forms of these doctrines were correct (see further Chapter 16). A good deal of the Christian writing from the second and third century is "in-house" literature directed against proponents of views deemed by the authors to be "heretical" rather than "orthodox" (on these terms, see Chapter 6). Among the best known authors of this period are such heresiologists as Irenaeus of Lyons, Hippolytus of Rome, Tertullian of Carthage, and Origen of Alexandria. All of these writers, of course, stood within the doctrinal tradition that eventually became dominant, and so declared itself "orthodox," by the end of the period. We can be sure, though, that Christians who took opposing views had a good deal to say for themselves, starting all the way back with Paul's opponents in Galatia and Corinth. But since the supporters of these alternative views lost the struggles, their writings were not preserved for us. As a result, we usually hear only one side of the argument.

It would be wrong to think, though, that this was the only side that was endorsed or that it necessarily proved to be the most persuasive for everyone everywhere. One of the most intriguing features of the Nag Hammadi library, as we will see, is that some of these Gnostic tractates attack proto-orthodox views for being completely misguided—"heretical"! Still, the vast preponderance of the surviving anti-heretical literature comes, naturally enough, from the pens of those who won the conflicts.

For Further Reading

Bauer, Walter. *Orthodoxy and Heresy in Earliest Christianity*, trans. Robert Kraft et. al, ed. Robert Kraft and Gerhard Krodel. Philadelphia: Fortress, 1971.

Ehrman, Bart D. *Lost Christianities: The Battles for Scripture and the Faiths We Never Knew.* New York: Oxford University Press, 2003.

Ehrman, Bart D. *The Orthodox Corruption of Scripture.* New York: Oxford University Press, 1993; esp. chapter 1.

Grant, Robert M. *Jesus After the Gospels: The Christ of the Second Century.* Louisville: Westminster/John Knox, 1990.

Pearson, Birger. "Anti-Heretical Warnings in Codex IX from Nag Hammadi," in *Essays on the Nag Hammadi Texts in Honour of Pahor Labib*, ed. M. Krause. NHS 6; Leiden: E. J. Brill, 1975; pp. 145–154.

Vallée, Gérard. *A Study in Anti-Gnostic Polemics: Irenaeus, Hippolytus, and Epiphanius.* Studies in Christianity and Judaism 1; Waterloo, Ontario: Wilfred Laurier University, 1981.

Wisse, Frederik. "The Nag Hammadi Library and the Heresiologists," *Vigiliae Christianae* 25 (1971) pp. 205–223.

PROTO-ORTHODOX HERESIOLOGISTS

The constant barrage of attacks on "heretical" views by the proto-orthodox of the first three Christian centuries should itself give us pause. If orthodox believers were always and everywhere in the solid majority, why were their opponents ubiquitous? And why were they so to be feared? Some scholars have suggested that the persistent proto-orthodox claims—for example, that heretical groups were pestiferous but small minorities—may themselves indicate otherwise.

A particularly striking feature of the early debates over orthodoxy is that various Christian groups were forced to fight simultaneously on a number of different fronts. For the proto-orthodox, at least, this situation resulted in a highly paradoxical set of beliefs. Against groups like the Ebionites, for example, who maintained that Christ was fully human but not at all divine, the proto-orthodox had to insist that he was God; at the same time, against some groups of Gnostics who maintained that Christ was fully divine but not human, they had to assert that he was a man. But how could he be both? And on yet a third front, other groups of Gnostics maintained that Christ was both human and divine because he was in fact two different entities: the man Jesus and the aeon Christ who temporarily indwelt him; in response, the proto-orthodox claimed that Jesus Christ was one being, not two. Out of these various conflicts, then, emerged the enigmatic doctrine of Christ that came to be embedded in the later orthodox creeds: Christ was fully human and fully divine, yet he was one person, not two.

The anti-heretical writings of the second and third centuries are among the most interesting and vitriolic literature of early Christianity. Much of the vitriol is reserved for the followers of Marcion and the Gnostics; we might assume that these groups were widely seen as the most threatening to the proto-orthodox. Although wide-ranging differences appear among the specific attacks of one heresiologist or another, their overall charges are fairly consistent:

1. The "heretics" subscribe to views that are absurdly complicated, self-contradictory, and contrary to "common sense." Often the heresiologists simply detail the myths told by such people and ridicule them as nonsense (as if the myths were meant to be taken as propositional truths).
2. The mind-boggling variety of heretical beliefs shows that none of them can possibly be true.
3. These absurd and contradictory views derive from faulty interpretations of the sacred Scriptures. Heretics are commonly attacked for not accepting a literal, straightforward understanding of the biblical text and for importing, instead, their own views by means of an allegorical reading.
4. The heretics cannot appeal to any apostolic authorization for their views; those who do so are either lying or deceived. According to the standard proto-orthodox position, Jesus delivered his true teachings to his apostles, who then entrusted them to the bishops of the churches they established. As a result, the leaders of the apostolic churches of the heresiologists' own day were said to stand in a direct

line of succession back to Jesus himself (this is the famous doctrine of "apostolic succession"). Anyone who disputed the teachings of these bishops, therefore, was charged with impugning Christ himself.

5. The alternative views fabricated by heretics become increasingly fantastic with the passing of time, as each new generation of heretics adds new perversions to the corrupt views of their forebears.

6. The perversion of the truth is closely tied to a perversion of morals. This is a constant weapon in the proto-orthodox arsenal: those who subscribe to heretical views engage in wild and profligate activities, immoral behavior that reflects the heretics' false beliefs.

As already pointed out, the opponents of these proto-orthodox writers certainly had plenty to say about each of these points. Unfortunately nearly all of their own attacks and counterattacks have been lost.

THE TEXTS

35. *Irenaeus: Against the Heresies*

Ireneaus was the bishop of Lyons (in Gaul) during the final quarter of the second century. Although he had predecessors among proto-orthodox heresiologists—he himself quotes Justin's tractate against Marcion—none of these earlier works survives intact. Irenaeus wrote his own lengthy treatise, "Refutation and Overthrow of Falsely-Called Gnosis," more widely known simply as "Against the Heresies," in Greek, around 180 CE. It is preserved in its entirety only in Latin translation.

The attack is principally against Valentinian Gnostics, whose myths Irenaeus mocks as completely implausible. Some scholars think that Irenaeus somewhat misunderstood his opponents, however, taking their myths as propositional and historical statements rather than mystical reflections on the meaning of the universe. In any event, a longish excerpt of his exposition is included below to provide a taste. Irenaeus attacks other, non-Valentinian, heretics in somewhat less detail, as seen in the excerpts on Marcus, Saturninus, Basilides, Carpocrates, Marcion, and others that follow.

Throughout his refutation Irenaeus maligns the heretics' emphasis on fragmentation and difference—within the divine realm, the world, and the church. In contrast, Irenaeus himself stresses unity: unity within the godhead (there is only one true God, unified in being and purpose), between God and creation, God and Christ, Jesus and Christ (he is one being, not two), Christ and the apostles, the apostles and the apostolic churches, and the apostolic churches with one another. Especially important for Irenaeus, in this connection, is his notion of the apostolic succession.

Irenaeus set the tone and provided the arguments for many of his heresiological successors, some of whom simply borrowed his descriptions and attacks for their own books. For another selection from "Against the Heresies," see Chapter 9.

Book 1

Preface

Certain people are discarding the truth and introducing deceitful myths and endless genealogies, which, as the Apostle says, "promote speculations rather than the divine training that is in faith."[1]

By specious argumentation, craftily patched together, they mislead the minds of the more ignorant and ensnare them by falsifying the Lord's words. Thus they become wicked interpreters of genuine words. They bring many to ruin by leading them, under the pretense of knowledge, away from him who established and adorned this universe, as if they had something more sublime and excellent to manifest than the God who made

---

1 1 Tim 1:4.

Irenaeus: Against the Heresies, Book 1, from *St. Irenaeus of Lyons against the Heresies*, ed. Dominic Unger. Mahwah: Paulist Press, 1992. Used by permission of Paulist Press; Book 3, from *The Ante-Nicene Fathers*, vol. 1. *The Apostolic Fathers with Justin Martyr and Irenaeus*, ed. A. Cleveland Coxe. Reprint; 2nd ed. Grand Rapids: Eerdmans, 1987.

heaven and . . . all things in heaven. By cleverness with words they persuasively allure the simple folk to this style of searching, but then, absurdly, bring them to perdition by trumping up their blasphemous and impious opinion against the Creator. In this matter they just cannot distinguish what is false from what is true.

2 Error, in fact, does not show its true self, lest on being stripped naked it should be detected. Instead, it craftily decks itself out in an attractive dress, and thus, by an outward false appearance, presents itself to the more ignorant, truer than truth itself, ridiculous as it is even to say this. With regard to such people, one greater than we has said: "An artful imitation in glass is a mockery to a precious stone, though it is an emerald and highly prized by some people, so long as no one is at hand to evaluate it and skillfully expose the crafty counterfeit. And when copper is alloyed to silver, what person, if he is unskilled, will readily be able to evaluate it." Therefore, we will see to it that it will not be our fault if some are snatched away, like sheep by wolves, whom they would fail to recognize because of the treachery of the sheepskin, since they speak the same language we do, but intend different meanings. Of such the Lord admonished us to beware. And so, after chancing upon the commentaries of the disciples of Valentinus—as they style themselves—and after conversing with some of them and becoming acquainted with their doctrine, we thought it necessary to inform you, our dear friend, about these portentous and profound "mysteries" which not all grasp, because not all have purged their brains. Thus, having learned of these mysteries yourself, you can make them clear to all your people and warn them to be on guard against this profundity of nonsense and of blasphemy against God. To the best of our ability we will give you a concise and clear report on the doctrine of these people who are at present spreading false teaching. We are speaking of the disciples of Ptolemaeus, an offshoot of the Valentinian school. We will also offer suggestions, to the best of our limited capacity, for refuting this doctrine, by showing how utterly absurd, inconsistent, and incongruous with the truth their statements are. Not that we are accustomed to writing books, or practiced in the art of rhetoric; but it is love that prompts us to acquaint you and all your people with the teachings which up till now have been kept secret, which, however, by the grace of God have at last come to light. "For nothing is covered that will not be revealed, and nothing hidden that will not be known."[2]

Chapter 1

1 They claim that in the invisible and unnameable heights there is a certain perfect Aeon that was before all, the First-Being, whom they also call First-Beginning, First-Father, and Profundity. He is invisible and incomprehensible. And, since he is incomprehensible and invisible, eternal and ingenerate, he existed in deep quiet and stillness through countless ages. Along with him there existed Thought, whom they also name Grace and Silence. At one time this Profundity decided to emit from himself the Beginning of all things. This emission would be as a "seed" which he decided to emit and deposit as it were in the womb of Silence, who coexisted with him. After she had received this "seed" and had become pregnant, she gave birth to Mind, who was both similar and equal to his Father who emitted him; and he alone comprehended his (Father's) greatness. This Mind they also call Only-begotten, Father, and Beginning of all things. Truth was emitted at the same time he [Mind] was. Thus these four constitute the first and principal Pythagorean Tetrad, for there are Profundity and Silence, then Mind and Truth. This [Tetrad] they also style the root of all things. But when this Only-begotten perceived for what things he was emitted, he in turn emitted Word and Life, since he was Father of all who were to come after him and the beginning and formation of the entire Fullness. Thereupon by the conjugal union of Word and Life, Man and Church were emitted. That is the

---

2 Matt 10:26.

principal Ogdoad, the root and the substance of all things, known among them by four names, Profundity, Mind, Word, and Man, because each of these is male and female; thus, in the first case, First-Father was united in marriage to Thought whom they call Grace and Silence; then Only-begotten, that is, Mind, to Truth; next Word, to Life; finally Man, to Church.

2 Since these Aeons themselves were emitted for their Father's glory, they in turn wished to glorify the Father by something of their own. So they sent forth emissions through conjugal unions. After Man and Church had been emitted, Word and Life emitted ten other Aeons, whose names are these: Profound and Mingling, Ageless and Union, Self-producing and Pleasure, Immobile and Blending, Only-begotten and Happiness. These are the ten Aeons which they assert were emitted by Word and Life. Moreover, Man himself, together with Church, emitted twelve Aeons, to whom they give these names: Advocate and Faith, Paternal and Hope, Maternal and Love, Praise and Understanding, Ecclesiastic and Blessedness, Desired and Wisdom.

3 Such are the thirty Aeons of their erroneous system. They are enveloped in silence and are known to no one. This indivisible and spiritual Fullness of theirs is tripartite, being divided into an Ogdoad, a Decad, and a Dodecad. And for this reason Savior—for they do not wish to call him Lord—did no work in public for thirty years,[3] thus manifesting the mystery of these Aeons. They also assert that these thirty Aeons are most plainly indicated in the parable of the laborers sent into the vineyard; for some are sent about the first hour, others about the third hour, others about the sixth hour, others about the ninth hour, others about the eleventh hour.[4] Now if the hours mentioned are added up, the sum total will be thirty; for one, three, six, nine, and eleven make thirty. Thus they hold that the Aeons have been indicated

by these hours. Besides, they claim that these are great and wonderful and unutterable mysteries, which they themselves bear as fruit. And if anywhere anything of the many things mentioned in the Scriptures can [be drawn to these things, they wish to] accommodate and adapt them to their fabrication.

Chapter 2

1 So they tell us that First-Father of theirs is known only to Only-begotten, that is, to Mind, who was born of him. To all the rest he is invisible and incomprehensible. According to them, Mind alone enjoyed himself in contemplating Father and exulted in considering his immeasurable greatness. He was thinking of communicating Father's greatness also to the rest of the Aeons, how vast and great he is, and that he is without beginning, immeasurable, and incapable of being seen. But at the will of Father, Silence restrained him, because she wished to get them all to have the mind and the desire to seek after their First-Father mentioned above. The rest of the Aeons, too, were in some manner quietly desiring to see the one who emitted their "Seed" and to be informed about their Root who was without beginning.

2 But the last and youngest Aeon of the Dodecad emitted by Man and Church, namely, Wisdom, advanced far ahead of all of them and suffered passion, though without the embrace of Desired, her consort. The passion began in Mind and Truth but spread as by infection to this estranged Aeon [Wisdom] under the pretense of love, but in reality out of temerity, because she had no fellowship with perfect Father, as even Mind did. The passion consisted in seeking after Father; for she wished, so they say, to comprehend his greatness. But then she was not able, inasmuch as she undertook an impossible affair, and she fell into extreme agony because of the immense height and unsearchable nature of Father and because of the affection for him. Since she was ever stretching forward to what was ahead, she would at last

---

3 Luke 3:23.

4 Matt 20:1–16.

have been swallowed up by his charm and resolved into the entire substance unless she had met the power that strengthens all things and safeguards them outside the unspeakable greatness. This power they also call Limit. By it they say she was restrained and strengthened, and when with difficulty she had been brought to her senses and was convinced that Father is unfathomable, she laid aside the first Intention together with the subsequent passion which had arisen from that amazing admiration [for Father].

3 Some of them, however, describe the passion and return of Wisdom in this mystical fashion. After she had undertaken the impossible and unattainable affair, she brought forth a formless substance, namely, such a nature as a woman could bring forth. When she looked at it, she was filled first with grief on account of the unfinished nature of her offspring, then with fear lest her very existence should come to an end. After that she was beside herself and perplexed as she sought the cause [of her offspring] and how she might conceal her. While involved in these passions, she changed her mind and tried to return to Father. When she had made the bold attempt for some time and her strength failed, she entreated Father. The other Aeons, too, especially Mind, made supplication together with her. Hence, they claim, material substance took its beginning from ignorance and grief, fear and bewilderment.

4 Afterwards Father, by means of Only-begotten, emitted the above-mentioned Limit as part of no conjugal couple, [but] bisexual. For they hold that sometimes Father emits with Silence as consort, then again he is above both male and female. This Limit they call Stake, Redeemer, Reaper, Limiter, and Restorer. They claim that Wisdom was purified by this Limit and strengthened and restored to her own consort [Desired]. For, after Intention, together with her subsequent passion, had been separated from her, she herself remained within the Fullness, but her Intention with her passion was separated by Limit and fenced out and kept outside of it. Intention is a spiritual substance, possessing some of the natural tendency of an Aeon, but she is formless and shapeless, because she had received nothing. For this reason they say she is a weak and feminine fruit.

5 After Intention had been separated outside the Fullness of the Aeons, and its Mother had been restored to her own conjugal partner, Only-begotten in accord with Father's forethought again emitted another conjugal couple, namely, Christ and Holy Spirit, for the stabilization and support of the Fullness, lest any of the Aeons have a similar misfortune [as Wisdom]. Through them they say the Aeons were perfected. For, they claim, Christ taught them the nature of their conjugal union, that they would be able to know the comprehension of Ingenerate. He also announced among them the knowledge of Father [Profundity], namely, that he is immeasurable and incomprehensible, and that he can be neither seen nor heard. He is known only by Only-begotten. Father's incomprehensible nature is primarily the cause for the permanent existence of the rest of the Aeons; but what can be comprehended of him, namely, his Son, is the cause of their origin and formation. These things, then, Christ performed among them as soon as he had been emitted.

6 The [one] Holy Spirit taught them to give thanks that they had all been made equal, and he introduced [them to] the true rest. They say that in this manner the Aeons were made equal in form and mind, since all became Minds and all Words and all Men and all Christs. In like manner, the female Aeons all became Truths and Lives and Spirits and Churches. Thereupon, they tell us, when all the Aeons had been strengthened and brought to perfect rest, they sang hymns amid much rejoicing to First-Father, who himself took part in the great exultation. Then, in gratitude for this benefit, the entire Fullness of the Aeons, with one will and mind, and with the consent of Christ and Spirit and the approval of their Father, collected and combined whatever most beautiful and brilliant each one had in himself. These things they fittingly blended together and carefully united into one. To the honor and glory of Profundity they made this emission the most perfect beauty and constellation of the Fullness, the most perfect fruit, Jesus. They also gave him the name Savior and Christ, and patronymically, Word, and All, because he is emitted from all. And as an honor to themselves, they emitted together with him Angels of the same nature to be his bodyguard.

Chapter 3

1 Such, then, are the dealings in the inner circle of the Fullness, as they tell them. Such, too, was the misfortune of the Aeon who suffered passion and nearly perished when, because of her search after Father, she was involved in much material substance. Such was the stabilization, after her agony, by Limit, Stake, Redeemer, Reaper, Limiter, and Restorer. Such was likewise the later origin of the Aeons, namely, of the first Christ and Holy Spirit, both of whom were emitted by Father after the repentance of Wisdom. Such was the formation of the second Christ—whom they also style Savior—a creation out of the combined contributions [of the Aeons]. These things, however, were not declared openly, because not all are capable of grasping this knowledge. They were pointed out mystically by Savior through parables to those who were able to understand them. Thus, the thirty Aeons are pointed out, as we said above, by the thirty years during which they say Savior did not work in public and by the parable of the workers in the vineyard. Paul, on his part, very clearly and frequently names these Aeons, and even preserves their rank, when he speaks thus: "To all generations of the age [aeon] of ages [aeons]."[5] Even we ourselves at the giving of thanks, when we say: "To the ages [aeons] of the ages [aeons]," are said to point out those Aeons. Finally, whenever the word Aeon or Aeons occurs [in Scripture], they maintain there is reference to their Aeons.

2 The emission of the Dodecad of the Aeons is indicated [they claim] by the fact that the Lord was twelve years old when he disputed with the teachers of the Law;[6] likewise, by the choice of the apostles. Besides, the other eighteen Aeons were revealed by the fact that after his resurrection from the dead, he is said to have spent eighteen months with his disciples. Likewise, the ten Aeons are pointed out by iota, the first letter of his name. For this reason Savior said: "Not one iota or one tittle shall be lost . . . till all is accomplished."[7]

3 Now the passion experienced by the twelfth Aeon is pointed out, they say, by the apostasy of Judas, the twelfth of the apostles, when the betrayal took place. Also by the fact that [Jesus] suffered in the twelfth month; for they profess that he preached one year after his baptism. Furthermore, this is most clearly manifested by the case of the woman with the hemorrhage, since, after she had suffered for twelve years, she was healed by Savior's coming, when she touched the hem of his cloak. And because of that, Savior said: "Who touched me?"[8] By this he taught the disciples the mystery that had taken place among the Aeons and the healing of the Aeon that had suffered passion. For that power was pointed out through her who had suffered for twelve years, inasmuch as she was straining forward and her material substance was flowing out into immensity, as they say. And unless she had touched that Son's cloak, that is, the Truth of the First Tetrad, which is indicated by the hem, she would have been resolved into the universal substance. But she stopped and rested from her passion; for, when the power of the Son went out—this they hold is the power of Limit—he healed her and removed the passion from her.

4 Moreover, they assert that Savior, who was made from all things, is the All. This is proved by the following passage: "Every male who opens the womb;"[9] for he, being the All, opened the womb of Intention of the Aeon who suffered passion when she was cast out of the Fullness. He also calls this

---

5 Eph 3:21.

6 Luke 2:41–51.

7 Matt 5:18.

8 Mark 5:30.

9 Exod 13:2; cf. Luke 2:23.

second Ogdoad, of which we shall speak a little later. They say that for this reason Paul said explicitly: "But he is all;"[10] and again: "To him and from him are all things;"[11] and further: "In him the whole fullness of deity dwells;"[12] and: "All things are recapitulated in Christ through God."[13] Thus they interpret these and similar passages. . . .

Chapter 8

1 Such is their system which neither the prophets preached, nor the Lord taught, nor the apostles handed down. They boast rather loudly of knowing more about it than others do, citing it from non-scriptural works; and, as people would say, they attempt to braid ropes of sand. They try to adapt to their own sayings in a manner worthy of credence, either the Lord's parables, or the prophet's sayings, or the apostles' words, so that their fabrication might not appear to be without witness. They disregard the order and the connection of the Scriptures and, as much as in them lies, they disjoint the members of the Truth. They transfer passages and rearrange them; and, making one thing out of another, they deceive many by the badly composed phantasy of the Lord's words that they adapt. By way of illustration, suppose someone would take the beautiful image of a king, carefully made out of precious stones by a skillful artist, and would destroy the features of the man on it and change around and rearrange the jewels, and make the form of a dog, or of a fox, out of them, and that a rather bad piece of work. Suppose he would then say with determination that this is the beautiful image of the king that the skillful artist had made, at the same time pointing to the jewels which had been beautifully fitted together by the first artist into the image of the king, but which had been badly changed by the second into

the form of a dog. And suppose he would through this fanciful arrangement of the jewels deceive the inexperienced who had no idea of what the king's picture looked like, and would persuade them that this base picture of a fox is that beautiful image of the king. In the same way these people patch together old women's fables, and then pluck words and sayings and parables from here and there and wish to adapt these words of God to their fables. We have already said how much of these words they adapt to the things within the Fullness. . . .

Chapter 10

1 The Church, indeed, though disseminated throughout the world, even to the ends of the earth, received from the apostles and their disciples the faith in one God the Father Almighty, the Creator of heaven and earth and the seas and all things that are in them; and in the one Jesus Christ, the Son of God, who was enfleshed for our salvation; and in the Holy Spirit, who through the prophets preached the Economies, the coming, the birth from a Virgin, the passion, the resurrection from the dead, and the bodily ascension into heaven of the beloved Son, Christ Jesus our Lord, and his coming from heaven in the glory of the Father to recapitulate all things, and to raise up all flesh of the whole human race, in order that to Christ Jesus, our Lord and God, Savior and King, according to the invisible Father's good pleasure, "Every knee should bow [of those] in heaven and on earth and under the earth, and every tongue confess him,"[14] and that he would exercise just judgment toward all; and that, on the other hand, he would send into eternal fire the spiritual forces of wickedness, and the angels who transgressed and became rebels, and the godless, wicked, lawless, and blasphemous people; but, on the other hand, by bestowing life on the righteous and holy and those who kept his commandments and who have persevered in his love—both those who did so from the beginning and those who did so after

---

10 Col 3:11.

11 Rom 11:36.

12 Col 2:9.

13 Eph 1:10.

---

14 Phil 2:10–11.

repentance—he would bestow on them as a grace the gift of incorruption and clothe them with everlasting glory.

2 The church, as we have said before, though disseminated throughout the whole world, carefully guards this preaching and this faith which she has received, as if she dwelt in one house. She likewise believes these things as if she had but one soul and the one and the same heart; she preaches, teaches, and hands them down harmoniously, as if she possessed but one mouth.

For, though the languages throughout the world are dissimilar, nevertheless the meaning of the tradition is one and the same. To explain, the churches which have been founded in Germany do not believe or hand down anything else; neither do those founded in Spain or Gaul or Libya or in the central regions of the world. But just as the sun, God's creation, is one and the same throughout the world, so too the light, the preaching of the truth, shines everywhere and enlightens all people who wish to come to the knowledge of the truth. Neither will any of those who preside in the churches, though exceedingly eloquent, say anything else (for no one is above the Master); nor will a poor speaker subtract from the tradition. For, since the faith is one and the same, neither he who can discourse at length about it adds to it, nor he who can say only a little subtracts from it. . . .

Chapter 22

1 The Rule of the Truth that we hold is this: There is one God Almighty, who created all things through his Word; he both prepared and made all things out of nothing, just as Scripture says: "For by the word of the Lord the heavens were made, and all their host by the breath of His mouth."[15] And again: "All things were made through Him and without Him was made not a thing."[16] From this "all" nothing is exempt. Now, it is the Father

who made all things through him, whether visible or invisible, whether sensible or intelligible, whether temporal for the sake of some dispensation or eternal. These he did not make through angels or some powers that were separated from his thought. For the God of all things needs nothing. No, he made all things by his Word and Spirit, disposing and governing them and giving all of them existence. This is the one who made the world, which indeed is made up of all things. This is the one who fashioned humans. This is the God of Abraham and Isaac and Jacob, above whom there is no other God, nor a Beginning, nor a Power, nor a Fullness. This is the Father of our Lord Jesus Christ, as we shall demonstrate. If, therefore, we hold fast this Rule, we shall easily prove that they have strayed from the truth, even though their statements are quite varied and numerous. It is true, nearly all the heretical sects, many as they are, speak of one God; but they alter him by their evilmindedness. They are thereby ungrateful to him who made them, just as the pagans by idolatry. Moreover, they hold in contempt God's handiwork by speaking against their own salvation; and they are thus their own most bitter accusers and false witnesses. Even though they do not wish to, they will surely rise again in the flesh in order to acknowledge the power of Him who raises them from the dead; they will, however, not be numbered with the righteous, because of their unbelief.

2 Since, therefore, the exposé and refutation of all the heretical sects is different and multiform, and since we have resolved to give an answer to everyone according to its own standard, we have deemed it necessary first of all to give an account of their source and root, in order that you may know their most sublime profundity, and understand the tree from which such fruits came forth.

Chapter 23

1 Simon, the Samaritan, was the famous magician of whom Luke, the disciple and follower of the apostles, said: "But there was a man named Simon, who had previously practiced magic in the

---

15 Ps 33:6.
16 John 1:3.

city and seduced the people of Samaria, saying that he himself was somebody great. They all gave heed to him, from the least to the greatest, saying, 'This man is that Power of God which is called Great.' And they gave heed to him, because for a long time he had bewitched them with his magic."[17] This Simon, then, feigned faith; he thought that even the apostles themselves affected cures by magic and not by God's power. He suspected that, when by the imposition of hands the apostles filled with the Holy Spirit those who believed in God through Jesus Christ who was announced by them, they were doing this through some greater knowledge of magic. But when he offered the apostles some money so that he too might receive this power of bestowing the Holy Spirit on whomever he willed, he heard this from Peter: "Keep your money to yourself, to perish with you, because you thought you could obtain the gift of God with money. You have neither part nor lot in this matter, for your heart is not right before God. For I see that you are in the gall of bitterness and in the bond of iniquity."[18] But he believed still less in God and greedily intended to rival the apostles so that he too might appear famous. So he made yet a deeper investigation into the entire art of magic to the amazement of the crowds of people. This happened during the reign of Emperor Claudius, who, so they say, also honored him with a stature because of his magic. So this man was glorified by many as a god. He taught that he himself was the one who appeared among the Jews as the Son of God, while in Samaria he descended as the Father, and among the other nations he came as the Holy Spirit. He also taught that he was the most sublime Power, that is, the Father who is above all things. He permitted himself to be called whatever people might call him.

2 Now Simon, the Samaritan, from whom all heresies got their start, proposed the following sort of heretical doctrine. Having himself redeemed a certain Helen from being a prostitute in Tyre, a city of Phoenicia, he took her with him on his rounds, saying that she was the first Thought of his mind, the Mother of all things, through whom in the beginning he conceived in his mind to make the Angels and Archangels. For he asserted that this Thought leaped forth from him, since she knew what her Father wanted, and descended to the lower regions and gave birth to Angels and Powers, by whom also this world was made. But after she had given birth to them, she was detained by them out of envy, since they did not wish to be considered the offspring of anyone else. For he was entirely unknown to them. His Thought, however, who was detained by the Powers and Angels that had been emitted by her, also suffered all kinds of contumely at their hands, so that she could not return to her Father on high. [She suffered] even to the extent of being imprisoned in a human body and of transmigrating for ages into other female bodies, as from one vessel into another. For example, she was in the famous Helen on account of whom the Trojan war was fought; for that reason Stesichorus who reviled her in his verses was struck blind, but after he repented and had written what are called palinodes, in which he sang her praises, his sight was restored. Thus, passing from one body into another, and always suffering insults from the body, she was at last a prostitute in a public house. She was the lost sheep.

3 He himself came for this reason that he might first take her to himself, free her from the bonds, and then bring salvation to humankind by his own knowledge. The angels governed the world badly, because each one desired to be sovereign. So he came, he said, to set matters right; having been transformed and made like the principalities and powers and angels, he appeared in turn as a man, though he was not a man. He appeared to suffer in Judea, though he really did not suffer. Moreover, the prophets uttered their prophecies by virtue of inspirations received from the angels who made the world. Wherefore, those who put their trust in Simon and his Helen do not give heed to them, but do whatever they will, since they are free. For they say that people are saved through his grace, and

---

17 Acts 8:9–11.

18 Acts 8:20–21, 23.

not through holy deeds, because deeds are holy not by nature but by accident. For example, the angels who made the world laid down precepts and through these made slaves of people. He, therefore, promised that the world would be destroyed so that those who belong to him would be freed from the domain of those who made the world.

4 The mystic priests of these people live licentious lives and practice magic, each one in whatever way he can. They make use of exorcisms and incantations, love-potions too and philters, and the so-called familiars, and dreamsenders. They diligently practice whatever other magic arts there may be. They also have a statue of Simon patterned after Jupiter, and one of Helen patterned after Minerva. They worship these statues. They also have a name for themselves, the "Simonians" derived from Simon the author of this most impious doctrine, from whom the falsely called knowledge took its origin, as one can learn from their assertions. . . .

Chapter 24

1 Saturninus, who was of Antioch near Daphne, and Basilides got their start from these heretics. Still they taught different doctrines, the one in Syria, the other in Alexandria. Saturninus, following Menander, assumed there is one Father who is unknown to all and who made the angels and archangels, virtues and powers. But the world and all that is in it was made by certain seven Angels. Humanity too is the work of angels. When a shining image appeared from above from the sovereign power and they were not able to hold fast to it because it immediately ascended again, he said that they exhorted each other, saying, "Let us make man after an image and likeness."[19] When this first-formed-man was made and was not able to stand erect because of the weakness of the angels, but wriggled on the ground as a worm, then the Power on high had pity on him, because he was made after its likeness, and he sent a spark of life

which raised him up and set him upright and made him live. This spark of life, then, he claims, returns to its own kind after a human's death, and the rest of the things out of which he was made are again resolved into these same things.

2 He assumed, furthermore, that Savior was unbegotten, incorporeal, and formless; still he was believed to have appeared as man. He says the God of the Jews is one of the angels. On this account, because his Father wished to destroy all the principalities, Christ came to destroy the God of the Jews and to bring salvation to those who believe in him. These are the ones who have in themselves the spark of life. In truth, he says that two kinds of humans were formed by the angels, the one wicked, the other good. And since the demons aided the wicked, Savior came for the destruction of the evil people and the demons, but for the salvation of the good. Besides, he said that to marry and to beget children comes from Satan. Most of his followers even abstain from animal food, misleading many by this false type of temperance. As for the prophecies, some were uttered by the angels who made the world, others by Satan, whom he assumed to be the very angel who opposes those who made the world, especially the God of the Jews. . . .

Chapter 25

1 Carpocrates and his disciples assert that the world and the things in it were made by angels who are far inferior to the ingenerate Father, and that Jesus was begotten by Joseph and, though he was made like humans, he was superior to the rest. Moreover, since his soul was vigorous and innocent, he remembered what he had seen within the sphere which belongs to the ingenerate God. For this reason, a power was sent down upon him by God, that by means of it he could escape from the makers of the world and that this [soul], having passed through all their domains and so remained free in all, might ascend to him [Father]. The souls that embrace things similar to it [Jesus' soul] will in like manner [ascend to him]. Furthermore,

---

19 Gen 1:26.

they say, the soul of Jesus, though trained according to the law in the practices of the Jews, despised them, and for this reason received power by which he destroyed the passions which were in people as a punishment.

2 The soul, therefore, which is like that of Jesus, is able to hold in contempt those rulers and makers of the world, receiving like Jesus a power to perform the same things that he performed. Wherefore, some of them advanced to such a pitch of pride that they claim to be like Jesus; others even claim that they are more powerful than Jesus; some again assert that they are superior to his disciples, as, for instance, Peter and Paul and the rest of the apostles. They claim that they are in no way inferior to Jesus. Really, their souls, they claim, descend from the same sphere, and because in like manner they hold in contempt the makers of the world, they have been deemed worthy of the same power and return again to the same place. If, however, anyone has despised the things here below more than he did, such a one can be better than he.

3 These people, too, practice magic and make use of incantations, philtres, spells, familiars, dreamsenders, and the rest of the evil magic. They assert that they have power even now to exercise dominion over the rulers and makers of this world; not only over them, but also over all the creatures in it. So some of them have been sent forth by Satan to the pagans to malign the holy name of the church, so that when people, in one way or another, hear their tenets and imagine that we all are like them, they would turn their ears from the preaching of the truth; or even as they see their conduct they would speak slander of us all. However, we have nothing in common with them in doctrine, morals, or daily conduct. On the contrary, they live licentious lives and hold godless doctrine. But they use the Name [of Jesus] only to veil their own wickedness. Their condemnation is just. They will be punished by God in keeping with the deserts of their deeds.

4 They have fallen into such unbridled madness that they boast of having in their power and of practicing every kind of impious and godless deed.

For they claim that deeds are good or bad only because of human opinion. Therefore, they say that the souls must have experience in every kind of life and in every act by means of transmigration from one body to another, unless some soul would preoccupy itself once and for all, and in an equivalent manner do in one coming [into this world] all the deeds—deeds which it is not only wrong for to us to speak of and to listen to, but which we may not even think or believe that such things are done among people who live in our cities. The purpose of this, according to their writings, is that the souls, having had every experience in life, may at their departure not be wanting in anything; moreover, they must take care lest they be again sent forth into a body because something was wanting to their liberation. For this reason they assert that Jesus uttered the following parable: "And as you with an accuser, make an effort to settle with him lest he drag you to the judge, and the judge hand you to the officer, and he put you in prison. Amen, I tell you, you will never get out till you have paid the very last copper."[20] They say that the adversary is one of the angels who are in the world. They call him Devil. They claim that he was made in order to lead from the world to the ruler those souls that perished. They also say he is the first of the authors of this world and he hands such souls over to another angel, who is his minister, that he might imprison them in other bodies; for the body is a prison, they assert. And this clause: "You will never get out till you have paid the very last copper," they interpret to mean that no one will escape from the power of the angels who made the world, but will always transmigrate from one body to another until he has had experience in absolutely every kind of action that exists in the world. And when nothing is wanting to him, his soul, having been liberated, escapes to the God who is above the angels, the makers of the world. In this manner all souls are saved—whether in one coming [into this world] they preoccupy themselves in being mixed up in every kind of action, whether they

---

20 Matt 5:25–26.

transmigrate from one body to another, or, what is the same, whether they have been sent into every kind of life. And having fulfilled the requirements and paid the debts, they are liberated, so that they no longer have to operate in a body.

5 Now, whether these impious, unlawful, and forbidden acts are really practiced by them, I would hardly believe. But in their writings it is so written, and they also explain it so. Jesus, they assert, spoke privately in mystery to his disciples and apostles and commissioned them to hand down privately these things to those who are worthy and believe; for they are saved by faith and love. But the other things are indifferent, some good, some bad, according to the view of people, inasmuch as nothing is bad by nature.

6 Some of them put a mark on their disciples, branding them on the underside of the lobe of the right ear. Marcellina belonged to their number. She came to Rome under Pope Anicetus and, since she belonged to this school, she led multitudes astray. They call themselves Gnostics and possess images, some of which are paintings, some made of other materials. They said Christ's image was copied by Pilate at the time that Jesus lived among humans. On these images they put a crown and exhibit them along with the images of the philosophers of the world, namely, with the image of Pythagoras, Plato, Aristotle, and the rest. Toward these [images] they observe other rites that are just like those of the pagans.

Chapter 26

1 A certain Cerinthus taught in Asia that the world was not made by the first God, but by some power which was separated and distant from the authority that is above all things, and which was ignorant of the God who is above all things. He proposes Jesus, not as having been born of a virgin—for this seemed impossible to him—but as having been born the son of Joseph and Mary like all other people, and that he excelled over every person injustice, prudence, and wisdom. After his baptism Christ descended on him in the shape of

a dove from the authority that is above all things. Then he preached the unknown Father and worked wonders. But at the end Christ again flew off from Jesus. Jesus indeed suffered and rose again from the dead, but Christ remained impassible, since he was spiritual.

2 The so-called Ebionites admit that the world was made by the true God, but in regard to the Lord they hold the same opinion as Cerinthus and Carpocrates. They use only the Gospel according to Matthew and reject the Apostle Paul, saying that he is an apostate from the law. The prophetical writings, however, they strive to interpret in a rather curious manner. They circumcise themselves and continue in the practices which are prescribed by the law and by the Judaic standard of living, so that they worship Jerusalem as the house of God. . . .

Chapter 27

1 A certain Cerdo also got his start from the disciples of Simon. He settled in Rome under Hyginus, who held the ninth place of the episcopacy by succession from the apostles. He taught that the God who had been proclaimed under the law and the prophets was not the Father of Our Lord Jesus Christ, for the former was known, but the latter was unknown; again, the former was just, whereas the latter was benevolent.

2 Marcion of Pontus succeeded Cerdo and amplified his doctrine. He uttered the impudent blasphemy that the God who was proclaimed by the law and the prophets was the author of evil, and desirous of war. He was inconsistent in his teaching and contradicted himself. Jesus, however, who has his origin in the Father who is above the God who made the world, came to Judea at the time when Pontius Pilate presided as procurator of Tiberius Caesar. He was manifested in the form of a man to those who were in Judea. He abolished the prophets and the law and all the works of the God who made the world, whom he also styled the World-Ruler. Besides all this, he mutilated the Gospel according to Luke, discarding all that is written about the birth of the Lord, and discarding also many of the Lord's discourses containing teaching in which it is most clearly written that the Lord confessed his Father as the Maker of the universe. Marcion persuaded his disciples that he was more truthful than the apostles who handed down the Gospel, though he gave them not the Gospel, but only a portion of the Gospel. In like manner, he mutilated the letters of Paul, removing whatever was clearly said by the apostle about the God who made the world inasmuch as he is the Father of our Lord Jesus Christ; for the apostle taught by quoting from the prophetical writings that foretold the Lord's coming.

3 Only those souls that had learned his doctrine would attain salvation. The body, on the contrary, since it was taken from the earth, is incapable of sharing in salvation. Besides the blasphemy against God, he added this one (thus truly speaking with the devil's mouth and uttering all things contrary to the truth): Cain and those like him, the Sodomites and the Egyptians and those like them, and all the pagans who walked in every mess of wickedness were all saved by the Lord when he descended into the netherworld and they met him, and he took them into his kingdom. But Abel, Enoch, Noah, and the rest of the righteous and the patriarchs who came from Abraham, together with all the prophets and those who pleased God, did not share in salvation, as the Serpent that was in Marcion proclaimed. For, he says, since these people know that their God always tempted them, they had a suspicion that he was tempting them at that time, and they did not go to meet Jesus, nor did they believe in his preaching. As a result their souls remained in the netherworld.

4 Now, since this man alone was openly so bold as to mutilate the Scriptures and to calumniate God more impudently than all others, we will answer him separately and expose him by his own writings, and also from the discourses of the Lord and the apostles which he himself kept and used; and thus with God's grace we shall overthrow him. We have necessarily made mention of him at present that you might know that all those who in

any way adulterate the truth and do injury to the preaching of the church are the disciples and successors of Simon, the magician of Samaria. For even though they do not acknowledge the name of their teacher in order to mislead others, yet it is his doctrine they teach. By proposing the name of Christ Jesus as a kind of incentive, they put many to death by wickedly disseminating their own teaching by means of the good name [Jesus], and by handing them the bitter and wicked poison of the Serpent, the author of the apostasy, under the guise of the delight and beauty of this name.

Book 3

Chapter 3

1 It is within the power of all, therefore, in every church, who may wish to see the truth, to contemplate clearly the tradition of the apostles manifested throughout the whole world; and we are in a position to reckon up those who were by the apostles instituted bishops in the churches, and [to demonstrate] the succession of these men to our own times; those who neither taught nor knew of anything like what these [heretics] rave about. For if the apostles had known hidden mysteries, which they were in the habit of imparting to "the perfect" apart and secretly from the rest, they would have delivered them especially to those to whom they were also committing the churches themselves. For they were desirous that these men should be very perfect and blameless in all things, whom also they were leaving behind as their successors, delivering up their own place of government to these men; which men, if they discharged their functions honestly, would be a great boon [to the church], but if they should fall away, the direst calamity.

2 Since, however, it would be very tedious, in such a volume, as this, to reckon up the successions of all the churches, we do put to confusion all those who, in whatever manner, whether by an evil self-pleasing, by vainglory, or by blindness and perverse opinion, assemble in unauthorized meetings; [we do this, I say,] by indicating that

tradition derived from the apostles, of the very great, the very ancient, and universally known church founded and organized at Rome by the two most glorious apostles, Peter and Paul; as also [by pointing out] the faith preached to people, which comes down to our time by means of the successions of the bishops. For it is a matter of necessity that every church should agree with this church, on account of its preeminent authority, that is, the faithful everywhere, inasmuch as the apostolical tradition has been preserved continuously by those [faithful men] who exist everywhere.

3 The blessed apostles, then, having founded and built up the Church, committed into the hands of Linus the office of the episcopate. Of this Linus, Paul makes mention in the Epistles to Timothy. To him succeeded Anacletus; and after him, in the third place from the apostles, Clement was allotted the bishopric. This man, as he had seen the blessed apostles, and had been conversant with them, might be said to have the preaching of the apostles still echoing [in his ears], and their traditions before his eyes. Nor was he alone [in this], for there were many still remaining who had received instructions from the apostles. In the time of this Clement, no small dissension having occurred among the brethren at Corinth, the Church in Rome despatched a most powerful letter to the Corinthians, exhorting them to peace, renewing their faith, and declaring the tradition which it had lately received from the apostles, proclaiming the one God, omnipotent, the Maker of heaven and earth, the Creator of humans, who brought on the deluge, and called Abraham, who led the people from the land of Egypt, spoke with Moses, set forth the law, sent the prophets, and who has prepared fire for the devil and his angels. From this document, whosoever chooses to do so, may learn that he, the Father of our Lord Jesus Christ, was preached by the churches, and may also understand the apostolical tradition of the church, since this Epistle is of older date than these people who are now propagating falsehood, and who conjure into existence another god beyond the Creator and the Maker of all existing things. To this Clement

there succeeded Evaristus. Alexander followed Evaristus; then, sixth from the apostles, Sixtus was appointed; after him, Telephorus, who was gloriously martyred; then Hyginus; after him, Pius; then after him, Anicetus. Soter having succeeded Anicetus, Eleutherius does now, in the twelfth place from the apostles, hold the inheritance of the episcopate. In this order, and by this succession, the ecclesiastical tradition from the apostles, and the preaching of the truth, have come down to us. And this is most abundant proof that there is one and the same vivifying faith, which has been preserved in the church from the apostles until now, and handed down in truth.

4 But Polycarp also was not only instructed by apostles, and conversed with many who had seen Christ, but was also, by apostles in Asia, appointed bishop of the church in Smyrna, whom I also saw in my early youth, for he tarried [on earth] a very long time, and, when a very old man, gloriously and most nobly suffering martyrdom, departed this life, having always taught the things which he had learned from the apostles, and which the Church has handed down, and which alone are true. To these things all the Asiatic Churches testify, as do also those men who have succeeded Polycarp down to the present time—a man who was of much greater weight, and a more steadfast witness of truth, than Valentinus, and Marcion, and the rest of the heretics. He it was who, coming to Rome in the time of Anicetus, caused many to turn away from the aforesaid heretics to the Church of God, proclaiming that he had received this one and sole truth from the apostles—that, namely, which is handed down by the church. There are also those who heard from him that John, the disciple of the Lord, going to bathe at Ephesus, and perceiving Cerinthus within, rushed out of the bath-house without bathing, exclaiming, "Let us fly, lest even the bath-house fall down, because Cerinthus, the enemy of the truth, is within." And Polycarp himself replied to Marcion, who met him on one occasion, and said, "Do you know me?" "I do know you, the first-born of Satan." Such was the

horror which the apostles and their disciples had against holding even verbal communication with any corrupters of the truth; as Paul also says, "A person that is an heretic, after the first and second admonition, reject; knowing that he that is such is subverted, and sins, being condemned of himself."[21] There is also a very powerful Epistle of Polycarp written to the Philippians, from which those who choose to do so, and are anxious about their salvation, can learn the character of his faith, and the preaching of the truth. Then, again, the Church in Ephesus, founded by Paul, and having John remaining among them permanently until the times of Trajan, is a true witness of the tradition of the apostles.

Chapter 4

1 Since therefore we have such proofs, it is not necessary to seek the truth among others which it is easy to obtain from the church; since the apostles, like a rich person [depositing his money] in a bank, lodged in her hands most copiously all things pertaining to the truth: so that every one, whosoever will, can draw from her the water of life. For she is the entrance to life; all others are thieves and robbers. On this account are we bound to avoid them, but to make choice of the things pertaining to the church with the utmost diligence, and to lay hold of the tradition of the truth. For how stands the case? Suppose there arise a dispute relative to some important question among us, should we not have recourse to the most ancient churches with which the apostles held constant intercourse, and learn from them what is certain and clear in regard to the present question? For how should it be if the apostles themselves had not left us writings? Would it not be necessary, [in that case,] to follow the course of the tradition which they handed down to those to whom they did commit the churches?

2 To which course many nations of those barbarians who believe in Christ do assent, having salvation written in their hearts by the Spirit, without paper or ink, and, carefully preserving the ancient tradition, believing in one God, the Creator of heaven and earth, and all things therein, by means of Christ Jesus, the Son of God; who, because of his surpassing love towards his creation, condescended to be born of the virgin, he himself uniting people through himself to God, and having suffered under Pontius Pilate, and rising again, and having been received up in splendor, shall come in glory, the Savior of those who are saved, and the Judge of those who are judged, and sending into eternal fire those who transform the truth, and despise his Father and his advent. Those who, in the absence of written documents, have believed this faith, are barbarians, so far as regards our language; but as regards doctrine, manner, and tenor of life, they are, because of faith, very wise indeed; and they do please God, ordering their conversation in all righteousness, chastity, and wisdom. If any one were to preach to these people the inventions of the heretics, speaking to them in their own language, they would at once stop their ears, and flee as far off as possible, not enduring even to listen to the blasphemous address. Thus, by means of that ancient tradition of the apostles, they do not suffer their mind to conceive anything of the [doctrines suggested by the] portentous language of these teachers, among whom neither church nor doctrine has ever been established.

3 For, prior to Valentinus, those who follow Valentinus had no existence; nor did those from Marcion exist before Marcion; nor, in short, had any of those malignant-minded people, whom I have above enumerated, any being previous to the initiators and inventors of their perversity. For Valentinus came to Rome in the time of Hyginus, flourished under Pius, and remained until Anicetus. Cerdo, too, Marcion's predecessor, himself arrived in the time of Hyginus, who was the ninth bishop. Coming frequently into the church, and making public confession, he thus remained, one time teaching in secret, and then again making public confession; but at last, having been

---

21 Tit 3:10.

denounced for corrupt teaching, he was excommunicated from the assembly of the brethren. Marcion, then, succeeding him, flourished under Anicetus, who held the tenth place of the episcopate. But the rest, who are called Gnostics, take rise from Menander, Simon's disciple, as I have shown; and each one of them appeared to be both the father and the high priest of that doctrine into which he has been initiated. But all these (the Marcosians) broke out into their apostasy much later, even during the intermediate period of the church.

36. Tertullian: Prescription of the Heretics

Tertullian was one of the most brilliant and wide-ranging Christian authors of the first three centuries, as we have already seen in Chapter 4 (see that Introduction). One of his most famous works is the heresiological treatise, "Prescription of the Heretics." As we will see in selection 65, the title refers to an established Roman legal practice, the "prescription," in which a lawyer could prevent a case from coming to trial on the basis of a legal technicality. Tertullian makes a metaphorical use of this strategy: heretics do not need to be given a fair hearing—their case does not even need to be put on the docket—because as those who have abandoned the church, they have forfeited their right to defend their views from the Scriptures that belong only to true Christians.

In the current selection, Tertullian introduces his treatise by indicating that it should come as no surprise that numerous heresies have arisen. Heresy, however, is sinful, forbidden by God, and demonic. True Christians follow the "Rule of Faith"— the set of orthodox doctrines that was handed down from the apostles themselves. Any other, contrary beliefs are to be ruled out of court.

Other significant ideas are developed in this treatise as well, including the notion that heretics have acquired their ideas from the pagan philosophers, that there is one rule of faith subscribed to by all true Christians, that heretics have modified the texts of Scripture to their own ends, and that their improper use of Scripture is paralleled by the undisciplined management of their churches. All in all, this is a brilliant tour de force composed early in Tertullian's career, possibly around 200 CE.

1 The times we live in provoke me to remark that we ought not to be surprised either at the occurrence of the heresies, since they were foretold, or at their occasional subversion of faith, since they occur precisely in order to prove faith by testing it. To be scandalized, as many are, by the great power of heresy is groundless and unthinking. What power could it have if it never

Tertullian: Prescription of the Heretics, from *Early Latin Theology: Selections from Tertullian, Cyprian, Ambrose and Jerome*, ed. S. L. Greenslade [The Library of Christian Classics, V]. London: SCM Press, 1956. Used with permission of SCM Press and Westminster John Knox Press.

occurred? When something is unquestionably destined to come into existence, it receives, together with the purpose of its existence, the force by which it comes to exist and which precludes its non-existence.

2 Fever, for example, we are not surprised to find in its appointed place among the fatal and excruciating issues which destroy human life, since it does in fact exist; and we are not surprised to find it destroying life, since that is why it exists. Similarly, if we are alarmed that heresies which have been produced in order to weaken and kill faith can actually do so, we ought first to be alarmed at their very existence. Existence and power are inseparable.

Faced with fever, which we know to be evil in its purpose and power, it is not surprise we feel, but loathing; and as it is not in our power to abolish it, we take what precautions we can against it. But when it comes to heresies, which bring eternal death and the heat of a keener fire with them, there are people who prefer to be surprised at their power rather than avoid it, although they have the power to avoid it. But heresy will lose its strength if we are not surprised that it is strong. . . .

6 I need say no more on that point, for it is the same Paul who elsewhere, when writing to the Galatians,[1] classes heresy among the sins of the flesh, and who counsels Titus to shun a heretic after the first reproof[2] because such a person is perverted and sinful, standing self-condemned. Besides, he censures heresy in almost every letter when he presses the duty of avoiding false doctrine, which is in fact the product of heresy. This is a Greek word meaning choice, the choice which anyone exercises when he teaches heresy or adopts it. That is why he calls a heretic self-condemned; he chooses for himself the cause of his condemnation. We Christians are forbidden to introduce anything on our own authority or to choose what

someone else introduces on his own authority. Our authorities are the Lord's apostles, and they in turn chose to introduce nothing on their own authority. They faithfully passed on to the nations the teaching which they had received from Christ. So we should anathematize even an angel from heaven if he were to preach a different gospel.[3] The Holy Ghost had already at that time foreseen that an angel of deceit would come in a virgin called Philumene, transforming himself into an angel of light, by whose miracles and tricks Apelles was deceived into introducing a new heresy.

7 These are human and demonic doctrines, engendered for itching ears by the ingenuity of that worldly wisdom which the Lord called foolishness, choosing the foolish things of the world to put philosophy to shame. For worldly wisdom culminates in philosophy with its rash interpretation of God's nature and purpose. It is philosophy that supplies the heresies with their equipment. From philosophy come the aeons and those infinite forms—whatever they are—and Valentinus's human trinity. He had been a Platonist. From philosophy came Marcion's God, the better for his inactivity. He had come from the Stoics. The idea of a mortal soul was picked up from the Epicureans, and the denial of the restitution of the flesh was taken over from the common tradition of the philosophical schools. Zeno taught them to equate God and matter, and Heracleitus comes on the scene when anything is being laid down about a god of fire. Heretics and philosophers perpend the same themes and are caught up in the same discussions. What is the origin of evil, and why? The origin of humans, and how? And—Valentinus's latest subject—what is the origin of God? No doubt in Desire and Abortion! A plague on Aristotle, who taught them dialectic, the art which destroys as much as it builds, which changes its opinions like a coat, forces its conjectures, is stubborn in argument, works hard at being contentious and is a burden even to itself. For it

1 Gal 5:20.
2 Tit 3:10.

3 Gal 1:8.

reconsiders every point to make sure it never finishes a discussion.

From philosophy come those fables and endless genealogies and fruitless questionings, those words that creep like a canker. To hold us back from such things, the Apostle testifies expressly in his letter to the Colossians that we should beware of philosophy. "Take heed lest anyone circumvent you through philosophy or vain deceit, after the tradition of humans,"[4] against the providence of the Holy Spirit. He had been at Athens where he had come to grips with the human wisdom which attacks and perverts truth, being itself divided up into its own swarm of heresies by the variety of its mutually antagonistic sects. What has Jerusalem to do with Athens, the Church with the Academy, the Christian with the heretic? Our principles come from the Porch of Solomon, who had himself taught that the Lord is to be sought in simplicity of heart. I have no use for a Stoic or a Platonic or a dialectic Christianity. After Jesus Christ we have no need of speculation, after the Gospel no need of research. When we come to believe, we have no desire to believe anything else; for we begin by believing that there is nothing else which we have to believe. . . .

13 The Rule of Faith—to state here and now what we maintain—is of course that by which we believe that there is but one God, who is none other than the Creator of the world, who produced everything from nothing through his Word, sent forth before all things; that this Word is called his Son, and in the Name of God was seen in divers ways by the patriarchs, was ever heard in the prophets and finally was brought down by the Spirit and power of God the Father into the Virgin Mary, was made flesh in her womb, was born of her and lived as Jesus Christ; who thereafter proclaimed a new law and a new promise of the kingdom of heaven, worked miracles, was crucified, on the third day rose again, was caught up into heaven and sat down at the

right hand of the Father; that he sent in his place the power of the Holy Spirit to guide believers; that he will come with glory to take the saints up into the fruition of the life eternal and the heavenly promises and to judge the wicked to everlasting fire, after the resurrection of both good and evil with the restoration of their flesh.

This Rule, taught (as will be proved) by Christ, allows of no questions among us, except those which heresies introduce and which make heretics. To know nothing against the Rule is to know everything. . . .

14 . . . Grant that heretics are not enemies of the truth, grant that we were not warned to avoid them, what is the good of conferring with people who themselves profess that they are still seeking? If they are indeed still seeking, they have still found nothing certain. Whatever they hold is only provisional. Their continual searching shows up their hesitation. And so when you, a seeker like them, look to people who are seekers themselves, the doubter to the doubters, the uncertain to the uncertain, then, blind yourself, you must needs be led by the blind into the ditch. But, in fact, it is only for the sake of deceiving us that they pretend to be still seeking. By first filling us with anxiety, they hope to commend their own views to us. The moment they get near us they begin to defend the very propositions which, they had been saying, need investigation. We must be as quick to refute them, making them understand that it is not Christ we deny, but themselves. In that they are still seeking, they do not yet hold any convictions. In that they possess no convictions, they have yet come to believe. In that they have not yet come to believe, they are not Christians.

An objection is raised. "They do hold convictions and believe, but assert the necessity of 'seeking' in order to defend their faith." Yes, but before they defend it they deny it, confessing by their seeking that they have not yet believed. Not Christians even to themselves, how can they be to us? What sort of faith are they arguing when they come with deceit? What truth are they vindicating

4 Col 2:8.

when they introduce it with a lie? Another objection. "They discuss and persuade on the basis of Scripture." Naturally. From what other source than the literature of the faith could they talk about the things of the faith?

15 So I reach the position I had planned. I was steering in this direction, laying the foundations by my introductory remarks. From this point onwards I shall contest the ground of my opponents' appeal. They plead Scripture, and some people are influenced from the outset by this audacious plea. Then, as the contest goes on, they weary even the strong, they capture the weak and send the waverers off torn with anxiety. Therefore I take my stand above all on this point: they are not to be admitted to any discussion of Scripture at all. If the Scriptures are to be their strong point (supposing they can get hold of them), we must first discover who are the rightful owners of the Scriptures, in case anyone is given access to them without any kind of right to them.

16 Do not suspect me of raising this objection from want of confidence or from a desire to enter upon the issues in some other way. My reason is primarily the obedience which our faith owes to the Apostle when he forbids us to enter upon questionings, to lend our ears to novel sayings, to associate with a heretic after one correction[5]—not, observe, after one *discussion*. In designating correction as the reason for meeting a heretic, he forbade discussion, and he says *one* correction because the heretic is not a Christian. He is to have no right to a second censure, like a Christian, before two or three witnesses, since he is to be censured for the very reason that forbids discussion with him. Besides, arguments about Scripture achieve nothing but a stomach-ache or a headache.

17 Any given heresy rejects one or another book of the Bible. What it accepts, it perverts with both additions and subtractions to suit

its own teaching, and if, in some cases, it keeps books unmaimed, it none the less alters them by inventing different interpretations from ours. False exegesis injures truth just as much as a corrupt text. Baseless assumptions naturally refuse to acknowledge the instrument of their own refutation. They rely on passages which they have put together in a false context or fastened on because of their ambiguity. What will you accomplish, most learned of biblical scholars, if the other side denies what you affirmed and affirms what you denied? True, you will lose nothing in the dispute but your voice; and you will get nothing from their blasphemy but bile.

18 You submit yourself to a biblical disputation in order to strengthen some waverer. Will he in fact incline to the truth any more than to heresy? He sees that you have accomplished nothing, the rival party being allowed equal rights of denial and affirmation and an equal status. As a result he will go away from the argument even more uncertain than before, not knowing which he is to count as heresy. The heretics too can retort these charges upon us. Maintaining equally that the truth is with them, they are compelled to say that it is we who introduce the falsifications of Scripture and the lying interpretations.

19 It follows that we must not appeal to Scripture and we must not contend on ground where victory is impossible or uncertain or not certain enough. Even if a biblical dispute did not leave the parties on a par, the natural order of things would demand that one point should be decided first, the point which alone calls for discussion now, namely, who holds the faith to which the Bible belongs, and from whom, through whom, when, and to whom was the teaching delivered by which people become Christians? For only where the true Christian teaching and faith are evident will the true Scriptures, the true interpretations, and all the true Christian traditions be found.

5 Tit 3:10.

20 Our Lord Jesus Christ, whoever he is—if he will permit me to speak in this way for the moment—of whatever God he is Son, of whatever matter Man and God, whatever faith he taught, whatever reward he promised, himself declared, while he lived on earth, what he was, what he had been, how he was fulfilling his Father's will, what he was laying down as a person's duty. He declared all this either openly to the people or privately to the disciples, twelve of whom he had specially attached to his person and destined to be the teachers of the nations. One of them was struck off. The remaining eleven, on his return to his Father after the resurrection, he ordered to go and teach the nations, baptizing them into the Father and into the Son and into the Holy Spirit.

At once, therefore, the apostles (whose name means "sent") cast lots and added a twelfth, Matthias, in the place of Judas, on the authority of the prophecy in a psalm of David; and having obtained the promised power of the Holy Spirit to work miracles and to speak boldly, they set out through Judaea first, bearing witness to their faith in Jesus Christ and founding churches, and then out into the world, proclaiming the same doctrine of the same faith to the nations. Again they set up churches in every city, from which the other churches afterwards borrowed the transmission of the faith and the seeds of doctrine and continue to borrow them every day, in order to become churches. By this they are themselves reckoned apostolic as being the offspring of apostolic churches. Things of every kind must be classed according to their origin. These churches, then, numerous as they are, are identical with that one primitive apostolic church from which they all come. All are primitive and all apostolic. Their common unity is proved by fellowship in communion, by the name of brother and the mutual pledge of hospitality—rights which are governed by no other principle than the single tradition of a common creed.

21 On this ground, therefore, we rule our prescription. If the Lord Christ Jesus sent the apostles to preach, none should be received as preachers except in accordance with Christ's institution. For no one knows the Father save the Son and the one to whom the Son has revealed him, nor is the Son known to have revealed him to any but the apostles whom he sent to preach—and of course to preach what he revealed to them. And I shall prescribe now that what they preached (that is, what Christ revealed to them) should be proved only through the identical churches which the apostles themselves established by preaching to them both *viva voce*, as one says, and afterwards by letters. If this is so, it follows that all doctrine which is in agreement with those apostolic churches, the wombs and sources of the faith, is to be deemed true on the ground that it indubitably preserves what the churches received from the apostles, the apostles from Christ, and Christ from God. It follows, on the other hand, that all doctrine which smacks of anything contrary to the truth of the churches and apostles of Christ and God must be condemned out of hand as originating in falsehood.

It remains for me to show whether this doctrine of ours, the Rule of which I have set out above, does originate in the tradition of the apostles and whether, in consequence, the other doctrines come from falsehood. We are in communion with the apostolic churches. That is not true of any other doctrine. This is evidence of truth. . . .

32 But if any heresies venture to plant themselves in the apostolic age, so that they may be thought to have been handed down by the apostles because they existed in their time, we can say, Let them exhibit the origins of their churches, let them unroll the list of their bishops, coming down from the beginning by succession in such a way that their first bishop had for his originator and predecessor one of the apostles or apostolic men; one, I mean, who continued with the apostles. For this is how the apostolic churches record their origins. The church of Smyrna, for example, reports that Polycarp was placed there by John, the church of Rome that Clement was ordained by Peter. In just the same way the other churches produced men who were appointed to the office of bishop by the apostles and so transmitted the apostolic seed to them.

Let the heretics invent something of the sort for themselves. Blasphemers already, they will have no scruples. But even if they do invent something, it will be useless to them. If their teaching is compared with the teaching of the apostles, the differences and contradictions between them will cry out that theirs is not the work of any apostle or apostolic person. For the apostles would not have differed from each other in their teaching and the apostolic persons would not have contradicted the apostles. Or are we to believe that the people who learned from the apostles preached something different? Consequently they will be challenged according to this standard by those churches which, though they can produce no apostle or apostolic person as their direct founder, since they are much later foundations (churches are being founded every day), yet, because they agree in the same faith, are reckoned to be no less apostolic through their kinship in doctrine. So, when the heresies are challenged by our churches according to these two standards, let them one and all show how they regard themselves as apostolic. But they are not, and they cannot prove themselves to be what they are not. Nor can they be received into peace and communion by churches which are in any way apostolic when they are in no way apostolic on account of their disagreement in creed. . . .

37 If therefore truth must be adjudged to us "as many as walk according to this rule"[6] which the church has handed down from the apostles, the apostles from Christ, and Christ from God, the principle which we propounded is established, the principle which ruled that heretics are not to be allowed to enter an appeal to Scripture, since, without using Scripture, we prove that they have nothing to do with Scripture. If they are heretics, they cannot be Christians, since the names which they accept come not from Christ but from the heretics whom they follow of their

own choice. So, not being Christians, they acquire no right to Christian literature, and we have every right to say to them: "Who are you? When did you arrive, and where from? You are not my people; what are you doing on my land? By what right are you cutting down my timber, Marcion? By whose leave are you diverting my waters, Valentinus? By what authority are you moving my boundaries, Apelles? This property belongs to me. And all the rest of you, why are you sowing and grazing here at your will? It is my property. I have been in possession for a long time, I came into possession before you appeared. I have good title-deeds from the original owners of the estate. I am heir to the apostles. As they provided in their will, as they bequeathed it in trust and confirmed it under oath, so, on their terms, I hold it. You they permanently disinherited and disowned as strangers and enemies." And how can heretics be strangers and enemies to the apostles except through their difference in doctrine, which each of them, on his own judgment, has either produced or received against the apostles?

38 Corruption of the Scriptures and of their interpretation is to be expected wherever difference in doctrine is discovered. Those who proposed to teach differently were of necessity driven to tamper with the literature of doctrine, for they could not have taught differently had they not possessed different sources of teaching. Just as their corruption of doctrine would not have been successful without their corruption of its literature, so our doctrinal integrity would have failed us without the integrity of the sources by which doctrine is dealt with.

Now, in our sources, what is there to contradict our teaching? What have we imported of our own making, that we should find it contradicted in Scripture, and remedy the defect by subtraction or addition or alteration? What we are, that the Scriptures have been from their beginning. We are of them, before there was any change, before you mutilated them. Mutilation must always be later than the original. It springs from hostility,

---

6 Gal 6:16.

which is neither earlier than, nor at home with, what it opposes. Consequently no person of sense can believe that it is we who introduced the textual corruptions into Scripture, we who have existed from the beginning and are the first, any more than he can help believing that it is they, who are later and hostile, who were the culprits. One man perverts Scripture with his hand, another with his exegesis. If Valentinus seems to have used the whole Bible, he laid violent hands on the truth with just as much cunning as Marcion. Marcion openly and nakedly used the knife, not the pen, massacring Scripture to suit his own material. Valentinus spared the text, since he did not invent scriptures to suit his matter, but matter to suit the Scriptures. Yet he took away, and added more, by taking away the proper meanings of particular words and by adding fantastic arrangements. . . .

41 I must not leave out a description of the heretics' way of life—futility, earthly, all too human, lacking in gravity, in authority, in discipline, as suits their faith. To begin with, one cannot tell who is a catechumen and who is baptized. They come in together, listen together, pray together. Even if any of the heathen arrive, they are quite willing to cast that which is holy to the dogs and their pearls (false ones!) before swine. The destruction of discipline is to them simplicity, and our attention to it they call affectation. They are in communion with everyone everywhere. Differences of theology are of no concern to them as long as they are all agreed in attacking the truth. They are all puffed up, they all promise knowledge. Their catechumens are perfect before they are fully instructed. As for the women of the heretics, how forward they are! They have the impudence to teach, to argue, to perform exorcisms, to promise cures, perhaps even to baptize. Their ordinations are hasty, irresponsible, and unstable. Sometimes they appoint novices, sometimes people tied to secular office, sometimes renegades from us, hoping to

bind them by ambition as they cannot bind them by the truth. Nowhere can you get quicker promotion than in the camp of the rebels, where your mere presence is a merit. So one man is bishop today, another tomorrow. The deacon of today is tomorrow's reader, the priest of today is tomorrow a layman. For they impose priestly functions even upon laymen.

42 What am I to say about the ministry of the word? Their concern is not to convert the heathen, but to subvert our folk. The glory they seek comes from bringing the upright down, not raising the fallen up. Since their work results from no constructive operations of their own, but from the destruction of the truth, they undermine our constructions to build their own. Take their complaints against the Law of Moses and the prophets and God the Creator away from them, and they have nothing to say. So it comes about that they find it easier to pull down standing buildings than to build up fallen ruins. In such labor only do they show themselves humble and suave and respectful. But they have no reverence for their own leaders. The reason why there are practically no schisms among the heretics is that when they occur they are not noticed, for their very unity is schism. I am much mistaken if among themselves they do not make alterations in their own rules of faith, each of them adapting what he has received to suit himself, just as the person who handed it down had put it together to suit himself. Its development does not belie its nature and the character of its origin. The Valentinians and Marcionites have taken the same liberty as Valentinus and Marcion themselves to make innovations in faith at their pleasure. In short, when heresies are closely examined, they are all found to be in disagreement on many points with their own founders. A great number of them even have no churches. Motherless and homeless, they wander about bereft of faith and banished from the truth.

37. Tertullian: On the Flesh of Christ

Although his "Prescription" maintains that heretical views do not need even to be considered, Tertullian himself attacked his Christian opponents at considerable length, summarizing, ridiculing, and refuting their views on the basis of the Christian Scriptures. In the present treatise he addresses those who maintained that Christ did not have real flesh—in other words, who taught that although Christ appeared to be human it was indeed all an appearance. This view is normally called "docetism," from the Greek word *dokeo*, "to seem" or "to appear."

A principal proponent of a docetic Christology was the mid–second-century thinker and evangelist Marcion, against whom Tertullian devoted an entire five-volume work elsewhere ("Against Marcion"). Taking his cue from Paul's letters, Marcion maintained that there was a sharp disjuncture between the Law of Moses and the Gospel of Christ; for him, in fact, the God who gave the Law to his people, the Jews, was not the God of Jesus. The Jewish God was harsh and vindictive ("an eye for an eye"); the God of Jesus was gracious and merciful ("turn the other cheek"). The Jewish God had created the world; the God of Jesus had never had anything to do with it—until he sent Jesus to save people from its harsh Judge. Since this world belonged to the creator God, Jesus had no ties to it; he was not really born and did not have real flesh. Marcion supported his views by appealing to his own version of the Christian Scriptures, comprising a Gospel comparable to Luke (from the New Testament) and ten of the Pauline epistles (excluding the Pastorals)—all edited by the removal of positive references to the Old Testament and its creator God.

In refuting Marcion's views, and those that he deemed similar, Tertullian makes extensive appeal to the words of his own New Testament (not just Luke and Paul) and offers some very interesting interpretations, including one of the earliest Christian expositions of the parallels between Eve and Mary.

1 They who are so anxious to shake that belief in the resurrection which was firmly settled before the appearance of our modern Sadducees, as even to deny that the expectation thereof has any relation whatever to the flesh, have great cause for besetting the flesh of Christ also with doubtful questions, as if it either had no existence at all, or possessed a nature altogether different from human flesh. For they cannot but be apprehensive that, if it be once determined that Christ's flesh was human, a presumption would immediately arise in opposition to them, that that flesh must by all means rise again, which has already risen in Christ. Therefore we shall have to guard our belief in the resurrection from the same armory, whence they get their weapons of destruction. Let us examine our Lord's bodily substance, for about his spiritual nature all are agreed. It is his flesh that is

Tertullian: On the Flesh of Christ, from *The Ante-Nicene Fathers*, vol. 3. *Latin Christianity: Its Founder, Tertullian*, ed. A. Cleveland Coxe. Reprint; 2d ed. Grand Rapids: Eerdmans, 1989.

in question. Its verity and quality are the points in dispute. Did it ever exist? Whence was it derived? And of what kind was it? If we succeed in demonstrating it, we shall lay down a law for our own resurrection. Marcion, in order that he might deny the flesh of Christ, denied also his nativity, or else he denied his flesh in order that he might deny his nativity; because, of course, he was afraid that his nativity and his flesh bore mutual testimony to each other's reality, since there is no nativity without flesh, and no flesh without nativity. As if indeed, under the prompting of that license which is ever the same in all heresy, he too might not very well have either denied the nativity, although admitting the flesh—like Apelles, who was first a disciple of his, and afterwards an apostate—or, while admitting both the flesh and the nativity, have interpreted them in a different sense, as did Valentinus, who resembled Apelles both in his discipleship and desertion of Marcion. At all events, he who represented the flesh of Christ to be imaginary was equally able to pass off his nativity as a phantom; so that the virgin's conception, and pregnancy, and child-bearing, and then the whole course of her infant too, would have to be regarded as putative. These facts pertaining to the nativity of Christ would escape the notice of the same eyes and the same senses as failed to grasp the full idea of his flesh.

2 Clearly enough is the nativity announced by Gabriel.[1] But what has he to do with the Creator's angel? The conception in the virgin's womb is also set plainly before us. But what concern has he with the Creator's prophet, Isaiah?[2] He will not brook delay, since suddenly (without any prophetic announcement) did he bring down Christ from heaven. "Away," says he, "with that eternal plaguey taxing of Caesar, and the scanty inn, and the squalid swaddling-clothes, and the hard stable. We do not care a jot for that multitude of the heavenly host which praised their Lord at night.

Let the shepherds take better care of their flock, and let the wise men spare their legs so long a journey; let them keep their gold to themselves. Let Herod, too, mend his manners, so that Jeremiah may not glory over him. Spare also the babe from circumcision, that he may escape the pain thereof; nor let him be brought into the temple, lest he burden his parents with the expense of the offering; nor let him be handed to Simeon, lest the old man be saddened at the point of death. Let that old woman also hold her tongue, lest she should bewitch the child."[3] After such a fashion as this, I suppose you have had, O Marcion, the hardihood of blotting out the original records (of the history) of Christ, that his flesh may lose the proofs of its reality. But on what grounds (do you do this)? Show me your authority. If you are a prophet, foretell us a thing; if you are an apostle, open your message in public; if a follower of apostles, side with apostles in thought; if you are only a (private) Christian, believe what has been handed down to us: if, however, you are nothing of all this, then (as I have the best reason to say) cease to live. For indeed you are already dead, since you are no Christian, because you do not believe that which by being believed makes people Christian—nay, you are the more dead, the more you are not a Christian; having fallen away, after you had been one, by rejecting what you formerly believed, even as you yourself acknowledge in a certain letter of yours, and as your followers do not deny, while our (brethren) can prove it. Rejecting, therefore, what you once believed, you have completed the act of rejection, by now no longer believing: the fact, however, of your having ceased to believe has not made your rejection of the faith right and proper; nay, rather, by your act of rejection you prove that what you believed previous to the said act was of a different character. What you believed to be of a different character, had been handed down just as you believed it. Now that which had been handed down was true, inasmuch as it had been transmitted by those whose duty it

1 Luke 1:26–38.

2 Isa 7:14.

3 Matt 1–2; Luke 1–2.

was to hand it down. Therefore, when rejecting that which had been handed down, you rejected that which was true. You had no authority for what you did. However, we have already in another treatise availed ourselves more fully of these prescriptive rules against all heresies. Our repetition of them here after that large (treatise) is superfluous, when we ask the reason why you have formed the opinion that Christ was not born.

3 Since you think that this lay within the competency of your own arbitrary choice, you must needs have supposed that being born was either impossible for God, or unbecoming to him. With God, however, nothing is impossible but what he does not will. Let us consider, then, whether he willed to be born (for if he had the will, he also had the power, and was born). I put the argument very briefly. If God had willed not to be born, it matters not why, he would not have presented himself in the likeness of a human. Now who, when he sees a human, would deny that he had been born? What God therefore willed not to be, he would in no wise have willed the seeming to be. When a thing is distasteful, the very notion of it is scouted; because it makes no difference whether a thing exist or do not exist, if, when it does not exist, it is yet assumed to exist. It is of course of the greatest importance that there should be nothing false (or pretended) attributed to that which really does not exist. But, say you, his own consciousness (of the truth of his nature) was enough for him. If any supposed that he had been born, because they saw him as a man, that was their concern. Yet with how much more dignity and consistency would he have sustained the human character on the supposition that he was truly born; for if he were not born, he could not have undertaken the said character without injury to that consciousness of his which you on your side attribute to his confidence of being able to sustain, although not born, the character of having been born even against his own consciousness! Why, I want to know, was it of so much importance, that Christ should, when perfectly aware

what he really was, exhibit himself as being that which he was not? You cannot express any apprehension that, if he had been born and truly clothed himself with human nature, he would have ceased to be God, losing what he was, while becoming what he was not. For God is in no danger of losing his own state and condition. But, say you, I deny that God was truly changed to a human in such wise as to be born and endued with a body of flesh, on this ground, that a being who is without end is also of necessity incapable of change. For being changed into something else puts an end to the former state. Change, therefore, is not possible to a Being who cannot come to an end. Without doubt, the nature of things which are subject to change is regulated by this law, that they have no permanence in the state which is undergoing change in them, and that they come to an end from thus wanting permanence, whilst they lose that in the process of change which they previously were. But nothing is equal with God; his nature is different from the condition of all things. If, then, the things which differ from God, and from which God differs, lose what existence they had while they are undergoing change, wherein will consist the difference of the Divine Being from all other things except in his possessing the contrary faculty of theirs—in other words, that God can be changed into all conditions, and yet continue just as he is? On any other supposition, he would be on the same level with those things which, when changed, lose the existence they had before; whose equal, of course, he is not in any other respect, as he certainly is not in the changeful issues of their nature. You have sometimes read and believed that the Creator's angels have been changed into human form, and have even borne about so veritable a body, that Abraham even washed their feet,[4] and Lot was rescued from the Sodomites by their hands;[5] an angel, moreover, wrestled with a man so strenuously with his

---

4 Gen 18:4.

5 Gen 19:12–23.

body, that the latter desired to be let loose, so tightly was he held.[6] Has it, then, been permitted to angels, which are inferior to God, after they have been changed into human bodily form, nevertheless to remain angels? and will you deprive God, their superior, of this faculty, as if Christ could not continue to be God, after his real assumption of the nature of a human? Or else, did those angels appear as phantoms of flesh? You will not, however, have the courage to say this; for if it be so held in your belief, that the Creator's angels are in the same condition as Christ, then Christ will belong to the same God as those angels do, who are like Christ in their condition. If you had not purposely rejected in some instances, and corrupted in others, the Scriptures which are opposed to your opinion, you would have been confuted in this matter by the Gospel of John, when it declares that the Spirit descended in the body of a dove, and sat upon the Lord.[7] When the said Spirit was in this condition, he was as truly a dove as he was also a spirit; nor did he destroy his own proper substance by the assumption of an extraneous substance. But you ask what becomes of the dove's body, after the return of the Spirit back to heaven, and similarly in the case of the angels. Their withdrawal was effected in the same manner as their appearance had been. If you had seen how their production out of nothing had been effected, you would have known also the process of their return to nothing. If the initial step was out of sight, so was also the final one. Still there was solidity in their bodily substance, whatever may have been the force by which the body became visible. What is written cannot but have been.

4 Since, therefore, you do not reject the assumption of a body as impossible or as hazardous to the character of God, it remains for you to repudiate and censure it as unworthy of him. Come now, beginning from the nativity itself, declaim against the uncleanness of the generative elements within the womb, the filthy concretion of fluid and blood, of the growth of the flesh for nine months long out of that very mire. Describe the womb as it enlarges from day to day—heavy, troublesome, restless even in sleep, changeful in its feelings of dislike and desire. Inveigh now likewise against the shame itself of a woman in labor, which, however, ought rather to be honored in consideration of that peril or to be held sacred in respect of (the mystery of) nature. Of course you are horrified also at the infant, which is shed into life with the embarrassments which accompany it from the womb; you likewise, of course, loathe it even after it is washed, when it is dressed out in its swaddling-clothes, graced with repeated anointing, smiled on with nurse's fawns. This reverend course of nature, you, O Marcion (are pleased to) spit upon; and yet, in what way were you born? You detest a human being at his birth; then after what fashion do you love anybody? Yourself, of course, you had no love of, when you departed from the church and the faith of Christ. But never mind, if you are not on good terms with yourself, or even if you were born in a way different from other people. Christ, at any rate, has loved even that person who was condensed in his mother's womb amidst all its uncleannesses, even that person who was brought into life out of the said womb, even that person who was nursed amidst the nurse's simpers. For his sake he came down (from heaven), for his sake he preached, for his sake "He humbled himself even unto death—the death of the cross."[8] He loved, of course, the being whom he redeemed at so great a cost. If Christ is the Creator's Son, it was with justice that he loved his own (creature); if he comes from another god, his love was excessive, since he redeemed a being who belonged to another. Well, then, loving the human he loved his nativity also, and his flesh as well. Nothing can be loved apart from that through which whatever exists has its existence. Either take away nativity, and then show us your human; or else withdraw the flesh, and then present to our view the being whom God

---

6 Gen 32:22–32.

7 John 1:33.

8 Phil 2:8.

has redeemed—since it is these very conditions which constitute the person whom God has redeemed. And are you for turning these conditions into occasions of blushing to the very creature whom he has redeemed, (censuring them), too, us unworthy of him who certainly would not have redeemed them had he not loved them? Our birth he reforms from death by a second birth from heaven; our flesh he restores from every harassing malady; when leprous, he cleanses it of the stain; when blind, he rekindles its light; when palsied, he renews its strength; when possessed with devils, he exorcises it; when dead, he reanimates it—then shall we blush to own it? If, to be sure, he had chosen to be born of a mere animal, and were to preach the kingdom of heaven invested with the body of a beast either wild or tame, your censure (I imagine) would have instantly met him with this demurrer: "This is disgraceful for God, and this is unworthy of the Son of God, and simply foolish." For no other reason than because one thus judges. It is of course foolish, if we are to judge God by our own conceptions. But, Marcion consider well this Scripture, if indeed you have not erased it: "God has chosen the foolish things of the world, to confound the wise."[9] Now what are those foolish things? Are they the conversion of people to the worship of the true God, the rejection of error, the whole training in righteousness, chastity, mercy, patience, and innocence? These things certainly are not "foolish." Inquire again, then, of what things he spoke, and when you imagine that you have discovered what they are will you find anything to be so "foolish" as believing in a God that has been born, and that of a virgin, and of a fleshly nature too, who wallowed in all the before-mentioned humiliations of nature? But some one may say, "These are not the foolish things; they must be other things which God has chosen to confound the wisdom of the world." And yet, according to the world's wisdom, it is more easy to believe that Jupiter became a bull or a swan, if we listen to Marcion, than that Christ really became a human.

5 There are, to be sure, other things also quite as foolish (as the birth of Christ), which have reference to the humiliations and sufferings of God. Or else, let them call a crucified God "wisdom." But Marcion will apply the knife to this doctrine also and even with greater reason. For which is more unworthy of God, which is more likely to raise a blush of shame, that God should be born, or that he should die? that he should bear the flesh, or the cross? be circumcised, or be crucified? be cradled, or be coffined? be laid in a manger, or in a tomb? Talk of "wisdom!" You will show more of *that* if you refuse to believe this also. But, after all, you will not be "wise" unless you become a "fool" to the world, by believing "the foolish things of God." Have you, then, cut away all sufferings from Christ, on the ground that, as a mere phantom, he was incapable of experiencing them? We have said that he might possibly have undergone the unreal mockeries of an imaginary birth and infancy. But answer me at once, you that murder truth: Was not God really crucified? And, having been really crucified, did he not really die? And, having indeed really died, did he not really rise again? Falsely did Paul "determine to know anything amongst us but Jesus and him crucified;"[10] falsely has he impressed upon us that he was buried; falsely inculcated that he rose again. False, therefore, is our faith also. And all that we hope for from Christ will be a phantom. O you most infamous of men, who acquits of all guilt the murderers of God! For nothing did Christ suffer from them, if he really suffered nothing at all. Spare the whole world's one only hope, you who are destroying the indispensable dishonor of our faith. Whatsoever is unworthy of God, is of gain to me. I am safe, if I am not ashamed of my Lord. "Whosoever," says He, "shall be ashamed of me, of him will I also be ashamed."[11] Other matters for shame find I none which can prove me to be shameless in a good

---

9 1 Cor 1:27.

10 1 Cor 2:2.

11 Mark 8:38.

sense, and foolish in a happy one, by my own contempt of shame. The Son of God was crucified; I am not ashamed because people must be ashamed of it. And the Son of God died; it is by all means to be believed, because it is absurd. And he was buried and rose again; the fact is certain, because it is impossible. But how will all this be true in him, if he was not himself true—if he really had not in himself that which might be crucified, might die, might be buried, and might rise again? I mean this flesh suffused with blood, built up with bones, interwoven with nerves, entwined with veins, a flesh which knew how to be born, and how to die, human without doubt, as born of a human being. It will therefore be mortal in Christ, because Christ is man and the Son of man. Else why is Christ man and the Son of man, if he has nothing of man, and nothing from man? Unless it be either that man is anything else than flesh, or man's flesh comes from any other source than man, or Mary is anything else than a human being, or Marcion's man is as Marcion's god. Otherwise Christ could not be described as being man without flesh, nor the Son of man without any human parent; just as he is not God without the Spirit of God, nor the Son of God without having God for his father. Thus the nature of the two substances displayed him as man and God—in one respect born, in the other unborn; in one respect fleshly, in the other spiritual; in one sense weak in the other exceeding strong; in one sense dying, in the other living. This property of the two states—the divine and the human—is distinctly asserted with equal truth of both natures alike, with the same belief both in respect of the Spirit and of the flesh. The powers of the Spirit, proved him to be God, his sufferings attested the flesh of man. If his powers were not without the Spirit in like manner, were not his sufferings without the flesh. If his flesh with its sufferings was fictitious, for the same reason was the Spirit false with all its powers. Why halve Christ with a lie? He was wholly the truth. Believe me, he chose rather to be born, than in any part to pretend—and that indeed to his own detriment—that he was bearing about a flesh

hardened without bones, solid without muscles, bloody without blood, clothed without the tunic of skin, hungry without appetite, eating without teeth, speaking without a tongue, so that his word was a phantom to the ears through an imaginary voice. A phantom, too, it was of course after the resurrection, when, showing his hands and his feet for the disciples to examine, he said, "Behold and see that it is I myself, for a spirit does not have flesh and bones, as you see that I have;"[12] without doubt, hands, and feet, and bones are not what a spirit possesses, but only the flesh. How do you interpret this statement, Marcion, you who tell us that Jesus comes only from the most excellent God, who is both simple and good? See how He rather cheats, and deceives, and juggles the eyes of all, and the senses of all, as well as their access to and contact with him! You ought rather to have brought Christ down, not from heaven, but from some troop of mountebanks, not as God besides humans, but simply as a human, a magician; not as the High Priest of our salvation, but as the conjurer in a show; not as the raiser of the dead, but as the misleader of the living,—except that, if he were a magician, he must have had a nativity!. . .

17 . . . Leaving Alexander with his syllogisms, which he so persuasively applies in his discussions, as well as with the hymns of Valentinus, which, with consummate assurance, he interpolates as the production of some respectable author, let us confine our inquiry to a single point—Whether Christ received flesh from the virgin?—that we may thus arrive at a certain proof that his flesh was human, if he derived its substance from his mother's womb, although we are at once furnished with clear evidences of the human character of his flesh, from its name and description as that of a human, and from the nature of its constitution, and from the system of its sensations, and from its suffering of death. Now, it will first be necessary to show what previous reason there was for the Son of God's being born of a virgin. He who was going to

---

12 Luke 24:39.

consecrate a new order of birth, must himself be born after a novel fashion, concerning which Isaiah foretold how that the Lord himself would give the sign. What, then, is the sign? "Behold a virgin shall conceive and bear a son."[13] Accordingly, a virgin did conceive and bear "Emmanuel, God with us."[14] This is the new nativity; a human is born in God. And in this human God was born, taking the flesh of an ancient race, without the help, however, of the ancient seed, in order that he might reform it with a new seed, that is, in a spiritual manner, and cleanse it by the removal of all its ancient stains. But the whole of this new birth was prefigured, as was the case in all other instances, in ancient type, the Lord being born as a human by a dispensation in which a virgin was the medium. The earth was still in a virgin state, reduced as yet by no human labor, with no seed as yet cast into its furrows, when, as we are told, God made man out of it into a living soul.[15] As, then, the first Adam is thus introduced to us, it is a just inference that the second Adam likewise, as the apostle has told us, was formed by God into a quickening spirit out of the ground—in other words, out of a flesh which was unstained as yet by any human generation. But that I may lose no opportunity of supporting my argument from the name of Adam, why is Christ called Adam by the apostle, unless it be

that, as a human, he was of that earthly origin? And even reason here maintains the same conclusion, because it was by just the contrary operation that God recovered his own image and likeness, of which he had been robbed by the devil. For it was while Eve was yet a virgin, that the ensnaring word had crept into her ear which was to build the edifice of death. Into a virgin's soul, in like manner, must be introduced that Word of God which was to raise the fabric of life; so that what had been reduced to ruin by this sex, might by the selfsame sex be recovered to salvation. As Eve had believed the serpent,[16] so Mary believed the angel. The delinquency which the one occasioned by believing, the other by believing effaced. But (it will be said) Eve did not at the devil's word conceive in her womb. Well, she at all events conceived; for the devil's word afterwards became as seed to her that she should conceive as an outcast, and bring forth in sorrow. Indeed she gave birth to a fratricidal devil; while Mary, on the contrary, bore one who was one day to secure salvation to Israel, his own brother after the flesh, and the murderer of himself. God therefore sent down into the virgin's womb his Word, as the good brother, who should blot out the memory of the evil brother. Hence it was necessary that Christ should come forth for the salvation of humans, in that condition of flesh into which humanity had entered ever since his condemnation.

13 Isa 7:14.

14 Matt 1:23.

15 Gen 2:7.

16 Gen 3:1–7.

38. Tertullian: Against Praxeas

Among second- and third-century Christians who accepted the basic proto-orthodox understanding of Christ as both human and divine, yet one being instead of two, there was a range of opinion about how to work out all the details. One popular view near the end of the second century was that Jesus was God the Father himself, become human. Only later did this view come to be widely acknowledged as a heresy; its opponents derisively labeled it "patripassianism" ("father-suffering"), for in it God the Father himself was said to have been crucified (see Chapter 16; the view is sometimes also called "Sabellianism" after one of its later proponents). Tertullian was among the first to attack this view, and he did so by spurning one of its leading proponents, a prominent Roman Christian whom he calls Praxeas.

The refutation is significant for several reasons, seen even in the short excerpt that follows: it shows how the debates over the person of Christ were becoming increasingly nuanced in the late second and early third centuries; it suggests how and why Christians began to think of the godhead in terms of a Trinity of beings, different in person but equal in substance (see Chapter 16); and it reveals Tertullian's own commitment to the Christian group known as the Montanists (after their leader, Montanus), who emphasized the ongoing revelatory work of the Holy Spirit and who were themselves later viewed as sectarian by the bulk of proto-orthodox Christians (see Selection 89).

For a further selection from this work, see Chapter 16.

1 In various ways has the devil rivalled and resisted the truth. Sometimes his aim has been to destroy the truth by defending it. He maintains that there is one only Lord, the Almighty Creator of the world, in order that out of this doctrine of the unity he may fabricate a heresy. He says that the Father himself came down into the virgin, was himself born of her, himself suffered, indeed was himself Jesus Christ. Here the old serpent has fallen out with himself, since, when he tempted Christ after John's baptism, he approached him as "the Son of God;" surely intimating that God had a Son, even on the testimony of the very Scriptures, out of which he was at the moment forging his temptation: "If you are the Son of God, command that these stones be made bread."[1] Again: "If you are the Son of God, cast yourself down from here; for it is written, He shall give his angels charge concerning you"—referring no doubt, to the Father—"and in their hands they shall bear up, that you do not strike your foot against a stone."[2] Or perhaps, after all, he was only reproaching the Gospels with a lie, saying in fact: "Away with Matthew; away with Luke! Why heed their words? In spite of them, I declare that it was God himself that I approached; it was the Almighty himself that I tempted face to face; and

1 Matt 4:3; Luke 4:3.

2 Matt 4:6; Luke 4:9–11.

Tertullian: Against Praxeas, from *The Ante-Nicene Fathers*; vol. 3. *Latin Christianity: Its Founder, Tertullian*, ed. A. Cleveland Coxe. Reprint; 2d ed. Grand Rapids: Eerdmans, 1989.

it was for no other purpose than to attempt him that I approached him. If, on the contrary, it had been only the Son of God, most likely I should never have condescended to deal with him." However, he is himself a liar from the beginning, and whatever person he instigates in his own way; as, for instance, Praxeas. For he was the first to import into Rome from Asia this kind of heretical pravity, a man in other respects of restless disposition, and above all inflated with the pride of confessorship simply and solely because he had to bear for a short time the annoyance of a prison; on which occasion, even "if he had given his body to be burned, it would have profited him nothing,"[3] not having the love of God, whose very gifts he has resisted and destroyed. For after the Bishop of Rome had acknowledged the prophetic gifts of Montanus, Prisca, and Maximilla, and, in consequence of the acknowledgment, had bestowed his peace on the churches of Asia and Phrygia, he, by importunately urging false accusations against the prophets themselves and their churches, and insisting on the authority of the bishop's predecessors in the see, compelled him to recall the pacific letter which he had issued, as well as to desist from his purpose of acknowledging the said gifts. By this Praxeas did a twofold service for the devil at Rome: he drove away prophecy, and he brought in heresy; he put to flight the Paraclete, and he crucified the Father. Praxeas' tares had been moreover sown, and had produced their fruit here also, while many were asleep in their simplicity of doctrine; but these tares actually seemed to have been plucked up, having been discovered and exposed by him whose agency God was pleased to employ. Indeed, Praxeas had deliberately resumed his old (true) faith, teaching it after his renunciation of error; and there is his own handwriting in evidence remaining among the carnally-minded, in whose society the transaction then took place; afterwards nothing was heard of him. We indeed, on our part, subsequently withdrew from the carnally-minded on our acknowledgment and maintenance

of the Paraclete. But the tares of Praxeas had then everywhere shaken out their seed, which having lain hid for some while, with its vitality concealed under a mask, has now broken out with fresh life. But again shall it be rooted up, if the Lord will, even now; but if not now, in the day when all bundles of tares shall be gathered together, and along with every other stumbling-block shall be burnt up with unquenchable fire.[4]

2 In the course of time, then, the Father forsooth was born, and the Father suffered—God himself, the Lord Almighty, whom in their preaching they declare to be Jesus Christ. We, however, as we indeed always have done (and more especially since we have been better instructed by the Paraclete, who leads people indeed into all truth), believe that there is one only God, but under the following dispensation, or economy, as it is called, that this one only God has also a Son, his word, who proceeded from himself, by whom all things were made, and without whom nothing was made. Him we believe to have been sent by the Father into the virgin, and to have been born of her—being both man and God, the Son of Man and the Son of God, and to have been called by the name of Jesus Christ; we believe him to have suffered, died, and been buried, according to the Scriptures, and, after he had been raised again by the Father and taken back to heaven, to be sitting at the right hand of the Father, and that he will come to judge the living and the dead; who sent also from heaven from the Father, according to his own promise, the Holy Spirit, the Paraclete, the sanctifier of the faith of those who believe in the Father, and in the Son, and in the Holy Spirit. That this rule of faith has come down to us from the beginning of the gospel, even before any of the older heretics, much more before Praxeas, a pretender of yesterday, will be apparent both from the lateness of date which marks all heresies, and also from the absolutely novel character of our new-fangled Praxeas. In this principle also we must

---

3 1 Cor 13:3.

4 Matt 13:30.

henceforth find a presumption of equal force against all heresies whatsoever—that whatever is first is true, whereas that is spurious which is later in date. But keeping this prescriptive rule inviolate, still some opportunity must be given for reviewing (the statements of heretics), with a view to the instruction and protection of divers persons; were it only that it may not seem that each perversion of the truth is condemned without examination, and simply prejudged; especially in the case of this heresy, which supposes itself to possess the pure truth, in thinking that one cannot believe in One Only God in any other way than by saying that the Father, the Son, and the Holy Spirit are the very selfsame person. As if in this way also one were not all, in that all are of one, by unit (that is) of substance; while the mystery of the dispensation is still guarded, which distributes the Unity into a Trinity, placing in their order the three Persons—the Father, the Son, and the Holy Spirit; three, however, not in condition, but in degree; not in substance, but in form; not in power, but in aspect; yet of one substance, and of one condition, and of one power, inasmuch as he is one God, from whom these degrees and forms and aspects are reckoned, under the name of the Father, and of the Son, and of the Holy Spirit. How they are susceptible of number without division, will be shown as our treatise proceeds.

GNOSTIC HERESIOLOGISTS

(See also Ptolemy's Letter to Flora in Chapter 10 and the Treatise on the Resurrection in Chapter 6)

It is a real loss not to have other sides of the debates over Christian heresy and orthodoxy more fully preserved. We are fortunate, though, to have two Nag Hammadi tractates that indicate how Gnostic heresiologists attacked their proto-orthodox opponents. The basic line of attack, not surprisingly, is that their opponents propounded absurd and ridiculous views about Christ based on a wooden, literalistic reading of sacred texts that, as divinely inspired, cannot simply be understood as bare-bones descriptions of divine realities. The inspired writings of the Old Testament and the events of Jesus' life are full of nuance and deeper meanings, far below the surface, and to understand them completely (rather than superficially, like the proto-orthodox opponents), one needs to be guided by divine revelation and recognize in them the truths about the nature of God and his relation to this world through Christ. Christians without gnosis have been misled by simple-minded bishops who wrangle over words whose depths they cannot perceive and discuss events (such as Jesus' crucifixion) whose meaning they cannot fathom.

THE TEXTS

39. *The Coptic Apocalypse of Peter*

There are three surviving apocalypses allegedly written by Simon Peter, the disciple of Jesus (for another one, see Chapter 8); the one given here was discovered at Nag Hammadi (see Chapter 6). The book contains a series of visions given by Jesus to Peter (hence the title "apocalypse" or "revelation"), which Peter then records in the first person. In these visions, Christ issues dire warnings against the teaching of heretics who propagate falsehoods. Strikingly, the heretics here are the bishops and deacons of the proto-orthodox churches, and their false teaching is that Jesus was himself the Christ who suffered a literal death on the cross. The author deems this staunchly orthodox view laughable; he labels its orthodox proponents blind.

For this author, the true significance of Jesus' death goes much deeper. Even though Jesus' flesh was killed, Christ himself was far removed from suffering; those who beheld the cross with full knowledge (gnosis) did not see the suffering Jesus but the living Christ, who was himself laughing at the entire proceeding. Jesus was merely his outer shell, and those who think that his death matters for salvation have simply seen the deceptive surface of the matter—not the deeper, more important truth.

Most scholars have dated this Gnostic treatise to the third century.

. . . When I said this, the Savior replied, "I have told you that these people are blind and deaf. Now listen to the things I am telling you in secret and keep them. Do not tell them to the children of this age. For they will denounce you during these ages, since they are ignorant of you, but they will praise you when there is knowledge.

"At first many will accept our words, but they will turn away again according to the will of the father of their error, because they have done his will, and the father of error will disclose them in his judgment as servants of the word. Those who have [74] associated with people of error will become their prisoners, since they are without perception. But the good person, who is pure and upright, will be handed over to the dealer in death, in the kingdom of those who praise a Christ of a future restored world. And they also praise people who preach this falsehood, people who will come after you. They will hold on to the name of a dead man, thinking that in this way they will become pure, but instead they will become more and more defiled. They will fall into a name of error and into the hand of an evil deceiver with complicated doctrines, and they will be dominated by heresy.

"Some of them will blaspheme the truth and proclaim evil teachings, and they will speak evil against each other. Some of them will give themselves a name, for they stand in the power of the rulers: the name of a man and a naked woman of

The Revelation of Peter, reproduced from Marvin Meyer, *The Nag Hammadi Scriptures*. San Francisco: HarperOne, 2007. Used with permission of HarperOne.

many forms and many sufferings. And [75] those who say all this will inquire into dreams, and if they claim that a dream came from a demon, which is appropriate for their error, they shall be granted perdition instead of incorruption.

"Evil cannot produce good fruit. Everything, wherever it comes from, produces what is like it. Not every soul is of the truth or of immortality. In our opinion, every soul of these present times is assigned to death and is always enslaved, since this soul is created to serve its own desires. These souls are destined for eternal destruction, in which they are and from which they are, for they love the creatures of matter that came into being with them.

"But immortal souls are not like these, Peter. Still, as long as the hour has not yet come, an immortal soul resembles mortal souls. It will not reveal its true nature: it alone is [76] immortal and contemplates immortality, and has faith, and desires to renounce these mortal souls.

"People do not gather figs from thistles or thorns, if they are wise, nor grapes from thornbushes. Something always stays in that state in which it exists. If something is in a bad state, that becomes destruction and death for the soul. But the soul abides in the eternal one, the source of life and immortality of life that these resemble.

"All that does not really exist will dissolve into nothingness, and those who are deaf and blind associate only with people like them.

"Others will wander from evil words and mysteries that lead people astray. Some who do not understand the mysteries and speak of what they do not understand will boast that the mystery of truth is theirs alone. In arrogance [77] they will embrace pride and will envy the immortal soul that has been used as down payment. For every authority, principality, and power of the ages wants to be with the immortal souls in the created world, in order that these powers, who do not come from what exists and have forgotten who they are, may be glorified by the immortal souls that do exist. The powers have not been saved or shown the way by them, though they always have wished to

become imperishable. For if an immortal soul is empowered by a spirit of thought, at once it is joined by one of those who were led astray.

"Many others, who oppose truth and are messengers of error, will ordain their error and their law against my pure thoughts. Since they see from one perspective only, they think that good and evil come from the same source. They do business in [78] my word. And they will establish harsh fate in which the generation of immortal souls will run in vain, until my return. For the immortal souls will surely remain among them. And I have forgiven the transgressions into which they have fallen through their adversaries, and I have redeemed them from their slavery, to give them freedom.

"Some will create a mere imitation of the remnant in the name of a dead man, who is Hermas, the firstborn of unrighteousness, in order that the little ones may not believe in the light that is. These are the workers who will be cast into the outer darkness, away from the children of light. For they will not enter, nor do they allow those who are going to their destination, for their deliverance, to enter.

"Still others among them endure suffering and think they will perfect [79] the wisdom of the brotherhood that really exists, the spiritual fellowship with those united in communion, through which the wedding of incorruptibility will be revealed. Instead, what will appear is a mere imitation, the kindred generation of the sisterhood. These people oppress their brothers and say to them, 'Through this fellowship our God has mercy, since salvation comes to us alone through this.' They do not know the punishment of those who rejoice at what was done to the little ones, those who watched when the little ones were taken captive.

"And there are others among those outside our number who call themselves bishops and deacons, as if they have received authority from God, but they bow before the judgment of the leaders. These people are dry canals."

I said, "I am afraid because of what you have told me. Although [80] there are only a few phonies among us, there are many others who lead astray and subdue multitudes of living ones. And when they speak your name, people will believe them."

The Savior replied, "For a specified time proportionate to their error, they will rule over the little ones. And after the completion of error, the being of immortal understanding, who does not grow old, will become new, and the little ones will rule over their rulers. That being will pull out their error by its root, and put it to shame and expose it for all the liberties it has taken. Peter, such people will never change.

"Come, let's proceed to the fulfillment of the good pleasure of the incorruptible Father. For look, those who will bring judgment on themselves are approaching and will put themselves to shame. They cannot touch me. Peter, you will stand in their midst, but don't be afraid, though you are fainthearted. [81] Their understanding will be gone, for the invisible one has taken a stand against them."

When he said this, I saw him apparently being arrested by them. I said, "What do I see, Lord? Is it really you they are seizing, and are you holding on to me? And who is the one smiling and laughing above the cross? Is it someone else whose feet and hands they are hammering?"

The Savior said to me, "The one you see smiling and laughing above the cross is the living Jesus. The one into whose hands and feet they are driving nails is his fleshly part, the substitute for him. They are putting to shame the one who came into being in the likeness of the living Jesus. Look at him and look at me."

When I looked, I said, "Lord, no one sees you. Let's get out of here."

He answered me, "I told you they are blind. Forget about them. Look at how they do not know what they are saying. [82] For they have put to shame the son of their own glory instead of the one who serves me."

Then I saw someone about to approach us who looked like the one laughing above the cross, but this one was intertwined with holy spirit, and

he was the Savior. And there was an unspeakably bright light surrounding them and a multitude of ineffable and invisible angels praising them. When the one who glorifies was revealed, I myself saw him.

He said to me, "Be strong, for these mysteries have been given to you so that you might know clearly that the one they crucified is the firstborn, the abode of demons, the stone vessel in which they live, the man of Elohim, the man of the cross, who is under the law. But the one who is standing near him is the living Savior, who was in him at first and was arrested but was set free. He is standing and observing with pleasure that those who did evil to him are divided among themselves. [83] And he is laughing at their lack of perception, knowing that they were born blind. The one capable of suffering must remain, since the body is the substitute, but what was set free was my bodiless body. I am the spirit of thought filled with radiant light. The one you saw approaching me is our fullness of thought, which unites the perfect light with my holy spirit.

"You are to present what you have seen to those who are strangers, who are not of this age. For there will be no grace among those who are not immortal, but only among those chosen because of their immortal nature, which has shown it can receive the one who gives in abundance.

"For this reason I have said, Whoever has will be given more, and this person will have in abundance. But whoever does not have—that is, the person of this world, who is completely dead, who derives from the planting of creation and procreation, [84] who thinks he can lay hold of someone else of immortal nature when such a person appears—this will be taken away from that person and added to whatever exists.

"So be courageous and fear nothing. For I shall be with you that none of your enemies may prevail over you. Peace be with you. Be strong."

When the Savior said these things, Peter came to his senses.

Revelation of Peter

40. The Second Treatise of the Great Seth

In the "Second Treatise of the Great Seth," Christ himself provides a first-hand description of how he descended into the man Jesus' body, occupied it for the length of his ministry, and then died only in appearance. It was not Christ himself who suffered the passion and crucifixion; the true Christ was completely separated from this suffering, and laughed at those who thought they could harm him. Those who ascribe to a literal understanding of Christ's death are said to proclaim "a doctrine of a dead man"; in so doing they subject themselves to "fear and slavery"; they are "small and ignorant."

As in the Coptic Apocalypse of Peter, these false believers are the proto-orthodox Christians, who foolishly believe that the Jewish Scriptures are true (from Adam to the Patriarchs, Moses, and the prophets) and that the Creator of the world is almighty. In fact, the ancient Jews and their God himself are all a "laughingstock." Those who do not see the deeper truths about God and Christ—those without gnosis—are "like dumb animals." They think that "they are advancing the name of Christ," especially in persecuting those who have been liberated (the Gnostics); but in fact they are completely ignorant.

The name Seth does not occur anywhere in the tractate except in the title. In the Old Testament, Seth is said to be the third son of Adam and Eve. As we have seen, some Gnostics maintained that he was the first to whom gnosis came, the progenitor of the Gnostics themselves. This book probably dates from the third century.

I approached a bodily dwelling and evicted the previous occupant, and I went in. The whole multitude of archons was upset, and all the material stuff of the rulers and the powers born of earth began to tremble at the sight of the figure with a composite image. I was in it, and I did not look like the previous occupant. He was a [52] worldly person, but I, I am from above the heavens. I did not defy them, and I became an anointed one, but neither did I reveal myself to them in the love coming from me. Rather, I revealed that I am a stranger to the regions below.

There was a great disturbance, with confusion and restlessness, in the whole world and in the council of the archons.

Some were convinced when they saw the mighty deeds I accomplished. They are of the generation of Adonaios and are descended from the one who fled from the throne to Sophia of hope, since she had previously given indication about us and all those with me. They all were moving about.

Others hurried to inflict every sort of punishment on me from the world ruler and his accomplices. They were restless of mind about what they would plot against me. They thought their majesty was everything, and they also told lies about the human being and all the Majesty [53] of the assembly. They were incapable of knowing the Father of truth, the human being of Majesty. They

The Second Discourse of Great Seth, reproduced from Marvin Meyer, *The Nag Hammadi Scriptures*. San Francisco: HarperOne, 2007. Used with permission of HarperOne.

usurped the name through corruption and igno-rance, <through> a flame of fire and a vessel cre-ated for the destruction of Adam, made to conceal all those who likewise are theirs.

The rulers from the realm of Yaldabaoth dis-closed the circuit of the angels. This is what hu-manity was seeking, that they might not know the true human, for Adam the modeled creature ap-peared to them. So throughout their dwelling place there was agitation and fear that the angels sur-rounding them might take a stand against them.

For those offering praise I died, though not really, that their archangel might be useless.

Then the voice of the world ruler announced to the angels, "I am God, and there is no other beside me." I laughed heartily when I reflected upon how conceited he was. He kept saying, over and over, "Who [54] is the human being?" The whole host of his angels, who had seen Adam and his dwelling place, laughed at its insignificance. Thus their thought turned away from the heavenly Majesty, who is the true human, whose name they perceived in the insignificance of a dwelling place. They are inferior, senseless in their empty thought, in their laughter, and so they were corrupted.

The entire Majesty of the Fatherhood of the Spirit was at rest in his realms, and I was with him, since I have a thought of a single emanation from the eternal and unknowable ones, undefiled and immeasurable. I disturbed and frightened the whole multitude of the angels and their ruler, and I placed a small thought in the world. I examined all with flame and fire through my thought, and all they did they did through me.

There was trouble and strife around the sera-phim and the cherubim, whose glory will perish, [55] and commotion around Adonaios, on every side, and around their dwelling place, all the way to the world ruler, who said, "Let us seize him." Others said, "This plan will never work out." For Adonaios knows me, through hope.

I was in the mouths of lions. They hatched a plot against me, to counter the destruction of their error and foolishness, but I did not give in to them as they had planned. I was not hurt at all. Though they punished me, I did not die in actuality but only in appearance, that I might not be put to shame by them, as if they are part of me. I freed myself of shame, and I did not become faint-hearted because of what they did to me. I would have become bound by fear, but I suffered only in their eyes and their thought, that nothing may ever be claimed about them. The death they think I suffered they suffered in their error and blind-ness. They nailed their man to their death. Their thoughts did not perceive [56] me, since they were deaf and blind. By doing these things they pro-nounce judgment against themselves. As for me, they saw me and punished me, but someone else, their father, drank the gall and the vinegar; it was not I. They were striking me with a scourge, but someone else, Simon, bore the cross on his shoul-der. Someone else wore the crown of thorns. And I was on high, poking fun at all the excesses of the rulers and the fruit of their error and conceit. I was laughing at their ignorance.

I brought all their powers into subjection. When I came down, no one saw me, for I kept changing my forms on high, transforming from shape to shape, so when I was at their gates, I as-sumed their likeness. I passed by them quietly. I saw their realms, but I was not afraid or ashamed, because I was pure. I was speaking with them and mingling with them, through those who are mine. Jealously I trampled on those who [57] are harsh toward them, and I put out the fire. I was doing all this by my will, to complete what I willed in the will of the Father above.

We brought the child of the Majesty, hidden in the region below, to the height. There I am, in the aeons that no one has seen or understood, where the wedding of the wedding robe is. It is the new wedding, not the old, and it does not perish, for the new bridal chamber is of the heavens, and it is perfect.

As I have revealed, there are three ways, and this is an undefiled mystery in the spirit of the eternal realm that is not destroyed or divided or even discussed, for it is indivisible, universal, and permanent.

The soul from on high will not discuss error here or carry herself away from these realms that are here. She will be carried forth when she is liberated and treated nobly in the world, and she stands [58] before the Father with no difficulty or fear, forever communing with the mind of ideal power. These will see me from every side with no animosity, for they see me, and they are seen, mingling with them. They did not put me to shame, and they were not ashamed. They were not afraid in my presence, and they will pass by every gate without fear and be perfected in the third glory.

The world was not receptive to my visible exaltation, my third immersion in an image that was perceptible. The flame of the seven authorities was extinguished, the sun of the powers of the rulers set, darkness overcame them, and the world became impoverished. They bound this one with many bonds and nailed him to the cross, and they secured him with four bronze nails. He ripped the temple veil with his own hands. An earthquake shook earth's chaos, for the souls of the dead were released and resurrected, and they walked out in the open. They laid aside [59] ignorant jealousy and lack of insight by the dead tombs, and they put on the new person. They had come to know the blessed, perfect one of the eternal, incomprehensible Father and the infinite light. That's what I am.

When I came to my own and united them with me, there was no need for many words. Our thought was one with their thought, so they understood what I was saying. We made plans for the destruction of the rulers, and in this I did the will of the Father. That's what I am.

When we left our home and came down to this world and became embodied in the world, we were hated and persecuted both by those who are ignorant and by those who claim to be enriched with the name of Christ, though they are vain and ignorant. Like irrational animals they do not know who they are. They hate and persecute those whom I have liberated. If these people would only shut their mouths for once, they would start weeping and groaning in futility, because [60] they have not really known me. Rather, they have served two masters—and even more.

You, however, will be winners in everything, in combat, fights, and schism with jealousy and anger. In the uprightness of our love, we are innocent, pure, and good, and we have the mind of the Father in an ineffable mystery.

It was a joke, I tell you, it was a joke. The rulers do not know that all this is an ineffable unity of undefiled truth like what is among the children of light. They have imitated it, and they proclaim the doctrine of a dead man, along with false teachings that mock the freedom and purity of the perfect assembly. In their doctrine they bind themselves to fear and slavery and worldly concerns and improper forms of worship, for they are ignorant and of no significance. They do not accept the nobility of truth. They hate the one to whom they belong, and they love the one to whom they do not belong.

They do not have the [61] knowledge of the Majesty, that it is from above, from the fountain of truth and not from slavery, jealousy, fear, and love of the material world. Boldly and freely they make use of what is not theirs and what is theirs. They do not covet because of their authority and their law that addresses what they desire. And those who are without the law are in dire straits: they do not have it and they still desire. These people mislead folks who through them resemble those who have the truth of their freedom, so as to place us under a yoke and coerce us with anxiety and fear. One person is subjected to bondage; another is controlled by God through threats and violent force.

Noble people of the fatherhood, however, are not controlled, since they control themselves by themselves, without command or force. They belong to the thought of the fatherhood, and they are one with their will, that the fatherhood may be perfect and inexpressible through [62] the living water.

Be wise among yourselves, not only in words that are heard but also in deeds, in words that are fulfilled. In this way those who are perfect are worthy to be established and united with me, and they will have no enmity. With good friendship I do everything through the one who is good, for this is the unity of truth, that people should have no adversary. If some cause division, they do not learn wisdom, because they cause division and are not friends. They are enemies. But those who live in the harmony and friendship of love of brother and sister, naturally and not only of necessity, completely and not merely in part, those truly reflect the will of the Father. This is universal and perfect love.

Adam was a joke. He was created by the ruler of the seventh realm in a phony way, in the shape of a human, as though he had become stronger than I and my siblings. We are blameless toward him, and we have not sinned.

Abraham was a joke, as were Isaac and Jacob, since they were called patriarchs in a phony way by the ruler of the seventh realm, as though [63] he had become stronger than I and my siblings. We are blameless toward him, and we have not sinned.

David was a joke, since his son was named Son of Humanity and was put in power by the ruler of the seventh realm, as though he had become stronger than I and my kin. We are blameless toward him; we have not sinned.

Solomon was a joke, since he became arrogant through the ruler of the seventh realm and thought he was the anointed, as though he had become stronger than I and my siblings. We are blameless toward him; I have not sinned.

The twelve prophets were a joke, since they appeared as imitations of the true prophets. They came in a phony way through the ruler of the seventh realm, as though he had become stronger than I and my siblings. We are blameless toward him, and we have not sinned.

Moses was a joke, called a faithful servant and friend. The testimony about him was wrong, since

he never knew me. He did not know me, and none of those before him, from Adam to Moses and John the Baptizer, knew me or [64] my siblings. They had instruction from angels to observe food laws and submit to bitter slavery. They never knew truth and they never will, because their souls are enslaved and they can never find a mind with freedom to know, until they come to know the Son of Humanity. On account of my Father, I was the one the world did not know, and for this reason it rose up against me and my siblings. But we are blameless toward it; we have not sinned.

The ruler was a joke, for he said, "I am God, and no one is greater than I. I alone am Father and Lord, and there is no other beside me. I am a jealous god, and I bring the sins of the fathers upon the children for three and four generations"—as though he had become stronger than I and my siblings. We are blameless toward him, and we have not sinned. In this way we mastered his doctrine, but he is conceited and does not agree with our Father. So through our friendship we overcame his doctrine, since he is arrogant and conceited and does not agree with our Father. He was a joke, with his [65] judgment and false prophecy.

O you who cannot see! You do not perceive that on account of your blindness this is one unknown. Neither did those people ever know or understand him. They would not listen to an accurate account of him, and so they practiced their lawless justice and raised their filthy, murderous hands against him as if they were beating the air. Those who are mindless and blind are always mindless, always slaves of law and worldly fear.

I am Christ, Son of Humanity, one from you who is within you. For you I am despised, that you may dismiss what is impermanent. Don't become female, lest you give birth to evil and what is related, jealousy, dissension, anger, wrath, dishonesty, and greed.

To you I am an ineffable mystery.

8

"Apostolic" Writings Outside the Canon
Early Christian Apocrypha

Early Christians chose to base their religious beliefs and practices on the writings of Jesus' apostles. It comes as no surprise, then, to find a large number of Christian writings forged in their names. We know of Christian forgeries even from within the New Testament itself: 2 Thessalonians 2:2 mentions a letter forged in Paul's name. Ironically enough, many scholars have suspected that 2 Thessalonians itself is falsely attributed to Paul—along with as many as five of the other New Testament letters that bear his name—and that both of the letters attributed to Peter are forgeries as well. Whether or not their view is right, there can be no doubt that the production of literary texts in the names of the apostles became something of a cottage industry in the second and third centuries. Numerous examples of such pseudonymous works still survive. They are known as the early Christian "Apocrypha."

The term *apocrypha* literally means "secret," and may be taken to refer to the secretive nature of the information conveyed in some of these works. But most of them are not at all esoteric, and so the term is not altogether apt. It has been customary to organize these books according to the genres preserved in the New Testament itself: as Gospels (roughly understood to be accounts of the words, deeds, or experiences of Jesus), Acts (the activities of his apostles), Epistles (letters written in their names), and Apocalypses (revelations of the heavenly truths that can explain mundane realities, including the truths about the future of the world, the end of time, or the nature of the afterlife).

The Christian authors who forged these writings were by no means anomalous in their wider Greco-Roman culture. Forgery was a widely practiced, though not widely appreciated, enterprise. We know of numerous other forgeries of all kinds that survive from this period, both pagan and Jewish; ancient authors sometimes comment on the practice, almost always disparagingly. Notwithstanding these strictures, there were always ample motivations for authors to forge documents: to make money by selling a famous author's "work" to a library (for instance, a treatise by Aristotle); to cast aspersions on an enemy (for example, by writing something scandalous in his name); or to authorize an important religious institution or practice (for example, by claiming a divine inspiration for it). Probably the most common reason for forging a document, however, was to receive a hearing for one's views. Anyone writing a philosophical treatise in his or her own name might not find much of a readership; that could quickly change if the work were signed by "Plato."

Since none of the early Christian authors who engaged in the practice left us any discussion of the matter, it is exceedingly difficult to know precisely what motivated them individually. Many of the surviving works appear to have been forged to allow the cherished views of the author to be more widely heard and/or to provide apostolic authority for perspectives that had become important in situations that had arisen after the death of the apostles. In other instances, though, it is difficult to believe that this was the motivating factor: many of these works appear to be told simply for the pleasure of the reading, essentially as entertainment for their hearers.

The following collection of some of the most interesting of these texts has been arranged according to genre; each group is provided with a separate introduction.

For Further Reading

Davies, Stevan. *The Revolt of the Widows: The Social World of the Apocryphal Acts*. Carbondale: Southern Illinois University, 1980.

Ehrman, Bart D. *Forged: Writing in the Name of God. Why the Bible's Authors Are Not Who We Think They Are*. San Francisco: HarperOne, 2011.

Ehrman, Bart D. *Forgery and Counterforgery: The Use of Literary Deceit in Early Christian Polemics*. New York: Oxford University Press, 2013.

Ehrman, Bart D. *Lost Christianities: The Battles for Scripture and the Faiths We Never Knew*. New York: Oxford University Press, 2003.

Ehrman, Bart D. and Zlatko Pleše (eds., trans.). *The Apocryphal Gospels: Texts and Translations*. New York: Oxford University Press, 2011.

Elliott, J. K., ed. *The Apocryphal New Testament*. Oxford: Clarendon, 1993.

Klauck, Hans-Josef. *Apocryphal Gospels: An Introduction*. New York: T&T Clark, 2003.

Klauck, Hans-Josef. *The Apocryphal Acts of the Apostles: An Introduction*. Waco: Baylor University Press, 2008.

Koester, Helmut. *Ancient Christian Gospels: Their History and Development*. London / Philadelphia: SCM Press Ltd / Trinity Press International, 1990.

Lapham, Fred. *An Introduction to the New Testament Apocrypha*. New York: T&T Clark, 2003.

MacDonald, Dennis R. *The Legend and the Apostle: The Battle for Paul in Story and Canon*. Philadelphia: Westminster, 1983.

Pervo, Richard. *The Making of Paul: Constructions of the Apostle in the Early Church*. Minneapolis: Fortress, 2010.

Apocryphal Gospels

(See also, for example, the Gospel of the Ebionites, the Secret Book of John, and the Gospel of Philip in Chapter 6)

Of the forty or so early Christian writings that can be classified as "Gospels," very few are structured like those of the New Testament, with portrayals of Jesus' public ministry of teaching and healing leading up to his passion and resurrection. Those that may have originally shared this form of narrative—for example, possibly, the Gospel of Peter (see below) and the Gospel according to the Ebionites (see Chapter 6)—have not survived in their entirety but only in fragments. Many of the noncanonical Gospels instead cover materials not found in the canonical four: the "lost" years of Jesus life (especially his infancy and childhood, and sometimes the events leading up to his miraculous conception), the mysterious revelations that he conveyed to his disciples after his resurrection, and other collections of previously unknown and secret teachings.

Most of these other Gospels appear to embody particular religious perspectives or doctrinal emphases that the author wanted to convey to his readers under divine authorization. Others of them (especially the stories of Jesus' childhood) may reflect pious and creative imaginations at work to entertain their readers and hearers. But even these were probably meant to guide their readers to a better understanding of who Jesus was, whether in his childhood, his adult life, or his "afterlife."

THE TEXTS

41. The Proto-Gospel of James

This book is called a "Proto-Gospel" because it narrates events that took place prior to Jesus' birth (although it includes an account of the birth as well). The manuscripts that preserve the book call it such things as "The Book of James" or "The Birth of Mary" or "The Narrative and History Concerning How the Very Holy Mother of God was Born for Our Salvation." Its author claims to be James, who is Jesus' brother known from the New Testament, here assumed to be Joseph's son by a previous marriage.

Focusing its attention on Jesus' mother, Mary, the book provides legendary accounts of (a) her miraculous birth to the wealthy Jew, Joachim, and his wife, Anna; (b) her sanctified upbringing in the Jerusalem Temple; (c) her marriage to Joseph, an old widower miraculously chosen to be her guardian; (d) her supernatural conception of Jesus through the Spirit; and (e) the miraculous events that happened soon thereafter. Parts of the book rely heavily on the infancy narratives of Matthew and Luke, but with numerous intriguing expansions, including information about Joseph's previous marriage and grown sons, Mary's work to produce the curtain in the temple, the birth of Jesus in a cave, and the skeptical post-partum inspection of Mary by a midwife named Salome, who learns that Mary had not only conceived but had also given birth as a virgin.

The book appears to have been known already to Origen in the early third century. It must then have been in circulation some time before that, so presumably in the late second century. It was destined to become enormously popular in later centuries.

The Birth of Mary. The Revelation of James.

1 In the "Histories of the Twelve Tribes of Israel" there was a very wealthy man Joachim, who used to offer a double portion of his gifts to the Lord, saying to himself, "The portion that is my surplus will be for all the people, and the portion that is for forgiveness will be for the Lord God as my atonement."

2 Now the great day of the Lord drew near, and the sons of Israel were offering their gifts. Reuben stood before him and said, "You are not allowed to offer your gifts first, since you have not produced any offspring in Israel."

3 Joachim was very upset and went away to consult the book of the twelve tribes of the people, saying to himself, "I will examine the Book of the Twelve Tribes of Israel to see if I am the only one not to produce offspring in Israel." And he searched and found that everyone who was righteous had raised up offspring in Israel. Then he remembered the patriarch Abraham, that at the end of his life the Lord God had given him a son, Isaac.

4 Joachim was very upset and did not appear to his wife, but went out to the wilderness and pitched his tent there. Joachim fasted for forty days and

"The Proto-Gospel of James" reproduced from Bart D. Ehrman and Zlatko Pleše, *The Apocryphal Gospels: Texts and Translations*. New York: Oxford University Press, 2011; used with permission of Oxford University Press.

nights, saying to himself, "I will not come down for either food or drink until the Lord my God visits me. My prayer will be my food and drink."[1]

2 Now his wife Anna wailed and mourned twice over, saying "I mourn for being a widow, I mourn for being childless."

2 The great day of the Lord drew near, and her servant Judith said to her, "How long will you humble your soul? See, the great day of the Lord is drawing near, and you are not allowed to lament. But take this headband that my supervisor gave me; I am not allowed to wear it, since I am your servant and it is of royal quality."

3 Anna replied, "Go away from me. I did none of these things and yet the Lord God has severely humbled me. For all I know, some scoundrel has given this to you, and you have come to implicate me in your sin."[2] Judith, her servant, said, "Why would I curse you, just because you have not listened to me? The Lord God has closed your womb to keep you from bearing fruit in Israel."

4 Anna was very upset, and took off her clothes of mourning; she then washed her face and put on her bridal clothes, and in midafternoon went down to walk in her garden. She saw a laurel tree and sat beneath it, and after resting a bit she prayed to the Master, saying, "O God of my fathers, bless me and hear my prayer, just as you blessed the womb of Sarah and gave her a son, Isaac."[3]

3 While Anna was gazing at the sky she saw a nest of sparrows in the laurel tree, and she mourned to herself, "Woe is me. Who gave me birth? What kind of womb bore me? I have been born as a curse before the sons of Israel and have been despised; they have mocked me and banished me from the Temple of the Lord my God.

2 Woe is me, what am I like? I am not like the birds of the sky, for even the birds of the sky are productive before you, O Lord. Woe is me, what

am I like? I am not like the senseless living creatures, for even the senseless living creatures are productive before you, O Lord. Woe is me, what am I like? I am not like the wild beasts of the earth, for even the wild beasts of the earth are productive before you, O Lord.

3 Woe is me, what am I like? I am not like these waters, for even these waters are tranquil yet prance about, and their fish bless you, O Lord. Woe is me. What am I like? I am not like this soil, for even this soil produces its fruit in its season and blesses you, O Lord."

4 Then, behold, an angel of the Lord appeared and said to her, "Anna, Anna, the Lord has heard your prayer. You will conceive a child and give birth,[4] and your offspring will be spoken of throughout the entire world." Anna replied, "As the Lord God lives, whether my child is a boy or a girl, I will offer it as a gift to the Lord my God, and it will minister to him its entire life."[5]

2 Behold, two angels came, saying to her, "See, your husband Joachim is coming with his flocks." For an angel of the Lord had descended to Joachim and said, "Joachim, Joachim, the Lord God has heard your prayer. Go down from here; see, your wife Anna has conceived a child."

3 Joachim immediately went down and called his shepherds and said, "Bring me here ten lambs without spot or blemish, and the ten lambs will be for the Lord God; and bring me twelve young calves, and the twelve calves will be for the priests and the council leaders, and bring a hundred male goats for all the people."

4 And behold, Joachim came with his flocks and Anna stood beside the gate and saw Joachim coming with his flocks; and running up to him she hung on his neck and said, "Now I know that the Lord God has blessed me abundantly. For see, the widow is no longer a widow and I who am childless have conceived a child." Then Joachim rested the first day in his home.

---

1 Cf. John 4:34.

2 The meaning of the exchange is obscure.

3 Gen 21:1–3.

4 Cf. Luke 1:13.

5 Cf. 1 Sam 1:11, 28; 2:11.

5 On the next day he brought his gifts as an offering, saying to himself, "If the Lord is gracious to me, the leafed plate of the priest's mitre[6] will make it known to me." And Joachim offered his gifts and looked closely at the priest's leafed mitre as he went up to the altar of the Lord; and he saw no sin in himself. Joachim then said, "Now I know that the Lord God has been gracious to me and forgiven me all my sins." He went down from the Temple of the Lord justified and came to his house.[7]

2 Some six months came to completion for Anna; and in the seventh month she gave birth. She asked the midwife, "What is it?" The midwife replied, "A girl." Anna said, "My soul is exalted today."[8] And she laid the child down. When the days came to completion, Anna washed off the blood of her impurity, gave her breast to the child, and named her Mary.

6 The child grew stronger every day. When she was six months old, her mother set her on the ground, to see if she could stand. She walked seven steps and came to her mother's bosom. Her mother lifted her up and said, "As the Lord my God lives, you will not walk at all on this ground until I have taken you up to the Temple of the Lord." Then she made a sanctuary in her bedroom and did not allow anything impure or unclean to pass through her lips. And she called the undefiled daughters of the Hebrews and they entertained her.

2 When the child had her first birthday, Joachim held a great feast and invited the chief priests, priests, scribes, council leaders, and all the people of Israel. Joachim brought the child out to the priests and they blessed her, saying, "O God of our fathers, bless this child and give her a name that will be famous forever, to all generations." And all the people replied, "Let it be so! Amen." They brought her to the chief priests, and they blessed her, saying, "O Most High God, look upon this child and bless her with an ultimate blessing, equal to none."

3 Her mother took her back to the sanctuary in her bedroom and nursed the child. And Anna made a song to the Lord God, saying, "I will sing a holy song to the Lord my God, for he has visited me and removed from me the reproach of my enemies.[9] The Lord my God has given me the fruit of his righteousness, unique and abundant before him. Who will report to the sons of Reuben that Anna is now nursing a child?[10] Listen closely, you twelve tribes of Israel; Anna is nursing a child!" And she laid her down to rest in the bedroom of her sanctuary and went out to serve the others, When the feast ended they descended happy, and they gave glory to the God of Israel.

7 Months passed for the child. When she became two, Joachim said, "Now we should take her up to the Temple of the Lord, to fulfill the promise we made;[11] otherwise the Master may send some harm our way and our gift be deemed unacceptable." Anna replied, "Let's wait until she is three; otherwise she may be homesick for her father and mother." Joachim agreed, "Let us wait."

2 When the child turned three, Joachim said, "We should call the undefiled daughters of the Hebrews and have each take a torch and set them up, blazing, that the child not turn back and her heart be taken captive away from the Temple of the Lord." They did this, until they had gone up to the Lord's Temple. And the priest of the Lord received her and gave her a kiss, blessing her and saying, "The Lord has made your name great among all generations. Through you will the Lord reveal his redemption to the sons of Israel at the end of time."

3 He set her on the third step of the altar, and the Lord God cast his grace down upon her. She danced on her feet, and the entire house of Israel loved her.

8 Her parents went away marveling, praising and glorifying God, the Master, that the child

---

6 Literally: the priest's leaf. The meaning is obscure.
7 Cf. Luke 18:14.
8 Cf. Luke 1:46.

9 Cf. 1 Sam 2:1.
10 Cf. Gen 21:7.
11 Cf. 1 Sam 1:21–28.

did not turn back. Mary was in the Temple of the Lord, cared for like a dove, receiving her food from the hand of an angel.

2 But when she reached her twelfth birthday, the priests held a council and said, "See, Mary has become twelve years old in the Lord's Temple. What then shall we do with her, to keep her from defiling the sanctuary of the Lord our God?" They said to the chief priest, "You have stood on the Lord's altar. Go in and pray about her, and we will do whatever the Lord God reveals to you."

3 The chief priest went in, taking the robe with twelve bells into the Holy of Holies; and he prayed about her. And behold, an angel of the Lord appeared and said to him, "Zacharias, Zacharias, go out and gather the widowers of the people, and have each of them bring a rod; she will become the wife of the one to whom the Lord God gives a sign."[12] The heralds went out to all the countryside of Judea and the trumpet of the Lord was blown, and see, everyone came running.

9 Joseph cast aside his carpenter's axe and went to their meeting. When they had gathered together they went to the priest, bringing their rods. When he had received the rods from them he went into the Temple and prayed. When he finished his prayer, he took the rods, went outside, and gave them back. And no sign appeared among them. But Joseph took the last rod, and behold! A dove came out of the rod and flew onto Joseph's head. The priest said to Joseph, "You have been chosen to take the Lord's virgin into your safe-keeping."

2 But Joseph refused, saying, "I have sons and am an old man; she is but a child. I do not want to become a laughingstock to the sons of Israel." The priest replied, "Fear the Lord your God, and remember everything that he did to Dathan, Abeira, and Core, how the earth split open and they were all swallowed up because of their dispute.[13] Now, Joseph, you should be afraid of this happening to your house as well."

3 Joseph was afraid and took her into his safe-keeping. He said to her, "Mary, I have received you from the Temple of the Lord. Now I am leaving you in my house, for I am going out to construct some buildings; later I will come back to you. The Lord will watch over you."

10 Then the priests held a council and said, "We should make a curtain for the Lord's Temple." The priest said, "Call to me the undefiled virgins from the tribe of David." The servants went out looking for them and found seven virgins. The priest then remembered that the child Mary was from the tribe of David, and that she was undefiled before God. The servants went out and led her back.

2 And they brought them into the Lord's Temple. And the priest said, "Cast lots before me to see who will spin the gold, the asbestos, the fine linen, the silk, the sapphire blue, the scarlet, and the true purple." Mary drew the lot for the true purple and the scarlet, and taking them she returned home. At that time Zacharias became silent.[14] Samuel took his place, until Zacharias spoke again. And Mary took the scarlet and began to spin it.

11 Mary took a pitcher and went out to fetch some water. And behold, she heard a voice saying, "Greetings, you who are favored! The Lord is with you. You are blessed among women."[15] Mary looked around, right and left, to see where the voice was coming from. She then entered her house frightened and set the pitcher down. Taking up the purple she sat on her chair and began to draw it out.

2 And behold, an angel of the Lord stood before her and said, "Do not fear, Mary. For you have found favor before the Master of all. You will conceive a child from his Word."[16] But when she heard this she asked herself, "Am I to conceive from the living Lord God and give birth like every other woman?"

12 Cf. Num 17:1–9.
13 Cf. Num 16:1, 31–33.

14 Cf. Luke 1:20–22, 64.
15 Cf. Luke 1:28.
16 Cf. Luke 1:30–31.

3 The angel of the Lord said to her, "Not so, Mary. For the power of God will overshadow you. Therefore the holy one born from you will be called the Son of the Highest.[17] And you will name him Jesus, for he will save his people from their sins."[18] Mary replied, "Behold the slave of the Lord is before him. May it happen to me as you have said."[19]

12 She made the purple and the scarlet, and brought them to the Temple. The priest took them and blessed her, "Mary, the Lord God has made your name great; you will be blessed among all the generations of earth."

2 Full of joy, Mary went off to her relative Elizabeth.[20] She knocked on the door; and when Elizabeth heard she cast aside the scarlet and ran to the door. When she opened it she blessed Mary and said, "How is it that the mother of my Lord should come to me? For see, the child in me leapt up and blessed you." But Mary forgot the mysteries that the archangel Gabriel had spoken to her, and gazed at the sky and said, "Who am I, Lord, that all the women of earth will bless me?"

3 She stayed with Elizabeth for three months. Day by day her own belly grew. Mary then returned home in fear, and hid herself from the sons of Israel. She was sixteen when these mysteries happened to her.

13 When she was in her sixth month, behold, Joseph returned from his buildings. As he came into the house he saw that she was pregnant. Striking his face he cast himself to the ground on sackcloth, weeping bitterly and saying, "How can I look upon the Lord God? How can I utter a prayer for this young girl? For I received her from the Temple of the Lord God as a virgin, but I did not watch over her. Who has preyed upon me? Who has done this wicked deed in my home and defiled the virgin? Has not the entire history of Adam been summed up in me? For just as Adam

was singing praise to God, when the serpent came and found Eve alone and led her astray,[21] so too has this now happened to me."

2 Joseph rose up from the sackcloth, called Mary, and said to her, "You who have been cared for by God: why have you done this? Have you forgotten the Lord your God? Why have you humiliated your soul—you who were brought up in the Holy of Holies and received your food from the hand of an angel?" (3) But she wept bitterly and said, "I am pure and have not had sex with any man."[22] Joseph replied to her, "How then have you become pregnant?" She said, "As the Lord my God lives, I do not know."

14 Joseph was very afraid and let her be, debating what to do about her. Joseph said, "If I hide her sin, I will be found to be fighting the Law of the Lord; if I reveal her condition to the sons of Israel, I am afraid that the child in her is angelic, and I may be handing innocent blood over to a death sentence. What then should I do with her? I will secretly divorce her."[23] Then night overtook him.

2 Behold, an angel of the Lord appeared to him in a dream and said, "Do not be afraid of this child. For that which is in her comes from the Holy Spirit. She will give birth to a son, and you will name him Jesus. For he will save his people from their sins."[24] Joseph rose up from his sleep and glorified the God of Israel who had bestowed favor on him; and he watched over her.

15 But Annas the scribe came to see him and said, "Joseph, why have you not appeared before our council?" Joseph replied, "I was tired from my journey and rested on my first day back." Annas then turned and saw that Mary was pregnant.

2 He left and ran off to the priest and said to him, "Joseph, the one you have vouched for, has committed a great sin." The priest replied, "What has he done?" He said, "He has defiled the virgin

---

17 Cf. Luke 1:35.

18 Cf. Matt 1:21.

19 Cf. Luke 1:38.

20 Cf. Luke 1:39–45.

21 Cf. Gen 3:13.

22 Cf. Luke 1:34.

23 Cf. Matt 1:19.

24 Cf. Matt 1:20–21.

he received from the Lord's Temple and has stolen her wedding rights.[25] And he has not revealed this to the sons of Israel." The priest asked, "Joseph, has done this?" Annas the scribe replied, "Send some servants, and you will find that the virgin is pregnant." The servants went off and found her just as he had said. They brought her back to the judgment hall, along with Joseph.

3 The high priest said to her, "Mary, why have you done this? Why have you humiliated your soul and forgotten the Lord your God? You who were brought up in the Holy of Holies and received your food from the hand of an angel, and heard his hymns, and danced before him—why have you done this?" But she wept bitterly and said, "As the Lord my God lives, I am pure before him and have not had sex with any man."

4 The priest then said, "Joseph, why have you done this?" Joseph replied, "As the Lord my God lives, and the witness of his truth, I am pure toward her," The priest said, "Do not bear false witness, but speak the truth. You have stolen her wedding rights[26] and not revealed it to the sons of Israel; and you have not bowed your head under the mighty hand that your offspring might be blessed." Joseph kept his silence.

16 The priest said, "Hand over the virgin you received from the Lord's Temple." And Joseph began to weep bitterly. The priest said, "I will have both of you drink the Lord's 'water of refutation,' and it will reveal your sin to your own eyes."[27]

2 The priest gave it to Joseph to drink, and sent him away to the wilderness. But he came back whole. He then gave it to Mary to drink and sent her off to the wilderness. And she came back whole. All the people were amazed that their sin was not revealed.

3 The priest said, "If the Lord God has not revealed your sin, neither do I judge you." And he released them. Joseph took Mary and returned home, rejoicing and glorifying the God of Israel.

25 Or: eloped with her.
26 Or: eloped with her.
27 Cf. Num 5:11–31.

17 An order went out from the king, Augustus, that everyone from Bethlehem of Judea was to be registered for a census.[28] Joseph said, "I will register my sons. But what should I do about this child? How should I register her? As my wife? I would be too ashamed. As my daughter? The sons of Israel know that she is not my daughter. This day of the Lord will turn out as he wishes."

2 He saddled the donkey and seated her on it; and his son led it along, while Samuel followed behind. When they approached the third milestone, Joseph turned and saw that she was gloomy. He said to himself, "Maybe the child in her is causing her trouble." Then Joseph turned again and saw her laughing. He said to her, "Mary, why is it that one time I see you laughing and at another time gloomy?" She replied, "Because my eyes see two peoples, one weeping and mourning and the other happy and rejoicing."

3 When they were halfway there, Mary said to him, "Joseph, take me down from the donkey. The child inside me is pressing on me to come out." He took her down from the donkey and said to her, "Where can I take you to hide your shame? For this place is a wilderness."

18 He found a cave there and took her into it. Then he gave his sons to her and went out to find a Hebrew midwife in the region of Bethlehem.

2 But I, Joseph, was walking, and I was not walking.[29] I looked up to the vault of the sky, and I saw it standing still, and into the air, and I saw that it was greatly disturbed, and the birds of the sky were at rest. I looked down to the earth and saw a bowl laid out for some workers who were reclining to eat. Their hands were in the bowl, but those who were chewing were not chewing; and those who were taking something from the bowl

28 Cf. Luke 2:1.
29 The Bodmer Papyrus V gives a much shorter version of chs. 18–21; the longer form of the text, generally regarded as older than the Bodmer version, is followed here, as reconstructed by de Strycher. Several witnesses report the vision of Joseph in ch. 18 in the third person.

were not lifting it up; and those who were bringing their hands to their mouths were not bringing them to their mouths. Everyone was looking up. I saw a flock of sheep being herded, but they were standing still. The shepherd raised his hand to strike them, but his hand remained in the air. I looked down at the torrential stream, and I saw some goats whose mouths were over the water, but they were not drinking. Then suddenly everything returned to its normal course.

19 I saw a woman coming down from the hill country, and she said to me, "O man, where are you going?" I replied, "I am looking for a Hebrew midwife." She asked me, "Are you from Israel?" I said to her, "Yes." She asked, "Who is the one who has given birth in the cave?" I replied, "My betrothed." She said to me, "Is she not your wife?" I said to her, "She is Mary, the one who was brought up in the Lord's Temple, and I received the lot to take her as my wife. She is not, however, my wife, but she has conceived her child by the Holy Spirit." The midwife said to him, "Can this be true?" Joseph replied to her, "Come and see." And the midwife went with him.

2 They stood at the entrance of the cave, and a bright cloud overshadowed it. The midwife said, "My soul has been magnified today, for my eyes have seen a miraculous sign: salvation has been born to Israel." Right away the cloud began to depart from the cave, and a great light appeared within, so that their eyes could not bear it. Soon that light began to depart, until an infant could be seen. It came and took hold of the breast of Mary, its mother. The midwife cried out, "Today is a great day for me, for I have seen this new wonder."

3 The midwife went out of the cave and Salome met her. And she said to her, "Salome, Salome, I can describe a new wonder to you. A virgin has given birth,[30] contrary to her natural condition." Salome replied, "As the Lord my God lives, if I do not insert my finger and examine her condition,[31] I will not believe that the virgin has given birth."

20 The midwife went in and said to Mary, "Brace yourself. For there is no small controversy concerning you." Then Salome inserted her finger in order to examine her condition, and she cried out, "Woe to me for my sin and faithlessness. For I have put the living God to the test, and see, my hand is burning, falling away from me."

2 She kneeled before the Master and said, "O God of my fathers, remember that I am a descendant of Abraham, Isaac, and Jacob. Do not make me an example to the sons of Israel, but deliver me over to the poor. For you know, O Master, that I have performed my services in your name and have received my wages from you."

3 And behold, an angel of the Lord appeared and said to her, "Salome, Salome, the Master of all has heard your prayer. Bring your hand to the child and lift him up; and you will find salvation and joy."

4 Salome joyfully came and lifted the child, saying, "I will worship him, for he has been born as a great king to Israel." Salome was immediately cured, and she went out of the cave justified. And behold a voice came saying, "Salome, Salome, do not report all the miraculous deeds you have seen until the child enters Jerusalem."

21 And behold, Joseph was ready to go into Judea. But there was a great disturbance in Bethlehem of Judea. For magi came saying, "Where is the king of the Jews? For we saw his star in the east, and we have come to worship him."[32]

2 When Herod heard, he was troubled; and he sent servants to the magi. He then summoned the high priests and asked them in the praetorium, "What does Scripture say about where the messiah is to be born?" They replied, "In Bethlehem of Judea, for that is what is found in Scripture." He then released them and asked the magi, "What sign did you see concerning the king who has been born?" The magi said, "We saw a magnificent star shining among these stars and overshadowing them, so that the other stars disappeared. And thus we knew that a king had been born in Israel, and we came to worship him." Herod replied, "Go

---

30 Cf. Isa 7:14.

31 Cf. John 20:25.

32 Cf. Matt 2:1–12

and look for him. If you find him, let me know, that I too may come to worship him."

3 The magi then left, and behold, the star they had seen in the east preceded them until they entered the cave, and it stood over the entrance of the cave. The magi saw the child with its mother, Mary, and they took from their packs gifts of gold, frankincense, and myrrh.

4 When they were warned by a revelation from an angel not to enter Judea, they went home another way.

22 When Herod realized that he had been duped by the magi, he grew angry and sent his murderers, saying to them, "Kill every infant, two years and under."[33]

2 When Mary heard that the infants were being killed, out of fear she took her child and wrapped him in swaddling clothes and placed him in a cattle manger.[34]

3 But when Elizabeth heard that they were looking for John, she took him and went up into the hill country looking for a place to hide him. But there was no hiding place. Then Elizabeth moaned and said, "Mountain of God, receive a mother with her child." For Elizabeth was not able to climb the mountain. And straight away the mountain split open and received her. And the mountain was shining a light on her, for an angel of the Lord was with them, protecting them.

23 Herod was looking for John, and he sent servants to Zacharias, saying, "Where have you hidden your son?" He answered them, "I am a minister of God, constantly attending his Temple. How could I know where my son is?"

2 The servants left and reported everything to Herod. Herod became angry and said, "His son is about to rule Israel." He sent his servants back to him to say, "Tell me the truth: where is your son? For you know that I can shed your blood with my hand." The servants went to report these things to him.

3 Zacharias responded, "I am God's witness if you shed my blood. For the Master will receive my spirit, since you will be shedding innocent blood in the forecourt of the Lord's Temple."[35] Zacharias was murdered around dawn, but the sons of Israel did not know that he was murdered.

24 But the priests came out at the time of greeting, and Zacharias did not come out to meet them with his blessing, as was the custom. The priests stood, waiting to greet Zacharias with a prayer and to glorify the Most High God.

2 When he did not come, everyone grew afraid. One of them took courage, entered the sanctuary, and saw blood congealed beside the altar of the Lord. He then heard a voice, "Zacharias has been murdered, and his blood will not be wiped away until the avenger comes." When he heard this word he was afraid and went outside to report to the priests what he had seen and heard.

3 Taking courage they entered and saw what had happened. The paneling around the Temple cried out and they ripped their clothes from top to bottom. They did not find his corpse, but they found his blood turned to stone. They left in fear, and reported to all the people that Zacharias had been murdered. All the tribes of the people heard and grieved for him, mourning for three days and nights.

4 After three days the priests deliberated whom to appoint in Zacharias's place, and the lot fell to Simeon. For this is the one who learned from a revelation of the Holy Spirit that he would not see death until he should see the Christ in the flesh.[36]

25 But I James, the one who has written this account in Jerusalem, hid myself away in the wilderness when there was a disturbance at the death of Herod, until the disturbance in Jerusalem came to an end. There I glorified God, the Master, who gave me the wisdom to write this account.

2 Grace be with all those who fear the Lord. Amen.

---

33 Cf. Matt 2:16–18.
34 Cf. Luke 2:7.

35 Cf. Matt 23:35.
36 Cf. Luke 2:26.

42. The Infancy Gospel of Thomas

The "Infancy Gospel of Thomas," not to be confused with the Coptic Gospel of Thomas from Nag Hammadi (see below), is one of the earliest legendary accounts of Jesus' life as a young boy. The author calls himself "Thomas, the Israelite." It is not clear whether he wanted himself to be recognized as Judas Thomas, allegedly Jesus' twin brother (see the Coptic Gospel of Thomas).

The narrative begins with Jesus as a supernaturally endowed and somewhat mischievous 5-year-old. Included are anecdotes of Jesus at play with his childhood companions (sometimes harming them with his divine power, sometimes healing them), in confrontation with his elders (usually bettering them), at school with his teachers (revealing their ignorance), and in the workshop with his father (miraculously correcting his mistakes). For modern readers it is difficult to know whether such stories were meant simply as speculative and entertaining episodes from the life of the youthful Son of God or, more probably, as serious accounts of Jesus' early years that were meant to foreshadow his character and activities as an adult. The book concludes with the story, familiar from the Gospel of Luke, of Jesus as a 12-year-old in the Temple.

Many scholars believe that such "infancy Gospels" began to circulate during the middle of the second century; the Infancy Gospel of Thomas may have been one of the earliest among them.

The Infancy Gospel of Thomas

1 I, Thomas the Israelite, make this report to all of you, my brothers among the Gentiles, that you may know the magnificent childhood activities of our Lord Jesus Christ—all that he did after being born in our country. The beginning is as follows:

2 When this child Jesus was five years old, he was playing by the ford of a stream; and he gathered the flowing waters into pools and made them instantly pure. These things he ordered simply by speaking a word.

2 He then made some soft mud and fashioned twelve sparrows from it. It was the Sabbath when he did this. There were also a number of other children playing with him.

3 When a certain Jew saw what Jesus was doing while playing on the Sabbath, he left right away and reported to his father, Joseph, "Look, your child is at the stream and he has taken mud and formed twelve sparrows. He has profaned the Sabbath!"

4 When Joseph came to the place and looked, he cried out to him, "Why are you doing what is forbidden on the Sabbath?" But Jesus clapped his hands and cried to the sparrows, "Be gone!" And the sparrows took flight and went off, chirping.

5 When the Jews saw this they were amazed; and they went away and reported to their leaders what they had seen Jesus do.

The Infancy Gospel of Thomas, reproduced from Bart D. Ehrman and Zlatko Pleše, *The Apocryphal Gospels: Texts and Translations*. New York: Oxford University Press, 2011. Used with permission of Oxford University Press.

3 Now the son of Annas the scribe was standing there with Joseph. He took a willow branch and scattered the water that Jesus had gathered.

2 Jesus was irritated when he saw what happened, and he said to him: "You unrighteous, irreverent idiot! What did the pools of water do to harm you? See, now you also will be withered like a tree, and you will never bear leaves or root or fruit."[1]

3 Immediately that child was completely withered. Jesus left and returned to Joseph's house. But the parents of the withered child carried him away, mourning his lost youth. They brought him to Joseph and began to accuse him, "What kind of child do you have who does such things?"

4 Somewhat later he was going through the village, and a child ran up and banged into his shoulder. Jesus was aggravated and said to him, "You will go no further on your way." Right away the child fell down and died. Some of those who saw what happened said, "Where was this child born? For everything he says is a deed accomplished!"

2 The parents of the dead child came to Joseph and blamed him, saying "Since you have such a child you cannot live with us in the village. Or teach him to bless and not to curse[2]—for he is killing our children!"

5 Joseph called to the child and admonished him privately, "Why are you doing such things? These people are suffering, they hate us and are persecuting us!" But Jesus replied, "I know these are not your words; nevertheless, I also will keep silent for your sake. But those others will bear their punishment." And immediately those who were accusing him were blinded.

2 Those who saw these things were greatly frightened and disturbed; they were saying about him, "Everything he has said, whether good or bad, has become an amazing deed." When Joseph saw what Jesus had done, he rose up, grabbed his ear, and yanked it hard.

3 The child was irritated and said to him, "It is enough for you to seek and not find; you have not acted at all wisely. Do you not know that I am yours? Do not grieve me."

6 Standing off to the side was an instructor named Zachaeus, who heard Jesus say these things to his father. He was greatly amazed that he was speaking such things, though just a child.

2 After a few days he approached Joseph and said to him, "You have a bright child with a good mind. Come, hand him over to me that he may learn his letters, and along with the letters I will teach him all knowledge, including how to greet all the elders and to honor them as his ancestors and fathers, and to love children his own age."

3 And he told him all the letters from Alpha to Omega, clearly and with great precision. But Jesus looked at the instructor Zachaeus and said to him, "Since you do not know the true nature of the Alpha, how can you teach anyone the Beta? You hypocrite! If you know it, first teach the Alpha, and then we will believe you about the Beta." Then he began to interrogate the teacher about the first letter, and he was not able to give him the answers.

4 While many others were listening, the child said to Zachaeus, "Listen, teacher, to the arrangement of the first letter of the alphabet; observe here how it has lines, and a middle stroke crossing both lines which you see, how they converge with the top projecting and turning back, three marks of the same kind, each principal and subordinate, of equal proportion.[3] Now you have the lines of the Alpha."[4]

---

1 Cf. Psalm 1:3.

2 Cf. Rom 12:14.

3 The Greek passage may be corrupt.

4 Irenaeus indicates that a Gnostic group known as the Marcosians had an apocryphal writing in which the young Jesus disputed with his teacher over the meaning of the Alpha and the Beta. It is difficult to know if Irenaeus was referring to the Infancy Gospel of Thomas. See Irenaeus, *Adv. Haer.* 1.20.1.

7 When the teacher Zachaeus heard the child setting forth so many such allegorical interpretations of the first letter, he was at a complete loss about this kind of explanation and his teaching, and he said to those standing there, "Woe is me! I am wretched and at a complete loss; I have put myself to shame, taking on this child.

2 I beg you, brother Joseph, take him away. I cannot bear his stern gaze or make sense of a single word. This child is not of this world; he can even tame fire. Maybe he was born before the world came into being. I cannot fathom what kind of uterus bore him or what kind of womb nourished him. Woe is me, friend. He befuddles me; I cannot follow his reasoning. I have fooled myself and am miserable three times over. I was struggling to have a student and have been found to have a teacher.

3 My friends, I know all too well my shame: though an old man, I have been defeated by a child. I may grow weak and die because of this child, for at this moment I cannot look him in the face. When everyone says that I have been defeated by a young child, what can I say? How can I explain the things he told me about the lines of the first letter? I have no idea, my friends, for I do not know its[5] beginning or end.

4 And so I ask you, brother Joseph, take him back home. What kind of great thing he could be—whether a divine being or an angel—I do not know even what to say."

8 While the Jews were giving Zachaeus advice, the child laughed aloud and said, "Now let what is yours bear fruit, and led the blind in heart see. I have come from above to curse them and call them to the realm above, just as the one who sent me for your sake commanded."

2 When the child stopped speaking, immediately all those who had fallen under his curse were healed. No one dared to anger him from that time on, fearing that he might cripple them with a curse.

9 Some days later Jesus was playing on a flat rooftop of a house, and one of the children playing with him fell from the roof and died. When the other children saw what had happened, they ran away, so that Jesus stood there alone.

2 When the parents of the one who died arrived they accused him of throwing him down. But Jesus said, "I certainly did not throw him down." But they continued to abuse him verbally.

3 Jesus leapt down from the roof and stood beside the child's corpse, and with a loud voice he cried out, "Zenon!" (for that was his name) "rise up and tell me: did I throw you down?" Right away he arose and said, "Not at all, Lord! You did not throw me down, but you have raised me up!" When they saw this they were astounded. The parents of the child glorified God for the sign that had occurred, and they worshiped Jesus.

10 A few days later there was a young man who was splitting wood in a secluded spot. The axe fell and split open the sole of his foot. He lost a lot of blood and was dying.

2 There was a disturbance and a crowd started to gather. The child Jesus also ran to the spot. Forcing his way through the crowd, he grabbed the young man's injured foot and immediately it was healed. He said to the young man, "Rise now, split the wood, and remember me."[6] When the crowd saw what had happened it worshiped the child, saying, "The Spirit of God truly resides within this child."

11 When he was six years old, his mother gave him a water jug and sent him to draw some water and bring it back home. But he was jostled by the crowd, and the water jug was shattered.

2 So Jesus unfolded the cloak he was wearing and filled it with water, and brought it to his mother. When his mother saw the sign that had happened, she kissed him. She kept to herself the mysterious deeds that she saw him do.[7]

---

5 Or: his

6 Cf. Gospel of Thomas 77.

7 Cf. Luke 2:19, 51.

12 When it later became time for sowing, the child went out with his father to sow wheat in their field. When his father sowed, the child Jesus also sowed a single grain of wheat.

2 When he harvested and threshed the grain, it produced a hundred large bushels.[8] He called all the poor people of the village to the threshing floor and gave them the wheat; and Joseph took what was left of it. He was eight years old when he did this sign.

13 Now his father was a carpenter, and at that time he used to make plows and yokes. He received an order from a certain rich man to make a bed for him. But when one of the bars, the so-called cross beam, came out too short, he did not know what to do. The child Jesus said to his father Joseph, "Place the two pieces of wood on the floor and line them up from the middle to one end."

2 Joseph did just as the child said. Then Jesus stood at the other end, grabbed the shorter board, and stretched it out to make it the same length as the other. His father Joseph saw what he had done and was amazed. He embraced the child and gave him a kiss, saying, "I am blessed that God has given me this child."

14 When Joseph observed the mind of the child and his age, and saw that he was starting to mature, he again resolved that he should not be unable to read, and so took him out and gave him over to another teacher. The teacher said to Joseph, "First I will teach him to read Greek, and then Hebrew." For the teacher knew of the child's learning and was afraid of him. Nonetheless, he wrote out the alphabet and practiced it for him for a long time; but the child gave him no response.

2 Then Jesus said to him, "If you are really a teacher and know the letters well, tell me the power of the Alpha, and I will tell you the power of the Beta." The teacher was aggravated and struck him

on the head. The child was hurt and cursed him; and immediately he fainted and fell to the ground on his face.

3 The child returned to Joseph's house. Joseph was smitten with grief and ordered his mother, "Do not let him out the door; for those who anger him die."

15 Some time later there was another instructor, a close friend of Joseph, who said to him, "Bring the child to me at the school. Maybe I can use flattery to teach him his letters." Joseph said to him, "If you are that courageous, brother, take him along with you." He took him with great fear and much anxiety, but the child went along gladly.

2 He entered the school with confidence and found a book lying on the reading desk. He picked it up, but instead of reading the words in it, he opened his mouth and began to speak in the Holy Spirit, teaching the Law to those who were standing there. A great crowd gathered and stood there listening to him; they were amazed at the beauty of his teaching and his carefully crafted words[9]— amazed that he could speak such things though still an infant.

3 But when Joseph heard about this he was frightened. He ran to the school, concerned that this instructor may also have proved inexperienced. But the instructor said to Joseph, "You should know, brother, that I took the child as a pupil; but he is filled with great grace and wisdom. Now I ask you, brother, take him home."

4 When the child heard these things, he immediately laughed at him and said, "Since you have rightly spoken and rightly borne witness, for your sake that other one who was struck down will be healed." And right away the other instructor was healed. Joseph took the child and returned home.

16 Now Joseph sent his son James to bundle some wood and bring it home. The child Jesus also followed him. While James was gathering the firewood, a snake bit his hand.

---

8 Cf. Matt 13:3–9; Mark 4:3–9; Luke 8:5–8; Gospel of Thomas 9.

9 Cf. Luke 4:16–22.

2 When he was stretched out on the ground dying, Jesus came up to him and breathed on the bite. The pain immediately stopped, the animal burst, and straight away James was returned to health.[10]

17 After these things, an infant in Joseph's neighborhood became sick and died; and his mother was weeping loudly. When Jesus heard the outburst of sorrow and the disturbance, he ran up quickly and found the child dead.[11] He touched its breast, saying "I say to you, young child, do not die but live, and be with your mother." Immediately the child opened its eyes and laughed. Jesus said to the woman, "Take him, give him milk, and remember me."

2 When the crowd standing there saw what had happened, it was amazed. The people said, "Truly this child is either a god or an angel of God, for his every word is an accomplished deed." Jesus then left from there to play with the other children.

18 Some time later a house was being built and there was a great disturbance. Jesus got up and went out to the place. He saw a man lying down, dead. Taking his hand he said, "I say to you, O man, rise up and do your work." Immediately he rose up and worshiped him.

2 When the crowd saw this, it was amazed and said, "This child comes from heaven. For he has saved many souls from death—for his entire life he is able to save them."

19 When he was twelve years old his parents made their customary trip to Jerusalem, in a caravan, for the Passover feast.[12] After the Passover they returned home. While they were returning, the child Jesus went back up to Jerusalem. But his parents thought he was in the caravan.

2 After their first day of travel, they began looking for him among their relatives and were upset not to find him. They returned again to the city to look for him. After the third day they found him sitting in the Temple in the midst of the teachers, both listening and asking them questions. Everyone was attending closely, amazed that though a child, he silenced the elders and teachers of the people, explaining the chief points of the Law and the parables of the prophets.

3 When his mother Mary came up to him she said, "Why have you done this to us, child? See, we have been distressed, looking for you." Jesus replied to them, "Why are you looking for me? Don't you know that I must be doing my Father's business?"[13]

4 The scribes and Pharisees said, "Are you the mother of this child?" She replied, "I am." They said to her, "You are most fortunate among women, because God has blessed the fruit of your womb.[14] For we have never seen or heard of such glory, such virtue and wisdom."

5 Jesus got up from there and followed his mother, and he was obedient to his parents. But his mother kept to herself all these things that had happened. And Jesus grew in wisdom and stature and grace.[15] To him be the glory forever and ever. Amen.

10 Cf. Acts 28:1–6.
11 Cf. Mark 5:22–43; Luke 7:11–17.
12 Luke 2:41–52.
13 Or: with those who are my Father's; or: in my Father's house.
14 Luke 1:42.
15 Luke 2:51–52.

43. The Gospel of Thomas

None of the fifty-two tractates discovered in the Nag Hammadi Library has attracted more attention than the Gospel of Thomas. This book of Jesus' sayings claims to have been written by Didymus Judas Thomas, who, according to Christian legend, was Jesus' own twin brother (see the Acts of Thomas in Chapter 2).

The book records 114 "secret teachings" of Jesus. Unlike the Gospels of the New Testament, it includes no other material: no miracles, no passion narrative, no stories of any kind. Jesus' death and resurrection thus appear to be of no concern to this author (since he never discusses them); what matters instead are the mysterious teachings that Jesus delivered. Indeed, the Gospel begins by stating that anyone who learns the interpretation of these words will have eternal life.

Many of the sayings—over half—closely approximate Jesus' words from the New Testament; for example, the warning against the "blind leading the blind" and the parables of the sower and the mustard seed. Others, however, are quite different and appear to presuppose some kind of Gnostic point of view (see Chapter 6 and the discussion of Thomasine Christians) in which people are understood to be spirits who have fallen from the divine realm and become entrapped in matter (i.e., in the prisons of their material bodies). Salvation, according to this perspective, comes to those who learn the truth of their plight and so are enabled to escape this impoverished material existence by acquiring the knowledge necessary for salvation. Jesus is the one who conveys this knowledge.

Some scholars maintain that the Gospel of Thomas is at least as old as the New Testament Gospels; but others point out that the theology of the more unusual "gnostic-like" sayings cannot be confidently dated prior to the beginning of the second century. Thus, while some of the Gospel's sayings may be quite old—may, in fact, go back to Jesus himself—the document as a whole was probably written somewhat after the New Testament Gospels (although perhaps independently of them), early in the second century.

The Gospel According to Thomas

These are the hidden sayings that the living Jesus spoke and Didymus Judas Thomas wrote down.

1 And he said, "Whoever finds the interpretation of these sayings will not taste death."[1]

2 Jesus said, "The one who seeks should not cease seeking until he finds.[2] And when he finds he will be disturbed; and when he is disturbed, he will marvel. And he will rule over the all."

3 Jesus said, "If your leaders say to you, 'Look, the kingdom is in the sky,' then the birds of the

---

1 Cf. John 8:51–52.

2 Cf. Matt 7:7–8; Luke 11:9–10.

The Gospel of Thomas, reproduced from Bart D. Ehrman and Zlatko Pleše, *The Apocryphal Gospels: Texts and Translations*. New York: Oxford University Press, 2011. Used with permission of Oxford University Press.

sky will precede you. If they say to you, 'It is in the sea,' then the fish will precede you. But the kingdom is within you,[3] and it is outside you. When you come to know yourselves, then you will be known, and you will understand that you are the children of the living Father. But if you will not know yourselves, then you are in poverty, and it is you who are the poverty."[4]

4 Jesus said, "A person advanced in days will not hesitate to ask a little child of seven days about the place of life, and that person will live. For many who are first will be last[5] and so become a single one."

5 Jesus said, "Know what is before your face, and what is hidden from you will be disclosed to you. For there is nothing hidden that will not be revealed."[6]

6 His disciples questioned him and said to him, "Do you want us to fast? And how should we pray? Should we give alms?[7] And what kind of diet should we observe?" Jesus said, "Do not tell lies and do not do what you hate, for they are all disclosed before heaven. For there is nothing hidden that will not be revealed, and nothing that is covered will remain undisclosed."[8]

7 Jesus said, "Blessed is the lion that the human will eat so that the lion becomes human. And cursed is the human whom the lion will eat, and the lion will become human."[9]

8 And he said, "The human being is like a wise fisherman, who cast his net into the sea and dragged it up from the sea, full of little fish. Among them the wise fisherman found a fine large fish. He cast all the small fish back into the sea and chose the large fish without any effort. The one who has ears to listen had better listen!"[10]

9 Jesus said, "Look, the sower came forth, took a handful, and cast. Now, some fell on the path, and the birds came and gathered them up. Others fell on the rock, and they did not take roots down into the ground and send up ears. And others fell on thorns, and they choked the seeds and the worm devoured them. And others fell on the good ground, and it sent up good fruit and yielded sixty per measure and a hundred twenty per measure."[11]

10 Jesus said, "I have cast a fire upon the world, and look, I am guarding it until it blazes."[12]

11 Jesus said, "This heaven will pass away, and the one above it will pass away.[13] And the dead are not alive, and the living will not die. In the days you ate what is dead you made it alive; (but) when you come to be in light, what will you do?[14] On the day when you were one, you became two; but when you become two, what will you do?"

12 The disciples said to Jesus, "We know that you will leave us. Who will be great among us?"[15] Jesus said to them, "Wherever you have come,[16] you will go to James the Righteous, for whose sake heaven and earth came to be."

13 Jesus said to his disciples, "Make a comparison and tell me: who am I like?"[17] Simon Peter said to him, "You are like a righteous angel." Matthew said to him, "You are like a wise philosopher." Thomas said to him, "Teacher, my mouth cannot let me say at all what you are like." Jesus said, "I am not your teacher, for you have drunk and become intoxicated from the bubbling spring that I myself have measured out." And he took him, withdrew, and said three sayings to him. Now, when Thomas came to his companions, they asked him, "What did Jesus say to you?" Thomas said to them, "If I tell you one of the sayings he said to me, you will take

---

3 Cf. Luke 17:20–21.

4 Cf. Gal 4:9.

5 Cf. Matt 19:30; 20:16; Mark 10:31; Luke 13:30.

6 Cf. Matt 10:26; Mark 4:22; Luke 8:17; 12:2.

7 Cf. Matt 6:1–8, 16–18.

8 Cf. Matt 10:26; Mark 4:22; Luke 8:17; 12:2.

9 Cf. Plato, Republic 9.588c7–589b6.

10 Cf. Matt 13:47–50.

11 Cf. Matt 13:3–9; Mark 4:3–9; Luke 8:5–8.

12 Cf. Luke 12:49.

13 Cf. Matt 24:35; Mark 13:31; Luke 21:33.

14 Cf. Hippolytus, Refut. 5.8.32.

15 Cf. Matt 18:1; Mark 9:34; Luke 9:46.

16 Or: "have come from."

17 Cf. Matt 16:13–17; Mark 8:27–30; Luke 9:18–21.

up stones and cast them at me, and fire will come out of the stones and burn you."

14 Jesus said to them, "If you fast, you will bring sin upon yourselves; and if you pray, you will be condemned; and if you give alms, you will do harm to your spirits.[18] And when you go into any land and walk in the countryside, if they receive you, eat whatever they place before you and heal the sick among them.[19] For whatever goes into your mouth will not defile you; rather, it is what comes out of your mouth that will defile you."[20]

15 Jesus said, "When you see one who was not born from woman, fall upon your faces and worship him: that one is your father."

16 Jesus said, "Perhaps people think that I have come to cast peace on the world, and they do not know that I have come to cast divisions on the earth; fire, sword, war. For there will be five in a house: three will be against two and two against three, the father against the son and the son against the father.[21] And they will stand as solitary ones."

17 Jesus said, "I will give you what eyes have not seen, and what ears have not heard, and what hands have not touched, and what has not arisen in the human heart."[22]

18 The disciples said to Jesus, "Tell us how our end will come about."[23] Jesus said, "Have you uncovered the beginning, then, that you are now seeking the end? For where the beginning is the end will come to be. Blessed is the one who stands at the beginning: that one will know the end and will not taste death."

19 Jesus said, "Blessed is the one who existed before coming to exist. If you exist as my disciples and listen to my sayings, these stones will serve you. For you have five trees in paradise that do not move in summer or winter, and whose leaves do not fall. Whoever knows them will not taste death."

20 The disciples said to Jesus, "Tell us: what is the kingdom of heaven like?" He said to them, "It is like a mustard seed. It is smallest of all seeds, but when it falls on tilled ground, it puts forth a great branch and becomes a shelter for the birds of the sky."[24]

21 Mary said to Jesus, "Whom are your disciples like?" He said, "They are like children[25] dwelling in a field that is not theirs. When the owners of the field come they will say, 'Surrender our field to us.' They, for their part, strip in their presence in order to surrender it to them and so give their field to them. For this reason I say, when the homeowner knows that the burglar is coming, he will keep watch before he comes, and will not let him dig through into his house, which belongs to his kingdom, to steal his possessions.[26] You, then, keep watch against the world. Gird your loins with great power,[27] so that the brigands may not find a way to come to you; for they will find the gain for which you are waiting.[28] Let there be among you a person of understanding. When the crop ripened, he came hastily with a sickle in his hand and reaped it.[29] The one who has ears to listen had better listen!"[30]

22 Jesus saw some infants being nursed. He said to his disciples, "These infants being nursed are like those entering the kingdom." They said to him, "Shall we then enter the kingdom by being infants?"[31] Jesus said to them, "When you make the two one, and make the inside like the outside

---

18 Cf. Matt 6:1–8, 16–18.

19 Cf. Luke 10:8–9.

20 Cf. Matt 15:11, 17–18; Mark 7:15, 18, 20.

21 Cf. Matt 10:34–35; Luke 12:51–53.

22 Cf. 1 Cor 2:9.

23 Cf. Matt 24:3; Mark 13:4; Luke 21:7.

24 Cf. Matt 13:31–32; Mark 4:20–32; Luke 13:18–19.

25 Or: "servants."

26 Cf. Matt 24:43–44; Luke 12:39–40.

27 Cf. Exod 12:11; Luke 12:35.

28 Or: "for they will find the necessities you are watching out for."

29 Cf. Mark 4:29.

30 Cf. Matt 13:9; Mark 4:9; Luke 8:8.

31 Cf. Matt 18:1–3; 19:13–15; Mark 9:33–36; 10:13–16; Luke 9:46–47; 18:15–17.

and the outside like the inside and the upper like the lower; and you make[32] the male and the female be a single one, with the male no longer being male and the female no longer female; when you make eyes in the place of an eye and a hand in the place of a hand and a foot in the place of a foot, an image in the place of an image—then you will enter the kingdom."

23 Jesus said, "I will choose you—one out of a thousand and two out of ten thousand. And they will stand as a single one."

24 His disciples said, "Show us the place where you are, since we must seek it." He said to them, "The one who has ears had better listen! There is light inside a person of light, and it[33] shines on the whole world. If it does not shine, it is dark."[34]

25 Jesus said, "Love your brother like your soul; guard him like the pupil of your eye."[35]

26 Jesus said, "You see the speck that is in your brother's eye, but you do not see the log that is in your eye. When you take the log out of your eye, then you will see well enough to take the speck out of your brother's eye."[36]

27 "If you do not fast from the world, you will not find the kingdom. If you do not make the Sabbath a sabbath,[37] you will not see the Father."

28 Jesus said, "I stood in the midst of the world and appeared to them in flesh.[38] I found them all drunk, and I did not find any of them thirsty. And my soul was anguished for the children of humankind, for they are blind in their hearts and do not see. For they came into the world empty, and

empty again they seek to depart from the world. Yet now they are drunk; when they shake off their wine, then they will repent."

29 Jesus said, "If the flesh came into being because of the spirit, it is a marvel. But if the spirit (came into existence) because of the body, it is a marvel of marvels. Yet I marvel at this, how this great wealth has come to dwell in this poverty."

30 Jesus said, "Where there are three gods, they are divine. Where there are two or one, I am with that one."[39]

31 Jesus said, "A prophet is not welcome in his village; a physician does not heal those who know him."[40]

32 Jesus said, "A city built upon a high mountain and fortified cannot fall, nor can it become hidden."[41]

33 Jesus said, "Whatever you hear with your ear, proclaim it into the other ear upon your rooftops.[42] For no one lights a lamp and places it under a bushel or sets it in a hidden place. But he puts it on the lampstand so that everyone who enters and leaves might see its light."[43]

34 Jesus said, "If a blind person leads a blind person, they both fall into a pit."[44]

35 Jesus said, "No one can enter the house of the strong and take it by force unless he binds his hands. Then he will plunder his house."[45]

36 Jesus said, "Do not be concerned from morning to evening and from evening to morning about what you will wear."[46]

37 His disciples said, "When will you appear to us and when shall we see you?" Jesus said, "When you strip naked without being ashamed and take

---

32 Lit. "and that you might make. . ."

33 Or: "and he . . . If he . . ."

34 Cf. Matt 6:22–23; 11:34–35.

35 Cf. Matt 22:39; Mark 12:31; Luke 10:27.

36 Cf. Matt 7:3–5; Luke 6:41–42.

37 The clause may mean two opposite things: either "if you do not observe the Sabbath day as a Sabbath," or "if you do not turn the Sabbath into a regular day (a sabbath)" that is, abstain from it. For the latter interpretation, see supra, sayings (6) and (14).

38 Cf. John 1:9–10, 14.

39 Cf. Matt 18:20.

40 Cf. Matt 13:57–58; Mark 6:4–5; Luke 4:24; John 4:44.

41 Cf. Matt 5:14.

42 Cf. Matt 10:27; Luke 12:3.

43 Cf. Matt 5:15; Mark 4:21; Luke 8:16; 11:33.

44 Cf. Matt 15:14; Luke 6:39.

45 Cf. Matt 12:29; Mark 3:27; Luke 11:21–22.

46 Cf. Matt 6:25; Luke 12:22.

your clothes and place them under your feet like little children and stamp on them, then you will see the Son of the Living One, and you will not be afraid."

38 Jesus said, "Many times you have desired to hear these sayings that I am speaking to you, and you have no one else to hear them from. Days will come when you will seek me, and you will not find me."[47]

39 Jesus said, "The Pharisees and the scribes have taken the keys of knowledge and hidden them. They have neither entered nor let those wishing to enter do so.[48] But you should be wise as snakes, and innocent as doves."[49]

40 Jesus said, "A grapevine has been planted outside of the Father. And since it is not strong, it will be pulled up by its root and perish."[50]

41 Jesus said, "The one who has something in his hand will be given (more); and the one who has nothing will have even the little that he has taken from him."[51]

42 Jesus said, "Become passersby."

43 His disciples said to him, "Who are you to say these things to us?" "You do not understand who I am from what I say to you.[52] Rather, you have become like the Jews; for they love the tree but hate its fruit; and they love the fruit but hate the tree."[53]

44 Jesus said, "Whoever blasphemes against the Father will be forgiven; and whoever blasphemes against the Son will be forgiven; but whoever blasphemes against the Holy Spirit will not be forgiven, either on earth or in heaven."[54]

45 Jesus said, "Grapes are not harvested from thorn bushes, nor are figs collected from thistles;

for they do not yield fruit. A good person brings something good from his storehouse; a bad person brings vile things from his evil storehouse inside his heart and speaks vile things. For from the abundance of the heart he brings forth vile things."[55]

46 Jesus said, "From Adam to John the Baptist, among those born of women there is no one greater than John the Baptist lest he should avert his eyes.[56] Yet I have said that whoever among you becomes a young child will know the kingdom; and he will become greater than John."[57]

47 Jesus said, "No person can mount two horses and string two bows; and no servant can serve two masters, or he will honor the one and insult the other.[58] No person drinks aged wine and immediately desires to drink new wine. And new wine is not put into old skins, or they might burst. And aged wine is not put into new skins, or it might go bad. An old patch is not sown on a new garment, for there would be a tear."[59]

48 Jesus said, "If two make peace with one another in a single house, they will say to the mountain, 'Move from here,' and it will move."[60]

49 Jesus said, "Blessed are the solitary ones and the elect, for you will find the kingdom. For you have come from it and you will return there."

50 Jesus said, "If they say to you, 'Where have you come from?' tell them 'We have come from the light, from the place where the light came to be on its own, established itself, and was revealed in their image.' If they say to you, 'Is it you?' say, 'We are its children, and we are the chosen of the living Father.' If they ask you, 'What is the sign of your Father in you?' say to them, 'It is movement and repose.' "

---

47 Cf. Matt 13:17; Luke 10:24; John 7:33–36.

48 Cf. Matt 23:13; Luke 11:52.

49 Cf. Matt 10:16.

50 Cf. Matt 15:13.

51 Cf. Matt 13:12; 25:29; Mark 4:25; Luke 18:18; 19:26.

52 Cf. John 14:9.

53 Cf. Matt 7:16–18; 12:33; Luke 6:43.

54 Cf. Matt 12:31–32; Mark 3:28–29; Luke 12:10.

55 Cf. Matt 7:16; 12:34–35; Luke 6:44–45.

56 Or: "lest he should keep his eyes down." Lit. "lest his eyes should be broken."

57 Cf. Matt 11:11; 18:3; Mark 10:15; Luke 7:28; 18:17.

58 Cf. Matt 6:24; Luke 16:13.

59 Cf. Matt 9:16–17; Mark 2:21–22; Luke 5:36–39.

60 Cf. Matt 17:20; 21:21; Mark 11:22–23; Luke 17:6.

51 His disciples said to him, "When will the repose of the dead take place? And when will the new world come?"[61] He said to them, "What you are looking for has come, but for your part you do not know it."[62]

52 His disciples said to him, "Twenty-four prophets spoke in Israel, and they all spoke about you." He said to them, "You have abandoned the one who lives in your presence and have spoken of the dead."

53 His disciples said to him, "Is circumcision beneficial or not?" He said to them, "If it were beneficial, their father would beget them already circumcised from their mother. But true circumcision in the spirit has become entirely profitable."[63]

54 Jesus said, "Blessed are the poor, for the kingdom of heaven is yours."[64]

55 Jesus said, "Whoever does not hate his father and his mother cannot be a disciple of mine; and whoever does not hate his brothers and his sisters and take up his cross the way I do, that person will not be worthy of me."[65]

56 Jesus said, "The one who has come to know the world has found a corpse; and the one who has found the corpse, the world is not worthy of that person."

57 Jesus said, "The kingdom of the Father is like a person having some good seed. His enemy came at night and sowed weeds among the good seed. The person did not allow them to pluck the weeds. He said to them, 'Otherwise, you might go to pluck the weeds and pluck the wheat with it. For on the harvest day the weeds will be plainly visible: they will be plucked and burned.' "[66]

58 Jesus said, "Blessed is the person who has suffered and found life."

59 Jesus said, "Look to the living one while you are living, or you might die and then seek to see him, and you will not be able to see."[67]

60 (They saw) a Samaritan carrying a lamb on his way to Judea. He said to his disciples, "That one is going around with the lamb." They said to him, "It is so he can kill it and eat it." He said to them, "While it is living he will not eat it, but only if he kills it and it becomes a corpse." They said, "He cannot do it otherwise." He said to them, "You, too, seek for yourselves a place for repose, lest you become a corpse and be eaten."

61 Jesus said, "Two will be resting on a couch: one will die, one will live."[68] Salome said, "Who are you, O man? As if you are from someone,[69] you have climbed onto my couch and eaten from my table." Jesus said to her, "I am the one who comes from what is whole.[70] I was given some of the things of my Father."[71] "I am your disciple." "For this reason I say that the one who is whole[72] will be full of light, but that the one who is divided will be filled with darkness."

62 Jesus said, "I am speaking my mysteries to those who are worthy of my mysteries.[73] Do not let your left hand understand what your right hand is doing."[74]

63 Jesus said, "There was a rich person who had many possessions. He said, 'I will use my possessions: I will sow, harvest, plant, and fill my storehouses with crops, so that I no longer need anything.' These things he was thinking in his heart, but that very night he died. The one who has ears had better listen!"[75]

---

61 Cf. Matt 24:3; Mark 13:4; Luke 21:7.

62 Cf. Luke 17:20–21.

63 Cf. Rom 2:25–29.

64 Cf. Matt 5:3; Luke 6:20.

65 Cf. Matt 10:37–38; 16:24; Mark 8:34; Luke 9:23; 14:26–27.

66 Cf. Matt 13:24–30.

67 Cf. John 7:33–36.

68 Cf. Matt 24:40; Luke 17:34.

69 Or: "as a stranger"; or "as from whom."

70 Or: "the sameness."

71 Cf. Matt 11:27; Luke 10:22.

72 Or: "destroyed"; or "desolate," following the ms. reading.

73 Cf. Matt 13:11; Mark 4:11; Luke 8:10.

74 Cf. Matt 6:3.

75 Cf. Luke 12:16–21.

64 Jesus said, "A person had some visitors. And when he prepared a dinner he sent his servant to invite the visitors. He went to the first and said to him, 'My master invites you.' He replied, 'Some merchants owe me money; they are coming to me this evening, and I must go to give them instructions. I ask to be excused from the dinner.' He went to another and said to him, 'My master has invited you.' He said to him, 'I have bought a house and need to be there for a day; I will not be free.' He went to another and said to him, 'My master invites you.' He said to him, 'My friend is getting married, and it is I who am to prepare the banquet. I cannot come; I ask to be excused from the dinner.' He went to another and said to him, 'My master invites you.' He said to him, 'I have bought an estate, and I am going to collect the rent. I cannot come: I ask to be excused.' The servant came and said to his master, 'The people you invited to the dinner have asked to be excused.' The master said to his servant, 'Go out to the streets; whomever you find, bring them in to have dinner.' Buyers and traders will not enter the places of my Father."[76]

65 He said, "A good man[77] owned a vineyard, and he leased it to tenant farmers so that they might work it and he might receive its produce from them. He sent his servant so the farmers might give him the produce of the vineyard. They seized the servant and beat him: they almost killed him. The servant went and told his master. The master said, 'Perhaps he did not know them.' He sent another servant, and the farmers beat this one as well. Then the master sent his son and said, 'Perhaps they will show respect to my son.' Since those farmers knew that he was the heir of the vineyard, they grabbed him and killed him. The one who has ears had better listen!"[78]

66 Jesus said, "Show me the stone that the builders have rejected: that is the cornerstone."[79]

67 Jesus said, "The one who knows the all but is lacking in himself lacks everything."[80]

68 Jesus said, "Blessed are you whenever they hate you and persecute you;[81] and wherever they have persecuted you, they will not find you there."

69 Jesus said, "Blessed are those who have been persecuted in their heart: it is they who have come to know the Father in truth. Blessed are those who are hungry, so that the stomach of the needy may be satisfied."[82]

70 Jesus said, "If you bring forth what is within you, what you have will save you; if you do not have that within you, what you do not have within you will kill you."

71 Jesus said, "I will destroy this house, and no one will be able to build it . . ."[83]

72 A person said to him, "Tell my brothers to divide my father's possessions with me." He said to him, "O man, who has made me a divider?" He turned to his disciples and said to them, "I am not a divider, am I?"[84]

73 Jesus said, "The harvest is plentiful, but the workers few. So pray to the Lord that he might send workers out to the harvest."[85]

74 He said, "Lord, there are many around the drinking trough, but there is nothing in the cistern."

75 Jesus said, "Many are standing at the door, but it is the solitary ones who will enter the bridal chamber."

76 Jesus said, "The kingdom of the Father is like a merchant who owned merchandise and then found a pearl. That merchant was wise; he sold the merchandise and bought for himself the single pearl.[86] You, too, seek his unfailing and enduring

---

76 Cf. Matt 22:1–10; Luke 14:15–24.

77 Or: "a usurer."

78 Cf. Matt 21:33–39; Mark 12:1–8; Luke 20:9–15.

79 Cf. Matt 21:42; Mark 12:10; Luke 20:17.

80 Or: "The one who knows the all but is deficient in one thing has been deficient in everything" (Emmel).

81 Cf. Matt 5:11; Luke 6:22.

82 Cf. Matt 5:6, 8, 10; Luke 6:21.

83 Cf. Matt 26:61; Mark 14:58.

84 Cf. Luke 12:13–14.

85 Cf. Matt 9:37–38; Luke 10:2.

86 Cf. Matt 13:44–46.

treasure, which no moth comes in to devour and no worm destroys."[87]

77 Jesus said, "It is I who am the light upon them all.[88] It is I who am the all. It is from me that the all has come, and to me that the all has extended.[89] Split a piece of wood: I am there. Lift up the stone and you will find me there."

78 Jesus said, "Why did you come out into the country? To see a reed moved by the wind? And to see a person dressed in soft clothes, like your kings and your dignitaries, who are dressed in soft clothes and are unable to know the truth?"[90]

79 A woman in the crowd said to him, "Blessed is the womb that bore you and the breasts that nourished you." He said to her, "Blessed are those who have heard the word of the Father and guarded it in truth. For days are coming when you will say, 'Blessed is the womb that has not conceived and the breasts that have not given milk.' "[91]

80 Jesus said, "The one who has come to know the world has found the body; and the one who has found the body—the world is not worthy of him."

81 Jesus said, "The one who has become rich, let him reign; and the one who has power, let him renounce (it)."

82 Jesus said, "The one who is near me is near the fire; and the one who is far from me is far from the kingdom."[92]

83 Jesus said, "The images are visible to humans. And the light that is within them is hidden in the image of the light of the Father. It[93] will be disclosed; and his image is hidden by his light."

84 Jesus said, "When you see your likeness, you rejoice. But when you see your images that came

into being before you and that neither die nor become revealed, how much you will bear!"[94]

85 Jesus said, "Adam came into being from a great power and a great wealth; and he did not become worthy of you. For had he been worthy, he would not have tasted death."

86 Jesus said, "The foxes have their dens and the birds their nests, but the Son of Man has no place to lay his head and rest."[95]

87 Jesus said, "Wretched is the body that depends on a body; and wretched is the soul that depends on these two."

88 Jesus said, "The angels[96] and the prophets are coming to you, and they will give you what you have. And you, too, give them what is yours and say to yourselves, 'When will they come and take what is theirs?' "

89 Jesus said, "Why do you wash the outside of the cup? Do you not realize that the one who made the inside is also the one who made the outside?"[97]

90 Jesus said, "Come to me, for my yoke is easy and my lordship is kind. And you will find repose for yourselves."[98]

91 They said to him, "Tell us who you are, so that we may believe in you." He said to them, "You evaluate the appearance of the sky and of the earth, yet you have not come to know the one who is before you, and you do not know how to evaluate this moment."[99]

92 Jesus said, "Seek and you will find.[100] Yet, the things you asked me about in the past and I did not tell you then, now I am willing to tell you, and you no longer seek after them."[101]

---

87 Cf. Matt 6:20; Luke 12:33.

88 Cf. John 8:12.

89 Cf. John 1:3.

90 Cf. Matt 11:7–8; Luke 7:24–25.

91 Cf. Matt 24:19; Mark 13:17; Luke 11:27–28; 21:23; 23:29.

92 Cf. Mark 12:34.

93 "It," viz. the hidden light. Or: "he."

94 Cf. Gen 1:26–27; Philo, Opif 69–71; LA 1.31–32.

95 Cf. Matt 8:20; Luke 9:58.

96 Or. "messengers."

97 Cf. Matt 23:25–26; Luke 11:39–40.

98 Cf. Matt 11:28–30.

99 Cf. Matt 16:1–3; Luke 12:56.

100 Cf. Matt 7:7; Luke 11:9.

101 Cf. John 16:4–5.

93 "Do not give holy things to dogs, or they might throw them on the dung heap. Do not throw pearls to swine, or else they might make it. . ."[102]

94 Jesus said, "The one who seeks will find; the one who knocks will have it opened."[103]

95 Jesus said, "If you have money, do not lend it at interest, but give it to the one from whom you will not get it back."[104]

96 Jesus said, "The kingdom of the Father is like a woman who took a small amount of yeast, hid it in dough, and made it into large loaves of bread. The one who has ears had better listen!"[105]

97 Jesus said, "The kingdom of the Father is like a woman who was carrying a jar full of meal. While she was walking a great distance on the road, the handle of the jar broke off and the meal poured out behind her on the road. She was not aware of it: she had noticed no trouble. When she reached her house, she set the jar down and found that it was empty."

98 Jesus said, "The kingdom of the Father is like a person who wanted to kill a dignitary. At home, he pulled the sword out and stuck it in the wall, to find out if his hand would be firm. Then he murdered the dignitary."

99 The disciples said to him, "Your brothers and your mother are standing outside." He said to them, "Those here who do the will of my Father, they are my brothers and my mother. It is they who will enter the kingdom of my Father."[106]

100 They showed Jesus a gold coin and said to him, "Caesar's people are demanding taxes from us." He said to them, "Give what is Caesar's to Caesar, and give what is God's to God; and what is mine, give it to me."[107]

101 "Whoever does not hate his father and his mother the way I do cannot be a disciple of mine.[108] And whoever does not love his father and his mother the way I do cannot be a disciple of mine. For my mother did . . .[109] But my true mother gave me life."

102 Jesus said, "Woe to the Pharisees, for they are like a dog sleeping in the cattle's feeding trough. For it neither eats nor lets the cattle eat."[110]

103 Jesus said, "Blessed is the person who knows at what point the robbers are entering, so that he may rise up, muster his estate, and arm himself before they enter."[111]

104 They said to Jesus, "Come, let us pray today and let us fast." Jesus said, "What is the sin that I have committed, or how have I been overcome? Rather, when the bridegroom comes out of the bridal chamber, then people should fast and pray."[112]

105 Jesus said, "Whoever knows the father and the mother will be called the child of a prostitute."

106 Jesus said, "When you make the two one, you will become children of humanity.[113] And when you say, 'Mountain, move away,' it will move."[114]

107 Jesus said, "The kingdom is like a shepherd who had a hundred sheep. One of them, the largest, wandered away. He left the ninety-nine and looked for the one until he found it. After all his labor, he said to the sheep, 'I love you more than the ninety-nine.' "[115]

108 Jesus said, "Whoever drinks from my mouth will become like me. I myself will become that person, and the hidden things will be revealed to that person."[116]

---

102 Cf. Matt 7:6. There are several possible restorations of the end of this saying: "or they might bring it to naught"; "or they might grind them to bits"; "or they might make mud of it."

103 Cf. Matt 7:8; Luke 11:10.

104 Cf. Matt 5:42; Luke 6:34–35.

105 Cf. Matt 13:33; Luke 13:20–21.

106 Cf. Matt 12:47; Mark 3:32; Luke 8:20–21.

107 Cf. Matt 22:16–21; Mark 12:14–17; Luke 20: 21–25.

108 Cf. Matt 10:37; Luke 14:26.

109 Possibly: "For my mother gave me falsehood."

110 Cf. Matt 23:13; Luke 11:52.

111 Cf. Matt 24:43; Luke 12:37–39.

112 Cf. Matt 9:14–15; Mark 2:18–20; Luke 5:33–35.

113 Or: "sons of man."

114 Cf. Matt 21:21; Luke 11:23.

115 Cf. Matt 18:12–13; Luke 16:4–6.

116 Cf. Matt 10:26; Luke 12:2.

109 Jesus said, "The kingdom is like a person who had a hidden treasure in his field without knowing it. And upon dying he left it to his son. The son did not know (about it). He took over the field and sold it. And the one who bought it came plowing and found the treasure. He began to lend out money at interest to whomever he wished."[117]

110 Jesus said, "Whoever finds the world and becomes rich, let him renounce the world."

111 Jesus said, "The heavens and the earth will roll up before you, and the one who is living from the living one will not see death." Does not Jesus say, "Whoever has found oneself, the world is not worthy of that person"?

112 Jesus said, "Woe to the flesh that depends on the soul. Woe to the soul that depends on the flesh."

113 His disciples said to him, "When will the kingdom come?"[118] "It will not come by waiting for it. It will not be said, 'Look, here it is,' or 'Look, it is there.' Rather, the kingdom of the Father is spread out upon the earth, and people do not see it."[119]

114 Simon Peter said to them, "Mary should leave us, for females are not worthy of the life." Jesus said, "Look, I am going to guide her in order to make her male, so that she too may become a living spirit resembling you males. For every female who makes herself male will enter the kingdom of heaven."

The Gospel according to Thomas

---

117 Cf. Matt 13:44.

118 Cf. Matt 24:3; Mark 13:4; Luke 21:7.

119 Cf. Luke 7:20–21.

44. The Gospel of Judas

The Gospel of Judas is the most recent Gospel to be published (2006), and is arguably the most important discovery of a Christian text since the Nag Hammadi library in 1945. It is a Sethian Gnostic text that contains a number of conversations between Jesus and his disciples immediately before his death (see Chapter 6 and the discussion of the Sethians). The Gospel is named after Judas Iscariot, Jesus' betrayer, because here he is portrayed as the one disciple who understands Jesus' identity and his message of revelation. The other disciples mistakenly think that Jesus belongs to the God who created this world—a view that Jesus, in this account, finds laughable. For this author, the world we live in and the human race itself was not made by the one, true God, but by lower divinities, one a blood-thirsty rebel and the other a fool.

There is a dispute among scholars whether Judas is portrayed as the good guy or the villain in this account. Possibly he is something in between. Unlike the other followers of Jesus, Judas knows the truth about Jesus. And it is to him that Jesus reveals the secrets of how the divine realm and this world came into being. This revelation may seem

---

The Gospel of Judas, reproduced from Bart D. Ehrman and Zlatko Pleše, *The Apocryphal Gospels: Texts and Translations*. New York: Oxford University Press, 2011. Used with permission of Oxford University Press.

very bizarre to modern readers, but it is thoroughly at home in the world of Sethian myth (see the Secret Book of John in Chapter 6). At the same time, it appears that even Judas will not be allowed to enter into the divine realm when he passes from this earth. Only the chosen (the Gnostics themselves) will be able to do so; this will come only through a full understanding of Jesus' revelation—not his death and resurrection, which are noticeably not narrated in the text.

Some form of this Gospel was known to the heresiologist Irenaeus, writing in 180 CE. It therefore appears that the Gospel was composed sometime in the middle of the second century.

The Gospel of Judas

33 The secret word of revelation that Jesus spoke with Judas Iscariot in the course of eight days, three days before he celebrated Passover.

When he appeared on earth, he performed signs and great miracles for the salvation of humankind. And since some walked on the path of righteousness and others walked in their transgression, the twelve disciples were called. He began to speak with them about the mysteries that are beyond the world and what will happen at the end. Oftentimes he would not disclose himself to his disciples, but when necessary,[1] you would find him in their midst.

One day he was in Judaea with his disciples, and he found them seated and assembled together, practicing godliness.[2] When he approached his disciples

34 as they were assembled together, seated and giving thanks over the bread, he laughed. But the disciples said to him, "Teacher, why are you laughing at our thanksgiving? Or what have we done? This is what is appropriate." He answered and said to them, "I am not laughing at you. You are not doing this out of your own will: rather, your god will receive praise through this." They said, "Teacher, you . . . are the son of God." Jesus said to them, "How do you know me? Truly I say to you that no generation will know me from the people that are among you."

Now when his disciples heard this, they began to feel irritated and angry, and to blaspheme against him in their hearts. And Jesus, when he saw their senselessness, said to them, "Why has this agitation produced wrath? Your god who is within you and his powers[3]

35 have become irritated together with your souls. Whoever is strong among you humans, let him bring out the perfect human being and stand before my face!"

And they all said, "We are strong." Yet their spirits could not dare to stand before him, except Judas Iscariot. He was able to stand before him, yet he could not look him in the eye, but rather turned his face away. Judas said to him, "I know who you are and where you have come from. You have come from the immortal aeon of Barbelo, and from the one that has sent you, whose name I am not worthy to utter." But Jesus, knowing that he was thinking of something lofty, said to him, "Separate from them, and I will tell you the mysteries of the kingdom, not so that you may go there, but that you may grieve greatly.

36 For someone else will take your place, so that the twelve disciples may again be complete with their god."[4] And Judas said to him, "When will you tell me these things, and when will the great [day] of light dawn for the . . . generation?" But when he said these things, Jesus left him.

---

1 Or: "you would find him as an apparition," or "as a child."

2 Cf. 1 Tim 4:7; or: "disputing issues concerning God."

3 Or: "servants."

4 Cf. Acts 1:15–26; John 17:13, 23.

The next morning, after this happened, he appeared to his disciples. They said to him, "Teacher, where did you go and what were you doing after you left us?" Jesus said to them, "I went to another generation, one that is great and holy." His disciples said to him, "Lord, which is the great generation that is superior to us and holy, but is not now in these aeons?"

When Jesus heard this, he laughed. He said to them, "Why are you thinking in your heart about the strong and holy generation?

37 Truly I say to you, no one born of this aeon will see that generation; and no angelic host of the stars will rule over that generation; and no human of mortal birth will be able to come along with it. For that generation is not from . . . that has come to be . . . but . . . the generation of people among you is from the generation of humanity . . . power, which . . . other powers . . . by which you rule."

When his disciples heard this, they each became disturbed in their spirit, and they did not find anything to say.

On another day Jesus came to them. They said to him, "Teacher, we have seen you in a vision; for we have seen great dreams this past night." He said, "Why have you . . . and have hidden yourselves away?"

38 They said, "We have seen a great house with a large altar in it, and twelve men— we would say they are the priests—and a name. A crowd attended at that altar until the priests were done presenting the offerings. As for us, we also were in attendance." Jesus said, "What are . . .[5] like?" They said, "Some . . .[6] two weeks, while others sacrifice their own children and others their wives, praising and humiliating each other. Some sleep with men, others perform murder, and

still others commit a multitude of sins and lawless acts; and the men who stand before the altar invoke your name.

39 And as they are occupied with all the actions of their sacrifice,[7] that altar becomes full."

When they said these things, they fell silent, for they were disturbed. Jesus said to them, "Why have you become disturbed? Truly I say to you, all the priests who stand before that altar call upon my name. I tell you again that my name has been written on this . . . of the generations of the stars by the generations of people, and they have shamefully planted trees without fruit in my name."

Jesus said to them, "It is you who are presenting the offerings at the altar you have seen. That one is the God you serve, and the twelve men you have seen are you. And the cattle brought in are the sacrifices you have seen—they are the crowd of people you lead astray

40 beside that altar. The . . .[8] will stand up and in this way use my name, and the generations of pious people will attend him. After him, another person will stand up for the fornicators, and another will stand up for the murderers of children, and yet another for those who sleep with men and those who fast, and the rest of the people of impurity, lawlessness, and error, and those who say, 'We are like angels.'[9] And they are the stars that bring everything to its end. For it has been said to the generations of people, 'Behold, God has received your sacrifice from the hands of the priests'—that is, the Minister of Error. Now, the Lord who commands is he who rules over the all.[10] On the last day they will be put to shame."

---

5 The lacuna may be filled with the "priests," the "crowd," or the "people."

6 Probably restore to "fast for," or "abstain for"; cf. infra, 40.

7 Or: "deficiency."

8 Possibly "the ruler of the world" (John 12:31; 14:30; 16:11), or "the great bishop."

9 Cf. Luke 20:36.

10 Or: "the universe."

41 Jesus said to them, "Stop sacrificing . . . that you have . . . upon the altar, since they are over your stars and your angels and have already come to their end there. So let them be . . . before you and go . . . the generations . . . A baker cannot feed all creation

42 that is under [heaven]." And when the disciples heard this they said to him, "Lord, help us and save us." Jesus said to them, "Stop contending with me. Each of you has his own star, and every one . . .

43 in the . . . he has not come . . . spring for the tree of . . . time of this aeon . . . after a while . . . . Rather, he has come to water God's paradise and the race that will last, for he will not defile the journey of that generation, but rather . . . for all eternity."

Judas said to him, "Rabbi, what fruit does this generation have?" Jesus said, "The souls of every human generation will die. But when these people bring the time of the kingdom to its end and the spirit parts from them, their bodies will die, but their souls will be alive and will be taken up."[11] Judas said, "Then what will the remaining generations of people do?" Jesus said, "It is impossible

44 to sow upon rock and receive fruit.[12] So also . . . the defiled race and the corruptible Sophia[13] . . . the hand that has fashioned mortal people, and their souls ascend to the aeons on high. Truly I say to you,[14] no . . . or angel or power can see those places, which this great, holy generation will see." After Jesus said these things, he departed.[15]

Judas said, "Teacher, just as you have listened to all of them, now also listen to me, for I have

seen a great vision." When Jesus heard (this), he laughed and said to him, "Why do you trouble yourself, O thirteenth daimon?[16] But speak up for yourself: I will bear with you."

Judas said to him, "I saw myself in the vision as the twelve disciples threw stones at me and

45 persecuted me zealously. And I came again to the place that . . . after you. I saw a house . . . and my eyes could not measure its size. Some great people were surrounding it, and that house (had a) grass rooftop,[17] and in the midst of the house there was a crowd . . . Teacher, take me inside, too, together with these people."

Jesus answered and said, "Your star has led you astray, Judas!" And further, "No person born of any mortal is worthy to enter the house you have seen. For that place is reserved for the holy, where neither the sun nor the moon will rule, nor will the day, but they will always stand there in the aeon with the holy angels. Look, I have told you the mysteries of the kingdom

46 and I have taught you about the error of the stars. And . . . send for . . . upon the twelve aeons."

Judas said, "Teacher, is it perhaps that my seed, too, is under the control of the rulers?" Jesus answered and said to him, "Come, I will . . . you, that . . . but that[18] you may come to grieve even more when you see the kingdom and its entire generation." When Judas heard these things, he said to him, "What gain is there for me, since you have set me apart from that generation?" Jesus answered and said, "You will become the thirteenth, and you will be cursed by the remaining generations, and you will come to rule over them.

---

11 See infra, 53.

12 Cf. Luke 8:6.

13 Or: "wisdom."

14 Plural form: the disciples are present as Jesus and Judas discuss the fate of human generations.

15 Or: "they departed."

16 Cf. infra, **46**. The number thirteen and the term *daimon* may have both positive and negative applications in the religious and philosophical texts of the period.

17 Cf. 4 Kgdms 19:16 LXX; Ps 128:6 LXX; Isa 37:27.

18 Probably "I will tell you, not that . . . but that . . ."

In the last days they will . . . you shall not ascend[19] on high

47 to the holy generation."
Jesus said, "Come, I will teach you about the things . . . that human . . . will see. For there exists a great and boundless aeon, whose size no angelic generation could see, in which is the great Invisible Spirit, that no eye of angel has seen and no thought of the mind comprehended,[20] and which was never called by any name.

And a luminous cloud appeared there. And he[21] said, 'Let an angel come into being as my attendant.' And from the cloud there came forth a great angel, the Self-Originate, the god of light. And because of him, another four angels came into being from another cloud, and they came to be as attendants for the angelic Self-Originate. And

48 the Self-Originate said, 'Let . . .[22] come into being,' and . . . came to be.[23] And he created the first luminary to rule over it,[24] and he said, 'Let angels come into being to serve it,' and countless myriads came to be.

And he said, 'Let a luminous aeon come into being,' and it came to be. He established the second luminary to rule over it, along with countless myriads of angels to render service. This is how he created the rest of the aeons of light, and he made them rule over them. And he created for them countless myriads of angels for their assistance.

And Adamas was in the first cloud of light, which no angel could see among all those called 'God.' And he did

49 . . . that . . . the image . . . and after the likeness of this angel he revealed the

incorruptible generation of Seth . . . the twelve . . . twenty-four . . . He revealed seventy-two luminaries in the incorruptible generation by the will of the Spirit. The seventy-two luminaries, for their part, revealed three hundred sixty luminaries in the incorruptible generation by the will of the Spirit, so that their numbers should be five for each.

And their Father consists of the twelve aeons of the twelve luminaries, with six heavens for each aeon, so that there might be seventy-two heavens for the seventy-two luminaries, and for each

50 of them five firmaments, so that there might be three hundred sixty firmaments.[25] They were granted authority and a great host of countless angels, for glory and service, and in addition virgin spirits as well, for glory and service of all the aeons and the heavens and their firmaments.

Now, the multitude of those immortal beings is called 'cosmos'—that is, corruption—by the Father and the seventy-two luminaries that are with the Self-Originate and his seventy-two aeons. There the first human being appeared together with his incorruptible powers.

Now, the aeon that appeared with his generation, the one in whom are the cloud of knowledge and the angel, is called

51 El.[26] . . . aeon . . . After these things he said . . .[27] 'Let twelve angels come into being to rule over chaos and the underworld.' And look, from the cloud there appeared an angel, whose face breathed out fire, and whose appearance was defiled with blood. His name was Nebro, meaning 'rebel' in translation,[28] but other people call him Ialdabaoth. And another angel, Saklas,

---

19 The meaning of this passage remains ambiguous.

20 Cf. 1 Cor 2:9.

21 Or: "it," viz., the Invisible Spirit.

22 Possibly "another aeon," or "Adamas."

23 Possibly "the procession occurred," or "it came to be as he said."

24 Or: "him."

25 All of these numbers have a clear astrological significance, denoting the hierarchy of heavenly beings.

26 Possibly a variant form of Eleleth.

27 Possibly Eleleth.

28 Possibly a reference to Nebruel from other Gnostic texts.

also came forth from the cloud. Nebro then created six angels, and Saklas,[29] to be attendants. And these gave birth to twelve angels in the heavens, and they each received a share in the heavens.

And the twelve rulers spoke with the twelve angels, 'Let each of you

52 ... and let them ... generation ... five angels.'

The first is Seth, who is called Christ;
the second is Harmathoth, who ...
the third is Galila;
the fourth is Iobel;
the fifth is Adonaios.

These are the five who have ruled over the underworld, and first over chaos.

Then Saklas said to his angels, 'Let us create a human being after the likeness and after the image.'[30] And they molded Adam and his wife Eve, who in the cloud is called 'Zoe.'[31] For by this name all generations greet him; and each of them calls her with their own names. Now, Saklas did not

53 command ... except ... the generations ... this ... And the ruler said to him, 'Your life shall belong ...[32] and your children for a time.' "[33]

Then Judas said to Jesus, "What is the longest that the human being will live?" Jesus said, "Why are you surprised that Adam, along with his generation, received his time numerically, considering that[34] he received his kingdom commensurably with his ruler?"

Judas said to Jesus, "Does the human spirit die?" Jesus said, "It is like this. God ordered Michael[35] to grant the spirits of people to them as a loan, while they serve. But the Great One ordered Gabriel to grant spirits to the great generation with no king—the spirit along with the soul.[36] For this reason, the rest of the souls

54 ... light ... chaos ... around ... spirit within you,[37] which you have made to dwell in this flesh from[38] the generations of angels. But God caused knowledge to be granted to Adam and those with him, so that the kings of chaos and the underworld might not rule over them."

Judas said to Jesus, "So what will those generations do?" Jesus said, "Truly I say to you,[39] the stars bring to completion all of them. And when Saklas completes his span of time that was allotted to him, their first star will come with the generations, and they will bring to fulfillment what has been said. Then they will fornicate in my name and slaughter their children,[40]

55 and they will ... and ...[41] from ... servants of Saklas ... all ... committing sins in my name.[42] And your star will rule over the thirteenth aeon."[43]

After that Jesus laughed. Judas said, "Teacher, why are you laughing at us?" Jesus answered and said, "I am not laughing at you, but rather at the error of the stars, that these six stars wander about

---

29 The Coptic text is unclear.
30 Cf. Gen 1:27.
31 Cf. Gen 3:20.
32 Probably "to you."
33 Cf. Gen 3:22.
34 Lit. "in the place where"; but see W. E. Crum, *A Coptic Dictionary* (1939) 154a–b.
35 Cf. Dan 10:31, 21; 12, 1.
36 Cf. supra, 43.
37 Plural.
38 Or: "among."
39 Plural.
40 Cf. supra, 38–39.
41 Possibly "and they will sleep with men, and they ..."
42 "From ... name"; recently restored by Wurst, "Gospel of Judas."
43 Cf. supra, 44, 46.

with these five warriors,[44] and they all will be destroyed together with their creations."

And Judas said to Jesus, "So what will those who have been baptized in your name do?" Jesus said, "Truly I say to you, this baptism

56 . . . in my name . . . I say to you, . . . human hand . . . to me. Truly I say to you, Judas, those who offer sacrifices to Saklas . . . everything that is evil. But you will surpass them all, for you will sacrifice the human being that bears me.[45]

Already your horn has been exalted,[46]
and your wrath has been kindled,[47]
and your star has passed through,
and your heart has become . . .

57 Truly I say to you, your last . . . become . . . grieve[48] . . . the ruler being destroyed.[49] And then the image[50] of the great generation of Adam will be exalted, for before the heaven, the earth, and the angels there exists that generation

from the aeons.[51] Look, you have been told everything. Lift up your eyes and see the cloud and the light in it, and the stars that surround it. And the star that leads the way is your star."

So Judas lifted up his eyes and saw the luminous cloud. And he[52] entered it. Those standing on the ground heard a voice coming from the cloud, saying,[53]

58 ". . . the great generation . . . image . . . and . . .

And their high priests murmured, for he had entered the guest room[54] for his prayer. Some scribes were there watching closely in order to arrest him during the prayer, for they were afraid of the people, since he was regarded by all as a prophet.[55] They approached Judas and said to him, "What are you doing here? You are Jesus' disciple."[56] He answered them as they wished.

And Judas received some money and handed him over to them.[57]

The Gospel of Judas

---

44 Cf. supra, 51–52; cf. Rev 12:5–7.

45 Scholars are divided over the meaning of this comment.

46 Cf. Ps 74:11; 88:18; 148:18 LXX.

47 Cf. Ps 2:12 LXX; or "your wrath has come to full," for which cf. Jer 6:11.

48 Cf. supra, 35, 46.

49 Or: "The ruler shall be destroyed."

50 Or: "the model."

51 Or: "from eternity."

52 "He," i.e., Judas, or possibly Jesus.

53 Cf. Mark 9:7.

54 Cf. Mark 14:14; Luke 22:11.

55 Cf. Matt 21:46; Luke 22:2.

56 Cf. Matt 26:14–15a; Mark 14:10; Luke 22:3–4; cf. also John 13:26–30.

57 Cf. Matt 26:15b–16; 27:3; Mark 14:11; Luke 22:5–6.

45. The Gospel of Peter

Although the Gospel of Peter was known and used as Scripture in some parts of the Christian church in the second century, its use was eventually disallowed by church leaders who considered some of its teachings heretical. Having fallen out of circulation, it was practically forgotten in all but name until a fragment of its text was discovered near the end of the nineteenth century in a tomb in Akhmim, Egypt.

The fragment narrates Jesus' passion and resurrection, beginning (in the middle of an episode) with Jesus' trial before Pilate. Although many of the stories are familiar from the New Testament, especially Matthew, some of the details are strikingly different, such as the statement that on the cross, Jesus was "silent as if he had no pain" (v. 10). Yet more striking are several episodes found nowhere else in any of our other Gospels, especially the impressive account of Jesus' emergence from his tomb as a giant, supported by two enormous angels and followed by a talking cross.

Scholars debate whether the Gospel of Peter consisted exclusively of a passion narrative or whether, like the New Testament Gospels, it simply ended with one. Nor is it clear whether the pseudonymous author derived his stories from the canonical accounts or, instead, from other sources and independently of them. What is clear is that his account, even more than the New Testament Gospels, goes out of its way to incriminate Jews for the death of Jesus (for example, v. 25). This strong anti-Judaic slant may help suggest a date from the early part of the second century.

The Gospel of Peter

1 . . . but none of the Jews washed his hands, nor did Herod or any of his judges.[1] Since they did not wish to wash, Pilate stood up.

2 Then King Herod ordered the Lord to be taken away and said to them, "Do everything that I ordered you to do to him."

3 Standing there was Joseph, a friend of both Pilate and the Lord. When he knew that they were about to crucify him, he came to Pilate and asked for the Lord's body for burial.[2]

4 Pilate sent word to Herod, asking for his body.

5 Herod said, "Brother Pilate, even if no one had asked for him we would have buried him, since the Sabbath is dawning.[3] For it is written in the Law that the sun must not set on one who has been killed."[4] And he delivered him over to the people[5] the day before their Feast of Unleavened Bread.[6]

6 Those who took the Lord began pushing him about, running up to him and saying, "Let us drag

---

1 Cf. Matt 27:24.

2 Cf. Matt 27:58; Mark 15:43; Luke 23:52; John 19:38.

3 Cf. Luke 23:54.

4 Deut 21:22–23; cf. John 19:31.

5 Cf. Matt 27:26; Mark 15:15; Luke 23:25; John 19:16.

6 Cf. Matt 26:17; Mark 14:12; Luke 22:7.

The Gospel of Peter, reproduced from Bart D. Ehrman and Zlatko Pleše, *The Apocryphal Gospels: Texts and Translations.* New York: Oxford University Press, 2011. Used with permission of Oxford University Press.

around the Son of God, since we have authority over him."

7 They clothed him in purple and sat him on the judgment seat, saying, "Give a righteous judgment, O King of Israel!"[7]

8 One of them brought a crown made of thorns and placed it on the Lord's head.

9 Others standing there were spitting in his face; some slapped his cheeks; others were beating him with a reed; and some began to flog him, saying, "This is how we should honor the Son of God!"[8]

10 They brought forward two evildoers and crucified the Lord between them. But he was silent, as if he had no pain.

11 When they had set the cross upright, they wrote an inscription: "This is the King of Israel."

12 Putting his clothes in front of him they divided them up and cast a lot for them.[9]

13 But one of the evildoers reviled them, "We have suffered like this for the evil things we did; but this one, the Savior of the people—what wrong has he done you?"[10]

14 They became angry at him and ordered his legs not be broken,[11] so that he would die in torment.

15 It was noon and darkness came over all of Judea. They were disturbed and upset that the sun may have already set while he was still alive; for their Scripture says that the sun must not set on one who has been killed.[12]

16 One of them said, "Give him gall mixed with vinegar to drink." And they made the mixture and gave it to him to drink.[13]

17 Thus they brought all things to fulfillment and completed all their sins on their heads.

18 But many were wandering around with torches, thinking that it was night; and they stumbled about.

19 And the Lord cried out, "My power, O power, you have left me behind!"[14] When he said this, he[15] was taken up.

20 At that hour, the curtain of the Temple in Jerusalem was ripped in half.[16]

21 Then they pulled the nails from the Lord's hands and placed him on the ground. All the ground shook and everyone was terrified.[17]

22 Then the sun shone and it was found to be three in the afternoon.[18]

23 But the Jews were glad and gave his body to Joseph that he might bury him, since he had seen all the good things he did.

24 He took the Lord, washed him, wrapped him in a linen cloth,[19] and brought him into his own tomb, called the Garden of Joseph.[20]

25 Then the Jews, the elders, and the priests realized how much evil they had done to themselves and began beating their breasts, saying "Woe to us because of our sins. The judgment and the end of Jerusalem are near."[21]

26 But I and my companions were grieving and went into hiding, wounded in heart. For we were being sought out by them as if we were evildoers who wanted to burn the Temple.

---

7 Cf. John 19:13.

8 Cf. Matt 26:67–68; 27:27–31; Mark 14:65; 15:16–20; Luke 22:63–65; John 19:2–3.

9 Cf. Matt 27:33–37; Mark 15:22–26; Luke 23:33–34; John 19:17–27.

10 Cf. Luke 23:39–43.

11 Cf. John 19:31–37.

12 Deut 21:22–23; cf. John 19:31.

13 Cf. Matt 27;34, 48; Mark 15:23, 36; Luke 23:36; John 29:28–30.

14 Cf. Matt 27:46; Mark 15:34.

15 Or: it.

16 Cf. Matt 27:51; Mark 15:38; Luke 23:45.

17 Cf. Matt 27:51, 54.

18 Cf. Matt 27;45; Mark 15:33; Luke 23:44.

19 Cf. Matt 27:59; Mark 14:46; Luke 23:53; John 19:40.

20 Cf. John 19:41.

21 Cf. Luke 23:48; esp. note the variant reading in the Latin ms g[1]: *saying, Woe to us! These things have happened today because of our sins. For the destruction of Jerusalem has drawn near.*

27 While these things were happening, we fasted and sat mourning and weeping, night and day, until the Sabbath.

28 The scribes, Pharisees, and elders gathered together and heard all the people murmuring and beating their breasts, saying, "If such great signs happened when he died, you can see how righteous he was!"[22]

29 The elders became fearful and went to Pilate and asked him,

30 "Give us some soldiers to guard his crypt for three days to keep his disciples from coming to steal him, Otherwise the people may assume he has been raised from the dead and then harm us."[23]

31 So Pilate gave them the centurion Petronius and soldiers to guard the tomb. The elders and scribes came with them to the crypt.

32 Everyone who was there, along with the centurion and the soldiers, rolled a great stone and placed it there before the entrance of the crypt.[24]

33 They smeared it with seven seals, pitched a tent there, and stood guard.[25]

34 Early in the morning, as the Sabbath dawned, a crowd came from Jerusalem and the surrounding area to see the sealed crypt.

35 But during the night on which the Lord's day dawned, while the soldiers stood guard two by two on their watch, a great voice came from the sky.

36 They saw the skies open and two men descend from there; they were very bright and drew near to the tomb.

37 That stone which had been cast before the entrance rolled away by itself and moved to one side; the tomb was open and both young men entered.[26]

38 When the solders saw these things, they woke up the centurion and the elders—for they were also there on guard.

39 As they were explaining what they had seen, they saw three men emerge from the tomb, two of them supporting the other, with a cross following behind them.

40 The heads of the two reached up to the sky, but the head of the one they were leading went up above the skies.

41 And they heard a voice from the skies, "Have you preached to those who are asleep?"[27]

42 And a reply came from the cross, "Yes."

43 They then decided among themselves to go off to disclose what had happened to Pilate.

44 While they were still making their plans, the skies were again seen to open, and a person descended and entered the crypt.

45 Those who were with the centurion saw these things and hurried to Pilate at night, abandoning the tomb they had been guarding, and explained everything they had seen. Greatly agitated, they said, "He actually was the Son of God."[28]

46 Pilate replied, "I am clean of the blood of the Son of God; you decided to do this."[29]

47 Then everyone approached him to ask and urge him to order the centurion and the soldiers to say nothing about what they had seen.

48 "For it is better," they said, "for us to incur a great sin before God than to fall into the hands of the Jewish people and be stoned."

49 And so Pilate ordered the centurion and the soldiers not to say a word.[30]

50 Now Mary Magdalene, a disciple of the Lord, had been afraid of the Jews, since they were inflamed with anger; and so she had not done at the Lord's crypt the things that women customarily do for loved ones who die. But early in the morning of the Lord's day

51 she took some of her women friends with her and came to the crypt where he had been buried.[31]

---

22 Cf. Luke 23:47–48.

23 Cf. Matt 27:62–66.

24 Cf. Matt 27:60; Mark 15:46; Luke 23:53.

25 Cf. Matt 27:66.

26 Cf. Matt 28:1–2.

27 Cf. 1 Pet 3:19.

28 Cf. Matt 27:54; Mark 15:39.

29 Cf. Matt 27:24.

30 Cf. Matt 28:11–15.

31 Cf. Matt 28:1; Mark 16:1–2, Luke 24:1; John 19:1.

52 And they were afraid that the Jews might see them, and they said, "Even though we were not able to weep and beat our breasts on the day he was crucified, we should do these things now at his crypt.

53 But who will roll away for us the stone placed before the entrance of the crypt, that we can go in, sit beside him, and do what we should?

54 For it was a large stone,[32] and we are afraid someone may see us. If we cannot move it, we should at least cast down the things we have brought at the entrance as a memorial to him; and we will weep and beat our breasts until we return home."

55 When they arrived they found the tomb opened. And when they came up to it they stooped down to look in, and they saw a beautiful young man dressed in a very bright garment, sitting in the middle of the tomb. He said to them,

32 Cf. Mark 16:3–4.

56 "Why have you come? Whom are you seeking? Not the one who was crucified? He has risen and left. But if you do not believe it, stoop down to look, and see the place where he was laid, that he is not there. For he has risen and left for the place from which he was sent."

57 Then the women fled out of fear.[33]

58 But it was the final day of the Feast of Unleavened Bread, and many left to return to their homes, now that the feast had ended.

59 But we, the twelve disciples of the Lord, wept and grieved; and each one returned to his home, grieving for what had happened.

60 But I, Simon Peter, and my brother Andrew, took our nets and went off to the sea.[34] And with us was Levi, the son of Alphaeus, whom the Lord. . . .

33 Cf. Mark 16:1–8.
34 Cf. John 21:1–14.

46. The Gospel of Mary

No one knew of the existence of a Gospel of Mary until a manuscript containing large portions of the text was discovered in 1896. Because of a series of unfortunate accidents, the book was not published until 1955. Over the past 20 years or so, though, the Gospel of Mary has become one of the most beloved and studied Gospels from outside the New Testament, in no small measure because the central figure is Jesus' follower Mary Magdalene, described here as one whom Jesus loved more than any of the male disciples.

The fragment of the text that survives begins in the middle of a conversation between Jesus and his disciples, in which he responds to a question about whether the material world will be destroyed or not. The Gnostic antimaterialist character of the text is clear already in his answer, as well as in the scene that follows. Jesus leaves the disciples; Peter then asks Mary to tell them the revelation that Jesus had given to

The Gospel of Mary, reproduced from Bart D. Ehrman and Zlatko Pleše, *The Apocryphal Gospels: Texts and Translations*. New York: Oxford University Press, 2011. Used with permission of Oxford University Press.

her, and her alone. Just when Mary begins to explain what Jesus had revealed to her, there is a large gap of four pages missing in the manuscript.

When it resumes, Mary is describing Jesus' revelation of how the human soul can ascend through the malevolent powers of this material world to return to its heavenly, spiritual home. When she finishes, an argument erupts among the male disciples over whether Jesus could possibly have revealed such truths to a woman, instead of to them, the men disciples. The dispute is eventually resolved in Mary's favor, and they all go forth to preach the gospel.

This Gospel was probably written in the mid to late second century.

The Gospel According to Mary

7 ... Will matter then be destroyed or not?" The Savior said, "Every nature, everything fashioned, and all creation exist together in one another, and they will dissolve again into their own root. For the nature of matter dissolves into what belongs to its own nature. The one who has ears to listen had better listen!"[1]

Peter said to him, "Since you have taught us everything, tell us also this thing. What is the sin of the world?"

The Savior said, "Sin does not exist; rather, it is you who produce sin when you do what is in accordance with the nature of adultery, which is called 'sin.'[2] For this reason, the good has come among you, to those of every nature, in order to restore each to its own root." He then continued by saying, "For this reason you are sick and are dying, because you love

8 that which deceives you. The one who understands should understand. Matter has given birth to a passion that has no resemblance, for it has come forth in a way contrary to nature. A disturbance then occurs in the entire body. This is why I told you, 'Be content at heart.'[3] And if you remain discontent, surely you should be content in the presence of each and every image of nature. The one who has ears to listen had better listen!"

When the blessed one had said these things, he greeted them all, saying, "Peace be to you, may my peace be born to you.[4] Be on guard so that no one leads you astray by saying, 'Look here' or 'Look over there.' For the Son of Man is within you.[5] Follow him! Those who seek him will find him. Go, then, and preach the gospel of the kingdom.[6] Do not

9 lay down any rules beyond what I have set for you, nor set forth any law like the lawgiver, or else you may be ruled by it."[7] When he said these things, he departed.

But they were distressed and wept greatly, saying, "How can we go to the gentiles and preach[8] the gospel of the kingdom of the Son of Man? If they did not spare him, how will they spare us?"

Then Mary arose and greeted them all, saying to her brothers, "Do not weep or grieve or be of two minds,[9] for his grace will be with all of you and will protect you. Rather, let us praise his

---

1 Matt 11:15; Mark 4:9.

2 Cf. Gos Phil. (NHC II.3) 61, 10–12: "Every union that has occurred between those unlike each other is adultery."

3 Cf. Luke 24:38; John 14:27.

4 Cf. Luke 24:37; John 14:27; 20:19, 21, 26.

5 Luke 17:21, 24.

6 Matt 4:23; 9:35; 24:14.

7 Cf. Matt 28:20. The Savior seems to condemn here the Mosaic law and its divine legislator.

8 Cf. Matt 28:19–20.

9 Cf. Matt 28:17.

greatness, for he has prepared us and made us human beings."

When Mary said these things, she turned their hearts toward the good, and they began to discuss the Savior's words.

10 Peter said to Mary, "Sister, we know that the Savior loved you more than the other women.[10] Tell us the words of the Savior that you remember, which you know and we do not, since we did not hear them."[11]

Mary replied, "What is hidden from you I will tell you." And she began speaking these words to them. "I," she said, "saw the Lord in a vision and said to him, 'Lord, I saw you in a vision today.' He answered me, 'You are blessed, because you do not falter at seeing me. For where the mind is, there is the treasure.'[12] I said to him, 'Now, Lord, does the one who sees a vision see it with the soul or with the spirit?' The Savior replied, 'He does not see it with the soul or with the spirit; but the mind that is between the two is what sees the vision, and it is that which . . .'"

15 . . . it.[13] And Desire said, 'I did not see you descending, but now I see you ascending. So why are you lying, since you belong to me!' The soul replied, 'I saw you. You did not see me, nor did you recognize me. You possessed me as a garment, and you did not know me.' When she said these things, she left, rejoicing greatly.

Again, she came to the third authority, which is called Ignorance. [It] examined the soul, saying, 'Where are you going? You have been ruled by wickedness. Surely you have been ruled, so do not

judge!' And the soul said, 'Why do you judge me, when I have not judged? I was ruled, without having ruled. I was not known, but I myself have come to know that all is being dissolved, both the things of earth

16 and those of heaven.'
When the soul had brought to naught the third authority, she ascended and saw the fourth authority. It took seven forms: the first form is Darkness; the second, Desire; the third, Ignorance, the fourth is the Envy of Death; the fifth is the Kingdom of the Flesh; the sixth is the Foolish Wisdom of the Flesh;[14] the seventh is the Wrathful Wisdom. These are the seven authorities of Wrath. They queried the soul, 'Where are you coming from, slayer of humans, and where are you going, destroyer of realms?' The soul replied, 'What has ruled me has been slain, and what has surrounded me has been destroyed, and my desire has been brought to an end, and my ignorance has died. In a world, I was set free

17 through another world, and in an image, through a superior image. The bond of forgetfulness is temporary; from now on, I shall receive repose in silence for the duration of the time of the age.'"

When Mary said these things, she fell silent, as though the Savior had spoken to her up to this point. Now Andrew[15] responded and said to his brothers, "Say what you will about what she has said, but I do not believe that the Savior said these things. For these teachings are strange thoughts indeed."[16] Peter replied and spoke about these things as follows, He asked them about the Savior, "Did he really speak with a woman secretly from us, not openly? Should we turn about, too, and all listen to her? Did he choose her over us?"[17]

---

10 Gospel of Phillip (NHC II.3) 63,30–64,9.

11 Cf. John 20:18.

12 Cf. Matt 6:21; Luke 12:34.

13 Or: "him." Mary's report on the Savior teaching resumes after a long lacuna with a description of the heavenly ascent of the soul. The name of the first authority, which is lost in the lacuna, is most likely "Darkness"; cf. the list of the seven forms of the fourth authority later.

---

14 Cf. 1 Cor 1:19–20, 26; 2 Cor 1:12.

15 On Andrew, see Matt 10:2; Mark 1:16–18; 3:18; Luke 6:14; John 1:35–42, 44; Acts 1:13.

16 Cf. Luke 24:10–11.

17 Cf. Gos Thom 114.

18 Then Mary wept and said to Peter, "My brother Peter, what are you thinking? Do you think that I have thought up these things alone in my heart or that I am telling lies about the Savior?" Levi[18] responded and said to Peter, "Peter, you are always angry. Now I see you disputing with this woman like the adversaries. If the Savior made her worthy, who are you then, for your part, to cast her aside? Surely the Savior knows her full well. That is why he has loved her more than us. Let us rather be ashamed, and put on the perfect human[19] and bring it forth for ourselves, just as he commanded us; and let us preach the Gospel, laying down no rule or law other than what the Savior has spoken." When

19 Levi said these things, they began to go out to teach and proclaim.

The Gospel according to Mary

18 On Levi, see Matt 9:9; Mark 2:14.

19 Cf. Gal 3:27; Eph 4:13; Col 1:28; Jas 3:2.

47. The Epistle of the Apostles

Completely unknown until the end of the nineteenth century, when a Coptic version of it was uncovered in Cairo, the "Epistle of the Apostles" gives a dialogue that Jesus allegedly had with his eleven remaining disciples after his resurrection (Judas having already hanged himself). The account is then passed along by them in a letter, written in the first person, to Christians around the world. This kind of "post-resurrection dialogue" was a genre highly favored among Gnostics (see the "Wisdom of Jesus Christ" in Chapter 6). But the orientation of this particular book is completely anti-Gnostic. In particular, it seeks to counter the views of Simon Magus and Cerinthus—two Gnostics most despised among the heresiologists of the second century—by insisting on the fleshly nature of Christ's body, the reality of his incarnation, death, resurrection, and future return in glory, and the importance of his followers' fleshly existence in this world and in the world to come (see Chapter 6).

The nature of its argument and the opponents that it names suggests that the book was written sometime in the mid–second century. Originally penned in Greek, the text is now preserved only in other languages. The following excerpt is drawn from the Ethiopic translation.

The Epistle of the Apostles, from *New Testament Apocrypha*, vol. 1, ed. Wilhelm Schneemelcher, 2d ed. Cambridge/Louisville: Lutterworth Press/Westminster John Knox Press, 1991. Used with permission of Lutterworth Press and Westminster John Knox Press.

1 What Jesus Christ revealed to his disciples as a letter, and how Jesus Christ revealed the letter of the council of the apostles, the disciples of Jesus Christ, to the Catholics; which was written because of the false apostles Simon and Cerinthus, that no one should follow them—for in them is deceit with which they kill people—that you may be established and not waver, not be shaken, and not turn away from the word of the Gospel that you have heard. As we have heard (it), kept (it), and have written (it) for the whole world, so we entrust (it) to you, our sons and daughters, in joy and in the name of God the Father, the ruler of the world, and in Jesus Christ. May grace increase upon you.

2 (We,) John and Thomas and Peter and Andrew and James and Philip and Bartholomew and Matthew and Nathanael and Judas Zelotes and Cephas, we have written to the churches of the East and West, towards North and South, recounting and proclaiming to you concerning our Lord Jesus Christ, as we have written; and we have heard and felt him after he had risen from the dead; and how he has revealed to us things great, astonishing, real. . . .

6 And these things our Lord and Savior revealed and showed to us, and likewise we to you, that you, reflecting upon eternal life, may be associates in the grace of the Lord and in our service and in our glory. Be firm, without wavering, in the knowledge and investigation of our Lord Jesus Christ, and he will prove gracious and will save always in all never-ending eternity.

7 Cerinthus and Simon have come to go through the world. But they are enemies of our Lord Jesus Christ, who in reality alienate those who believe in the true word and deed, namely Jesus Christ. Therefore take care and beware of them, for in them is affliction and contamination and death, the end of which will be destruction and judgment.

8 Because of that we have not hesitated with the true testimony of our Lord and Savior Jesus Christ, how he acted while we saw him, and how he constantly both explained and caused our thoughts within us.

9 He of whom we are witnesses we know as the one crucified in the days of Pontius Pilate and of the prince Archelaus, who was crucified between two thieves;[1] and was taken down from the wood of the cross together with them; and he was buried in a place which is called the place of the skull, to which three women came, Sarah, Martha, and Mary Magdalene. They carried ointment to pour out upon his body, weeping and mourning over what had happened. And they approached the tomb and found the stone where it had been rolled away from the tomb, and they opened the door and did not find his body.

10 And as they were mourning and weeping, the Lord appeared to them and said to them, "Do not weep; I am he whom you seek. But let one of you go to your brothers and say to them, 'Come, our Master has risen from the dead.' "

And Mary came to us and told us. And we said to her, "What have we to do with you, O woman? He that is dead and buried, can he then live?" And we did not believe her, that our Savior had risen from the dead.

Then she went back to our Lord and said to him, "None of them believed me concerning your resurrection." And he said to her, "Let another one of you go saying this again to them." And Sarah came and gave us the same news, and we accused her of lying. And she returned to our Lord and spoke to him as Mary had.

11 And then the Lord said to Mary and to her sisters, "Let us go to them." And he came and found us inside, veiled. And we doubted and did not believe. He came before us like a ghost and we did not believe that it was he. But it was he. And thus he said to us. "Come, and do not be afraid. I am your teacher whom you, Peter, denied

---

1 Matt 27–28; Mark 15–16; Luke 23–24; John 19–21.

three times before the cock crowed, and now do you deny again?" And we went to him, thinking and doubting whether it was he. And he said to us, "Why do you doubt and why are you not believing that I am he who spoke to you concerning my flesh, my death, and my resurrection? And that you may know that it is I, lay your hand, Peter (and your finger) in the nailprint of my hands; and you, Thomas, in my side; and also you, Andrew, see whether my foot steps on the ground and leaves a footprint. For it is written: 'But a ghost, a demon, leaves no print on the ground.'"

12 But now we felt him, that he had truly risen in the flesh. And then we fell on our faces before him, asked him for pardon, and entreated him because we had not believed him. Then our Lord and Savior said to us, "Stand up and I will reveal to you what is on earth, and what is above heaven, and your resurrection that is in the kingdom of heaven, concerning which my Father has sent me, that I may take up you and those who believe in me."

13 And what he revealed is this, as he said to us, "While I was coming from the Father of all, passing by the heavens, wherein I put on the wisdom of the Father and by his power clothed myself in his power, I was like the heavens. And passing by the angels and archangels in their form and as one of them, I passed by the orders, dominions, and princes, possessing the measure of the wisdom of the Father who sent me. And the archangels Michael and Gabriel, Raphael and Uriel followed me until the fifth firmament of heaven, while I appeared as one of them. This kind of power was given me by the Father. Then I made the archangels to become distracted with the voice and go up to the altar of the Father and serve the Father in their work until I should return to him. I did this thus in the likeness of his wisdom. For I became all in all with them, that I, fulfilling the will of the mercy of the Father and the glory of him who sent me, might return to him.

14 "Do you know that the angel Gabriel came and brought the message to Mary?" And we said to him, "Yes, O Lord." And he answered and said to us, "Do you not remember that I previously said to you that I became like an angel to the angels?" And we said to him, "Yes, O Lord." And he said to us, "At that time I appeared in the form of the archangel Gabriel to the virgin Mary and spoke with her, and her heart received (me); she believed and laughed; and I, the Word, went into her and became flesh; and I myself was servant for myself; and in the likeness of an angel, like him will I do, and after it I will go to my Father.

15 "And you therefore celebrate the remembrance of my death, which is the Passover; the one who stands beside me will be thrown into prison for my name's sake, and he will be very grieved and sorrowful, for while you celebrate the passover he who is in custody did not celebrate it with you. And I will send my power in the form of (my) angel, and the door of the prison will open, and he will come out and come to you to watch with you and to rest. And when you complete my Agape and my remembrance at the crowing of the cock, he will again be taken and thrown in prison for a testimony, until he comes out to preach, as I have commanded you." And we said to him, "O Lord, have you then not completed the drinking of the passover? Must we, then, do it again?" And he said to us, "Yes, until I come from the Father with my wounds."

16 And we said to him, "O Lord, great is this that you say and reveal to us. In what kind of power and form are you about to come?" And he said to us, "Truly I say to you, I will come as the sun which bursts forth; thus will I, shining seven times brighter than it in glory, while I am carried on the wings of the clouds in splendor with my cross going on before me, come to the earth to judge the living and the dead."

17 And we said to him, "O Lord, how many years yet?" And he said to us, "When the hundred and fiftieth year is completed, between pentecost and passover will the coming of my Father take place." And we said to him, "O Lord, now you said to us, 'I will come,' and then you said, 'he who sent me will come.' " And he said to us, "I am wholly in the Father and the Father in me."[2] Then we said to him, "Will you really leave us until your coming? Where will we find a teacher?" And he answered and said to us, "Do you not know that until now I am both here and there with him who sent me?" And we said to him, "O Lord, is it possible that you should be both here and there?" And he said to us, "I am wholly in the Father and the Father in me after his image and after his likeness and after his power and after his perfection and after his light, and I am his perfect word."

18 This is, when he was crucified, had died and risen again, as he said this, and the work that was thus accomplished in the flesh, that he was crucified, and his ascension—this is the fulfilling of the number. "And the wonders and his image and everything perfect you will see in me with respect to redemption which takes place through me, and while I go to the Father and into heaven. . . ."

23 And we said again to him, "O Lord, but it is necessary, since you have commanded us to preach, prophesy, and teach, that we, having heard accurately from you, may be good preachers and may teach them, that they may believe in you. Therefore we question you."

24 He answered and said to us, "Truly I say to you, the flesh of every one will rise with his soul alive and his spirit." And we said to him, "O Lord, then can what is departed and scattered become alive? Not as if we deny it do we ask; rather we believe that what you say has happened and will happen." And he said to us, being angry,

"You of little faith, how long yet do you ask me? And inquire (only) without anguish after what you wish to hear.

"Keep my commandments, and do what I tell you, without delay and without reserve and without respect of persons; serve in the strait, direct, and narrow way. And thereby will the Father in every respect rejoice concerning you."

25 And we said again to him, "O Lord, look; we have you to derision with the many questions." And he said to us, "I know that in faith and with your whole heart you question me. And I am glad because of you. Truly I say to you I am pleased, and my Father in me rejoices, that you thus inquire and ask. Your boldness makes me rejoice, and it affords yourselves life." And when he had said this to us, we were glad, for he had spoken to us in gentleness. And we said again to him, "Our Lord, in all things you have shown yourself gracious toward us and grant us life; for all we have asked you you have told us." Then he said to us, "Does the flesh or the spirit fall away?" And we said to him, "The flesh." And he said to us, "Now what has fallen will arise, and what is ill will be sound, that my Father may be praised therein; as he has done to me, so I (will do) to you and to all who believe in me.

26 "Truly I say to you, the flesh will rise with the soul, that they may confess and be judged with the work which they have done, whether it is there may be a selection and exhibition for those who have believed and have done the commandment of my Father who sent me. Then will the righteous judgment take place; for thus my Father wills, and he said to me, 'My son, on the day of judgment you will not fear the rich and not spare the poor; rather deliver each one to eternal punishment according to his sins.' But to those who have loved me and do love me and who have done my commandment I will grant rest in life in the kingdom of my heavenly Father."

---

2 John 10:38; 14:10–21.

APOCRYPHAL ACTS

(See also the Acts of John and the Acts of Thomas in Chapter 2 and the Acts of Thecla in Chapter 14)

In addition to extracanonical accounts of Jesus' words and deeds, we have a number of accounts of the activities and experiences of his apostles after his death. Some of these may have been modeled on the canonical Acts of the Apostles, but in most instances the noncanonical accounts concern the missionary exploits of only one or the other of the apostolic band, such as Thomas, Peter, or John. Most of them do appear to be written for didactic or hortatory purposes—for example, to urge a life of strict asceticism or the need of martyrdom. Only on occasion do they push for one doctrinal idea or another. By and large, they appear to be chiefly intent on providing entertaining accounts of the miraculous lives of Jesus' apostles, their passion for spreading the Gospel, and the supernatural support they receive from God himself in exchange for their devotion to his work.

THE TEXTS

48. The Acts of Thomas

We have already seen some of the Acts of Thomas in Chapter 2. The following selection comes from the beginning of the narrative where Jesus, after his resurrection, pulls a trick on his twin brother in order to compel him to go, unwilling as he is, to India in order to spread the Gospel there. Along the way Thomas finds himself in the midst of a royal wedding ceremony, to which he is opposed as a good ascetic Christian intent on denying the pleasures of the flesh. In this episode his status as the identical twin of Jesus plays a central role, with somewhat amusing results; when Thomas proves unable to stop the wedded couple from consummating their marriage, his twin Jesus appears and proves to be far more persuasive.

1 At that time we apostles were all in Jerusalem—Simon called Peter, and Andrew his brother, James the son of Zebedee, and John his brother, Philip and Bartholomew, Thomas and Matthew the taxgatherer, James the son of Alphaeus and Simon the Cananaean, and Judas the son of James—and we portioned out the regions of the world, in order that each one of us might go into the region that fell to him by lot, and to the nation to which the Lord had sent him. By lot India fell to Judas Thomas, also called Didymus. And he did not wish to go, saying that he was not able to travel on account of the weakness of his body. He said, "How can I, being a Hebrew, go among the Indians to proclaim the truth?" And while he was considering this and speaking, the Saviour appeared to him during the night and said to him, "Fear not, Thomas, go away to India and preach the word there, for my grace is with you." But he would not obey saying, "Wherever you wish to send me, send me, but elsewhere. For I am not going to the Indians."

2 And as he was thus speaking and considering, it happened that a merchant named Abban, who had come from India, was there, sent from King Gundaphorus, having received an order from him to buy a carpenter and bring him to him. And the Lord, having seen him walking about in the market at noon, said to him, "Do you wish to buy a carpenter?" He replied, "Yes." And the Lord said to him, "I have a slave who is a carpenter, and I wish to sell him." And having said this he showed him Thomas from a distance and agreed with him for three pounds of uncoined silver, and wrote a bill of sale saying, "I, Jesus, son of the carpenter Joseph, declare that I have sold my slave, Judas by name, to you, Abban, a merchant of Gundaphorus, king of the Indians." When the purchase was completed the Saviour took Judas, also called Thomas, and led him to Abban, the merchant. When Abban saw him he said to him, "Is this your master?" The apostle answered and said, "Yes, he is my Lord." And he said,

The Acts of Thomas, reproduced from J. K. Elliott, *Apocryphal New Testament*. Oxford: Clarendon Press, 1993. Used with permission of Oxford University Press.

"I have bought you from him." And the apostle held his peace.

3 On the following morning the apostle prayed and entreated the Lord, saying, "I go wherever you wish, O Lord Jesus, your will be done."[1] And he went to the merchant Abban, carrying nothing at all with him, but only his price. For the Lord had given it to him, saying, "Let your worth also be with you along with my grace, wherever you may go." And the apostle came up with Abban, who was carrying his luggage into the boat. He too began to carry it along with him. And when they had gone on board and sat down, Abban questioned the apostle, saying, "What kind of work do you know?" And he said, "In wood, ploughs and yokes and balances and ships and boats" oars and masts and small blocks; in stone, pillars and temples and royal palaces." And Abban the merchant said to him, "We need such a workman." They began their voyage. And they had a fair wind; and they sailed cheerfully till they came to Andrapolis, a royal city.

4 And leaving the boat they went into the city. And behold, the sounds of flute-players and water-organs and trumpets echoed round them. And the apostle inquired saying, "What festival is it in this city?" And the inhabitants there answered, "The gods have brought you to keep festival in this city. For the king has an only daughter and now he is going to give her to a husband in marriage. This festival, then, which you see today, is the rejoicing and public assembly for the marriage. And the king has sent forth heralds to proclaim everywhere that all are to come to the marriage, rich and poor, bond and free, strangers and citizens. But if anyone should refuse and not come to the marriage, he is answerable to the king. And Abban, having heard this, said to the apostle, "Let us also go so that we give no offence to the king, especially as we are strangers." And he said, "Let us go." And having obtained lodgings at the inn and rested a little they went to the wedding. And the apostle, seeing them all reclining, reclined also in their midst. And they all looked at him as at a stranger, a man coming from a foreign land. And Abban the merchant, being the master, reclined in another place.

5 And whilst they were eating and drinking, the apostle tasted nothing. Those about him said to him, "Why have you come here, neither eating nor drinking?" And he answered and said to them, "For something greater than food or even drink have I come here, that I might accomplish the will of the king. For the heralds proclaim the wishes of the king, and whoever will not hear the heralds will be liable to the judgement of the king." When they had dined and drunk, and crowns and perfumes had been brought, each took perfume, and one anointed his face, another his beard, and others different parts of the body. And the apostle anointed the crown of his head, and put a little of the ointment in his nostrils, and dropped it also in his ears, and applied it also to his teeth, and carefully anointed the parts round about his heart; but the crown that was brought to him, wreathed with myrtle and other flowers, he put on his head, and he took a branch of reed in his hand and held it. And the flute-girl, holding her flute in her hand, went round them all; and when she came to the place where the apostle was she stood over him, playing the flute over his head a long time. And that flute-girl was a Hebrew by race.

6 And as the apostle looked to the ground, one of the cupbearers stretched forth his hand and struck him. And the apostle, having raised his eyes, looked at the man who had struck him, saying, "My God will forgive you for this wrong in the world to come, but in this world he will show his wonders, and I shall soon see that hand that struck me dragged along by dogs." And having spoken he began to sing this song:

"The maiden is the daughter of the light,
    On whom rests the majestic splendour of
        kings;

---

1 Matt 6:10; Luke 22:42.

Delightful is the sight of her,
Resplendent with brilliant beauty.
Her garments are like spring flowers
Sending forth sweet fragrance.
On the crown of her head the king is seated
Feeding with his own ambrosia those who
    live under him.
Truth rests upon her head,
Joy she shows forth with her feet.
Her mouth is opened, and becomingly.[2]
Thirty-and-two are they who praise her.
Her tongue is like a door-curtain,
Drawn back for those who go in.[3]
Made by the first creator.
Her two hands point and make secret signs
    predicting the chorus of the blessed ages,
Her fingers show the gates of the city.
Her chamber is bright,
Breathing forth scent from balsam and every
    perfume,
Sending forth a sweet smell of myrrh and herbs.
Within are strewn myrtle-branches and all
    manner of sweet-smelling flowers,
The portal is adorned with reeds.

7 She is surrounded by her groomsmen, seven
in number,

Chosen by herself;
Her bridesmaids are seven,
Who dance before her.
Twelve in number are they who minister
    before her
And are at her bidding.
Their gaze is attentively directed at the
    bridegroom,
That they be enlightened by his sight,
And be for ever with him in that everlasting
    joy,
And sit down at that wedding to which the
    princes assemble,

And abide at the supper, of which the eternal
    ones are deemed worthy,
And put on royal garments, and be dressed in
    splendid robes
That both may rejoice and exult
And praise the Father of all,
Whose majestic light they have received
And have been enlightened by the sight of
    their Lord,
Whose ambrosial food they received,
Of which there is no deficiency,
And drank also of his wine,
Which brings to them neither thirst nor
    desire,
And they praised and glorified with the living
    spirit
The Father of truth and the mother of wisdom."

8 And when he had finished this song all who
were present looked at him. He kept silence.
They also saw his form changed, but they did not
understand his words, as he was a Hebrew and his
words were spoken in Hebrew. Only the flute-girl
understood him, being of the Hebrew race; and
leaving him she played the flute to the others, but
repeatedly looked back and gazed at him.

For she loved him as one belonging to her
race, and he was also beautiful in appearance above
all who were there. And when the flute-girl had
finished her flute-playing, she sat down opposite
him, and looked steadily at him. But he looked at
no one at all, neither did he pay attention to any
one, but kept his eyes only on the ground, waiting
until he could depart. And the cupbearer that
struck him came down to the fountain to draw
water. And there happened to be a lion there
which killed him and left him lying in the place,
after tearing his limbs asunder. And dogs immediately seized his limbs, among them a black dog,
which grasped his right hand in his mouth and
brought it to the place of the banquet.

9 When they all saw it they were frightened and
inquired who was absent. And when it became
known that it was the hand of the cupbearer that

---

2 Syriac adds "She sings loud songs of praise".

3 Syriac adds "Her neck ascends like steps".

struck the apostle, the flute-girl broke her flute and threw it away, and went and sat at the feet of the apostle, saying, "This man is either God or God's apostle. For I heard him say in Hebrew to the cup-bearer, 'I shall soon see the hand that struck me dragged about by dogs.' This you have now seen. For just as he said, so also it has come to pass." Some believed her, and some not. And when the king heard of it he came and said to the apostle, "Rise up and go with me, and pray for my daughter. For she is my only child and to-day I give her away in marriage." And the apostle would not go with him, for the Lord had not yet been revealed to him there. But the king took him away against his will to the bridal chamber, that he might pray for them.

10 And the apostle stood and began to pray and speak thus: "My Lord and my God,[4] who accompanies his servants, guide and leader of those who believe in him, refuge and repose of the afflicted, hope of the poor and deliverer of the captives, physician of the souls laid low by disease, and saviour of every creature, who gives life to the world and strengthens the souls, you know the future and accomplish it through us; you, Lord, who reveal hidden mysteries and declare secret words; you, Lord, are the planter of the good tree and by your hand all good works are produced; you, Lord, are in all, and come through all, and exist in all your works and make yourself manifest through the working of them all; Jesus Christ, the Son of compassion and perfect Saviour; Christ, Son of the living God, the undaunted power which has overthrown the enemy; the voice, heard by the rulers, which shook all their powers; messenger, sent from on high, who went down even to Hades; who also, having opened the doors, brought out from there those who had been shut in for many ages in the treasuries of darkness, and showed them the way that leads up on high—I beseech you, Lord Jesus, offering you supplication for these young persons, that you may do to them what helps, benefits, and is profitable for them." And having laid his hands

---

4 John 20:28.

on them and said, "The Lord be with you", he left them in that place and went away.

11 The king requested the groomsmen to leave the bridal chamber. When all had left, and the doors were shut, the bridegroom raised the curtain of the bridal chamber, that he might bring the bride to himself. And he saw the Lord Jesus talking with the bride. He had the appearance of Judas Thomas, the apostle, who shortly before had blessed them and departed; and he said to him, "Did you not go out before them all? And how is it that you are here now?" And the Lord said to him, "I am not Judas Thomas, I am his brother." And the Lord sat down on the bed and ordered them to sit down on couches, and he began to speak to them.

12 "Remember, my children, what my brother said to you, and to whom he commended you; and know that if you refrain from this filthy intercourse you become temples holy and pure, being released from afflictions and troubles, known and unknown, and you will not be involved in the cares of life and of children, whose end is destruction. But if you get many children, for their sakes you become grasping and avaricious, plundering orphans and deceiving widows, and by doing this you subject yourselves to most grievous punishments. For most children become unprofitable, being possessed by demons, some openly and some secretly. For they become either lunatics or half-withered or crippled or deaf or dumb or paralytics or idiots. And though they be healthy, they will be again good-for-nothing, doing unprofitable and abominable works. For they will be detected either in adultery or in murder or in theft or in unchastity, and by all these you will be afflicted. But if you obey and preserve your souls pure to God, there will be born to you living children, untouched by these hurtful things, and you will be without care, spending an untroubled life, free from grief and care, looking forward to receive that incorruptible and true marriage, and you will enter as groomsmen into that bridal chamber full of immortality and light."

13 And when the young people heard this, they believed the Lord and gave themselves over to him and refrained from filthy lust, and remained thus spending the night in the place. And the Lord went away from them saying, "The grace of the Lord be with you!"[5] And when dawn came the king arrived, and having furnished the table brought it in before the bridegroom and the bride. And he found them sitting opposite each other, and he found the face of the bride uncovered, and the bridegroom was very cheerful. And the mother came in and said to the bride, "Why do you sit thus, child, and are not ashamed, but act as if you had lived for a long time with your own husband?" And her father said, "Is it because of your great love to your husband that you are unveiled?"

14 The bride answered and said, "Truly, father, I am in great love, and I pray to my Lord that the love which I have experienced this night may remain, and that I obtain that man whom I have experienced today. That I do not veil myself is because the mirror of shame has been taken away from me; I am no longer ashamed or abashed, since the work of shame and bashfulness has been removed far from me. And that I am not frightened is because alarm did not abide in me. And that I am cheerful and glad is because the day of joy has not been disturbed. And that I have set at naught this husband and these nuptials which have passed away from before my eyes is because I have been joined in a different marriage. And that I had no conjugal intercourse with a temporary husband, whose end is repentance and bitterness of soul, is because I have been united to the true husband."

15 And when the bride was saying even more, the bridegroom answered and said, "I thank you, Lord, who have been proclaimed by the stranger and found in us; who have put corruption far from me, and have sown life in me, who have delivered me from this disease, hard to heal, hard to cure and abiding for ever, and established in me sound health;

who have shown yourself to me, and have revealed to me my condition, in which I am; who have redeemed me from falling, and have led me to something better, and who have released me from things temporary, but have deemed me worthy of things immortal and everlasting; who have humbled yourself to me and my weakness, to place me beside your greatness and to unite with you; who have not kept your compassion from me, who was lost, but have shown me how to seek myself, and to know who I was and who and how I now am, that I may become again what I was; whom I did not know, but you have sought me out; of whom I did not know, but you stood by me; whom I have experienced and am not able to forget; whose love is fervent in me and of whom I cannot speak as I ought. But what I have to say about him is short and very little, and is not in proportion to his glory; but he does not find fault with me if I dare to tell him even what I know not; for it is out of love to him I say this."

16 And when the king heard these things from the bridegroom and the bride, he rent his garments and said to those standing near him, "Go out quickly, and search the whole city, and seize and bring that man, the sorcerer, who has come by evil chance into this city. For I led him with my own hands into my house, and I told him to pray for my most unfortunate daughter. Whoever shall find him and bring him to me, I give him whatever he shall ask of me." They departed, therefore, and went round seeking him, and did not find him; for he had set sail. They also went into the inn where he had stayed, and found there the flute-girl weeping and in distress, because he had not taken her with him. And when they told her what had taken place with the young people, she rejoiced greatly upon hearing it, setting aside her grief, and said, "Now I also have found repose here!" And she arose and went to them, and was with them a long time, until they had instructed the king also. And many of the brethren also met there, until the rumour had spread that the apostle had gone to the cities of India, and was teaching there. And they went away and joined him.

5 1 Cor 16:23.

49. *The Acts of Peter*

Closely related to the tales about Peter found in the "Homilies of Clement" (see Chapter 6), the Acts of Peter provides a number of entertaining accounts of the escapades of the leader of the apostles, including several of his sermons and a number of his miracles (see also Chapter 14). Much of the narrative concerns a series of contests between Peter and his nemesis, the Satanically inspired sorcerer Simon Magus, who presents himself as the true representative of God on earth. The same Simon is elsewhere portrayed as the first Gnostic and arch-heretic (see, for example, the Epistle of the Apostles, above), although here there is less attention paid to his theology than to his claims of divine superiority. These claims are completely refuted by Peter, who, through the true power of God, is able to make dogs and newborn infants speak and to restore smoked tunas and dead people back to life. The contests reach a climax in a passage not excerpted here, when Simon uses his powers to fly like a bird over the temples and hills of Rome; Peter responds by calling upon God to smite him in midair. When Simon crashes to the ground, the crowds, convinced of Peter's superior power, rush to the scene to stone Simon and leave him for dead.

This account appears to have been in circulation some time before the end of the second century.

4 After a few days there was a great commotion in the congregation, for some said that they had seen things done by a man named Simon, who was at Aricia. They also added, "He claims to be the great power of God, doing nothing without God. Is he then Christ? We, however, believe in him whom Paul has preached to us. For through him we saw the dead raised and some healed from various diseases. This power seeks conflicts, we know. For it is no small disturbance that has come upon us. Perhaps he has already come to Rome. For yesterday he was invited with great acclamation to do so, being told, 'You are God in Italy, you are the savior of the Romans; hasten to Rome as quickly as possible.' And Simon addressed the people and said with a shrill voice, 'On the following day about the seventh hour you shall see me fly over the gate of the city in the same form in which I now speak to you.' Wherefore, brethren, if you agree, let us go and diligently await the end of the matter." And they all went out and came to the gate. About the seventh hour there suddenly appeared afar off a dust-cloud in the sky, looking like smoke shining with a glare of fire. And when it reached the gate it suddenly disappeared. Then he appeared standing in the midst of the people. They all worshipped him and knew that it was he whom they had seen the day before. And the brethren were exceedingly disturbed, especially as Paul was not at Rome, nor Timothy and Barnabas, whom Paul had sent to Macedonia, nor anyone who could strengthen us (*sic*) in the faith, especially the neophytes. As Simon's authority grew more and more, some of those among whom

The Acts of Peter, from *The Apocryphal New Testament*, ed. J. K. Elliott. © Oxford University Press, 1993. Reprinted by permission of Oxford University Press.

he worked in their daily conversations called Paul a sorcerer and a deceiver and all of the great multitude which had been confirmed in the faith were led astray, excepting the presbyter Narcissus, and two women in the hospice of the Bithynians, and four others who could not leave their house; and day and night they entreated the Lord either that Paul might return as soon as possible or that some one else might come to care for his servants, whom the devil by his wickedness had perverted.

5 While they were grieving and fasting God was already preparing Peter at Jerusalem for the future. After the twelve years had passed, according to the direction of the Lord to Peter, Christ showed to him the following vision, saying, "Peter, Simon, whom you expelled from Judaea after having exposed him as a magician, has forestalled you at Rome. And in short, all who believed in me he has perverted by the cunning and power of Satan, whose agent he proves to be. But do not delay. Go tomorrow to Caesarea, and there you will find a ship ready to sail to Italy. And within a few days I will show you my grace which is boundless." Instructed by this vision, Peter did not delay to mention it to the brethren and said, "I must go up to Rome to subdue the enemy and opponent of the Lord and of our brethren." And he went down to Caesarea and at once boarded the ship, which was ready to sail, without having obtained for himself any provisions. But the steersman, named Theon, looked at Peter and said, "What we have belongs to you. For what grace is it for us in receiving a man like ourselves in difficult circumstances, without sharing with him what we have? Let us have a safe journey." Peter thanked him for his offer. And he fasted in the ship, being dejected, and yet again comforted because God regarded him as a servant worthy of his service. A few days later the captain got up at meal time and asked Peter to eat with him, saying to him, "Whoever you are, I hardly know you. You are either a God or a man. But as far as I can see, I think that you are a servant of God. As I was steering my ship in the middle of the night I fell asleep. It seemed to me as

if a human voice from heaven said to me, "Theon, Theon!" Twice it called me by name and said to me, 'Amongst all the passengers treat Peter in the most honorable way. For, with his help, you and the rest will escape safe from an unexpected incident.' " Peter, however, thinking that God wished to show his providence to all those who were in the ship, began at once to speak to Theon of the great deeds of God, and how the Lord had chosen him among the apostles and for what cause he was sailing to Italy. Daily he spoke to him the word of God. After they had become better acquainted Peter found out that Theon was one with him in the faith and a worthy servant. When the ship was detained by the calm of the Adriatic Sea, Theon remarked on the calm to Peter and said, "If you think me worthy to be baptized with the sign of the Lord, you have the chance now." All the others in the ship were in a drunken stupor. Peter let himself down by a rope and baptized Theon in the name of the Father and of the Son and of the Holy Spirit. He came up out of the water rejoicing with great joy. Peter also had become more cheerful because God had deemed Theon worthy of his name. And it happened that in the same place where Theon was baptized, a young man, radiant in splendor, appeared and said to them, "Peace be with you." And both Peter and Theon immediately went up and entered the cabin; and Peter took bread and gave thanks to the Lord, who had deemed him worthy of his holy service, and because a young man had appeared to them saying, "Peace be with you." Peter said, "Most excellent and the only Holy One, for you appeared to us, O God Jesus Christ. In your name I have spoken, and he was signed with your holy sign. Therefore also I give to him, in your name, your eucharist, that he may for ever be your servant, perfect and without blemish." When they were eating and rejoicing in the Lord, suddenly a moderate wind, not a violent one, arose at the prow of the ship and lasted six days and six nights till they came to Puteoli.

6 Having landed at Puteoli, Theon left the ship and went to the inn where he usually stayed,

to make preparations for the reception of Peter. The inn-keeper's name was Ariston, a God-fearing man, and to him he went for the sake of the Name. And when he had come to the inn and found Ariston, Theon said to him, "God, who counted you worthy to serve him, has also made known to me his grace through his holy servant Peter, who has just arrived with me from Judaea, being bidden by our Lord to go to Italy." When Ariston heard this, he fell upon Theon's neck, embraced him and asked him to bring him to the ship and show Peter to him. For Ariston said, "Since Paul has gone to Spain there was not one of the brethren who could strengthen me. Besides, a certain Jew named Simon has invaded the city. By means of his magical sayings and his wickedness he has completely perverted the entire fraternity, so that I have fled from Rome hoping for the arrival of Peter. For Paul had spoken of him, and I saw many things in a vision. Now I believe in my Lord, that he will again establish his ministry, that all deception be extinguished from his servants. For our Lord Jesus Christ is faithful, and he can renew our thoughts." When Theon heard this from the weeping Ariston, his confidence was restored, and he was even more strengthened in his faith, knowing that he believed in the living God. When they came to the ship, Peter saw them and, filled with the Spirit, he smiled, so that Ariston fell upon his face to the feet of Peter and said, "Brother and Lord, who makes known the sacred mysteries and teaches the right way, which is in the Lord Jesus Christ, our God, through you he has shown us his coming. All whom Paul entrusted to us we have lost through the power of Satan. But now I trust in the Lord, who sent his messenger and told you to hasten to us, that he has deemed us worthy to see his great and wonderful deeds done by your hands. I therefore beg you, come quickly to the city. For I left the brethren who had stumbled, whom I saw fall into the snares of the devil, and fled here saying to them, 'Brethren, stand firm in the faith; for it is to be that within the next two months the mercy of our Lord will bring you his servant.' I saw a vision of Paul speaking to me and saying, 'Ariston, flee from the city.' Having heard this, I believed without wavering, departed from the city in the Lord, and though the flesh which I bear is weak, yet I came here, stood daily by the shore, and asked the sailors, 'Has Peter come with you?' And now that the grace of the Lord abounds, I beseech you to go up to Rome without delay, lest the teaching of the wicked man increases still more." When Ariston had spoken amidst tears Peter gave him his hand and lifted him up from the ground, and said with tears and sighs, "He who tempts the world by his angels forestalled us; but he who has the power to deliver his servants from all temptation will destroy his deceits and put them under the feet of those who believe in Christ, whom we preach." And when they entered by the gate Theon entreated Peter and said, "During the long sea voyage you never refreshed yourself on the ship, and now will you go from the ship on such a rough road? No, stay, refresh yourself and then go. From here to Rome the road is rocky, and I fear you might hurt yourself with the shaking." But Peter answered and said to them, "But what would have happened if about my neck and that of the enemy of the Lord a millstone were hanged (as my Lord said to us, if any one should offend one of the brethren[1]), and we be drowned in the depths of the sea? Not only would it be a millstone, but what is worse, I the opponent of this persecutor of his servants would die far away from those who have believed in the Lord Jesus Christ." In no way could Theon persuade him to remain a day longer. Whereupon Theon gave everything that was in the ship to be sold at a fair price, and followed Peter to Rome, and accompanied Ariston to the house of the presbyter Narcissus.

7 Soon it became known among the scattered brethren of the city that Peter had come to Rome on account of Simon, to prove that he was a seducer and persecutor of the good. And the whole multitude came together to see the apostle

---

1 Matt 18:6.

of the Lord, confirming the congregation in Christ. When they gathered on the first day of the week to meet Peter he began to speak with a loud voice, "You people who are here, hoping in Christ, you who suffered a brief temptation, learn why God sent his Son into the world, or why he begot him by the virgin Mary, if it were not to dispense some mercy or means of salvation. For he meant to annul every offence and every ignorance and every activity of the devil, his instigations and powers, by means of which he once had the upper hand, before our God shone forth in the world. Since with their many and manifold weaknesses they fell to death by their ignorance, Almighty God had compassion and sent his Son into the world, and I was with him. And I walked on the water and survive as a witness; I confess I was there when he was at work in the world performing signs and wonders. Dearest brethren, I denied our Lord Jesus Christ, not once, but thrice; for those who ensnared me were wicked gods, just as the prophet of the Lord said. But the Lord did not lay it to my charge; he turned to me and had mercy on the weakness of my flesh, so that I wept bitterly; and I mourned for my little faith, having been deceived by the devil and disobeyed the word of my Lord. And now I tell you, men and brethren, who are convened in the name of Jesus Christ, Satan the deceiver sends his arrows upon you too, to make you leave the way. But do not be disloyal, brethren, nor fail in your mind, but strengthen yourselves, stand fast, and doubt not. For if Satan has subverted me, whom the Lord esteemed so highly, so that I denied the light of my hope, causing me to fall and persuading me to flee as if I believed in a man, what do you think will happen to you, who have just become converted? Do you imagine that he will not subvert you to make you enemies of the Kingdom of God and to bring you by the worst error into perdition? For every one whom he deprives of the hope in our Lord Jesus Christ is a child of perdition for all eternity. Repent, therefore, brethren whom the Lord has chosen, and be firmly established in the Almighty Lord, the Father of our Lord Jesus Christ, whom

no one has ever seen nor can see except he who believes in him. Understand whence the temptation has come for you. For I came not only for the sake of convincing you with words that he whom I preach is the Christ, but by reason of miraculous deeds and powers I exhort you by faith in Jesus Christ. Let no one wait for another savior besides him who was despised and whom the Jews reviled, this crucified Nazarene, who died and rose again on the third day."

8 The brethren repented and asked Peter to overcome Simon's claim that he was the power of God. Simon was staying at the house of the senator Marcellus whom he had won over by his magic. "Believe us, brother Peter", they said, "none among humans was so wise as this Marcellus. All the widows who hoped in Christ took their refuge in him; all the orphans were fed by him. Will you know more, brother? All the poor called Marcellus their patron; his house was called the house of the pilgrims and poor. To him the emperor said, 'I will give you no office, lest you rob the provinces to benefit the Christians.' To this Marcellus replied, 'Yet everything that is mine is yours,' Caesar said to him, 'It would be mine if you kept it for me, but now it is not mine, since you give it to whom you please, and who knows to what low people?' This, brother Peter, we know and report to you, now that the great benevolence of the man has been turned into blasphemy. For had he not been changed we certainly should not have left the holy faith in God our Lord. Now this Marcellus is enraged and repents of his good deeds and says, 'So much wealth have I spent for such a long time in the foolish belief that I spent it for the knowledge of God.' In his rage he even goes so far that when a pilgrim comes to the door of his house he beats him with a stick or has him driven off and says, 'If only I had not spent so much money on those imposters!' And he utters many more blasphemies. But if you have something of the compassion of our Lord in you and the goodness of his commandments, help this man in his error for he has shown goodness to a

great many of God's servants." When Peter learned this he was very greatly moved and said, "Oh, the manifold arts and temptations of the devil! Oh, the cunnings and devices of the evil one, treasuring up to himself the great fire in the day of wrath, destruction of simple people, a ravening wolf devouring and destroying eternal life! You enticed the first man to evil lust and by your former wickedness and bodily bond bound him to you. You are the fruit of bitterness, which is entirely bitter, inducing various desires. You have forced my fellow disciple and co-apostle Judas to act wickedly and betray our Lord Jesus Christ; you must be punished. You hardened the heart of Herod and kindled Pharaoh and made him fight against Moses, the holy servant of God; you emboldened Caiaphas to deliver our Lord Jesus Christ to the cruel multitude; and now you are still firing your poisonous arrows at innocent souls. You wicked foe of all, you shall be cursed from the church of the Son of the holy, almighty God and extinguished like a firebrand thrown from the fireplace by the servants of our Lord Jesus Christ. Let your blackness turn against you and against your sons, the wicked seed; let your wickedness turn against you, also your threats, and let your temptations turn against you and your angels, you beginning of iniquity, abyss of darkness! Let the darkness which you have be with you and your vessels which you own. Depart, therefore, from those who shall believe in God; depart from the servants of Christ and from those who will serve in his army. Keep for yourself your garments of darkness; without cause you knock at strange doors which belong not to you but to Christ Jesus who keeps them. For you, ravening wolf, will carry off the sheep which do not belong to you but to Christ Jesus, who keeps them with the greatest diligence."

9 When Peter had spoken with great sorrow of soul many more believers were added to the congregation. And the brethren entreated Peter to fight with Simon and not allow him to disturb the people any longer. And without delay Peter left the meeting and went to the house of Marcellus where Simon was staying. And a great multitude followed him. When he came to the door he summoned the keeper and said to him, "Go and tell Simon, 'Peter, on whose account you left Judaea, awaits you at the door!' " The door-keeper answered and said to Peter, "I do not know, sir, if you are Peter. But I have instructions. Knowing that you arrived yesterday in the city, he said to me, 'Whether he comes in the day or at night or at whatever hour, say that I am not at home.' " But Peter said to the young man, "You were right to tell me this, although you have been forced by him not to tell me." And Peter, turning around to the people, who followed him, said, "You are about to see a great and wonderful sign." And Peter saw a big dog, tied by a big chain, and he went and loosened him. The dog, being loosed, became endowed with a human voice and said to Peter, "What will you have me do, servant of the ineffable living God?" to which Peter said, "Go inside and tell Simon in the presence of the people, 'Peter sends word to you to come outside. For on your account I have come to Rome, you wicked man and destroyer of simple souls.' " And the dog ran away at once and went into the midst of the people who were with Simon, and lifting his front legs he said with a very loud voice, "Simon, Peter, who stands at the door, bids you to come outside in public; for he says 'On your account have I come to Rome, you wicked man and destroyer of simple souls.' " When Simon heard this and saw the incredible occurrence he lost the words with which he was deceiving the onlookers, and all were amazed.

10 When Marcellus saw this he ran outside and fell down before Peter and said, "Peter, holy servant of the holy God, I embrace your feet. I have committed many sins; do not punish my sins if you have some true faith in Christ, whom you preach. If you remember the commandments, to hate none, to do no evil to anyone, as I have learned from your fellow-apostle Paul, do not consider my sins but pray for me to the Lord, the holy Son of God, whom I angered by persecuting his servants. Pray, therefore, for me, like a good advocate of God, that I may not be given over with the sins of Simon to the everlasting fire. For by his persuasion it came about that I erected a statue to him with the following inscription: 'To Simon, the young god.' If I knew, Peter, that you could be won over with money I would give you all my property. I would give it to you, to save my soul. If I had sons I would esteem them for nothing if only I could believe in the living God. I confess, however, that he seduced me only because he said that he was the power of God. Nevertheless I will tell you, dearest Peter: I was not worthy to hear you, servant of God, and I was not firmly established in the belief in God which is in Christ: for this reason I was made to stumble. I pray you, therefore, be not angry at what I am about to say. Christ our Lord, whom you preach in truth, said to your fellow-apostles in your presence, 'If you have faith like a grain of mustard-seed, you will say to this mountain: Remove yourself, and at once it shall move.'[2] But this Simon called you, Peter, an unbeliever, because you lost faith on the water. And I heard that he also said, 'Those who are with me understood me not.' If, therefore, you, upon whom he laid his hands, whom he has also chosen, with whom he even performed miraculous deeds—if you doubted, therefore I also repent, and relying upon his testimony I resort to your intercession. Receive me, who have fallen away from our Lord and his promise. But I believe that by repenting he will have mercy on me. For the Almighty is faithful to forgive my sins." And Peter said with a loud voice, "Glory and praise be unto our Lord, Almighty God, Father of our Lord Jesus Christ. To you be praise and honor for ever and ever. Amen. Since you have now fully strengthened us and fully established us in you in the sight of all who see it, holy Lord, confirm Marcellus and give him and his house your peace today. But all who are lost or erring, you alone can restore. We worship you, O Lord, the Shepherd of the sheep which once were scattered, but now will be brought together through you. So receive Marcellus also as one of your sheep, and do not permit him to walk about any longer in error or in ignorance but receive him among the number of your sheep. Yes, Lord, receive him, since he beseeches you with sorrow and with tears."

11 Having thus spoken, and having embraced Marcellus, Peter turned to the multitude who stood beside him, when he saw one man laughing, in whom was a very bad devil. Peter said to him, "Whoever you are who have been laughing, show yourself in public." When the young man heard this he ran into the courtyard of the house, cried with a loud voice, threw himself against the wall, and said, "Peter, there is a mighty contest between Simon and the dog, which you sent inside. For Simon says to the dog, 'Say I am not here.' But the dog tells him more things than you commanded. And when he has fulfilled your wish he will die at your feet." And Peter said, "Demon, whoever you are, in the name of our Lord Jesus Christ depart from this young man without hurting him. Show yourself to all present." When the young man heard this he rushed forward, took hold of a large marble statue, which stood in the courtyard of the house, and kicked it to pieces. It was a statue of Caesar. When Marcellus saw this he beat his forehead and said to Peter, "A great crime has been committed, for should Caesar hear of it through one of his spies he will greatly punish us." Peter answered, "I see that you are not the man you were a short time ago when you said you were ready to spend everything for the salvation of your soul. But if you are truly repentant and believe in Christ with all your heart, take running water into your hands and, beseeching the Lord, sprinkle it in his name on the pieces of the statue and it shall be a whole as before." Marcellus did not doubt, but believed with his whole heart, and before taking the water he lifted up his hands and said, "I believe in you, Lord Jesus Christ. For your apostle Peter has examined me whether I truly believe in your holy name. Therefore I take water in my hands and sprinkle these

---

2 Matt 17:20.

stones in your name that the statue become whole again as before. If it is your will, O Lord, that I live and receive no punishment from Caesar, let this statute be whole as before." And he sprinkled water on the stones, and the statue became whole, Peter, therefore, exulted that he had not hesitated to petition the Lord, and Marcellus also rejoiced in the Spirit, that the first miracle took place by his hands. He believed therefore, with all his heart in the name of Jesus Christ, the Son of my God, by whom all things impossible become possible.

12 And Simon, being inside, spoke thus to the dog, "Tell Peter that I am not in." But the dog said to him in the presence of Marcellus, "You most wicked and shameless man, worst enemy of all who live and believe in Christ Jesus. A dumb animal, which received a human voice, has been sent to you to convict you and to prove that you are a cheat and deceiver. Did it require so many hours for you to say, 'Say I am not here!' You have not been ashamed to lift up your weak and useless voice against Peter, the servant and apostle of Christ, as if you could be hidden from him who told me to speak to your face. And this is not for your sake, but on account of those whom you deceived and brought to perdition. You shall therefore be accursed, enemy and destroyer of the way of Christ's truth. He shall punish your iniquities, which you have done, with imperishable fire and you shall be in outer darkness." Having spoken these words the dog ran away. And the multitude followed so that Simon remained alone. And the dog came to Peter who was with the crowd who had come to see the face of Peter; and the dog reported what had happened with Simon. To the messenger and apostle of the true God the dog said as follows, "Peter, you shall have a hard fight with Simon, the enemy of Christ, and with his adherents, but many whom he deceived you shall convert to the faith. For this you shall receive a reward for your work from God." Having thus spoken the dog fell at the feet of Peter and expired. When the multitude with great astonishment saw the talking dog, many fell down at the feet of

Peter, but others said, "Show us another miracle that we may believe in you as a servant of the living God, for Simon too did many wonders in our presence, and on that account we followed him."

13 And Peter turning around saw a smoked tuna fish hanging in a window. He took it, saying to the people, "When you see this swimming in water like a fish, will you be able to believe in him whom I preach?" And all said with one voice, "Indeed we shall believe you." So he went to the pond near by, saying, "In your name, O Jesus Christ, in whom they do not yet believe, I say, 'Tuna, in the presence of all these, live and swim like a fish.' " And he cast the tuna into the pond, and it became alive and began to swim. The multitude saw the swimming fish and he made it swim not only for that hour but, lest they said that it was a deception, he made it swim longer, thereby attracting crowds from all parts and showing that the smoked tuna had again become a living fish. The success was such that many threw pieces of bread into the water, seeing that the fish was whole. Very many who had witnessed this followed Peter and believed in the Lord, and met day and night in the house of Narcissus the presbyter. And Peter spoke to them of the prophetical writings and of the things done by our Lord Jesus Christ in word and deed.

14 Marcellus was more firmly established in the faith, seeing the signs which Peter did by the grace of Jesus Christ, which was given to him. And Marcellus attacked Simon, who sat in the dining-room of his house. Cursing him, he said to him, "O you most malevolent and most pestilential of men, destroyer of my soul and of my house, who intended to lead me away from Christ, my Lord and Savior." And he laid his hand on him and ordered that he be thrown out of his house. And the servants, having obtained permission, treated him in the most shameful way; some struck him in the face, some beat him with a rod, some flung stones at him, some emptied vessels containing filth over his head. Those who, for his sake, had left their master and were imprisoned, and other servants whom he had maligned to their master, reviled him and said to him, "Now we repay to you the worthy reward, according to the will of God, who had mercy upon us and upon our master." And Simon, thus treated, left the house and went to the house in which Peter was staying. Standing at the door of the house of the presbyter Narcissus, he cried, "Behold, here am I, Simon. Come down, Peter, and I will prove that you believed in a Jewish man and the son of a carpenter."

15 When Peter heard these things he sent to him a woman with her suckling child and said to her, "Go down quickly and you shall see someone seeking me. As for you, do not speak, but keep silent and listen to what the child which you hold will say to him." And the woman went down. And her baby was seven months old. Assuming a manly voice it said to Simon, "You abomination before God and people, O destroyer of truth and most wicked seed of corruption, O unfaithful fruit of nature! After only a little while an everlasting punishment awaits you. Son of a shameless father, never taking root in good soil but in poison; unfaithful creature, destitute of all hope: when the dog accused you, you were not ashamed. I, a child, am forced by God to speak and still you do not blush. But against your will, on the coming Sabbath day, another shall lead you to the forum of Julius that you may be shown what you are. Leave by the doorway at which the saints enter. For no more shall you corrupt innocent souls whom you perverted and led away from Christ. Your whole evil nature will therefore be manifested, and your machinations will be spoiled. Now I say to you a last word: Jesus Christ says to you, 'Be speechless by the power of my name and leave Rome till the coming Sabbath.'"

At once he became speechless, and being constrained he left Rome till the next Sabbath and lodged in a stable. The woman returned to Peter with the baby and told Peter and the other brethren what the child had said to Simon. And

they praised the Lord who had shown these things to humans.

16 When night came Peter, still awake, saw Jesus clothed with a shining garment, smiling and saying to him, "The greatest part of the brethren has already come back through me and through the signs which you have made in my name. But on the coming Sabbath you shall have a contest of faith, and many more Gentiles and Jews shall be converted in my name to me who was reviled, despised, and spat upon. For I shall show myself to you when you shall ask for signs and wonders and you shall convert many, but you will have Simon opposing you through the works of his father. But all his doings shall be manifested as sorcery and magical deception. And do not delay and you shall confirm in my name all those whom I shall send to you." When it was day he told the brethren how the Lord had appeared to him and what he had commanded him. . . .

20 When Peter had entered he saw one of the old women who was blind, and her daughter led her by the hand and conducted her into the house of Marcellus. And Peter said to her, "Come here, mother; from this day Jesus gives you his right hand; through him we have light unapproachable which darkness cannot hide. Through me he says to you, 'Open your eyes, see and walk on your own.'" And the widow at once saw Peter put his hand upon her. When Peter came into the dining-room he saw that the gospel was being read. And rolling it up he said, "People, who believe in Christ and hope in him, you shall know how the holy scriptures of our Lord must be explained. What we have written down according to his grace, though it may seem to you as yet so little, contains what is endurable to be understood by humanity. It is necessary that we first know God's will or his goodness; for when deceit was spread and many thousands of people were plunging into perdition the Lord was moved by compassion to show himself in another form and to appear in the image of man, by whom neither the Jews nor we are worthy to be enlightened. For each of us saw him as his capacity permitted. Now, however, I will explain to you that which has been read to you. Our Lord wished to let me see his majesty on the holy mountain;[3] but when I with the sons of Zebedee saw his brightness I fell at his feet as dead, closed my eyes, and heard his voice in a manner which I cannot describe. I imagined I had been deprived of my eyesight by his splendor. I recovered a little and said to myself, 'Perhaps the Lord has brought me here to deprive me of my eyesight.' And I said, 'If such is your will, O Lord, I shall not resist.' And he took me by the hand and lifted me up. And when I arose I saw him again in a form which I could not comprehend. So the merciful God, most beloved brethren, has borne our infirmities and carried our transgressions, as the prophet says, 'He bears our griefs; and is afflicted for us; yet we did esteem him stricken and afflicted.'[4] For he is in the Father and the Father in him; in him also is the fullness of all majesty, who has shown us all his benefits. He ate and drank on our account though he was neither hungry nor thirsty; he suffered and bore reproaches for us, he died and rose for us. He also defended and strengthened me through his greatness when I sinned; he will also comfort you, so that you may love him, this Great and Small One, this Beautiful and Ugly One, this Young Man and Old Man, appearing in time, yet utterly invisible in eternity; whom a human hand has not grasped, yet is held by his servants; whom flesh has not seen and now sees; who has not been heard, but is known now as the word which is heard; never chastised, but now chastised; who was before the world and is now perceived in time, beginning greater than all dominion, yet delivered to the princes; glorious, but lowly among us; ugly, yet foreseeing. This Jesus you have, brethren, the door, the light, the way, the bread, the water, the life, the resurrection, the refreshment, the pearl, the treasure, the seed, the abundance, the grain of mustard seed, the vine, the plough, the grace, the faith, the word: he is everything, and there is none greater than he; to him be praise in all eternity. Amen.". . .

23 The brethren and all who were in Rome came together, and on payment of a piece of gold each occupied a seat. Senators and prefects and officers also assembled. But when Peter came in he stood in the center. All cried aloud, "Show us, Peter, who your God is or which majesty it is which gave you such confidence. Be not disaffected to the Romans; they are lovers of the gods. We have had evidence from Simon, let us have yours also; show us, both of you, whom we must believe." And when they had spoken Simon also came. Dismayed, he stood by the side of Peter gazing closely at him. After a long silence Peter said, "Roman men, you shall be our true judges. I say that I believe in the living and true God, of whom I will give you proof already known to me, and to which many among you testify. You see that this man is silent because he has been refuted and because I have driven him from Judaea on account of the frauds perpetrated upon Eubola, a highly respected but simple woman, by means of his magic. Having been expelled by me from there, he has come here believing that he could remain hidden among you; and now here he stands face to face with me. Tell me, Simon, did you not fall at my feet and those of Paul, when in Jerusalem you saw the miraculous cures which took place by our hands, and say, 'I pray you, take as much money from me as you wish, that I too by laying on of hands may perform such deeds'? And when we heard this from you, we cursed you: do you think that we try to possess money? And now are you afraid? My name is Peter, because the Lord Christ had the grace to call me to be ready for every cause. For I believe in the living God, through whom I shall destroy your magic arts. Let Simon perform in your presence the wonderful things which he used to do. And will you not believe me what I just told you about him?" And Simon said, "You have the impudence to speak of

---

3 Mark 9:2–8.

4 Isa 53:4.

Jesus the Nazarene, the son of a carpenter, himself a carpenter, whose family is from Judaea. Listen Peter. The Romans have understanding, they are no fools." And turning to the people he said, "Men of Rome, is a God born? Is he crucified? Whoever has a master is no God." And when he spoke, many said, "You are right, Simon."

24 And Peter said, "Cursed be your words against Christ. You spoke in these terms whereas the prophet says of him, 'Who shall declare his generation?'[5] And another prophet says, 'And we have seen him, and he had no form nor beauty.'[6] And 'In the last days a child shall be born of the Holy Spirit; his mother knows not a man and no one claims that he is his father.' And again he says, 'She has given birth and has not given birth.' And again, 'Is it a very little thing for you to go to battle? Behold, in the womb a virgin shall conceive.'[7] And another prophet says in honor of the Father, 'We neither heard her voice, nor did a midwife come.'[8] Another prophet says, 'He came not out of the womb of a woman but descended from a heavenly place,' and 'A stone cut out without hands and has broken all kingdoms,'[9] and 'The stone which the builders rejected has become the headstone of the corner,'[10] and he calls him 'the tried, precious' stone.[11] And again, the prophet says of him, 'I saw him come on a cloud like the Son of man.'[12] And what more shall I say? Men of Rome, if you knew the prophetical writings I would explain everything to you. It was necessary that through them it should be a mystery and the Kingdom of God be completed. But these things

---

5 Isa 53:8

6 Isa 53:2.

7 Isa 7:14.

8 Asc of Isa 11:13.

9 Dan 2:34.

10 Ps 118:22; Mark 12:10.

11 Isa 28:16.

12 Dan 7:13.

shall be revealed to you afterwards. Now I turn to you, Simon; do one of the signs whereby you deceived them before and I shall frustrate it through my Lord Jesus Christ." Simon took courage and said, "If the prefect permits."

25 The prefect wished to show his impartiality to both, so that he might not appear to be acting unjustly. And the perfect summoned one of his slaves and spoke to Simon, "Take him and kill him." To Peter he said, "And you revive him." And to the people the prefect said, "It is for you to decide which of these is accepted before God, he who kills, or he who revives." And Simon whispered something into the ear of the slave and made him speechless, and he died. But when the people began to murmur, one of the widows who had been cared for by Marcellus cried out, "Peter, servant of God, my son also is dead, the only one I had." The people made room for her, and they brought her to Peter. And she fell down at his feet and said, "I had only one son; by the labor of his hands he provided for me; he lifted me up, he carried me. Now he is dead, who will give me a hand?" Peter said to her, "In the presence of these witnesses go and bring your son, that they may be able to see and believe that he was raised up by the power of God; the other shall see it and perish." And Peter said to the young men, "We need young men such as shall believe." And at once thirty young men offered themselves to carry the widow and to fetch her dead son. When the widow had recovered, the young men lifted her up. But she cried and said, "Behold my son, the servant of Christ has sent for you," and she tore her hair and scratched her face. And the young men who had come examined the nose of the boy to see if he were really dead. When they perceived that he was dead they comforted his mother and said, "If you really believe in the God of Peter, we will lift him up and bring him to Peter, that he may revive him and restore him to you."

26 While the young men were saying this the prefect in the forum looked at Peter and said, "What do you say, Peter? Behold, the lad is dead; the emperor liked him, and I spared him not. I had indeed many other young men; but I trusted in you and in your Lord whom you proclaim, if indeed you are sure and truthful: therefore I allowed him to die." And Peter said, "God is neither tempted nor weighed in the balance. But he is to be worshipped with the whole heart by those whom he loves and he will hear those who are worthy. Since, however, my God and Lord Jesus Christ is now tempted among you, he is doing many signs and miracles through me to turn you from your sins. In your power, revive now through my voice, O Lord, in the presence of all, him whom Simon killed by his touch." And Peter said to the master of the lad, "Come, take hold of him by the right hand and you shall have him alive and walking with you." And the prefect Agrippa ran and came to the lad, took his hand, and restored him to life. And when the multitude saw this they cried, "There is only one God, the God of Peter."

27 Meanwhile the widow's son was brought in on a bier by the young men. The people made room, and they brought him to Peter. Peter, however, lifted up his eyes towards heaven, stretched forth his hands, and said, "Holy Father of your Son Jesus Christ who has given us power to ask and to obtain through you and to despise everything that is in this world and follow you only, who are seen by few and wish to be known by many; shine round, O Lord, enlighten, appear, revive the son of the aged widow, who is helpless without him. And I take the word of my Lord Christ and say to you, 'Young man, arise and walk with your mother as long as you can be of use to her. Afterward you shall be called to a higher ministry and serve as deacon and bishop.' " And the dead man rose immediately, and the multitude saw and were amazed, and the people cried, "You, God the Savior, you, God of Peter, invisible God and Savior." And they spoke with one another and wondered at the power of a man who with his word called upon his Lord, and they accepted what had taken place for their sanctification.

28 When the news had spread through the entire city, the mother of a senator came, and making her way through the multitude she threw herself at Peter's feet and said, "I heard many people say that you are a minister of the merciful God and that you impart his mercy to all who desire this light. Bestow, therefore, also to my son this light, since I have learned that you are not ungenerous towards any one; do not turn way from a lady, who entreats you." Peter said to her, "Do you believe in my God through whom your son shall rise?" And the mother, weeping, said with a loud voice, "I believe, Peter, I believe." The whole multitude cried out, "Give the mother her son." And Peter said, "Let him be brought here into the presence of all." And Peter, turning to the people, said, "Men of Rome, I, too, am one of you! I have human flesh and I am a sinner, but I have obtained mercy. Do not imagine that what I do, I do in my own power; I do it in the power of my Lord Jesus Christ who is the judge of the living and the dead. I believe in him, I have been sent by him, and I dare to call upon him to raise the dead. Go, therefore, woman, and have your son brought here and have him raised." And the woman made her way through the multitude, ran into the street with great joy, and believed with her heart; coming to the house she made her slaves carry him and came back to the forum. And she told the young men to cover their heads and go before the bier and carry everything that she intended to spend on the body of her son in front of the bier, so that Peter, seeing this, might have pity on the body and on her. With them all as mourners she came to the assembly, followed by a multitude of senators and ladies who came to see God's wonderful deeds. And Nicostratus (the man who had died) was very noble and respected in the senate. They brought him and placed him before Peter. And Peter asked them to be silent and said with a very loud voice, "Romans, let a righteous judgment now take place between me and Simon, and judge which of us believes in the living God, he or I. Let him revive the body which is before us, and believe in him as an angel of God. If he is not able

I will call upon my God. I will restore the son alive to his mother and then you shall believe that he is a sorcerer and deceiver, this man who enjoys your hospitality." When they heard this, it seemed right to them what Peter had said. They encouraged Simon saying, "Show yourself publicly what you can do; either you convince us or you shall be convicted. Why do you stand still? Commence."

When Simon perceived that they all pushed him, he stood in silence. When the people had become quiet and were looking at him, Simon cried out and said, "Romans, when you see that the dead man is raised, will you cast Peter out of the city?" And the whole multitude said, "We shall not only cast him out but also burn him at once." Simon came to the head of the dead man, bowed three times, and he showed the people how the dead man had lifted up his head and moved it, and opened his eyes and lightly bowed to Simon. And immediately they began to gather wood to burn Peter. But Peter, having received the power of Christ, lifted up his voice and said to those who were shouting against him, "Now I see, Romans, that I must not call you foolish and silly so long as your eyes and your ears and your senses are blinded. So long as your mind is darkened you do not perceive that you are bewitched, since you seemingly believe that a dead man rose who has not risen. I would have been content, Romans, to keep silent and to die in silence and to leave you among the illusions of this world. But the punishment of the unquenchable fire is before my eyes. If you agree, let the dead man speak, let him rise; if he is alive, let him untie the band from his chin, let him call his mother and say to you, 'Bawlers, why are you crying?' Let him beckon to you with his hand. If, therefore, you wish to see that he is dead and you are spellbound, let this man step back from the bier, this one who persuaded you to withdraw from Christ, and you shall see the dead man as you saw him when you brought him in." And the prefect Agrippa could no longer restrain himself but rose and with his own hand pushed Simon away. And the dead man looked as he had before. And the people were enraged and,

converted from the magical spell of Simon, began to cry, "Hear, O Caesar, should the dead not rise let Simon be burned instead of Peter, because he has really deceived us." But Peter stretched forth his hand and said, "Romans, be patient. I do not say that Simon should be burned if the boy is restored; it is only when I tell you to do it, that you will." And the people cried, "Even if you should not wish it, Peter, we shall do it." Peter said to them, "If you continue, the boy shall not rise. We have learned not to recompense evil for evil, but we have learned to love our enemies and to pray for those who persecute us. For should even he repent, it is better. For God will not remember the evil. Let him, therefore, come to the light of Christ. But if he cannot, let him inherit the portion of his father, the devil. But do not let your hands be contaminated." Having thus spoken to the people he came to the boy, and before raising him he said to his mother, "These young men, whom you set free in honor of your son, can as free men obey their living master. For I know that the souls of some among them will be wounded when they see your risen son and serve again as slaves. But let them all be free and receive their subsistence as before—for your son shall rise again—and let them be with him." And Peter looked at her for some time awaiting the answer. And the mother of the boy said, "How can I do otherwise? Therefore I declare before the prefect that they should possess all that which I had to spend on the corpse of my son." Peter said to her, "Let the rest be divided among the widows." And Peter rejoiced in his soul and said in the spirit, "O Lord, who are merciful, Jesus Christ, manifest yourself to your servant Peter who calls upon you, as you always show mercy and goodness. In the presence of all these who have been set free, that they may be able to serve, let Nicostratus now arise." And Peter touched the side of the lad and said, "Arise." And the lad arose, took up his garment and sat and untied his chin, asked for other garments, came down from the bier, and said to Peter, "I beg you, man, let us go to our Lord Christ, whom I heard speak to you; he said to you, pointing at me,

'Bring him here, for he belongs to me.' " When Peter heard this he was still more strengthened in the spirit by the help of the Lord and said to the people, "Romans, thus the dead are awakened, thus they speak, thus they walk when they are raised; they live for so long as it pleases God. But now I turn to you who came to see the spectacle. If you repent now from your sins and from all your human-made gods and from all uncleanness and lust, you shall receive the communion of Christ in faith so that you may obtain life for eternity."

29 From that hour on they worshipped him like a god, and the sick, whom they had at home, they brought to his feet to be cured by him. And when the prefect perceived that such a great multitude adhered to Peter he asked him to depart. And Peter bade the people come into the house of Marcellus. And the mother of the lad asked Peter to come to her house. But Peter had arranged to go to Marcellus on Sunday to see the widows, as Marcellus had promised, so that he might minister to them with his own hand. And the lad who had been raised said, "I shall not leave Peter." And his mother returned joyfully and cheerfully to her house. And on the day after the Sabbath she came into the house of Marcellus and brought two thousand pieces of gold and said to Peter, "Divide these among the virgins of Christ who minister to him." But the lad who had been raised, perceiving that he had not yet given anything to anyone, ran to his house, opened a chest, and brought four thousand pieces of gold, and said to Peter, "See, I also, who have been raised, offer the double gift and present myself from now on as a living sacrifice to God."

50. The Acts of Paul

The Acts of Paul is not preserved in its entirety, but only in large fragments that are difficult to piece together. The complete book is usually thought to have included the Acts of Thecla (see Chapter 14) and the pseudonymous letter of 3 Corinthians (see selection 53). Together, the various fragments narrate legendary episodes from Paul's life, including the account, not excerpted here, of a talking lion whom Paul converts and baptizes, who then, at a later time, spares the apostle when loosed upon him in the arena.

The following extract was no doubt the conclusion of the book, for it describes Paul's martyrdom. Put on trial before the evil emperor, Nero, Paul announces that if executed, he will reappear as proof that he can never really die but will live forever. When Paul is then beheaded, milk (a symbol of life?) rather than blood squirts from his wound. Then, after his death, Paul fulfills his word by appearing to Nero and pronouncing the emperor's imminent doom.

Many scholars identify the Acts of Paul with a book known to the church father Tertullian, who, around 200 CE, claimed that it had been fabricated by a presbyter of Asia Minor, who, after being caught, indicated that he had done it "out of love for Paul."

The Acts of Paul, from *The Apocryphal New Testament*, ed. J. K. Elliott. © Oxford University Press, 1993. Reprinted by permission of Oxford University Press.

1 Luke, who had come from Gaul, and Titus, who had come from Dalmatia, expected Paul at Rome. When Paul saw them he rejoiced and rented a barn outside Rome where he and the brethren taught the word of truth. He became famous and many souls were added to the Lord, so that it was noised about in Rome and a great many from the house of the emperor came to him and there was much joy.

A certain Patroclus, a cupbearer of the emperor, who had come too late to the barn and could not get near to Paul on account of the throng of the people sat on a high window, and listened as he taught the word of God. But Satan, being wicked, became jealous of the love of the brethren and Patroclus fell down from the window and died; speedily it was reported to Nero. Paul, however, having learned it by Spirit said, "Brethren, the evil one has obtained a way to tempt you; go forth and you will find a boy who has fallen down and is dying. Lift him up and bring him here." This they did. When the people saw him they were frightened. Paul said to them, "Now, brethren, show your faith. Come, let us mourn to our Lord Jesus Christ, that the boy might live and we remain unharmed." When all began to lament, the boy took breath and, having put him on an animal, they sent him away alive with all those who were of the emperor's house.

2 And Nero, having heard of Patroclus' death, became very sad, and as he came out from his bath he ordered another to be appointed for the wine. But his servants said, "Emperor, Patroclus is alive and stands at the sideboard." When the emperor heard that Patroclus was alive he was frightened and would not come in. But when he came in and saw Patroclus he cried out, "Patroclus, are you alive?" He answered, "I am alive, Caesar." But he said, "Who is he who made you alive?" And the boy, uplifted by the confidence of faith, said, "Christ Jesus, the king of the ages." The emperor asked in dismay, "Is he to be king of the ages and destroy all kingdoms?" Patroclus said to him, "Yes, he destroys all kingdoms under

heaven, and he alone shall remain in all eternity, and there will be no kingdom which escapes him." And he struck his face and cried out, "Patroclus, are you also fighting for that king?" He answered, "Yes, my lord and Caesar, for he has raised me from the dead."

And Barsabas Justus the flat-footed and Urion the Cappadocian and Festus of Galatia, the chief men of Nero, said, "And we, too, fight for him, the king of the ages." After having tortured those men whom he used to love he imprisoned them and ordered that the soldiers of the great king be sought, and he issued an edict that all Christians and soldiers of Christ that were found should be executed.

3 And among the many Paul also was brought in fetters. Those who were imprisoned with him looked at him, so that the emperor observed that he was the leader of the soldiers. And he said to him, "Man of the great king, now my prisoner, what induced you to come secretly into the Roman empire and to enlist soldiers in my territory?" But Paul, filled with the Holy Spirit, said in the presence of all, "Caesar, we enlist soldiers not only in your territory but in all lands of the earth. For thus we are commanded to exclude none who wishes to fight for my king. If it seems good to you, serve him, for neither riches nor the splendors of this life will save you; but if you become his subject and beseech him you shall be saved. For in one day he will destroy the world."

Having heard this Nero commanded all the prisoners to be burned with fire, but Paul to be beheaded according to the law of the Romans. But Paul was not silent and communicated the word to Longus the prefect and Cestus the centurion. And Nero, being instigated by the evil one, raged in Rome and had many Christians executed without trial, so that the Romans stood before the palace and cried, "It is enough, Caesar; these people are ours. You destroy the strength of the Romans." Being thus convinced, he desisted and commanded that no Christian was to be touched till his case had been investigated.

4 After the issuing of the edict Paul was brought before him, and he insisted that he should be executed. And Paul said, "Caesar, I live not merely for a short time for my king; and if you have me executed I shall do the following: I will rise again and appear to you, for I shall not be dead but alive to my king, Christ Jesus, who shall come to judge the earth."

And Longus and Cestus said to Paul, "Whence have you this king that you believe in him without changing your mind even at point of death?" And Paul answered and said, "You men, who are now ignorant and in error, change your mind and be saved from the fire which comes over the whole earth. For we fight not, as you suppose, for a king who is from the earth but for one who is from heaven: he is the living God who comes as judge because of the lawless deeds which take place in this world. And blessed is he who will believe in him and live in eternity when he shall come with fire to purge the earth." And they besought him and said, "We entreat you, help us, and we will release you." But he answered, "I am not a deserter from Christ but a faithful soldier of the living God. If I knew that I should die I would still have done it, Longus and Cestus, but since I live to God and love myself I go to the Lord that I may come again with him in the glory of his Father." And they said to him, "How can we live after you have been beheaded?"

5 And while they were speaking Nero sent a certain Parthenius and Pheretas to see whether Paul had already been beheaded. And they found him still alive. He summoned them beside him and said, "Believe in the living God who will raise me, as well as all those who believe in him, from the dead." But they said, "We will now go to Nero but when you have died and have been raised up we will believe in your God."

But when Longus and Cestus continued to ask about salvation he said to them, "In the early dawn come quickly to my grave and you will find two men at prayer, Titus and Luke; they will give you the seal in the Lord."

And turning toward the east, Paul lifted up his hands to heaven and prayed at length; and after having conversed in Hebrew with the fathers during prayer he bent his neck, without speaking any more. When the executioner cut off his head milk splashed on the tunic of the soldier. And the soldier and all who stood near by were astonished at this sight and glorified God who had thus honored Paul. And they went away and reported everything to Caesar.

6 When he heard of it he was amazed and did not know what to say. While many philosophers and the centurion were assembled with the emperor, Paul came about the ninth hour, and in the presence of all he said, "Caesar, behold, here is Paul, the soldier of God; I am not dead but live in my God. But upon you, unhappy one, many evils and great punishment will come because you have unjustly shed the blood of the righteous not many days ago." And having spoken this Paul departed from him. When Nero had heard, he commanded that the prisoners be released, Patroclus as well as Barsabas with his friends.

7 And, as Paul had told them, Longus and Cestus, the centurion, came in fear very early to the grave of Paul. And when they drew near they found two men in prayer and Paul with them, and they became frightened when they saw the unexpected miracle, but Titus and Luke, being afraid at the sight of Longus and Cestus, turned to run away.

But they followed and said to them, "We follow you not in order to kill you, blessed men of God, as you imagine, but in order to live, that you may do to us as Paul promised us. We have just seen him in prayer beside you." Upon hearing this Titus and Luke gave them joyfully the seal in the Lord, glorifying God and the Father of our Lord Jesus Christ to whom be glory for ever and ever. Amen.

51. The Acts of John

Some of the most entertaining stories found among the apocryphal accounts of the apostles are in the "Acts of John," stories of the exploits of the son of Zebedee, the disciple commonly regarded as Jesus' closest companion. Two of the book's episodes have already been excerpted in Chapter 2. Like those earlier accounts, the stories below demonstrate the uncanny power of God at work within his great apostle. The first is the amusing tale of the obedient bed bugs, who leave John in peace to allow him to get some much-needed rest. The second is a gripping story of passion gone awry, in a love triangle involving the beautiful but ascetic Christian, Drusiana, her loving husband, Andronicus, and the unbeliever Callimachus, whose unsatisfied lust becomes known to Drusiana, causing her to die of grief for being the object of temptation. In a fit of passion, however, Callimachus bribes his way into the burial vault, where he plans to fulfill his passion on Drusiana's corpse, only to be attacked by a preternatural serpent that stands as her guardian.

Razor-sharp in its contrast between ascetic virtue and lustful vice, this intriguing account stresses both the need for purity before God and the power of the apostle, who is able to raise the dead and to right all that has gone wrong in the world. The pure Drusiana, too, it should be noted, performs a resurrection in the account. The account was probably composed during the second half of the second century.

60 On the first day we came to a lonely inn, and when we were trying to find a bed for John we experienced a strange event. There was one bedstead with covers over which we spread our cloaks which we had brought and requested him to lie down and to rest, whilst we slept on the floor. He had hardly lain down, when he was molested by bugs. But as they became more and more troublesome, and as it was midnight already, we all heard him say to them, "I say to you, you bugs, be considerate; leave your home for this night and go to rest in a place which is far away from the servants of God!" And while we laughed and talked, John fell asleep. And we conversed quietly, and thanks to him we remained undisturbed.

61 When it was day, I rose first, and with me Verus and Andronicus. And in the door of the room which we had taken was a mass of bugs. And having called all the brethren, we went outside to have a full view of them. John was still asleep. When he woke up we showed him what we had seen. And sitting up in bed and seeing them, he said, "Since you have been wise to heed my warning, go back to your place!" When he had spoken and had risen from the bed, the bugs hastened from the door to the bed, ran up the legs into the joints and disappeared. And John said again, "This creature heard the voice of a man and kept quiet and was obedient. We, however, hear God's voice, and yet irresponsibly transgress his commandments. And how long will this go on?"

62 After this we came to Ephesus. And when the brethren who lived there had learned that John had returned after this long time, they

The Acts of John, from *The Apocryphal New Testament*, ed. J. K. Elliott. © Oxford University Press, 1993. Reprinted by permission of Oxford University Press.

met in the house of Andronicus, where he was also staying, grasped his feet, put his hands to their faces, and kissed them because they had touched his clothes.

63 And while great love and endless joy prevailed among the brethren, one, a servant of Satan, coveted Drusiana, although he saw and knew that she was the wife of Andronicus. Very many people remonstrated with him, "It is impossible for you to obtain this woman, especially since she has separated even from her husband out of piety. Or do you alone not know that Andronicus, who was not the godly man he now is, had locked her up in a tomb, saying, 'Either I'll have you as a wife, as I had you before, or you must die?' And she preferred to die rather than to commit the repugnant act. Now, if out of piety she withheld her consent to sexual intercourse with her husband and master, but persuaded him to become likeminded, should she consent to you, who wish to commit adultery with her? Desist from your passion, which gives you no rest! Desist from your scheme, which you cannot accomplish!"

64 Though his intimate friends remonstrated with him, they could not persuade him. He was even so impudent as to send word to her. When Drusiana heard of his disgraceful passion and shameless demands, she became very despondent, and after two days she was feverish. She said, "Oh, if I only had not come back to my native city where I have become a stumbling-block to a man who believes not in the worship of God! For if he were filled with God's word, he would not fall into such a passion. Therefore, O Lord, since I have become accessory to a blow which struck an ignorant soul, deliver me from this prison and take me soon to you!" And without being understood by anyone Drusiana departed this life in the presence of John, not rejoicing but sorrowing over the physical trouble of that man.

65 And Andronicus was sad and carried a hidden sorrow in his heart, and wept bitterly,

so that John could only silence him by saying to him, "Drusiana has departed this unjust life for a better hope." To this answered Andronicus, "Of this I am certain, John, and I have no doubt in the belief in my God. My hopes are grounded on the fact, that she departed this life pure."

66 After she was interred, John took Andronicus aside, and having learned of the cause he sorrowed more than Andronicus. And he kept silence, considering the threats of the enemy, and sat still a little. When the brethren were assembled to hear which words he would say concerning the departed, he began to speak:

67 "When the helmsman who crosses the ocean has landed with the ship and passengers in a quiet haven free from storms, he feels secure. The husbandman who sowed the seed-grains in the ground and cared for them with great pains is only then to enjoy a rest from his labors when he has harvested abundant corn in his barns. Whoever promises to take part in a race should rejoice only when he has obtained the prize. He whose name is entered on the list of prize-fighting should triumph only after he receives the crowns. And thus it is with all races and skills, when they do not fail at the end, but are carried out, as they were intended.

68 "So I think it is with the faith which every one of us practises, and which can only be decided as having been the true one when it remains the same to the end of life. For there are many obstacles which cause unrest to human reasoning: cares, children, parents, glory, poverty, flattery, youth, beauty, boasting, desire for riches, anger, pride, frivolity, envy, passion, carelessness, violence, lust, slaves, money, pretence, and all the other similar obstacles which exist in life; it is the same for the helmsman who takes his course for a quiet journey and is opposed by the adverse winds and a great tempest and a mighty wave, when the heaven is serene; it is the same for the husbandman who is opposed by untimely weather and blight and creeping worms appearing from the ground; for the athletes, the near miss, and for the craftsman the obstacles to their skills.

69 "The believer must above all things consider the end and carefully examine how it will come, whether energetic and sober and without impediment, or in confusion and flattering worldly things and bound by passions. Thus one can praise the beauty of the body only when it is completely naked; and the greatness of the general when he has happily finished the whole campaign as he promised; and the excellence of the physician when he has succeeded in every cure; and so one praises a soul filled with faith and worthy of God if it has happily accomplished that which it promised, not one of which made a good beginning, and gradually descended into the errors of life and became weak, nor the numb soul which made an effort to attain higher things and was afterwards reduced to perishable, nor that which loved the temporal more than the eternal, nor that which exchanged the perishable for the lasting, nor that which honored what was not to be honored and loved works of dishonor, nor that which accepted pledges from Satan and received the serpent into its house, nor one which was reviled for God's sake and afterwards was ashamed, nor one which consented with the mouth but did not show it by the deed; but we praise one which refused to be inflamed by filthy lust, to succumb to levity, to be ensnared by thirst after money, or to be betrayed by the strength of the body and anger."

70 While John continued to preach to the brethren that they despise earthly goods for the sake of the eternal ones, the lover of Drusiana, inflamed by the influence of the polymorphous Satan to the most ardent passions, bribed the greedy steward of Andronicus with money. And he opened the tomb of Drusiana and left him to accomplish on the body that which was once denied to him. Since he had not procured her during her lifetime, he continually thought of her body after she was dead, and exclaimed, "Although

when living you refused to unite with me in love, after your death I will dishonor your corpse." Being in such a frame of mind he obtained the opportunity to execute his impious plan through the accursed steward, and both went to the tomb. Having opened the door, they began to take the graveclothes from the corpse, and said, "What have you gained, unhappy Drusiana? Could you not have done this while you were alive? It need not have grieved you if you had done it willingly."

71 While they spoke and only the shift remained, there appeared something wonderful, which people that do such things deserve to experience. A serpent appeared from somewhere, bit the steward, and killed him. And the serpent did not bite the young man, but encircled his feet, hissing fearfully, and when he fell down, the serpent sat on him.

72 On the following day John and Andronicus and the brethren went at the break of day to the tomb in which Drusiana had been for three days, so that we might break bread there. And when we were about to start, the keys were not to be found. And John said to Andronicus, "It is right that they are lost, for Drusiana is not in the tomb. Nevertheless, let us go, that you do not appear neglectful, and the doors will open of themselves, since the Lord has already given us many other things."

73 When we came to the place, the doors opened at the master's behest, and at the tomb of Drusiana we saw a beautiful youth smiling. When John saw him, he exclaimed and said, "Do you come before us here also, noble one? And why?" And he heard a voice saying to him, "For the sake of Drusiana, whom you are to raise up. I found her almost defiled on account of the dead man lying near the tomb." And when the noble one had thus spoken to John he ascended to heaven before the eyes of all. And John turned to the other side of the tomb and saw a young man, the very prominent Ephesian Callimachus—for this is what he was called—and on him a huge snake sleeping, also the steward of Andronicus, named Fortunatus, dead. On seeing both, he stood helpless and said to the brethren, "What does all this mean? Or why did the Lord not reveal to me what took place here, for he was always concerned for me?"

74 When Andronicus saw these bodies, he jumped up and went to the tomb of Drusiana. And when he saw her in her shift, he said to John, "I understand what took place, blessed servant of God. This Callimachus loved my sister. And as he could not get her, although he tried it often, he no doubt bribed this accursed steward of mine with a great sum of money with the intention—as one can now see—to accomplish his purpose through him. For this Callimachus said to many, 'If she will not yield to be me alive, rape shall be committed on her death.' This, O master, the noble one saw and did not allow her earthly remains to be violated. That is why those who engineered this are dead. And the voice which came to you 'Raise Drusiana!' foretold this. For she departed this life through sorrow. And I believe him who said that this is one of the men who was led astray. For you were asked to raise him. As for the other I know that he does not deserve salvation. But one thing I ask of you. Raise Callimachus first, and he shall confess what took place."

75 And John looked at the corpse and said to the poisonous snake, "Depart from him who is to serve Jesus Christ!" Then he rose and prayed, "God, whose name is rightly praised by us; God, who overcomes each harmful work; God, whose will is done, who always hears us, make your grace now efficacious on this youth! And if through him some dispensation is to take place, make it known to us, when he is raised!" And the young man immediately arose and kept silence for a whole hour.

76 When the man had regained his senses, John asked what his intrusion into the tomb meant. And having learned from him what Andronicus had already told him, how he passionately loved Drusiana, John asked further whether he had accomplished his wicked design to commit rape on the holy earthly remains. And he replied, "How could I have accomplished this when this fearful beast killed Fortunatus with one bite before my eyes? And this deservedly so, for he encouraged me to such madness, after I had already desisted from the ill-timed and dreadful frenzy—but he frightened me and put me in the state in which you saw me, before I arose. But I will tell you another great miracle, which nearly slew me and almost killed me. When my soul was seized with mad passion and the incurable disease was troubling me, when I had already robbed her of the grave-clothes with which she was dressed, and went from the grave to put them down as you see, I turned back to perpetrate the abominable deed. And I saw a beautiful youth covering her with this cloak. Rays of light fell from his face upon hers, and he turned to me also and said, "Callimachus, die, that you may live." Who it was, I knew not, servant of God. Since you have come here, I know that it was an angel of God. And this I truly know, that the true God is preached by you; and I am sure of it. But I pray you, see to it that I may be delivered from this fate and dreadful crime, and bring me to your God as a man who had gone astray in scandalous, abominable, deceit. On my knees I ask for your help. I will become one of those who hope in Christ so that the voice may also prove true, which spoke here to me, 'Die to live!' And it is already fulfilled. For that unbeliever, godless, lawless man, is dead; I am raised by you as a believer, faithful and godly, that I may know the truth, which I ask of you to reveal to me."

77 And John, rejoicing, contemplated the whole spectacle of the salvation of people and said, "O Lord Jesus Christ, I do not know what your power is. I am amazed at your great mercy and endless forbearance. Oh, what greatness descended to servitude! O unspeakable freedom, which was enslaved by us! O inconceivable glory, which has come upon us! You have kept the grave from shame, and redeemed that man who contaminated himself with blood, and taught him to be chaste who meant to violate dead bodies. Father, full of mercy and compassion toward him who disregarded you, we praise, glorify, and honor you and thank you for your great goodness and long-suffering, holy Jesus, for you alone are God and none else; you against whose power all devices can do nothing now and in all eternity! Amen!"

78 After these words, John took Callimachus, kissed him, and said, "Glory be to our God, who had mercy upon you, child, and deemed me worthy to praise his power, and delivered you by a wise method from that madness and intoxication and called you to rest and renewal of life."

79 When Andronicus saw that Callimachus had been raised from the dead, he and the brethren besought John to raise Drusiana also, and said, "John, let her be raised and happily complete life's short space, which she gave up out of sorrow for Callimachus, because she thought she was a temptation to him! And when it pleases the Lord, he will take her to himself." And without delay John went to the grave, seized her hand and said, "You who alone are God, I call upon you, the immense, the unspeakable, the incomprehensible, to whom all worldly power is subject, before whom every authority bows, before whom every pride falls down and is silent, before whose voice the demons are confounded, at whose contemplation the whole creation surrenders in quiet meditation. Your name will be hallowed by us. Raise Drusiana that Callimachus be still further strengthened in you who alone can do what is wholly impossible with man, and have given salvation and resurrection, and let Drusiana come out comforted because, in consequence of the conversion of the youth, she no more has the least impediment to long for you!"

80 Having spoken thus John said, "Drusiana, arise!" And she arose and came from the

tomb. And when she saw that she wore nothing but her shirt, she was perplexed how to explain what had happened. Having learned everything from Andronicus, while John was upon his face and Callimachus with tears praised God, she also rejoiced and praised God.

81 Having dressed herself and looked around, she saw Fortunatus. And she said to John, "Father, he too shall rise, though he tried so much to become my betrayer." When Callimachus heard her speaking thus, he said, "No, I beg you, Drusiana. For the voice which I heard did not mention him, but only concerned you, and when I saw I believed. If he were good, God out of mercy would have certainly raised him through the blessed John. He knew that the man should have a bad death." And John answered him, "My son, we have not learnt to recompense evil with evil. For God has not recompensed the evil which we have done to him, but has given us repentance. And although we did not know his name, he did not forget us, but had mercy upon us. And when we reviled him, he forsook us not, but was merciful. And when we were disbelieving, he remembered not the evil. And when we persecuted his brethren, he did not requite us, but made us repent, turn away from sin, and called us to himself, as he called you also, child Callimachus, and, without remembering your former sins, made you his servant through his long-suffering mercy. If you do not wish me to raise Fortunatus, let Drusiana do it."

82 Without wavering, but in the joy of her spirit and soul, she went to the body of Fortunatus and said, "God of the ages, Jesus Christ, God of truth, you allowed me to see signs and wonders and granted me to partake of your name. You breathed into me your spirit with your polymorphous face, and showed much compassion. With your rich goodness, you protected me when my former husband, Andronicus, did violence to me, and gave me your servant Andronicus as a brother. Until now you have kept me, your maiden, pure. You raised me when I was dead through your servant John. To me, risen and freed from offence, you showed me him who was offended at me. You gave me perfect rest in you, and delivered me from the secret madness. I love you with all my heart. I beseech you, Christ, not to dismiss Drusiana's petition, who asks of you the resurrection of Fortunatus, though he tried so much to become my betrayer."

83 And she took the hand of the dead man and said, "Rise, Fortunatus, in the name of our Lord Jesus Christ!" And Fortunatus rose up. And seeing John in the tomb and Andronicus and Drusiana risen from the dead and Callimachus now a believer, he said, "O how far the power of these awful people has spread! I wish I were not raised, but remained dead, so as not to see them." And with these words he ran from the tomb.

84 And when John perceived the unchangeable soul of Fortunatus, he said, "O nature, unchanged for the better! O source of the soul, remaining in the filth! O essence of corruption, full of darkness! O death, dancing among those belonging to you! O fruitless tree, full of fire! O wood, producing coal as fruit! O forest, with trees full of unhealthy shoots, neighbor of unbelief! You showed us who you are, and you will always be convicted with your children. And the power of praising higher things is unknown to you, for you do not have it. Therefore as your issue is, so is your root and nature. Vanish away from those who hope in the Lord—from their thoughts, from their mind, from their souls, from their bodies, from their action, from their life, from their conversation, from their activity, from their deeds, from their counsel, from their resurrection to God, from their fragrance which you will share, from their fastings, from their prayers, from their holy baptism, from their eucharist, from the nourishment of

their flesh, from their drink, from their dress, from their agape, from their acts of mourning, from their continence, and from their righteousness. From all these, most unholy and abominable Satan, shall Jesus Christ, our God and judge of those who are like you and your nature, remove you."

85 After these words John prayed, fetched a loaf of bread to the tomb to break it, and said, "We praise your name, who have converted us from error and unmerciful lusts. We praise you who have brought before our eyes that which we saw. We bear witness to your goodness manifested to us in various ways. We hallow your gracious name, Lord, and thank you who have convicted those who are convicted by you. We thank you, Lord Jesus Christ, that we believe in your unchangeable mercy. We thank you that you are in need of a saved human nature. We thank you that you gave this sure faith, that you alone are God, now and for ever. We, your servants, thank you, O holy One, we who are assembled with good reason and risen from the dead."

86 Having thus prayed and praised God, he made all the brethren partake of the eucharist of the Lord and then left the tomb. And when he had come into the house of Andronicus, he said to the brethren, "Dear brethren, a spirit within me has prophesied that, in consequence of the bite of the serpent, Fortunatus would die of blood-poisoning. Let someone make haste and inquire whether it is so!" And one of the young men ran and found him dead already, the poison having spread and reached his heart. And he returned to John, reporting that he had been dead three hours already. And John said, "You have your child, devil!"

Thus John rejoiced with the brethren in the Lord.

APOCRYPHAL EPISTLES

(See also the Letter of the Apostles, above, and the Letter of Peter to James, Chapter 6)

Although the earliest Christian pseudepigrapha were epistles (for example, the disputed Pauline epistles in the New Testament), apocryphal epistles are not particularly numerous. Of the ones that do survive, some are clearly meant to advance a particular doctrinal perspective or to oppose the doctrinal views of others (for example, 3 Corinthians, directed explicitly against certain Gnostics), others serve to promote the status and importance of a particular apostolic hero (for example, the forged correspondence between Paul and the Roman philosopher Seneca), and yet others claim to be otherwise lost letters referred to elsewhere in our literature (for example, Paul's letter to the Laodiceans). One of them, our first selection below, claims to be a correspondence between Jesus himself and a nearby king.

The Texts

52. *The Letters of Abgar and Jesus*

The letters between King Abgar and Jesus provide the earliest known instance in which Jesus is said to have written anything (the story of his writing on the ground in the account of the "woman taken in adultery" [John 7:53–8:11] is not original to the Gospel of John, but is found only in later manuscripts). His letter is a response to a written request from Abgar "the Black," king of the city of Edessa in Syria. Even though there actually was a King Abgar there (4 BCE–7 CE and 13–50 CE), this letter is obviously a fiction. In it he acknowledges that Jesus is a great miracle-worker, and he asks him to come to Edessa to heal him of an unspecified illness. He adds that the trip would be beneficial to Jesus as well, since it would allow him to escape the animosity of the Jews in his homeland.

In his reply, Jesus blesses Abgar for believing in him sight unseen (an allusion to John 20:29), but he informs the king that he cannot come. He needs instead to stay where he is, in order to fulfill his mission (to be crucified). But after he ascends to heaven, he will send an apostle to heal the king.

We first learn of these letters in the *Ecclesiastical History* of Eusebius, who discusses them and quotes them in the form found here. They were evidently composed in the early third century.

Jesus' Correspondence with Abgar
(Eusebius, *Ecclesiastical History* I, 13)

Copy of the Letter Written by the Ruler Abgar to Jesus, and Sent by Him to Jerusalem through His Courier Ananias

The Ruler Abgar Uchama,[1] to Jesus the good Savior who has appeared in the region of Jerusalem, greetings. I have heard about you and your healings, which you perform without medications or herbs. As the report indicates, you make the blind see again and the lame walk, you cleanse lepers, you cast out unclean spirits and demons, you heal the chronically sick, and you raise the dead. Having heard all these things about you, I have concluded one of two things: either you are God and do these things having descended from heaven, or you do them as the Son of God. For this reason now I am writing you, asking that you take the trouble to come to me and heal my illness.[2] For I have also heard that the Jews are

---

1 *Uchama* is a Syriac word that means "black." It is often used in texts to refer to people with African roots. Some manuscripts omit the word.

2 Cf. 2 Kings 5:1–19.

---

murmuring against you and wish to harm you.[3] My city is very small and esteemed, and it can accommodate us both.

The Reply Sent by Jesus to the Ruler Abgar through the Courier Ananias

Blessed are you who have believed in me without seeing me.[4] For it is written about me that those who see me will not believe in me, and that those who do not see me will believe and live.[5] But concerning your request for me to come to you: I must accomplish everything I was sent here to do, and after accomplishing them ascend to the One who sent me. After I have ascended I will send you one of my disciples to heal your illness and to provide life both to you and to those who are with you.

---

3 Cf. John 6:41.
4 Cf. John 20:29.

5 Cf. Isa 6:9; Matt 13:14–17; John 9:39; 12:39–40.

53. Paul's Third Letter to the Corinthians

The letter traditionally called 3 Corinthians is a pseudonymous reply of "Paul" to a letter from the Christians in Corinth, sent to him while he was in prison in Philippi. Both letters eventually came to be incorporated into the apocryphal Acts of Paul (see above).

The letter from the Corinthians asks for Paul's advice about the teachings of two heretics, Simon (Magus?) and Cleobius, who maintain, among other things, that (a) God was not the creator, (b) the Jewish prophets were not from God, (c) Jesus did not come in the flesh, and (d) the flesh will not be raised. All of these are clearly Gnostic ideas (see Chapter 6). The pseudonymous author of 3 Corinthians replies by refuting each of them in turn. The letter concludes with dire warnings of eternal torment for those who embrace the heretical teachings of Paul's opponents.

If, as most scholars now think, these letters were originally composed and transmitted independently of the Acts of Paul, they must have been in circulation no later than the middle of the second century.

Letter of the Corinthians to Paul

1 Stephanus and his fellow-presbyters Daphnus and Eubulus and Theophilus and Zeno to Paul, the brother in the Lord—greeting!

2 Two individuals have come to Corinth, named Simon and Cleobius, who overthrow the faith of some through pernicious words.

3 These you shall examine yourself.

4 For we never heard such things either from you or from the other apostles.

5 But we keep what we have received from you and from the others.

6 Since the Lord has shown us mercy, while you are still in the flesh we should hear this from you once more.

---

7 Come to us or write to us.

8 For we believe, as it has been revealed to The-onoe, that the Lord has delivered you from the hands of the godless.

9 What they say and teach is as follows:

10 They assert that one must not appeal to the prophets

11 and that God is not almighty,

12 there is no resurrection of the body,

13 man has not been made by God,

14 Christ has neither come in the flesh, nor was he born of Mary,

15 and the world is not the work of God but of angels.

16 Wherefore we beseech you, brother, be diligent to come to us that the Corinthian church may remain without stumbling and the foolishness of these men be confounded. Farewell in the Lord!...

Paul's Epistle to the Corinthians

1 Paul, the prisoner of Jesus Christ, to the brethren at Corinth—greeting!

2 Being in many afflictions, I marvel not that the teachings of the evil one had such rapid success.

3 For my Lord Jesus Christ will quickly come, since he is rejected by those who falsify his teaching.

4 For I delivered to you first of all what I received from the apostles before me who were always with Jesus Christ,

5 that our Lord Jesus Christ was born of Mary of the seed of David, the Father having sent the spirit from heaven into her

6 that he might come into this world and save all flesh by his own flesh and that he might raise us in the flesh from the dead as he has presented himself to us as our example.

7 And since humankind is created by his Father,

8 for this reason was he sought by him when he was lost, to become alive by adoption.

9 For the almighty God, maker of heaven and earth, sent the prophets first to the Jews to deliver them from their sins,

10 for he wished to save the house of Israel; therefore he took from the spirit of Christ and poured it out upon the prophets who proclaimed the true worship of God for a long period of time.

11 For the wicked prince who wished to be God himself laid his hands on them and killed them and bound all flesh of humans to his pleasure.

12 But the almighty God, being just, and not wishing to repudiate his creation had mercy

13 and sent his Spirit into Mary the Galilean,

15 that the evil one might be conquered by the same flesh by which he held sway, and be convinced that he is not God.

16 For by his own body Jesus Christ saved all flesh,

17 presenting in his own body a temple of righteousness

18 through which we are saved.

19 They who follow them are not children of righteousness but of wrath, who despise the wisdom of God and in their disbelief assert that heaven and earth and all that is in them are not a work of God.

20 They have the accursed belief of the serpent.

21 Turn away from them and keep aloof from their teaching.

24 And those who say that there is no resurrection of the flesh shall have no resurrection,

25 for they do not believe him who had thus risen.

26 For they do not know, O Corinthians, about the sowing of wheat or some other grain that it is cast naked into the ground and having perished rises up again by the will of God in a body and clothed.

27 And he not only raises the body which is sown, but blesses it manifold.

28 And if one will not take the parable of the seeds

29 let him look at Jonah, the son of Amathios who, being unwilling to preach to the Ninevites, was swallowed up by the whale.

30 And after three days and three nights God heard the prayer of Jonah out of deepest hell, and

nothing was corrupted, not even a hair nor an eyelid.

31 How much more will he raise you up, who have believed in Christ Jesus, as he himself was raised up.

32 When a corpse was thrown on the bones of the prophet Elisha by one of the children of Israel the corpse rose from death; how much more shall you rise up on that day with a whole body, after you have been thrown upon the body and bones and Spirit of the Lord.

34 If, however, you receive anything else let no one trouble me,

35 for I have these bonds on me that I may win Christ, and I bear his marks that I may attain to the resurrection of the dead.

36 And whoever accepts this rule which we have received by the blessed prophets and the holy gospel, shall receive a reward,

37 but for whomsoever deviates from this rule fire shall be for him and for those who preceded him therein

38 since they are Godless people, a generation of vipers.

39 Resist them in the power of the Lord.

40 Peace be with you.

54. Paul's Letter to the Laodiceans

The New Testament book of Colossians mentions a letter sent by Paul to the church of Laodicea in Asia Minor (Colossians 4:16). No letter addressed to the Laodiceans survives from Paul's own hand, but we know that one had been placed in circulation already in the second century, since the Muratorian canon (see Chapter 9) warns against it as a Marcionite forgery (on Marcion, see Chapter 7). The letter given here is almost certainly not the one mentioned in the Muratorian canon, for even though it shares its name, it shows no clear Marcionite tendencies. It may be that this letter was written by a proto-orthodox author precisely in order to counter the Marcionite forgery: those who knew of its existence could claim that *this* was the letter Paul had been referring to.

The letter has struck many scholars as rather banal and insipid, showing few tendencies of any kind. It instead represents a kind of pastiche of statements drawn from Paul's canonical writings, especially Philippians: it evidences no specific occasion and addresses no clear theological or ethical issues. Nonetheless, the letter came to be widely copied by Latin scribes, and it is included in a number of Latin manuscripts of the New Testament itself.

It is difficult to determine the date of this letter, but it appears to have been written sometime during the second or third centuries.

1 Paul, an apostle not of humans and not through humans, but through Jesus Christ, to the brethren who are in Laodicea:

2 Grace to you and peace from God the Father and the Lord Jesus Christ.

3 I thank Christ in all my prayer that you continue in him and persevere in his works, in expectation of the promise at the day of judgment.

4 And may you not be deceived by the vain talk of some people who tell tales that they may lead you away from the truth of the gospel which is proclaimed by me.

5 And now may God grant that those who come from me for the furtherance of the truth of the gospel (. . .) may be able to serve and to do good works for the well-being of eternal life.

6 And now my bonds are manifest, which I suffer in Christ, on account of which I am glad and rejoice.

7 This to me leads to eternal salvation, which itself is brought about through your prayers and by the help of the Holy Spirit, whether it be through life or through death.

8 For my life is in Christ and to die is joy.

9 And his mercy will work in you, that you may have the same love and be of one mind.

10 Therefore, beloved, as you have heard in my presence, so hold fast and work in the fear of God, and eternal life will be yours.

11 For it is God who works in you.

12 And do without hesitation what you do.

13 And for the rest, beloved, rejoice in Christ and beware of those who are out for sordid gain.

14 May all your requests be manifest before God, and be steadfast in the mind of Christ.

15 And do what is pure, true, proper, just and lovely.

16 And what you have heard and received, hold in your heart, and peace will be with you.

17 Salute all the brethren with the holy kiss.

18 The saints salute you.

19 The grace of the Lord Jesus Christ be with your spirit.

20 And see that (this epistle) is read to the Colossians and that of the Colossians to you.

55. The Correspondence Between Paul and Seneca

In an effort to heighten the worldly significance of Paul, who in fact is never mentioned in any of the writings of his Jewish and Roman contemporaries, an unknown Christian author forged a series of fourteen letters between the apostle and the well-known philosopher and statesman, Seneca. Seneca, the most famous philosopher of his day, had been the tutor of the young Nero; when Nero later became emperor of Rome, he appointed Seneca to be his political advisor. The pseudonymous correspondence between Seneca and Paul presupposes that historical context, as Seneca indicates that he has shown Paul's letters to the emperor, who was extremely impressed. Apart from a show of mutual admiration, there is little of substance in the correspondence, with the exception of letter eleven, which mentions the fire in Rome allegedly started by Nero but blamed on the Christians (see Chapter 3). This letter was probably composed by a different author.

The Correspondence between Paul and Seneca, from *New Testament Apocrypha*, vol. 2, ed. Wilhelm Schneemelcher, 2d ed. Cambridge/Louisville: Lutterworth Press/Westminster John Knox Press, 1991. Used with permission of Lutterworth Press and Westminster John Knox Press.

This entire correspondence is often thought to have been produced sometime in the middle of the fourth century. The following are the final eight letters, given in their entirety.

Letter 7: From Seneca

I confess that I was much taken with the reading of your letters which you sent to the Galatians, the Corinthians, and the Achaeans, and let us both live in the spirit which with sacred awe you show in them. For the Holy Spirit is in you and above all exalted ones gives expression by your sublime speech to the most venerable thoughts. I could wish therefore that when you express such lofty thoughts a cultivated form of discourse should not be lacking to their majesty. And that I may conceal nothing from you, brother, or burden my conscience, I confess that the emperor was moved by your sentiments. When I had read to him about the origin of the power in you, he said that he could only wonder that a man who had not enjoyed the usual education should be capable of such thoughts. To which I answered that the gods are wont to speak through the mouths of the innocent, not of those who by their education are able to prevaricate. I gave him the example of Vatienus, an uneducated countryman, to whom two men appeared in a field at Reate who afterwards are named as Castor and Pollux; with that he seems sufficiently instructed. Farewell.

Letter 8: From Paul

I am not unaware that our emperor, if ever he is despondent, is a lover of marvellous things; however, he allows himself not to be injured, but only admonished. For I think you have gravely erred that you have wished to bring to his notice what is contrary to his belief and tenets. Since he worships the gods of the nations, I do not see what was your purpose in wishing him to know this, unless I am to think that you are doing this out of undue love for me. I beg you for the future not to do it. For you must beware lest in loving me you

cause offence to the empress, whose displeasure will indeed only do harm if it persists, but also will be of no profit if that is not so. Even if as empress she is not affronted, as a woman she will be offended. Farewell.

Letter 9: From Seneca

I know that you are not so much disturbed for your own sake by the letter which I wrote to you about the giving of your letters to the emperor as by the nature of things which so hold back the minds of people from all arts and right customs. Today I do not wonder, especially since I now know it well from many documents. Therefore let us make a new beginning, and if in the past anything has been done too lightly, you will grant me forgiveness. I have sent you a book on "verbosity." Farewell, most beloved Paul.

Letter 10: From Paul

As often as I write to you and set my name behind yours, I commit a serious fault which is not congruent with my religion. For I ought, as I have often professed, to be all things to all people, and as concerns your person to observe what Roman law has conceded to the honor of the Senate, namely after perusal of a letter to choose the last place, that I may not with embarrassment and shame seek to do what was within my power. Farewell, my highly revered teacher.

Given on 27 June in the consulship of Nero (for the third time) and Messala (58 CE).

Letter 11: From Seneca

Greetings, my dearest Paul! Do you think that I am not saddened and distressed that capital punishment is still visited upon your innocence? And also that all the populace judges you people so hardhearted and so ready for any crime, believing that whatever happens amiss in the city is done by you? But let us bear with equanimity and make use of the forum which fate provides, until invincible good fortune makes an end of evils. The time of the ancients suffered the Macedonian, the son of Philip, the Cyruses, Darius, and Dionysius, our own time also Gaius Caesar (= Caligula), men for whom all that they wished was legitimate. It is clear at whose hands the city of Rome so often suffers burning. But if human humility could declare what is the cause of it, and in this darkness was free to speak with impunity, then all would see everything. Christians and Jews are—forsooth!—executed as fire-raisers, as a matter of common custom. Whoever that delinquent is, who takes pleasure in murder and uses lies as a disguise, his days are numbered, and just as the best is sometimes offered up as one life for many, so also will this accursed one be burned in the fire for all. 132 palaces, 4000 apartment houses were burned in six days; the seventh brought a pause. I wish you good health, brother.

Given on 28 March in the consulship of Frugi and Bassus (64 CE).

Letter 12: From Seneca

Greetings, my dearest Paul! If a man so distinguished as you and in every way beloved by God is, I do not say united but of necessity interwoven with me and my name, then it will be for the best with your Seneca. Since you are the crown and peak of all most lofty mountains, do you not wish me to rejoice that I am so close to you that I may be thought your second self? You should therefore not think that you are unworthy to be named in the first place in the letters, that you may not seem to tempt rather than to praise me, especially since you know yourself to be a Roman citizen. For I could wish that my place could be yours in your letters and yours mine. Fare well, dearest Paul.

Given on 23 March in the consulship of Apronianus and Capito (59 CE).

Letter 13: From Seneca

Many things are brought together by you, allegorically and enigmatically, from every quarter, and therefore the great power granted to you, in your material and in your office, ought to be adorned not with verbal trappings but with a certain refinement. Nor should you be afraid—as I recall, I have said this often already—that many who concern themselves with such things may corrupt the sense and weaken the power of the material. Certainly I could wish that you make me the concession to have regard for the Latinity and with noble words find the proper form, that you may worthily fulfil the honorable task entrusted to you. Fare well.

Given on 6 July in the consulship of Lurco and Sabinus (58 CE).

Letter 14: From Paul

In your reflection things have been revealed to you which the Deity has granted only to a few. With assurance therefore I sow in a field already fertile most powerful seed, not indeed matter that seems to be decaying but the firm word of God, the outflow of him who grows and abides for ever. What your discernment has grasped must remain unfailing: that the observances of the Gentiles and the Jews are to be avoided. Make yourself a new herald of Christ Jesus, showing by your rhetorical proclamations the irrefutable wisdom which you have almost attained. This you will teach to the temporal king and his servants and faithful friends. For them persuasion will be hard and above their capacity, for several of them are but little swayed by your expositions. But if the word of God is instilled in them as a vital blessing, it begets a new person without corruption, an animal ever in motion, which hastens hence towards God. Farewell, Seneca most dear to us!

Given on 1 August in the consulship of Lurco and Sabinus (58 CE).

APOCRYPHAL APOCALYPSES

Apocalypses were a popular kind of writing in ancient Judaism and Christianity. Most apocalypses present a first-person narrative of revelations given by God to a prophet through an angelic mediator (and interpreter); these revelations are of either the future course of world events or of the heavenly truths that explain the realities of life on earth. Normally they are given in wild dreams or visions loaded with bizarre (though sometimes transparent) symbolism; often they have a triumphalistic progression, providing hope that the horrible suffering of the present is simply a prelude to the glorious end that God has planned for his people from eternity past.

Like the Jewish apocalypses from the period, the noncanonical Christian apocalypses are, as a rule, written pseudonymously (unlike the Revelation to John in the New Testament, whose author does not claim to be any John in particular). Many of these books are concerned not so much with the course of future events on earth as with the fate of souls after death (cf. the Acts of John in Chapter 2). The typical narrative framework involves an apostle's journey through heaven and hell to witness the glorious afterlife of the saved and the cruel torments of the damned. The hortatory purpose of these accounts is clear: to ensure the blessings of heaven and avoid the tortures of hell, one must follow Christ and live an upright and moral life. Other apocalypses are concerned with other heavenly visions, as seen in the selection taken from the Ascension of Isaiah.

THE TEXTS

56. The Apocalypse of Peter

Three different Christian apocalypses claim to have been written by Jesus' disciple Peter (for one of the others, see Chapter 7). The one given here was discovered in 1886 in a tomb in Akhmim Egypt, along with the Gospel of Peter (see above). It was subsequently found in a fuller Ethiopic translation. Written in the early second century, the book was considered canonical in some proto-orthodox churches.

The bulk of the account gives Jesus' response to a query by Peter about the coming judgment, in which he describes the terrors of the last days, details the torments of the damned, and describes (more briefly) the blessings of the saved. It is not clear whether Jesus actually takes Peter on a journey of these two abodes of the dead or simply depicts them in such vivid detail that it seems as if Peter is seeing them. There is no ambiguity, however, concerning the ecstasies and torments awaiting those destined for one place or the other —particularly those in hell, whose horrific punishments are often made to fit their crimes. The book ends with Peter's first-hand description of what he saw on the Mount of Transfiguration (not excerpted here), possibly given in order to validate the legitimacy of the rest of his vision (cf. 2 Peter 1:17–18).

The following excerpt gives the entire first fourteen chapters, from the Ethiopic version.

1 And when he was seated on the Mount of Olives, his own came to him, and we entreated and implored him severally and besought him, saying to him, "Make known to us what are the signs of your Parousia and of the end of the world, that we may perceive and mark the time of your Parousia and instruct those who come after us, to whom we preach the word of your gospel and whom we install in your Church, in order that they, when they hear it, may take heed to themselves that they mark the time of your coming."[1]

And our Lord answered and said unto us, "Take heed that people deceive you not and that you do not become doubters and serve other gods. Many will come in my name saying 'I am Christ.' Believe them not and draw not near unto them. For the coming of the Son of God will not be manifest, but like the lightning that flashes from the east to the west, so shall I come on the clouds of heaven with a great host in my glory; with my cross going before my face will I come in my glory, shining seven times as bright as the sun will I come in my glory, with all my saints, my angels, when my Father will place a crown upon my head,

---

1 See Matt 24; Mark 13; Luke 21.

The Apocalypse of Peter, from *New Testament Apocrypha*, vol 2; ed. Wilhelm Schneemelcher, 2d ed. Cambridge/ Louisville: Lutterworth Press/Westminster John Knox Press, 1991. Used with permission of Lutterworth Press and Westminster John Knox Press.

that I may judge the living and the dead and recompense every one according to his work.

2 "And you, receive the parable of the fig-tree: as soon as its shoots have gone forth and its boughs have sprouted, the end of the world will come."[2] And I, Peter, answered and said to him, "Explain to me concerning the fig-tree, and how we shall perceive it, for throughout all its days does the fig-tree sprout and every year it brings forth its fruit for its master. What does the parable of the fig-tree mean? We know it not."—And the Master answered and said to me, "Do you not understand that the fig-tree is the house of Israel? Even as a person planted a fig-tree in his garden and it brought forth no fruit, and he sought its fruit for many years. When he found it not, he said to the keeper of his garden, 'Uproot the fig-tree that our land may not be unfruitful for us.' And the gardener said to God, 'We your servants wish to clear it (of weeds) and to dig the ground around it and to water it. If it does not then bear fruit, we will immediately remove its roots from the garden and plant another one in its place.' Have you not grasped that the fig-tree is the house of Israel? Truly, I say to you, when its boughs have sprouted at the end, then shall deceiving Christs come, and awaken hope (with the words): 'I am the Christ, who am (now) come into the world.' And when they shall see the wickedness of his (the false Messiah's) deeds, they shall turn away after them and deny him to whom our fathers gave praise, who crucified the first Christ and thereby sinned exceedingly. But this deceiver is not the Christ. And when they reject him, he will kill with the sword (dagger) and there shall be many martyrs. Then shall the boughs of the fig-tree, i.e., the house of Israel, sprout, and there shall be many martyrs by his hand: they shall be killed and become martyrs. Enoch and Elias will be sent to instruct them that this is the deceiver who must come into the world and do signs and wonders in order to deceive. And therefore shall they that are slain by his hand be martyrs and shall

be reckoned among the good and righteous martyrs who have pleased God in their life."

3 And he showed me in his right hand the souls of all (people) and on the palm of his right hand the image of that which shall be fulfilled at the last day; and how the righteous and the sinners shall be separated and how those will do who are upright in heart, and how the evil-doers will be rooted out for all eternity. We saw how the sinners wept in great distress and sorrow, until all who saw it with their eyes wept, whether righteous, or angels, or himself also. And I asked him and said, "Lord, allow me to speak your word concerning these sinners: 'It were better for them that they had not been created.' "[3] And the Savior answered and said "O Peter, why speak thus, 'that not to have been created were better for them'? You resist God. You would not have more compassion than he for his image, for he has created them and has brought them forth when they were not. And since you have seen the lamentation which sinners shall encounter in the last days, therefore your heart is saddened; but I will show you their works in which they have sinned against the Most High.

4 "Behold now what they shall experience in the last days, when the day of God comes. On the day of the decision of the judgment of God, all the children of mortals from the east unto the west shall be gathered before my Father who ever lives, and he will command hell to open its bars of steel and to give up all that is in it. And the beasts and the fowls shall he command to give back all flesh that they have devoured, since he desires that people should appear (again); for nothing perishes for God, and nothing is impossible with him, since all things are his. For all things (come to pass) on the day of decision, on the day of judgment, at the word of God, and as all things came to pass when he created the world and commanded all that is therein, and it was all done—so shall it

2 Mark 13:28–29.

3 Mark 14:21.

be in the last days; for everything is possible with God, and he says in the Scripture: 'Son of man, prophesy upon the several bones, and say to the bones—bone unto bone in joints, sinews, nerves, flesh and skin and hair thereon.[4] And soul and spirit shall the great Uriel give at the command of God. For him God has appointed over the resurrection of the dead on the day of judgment. Behold and consider the corns of wheat which are sown in the earth. As something dry and without a soul does a person sow (them) in the earth; and they live again, bear fruit, and the earth gives (them) back again as a pledge entrusted to it. And this which dies, which is sown as seed in the earth and shall become alive and be restored to life, is humanity. How much more shall God raise up on the day of decision those who believe in him and are chosen by him and for whom he made (the earth); and all this shall the earth give back on the day of decision, since it shall be judged with them, and the heaven with it.

5 "And these things shall come to pass in the day of judgment of those who have fallen away from faith in God and have committed sin: cataracts of fire shall be let loose; and obscurity and darkness shall come up and cover and veil the entire world, and the waters shall be changed and transformed into coals of fire, and all that is in it (the earth?) shall burn and the sea shall become fire; under the heaven there shall be a fierce fire that shall not be put out and it flows for the judgment of wrath. And the stars shall be melted by flames of fire, as if they had not been created, and the fastnesses of heaven shall pass away for want of water and become as though they had not been created. And the lightnings of heaven shall be no more and, by their enchantment, they shall alarm the world. And the spirits of the dead bodies shall be like to them and at the command of God will become fire. And as soon as the whole creation is dissolved, the people who are in the east shall flee to the west [and those in the west] to the east;

those that are in the south shall flee to the north and those in the [north to the] south, and everywhere will the wrath of the fearful fire overtake them; and an unquenchable flame shall drive them and bring them to the judgment of wrath in the stream of unquenchable fire which flows, flaming with fire, and when its waves separate one from another, seething, there shall be much gnashing of teeth among the children of mortals.

6 "And all will see how I come upon an eternal shining cloud, and the angels of God who will sit with me on the throne of my glory at the right hand of my heavenly Father. He will set a crown upon my head. As soon as the nations see it, they will weep, each nation for itself. And he shall command them to go into the river of fire, while the deeds of each individual one of them stand before them. [Recompense shall be given] to each according to his work. As for the elect who have done good, they will come to me and will not see death by devouring fire. But the evil creatures, the sinners and the hypocrites will stand in the depths of the darkness that passes not away, and their punishment is the fire, and angels bring forward their sins and prepare for them a place wherein they shall be punished for ever, each according to his offence. The angel of God, Uriel, brings the souls of those sinners who perished in the flood, and of all who dwell in all idols, in every molten image, in every love and in paintings, and of them that dwell on all hills and in stones and by the wayside, (whom) people call gods: they shall be burned with them (i.e., the objects in which they lodge) in eternal fire. After all of them, with their dwelling places, have been destroyed, they will be punished eternally.

7 "Then will men and women come to the place prepared for them. By their tongues with which they have blasphemed the way of righteousness will they be hung up. There is spread out for them unquenchable fire. . . .

"And behold again another place: this is a great pit filled, in which are those who have denied

---

4 Ezek 37:4–8.

righteousness; and angels of punishment visit (them) and here do they kindle upon them the fire of their punishment. And again two women: they are hung up by their neck and by their hair and are cast into the pit. These are they who plaited their hair, not to create beauty, but to turn to fornication, and that they might ensnare the souls of men to destruction. And the men who lay with them in fornication are hung by their thighs in that burning place, and they say to one another, 'We did not know that we would come into everlasting torture.'

"And the murderers and those who have made common cause with them are cast into the fire, in a place full of venomous beasts, and they are tormented without rest, as they feel their pains, and their worms are as numerous as a dark cloud. And the angel Ezrael will bring forth the souls of them that have been killed and they shall see the torment [of those who] killed [them] and shall say to one another, 'Righteousness and justice is the judgment of God. For we have indeed heard, but did not believe that we would come to this place of eternal judgment.'

8 "And near this flame there is a great and very deep pit and into it there flow all kinds of things from everywhere: judgment, horrifying things, and excretions. And the women (are) swallowed up (by this) up to their necks and are punished with great pain. These are they who have procured abortions and have ruined the work of God which he has created. Opposite them is another place where the children sit, but both alive, and they cry to God. And lightnings go forth from those children which pierce the eye of those who, by fornication, have brought about their destruction. Other men and women stand above them naked. And their children stand opposite to them in a place of delight. And they sigh and cry to God because of their parents, 'These are they who neglected and cursed and transgressed your commandment. They killed us and cursed the angel who created (us) and hung us up. And they withheld from us the light which you have appointed for all.' And the milk of the mothers

flows from their breasts and congeals and smells foul, and from it come forth beasts that devour flesh, which turn and torture them for ever with their husbands, because they forsook the commandment of God and killed their children. And the children shall be given to the angel Temlakos. And those who slew them will be tortured for ever, for God wills it to be so.

9 "Ezrael, the angel of wrath, brings men and women with the half of their bodies burning and casts them into a place of darkness, the hell of humans; and a spirit of wrath chastises them with all manner of chastisement, and a worm that never sleeps consumes their entrails. These are the persecutors and betrayers of my righteous ones.

"And near to those who live thus were other men and women who chew their tongues, and they are tormented with red hot irons and have their eyes burned. These are the slanderers and those who doubt my righteousness.

"Other men and women—whose deeds (were done) in deception—have their lips cut off and fire enters into their mouths and into their entrails. [These are those] who slew the martyrs by their lying.

"In another place situated near them, on the stone pillar of fire, and the pillar is sharper than swords—men and women who are clad in rags and filthy garments, and they are cast upon it, to suffer the judgment of unceasing torture. These are they which trusted in their riches and despised widows and the woman (with) orphans . . . in the sight of God.

10 "And into another place near by, saturated with filth, they throw men and women up to their knees. These are they who lent money and took usury.

"And other men and women thrust themselves down from a high place and return again and run, and demons drive them. These are the worshippers of idols, and they drive them to the end of their wits (the slope?) and they plunge down from there. And this they do continually and are tormented for ever. These are they who have cut their flesh as apostles of a man, and the women who were with them . . . and thus are the men who defiled themselves with one another in the fashion of women.

"And beside them . . . [an untranslatable word], and beneath them the angel Ezrael prepares a place of much fire, and all the golden and silver idols, all idols, the works of human hands, and what resembles the images of cats and lions, of reptiles and wild beasts, and the men and women who manufactured the images, shall be in chains of fire; they shall be chastised because of their error before them (the images) and this is their judgment for ever. And near them other men and women who burn in the flames of the judgment, whose torture is for ever. These are they who have forsaken the commandment of God and followed . . . (unknown word) of the devils.

11 "And another very high place . . . (some unintelligible words), the men and women who make a false step go rolling down to where the fear is. And again, while the (fire) that is prepared flows, they mount up and fall down again and continue their rolling. They shall be punished thus for ever. These are they who have not honored their father and mother, and of their own accord withdrew themselves from them. Therefore shall they be punished eternally. Furthermore the angel Ezrael brings children and maidens to show to them those who are punished. They will be punished with pain, with hanging up and with many wounds which flesh-eating birds inflict. These are they that have confidence in their sins, are not obedient to their parents, and do not follow the instruction of their fathers and do not honor those who are older than they. Beside them, maidens clad in darkness for raiment, and they shall be seriously punished and their flesh will be torn in pieces. These are they who retained not their virginity till they were given in marriage; they shall be punished with these tortures, while they feel them.

"And again other men and women who ceaselessly chew their tongues and are tormented with eternal fire. These are the slaves who were not obedient to their masters. This then is their judgment for ever.

12 "And near to this torment are blind and dumb men and women whose raiment is white. They are packed closely together and fall on coals of unquenchable fire. These are they who give alms and say, 'We are righteous before God,' while they have not striven for righteousness.

"The angel of God, Ezrael, allows them to come forth out of this fire and sets forth a judgment of decision (?). This then is their judgment. (And) a stream of fire flows and all those judged are drawn into the midst of the stream. And Uriel sets them down (there). And there are wheels of fire, and men and women hung thereon by the power of their whirling. Those in the pit burn. Now these are the sorcerers and sorceresses. These wheels (are) in all decision by fire without number (?).

13 "Then the angels brought my elect and righteous, who are perfect in all righteousness, bearing them on their hands, clothed with the garments of eternal life. They shall see (their desire) on those who hated them, when he punishes them. Torment for every one (is) forever according to his deeds. And all those who are in torment will say with one voice, 'Have mercy upon us, for now we know the judgment of God, which he declared to us beforehand, and we did not believe.' And the angel Tatirokos (= Tartarouchos) will come and chasten them with even greater torment and will say unto them, 'Now do you repent when there is no more time for repentance, and nothing of life remains.' And all shall say, 'Righteous is the judgment of God; for we have heard and perceived that his judgment is good, since we are punished according to our deeds.'

14 "Then will I give to my elect and righteous the baptism and the salvation for which they have besought me, in the field Akrosja (= Acherusia) which is called Aneslesleja (= Elysium). They shall adorn with flowers the portion of the righteous and I will go. . . . I will rejoice with them. I will cause the nations to enter into my eternal kingdom and show to them that eternal thing to which I have directed their hope, I and my heavenly Father. I have spoken it to you, Peter, and make it known to you. Go forth then and journey to the city in the west in the vineyard which I will tell you of . . . by the hand of my Son who is without sin, that his work . . . of destruction may be sanctified. But you are chosen in the hope which I have given to you. Spread my gospel throughout the whole world in peace! For there will be rejoicing (?) at the source of my word, the hope of life, and suddenly the world will be carried off."

57. The Apocalypse of Paul

In a well-known passage from 2 Corinthians 12, Paul claims that he had once been caught up into heaven to behold a vision of things that could not be uttered. A later Christian nonetheless decided to give utterance to these things, and the present apocalypse is the result. The book describes Paul's ascent into heaven to receive a revelation concerning the fate of individual souls after death. He observes souls who leave their bodies to appear before God, who knows every detail about their lives and metes out rewards or punishments accordingly. The vision continues with a narrative description of Paradise and a graphic portrayal of the torments of the damned, which parallel in many ways those found in the Apocalypse of Peter (see above).

The Apocalypse of Paul in its present form dates from the end of the fourth century, but it contains materials that were composed earlier, as they are apparently alluded to by Origen in the early third century. The portions excerpted here may be among the older portions of the book.

In the consulship of Theodosius Augustus the Younger and Cynegius, a certain nobleman was then living in Tarsus, in the house which was that of Saint Paul; an angel appeared in the night and revealed it to him, saying that he should open the foundations of the house and should publish what he found, but he thought that these things were dreams.

2 But the angel coming for the third time beat him and forced him to open the foundation.

And digging he found a marble box, inscribed on the sides; there was the revelation of Saint Paul, and his shoes in which he walked teaching the word of God. But he feared to open that box and brought it to the judge; when he had received it, the judge, because it was sealed with lead, sent it to the emperor Theodosius, fearing lest it might be something else; when the emperor had received it he opened it, and found the revelation of Saint Paul, a copy of which he sent to Jerusalem, and retained the original himself.

The Apocalypse of Paul, from *The Apocryphal New Testament*, ed. J. K. Elliott © Oxford University Press, 1993. Reprinted by permission of Oxford University Press.

3 While I was in the body in which I was snatched up to the third heaven, . . .

14 And I said to the angel, "I wish to see the souls of the just and of sinners, and to see in what manner they go out of the body." And the angel answered and said to me, "Look again upon the earth." And I looked and saw all the world, and people were as naught and growing weak; and I looked carefully and saw a certain man about to die, and the angel said to me, "This one whom you see is a just man." And I looked again and saw all his works, whatever he had done for the sake of God's name, and all his desires, both what he remembered, and what he did not remember; they all stood in his sight in the hour of need; and I saw the just man advance and find refreshment and confidence, and before he went out of the world the holy and the impious angels both attended; and I saw them all, but the impious found no place of habitation in him, but the holy angels took possession of his soul, guiding it till it went out of the body; and they roused the soul saying, "Soul, know the body you leave, for it is necessary that you should return to the same body on the day of the resurrection, that you may receive the things promised to all the just." Receiving therefore the soul from the body, they immediately kissed as if it were familiar to them, saying to it, "Be of good courage, for you have done the will of God while placed on earth." And there came to meet it the angel who watched it every day, and said to it, "Be of good courage, soul; I rejoice in you, because you have done the will of God on earth; for I related to God all your works just as they were." Similarly also the spirit proceeded to meet it and said, "Soul, fear not, nor be disturbed, until you come to a place which you have never known, but I will be a helper to you: for I found in you a place of refreshment in the time when I dwelt in you, while I was on earth." And his spirit strengthened it, and his angel received it, and led it into heaven; and an angel said, "Where are you running to, O soul, and do you dare to enter heaven? Wait and let us see if there is anything of ours in you; and behold

we find nothing in you. I see also your divine helper and angel, and the spirit is rejoicing along with you, because you have done the will of God on earth." And they led it along till it should worship in the sight of God. And when it had ceased, immediately Michael and all the army of angels, with one voice, adored the footstool of his feet and his doors, saying at the same time to the soul, "This is your God of all things, who made you in his own image and likeness." Moreover, the angel ran on ahead and pointed him out, saying, "God, remember his labors; for this is the soul, whose works I related to you, acting according to your judgment." And the spirit said likewise, "I am the spirit of vivification inspiring it; for I had refreshment in it, in the time when I dwelt in it, acting according to your judgment." And there came the voice of God and said, "In as much as this man did not grieve me, neither will I grieve him; as he had pity, I also will have pity. Let it therefore be handed over to Michael, the angel of the Covenant, and let him lead it into the Paradise of joy, that it may become coheir with all the saints." And after these things I heard the voices of a thousand thousand angels and archangels and cherubim and twenty-four elders, saying hymns and glorifying the Lord and crying, "You are just, O Lord, and just are your judgments, and there is no respect of persons with you, but you reward every one according to your judgment." And the angel answered and said to me, "Have you believed and known that whatever each one of you has done he sees in the hour of need?" And I said, "Yes, sir."

15 And he said to me, "Look again down on the earth, and watch the soul of an impious man going out of the body, which grieved the Lord day and night, saying, "I know nothing else in this world, I eat and drink, and enjoy what is in the world; for who is there who has descended into hell and, ascending, has declared to us that there is judgment there!' " And again I looked carefully, and saw all the scorn of the sinner, and all that he did, and they stood together before him in the hour of need; and it was done to him in that

hour, when he was led out of his body at the judgment, and he said, "It were better for me if I had not been born." And after these things, there came at the same time the holy angels and the evil angels, and the soul of the sinner saw both and the holy angels did not find a place in it. Moreover the evil angels cursed it; and when they had drawn it out of the body the angels admonished it a third time, saying, "O wretched soul, look upon your flesh from which you have come out; for is it necessary that you should return to your flesh in the day of resurrection, that you may receive what is the due for your sins and your impieties."

16 And when they had led it forth the guardian angel preceded it, and said to it. "O wretched soul, I am the angel belonging to you, relating daily to the Lord your evil works, whatever you did by night or day; and if it were in my power, not for one day would I minister to you, but none of these things was I able to do: the judge is full of pity and just, and he himself commanded us that we should not cease to minister to the soul till you should repent, but you have lost the time of repentance. I have become a stranger to you and you to me. Let us go on then to the just judge; I will not dismiss you before I know from today I am to be a stranger to you." And the spirit afflicted it, and the angel troubled it. When they had arrived at the powers, when it started to enter heaven, a burden was imposed upon it, above all other burden: error and oblivion and murmuring met it, and the spirit of fornication, and the rest of the powers, and said to it, "Where are you going, wretched soul, and do you dare to rush into heaven? Hold, that we may see if we have our qualities in you, since we do not see that you have a holy helper." And after that I heard voices in the height of heaven saying, "Present that wretched soul to God, so it may know that it is God whom it despised." When, therefore, it had entered heaven all the angels saw it; a thousand thousand exclaimed with one voice, all saying, "Woe to you, wretched soul, for the sake of your works which you did on earth; what answer are you about to

give to God when you have approached to adore him?" The angel who was with it answered and said, "Weep with me, my beloved, for I have not found rest in this soul." And the angels answered him and said, "Let such a soul be taken away from our midst, for from the time it entered the stink of it crosses to us angels." And after these things it was presented, that it might worship in the sight of God, and an angel of God showed it God who made it after his own image and likeness. Moreover its angel ran before it saying, "Lord God Almighty, I am the angel of this soul, whose works I presented to you day and night, not acting in accordance with your judgment." And the spirit likewise said, "I am the spirit who dwelt in it from the time it was made; in itself I know it, and it has not followed my will; judge it, Lord, according to your judgment." And there came the voice of God to it and said, "Where is your fruit which you have made worthy of the goods which you have received? Have I put a distance of one day between you and the just person? Did I not make the sun to arise upon you as upon the just?" But the soul was silent, having nothing to answer, and again there came a voice saying, "Just is the judgment of God, and there is no respect of persons with God, for whoever shall have done mercy, on him shall he have mercy, and whoever shall not have been merciful, neither shall God pity him. Let it therefore be handed over to the angel Tartaruchus, who is set over the punishments, and let him cast it into outer darkness, where there is weeping and gnashing of teeth, and let it be there till the great day of judgment." And after these things I heard the voice of angels and archangels saying, "You are just, Lord, and your judgment is just."

17 And again I saw and, behold, a soul which was led forward by two angels, weeping and saying, "Have pity on me, just God, God the judge, for today it is seven days since I went out of my body, and I was handed over to these two angels, and they brought me to those places which I had never seen." And God, the just judge, said to it, "What have you done? For you never showed mercy, therefore you were handed over to such angels as have no mercy, and because you did no right, so neither did they act compassionately with you in your hour of need. Confess your sins which you committed when placed in the world." And it answered and said, "Lord, I did not sin." And the Lord, the just Lord, was angered in fury when it said, "I did not sin," because it lied; and God said, "Do you think you are still in the world where any one of you, sinning, may conceal and hide his sin from his neighbor? Here nothing whatever shall be hidden, for when the souls come to worship in sight of the throne both the good works and the sins of each one are made manifest." And hearing these things the soul was silent, having no answer. And I heard the Lord God, the just judge, again saying, "Come, angel of this soul, and stand in the midst." And the angel of the sinful soul came, having in his hands a document, and said, "These, Lord, in my hands, are all the sins of this soul from its youth till today, from the tenth year of its birth; and if you command, Lord, will also relate its acts from the beginning of its fifteenth year." And the Lord God, the just judge, said, "I say to you, angel, I do not expect of you an account of it since it began to be fifteen years old, but state its sins for five years before it died and before it came hither." And again God, the just judge, said, "For by myself I swear, and by my holy angels, and by my virtue, that if it had repented five years before it died, on account of a conversion one year old, oblivion would now be thrown over all the evils which it sinned before, and it would have indulgence and remission of sins; now indeed it shall perish." And the angel of the sinful soul answered and said, "Lord, command that angel to exhibit those souls."

18 And in that same hour the souls were exhibited in the midst, and the soul of the sinner knew them; and the Lord said to the soul of the sinner, "I say to you, soul, confess your work which you wrought in these souls whom you see, when they were in the world." And it answered and said, "Lord, it is not yet a full year since I slew this one and poured his blood upon the ground,

and with another I committed fornication; not only this, but I also greatly harmed her in taking away her goods." And the Lord God, the just judge, said, "Did you not know that if someone does violence to another and the person who sustains the violence dies first, he is kept in this place until the one who was committed the offence dies, and then both stand in the presence of the judge, and now each receives according to his deed." And I heard a voice of one saying, "Let that soul be delivered into the hands of Tartarus, and led down into hell; he shall lead it into the lower prison, and it shall be put in torments and left there till the great day of judgment." And again I heard a thousand thousand angels saying hymns to the Lord, and crying, "You are just, O Lord, and just are your judgments."

19 The angel answered and said to me, "Have you perceived all these things?" And I said, "Yes, sir." And he said to me, "Follow me again, and I will take you, and show you the places of the just." And I followed the angel, and he raised me to the third heaven and placed me at the entry of the door; and looking, I saw that the door was of gold, and two columns of gold above it full of golden letters, and the angel turned again to me and said, "Blessed are you if you enter through these doors, for it is not permitted for any to enter except those who have goodness and purity of body in all things. . . ."

22 And I looked around upon that land, and I saw a river flowing with milk and honey, and there were trees planted by the bank of that river, full of fruit; moreover, each single tree bore twelve fruits in the year, having various and diverse fruits; and I saw the created things which are in that place and all the work of God, and I saw there palms of twenty cubits, but others of ten cubits; and that land was seven times brighter than silver. And there were trees full of fruits from the roots to the highest branches, of ten thousand fruits of palms upon ten thousand fruits. The grapevines had ten thousand plants. Moreover in

the single vines there were ten thousand thousand bunches and in each of these a thousand single grapes; moreover these single trees bore a thousand fruits. And I said to the angel, "Why does each tree bear a thousand fruits?" The angel answered and said to me, "Because the Lord God gives an abounding profusion of gifts to the worthy and because they of their own will afflicted themselves when they were placed in the world doing all things on account of his holy name." And again I said to the angel, "Sir, are these the only promises which the Most Holy God makes?" And he answered and said to me, "No! There are seven times greater than these. But I say to you that when the just go out of the body they shall see the promises and the good things which God has prepared for them. Till then, they shall sigh and lament, saying, "Have we uttered any word from our mouth to grieve our neighbor even on one day?' " I asked and said again, "Are these alone the promises of God?" And the angel answered and said to me, "These whom you now see are the souls of the married and those who kept the chastity of their nuptials, controlling themselves. But to the virgins and those who hunger and thirst after righteousness and those who afflicted themselves for the sake of the name of God, God will give seven times greater than these, which I shall now show you.". . .

26 Again he led me where there is a river of milk, and I saw in that place all the infants whom Herod slew because of the name of Christ, and they greeted me, and the angel said to me, "All who keep their chastity and purity, when they have come out of the body, after they adore the Lord God are delivered to Michael and are led to the infants, and they greet them, saying that they are our brothers and friends and members; among them they shall inherit the promises of God."

27 Again he took me up and brought me to the north of the city and led me where there was a river of wine, and there I saw Abraham and Isaac and Jacob, Lot and Job and other

saints, and they greeted me; and I asked and said, "What is this place, my lord?" The angel answered and said to me, "All who have given hospitality to strangers when they go out of the world first adore the Lord God, and are delivered to Michael and by this route are led into the city, and all the just greet them as son and brother, and say to them, 'Because you have observed humanity and helped pilgrims, come, have an inheritance in the city of the Lord our God: every righteous person shall receive good things of God in the city, according to his own action.' "

28 And again he carried me near the river of oil on the east of the city. And I saw there men rejoicing and singing psalms, and I said, "Who are those, my lord?" And the angel said to me, "These are they who devoted themselves to God with their whole heart and had no pride in themselves. For all those who rejoice in the Lord God and sing psalms to the Lord with their whole heart are here led into this city. . . ."

31 When he had ceased speaking to me, he led me outside the city through the midst of the trees and far from the places of the land of the good, and put me across the river of milk and honey; and after that he led me over the ocean which supports the foundations of heaven.

The angel answered and said to me, "Do you understand why you go hence?" And I said, "Yes, sir." And he said to me, "Come and follow me, and I will show you the souls of the godless and sinners, that you may know what manner of place it is." And I went with the angel, and he carried me towards the setting of the sun, and I saw the beginning of heaven founded on a great river of water, and I asked, "What is this river of water?" And he said to me, "This is the ocean which surrounds all the earth." And when I was at the outer limit of the ocean I looked, and there was no light in that place, but darkness and sorrow and sadness; and I sighed.

And I saw there a river boiling with fire, and in it a multitude of men and women immersed up to the knees, and other men up to the navel, others even up to the lips, others up to the hair. And I asked the angel and said, "Sir, who are those in the fiery river?" And the angel answered and said to me, "They are neither hot nor cold, because they were found neither in the number of the just nor in the number of the godless. For those spent the time of their life on earth passing some days in prayer, but others in sins and fornications, until their death." And I asked him and said, "Who are these, sir, immersed up to their knees in fire?" He answered and said to me, "These are they who when they have gone out of church occupy themselves with idle disputes. Those who are immersed up to the navel are those who, when they have taken the body and blood of Christ, go and fornicate and do not cease from their sins till they die. Those who are immersed up to the lips are those who slander each other when they assemble in the church of God; those up to the eyebrows are those who nod to each other and plot spite against their neighbor."

32 And I saw to the north a place of various and diverse punishments full of men and women, and a river of fire ran down into it. I observed and I saw very deep pits and in them several souls together, and the depth of that place was about three thousand cubits, and I saw them groaning and weeping and saying, "Have pity on us, O Lord!", and no one had pity on them. And I asked the angel and said, "Who are these, sir?" And the angel answered and said to me, "These are they who did not hope in the Lord, that they would be able to have him as their helper." And I asked and said, "Sir, if these souls remain for thirty or forty generations thus one upon another, I believe the pits would not hold them unless they were dug deeper." And he said to me, "The Abyss has no measure, for beneath it there stretches down below that which is below it; and so it is that if perchance anyone should take a stone and throw it into a very deep well after many hours it would reach the bottom, such is the abyss. For when the souls are thrown in there, they hardly reach the bottom in fifty years."

33 When I heard this, I wept and groaned over the human race. The angel answered and said to me, "Why do you weep? Are you more merciful than God? For though God is good, he knows that there are punishments, and he patiently bears with the human race, allowing each one to do his own will in the time in which he dwells on the earth."

34 I observed the fiery river and saw there a man being tortured by Tartaruchian angels having in their hands an iron instrument with three hooks with which they pierced the bowels of that old man; and I asked the angel and said, "Sir, who is that old man on whom such torments are imposed?" And the angel answered and said to me, "He whom you see was a presbyter who did not perform his ministry well: when he had been eating and drinking and committing fornication he offered the host to the Lord at his holy altar."

35 And I saw not far away another old man led on by evil angels running with speed, and they pushed him into the fire up to his knees, and they struck him with stones and wounded his face like a storm and did not allow him to say, "Have pity on me!" And I asked the angel, and he said to me, "He whom you see was a bishop and did not perform his episcopate well, who indeed accepted the great name but did not enter into the witness of him who gave him the name all his life, seeing that he did not give judgment and did not pity widows and orphans, but now he receives retribution according to his iniquity and his works."

36 And I saw another man in the fiery river up to his knees. His hands were stretched out and bloody, and worms proceeded from his mouth and nostrils, and he was groaning and weeping, and crying he said, "Have pity on me! For I am hurt more than the rest who are in this punishment." And I asked, "Sir, who is this?" And he said to me, "This man whom you see was a deacon who devoured the oblations and committed fornication and did not do right in the sight of God; for this cause he unceasingly pays this penalty."

And I looked closely and saw alongside of him another man, whom they delivered up with haste and cast into the fiery river, and he was in it up to the knees; and the angel who was set over the punishments came with a great fiery razor, and with it he cut the lips of that man and the tongue likewise. And sighing, I lamented and asked, "Who is that, sir?" And he said to me, "He whom you see was a reader and read to the people, but he himself did not keep the precepts of God; now he also pays the proper penalty."

37 And I saw another multitude of pits in the same place, and in the midst of it a river full with a multitude of men and women, and worms consumed them. But I lamented, and sighing asked the angel and said, "Sir, who are these?" And he said to me, "These are those who exacted interest on interest and trusted in their riches and did not hope in God that he was their helper."

And after that I looked and saw another place, very narrow, and it was like a wall, and fire round about it. And I saw inside men and women gnawing their tongues, and I asked, "Sir, who are these?" And he said to me, "These are they who in church disparage the Word of God, not attending to it, but as it were making naught of God and his angels; for that reason they now likewise pay the proper penalty."

38 And I observed and saw another pool in the pit and its appearance was like blood, and I asked and said, "Sir, what is this place?" And he said to me, "Into that pit stream all the punishments." And I saw men and women immersed up to the lips, and I asked, "Sir, who are these?" And he said to me, "These are the magicians who prepared for men and women evil magic arts and did not cease till they died."

And again I saw men and women with very black faces in a pit of fire, and I sighed and lamented and asked, "Sir, who are these?" And he said to me, "These are fornicators and adulterers who

committed adultery, having wives of their own; likewise also the women committed adultery, having husbands of their own; therefore they unceasingly suffer penalties."

39 And I saw there girls in black raiment, and four terrifying angels having in their hands burning chains, and they put them on the necks of the girls and led them into darkness; and I, again weeping, asked the angel, "Who are these, sir?" And he said to me, "These are they who, when they were virgins, defiled their virginity unknown to their parents; for which cause they unceasingly pay the proper penalties."

And again I observed there men and women with hands cut and their feet placed naked in a place of ice and snow, and worms devoured them. Seeing them I lamented and asked, "Sir, who are these?" And he said to me, "These are they who harmed orphans and widows and the poor, and did not hope in the Lord, for which cause they unceasingly pay the proper penalties."

And I observed and saw others hanging over a channel of water, and their tongues were very dry, and many fruits were placed in their sight, and they were not permitted to take of them, and I asked, "Sir, who are these?" And he said to me, "These are they who broke their fast before the appointed hour; for this cause they unceasingly pay these penalties."

And I saw other men and women hanging by their eyebrows and their hair, and a fiery river drew them, and I said, "Who are these, sir?" And he said to me, "These are they who join themselves not to their own husbands and wives but to whores, and therefore they unceasingly pay the proper penalties."

And I saw other men and women covered with dust, and their countenance was like blood, and they were in a pit of pitch and sulphur running in a fiery river, and I asked, "Sir, who are these?" And he said to me, "These are they who committed the iniquity of Sodom and Gomorrah, the male with the male, for which reason they unceasingly pay the penalties.". . .

58. The Ascension of Isaiah

The Ascension of Isaiah is a highly unusual Christian text, in that it is written about a great prophet of the Old Testament rather than a Christian saint. Parts of the text, in fact, claim to be written by Isaiah himself. The first portion of the account, which is not cited here, describes the (legendary) martyrdom of Isaiah and includes a description of Isaiah's prophecy of the coming of Christ. The second portion (given here) is an apocalypse in which Isaiah, prior to his martyrdom, is said to ascend through the seven heavens, observing the angels inhabiting each level, until he reaches the highest heaven, the realm of God himself.

From this exalted sphere, Isaiah observes and describes the descent of Christ—who is called 'the Beloved'—down through each of the heavenly realms. At each level Christ takes on an angelic disguise so as not to be recognized by the rulers of these spheres and provides the passwords that he needs in order to be allowed to pass by their realm. Once he reaches the earth, he experiences his incarnation and crucifixion. He is then able to re-ascend to the realm of God—to the surprise of the angelic beings of the lower heavens who never suspected that he had previously passed their way.

As with most apocalypses, it is difficult to date this account with any certainty, but it appears to have been written in the early or mid–second century.

7 Now the vision which he had seen Isaiah narrated to Hezekiah, his son Jasub, Micaiah and the rest of the prophets saying,

2 "In that moment when I was prophesying according to things heard by you, I saw a sublime angel and he was not like the glory of the angels which I was accustomed [already] to see, but he possessed great glory and honour, so that I cannot describe the glory of this angel.

3 And he took hold of me by my hand and then I saw (*Slav*: he led me on high); and I said to him, 'Who art thou, and what is thy name, and wherefore dost thou lead me on high?', for strength was granted to me to speak with him.

4 And he said to me: 'When I have led thee on high by degrees and have shown thee the vision for which I have been sent to thee, then wilt thou know who I am,

5 but my name thou shalt not find out, since thou must return to this thy body. But whither I would raise thee on high, thou shalt see, since for this purpose I have been sent.'

6 And I rejoiced because he spoke amiably with me.

7 And he said to me: 'Dost thou rejoice because I have spoken amiably to thee?'; and he went on, 'Thou wilt see one who is greater than I, who will speak amiably and peaceably with thee;

8 and his Father also who is greater wilt thou see, because for this purpose have I been sent from the seventh heaven to explain all these things for thee.'

The Ascension of Isaiah, reproduced from William Schneemelcher, ed., *New Testament Apocrypha*, revised edition, vol.2. Cambridge/Luisville: Lutterworth Press/Westminster John Knox, 1991. Used with permission of Westminster John Knox Press.

9 And we ascended to the firmament, I and he, and there I saw Sammael and his hosts, and a great struggle was taking place against him, and the angels of Satan were envious of one another.

10 And as it is above, so is it also on the earth, for the likeness of that which is in the firmament is also on the earth.

11 And I said to the angel. '(What is this struggle) and what is this envy?'

12 And he said to me, 'So it has been, since this world began until now, and this struggle [will continue] till he whom thou shalt see shall come and destroy him [Satan].'

13 And after this he brought me up above the firmament, which is the (first) heaven.

14 And there I saw a throne in the midst, and on the right and on the left of it were angels.

15 And (the angels on the left) were not like the angels who stood on the right, for those on the right possessed a greater glory, and they all praised with one voice; and there was a throne in the midst; and likewise those on the left sang praises after them, but their voice was not such as the voice of those on the right, nor their praise like their praise.

16 And I asked the angel who led me and said unto him, 'To whom is this praise given?'

17 And he said to me, '[It is] for the praise (of him who is in) the seventh heaven, for him who rests [in] eternity among his saints, and for his Beloved, whence I have been sent unto thee. (Thither is it sent).'

18 And again he caused me to ascend to the second heaven, and the height of that heaven is the same as from heaven to earth (and to the firmament).

19 And (I saw there as) in the first heaven, angels on the right and on the left and a throne in the midst and the praise of the angels in the second heaven; and he who sat on the throne in the second heaven had a greater glory than all [the rest].

20 And there was much [more] glory in the second heaven, and their praise was not like the praise of those in the first heaven.

21 And I fell on my face to worship him, and the angel who conducted me did not allow me, but

said to me, 'Worship neither angel nor throne which belongs to the six heavens—for this reason was I sent to conduct thee—till I tell thee in the seventh heaven.

22 For above all the heavens and their angels is thy throne set, and thy garments and thy crown which thou shalt see.'

23 And I rejoiced greatly that those who love the Most High and his Beloved will at their end ascend thither by the angel of the Holy Spirit.

24 And he brought me up to the third heaven, and in like manner I saw those on the right and on the left, and there stood there also a throne in the midst but the remembrance of this world is not known there.

25 And I said to the angel who was with me, for the glory of my countenance was being transformed as I ascended from heaven to heaven, 'Nothing of the vanity of that world is here named.'

26 And he answered and said to me, 'Nothing is named by reason of its weakness, and nothing is hidden here [of what] took place.'

27 And I desired to find out how it is known, but he answered and said to me, 'When I have brought thee to the seventh heaven whence I was sent, high above these, then shalt thou know that nothing is hidden from the thrones and from those who dwell in the heavens and from the angels.' And great were the praises they sang and the glory of him who sat on the throne, and the angels on the right and on the left possessed a greater glory than those in the heaven beneath them.

28 And again he carried me upwards to the fourth heaven, and the distance from the third heaven to the fourth is greater than that from earth to the firmament.

29 And there once more I saw those on the right and on the left, and he who sat on the throne was in the midst, and here also they sang their praises.

30 And the praise and glory of the angels on the right was greater than that of those on the left,

31 and again the glory of him who sat on the throne was greater than that of the angels on the right, and their glory was greater than that of those who were below.

32 And he brought me up to the fifth heaven.

33 And again I saw those on the right and those on the left and him who sat on the throne, possessing greater glory than those in the fourth heaven.

34 And the glory of those on the right surpassed that of those on the left.

35 And the glory of him who sat on the throne was greater than the glory of the angels on the right,

36 and their praises were more glorious than those in the fourth heaven.

37 And I praised the unnamed one and the only one, who dwells in the heavens, whose name is unfathomable for all flesh, who has bestowed such a glory from heaven to heaven, who makes great the glory of the angels and makes greater the glory of him who sits on the throne.

8 And again he raised me up into the air of the sixth heaven, and I saw there a glory such as I had not seen in the fifth heaven,

2 as I ascended, namely, angels in greater glory;

3 and there was a holy and wonderful song of praise there.

4 And I said to the angel who conducted me, 'What is this that I see, my Lord?'

5 And he said, 'I am not thy Lord, but thy companion.'

6 And once more I asked him saying, 'Why are the angels not [any longer] in two groups?'

7 And he said, 'From the sixth heaven and upwards there are no longer any angels on the left, nor is there a throne in the midst, but (they receive their arrangement) from the power of the seventh heaven, where the unnamed one dwells and his Elect one whose name is unfathomable and cannot be known by the whole heaven,

8 for it is he alone to whose voice all the heavens and thrones give answer. Thus I have been empowered and sent to bring thee up here to see the glory,

9 and to see the Lord of all those heavens and these thrones

10 being transformed till he comes to your image and likeness.

11 But I say to thee, Isaiah, that no one who has to return to a body in this world has ascended or seen or perceived what thou hast perceived and what thou shalt [yet] see;

12 for it is appointed unto thee in the lot of the Lord (the lot of [the cross of] wood,) to come hither (, and from hence comes the power of the sixth heaven and the air).'

13 And I extolled my Lord with praise that I through his lot should come hither.

14 And he said, 'Hear then this from thy companion: when thou by the will of God hast ascended here from the body as a spirit, then shalt thou receive the garment which thou shalt see, and the other garments as well, numbered and stored up, thou shalt see;

15 and then shalt thou resemble the angels in the seventh heaven.'

16 And he brought me up into the sixth heaven and there was no one on the left and no throne in the midst, but all had one appearance and their song of praise was the same. And (power) was given to me and I sang praise with them, and that angel also, and our praise was like theirs.

18 And there they all named the primal Father and his Beloved, Christ, and the Holy Spirit, all with one voice,

19 but it was not like the voice of the angels in the fifth heaven,

20 nor like their speech, but another voice resounded there, and there was much light there.

21 And then, when I was in the sixth heaven, I considered that light which I had seen in the five heavens as darkness.

22 And I rejoiced and praised him who has bestowed such light on those who wait for his promise.

23 And I besought the angel who conducted me that he would no more take me back to the world of the flesh.

24 I say to you, Hezekiah and Jasub my son and Micaiah, that there is much darkness here.

25 And the angel who conducted me perceived what I thought and said, 'If thou dost rejoice already in this light, how much wilt thou rejoice when, in the seventh heaven, thou seest that light where God and his Beloved are, whence I have been sent, (who in the world will be called "Son".

26 Not yet is he revealed who shall be in this corrupted world), and the garments, thrones and crowns which are laid up for the righteous, for those who believe in that Lord who shall descend in your form. For the light there is great and wonderful.

27 As far as thy [wish] not to return to the flesh is concerned, thy days are not yet fulfilled that thou mayest come here.'

28 When I heard that, I was sad; but he said, 'Do not be sad.'

9 And he conveyed me into the air of the seventh heaven and I heard again a voice saying, 'How far shall he ascend who dwells among aliens?' And I was afraid and began to tremble.

2 And when I trembled, behold, there came another voice, sent forth thence, and said, 'It is permitted to the holy Isaiah to ascend hither, for his garment is here.'

3 And I asked the angel who was with me and said, 'Who is he who forbade me, and who is this who has permitted me to ascend?'

4 And he said unto me, 'He who forbade thee is he who [is placed] over the praise of the sixth heaven,

5 and he who gave permission is thy Lord, God, the Lord Christ, who will be called Jesus on earth, but his name thou canst not hear till thou hast ascended out of thy body.'

6 And he caused me to ascend into the seventh heaven and I saw there a wonderful light and angels without number.

7 And there I saw all the righteous from Adam.

8 And I saw there the holy Abel and all the righteous.

9 And there I saw Enoch and all who were with him, stripped of the garment of the flesh, and I saw them in their higher garments, and they were like the angels who stand there in great glory.

10 But they did not sit on their thrones, nor were their crowns of glory on their heads.

11 And I asked the angel who was with me, 'How is it that they have received their garments, but are without their thrones and their crowns?'

12 And he said to me, 'Crowns and thrones of glory have they not yet received, [but] only when the Beloved shall descend in the form in which you will see him descend; –

13 that is to say, in the last days the Lord, who will be called Christ, will descend into the world. – Nevertheless, they see the thrones and know to whom they shall belong and to whom the crowns shall belong after he has descended and become like you in appearance, and it will be thought that he is flesh and a man.

14 And the god of that world will stretch forth his hand against the Son, and they will lay hands on him and crucify him on a tree, without knowing who he is.

15 So his descent, as thou wilt see, is hidden from the heavens so that it remains unperceived who he is.

16 And when he has made spoil of the angel of death, he will arise on the third day and will remain in that world 545 days;

17 and then many of the righteous will ascend with him, whose spirits do not receive their garments till the Lord Christ ascends and they ascend with him.

18 Then indeed will they receive (their garments and) thrones and crowns when he shall have ascended into the seventh heaven.'

19 And I said unto him, 'As I asked thee in the third heaven,

20 show me (*Ethiop.* instead: And he said to me) how what happens in the world becomes known here.'

21 And while I was still talking with him, behold, [there came] one of the angels who stood by, more glorious than the glory of that angel who had brought me up from the world,

22 and he showed me books (but not like books of this world) and he opened them and the books were written, but not like books of this world. And he gave them to me and I read them and behold, the deeds of the children of Israel were recorded therein, and the deeds of those whom I know (*Eth.*: thou knowest) not (*missing in Eth.*), my son Jasub.

23 And I said, 'Truly there is nothing hidden in the seventh heaven of that which happens in the world.'

24 And I saw there many garments stored up, and many thrones and many crowns,

25 and I said to the angel who conducted me, 'To whom do these garments and thrones and crowns belong?'

26 And he said to me, 'These garments shall many from that world receive, if they believe on the words of that one who, as I have told thee, shall be named, and observe them and believe therein, and believe in his cross. For them are these laid up.'

27 And I saw one standing whose glory surpassed that of all, and his glory was great and wonderful.

28 And after I had beheld him, all the righteous whom I had seen and all the angels whom I had seen came unto him, and Adam, Abel and Seth and all the righteous approached first, worshipped him and praised him, all with one voice, and I also sang praise with them, and my song of praise was like theirs.

29 Then all the angels drew near and worshipped and sang praise.

30 And [again] I was transformed (*Eth.*: he transformed) and became like an angel

31 Then the angel who conducted me said to me, 'Worship this one'; so I worshipped and praised.

32 And the angel said to me, 'This is the Lord of all glory whom thou hast seen.'

33 And while he [the angel] was still speaking, I saw another glorious one, like to him, and the righteous drew near to him, worshipped and sang praise, and I too sang praise with them, but my glory was not transformed in accordance with their appearance.

34 And thereupon the angels approached and worshipped.

35 And I saw the Lord and the second angel, and they were standing; but the second one whom I saw was on the left of my Lord.

36 And I asked, 'Who is this?', and he said to me, 'Worship him, for this is the angel of the holy Spirit, who speaks (*Eth.*: has spoken) through thee and the rest of the righteous.'

37 And I beheld the great glory, for the eyes of my spirit were open, and I was not thereafter able to see either the angel who was with me or all the angels whom I had seen worshipping my Lord.

38 But I saw the righteous beholding with great power the glory of that One.

39 So my Lord drew near to me, and the angel of the Spirit, and said, 'Behold, now it is granted to thee to behold God, and on thy account is power given to the angel with thee.'

40 And I saw how my Lord worshipped, and the angel of the Holy Spirit, and how both together praised God.

41 Thereupon all the righteous drew near and worshipped,

42 and the angels approached and worshipped, and all the angels sang praise.

10 And thereupon I heard the voices and the hymns of praise which I had heard ascending in each of the six heavens (and they were audible) here.

2 And they were all directed to the glorious One whose glory I could not see.

3 And I myself heard and saw the praise for him.

4 And the Lord and the angel of the spirit beheld all and heard all;

5 and all the praises which were sent forth from the six heavens were not only heard but were also visible.

6 And I heard the angel who led me, how he said, 'This is the Most High of the High ones, who dwells in the holy world and rests with the holy ones, who will be called by the holy Spirit, through the mouth of the righteous, the Father of the Lord.'

7 And I heard the words of the Most High, the Father of my Lord, as he spoke to my Lord Christ who shall be called Jesus:

8 'Go and descend through all the heavens; descend to the firmament and to that world, even to the angel in the realm of the dead; but to Hell thou shalt not go.

9 And thou shalt become like to the form of all who are in the five heavens;

10 and with carefulness thou shalt resemble the form of the angels of the firmament and the angels also who are in the realm of the dead.

11 And none of the angels of this world will know that thou, along with me, art the Lord of the seven heavens and of their angels.

12 And they will not know that thou art mine till with the voice of heaven I have summoned their angels and their lights, and the mighty voice be made to resound to the sixth heaven, that thou mayest judge and destroy the prince and his angels and the gods of this world and the world which is ruled by them,

13 for they have denied me and said "We alone are, and there is none beside us."

14 And afterwards thou wilt ascend from the angels of death to thy place, and thou wilt not be transformed in each heaven, but in glory thou wilt ascend and sit on my right hand.

15 And the princes and powers of this world will worship thee.'

16 Thus I heard the great glory give command to my Lord.

17 Then I saw that my Lord went forth from the seventh heaven to the sixth heaven.

18 And the angel who conducted me (from this world was with me and) said, 'Attend, Isaiah, and behold, that thou mayest see the transformation of the Lord and his descent.'

19 And I beheld and when the angels who are in the sixth heaven saw him they praised and extolled him, for he had not yet been transformed into the form of the angels there, and they praised him, and I also praised with them.

20 And I saw how he descended into the fifth heaven, and in the fifth heaven took the appearance of the angels there, and they did not praise him, for his appearance was like theirs.

21 And immediately he descended into the fourth heaven and took the form of the angels there;

22 and when they saw him, they did not praise and laud him, for his appearance was as theirs.

23 And again I beheld how he descended into the third heaven and took the form of the angels of the third heaven.

24 And the guardians of the gate of this heaven demanded the pass-word and the Lord gave it to them in order that he should not be recognised, and when they saw him they did not praise and extol him, for his appearance was as theirs.

25 And again I beheld how he descended into the second heaven, and again he gave the pass-word there, for the door-keepers demanded it and the Lord gave it.

26 And I saw how he took the form of the angels in the second heaven; they saw him but did not praise him, since his form was like theirs.

27 And again I beheld how he descended into the first heaven and also gave the pass-word to the door-keepers there, and took the form of the angels who are on the left of that throne; and they did not praise or laud him, for his appearance was as theirs.

28 But no one asked me, on account of the angel who conducted me.

29 And again he descended into the firmament where the prince of this world dwells, and he gave the pass-word to those on the left, and his form was like theirs, and they did not praise him there, but struggled with one another in envy, for there the power of evil rules, and envying about trifles.

30 And I beheld, how he descended and became like the angels of the air and was like one of them.

31 And he gave no pass-word for they were plundering and doing violence to one another.

11 And after this, I beheld, and the angel who talked with me and conducted me said to me, 'Attend, Isaiah, son of Amoz, because for this purpose have I been sent from God.'

2 And I saw of the family of David the prophet a *woman named Mary*, who was a *virgin, and betrothed to a man called Joseph,* a carpenter, and he also was of the seed and family of the righteous David, of Bethlehem in Judah.

3 And he came to his portion. And *when she was betrothed, it was found that she was with child, and Joseph, the carpenter, wished to put her away.*

4 But the *angel* of the Spirit *appeared* in this world, and after that Joseph did not put Mary away, but kept her, but he did not reveal the matter to anyone.

5 And he did not approach Mary, but kept her as a holy virgin, although she was with child.

6 And he did not [yet] live with her for two months.

7 And after two months, when Joseph was in his house, and his wife Mary, but both alone,

8 it came to pass, while they were alone, that Mary straightway beheld with her eyes and saw a small child, and she was amazed.

9 And when her amazement wore off, her womb was found as it was before she was with child.

10 And when her husband Joseph said to her, 'What made thee amazed?' his eyes were opened and he saw the child and praised God, that the Lord had come to his portion.

11 And a voice came to them: 'Tell this vision to no one.'

12 And the report was noised abroad in Bethlehem.

13 Some said, 'The virgin Mary has given birth before she was married two months',

14 and many said, 'She has not given birth: the midwife has not gone up [to her] and we have heard no cries of pain.' And they were all in the dark concerning him, and they all knew of him, but no one knew whence he was.

15 And they took him and came *to Nazareth* in *Galilee.*

16 And I saw, O Hezekiah and Jasub my son, and declare before the other prophets who stand [here] that this was hidden from all the heavens and all the princes and every god of this world.

17 And I saw: in Nazareth he sucked the breast like a baby, as was customary, so that he would not be recognised.

18 And when he grew up he performed great signs and wonders in the land of Israel and in Jerusalem.

19 And after this the adversary envied him and roused the children of Israel against him, not knowing who he was, and they delivered him to the king and crucified him, and he descended to the angel [of the underworld].

20 In Jerusalem indeed I saw how he was crucified on the tree,

21 and how he was raised after three days and remained [still many] days.

22 And the angel who conducted me said to me, 'Attend, Isaiah.' And I saw how he sent out his twelve apostles and ascended.

23 And I saw him and he was in the firmament, but he had not changed to their form, and all the angels of the firmament and the Satan saw him, and they worshipped him.

24 And great sorrow was occasioned there, while they said, 'How did our Lord descend in our midst and we perceived not the glory (which was upon him) which, as we see, was found on him from the sixth heaven?'

25 And he ascended into the second heaven and was not changed, but all the angels on the right and on the left and the throne in the midst

26 worshipped him and praised him saying 'How did our Lord remain hidden from us when he descended, and we perceived not?'

27 And in like manner he ascended to the third heaven and they sang praise and spoke in the same way.

28 And in the fourth and the fifth heavens they spoke exactly in the same manner,

29 there was rather one song of praise and [even] after that he was not changed.

30 And I saw how he ascended to the sixth heaven, and they worshipped him and praised him,

31 but in all the heavens the song of praise increased.

32 And I saw how he ascended into the seventh heaven, and all the righteous and all the angels praised him. And then I saw how he sat down on the right hand of that great glory, whose glory, as I told you, I was not able to behold.

33 And also I saw the angel of the holy Spirit sitting on the left.

34 And this angel said to me, 'Isaiah, son of Amoz, it is enough for thee, for these are great things; for thou hast seen what none born of flesh has yet seen,

35 and thou wilt return into thy garment till thy days are fulfilled: then thou wilt come hither.' This have I seen."

36 And Isaiah told it to all who stood before him, and they sang praise. And he spoke to king Hezekiah and said, "Such things have I spoken,

37 and the end of this world

38 and all this vision will be consummated in the last generation."

39 And Isaiah made him swear that he would not tell this to the people of Israel, nor permit any man to write down the words.

9

The New Scriptures
Canonical Lists in Early Christianity

Christianity started out as a religion that revered a sacred book. The Hebrew Bible (at least part of it, including the Torah) was accepted, interpreted, and taught by Jesus and his followers. As the Christian movement developed away from its Jewish roots (see Chapter 5), it maintained its literary emphasis, both reinterpreting the Jewish Scriptures in light of its own emerging theology and producing and accepting other writings as standing on a par with them. The movement to adopt a new authority may have started as soon as Christians began to accept Jesus' own words as authoritative. Clearly his teachings functioned this way for the earliest Christian communities (see 1 Corinthians 7:10; 9:14); by the end of the first century they were sometimes quoted as "Scripture" (1 Timothy 5:18). Moreover, the writings of Jesus' apostles were also seen as carrying particular weight; they were read in early Christian worship services and, by the close of the New Testament period, were occasionally referred to as Scripture (1 Peter 3:16).

The second and third centuries saw a movement within Christian circles to establish a fixed "canon" of Scripture. The word *canon* comes from the Greek, and literally means "straight edge" or "ruler"; it is used to refer to a normative collection of writings, in this case an authoritative collection of authoritative books. Several factors facilitated this movement toward a canon, including the following: (a) the desire of Christians to have their own authorities in addition to those inherited from their mother religion (Judaism) and thereby to differentiate themselves from non-Christian Jews; (b) the widely perceived need to have an authoritative basis for the doctrines and practices central to the religion, and the concomitant sense that the "right" beliefs and practices required a foundation in the "right" books (i.e., those produced by Jesus' own apostles); and (c) the production of documents falsely claiming to be written by Jesus' apostles and embracing alternative views of belief and practice (see Chapter 8).

Many people do not realize that the formation of the New Testament was a long and drawn out process. The 27-book canon familiar today did not come into being immediately at the end of the first century. For several hundred years, Christians debated over which books to include. The first Christian known to make an authoritative pronouncement on the canon was Marcion (see Chapter 7), who maintained that the Christian Scriptures comprised the Gospel of Luke and ten of Paul's letters (all severely edited)—no other apostolic writings and none of the Old Testament. Other Christian groups had other favorite books, some preferring one or the other Gospel that eventually made it into the New Testament, possibly with the addition of other books like the Gospel of Peter or the Gospel of Thomas. Others of them favored a kind of mega-Gospel produced in the middle of the second century by a Christian named Tatian, whose work, the Diatessaron ("Through the Four") compiled the stories of all four Gospels into one. Even among proto-orthodox groups there was no firm agreement, although by the end of the second century most such Christians accepted Matthew, Mark, Luke, and John, along with the book of Acts, the thirteen letters of Paul, 1 Peter, and 1 John. But even then, there continued to be wide-ranging disputes concerning the status of such books as Hebrews, Revelation, the Shepherd of Hermas, and the Letter of Barnabas.

Christians engaged in these disputes generally appealed to several considerations. It was widely conceded that to be accepted as Scripture, a book needed to be (a) ancient: not representing any recent innovations; (b) apostolic: written by an apostle or one of their own followers; (c) catholic: used widely among Christian churches everywhere; and, perhaps most important, (d) orthodox: presenting the "right" beliefs as opposed to the wrong ones. What those beliefs were, of course, varied from one Christian group to another.

The canonical debates raged far beyond our period. The first known instance of any Christian author of any kind insisting on the 27 books now in the canon, and only these 27, came in 367 CE—nearly 300 years after much of the New Testament had been written—in a letter sent to his churches by Athanasius, the powerful and influential bishop of Alexandria. Even then, however, the matter was far from resolved; orthodox Christians continued to dispute the fringes of the canon for well over a century.

The following are several of the canon lists of the second and third centuries, lists of books considered canonical by various authors of the period.

For Further Reading

Barton, John. *Holy Writings, Sacred Text. The Canon in Early Christianity*. Louisville: Westminster John Knox Press, 1997.

Campenhausen, Hans von. *The Formation of the Christian Bible*, trans. J. A. Baker. Philadelphia: Fortress, 1972.

Dungan, D. L. *Constantine's Bible. Politics and the Making of the New Testament*. Minneapolis: Fortress Press, 2007.

Ehrman, Bart. *Lost Christianities: The Battles for Scripture and the Faiths We Never Knew*. New York: Oxford University, 2003.

Gamble, Harry. *The New Testament Canon: Its Making and Meaning*. Philadelphia: Fortress, 1985.

Gamble, Harry. "The Canon of the New Testament," *Anchor Bible Dictionary*. ed. David Noel Freedman. New York: Doubleday, 1992; I.852–61.

Metzger, Bruce M. *The Canon of the New Testament: Its Origin, Development, and Significance*. Oxford: Clarendon, 1987.

THE TEXTS

59. The Muratorian Canon

Named after L. A. Muratori, the Italian scholar who discovered it in the early eighteenth century, the Muratorian Canon is the earliest list of New Testament books known to exist. Written on a fragmentary manuscript in ungrammatical Latin, the list begins in mid-sentence by describing the production of an unnamed Gospel; since it continues by explicitly calling Luke the "third book of the Gospel" and John, then, the "fourth," the list evidently began with Matthew and Mark.

Twenty-two of the twenty-seven books of the New Testament canon are included here, with the exceptions of Hebrews, James, 1 & 2 Peter, and 3 John. The author also accepts the Wisdom of Solomon and the Apocalypse of Peter (see Chapter 8). The Shepherd of Hermas is accepted for reading but not as part of sacred Scripture for the church; the author explicitly rejects "Paul's" letters to Laodicea and Alexandria as Marcionite forgeries and condemns many others that he does not name.

The time and place of composition of this list is in great dispute, but since the author shows a particular concern with the false teachings of Marcion, Valentinus, Basilides, and others who lived in the middle of the second century, and knows something of the family of bishop Pius of Rome (d. 154), many scholars think he was living in the latter half of the second century, possibly in Rome.

But he was present among them, and so he put [the facts down in his Gospel.] The third book of the Gospel [is that] according to Luke. Luke, the physician, after the ascension of Christ, when Paul had taken him with him as a companion of his traveling, [and after he had made] an investigation, wrote in his own name—but neither did he see the Lord in the flesh—and thus, as he was able to investigate, so he also begins to tell the story [starting] from the nativity of John. The fourth [book] of the Gospels is that of John, [one] of the disciples. When his fellow-disciples and bishops urged [him], he said: "Fast together with me today for three days and, what shall be revealed to each, let us tell [it] to each other." On the same night it was revealed to Andrew, [one] of the Apostles, that, with all of them reviewing [it], John should describe all things in his own name. And so, although different beginnings might be taught in the separate books of the Gospels, nevertheless it makes no difference to the faith of believers, since all things in all [of them] are declared by the one sovereign Spirit—concerning [his] nativity, concerning [his] passion, concerning [his] resurrection, concerning [his] walk with his disciples, and concerning his double advent: the first in humility when he was despised, which has been; the second in royal power, glorious, which is to be. What

---

The Muratorian Canon, from *Evidence of Tradition*, ed. Daniel J. Theron. 2nd ed. Grand Rapids: Baker Book House, 1980.

marvel, therefore, if John so constantly brings forward particular [matters] also in his Epistles, saying of himself: "What we have seen with our eyes and have heard with [our] ears and our hands have handled, these things we have written to you."[1] For thus he declares that he was not only an eyewitness and hearer, but also a writer of all the wonderful things of the Lord in order.

The Acts of all the Apostles, however, were written in one volume. Luke described briefly "for" most excellent Theophilus particular [things], which happened in his presence, as he also evidently relates indirectly the death of Peter (?) and also Paul's departure from the city as he was proceeding to Spain.

The Epistles of Paul themselves, however, show to those, who wish to know, which [they are], from what place, and for what cause they were sent. First of all he wrote to the Corinthians, admonishing against schism of heresy; thereupon to the Galatians [admonishing against] circumcision; to the Romans, however, [he wrote] rather lengthily pointing out with a series of Scripture quotations that Christ is their main theme also. [But] it is necessary that we have a discussion singly concerning these, since the blessed Apostle Paul himself, imitating the example of his predecessor, John, wrote to seven churches only by name [and] in this order: The first [Epistle] to the Corinthians, the second to the Ephesians, the third to the Philippians, the fourth to the Colossians, the fifth to the Galatians, the sixth to the Thessalonians, and the seventh to the Romans.

---

1 1 John 1:1.

But, although he wrote twice to the Corinthians and to the Thessalonians, for reproof, nevertheless [it is evident that] one Church is made known to be diffused throughout the whole globe of the earth. For John also, though he wrote in the Apocalypse to seven churches, nevertheless he speaks to them all. But he [wrote] one [letter] to Philemon and one to Titus, but two to Timothy for the sake of affection and love. In honor of the General Church, however, they have been sanctified by an ordination of the ecclesiastical discipline. There is extant also [an epistle] to the Laodiceans, and another to the Alexandrians, forged in the name of Paul according to the heresy of Marcion. There are also many others which cannot be received in the General Church, for gall cannot be mixed with honey.

The Epistle of Jude indeed and the two with the superscription, "Of John," are accepted in the General [Church]—so also the Wisdom of Solomon written by friends in his honor. We accept only the Apocalypses of John and of Peter, although some of us do not want it to be read in the Church. But Hermas composed The Shepherd quite recently in our times in the city of Rome, while his brother, Pius, the bishop, occupied the [episcopal] seat of the city of Rome. And therefore, it should indeed be read, but it cannot be published for the people in the Church, neither among the Prophets, since their number is complete, nor among the Apostles for it is after their time.

But we accept nothing at all of Arsinoes, or Valentinus, or Metiades. Those also [are rejected] who composed a new book of Psalms for Marcion together with Basilides and the Cataphrygians of Asia. . . .

60. Irenaeus: Against the Heresies

Writing in 180 CE in Gaul, the great proto-orthodox heresiologist Irenaeus (see Chapter 7) did not provide a complete list of books that he considered to be canonical. But he did attack various heretical groups for accepting only one or the other of the Gospels (while maintaining that the heretics would not have gone astray had they correctly interpreted even the one book they accepted). Irenaeus then mounted the following argument for his own view that there were four and only four Gospels, an argument that many interpreters suspect was convincing chiefly to those who already agreed with it.

So firm is the ground upon which these Gospels rest, that the very heretics themselves bear witness to them, and, starting from these [documents], each one of them endeavours to establish his own peculiar doctrine. For the Ebionites, who use Matthew's Gospel only, are confuted out of this very same, making false suppositions with regard to the Lord. But Marcion, mutilating that according to Luke, is proved to be a blasphemer of the only existing God, from those [passages] which he still retains. Those, again, who separate Jesus from Christ, alleging that Christ remained impassible, but that it was Jesus who suffered, preferring the Gospel by Mark, if they read it with a love of truth, may have their errors rectified. Those, moreover, who follow Valentinus, making copious use of that according to John, to illustrate their conjunctions, shall be proved to be totally in error by means of this very Gospel, as I have shown in the first book. Since, then, our opponents do bear testimony to us, and make use of these [documents], our proof derived from them is firm and true.

It is not possible that the Gospels can be either more or fewer in number than they are. For, since there are four zones of the world in which we live, and four principal winds, while the church is scattered throughout all the world, and the pillar and ground of the church is the Gospel and the spirit of life; it is fitting that she should have four pillars, breathing out immortality on every side, and vivifying afresh. From which fact, it is evident that the Word, the Artificer of all, he that sits upon the cherubim, and contains all things, he who was manifested to humans, has given us the Gospel under four aspects, but bound together by one Spirit.

Irenaeus's Gospel Canon, from *The Ante-Nicene Fathers*, vol. 1. *The Apostolic Fathers with Justin Martyr and Irenaeus*, ed. A. Cleveland Coxe. Reprint; 2nd ed. Grand Rapids: Eerdmans, 1987.

61. Origen of Alexandria

Nonone of the surviving writings of Origen, the great Christian scholar of Alexandria (see Chapter 4), provides a full listing of the books that he considered to be part of the New Testament canon. Origen does make scattered references to the canon, however. The following partial lists are drawn from his Commentaries on Matthew and John and his Homilies on the Epistle to the Hebrews. As can be seen, Origen accepted the four Gospels that were eventually agreed upon, along with the Pauline epistles (which he does not enumerate in this fragment); one letter of Peter, allowing for the possibility of a second; one letter of John and possibly two more; and the Apocalypse to John. In the final fragment given here, he addresses the problem posed by the book of Hebrews, accepting it as canonical but expressing his doubts over whether Paul was actually its author.

These excerpts are drawn from the *Ecclesiastical History* of Eusebius (see selection 62), who devoted a significant portion of an entire volume of his history to the life and work of Origen.

1. From Origen's *Commentary on Matthew*

I accept the traditional view of the four Gospels which alone are undeniably authentic in the church of God on earth. First to be written was that of the one-time exciseman who became an apostle of Jesus Christ—Matthew; it was published for believers of Jewish origin, and was composed in Aramaic. Next came that of Mark, who followed Peter's instructions in writing it, and who in Peter's general epistle was acknowledged as his son: "Greetings to you from the church in Babylon, chosen like yourselves, and from my son Mark."[1] Next came that of Luke, who wrote for Gentile converts the Gospel praised by Paul. Last of all came John's.

2. From Origen's *Commentary on John*

The man who was enabled to become a minister of the New Covenant, not of the letter but of the spirit, Paul, proclaimed the Gospel from Jerusalem, in a wide sweep as far as Illyricum. But he did not write to all the churches he had taught; and to those to which he did write he sent only a few lines. Peter, on whom is built Christ's Church, over which the gates of Hades shall have no power, left us one acknowledged epistle, possibly two—though this is doubtful. Need I say anything about the man who leant back on Jesus' breast, John? He left a single Gospel, though he confessed that he could write so many that the whole world would not hold them.[2] He also wrote

---

1 1 Pet 1:13.

2 John 21:25.

Origen's New Testament Canon, from *Eusebius: The History of the Church from Christ to Constantine*, trans. G. A. Williamson, rev. Andrew Louth (Penguin Classics 1965, rev. ed. 1989). Copyright © G. A. Williamson, 1965. Revisions copyright © Andrew Louth, 1989. Used with permission.

the Revelation, but was ordered to remain silent and not write the utterances of the seven thunders.[3] In addition, he left an epistle of a very few lines, and possibly two more, though their authenticity is denied by some. Anyway, they do not total a hundred lines between them.

3. From Origen's
Homilies on Hebrews

In the epistle entitled *To the Hebrews* the diction does not exhibit the characteristic roughness of speech or phraseology admitted by the Apostle himself, the construction of the sentences is closer to Greek usage, as anyone capable of recognizing

---

3 Rev 10:3–4.

differences of style would agree. On the other hand the matter of the epistle is wonderful, and quite equal to the Apostle's acknowledged writings: the truth of this would be admitted by anyone who has read the Apostle carefully. . . . If I were asked my personal opinion, I would say that the matter is the Apostle's but the phraseology and construction are those of someone who remembered the Apostle's teaching and wrote his own interpretation of what his master had said. So if any church regards this epistle as Paul's, it should be commended for so doing, for the primitive Church had every justification for handing it down as his. Who wrote the epistle is known to God alone: the accounts that have reached us suggest that it was either Clement, who became Bishop of Rome, or Luke, who wrote the Gospel and the Acts.

62. *Eusebius: Ecclesiastical History*

As noted in Chapter 1, Eusebius of Caesarea, commonly known as the "Father of Church History," wrote in the early decades of the fourth century, immediately after the period otherwise represented here. But it may be useful to include at least one brief passage from his book, the *Ecclesiastical History,* to show that the debates over the canon had not been resolved, even within proto-orthodox circles, some 200 years after the last of the books of the New Testament had been produced. Of particular interest in Eusebius's list is his categorization of apostolic books as (a) "recognized," that is, accepted as canonical by all churches; (b) "disputed," that is, recognized by some churches but not others (some of these books he labels "spurious," i.e., orthodox but pseudonymous and so not to be accepted); and (c) rejected, that is, heretical forgeries.

Eusebius's New Testament Canon, from *Eusebius: The History of the Church from Christ to Constantine,* trans. by G. A. Williamson, rev. Andrew Louth (Penguin Classics 965, rev. ed. 1989). Copyright © G. A. Williamson, 1965. Revisions copyright © Andrew Louth, 1989. Used with permission.

It will be well, at this point, to classify the New Testament writings already referred to. We must, of course, put first the holy quartet of the Gospels, followed by the Acts of the Apostles. The next place in the list goes to Paul's epistles, and after them we must recognize the epistle called 1 John; likewise 1 Peter. To these may be added, if it is thought proper, the Revelation of John, the arguments about which I shall set out when the time comes. These are classed as Recognized Books. Those that are disputed, yet familiar to most, include the epistles known as James, Jude, and 2 Peter, and those called 2 and 3 John, the work either of the evangelist or of someone else with the same name.

Among Spurious Books must be placed the "Acts" of Paul, the "Shepherd," and the "Revelation of Peter"; also the alleged "Epistle of Barnabas," and the "Teachings of the Apostles," together with the Revelation of John, if this seems the right place for it: as I said before, some reject it, others include it among the Recognized Books. Moreover, some have found a place in the list for the "Gospel of Hebrews," a book which has a special appeal for those Hebrews who have accepted Christ. These would all be classed with the Disputed Books, but I have been obliged to list the latter separately, distinguishing those writings which according to the tradition of the Church are true, genuine, and recognized, from those in a different category, not canonical but disputed, yet familiar to most church people; for we must not confuse these with the writings published by heretics under the name of the apostles, as containing either Gospels of Peter, Thomas, Matthias, and several others besides these, or Acts of Andrew, John, and other apostles. To none of these has any church person of any generation ever seen fit to refer in his writings. Again, nothing could be farther from apostolic usage than the type of phraseology employed, while the ideas and implications of their contents are so irreconcilable with true orthodoxy that they stand revealed as the forgeries of heretics. It follows that so far from being classed even among Spurious Books, they must be thrown out as impious and beyond the pale.

10

Text and Meaning

The Interpretation of Scripture in Early Christianity

As we observed in Chapter 9, the Bible was important from the very beginnings of the early Christian movement. Whatever else the historical Jesus may have been—charismatic holy man, Jewish cynic philosopher, political revolutionary, apocalyptic prophet—he was certainly a Galilean Jew who was deeply committed to the Jewish Scriptures, and he was fundamentally understood by his followers to have been an interpreter of the Bible. In fact, he was the interpreter par excellence, the one whose understanding of the Torah of God could show the way to ultimate salvation.

The importance of interpreting Scripture continued on after Jesus' death as his followers soon began to believe that he himself had come as the fulfillment of the Law and the prophets, that in fact the entire point of the Jewish Bible was to point forward to Jesus' life, death, and resurrection as the fore-ordained goal of all God's promises to his chosen people, beginning with Moses. Scriptural interpretation played a highly significant role in the ministry and writings of our earliest Christian author, Paul—who, although he was writing to Christians who had converted not out of the Jewish tradition but out of paganism, nonetheless appealed to the writings of Scripture to justify his understanding of the gospel. For Paul, Christ was not only the fulfillment of the Law given to Moses, he also brought an end to that Law—at least to its utility for the purposes of salvation (Romans 10:4). But, somewhat ironically, Paul insisted that this advocacy of salvation apart from the Law is precisely what the Law itself taught (Romans 3:21, 31).

In many ways Paul set the stage for what was yet to come within the Christian tradition, in that he wrestled mightily with the meaning of the Scriptures and was open to understanding these texts not only in literal ways but also allegorically. On the literal level, as an example, since God made a covenant with Abraham to be the father of the people of God some 430 years before giving the Law of Moses, then the Law is obviously not the key to participating in the promise made to Abraham (Galatians 3:15–18). On the allegorical level, one finds occasional off-the-cuff comments such as 1 Corinthians 10:4, that the rock that provided Moses and the children of Israel the water they needed during their wanderings in the wilderness was none other than Christ himself. And sometimes Paul launches into a detailed exposition of a text using nonliteral renderings, as when he pronounces that the two sons of Abraham, one by a free woman and the other by a slave, are in fact "allegories" meant to teach Paul's law-free gospel (Galatians 4:21–31).

In making these exegetical moves, Paul was simply following established Jewish principles of interpretation. But they ended up created very large difficulties for later interpreters who understood themselves to stand within the Pauline tradition. As the Christian church grew and various factions claimed to represent the "true" form of the religion (see Chapters 7 and 8), all could insist that their interpretation of the tradition was not just valid but God-given, and they could appeal to the Scriptures, interpreted variously, in support. The debates over orthodoxy and heresy were not merely rooted in claims for one set of sacred books over another. As the participants in these debates knew so well, accepting the authority of a book is not at all the same thing as understanding the book's authoritative teaching. Various Christian groups might agree that this, that, or the other book was an authoritative text, whether "Old" Testament or "New" Testament. But if the book was interpreted in radically different ways, the authoritative teachings of the book could shift radically as well.

We do not have extensive evidence for the "rules of interpretation" of most early Christian groups—for example Jewish Christians, Sethians, Valentinians, Thomasines, other Gnostics, Marcionites, Montanists, the proto-orthodox, and so on, let alone, of course, for groups about whom we hear only hints and murmurs or about whom we know nothing at all. In the best of these cases, all we have are their direct or indirect expositions of Scripture, where we can see their own exegetical practices in action.

We do see enough of the Valentinian and Sethian exegesis of texts to recognize that it was a complicated affair (see selection 66), and we have a clear exposition of an understanding of Scripture in a tractate by one prominent Valentinian, Ptolemy, in his letter to Flora (selection 63). Based on the surviving exegetical treatises, it is abundantly clear that various Gnostic groups were adept at allegorical readings of texts. And it is more than obvious from proto-orthodox polemics (for example, Irenaeus) that one counterattack to dispute these readings involved insisting on the primacy of a literal reading; that is, one governed by established historical/grammatical principles of determining the meaning of words without allowing allegorical renderings that make the text mean something other than it says (Paul's precedent notwithstanding).

Some other groups—notably the Marcionites—were hard-core literalists. With proto-orthodox authors, however, it is clear that when not concerned to ward off the "aberrant" interpretations of one exegete or another, they were not at all averse to using more figurative methods for themselves. We see such figurative exegesis already in an Apostolic Father such as Barnabas (see selection 18 in Chapter 5); it recurs throughout our period as well, for example, in that virulent proponent of all things orthodox, including the literal readings of text, Tertullian.

It is not until Origen, however, that a systematic attempt was made at establishing an orthodox hermeneutical method. In the long selection taken from *On First Principles* (selection 67), it becomes clear that even though Origen insisted on the importance of the literal reading of a text when possible (an importance that some interpreters have overlooked), there are grounds for understanding texts in deeper, more figurative senses as well. By explaining how this is to be done, Origen opened the door for the development of more sophisticated methods of interpretation to be developed by Christian thinkers after the period under consideration here.

For Further Reading

Clark, Elizabeth A. *Reading Renunciation: Asceticism and Scripture in Early Christianity.* Princeton: Princeton University Press, 1999.

Dawson, David. *Allegorical Readers and Cultural Revision in Ancient Alexandria.* Berkeley: University of California, 1992.

Froehlich, Karlfried. *Biblical Interpretation in the Early Church.* Philadelphia: Fortress, 1984.

Grant, Robert M. *A Short History of the Interpretation of the Bible*, revised ed. by David Tracy. Philadelphia: Fortress, 1983.

Hauser, Alan J. and Duane F. Watson, eds., *A History of Interpretation*; vol. 1 *The Ancient Period.* Grand Rapids: Eerdmans, 2003.

Kugel, James L., and Rowan A. Greer. *Early Biblical Interpretation.* Philadelphia: Westminster Press, 1986.

Paget, James C. and Joachim Schapter. *The New Cambridge History of the Bible: From the Beginnings to 600.* Cambridge: Cambridge University, 2013.

Simonetti, Manlio. *Biblical Interpretation in the Early Church: An Historical Introduction to Patristic Exegesis.* trans. J. A. I. Hughes. Edinburgh: T&T Clark, 1994.

THE TEXTS

(See also the Epistle of Barnabas in Chapter 5)

63. *Ptolemy's Letter to Flora*

One of the most famous disciples of Valentinus (see Chapter 6) was Ptolemy, a renowned Gnostic teacher who lived in Rome in the mid–second century. From Ptolemy's own hand comes one of the clearest expositions of Valentinian ideas, in a letter addressed to a woman named Flora, a non-Gnostic Christian whom Ptolemy is concerned to educate into the higher realms of knowledge of the faith. The letter is just the beginning of Ptolemy's instruction (regrettably, his subsequent lessons have been lost), but it concerns a central component of his Gnostic views: his understanding of the Bible.

The proper interpretation of the Bible, Ptolemy avers, depends on understanding the nature of its divine inspiration. Those who maintain that it was authored by the Perfect God and Father (for example, the proto-orthodox Christians) err, because a perfect being could not inspire laws that are imperfect. Those who claim that it was written by his adversary, the Devil (for example, other groups of Gnostics?) also err, because an evil deity could not inspire laws that are just. Instead, there is a god intermediate between these two, the just but imperfect (and harsh) god who created the world; it was he who inspired parts of the Bible. Other parts, though, derive from Moses himself, and yet others from the elders around him. Those that are from god can themselves be divided into three parts: those that Jesus fulfilled (for example, the Ten Commandments), those that he abolished (for example, "an eye for an eye"), and those that he has symbolically transformed (for example, ceremonial laws). Ptolemy explicitly claims to base his views on the teachings of Paul and, especially, Jesus himself.

This letter was not present among the Nag Hammadi writings and has not been transmitted independently, but can be found only in quotations in the writings of the fourth-century heresiologist Epiphanius (Book 33 of *The Medicine Chest*).

3 The law established by Moses, my dear sister Flora, has in the past been misunderstood by many people, for they were not closely acquainted with the one who established it or with its commandments. I think you will see this at once if you study their discordant opinions on this topic.

---

2 For some say that this law has been ordained by god the father; while others, following the opposite course, stoutly contend that it has been established by the adversary, the pernicious devil; and so the latter school attributes the craftsmanship of the world to the devil, saying that he is "the father and maker of the universe."[1]

3 <But> they are <utterly> in error, they disagree with one another, and each of the schools utterly misses the truth of the matter.

4 Now, it does not seem that the law was established by the perfect god and father: for, it must be of the same character as its giver; and yet it is imperfect and needful of being fulfilled by another and contains commandments incongruous with the nature and intentions of such a god.

5 On the other hand to attribute a law that abolishes injustice to the injustice of the adversary is the false logic of those who do not comprehend the principle of which the savior spoke. For our savior declared that a house or city divided against itself will not be able to stand.

6 And, further, the apostle states that the craftsmanship of the world is his, and that "all things were made through him, and without him was not anything made,"[2] thus anticipating these liars' flimsy wisdom. And the craftsmanship is that of a god who is just and hates evil, not a pernicious one as believed by these thoughtless people, who take no account of the craftsman's forethought and so are blind not only in the eye of the soul but even in the eyes of the body.

7 Now, from what has been said it should be clear to you (sing.) that these (schools of thought) utterly miss the truth, though each does so in its own particular way: one (school) by not being acquainted with the god of righteousness, the other by not being acquainted with the father of the entirety, who was manifested by him alone who came and who alone knew him.

8 It remains for us, who have been deemed worthy of <acquaintance> with both, to show you

(sing.) exactly what sort of law the law is, and which legislator established it. We shall offer proofs of what we say by drawing from our savior's words, by which alone it is possible to reach a certain apprehension of the reality of the matter without stumbling.

4 Now, first you must learn that, as a whole, the law contained in the Pentateuch of Moses was not established by a single author, I mean not by god alone: rather, there are certain of its commandments that were established by human beings as well. Indeed, our savior's words teach us that the Pentateuch divides into three parts.

2 For one division belongs to god himself and his legislations; while <another division> belongs to Moses—indeed, Moses ordained certain of the commandments not as god himself ordained through him, rather based upon his own thoughts about the matter; and yet a third division belongs to the elders of the people, <who> likewise in the beginning must have inserted certain of their own commandments.

3 You will now learn how all this can be demonstrated from the savior's words.

4 When the savior was talking with those who were arguing with him about divorce—and it has been ordained (in the law) that divorce is permitted—he said to them: "For your (pl.) hardness of heart Moses allowed divorce of one's wife. Now, from the beginning it was not so."[3] For god, he says, has joined together this union, and "what the lord has joined together, let no man put asunder."[4]

5 Here he shows that <the> law of god is one thing, forbidding a woman to be put asunder from her husband; while the law of Moses is another, permitting the couple to be put asunder because of hard-heartedness.

6 And so, accordingly, Moses ordains contrary to what god ordains; for <separating> is contrary to not separating.

---

1 Plato *Timaeus* 28e.

2 John 1:3.

3 Matt 19:8.

4 Matt 19:6.

Yet if we also scrutinize Moses' intentions with which he ordained this commandment, we find that he created the commandment not of his own inclination but of necessity because of the weakness of those to whom it was ordained.

7 For the latter were not able to put into practice god's intentions, in the matter of their not being permitted to divorce their wives. Some of them were on very bad terms with their wives, and ran the risk of being further diverted into injustice and from there into their destruction.

8 Moses, wishing to excise this unpleasant element through which they also ran the risk of being destroyed, ordained for them of his own accord a second law, the law of divorce, choosing under the circumstances the lesser of two evils, as it were,

9 so that if they were unable to keep the former (that is, god's law) they could keep at least the latter and so not be diverted into injustice and evil, through which utter destruction would follow in consequence.

10 These are Moses' intentions, with which we find him ordaining laws contrary to those of god. At any rate, even if we have for the moment used only one example in our proof, it is beyond doubt that, as we have shown, this law is of Moses himself and is distinct from god's.

11 And the savior shows also that there are some traditions of the elders interwoven in the law. He says, "For god spoke: 'Honor your father and your mother, that it may be well with you.'

12 But you have declared," the savior says, addressing the elders, "'What you would have gained from me is given to god.' And for the sake of your tradition, O ancients, you have made void the law of god."[5]

13 And Isaiah declared this by saying, "This people honors me with their lips, but their heart is far from me; in vain do they worship me, teaching as doctrines the precepts of men."[6]

14 Thus it has been clearly shown from these passages that, as a whole, the law is divided into three parts. For we have found in it legislations belonging to Moses himself, to the elders, and to god himself. Moreover, the analysis of the law as a whole, as we have divided it here, has made clear which part of it is genuine.

5 Now, what is more, the one part that is the law of god himself divides into three subdivisions.

The first subdivision is the pure legislation not interwoven with evil, which alone is properly called law, and which the savior did not come to abolish but to fulfill. For what he fulfilled was not alien to him, <but stood in need of fulfillment>: for it did not have perfection.

And the second subdivision is the part interwoven with the inferior and with injustice, which the savior abolished as being incongruous with his own nature.

2 Finally, the third subdivision is the symbolic and allegorical part, which is after the image of the superior, spiritual realm: the savior changed (the referent of) this part from the perceptible, visible level to the spiritual, invisible one.

3 The first, the law of god that is pure and not interwoven with the inferior, is the decalogue of Ten Commandments inscribed on two stone tablets; they divide into the prohibition of things that must be avoided and the commanding of things that must be done. Although they contain pure legislation they do not have perfection, and so they were in need of fulfillment by the savior.

4 The second, which is interwoven with injustice, is that which applies to retaliation and repayment of those who have already committed a wrong, commanding us to pluck out an eye for an eye and a tooth for a tooth and to retaliate for murder with murder.[7] This part is interwoven with injustice, for the one who is second to act unjustly still acts unjustly, differing only in the relative order in which he acts, and committing the very same act.

5 But otherwise, this commandment both was and is just, having been established as a deviation from the pure law because of the weakness of

---

5 Matt 15:4–5.

6 Isa 29:3; Matt 15:8.

---

7 Lev 24:17, 20.

those to whom it was ordained; yet it is incongruous with the nature and goodness of the father of the entirety.

6 Now perhaps this was apt; but even more, it was a result of necessity. For when one who does not wish even a single murder to occur—by saying, "You shall not kill"—when, I say, he ordains a second law and commands the murderer to be murdered,[8] acting as judge between two murders, he who forbade even a single murder[9] has without realizing it been cheated by necessity.

7 For this reason, then, the son who was sent from him abolished this part of the law, though he admits that it too belonged to god: this part is reckoned as belonging to the old school of thought, both where he says, "For god spoke: 'He who speaks evil of father or mother, let him surely die'"[10] and elsewhere.

8 And the third subdivision of god's law is the symbolic part, which is after the image of the superior, spiritual realm: I mean, what is ordained about offerings, circumcision, the Sabbath, fasting, Passover, the Feast of Unleavened Bread, and the like.

9 Now, once the truth had been manifested, the referent of all these ordinances was changed, inasmuch as they are images and allegories. As to their meaning in the visible realm and their physical accomplishment they were abolished; but as to their spiritual meaning they were elevated, with the words remaining the same but the subject matter being altered.

10 For the savior commanded us to offer offerings, but not dumb beasts or incense: rather, spiritual praises and glorifications and prayers of thanksgiving, and offerings in the form of sharing and good deeds.

11 And he wishes us to perform circumcision, but not circumcision of the bodily foreskin, rather of the spiritual heart;

12 and to keep the Sabbath, for he wants us to be inactive in wicked acts;

13 and to fast, though he does not wish us to perform physical fasts, rather spiritual ones, which consist of abstinence from all bad deeds.

Nevertheless, fasting as to the visible realm is observed by our adherents, since fasting, if practiced with reason, can contribute something to the soul, so long as it does not take place in imitation of other people or by habit or because fasting has been prescribed <for> a particular day.

14 Likewise, it is observed in memory of true fasting, so that those who are not yet able to observe true fasting might have a remembrance of it from fasting according to the visible realm.

15 Likewise, the apostle Paul makes it clear that Passover and the Feast of Unleavened Bread were images, for he says that "Christ, our paschal lamb, has been sacrificed"[11] and, he says, be without leaven, having no share in leaven—now, by "leaven" he means evil—but rather "be fresh dough."

6 And so it can be granted that the actual law of god is subdivided into three parts. The first subdivision is the part that was fulfilled by the savior: for "you shall not kill," "you shall not commit adultery," "you shall not swear falsely" are subsumed under not being angry, not looking lustfully at another, and not swearing at all.[12]

2 The second subdivision is the part that was completely abolished. For the commandment of "an eye for an eye and a tooth for a tooth,"[13] which is interwoven with injustice and itself involves an act of injustice, was abolished by the savior with injunctions to the contrary,

3 and of two contraries one must "abolish" the other: "For I say to you (pl.), Do not in any way resist one who is evil. But if any one strikes you (sing.), turn to him the other cheek also."[14]

4 And the third subdivision is the part whose referent was changed and which was altered from the physical to the spiritual—the allegorical part,

---

8 Exod 20:13.

9 Exod 21:12.

10 Matt 15:4.

11 1 Cor 5:7.

12 Matt 5:21, 27, 33.

13 Lev 24:20.

14 Matt 5:39.

which is ordained after the image of the superior realm.

5 Now, the images and allegories are indicative of other matters, and they were well and good while truth was not present. But now that truth is present, one must do the works of truth and not those of its imagery.

6 His disciples made these teachings known, and so did the apostle Paul: he makes known to us the part consisting of images, through the passage on the paschal lamb and the unleavened bread, which we have already spoken of. The part consisting of a law interwoven with injustice, he made known by speaking of "abolishing the law of commandments and ordinances";[15] and the part not interwoven with the inferior, when he says, "The law is holy, and the commandment is holy and just and good."[16]

7 Thus I think I have shown you, as well as possible in a brief treatment, both that there is human legislation which has been slipped into the law and that the law of god himself divides into three subdivisions.

2 Now it remains for us to say what sort of being this god is, who established the law. But this too I believe I have demonstrated to you (sing.) in what I have already said, providing you have followed carefully.

3 For since this division of the law (that is, god's own law) was established neither by the perfect god, as we have taught, nor surely by the devil—which it would be wrong to say—then the establisher of this division of the law is distinct from them.

4 And he is the craftsman and maker of the universe or world and of the things within it. Since he is different from the essences of the other two <and> (rather) is in a state intermediate between them, he would rightfully be described by the term intermediateness.

5 And if the perfect god is good according to his nature—as indeed he is, for our savior showed that "one only is there who is good,"[17] namely his father whom he manifested—and if furthermore the law belonging to the nature of the adversary is both evil and wicked and is stamped in the mold of injustice, then a being that is in a state intermediate between these and is neither good, nor evil or unjust, might well be properly called just, being a judge of the justice that is his.

6 And on the one hand this god must be inferior to the perfect god and less than his righteousness precisely because he is engendered and not unengendered—for "there is one unengendered father, from whom are all things,"[18] or more exactly, from whom all things depend; and on the other hand, he must have come into being as better and more authoritative than the adversary; and must be born of an essence and nature distinct from the essences of the other two.

7 For the essence of the adversary is both corruption and darkness, for the adversary is material and divided into many parts; while the essence of the unengendered father of the entirety is both incorruptibility and self-existent light, being simple and unique. And the essence of this intermediate produced a twofold capacity, for he is an image of the better god.

8 And now, given that the good by nature engenders and produces the things that are similar to itself and of the same essence, do not be bewildered as to how these natures—that of corruption and <that> of intermediateness—which have come to be different in essence, arose from a single first principle of the entirety, a principle that exists and is confessed and believed in by us, and which is unengendered and incorruptible and good.

9 For, god permitting, you will next learn about both the first principle and the generation of these two other gods, if you are deemed worthy of the apostolic tradition, which even we have received

---

15 Eph 2:15.
16 Rom 7:12.

17 Matt 19:17.
18 1 Cor 8:6.

by succession; and along with this you will learn how to test all the propositions by means of our savior's teaching.

10 I have not failed, my sister Flora, to state these matters to you briefly. And what I have just written is a concise account, though I have treated the subject adequately. In the future these teachings will be of the greatest help to you—at least if, like good rich soil that has received fertile seeds, you bear fruit.

64. Irenaeus: Against the Heresies

We have seen an excerpt from Irenaeus's five-volume heresiological work, *Against the Heresies*, already in Selection 35 in Chapter 7. In the selection given here, Irenaeus attacks his Valentinian Gnostic opponents for how they used Scripture to support their theological views. Irenaeus considers the Gnostic methods of interpretation bizarre, arbitrary, and even laughable, and he does his best both to mock them and to show their inadequacies. In his view, the Valentinians employ symbolic interpretations of texts that have no relationship at all to their literal meanings; and they rearrange the words of a text to make it say something completely at odds with what the author literally meant. In a famous image, Irenaeus likens this latter interpretative approach to someone who takes a mosaic portrait of a great king and rearranges all the small pebbles of the portrait to make them resemble a wild dog, claiming that this is what the author had in mind all along.

In the final section, Irenaeus argues that his Valentinian opponents string together unrelated texts willy-nilly in order to create an entirely new text that ends up saying something that cannot be found anywhere in the Scripture, but only in their own fertile imaginations.

III

1 Such, then, is the account they give of what took place within the Pleroma; such the calamities that flowed from the passion which seized upon the Æon who has been named, and who was within a little of perishing by being absorbed in the universal substance, through her inquisitive searching after the Father; such the consolidation [of that Æon] from her condition of agony by Horos, and Stauros, and Lytrotes, and Carpistes, and Horothetes, and Metagoges. Such also is the account of the generation of the later Æons, namely of the first Christ and of the Holy Spirit, both of whom were produced by the Father after the repentance [of Sophia], and of the second Christ (whom they also style Saviour), who owed his being to the joint contributions [of the Æons]. They tell us, however, that this knowledge has not been openly divulged, because all are not capable of receiving it, but has been mystically revealed by

Irenaeus Against the Heresies, reproduced from *The Ante-Nicene Fathers*; vol. 1, ed. A. Cleveland Coxe. Reprint; 2nd ed. Grand Rapids: Eerdmans, 1989.

the Saviour through means of parables to those qualified for understanding it. This has been done as follows. The thirty Æons are indicated (as we have already remarked) by the thirty years during which they say the Saviour performed no public act, and by the parable of the labourers in the vineyard. Paul also, they affirm, very clearly and frequently names these Æons, and even goes so far as to preserve their order, when he says, "To all the generations of the Æons of the Æon." Nay, we ourselves, when at the giving of thanks we pronounce the words, "To Æons of Æons" (for ever and ever), do set forth these Æons. And, in fine, wherever the words *Æon* or *Æons* occur, they at once refer them to these beings.

2 The production, again, of the Duodecad of the Æons, is indicated by the fact that the Lord was *twelve* years of age when He disputed with the teachers of the law, and by the election of the apostles, for of these there were twelve. The other eighteen Æons are made manifest in this way: that the Lord, [according to them,] conversed with His disciples for eighteen months after His resurrection from the dead. They also affirm that these eighteen Æons are strikingly indicated by the first two letters of His name ['Ἰησοῦς], namely *Iota* and *Eta*. And, in like manner, they assert that the ten Æons are pointed out by the letter *Iota*, which begins His name; while, for the same reason, they tell us the Saviour said, "One *Iota*, or one tittle, shall by no means pass away until all be fulfilled."

3 They further maintain that the passion which took place in the case of the twelfth Æon is pointed at by the apostasy of Judas, who was the twelfth apostle, and also by the fact that Christ suffered in the twelfth month. For their opinion is, that He continued to preach for one year only after His baptism. The same thing is also most clearly indicated by the case of the woman who suffered from an issue of blood. For after she had been thus afflicted during twelve years, she was healed by the advent of the Saviour, when she had touched the border of His garment; and on this account the Saviour said, "Who touched me?"—teaching his disciples the mystery which had occurred among

the Æons, and the healing of that Æon who had been involved in suffering. For she who had been afflicted twelve years represented that power whose essence, as they narrate, was stretching itself forth, and flowing into immensity; and unless she had touched the garment of the Son, that is, Aletheia of the first Tetrad, who is denoted by the hem spoken of, she would have been dissolved into the general essence [of which she participated]. She stopped short, however, and ceased any longer to suffer. For the power that went forth from the Son (and this power they term Horos) healed her, and separated the passion from her.

4 They moreover affirm that the Saviour is shown to be derived from all the Æons, and to be in Himself *everything* by the following passage: "Every male that openeth the womb." For He, being everything, opened the womb[19] of the enthymesis of the suffering Æon, when it had been expelled from the Pleroma. This they also style the second Ogdoad, of which we shall speak presently. And they state that it was clearly on this account that Paul said, "And He Himself is all things;" and again, "All things are to Him, and of Him are all things;" and further, "In Him dwelleth all the fulness of the Godhead;" and yet again, "All things are gathered together by God in Christ." Thus do they interpret these and any like passages to be found in Scripture.

5 They show, further, that that Horos of theirs, whom they call by a variety of names, has two faculties,—the one of supporting, and the other of separating; and in so far as he supports and sustains, he is Stauros, while in so far as he divides and separates, he is Horos. They then represent the Saviour as having indicated this twofold faculty: first, the sustaining power, when He said, "Whosoever doth not bear his cross (Stauros), and follow after me, cannot be my disciple;" and again, "Taking up the cross, follow me;" but the separating power when He said, "I came not to send peace, but a sword." They also maintain that John indicated the same thing when he said, "The fan is

---

19 Luke 2:23.

in His hand, and He will thoroughly purge the floor, and will gather the wheat into His garner; but the chaff He will burn with fire unquenchable." By this declaration He set forth the faculty of Horos. For that fan they explain to be the cross (Stauros), which consumes, no doubt, all material objects, as fire does chaff, but it purifies all them that are saved, as a fan does wheat. Moreover, they affirm that the Apostle Paul himself made mention of this cross in the following words: "The doctrine of the cross is to them that perish foolishness, but to us who are saved it is the power of God."[20] And again: "God forbid that I should glory in anything save in the cross of Christ, by whom the world is crucified to me, and I unto the world."

6 Such, then, is the account which they all give of their Pleroma, and of the formation of the universe, striving, as they do, to adapt the good words of revelation to their own wicked inventions. And it is not only from the writings of the evangelists and the apostles that they endeavour to derive proofs for their opinions by means of perverse interpretations and deceitful expositions: they deal in the same way with the law and the prophets, which contain many parables and allegories that can frequently be drawn into various senses, according to the kind of exegesis to which they are subjected. And others of them, with great craftiness, adapted such parts of Scripture to their own figments, lead away captive from the truth those who do not retain a stedfast faith in one God, the Father Almighty, and in one Lord Jesus Christ, the Son of God.

IV

1 Such, then, is their system, which neither the prophets announced, nor the Lord taught, nor the apostles delivered, but of which they boast that beyond all others they have a perfect knowledge. They gather their views from other sources than the Scriptures; and, to use a common proverb, they strive to weave ropes of sand, while they endeavour to adapt with an air of probability to their

own peculiar assertions the parables of the Lord, the sayings of the prophets, and the words of the apostles, in order that their scheme may not seem altogether without support. In doing so, however, they disregard the order and the connection of the Scriptures, and so far as in them lies, dismember and destroy the truth. By transferring passages, and dressing them up anew, and making one thing out of another, they succeed in deluding many through their wicked art in adapting the oracles of the Lord to their opinions. Their manner of acting is just as if one, when a beautiful image of a king has been constructed by some skilful artist out of precious jewels, should then take this likeness of the man all to pieces, should re-arrange the gems, and so fit them together as to make them into the form of a dog or of a fox, and even that but poorly executed; and should then maintain and declare that *this* was the beautiful image of the king which the skilful artist constructed, pointing to the jewels which had been admirably fitted together by the first artist to form the image of the king, but have been with bad effect transferred by the latter one to the shape of a dog, and by thus exhibiting the jewels, should deceive the ignorant who had no conception what a king's form was like, and persuade them that that miserable likeness of the fox was, in fact, the beautiful image of the king. In like manner do these persons patch together old wives' fables, and then endeavour, by violently drawing away from their proper connection, words, expressions, and parables whenever found, to adapt the oracles of God to their baseless fictions. We have already stated how far they proceed in this way with respect to the interior of the Pleroma.

IX

1 You see, my friend, the method which these men employ to deceive themselves, while they abuse the Scriptures by endeavouring to support their own system out of them. For this reason, I have brought forward their modes of expressing themselves, that thus thou mightest understand the

---

20 1 Cor 1:18.

deceitfulness of their procedure, and the wickedness of their error. For, in the first place, if it had been John's intention to set forth that Ogdoad above, he would surely have preserved the order of its production, and would doubtless have placed the primary Tetrad first, as being, according to them, most venerable, and would then have annexed the second, that, by the sequence of the names, the order of the Ogdoad might be exhibited, and not after so long an interval, as if forgetful for the moment; and then again calling the matter to mind, he, last of all, made mention of the primary Tetrad. In the next place, if he had meant to indicate their conjunctions, he certainly would not have omitted the name of Ecclesia; while, with respect to the other conjunctions, he either would have been satisfied with the mention of the male [Æons] (since the others [like Ecclesia] might be understood), so as to preserve a uniformity throughout; or if he enumerated the conjunctions of the rest, he would also have announced the spouse of Anthropos, and would not have left us to find out her name by divination.

2 The fallacy, then, of this exposition is manifest. For when John, proclaiming one God, the Almighty, and one Jesus Christ, the Onlybegotten, by whom all things were made, declares that this was the Son of God, this the Onlybegotten, this the Former of all things, this the true Light who enlighteneth every man, this the Creator of the world, this He that came to His own, this He that became flesh and dwelt among us,—these men, by a plausible kind of exposition, perverting these statements, maintain that there was another Monogenes, according to production, whom they also style Arche. They also maintain that there was another Saviour, and another Logos, the son of Monogenes, and another Christ produced for the re-establishment of the Pleroma. Thus it is that, wresting from the truth every one of the expressions which have been cited, and taking a bad advantage of the names, they have transferred them to their own system; so that, according to them, in all these terms John makes no mention of the Lord Jesus Christ.

For if he has named the Father, and Charis, and Monogenes, and Aletheia, and Logos, and Zoe, and Anthropos, and Ecclesia, according to their hypothesis, he has, by thus speaking, referred to the primary Ogdoad, in which there was as yet no Jesus, and no Christ, the teacher of John. But that the apostle did not speak concerning their conjunctions, but concerning our Lord Jesus Christ, whom he also acknowledges as the Word of God, he himself has made evident. For, summing up his statements respecting the Word previously mentioned by him, he further declares, "And the Word was made flesh, and dwelt among us."[21] But, according to their hypothesis, the Word did not become flesh at all, inasmuch as He never went outside of the Pleroma, but that Saviour [became flesh] who was formed by a special dispensation [out of all the Æons], and was of later date than the Word.

3 Learn then, ye foolish men, that Jesus who suffered for us, and who dwelt among us, is Himself the Word of God. For if any other of the Æons had become flesh for our salvation, it would have been probable that the apostle spoke of another. But if the Word of the Father who descended is the same also that ascended, He, namely, the Only-begotten Son of the only God, who, according to the good pleasure of the Father, became flesh for the sake of men, the apostle certainly does not speak regarding any other, or concerning any Ogdoad, but respecting our Lord Jesus Christ. For, according to them, the Word did not originally become flesh. For they maintain that the Saviour assumed an animal body, formed in accordance with a special dispensation by an unspeakable providence, so as to become visible and palpable. But *flesh* is that which was of old formed for Adam by God out of the dust, and it is this that John has declared the Word of God became. Thus is their primary and first-begotten Ogdoad brought to nought. For, since Logos, and Monogenes, and Zoe, and Phōs, and Soter, and Christus, and the Son of God, and He who

---

21 John 1:14.

became incarnate for us, have been proved to be one and the same, the Ogdoad which they have built up at once falls to pieces. And when this is destroyed, their whole system sinks into ruin,—a system which they falsely dream into existence, and thus inflict injury on the Scriptures, while they build up their own hypothesis.

4 Then, again, collecting a set of expressions and names scattered here and there [in Scripture], they twist them, as we have already said, from a natural to a non-natural sense. In so doing, they act like those who bring forward any kind of hypothesis they fancy, and then endeavour to support them out of the poems of Homer, so that the ignorant imagine that Homer actually composed the verses bearing upon that hypothesis, which has, in fact, been but newly constructed; and many others are led so far by the regularly-formed sequence of the verses, as to doubt whether Homer may not have composed them. Of this kind is the following passage, where one, describing Hercules as having been sent by Eurystheus to the dog in the infernal regions, does so by means of these Homeric verses,—for there can be no objection to our citing these by way of illustration, since the same sort of attempt appears in both: —

"Thus saying, there sent forth from his house deeply groaning."—*Od.*, x. 76.

"The hero Hercules conversant with mighty deeds."—*Od.*, xxi. 26.

Eurystheus, the son of Sthenelus, descended from Perseus."—*Il.*, xix. 123.

"That he might bring from Erebus the dog of gloomy Pluto."—*Il.*, viii. 368.

"And he advanced like a mountain-bred lion confident of strength."—*Od.*, vi. 130.

"Rapidly through the city, while all his friends followed."—*Il.*, xxiv. 327.

"Both maidens, and youths, and much-enduring old men."—*Od.*, xi. 38.

"Mourning for him bitterly as one going forward to death."—*Il.*, xxiv. 328.

"But Mercury and the blue-eyed Minerva conducted him."—*Od.*, xi. 626.

"For she knew the mind of her brother, how it laboured with grief."—*Il.*, ii. 409.

Now, what simple-minded man, I ask, would not be led away by such verses as these to think that Homer actually framed them so with reference to the subject indicated? But he who is acquainted with the Homeric writings will recognise the verses indeed, but not the subject to which they are applied, as knowing that some of them were spoken of Ulysses, others of Hercules himself, others still of Priam, and others again of Menelaus and Agamemnon. But if he takes them and restores each of them to its proper position, he at once destroys the narrative in question. In like manner he also who retains unchangeable in his heart the rule of the truth which he received by means of baptism, will doubtless recognise the names, the expressions, and the parables taken from the Scriptures, but will by no means acknowledge the blasphemous use which these men make of them. For, though he will acknowledge the gems, he will certainly not receive the fox instead of the likeness of the king. But when he has restored every one of the expressions quoted to its proper position, and has fitted it to the body of the truth, he will lay bare, and prove to be without any foundation, the figment of these heretics.

65. Tertullian: Prescription of the Heretics and Against Marcion

We have already seen a selection from Tertullian's biting attack on people he considered to be heretical, his *Prescription of the Heretics* (see selection 36, Chapter 7). As mentioned in the introduction there, when Tertullian entitled his attack a "prescription" he was using an established legal term. In a court of law, it was possible to raise an objection to a case even before it had been brought to court, on technical grounds. This kind of preemptive objection—in which a case was literally ruled out of court—was called a "prescription." In this treatise Tertullian issues a prescription against the case that heretics want to make for the Scriptural justification of their views. Tertullian will not even allow them to argue their position, but rules that it is completely illegitimate on legal grounds. The heretics have no right to use the Scripture, or to claim that their interpretations of Scripture are correct, because the Scripture does not belong to them. The Scripture belongs only to those to whom it has been given by the apostles of Jesus: only faithful members of the church at large—not a heretical offshoot. Since the heretics have abandoned they church, they are not Christians; and since they are not Christians, they have no right to appeal to the Christian Scriptures.

In the second, brief, selection, taken from Tertullian's five-volume work *Against Marcion*, we see that despite the occasional proto-orthodox objection to figurative interpretations of texts (see selection 64 from Irenaeus), the proto-orthodox could as well employ creative figurative strategies for reading Scripture, when it suited their purpose, making the text say something other than would be suggested by a literal reading.

XIV

(Suppose) that heretics were not enemies to the truth, so that we were not forewarned to avoid them, what sort of conduct would it be to agree with men who do themselves confess that they are still seeking? For if they are still seeking, they have not as yet found anything amounting to certainty; and therefore, whatever they seem for a while to hold, they betray their own scepticism, whilst they continue seeking. You therefore, who seek after their fashion, looking to those who are themselves ever seeking, a doubter to doubters, a waverer to waverers, must needs be "led, blindly by the blind, down into the ditch." But when, for the sake of deceiving us, they pretend that they are still seeking, in order that they may palm their essays upon us by the suggestion of an anxious sympathy,—when, in short (after gaining an access to us), they proceed at once to insist on the necessity of our inquiring into such points as they were in the habit of advancing, then it is high time for us in moral obligation to repel them, so that they may know that it is not Christ, but themselves, whom we

Writings of Tertullian reproduced from *The Ante-Nicene Fathers*; vol. 3, ed. A. Cleveland Coxe. Reprint; 2nd ed. Grand Rapids: Eerdmans, 1989.

disavow. For since they are still seekers, they have no fixed tenets yet; and being not fixed in tenet, they have not yet believed; and being not yet believers, they are not Christians. But even though they have their tenets and their belief, they still say that inquiry is necessary in order to discussion. Previous, however, to the discussion, they deny what they confess not yet to have believed, so long as they keep it an object of inquiry. When men, therefore, are not Christians even on their own admission, how much more (do they fail to appear such) to us! What sort of truth is that which they patronize, when they commend it to us with a lie? Well, but they actually treat of the Scriptures and recommend (their opinions) out of the Scriptures! To be sure they do. From what other source could they derive arguments concerning the things of the faith, except from the records of the faith?

XV

We are therefore come to (the gist of) our position; for at this point we were aiming, and for this we were preparing in the preamble of our address (which we have just completed),—so that we may now join issue on the contention to which our adversaries challenge us. They put forward the Scriptures, and by this insolence of theirs they at once influence some. In the encounter itself, however, they weary the strong, they catch the weak, and dismiss waverers with a doubt. Accordingly, we oppose to them this step above all others, of not admitting them to any discussion of the Scriptures.

If in these lie their resources, before they can use them, it ought to be clearly seen to whom belongs the possession of the Scriptures, that none may be admitted to the use thereof who has no title at all to the privilege.

XVI

I might be thought to have laid down this position to remedy distrust in my case, or from a desire of entering on the contest in some other way, were there not reasons on my side, especially this, that our faith owes deference to the apostle, who forbids us to enter on "questions," or to lend our ears to new-fangled statements, or to consort with a heretic "after the first and second admonition," not, (be it observed,) after discussion. Discussion he has inhibited in this way, by designating *admonition* as the purpose of dealing with a heretic, and the *first* one too, because he is not a Christian; in order that he might not, after the manner of a Christian, seem to require correction again and again, and "before two or three witnesses," seeing that he ought to be corrected, for the very reason that he is not to be disputed with; and in the next place, because a controversy over the Scriptures can, clearly, produce no other effect than help to upset either the stomach or the brain.

XVII

Now this heresy of yours does not receive certain Scriptures; and whichever of them it does receive, it perverts by means of additions and diminutions, for the accomplishment of it own purpose; and such as it does receive, it receives not in their entirety; but even when it does receive any up to a certain point as entire, it nevertheless perverts even these by the contrivance of diverse interpretations. Truth is just as much opposed by an adulteration of its meaning as it is by a corruption of its text. Their vain presumptions must needs refuse to acknowledge the (writings) whereby they are refuted. They rely on those which they have falsely put together, and which they have selected, because of their ambiguity. Though most skilled in the Scriptures, you will make no progress, when everything which you maintain is denied on the other side, and whatever you deny is (by them) maintained. As for yourself, indeed, you will lose nothing but your breath, and gain nothing but vexation from their blasphemy.

XVIII

But with respect to the man for whose sake you enter on the discussion of the Scriptures, with the view of strengthening him when afflicted with doubts, (let me ask) will it be to the truth, or rather to heretical opinions that he will lean? Influenced by the very fact that he sees you have made no progress, whilst the other side is on an equal footing (with yourself) in denying and in defence, or at any rate on a like standing he will go away confirmed in his uncertainty by the discussion, not knowing which side to adjudge heretical. For, no doubt, they too are able to retort these things on us. It is indeed a necessary consequence that they should go so far as to say that adulterations of the Scriptures, and false expositions thereof, are rather introduced by ourselves, inasmuch as they, no less than we maintain that truth is on their side.

XIX

Our appeal, therefore, must not be made to the Scriptures; nor must controversy be admitted on points in which victory will either be impossible, or uncertain, or not certain enough. But even if a discussion from the Scriptures should not turn out in such a way as to place both sides on a par, (yet) the natural order of things would require that this point should be first proposed, which is now the only one which we must discuss: "With whom lies that very faith to which the Scriptures belong. From what and through whom, and when, and to whom, has been handed down that rule, by which men become Christians?" For wherever it shall be manifest that the true Christian rule and faith shall be, *there* will likewise be the true Scriptures and expositions thereof, and all the Christian traditions.

XXXVII

Since this is the case, in order that the truth may be adjudged to belong to us, "as many as walk according to the rule," which the church has handed down from the apostles, the apostles from Christ, *and* Christ from God, the reason of our position is clear, when it determines that heretics ought not

to be allowed to challenge an appeal to the Scriptures, since we, without the Scriptures, prove that they have nothing to do with the Scriptures. For as they are heretics, they cannot be true Christians, because it is not from Christ that they get that which they pursue of their own mere choice, and from the pursuit incur and admit the name of heretics. Thus, not being Christians, they have acquired no right to the Christian Scriptures; and it may be very fairly said to them, "Who are you? When and whence did you come? As you are none of mine, what have you to do with that which is mine? Indeed, Marcion, by what right do you hew my wood? By whose permission, Valentinus, are you diverting the streams of my fountain? By what power, Apelles, are you removing my landmarks? This is my property. Why are you, the rest, sowing and feeding here at your own pleasure? This (I say) is my property. I have long possessed it; I possessed it before you. I hold sure title-deeds from the original owners themselves, to whom the estate belonged. I am the heir of the apostles. Just as they carefully prepared their will and testament, and committed it to a trust, and adjured (the trustees to be faithful to their charge), even so do I hold it. As for you, they have, it is certain, always held you as disinherited, and rejected you as strangers—as enemies. But on what ground are heretics strangers and enemies to the apostles, if it be not from the difference of their teaching, which each individual of his own mere will has either advanced or received in opposition to the apostles?"

XXXVIII

Where diversity of doctrine is found, *there,* then, must the corruption both of the Scriptures and the expositions thereof be regarded as existing. On those whose purpose it was to teach differently, lay the necessity of differently arranging the instruments of doctrine. They could not possibly have effected their diversity of teaching in any other way than by having a difference in the means whereby they taught. As in their case, corruption in doctrine could not possibly have succeeded without a corruption also of its instruments, so to ourselves also integrity of doctrine could not have accrued, without integrity in those means by which doctrine is managed. Now, what is there in our Scriptures which is contrary to us? What of our own have we introduced, that we should have to take it away again, or else add to it, or alter it, in order to restore to its natural soundness anything which is contrary to it, and contained in the Scriptures? What we are ourselves, that also the Scriptures are, (and have been) from the beginning. Of them we have our being, before there was any other way, before they were interpolated by you. Now, inasmuch as all interpolation must be believed to be a later process, for the express reason that it proceeds from rivalry which is never in any case previous to nor home-born with that which it emulates, it is as incredible to every man of sense that we should seem to have introduced any corrupt text into the Scriptures, existing, as we have been, from the very first, and being the first, as it is that they have not in fact introduced it, who are both later in date and opposed (to the Scriptures). One man perverts the Scriptures with his hand, another their meaning by his exposition. For although Valentinus seems to use the entire volume, he has none the less laid violent hands on the truth only with a more cunning mind and skill than Marcion. Marcion expressly and openly used the knife, not the pen, since he made such an excision of the Scriptures as suited his own subject-matter. Valentinus, however, abstained from such excision, because he did not invent Scriptures to square with his own subject-matter, but adapted his matter to the Scriptures; and yet he took away more, and added more, by removing the proper meaning of every particular word, and adding fantastic arrangements of things which have no real existence.

66. Origen: Commentary on John

Among Origen's vast number of writings, his commentary on the Gospel of John is particularly interesting, in no small measure because it occasionally offers a point-by-point refutation of the interpretations of this Gospel set forth in an earlier writing by a Valentinian Gnostic named Heracleon. It is indeed a striking fact of Christian history that Heracleon's work is the first known commentary of any kind written by a Christian on any text of Scripture—written not by a proto-orthodox believer but by one later deemed to have been a Gnostic heretic. We are fortunate indeed that Origen occasionally quotes Heracleon's understanding of the text, verse by verse, before giving his "correction" of it or even, on occasion, his approbation. These quotations appear to be accurate, so that through them we can see how a Valentinian would approach this book of Scripture, the Gospel most in favor among Valentinians and, evidently, other kinds of Gnostic as well. In turn, Origen's responses to these interpretations show an unusually sharp and intelligent mind at work, revealing how a proto-orthodox author would go about interpreting difficult texts in line with his own theological beliefs.

Origen: Commentary on John, reproduced from Ronald Heine, *Origen: Commentary on the Gospel according to John*. Washington, DC: Catholic University Press, 1967. Used with permission.

100 Heracleon, who is said to be a disciple of Valentinus, in explaining the statement, "All things were made through him,"[1] has, in my opinion, violently and without proof understood "all things" to mean the cosmos and what is in it. At the same time, to suit his own purpose, he excludes from "all things," those things which exceed the world and the things in it. For he says: "Neither the aeon nor the things in the aeon have been made through the Word." He thinks these things were made before the Word. And he adopts a rather shameless attitude to the statement, "And without him nothing was made,"[2] because he does not respect the saying, "Add not to his words, lest he reprove you and you be a liar."[3] He adds to "nothing" the words, "of the things in the cosmos and in the creation."

101 And since it is clear that his statements are exceedingly distorted and made contrary to manifest facts, if what is divine according to his way of thinking is excluded from the "all things," but those things which are utterly destroyed, as he thinks, are properly called "all things," we must not spend more time refuting statements which are obviously absurd. For example, when Scripture says, "Without him nothing was made," he adds, without warrant from Scripture, the words, "of the things in the cosmos and in the creation." Nor does he prove this with plausible argument, since he considers himself worthy to be believed like the prophets or apostles who, in an authoritative manner and beyond criticism, left writings of salvation for their contemporaries and those who would come after themselves.

102 Furthermore, he also understands "all things were made through him" in a peculiar way when he says, "The one who provided the creator with the cause for making the world, that is the Word, is not the one 'from whom,' or 'by whom,' but the one 'through whom', taking what has been written contrary to the customary usage of the phrase. For if the truth of things were as he understands it, it would have had to be written that all things have been made by the Word through the creator, and not contrariwise through the Word by the creator.

103 We, on the one hand, by using the phrase "through whom" properly in its customary usage have not left our interpretation unattested. He, however, by not having supported his private understanding from the divine Scriptures, appears both to have suspected the truth and to have opposed it shamelessly. For he says, "The Word himself did not create as though under the impulse of another, that the phrase, 'through him,' should be understood in this way, but another created under his impulse."

104 But this is not the time to prove that the Creator did not become the servant of the Word and make the world, and to show that the Word became the servant of the creator and prepared the world. For according to the prophet David, "God spoke and they were made; he commanded and they were created."[4] For the uncreated God "commanded" the firstborn of all creation[5] and "they were created." This includes not only the cosmos and the things in it, but also all that remains, "whether thrones, or dominations, or principalities, or powers; for all things have been created through him and for him, and he is before all things."[6]

137 But when Heracleon came to the passage, "What was made in him was life,"[7] he took "in him" in a very forced manner to mean "in spiritual men," as though he thought the Word and spiritual men were the same, although he did not say this explicitly. And as if to give a reason, he says, "For he himself furnished their first form at their origin when he brought the things sown by another into form and illumination and their own individuality, and brought them forth."

---

1 John 1:3.

2 Ibid.

3 Prov 30:6.

---

4 Cf. Ps 148:5.

5 Cf. Col 1:15.

6 Cf. Col 1:16–17.

7 John 1:4.

138 He did not, however, also observe carefully what Paul says about spirituals, namely that he left unsaid that they are men. "The natural man does not accept the things of the spirit of God, for they are foolishness to him. But the spiritual judges all things."[8] We say that it is no accident that he has not added the noun "man" in the case of the spiritual. For the spiritual is better than "man," since man is characterized either by soul or body or both of these together, but not also by spirit which is more divine than these. The spiritual receives this title in accordance with his predominate participation in the spirit.

139 At the same time, however, the elements of such an hypothesis are declared without even an apparent proof, nor was he able to arrive at ordinary persuasiveness in his argument concerning these matters. Enough about Heracleon.

194 But Heracleon says the statement, "He stands in your midst"[9] is the equivalent of: He is already present and is in the world and among men, and is already manifest to all of you. In this way he nullifies what we have shown about him permeating the whole world.

195 We must reply, When is he not present? And when is he not in the world? Even the gospel says as much: "He was in the world, and the world was made through him."[10] It is for this reason too that these to whom the Word is he "whom you do not know,"[11] do not know him, because they have not yet gone out of the world, and "the world did not know him."[12]

196 At what time did he interrupt his sojourn among men? Was he not in Isaias when he said, "The spirit of the Lord is upon me, because he has anointed me,"[13] and "I became manifest to those who were not seeking me"?[14] Let them say if he was not also in David when he said, not on his own, "But I was appointed king by him over Sion his holy mountain,"[15] and as many other words as have been recorded in the Psalms in the person of Christ.

197 And why must I demonstrate in detail that he was always among men? The statements which are capable of showing this clearly would be difficult to enumerate. Must I refute what was not stated correctly—namely "He is already present and is in the world and among men"—as Heracleon's interpretation of the words: "He has stood in your midst"?[16]

His statement, however, is not unconvincing that the words, "who comes after me,"[17] reveal that John is the forerunner of the Christ: For he is truly like a servant running before his master.

198 Heracleon has, however, taken the statement, "I am not worthy to loose the thong of his shoes,"[18] much too simply, in the sense that the Baptist confesses through these words that he is not worthy even of the lowliest service to the Christ. But after this interpretation he has suggested rather plausibly this view: I am not sufficient that for my sake he should descend from his greatness and receive flesh as a shoe, of which I can give no account or description or explain the plan concerning it.

199 The same Heracleon, after taking the shoe as the world in a very powerful and ingenious manner, changed his position to declare very impiously that all these words must be understood also about that person who is indicated by John. For he thinks that the Creator of the world, who is inferior to Christ, acknowledges this fact through these words. This is the greatest of all impieties. For the Father who sent him, the God of the living, as Jesus himself testifies, being God of Abraham,

---

8 Cf. 1 Cor 2:14–15.

9 Cf. John 1:26.

10 John 1:10.

11 John 1:26.

12 Cf. John 1:10.

13 Isa 61:1.

14 Isa 65:1; cf. Rom 10:20.

15 Ps 2:6.

16 John 1:26.

17 John 1:27.

18 Ibid.

and of Isaac, and of Jacob,[19] the Lord of heaven and earth because he has made them, is alone good and greater than the one who was sent.

201 But even if, as we said previously, Heracleon has taken all the world in a very powerful manner to be the shoe of Jesus, I do not think we must agree. For how will the saying, "Heaven is my throne and the earth my footstool,"[20] which Jesus attested to be said of the Father, be retained with such an interpretation? For "swear not by heaven," he said, "because it is the throne of God, nor by the earth, for it is his footstool."[21]

202 And how will it be possible to set the text, "'Do not I fill heaven and earth?' says the Lord,"[22] side by side with the whole world understood as Jesus' shoe? It is worthwhile, however, to give attention to whether we must understand the words in relation to the fact that the Word and Wisdom have permeated the whole world, and the Father is in the Son, as we presented it, or he who first girded himself with all creation, because the Son was in him, granted to the Savior, since he was second after him and God the Word, to pervade the whole creation.

203 It will be especially worthwhile for those who can comprehend the ceaseless movement of so great a heaven which brings so great a multitude of stars around with itself from east to west to inquire into what immanent power is so great and ancient in all the world. It may, perhaps, be impious to dare say that this power is different from the Father and the Son.

57 Let us also see what Heracleon says on these passages. He says that the [fountain and] the life and glory pertaining to it was insipid, temporary, and deficient, for it was physical. And he thinks he produces proof that it was physical from the fact that Jacob's cattle drank from it.[23]

58 Now we would not object, if he took the knowledge that is in part[24] to be insipid, temporary, and deficient, or that which is from the Scriptures in comparison with the words that cannot be spoken, that "it is not permitted to man to speak,"[25] [or] all the present knowledge that is "through a mirror and a riddle"[26] and is set aside when that which is perfect comes. But he would be culpable if he does this to slander the ancient words.

59 He is not wrong, however, when he says that the water that the Savior gives is of his spirit and power.

60 And he has explained the statement, "But he shall not thirst forever,"[27] as follows with these very words: For the life he gives is eternal and never perishes, as, indeed, does the first life which comes from the well; the life he gives remains. For the grace and the gift of our Savior is not to be taken away, nor is it consumed, nor does it perish, when one partakes of it.

61 He would be correct when he grants that the first life perishes if he meant that life which is according to the letter, when it seeks and discovers the life according to the Spirit by the removal of the veil. But, if he is accusing the ancient words of passing out of existence all together, it is clear that he does this because he does not perceive that those good words contain the shadow of future things.

62 Now his interpretation of the "leaping water"[28] is not unconvincing. He takes it to refer to those who partake of that which is richly supplied to them from above and who themselves cause what is supplied to them to gush out for the eternal life of others.

63 But he also praises the Samaritan woman because she demonstrated a faith that was unhesitating

19 Cf. Matt 22:32.
20 Isa 66:1; Acts 7.49.
21 Cf. Matt 5:34–35.
22 Jer 23:24.
23 Cf. John 4:12.

24 Cf. 1 Cor 13:9.
25 2 Cor 12:4.
26 Cf. 1 Cor 13:12.
27 Cf. John 4:14.
28 Cf. John 4:14.

and appropriate to her nature, when she had no doubt about what he said to her.[29]

64 We too would agree, then, if he were admitting that she had free choice and not hinting that her nature was more excellent. But if he is referring the cause of her consent to her natural state, as something not present in all people, his argument must be refuted.

65 And I do not know how Heracleon, by taking note of what has not been written, says on the statement, "Give me this water,"[30] that, therefore, when the Samaritan woman had been pricked a little by his word, she hated henceforth even the place of the so-called living water.

66 And furthermore, on the saying, "Give me this water that I may not thirst nor come here to draw,"[31] he says that the woman says this to show that the water is burdensome, hard to procure, and lacks nourishment. From what source can he demonstrate that Jacob's water lacks nourishment?

67 And further, in reference to the clause, "He says to her,"[32] Heracleon says that it is clear that he is saying something like this: If you wish to receive this water, go call your husband. Now he thinks that the one the Savior calls the Samaritan woman's husband is her pleroma, and that by coming to the Savior with him she might be able to acquire power, unity, and union with her pleroma from him. For Heracleon says that he did not ask her to summon a physical husband, since indeed he would not have been ignorant of the fact that she did not have a lawful husband.

68 But here he clearly distorts the text when he says that the Savior said to her, "Call your husband and come here,"[33] meaning her consort from the pleroma. For if this were so, he would have to explain in what manner she must summon her husband that she might come to the Savior with him.

69 But since, as Heracleon says, she was ignorant of her own husband at the spiritual level, and at the literal level she was ashamed to say that she had an adulterer, and not a husband, will he not issue a vain command who says, "Go, call your husband and come here"?[34]

70 Then, on the statement, "You have said truly that you do not have a husband," Heracleon says that these words were spoken because the Samaritan woman did not have a husband in the world, for her husband was in the aeon.

71 We have read: "You have had five husbands," but in Heracleon we have found: You have had six husbands.

72 And he takes the six husbands to mean all material evil. These were the husbands with whom the Samaritan woman was united and with whom she associated contrary to reason, committing fornication, being insulted, rejected, and forsaken by them.

73 But we must reply that if the spiritual [nature] committed fornication, the spiritual [nature] sinned. And if the spiritual [nature] sinned, the spiritual [nature] was not a good tree. For according to the Gospel, "A good tree cannot bear evil fruit."[35]

74 It is clear that the making of fables is their undoing. But if it is impossible for a good tree to bear evil fruit, and the Samaritan woman was a good tree because she happened to be spiritual, it is fitting to say to him that either her fornication was not sin or she did not commit fornication.

---

29 See FOTC 80:25–26.

30 John 4:15.

31 John 4:15.

32 Cf. John 4:16.

33 Cf. John 4:16.

34 John 4:16.

35 Cf. Matt 7:18.

67. Origen: On First Principles

One of Origen's most significant books was called *On First Principles* (for another excerpt, see Chapter 16). This was the first known "systematic theology" from the early Christian church, an attempt to systematize the important Christian doctrines about God, Christ, the Spirit, the Creation, and so on. Origen also spends considerable time discussing the Christian Scriptures and, in particular, how they are to be interpreted.

In the selection given here, taken from Book IV of the work, Origen explains how the text of Scripture is susceptible of various kinds of interpretation. Just as the human being comprises body, soul, and spirit, so too does Scripture. Some passages, of course, are to be interpreted as meaning just what, on close and careful examination, they appear to say literally (a kind of "bodily" interpretation). But other passages are problematic because they say things that cannot be literally true or because they contradict what is said in other texts of Scripture. All Scripture is inspired by the Holy Spirit, however. That means that in these problematic passages the Spirit has intended the informed reader to understand the deeper, figurative significance of the text (its "soulish" or "spiritual" meaning)—not simply or even principally its literal meaning.

Book IV

1 Now that we have spoken cursorily about the inspiration of the divine scriptures it is necessary to discuss the manner in which they are to be read and understood, since many mistakes have been made in consequence of the method by which the holy documents ought to be interpreted not having been discovered by the multitude. For the hard-hearted and ignorant members of the circumcision have refused to believe in our Saviour because they think that they are keeping closely to the language of the prophecies that relate to him, and they see that he did not literally 'proclaim release to captives' or build what they consider to be a real 'city of God' or 'cut off the chariots from Ephraim and the horse from Jerusalem' or 'eat butter and honey, and choose the good before he knew or preferred the evil.'[1]

Further, they think that it is the wolf, the four-footed animal, which is said in prophecy to be going to 'feed with the lamb, and the leopard to lie down with the kid, and the calf and bull and lion to feed together, led by a little child, and the ox and the bear to pasture together, their young ones growing up with each other, and the lion to eat straw like the ox';[2] and having seen none of these events literally happening during the advent of him whom we believe to be Christ they did not

---

1 For these passages see Isa 61:1 (Luke 4:19); Ps 46:4; Ezek 48:15 ff; Zech 9:10; Isa 7:15.

2 See Isa 11:6, 7

Origen: On First Principles, reproduced from G.W. Butterworth, trans. *Origen On First Principles*. London: SPCK, 1973; used with permission of SPCK.

accept our Lord Jesus, but crucified him on the ground that he had wrongly called himself Christ.

And the members of the heretical sects, reading the passage, 'A fire has been kindled in mine anger';[3] and 'I am a jealous God, visiting the sins of the fathers upon the children to the third and fourth generation';[4] and 'It repenteth me that I have anointed Saul to be king';[5] and 'I, God, make peace and create evil';[6] and elsewhere, 'There is no evil in a city, which the Lord did not do';[7] and further, 'Evils came down from the Lord upon the gates of Jerusalem';[8] and 'An evil spirit from the Lord troubled Saul';[9] and ten thousand other passages like these, have not dared to disbelieve that they are the writings of God, but believe them to belong to the Creator, whom the Jews worship.[10] Consequently they think that since the Creator is imperfect and not good, the Saviour came here to proclaim a more perfect God who they say is not the Creator, and about whom they entertain diverse opinions. Then having once fallen away from the Creator, who is the sole unbegotten God, they have given themselves up to fictions, fashioning mythical hypotheses according to which they suppose that there are some things that are seen and others that are not seen, all of which are the fancies of their own minds.

Moreover, even the simpler of those who claim to belong to the Church, while believing indeed that there is none greater than the Creator, in which they are right, yet believe such things about him as would not be believed of the most savage and unjust of men.

2 Now the reason why all those we have mentioned hold false opinions and make impious or ignorant assertions about God appears to be nothing else but this, that scripture is not understood in its spiritual sense, but is interpreted according to the bare letter. On this account we must explain to those who believe that the sacred books are not the works of men, but that they were composed and have come down to us as a result of the inspiration of the Holy Spirit by the will of the Father of the universe through Jesus Christ, what are the methods of interpretation that appear right to us, who keep to the rule of the heavenly Church of Jesus Christ through the succession from the Apostles.

That there are certain mystical revelations made known through the divine scriptures is believed by all, even by the simplest of those who are adherents of the word; but what these revelations are, fair-minded and humble men confess that they do not know. If, for instance, an inquirer were to be in a difficulty, about the intercourse of Lot with his daughters,[11] or the two wives of Abraham,[12] or the two sisters married to Jacob,[13] or the two hand-maids who bore children by him,[14] they can say nothing except that these things are mysteries not understood by us.

But when the passage about the equipment of the tabernacle is read,[15] believing that the things described therein are types, they seek for ideas which they can attach to each detail that is mentioned in connexion with the tabernacle. Now so far as concerns their belief that the tabernacle is a type of something they are not wrong; but in rightly attaching the word of scripture to the particular idea of which the tabernacle is a type, here they sometimes fall into error. And they declare that all narratives that are supposed to speak

---

3 Deut 32:22; Jer 15:14.

4 Exod 20:5.

5 1 Sam 15:11.

6 Isa 45:7.

7 Amos 3:6.

8 Micah 1:12.

9 1 Sam 18:10.

10 See On First Principles 2.5.1.

11 See Gen 19:30 ff.

12 See Gen 16.

13 See Gen 29:21 ff.

14 Gen 30:1–13.

15 See Exod 25: ff.

about marriage or the begetting of children or wars or any other stories whatever that may be accepted among the multitude are types; but when we ask, of what, then sometimes owing to the lack of thorough training, sometimes owing to rashness, and occasionally, even when one is well trained and of sound judgment, owing to man's exceedingly great difficulty in discovering these things, the interpretation of every detail is not altogether clear.

3 And what must we say about the prophecies, which we all know are filled with riddles and dark sayings?[16] Or if we come to the gospels, the accurate interpretation even of these, since it is an interpretation of the mind of Christ, demands that grace that was given to him who said, 'We have the mind of Christ, that we may know the things that were freely given to us by God. Which things also we speak, not in words which man's wisdom teacheth, but which the Spirit teacheth.'[17] And who, on reading the revelations made to John, could fail to be amazed at the deep obscurity of the unspeakable mysteries contained therein, which are evident even to him who does not understand what is written? And as for the apostolic epistles, what man who is skilled in literary interpretation would think them to be plain and easily understood, when even in them there are thousands of passages that provide, as if through a window, a narrow opening leading to multitudes of the deepest thoughts?

Seeing, therefore, that these things are so, and that thousands of men make mistakes, it is dangerous for us when we read to declare lightly that we understand things for which the 'key of knowledge' is necessary, which the Saviour says is with 'the lawyers'.[18] And as for those who are unwilling to admit that these men held the truth before the coming of Christ, let them explain to us how it is that our Lord Jesus Christ says that the 'key of knowledge' was with them, that is, with

men who as these objectors say, had no books containing the secrets of knowledge and the all-perfect mysteries.[19] For the passage runs as follows: 'Woe unto you lawyers, for ye have taken away the key of knowledge. Ye entered not in yourselves, and them that were entering in ye hindered.'[20]

4 The right way, therefore, as it appears to us, of approaching the scriptures and gathering their meaning, is the following, which is extracted from the writings themselves. We find some such rule as this laid down by Solomon in the Proverbs concerning the divine doctrines written therein: 'Do thou pourtray them threefold in counsel and knowledge, that thou mayest answer words of truth to those who question thee'.[21]

One must therefore pourtray the meaning of the sacred writings in a threefold way upon one's own soul, so that the simple man may be edified by what we may call the flesh of the scripture, this name being given to the obvious interpretation; while the man who has made some progress may be edified by its soul, as it were; and the man who is perfect and like those mentioned by the apostle: 'We speak wisdom among the perfect; yet a wisdom not of this world, nor of the rulers of this world, which are coming to nought; but we speak God's wisdom in a mystery, even the wisdom that hath been hidden, which God foreordained before the worlds unto our glory'[22]—this man may be edified by the spiritual law,[23] which has 'a shadow of the good things to come'[24] For just as man consists of body, soul and spirit, so in the same way does the scripture, which has been prepared by God to be given for man's salvation.

We therefore read in this light the passage in The Shepherd, a book which is despised by some,

---

16 See Prov 1:6 and Origen, *Con Celsum* 3:45; 7:10.

17 1 Cor 2:16, 12, 13.

18 See Luke 11:52.

19 Books, that is, such as the Gnostics claimed to possess.

20 Luke 11:52.

21 Prov 22:20, 21.

22 1 Cor 2:6, 7.

23 See Rom 7:14.

24 See Heb 10:1.

where Hermas is bidden to 'write two books', and after this to 'announce to the presbyters of the Church' what he has learned from the Spirit. This is the wording: 'Thou shalt write two books, and shalt give one to Clement and one to Grapte. And Grapte shall admonish the widows and the orphans. But Clement shall send to the cities without, and thou shalt announce to the presbyters of the Church.'

Now Grapte, who admonishes the widows and orphans, is the bare letter, which admonishes those child souls that are not yet able to enrol God as their Father and are on this account called orphans, and which also admonishes those who while no longer associating with the unlawful bridegroom are in widowhood because they have not yet become worthy of the true one. But Clement, who has already gone beyond the letter, is said to send the sayings 'to the cities without', as if to say, to the souls that are outside all bodily and lower thoughts; while the disciple of the Spirit is bidden to announce the message in person, no longer through letters but through living words, to the presbyters or elders of the whole Church of God, to men who have grown grey through wisdom.

5 But since there are certain passages of scripture which, as we shall show in what follows, have no bodily sense at all, there are occasions when we must seek only for the soul and the spirit, as it were, of the passage. And possibly this is the reason why the waterpots which, as we read in the gospel according to John, are said to be set there 'for the purifying of the Jews', contain two or three firkins apiece.[25] The language alludes to those who are said by the apostle to be Jews 'inwardly',[26] and it means that these are purified through the word of the scriptures, which contain in some cases 'two firkins', that is, so to speak, the soul meaning and the spiritual meaning, and in other cases three, since some passages possess, in addition to those before-mentioned, a bodily sense as well, which is capable of edifying the hearers. And six waterpots may reasonably allude to those who are being purified in the world, which was made in six days, a perfect number.

6 That it is possible to derive benefit from the first, and to this extent helpful meaning, is witnessed by the multitudes of sincere and simple believers. But of the kind of explanation which penetrates as it were to the soul an illustration is found in Paul's first epistle to the Corinthians. 'For,' he says, 'it is written; thou shalt not muzzle the ox that treadeth out the corn'. Then in explanation of this law he adds, 'Is it for the oxen that God careth? Or saith he it altogether for our sake? Yea, for our sake it was written, because he that ploweth ought to plow in hope, and he that thresheth, to thresh in hope of partaking.'[27] And most of the interpretations adapted to the multitude which are in circulation and which edify those who cannot understand the higher meanings have something of the same character.

But it is a spiritual explanation when one is able to show of what kind of 'heavenly things' the Jews 'after the flesh' served a copy and a shadow, and of what 'good things to come' the law has a 'shadow'.[28] And, speaking generally, we have, in accordance with the apostolic promise, to seek after 'the wisdom in a mystery, even the wisdom that hath been hidden, which God foreordained before the worlds unto the glory' of the righteous, 'which none of the rulers of this world knew'.[29] The same apostle also says somewhere, after mentioning certain narratives from Exodus and Numbers, that 'these things happened unto them figuratively, and they were written for our sake, upon whom the ends of the ages are come.'[30] He also gives hints to show what these things were figures of, when he says: 'For they drank of that spiritual rock that followed them, and that rock was Christ.'[31]

---

25 See John 2:6.

26 See Rom 2:29.

27 1 Cor 9:9, 10 (Deut 25:4).

28 See Heb 8:5; Rom 8:5; Heb 10:7.

29 See 1 Cor 2:7, 8.

30 1 Cor 10:11.

31 1 Cor 10:4.

In another epistle, when outlining the arrangements of the tabernacle he quotes the words: 'Thou shalt make all things according to the figure that was shown thee in the mount.'[32] Further, in the epistle to the Galatians, speaking in terms of reproach to those who believe that they are reading the law and yet do not understand it, and laying it down that they who do not believe that there are allegories in the writings do not understand the law, he says: 'Tell me, ye that desire to be under the law, do ye not hear the law? For it is written, that Abraham had two sons, one by the handmaid and one by the free woman. Howbeit the son by the handmaid is born after the flesh; but the son by the free woman is born through promise. Which things contain an allegory; for these women are two covenants',[33] and what follows. Now we must carefully mark each of the words spoken by him. He says, 'Ye that desire to be under the law' (not, 'ye that are under the law') 'do ye not hear the law?' hearing being taken to mean understanding and knowing.

And in the epistle to the Colossians, briefly epitomising the meaning of the entire system of the law, he says: 'Let no man therefore judge you in meat or in drink or in respect of a feast day or a new moon or a sabbath, which are a shadow of the things to come.'[34] Further, in the epistle to the Hebrews, when discoursing about those who are of the circumcision, he writes: 'They who serve that which is a copy and shadow of the heavenly things.'[35] Now it is probable that those who have once admitted that the apostle is a divinely inspired man will feel no difficulty in regard to the five books ascribed to Moses; but in regard to the rest of the history they desire to learn whether those events also 'happened figuratively.'[36] We must note the quotation in the epistle to the Romans: 'I have left for myself seven thousand men, who have not bowed the knee to Baal,'[37] found in the third book of the Kings. Here Paul has taken it to stand for those who are Israelites 'according to election',[38] for not only are the gentiles benefited by the coming of Christ, but also some who belong to the divine race.

7 This being so, we must outline what seems to us to be the marks of a true understanding of the scriptures. And in the first place we must point out that the aim of the Spirit who, by the providence of God through the Word who was 'in the beginning with God',[39] enlightened the servants of the truth, that is, the prophets and apostles, was pre-eminently concerned with the unspeakable mysteries connected with the affairs of men—and by men I mean at the present moment souls that make use of bodies—his purpose being that the man who is capable of being taught might by 'searching out' and devoting himself to the 'deep things'[40] revealed in the spiritual meaning of the words become partaker of all the doctrines of the Spirit's counsel.

And when we speak of the needs of souls, who cannot otherwise reach perfection except through the rich and wise truth about God, we attach of necessity pre-eminent importance to the doctrines concerning God and His only-begotten Son: of what nature the Son is, and in what manner he can be the Son of God, and what are the causes of his descending to the level of human flesh and completely assuming humanity; and what, also, is the nature of his activity, and towards whom and at what times it is exercised. It was necessary, too, that the doctrines concerning beings akin to man and the rest of the rational creatures, both those that are nearer the divine and those that have fallen from blessedness, and the causes of the fall of these latter, should be included in the accounts of the

---

32 Heb 8:5 (Exod 25:40).

33 Gal 4:21–24.

34 Col 2:16, 17.

35 Heb 8:5.

36 See 1 Cor 10:11.

37 Rom 11:4 (1 Kings 19:18).

38 See Rom 11:5.

39 See John 1:1.

40 See 1 Cor 2:10.

divine teaching; and the question of the differences between souls and how these differences arose, and what the world is and why it exists, and further, how it comes about that evil is so widespread and so terrible on earth, and whether it is not only to be found on earth but also in other places—all this it was necessary that we should learn.

8 Now while these and similar subjects were in the mind of the Spirit who enlightened the souls of the holy servants of the truth, there was a second aim, pursued for the sake of those who were unable to endure the burden of investigating matters of such importance. This was to conceal the doctrine relating to the before-mentioned subjects in words forming a narrative that contained a record dealing with the visible creation, the formation of man and the successive descendants of the first human beings until the time when they became many; and also in other stories that recorded the acts of righteous men and the sins that these same men occasionally committed, seeing they were but human, and the deeds of wickedness, licentiousness and greed done by lawless and impious men.

But the most wonderful thing is, that by means of stories of wars and the conquerors and the conquered certain secret truths are revealed to those who are capable of examining these narratives; and, even more marvellous, through a written system of law the laws of truth are prophetically indicated, all these having been recorded in a series with a power which is truly appropriate to the wisdom of God. For the intention was to make even the outer covering of the spiritual truths, I mean the bodily part of the scriptures, in many respects not unprofitable but capable of improving the multitude in so far as they receive it.

9 But if the usefulness of the law and the sequence and ease of the narrative were at first sight clearly discernible throughout, we should be unaware that there was anything beyond the obvious meaning for us to understand in the scriptures. Consequently the Word of God has arranged for certain stumbling-blocks, as it were, and hindrances and impossibilities to be inserted in the midst of the law and the history, in order that we may not be completely drawn away by the sheer attractiveness of the language, and so either reject the true doctrines absolutely, on the ground that we learn from the scriptures nothing worthy of God, or else by never moving away from the letter fail to learn anything of the more divine element.

And we must also know this, that because the principal aim was to announce the connexion that exists among spiritual events, those that have already happened and those that are yet to come to pass, whenever the Word found that things which had happened in history could be harmonised with these mystical events he used them, concealing from the multitude their deeper meaning. But wherever in the narrative the accomplishment of some particular deeds, which had been previously recorded for the sake of their more mystical meanings, did not correspond with the sequence of the intellectual truths, the scripture wove into the story something which did not happen, occasionally something which could not happen, and occasionally something which might have happened but in fact did not. Sometimes a few words are inserted which in the bodily sense are not true, and at other times a greater number.

A similar method can be discerned also in the law, where it is often possible to find a precept that is useful for its own sake, and suitable to the time when the law was given. Sometimes, however, the precept does not appear to be useful. At other times even impossibilities are recorded in the law for the sake of the more skilful and inquiring readers, in order that these, by giving themselves to the toil of examining what is written, may gain a sound conviction of the necessity of seeking in such instances a meaning worthy of God.

And not only did the Spirit supervise the writings which were previous to the coming of Christ, but because he is the same Spirit and proceeds from the one God he has dealt in like manner with the gospels and the writings of the apostles. For the history even of these is not everywhere pure, events being woven together in the bodily sense without having actually happened; nor do the law and the commandments contained therein entirely declare what is reasonable.

1 Now[41] what man of intelligence will believe that the first and the second and the third day, and the evening and the morning existed without the sun and moon and stars? And that the first day, if we may so call it, was even without a heaven?[42] And who is so silly as to believe that God, after the manner of a farmer, 'planted a paradise eastward in Eden', and set in it a visible and palpable 'tree of life', of such a sort that anyone who tasted its fruit with his bodily teeth would gain life; and again that one could partake of 'good and evil' by masticating the fruit taken from the tree of that name? And when God is said to 'walk in the paradise in the cool of the day' and Adam to hide himself behind a tree, I do not think anyone will doubt that these are figurative expressions which indicate certain mysteries through a semblance of history and not through actual events.[43]

Further, when Cain 'goes out from the face of God' it seems clear to thoughtful men that this statement impels the reader to inquire what the 'face of God' is and how anyone can 'go out' from it.[44] And what more need I say, when those who are not altogether blind can collect thousands of such instances, recorded as actual events, but which did not happen literally?

Even the gospels are full of passages of this kind, as when the devil takes Jesus up into a 'high mountain' in order to show him from thence 'the kingdoms of the whole world and the glory of them'.[45] For what man who does not read such passages carelessly would fail to condemn those who believe that with the eye of the flesh, which

requires a great height to enable us to perceive what is below and at our feet, the kingdoms of the Persians, Scythians, Indians and Parthians were seen, and the manner in which their rulers are glorified by men? And the careful reader will detect thousands of other passages like this in the gospels, which will convince him that events which did not take place at all are woven into the records of what literally did happen.

2 And to come to the Mosaic legislation, many of the laws, so far as their literal observance is concerned, are clearly irrational, while others are impossible. An example of irrationality is the prohibition to eat vultures, seeing that nobody even in the worst famine was ever driven by want to the extremity of eating these creatures.[46] And in regard to the command that children of eight days old who are uncircumcised 'shall be destroyed from among their people',[47] if the law relating to these children were really meant to be carried out according to the letter, the proper course would be to order the death of their fathers or those by whom they were being brought up. But as it is the Scripture says: 'Every male that is uncircumcised, who shall not be circumcised on the eighth day, shall be destroyed from among his people'.[48]

And if you would like to see some impossibilities that are enacted in the law, let us observe that the goat-stag, which Moses commands us to offer in sacrifice as a clean animal, is a creature that cannot possibly exist; while as to the griffin,[49] which the lawgiver forbids to be eaten, there is no record that it has ever fallen into the hands of man. Moreover in regard to the celebrated sabbath, a careful reader will see that the command, 'Ye shall sit each one in your dwellings; let none of you go out from his place on the sabbath day,'[50] is an impossible one

---

41 See Gen 1:5–13.

42 See Gen 2:8, 9. and cp. Philo, *Legis alleg.* 1:14. 'Let not our reasoning admit such gross impiety as to suppose that God works as a farmer and plants gardens.'

43 See Gen 3:8.

44 See Gen 4:16 and Philo, *De poster. Cain* 1:1.

45 See Matt 4:8.

---

46 Lev 11:14. Rufinus has omitted this example.

47 See Gen 17:14 (Sept.).

48 See Gen 17:14 (Sept.).

49 Gr. *gryps,* a variety of eagle. Levit 11:13; Deut 14:12.

50 Exod 16:29.

to observe literally, for no living creature could sit for a whole day and not move from his seat.

Consequently the members of the circumcision and all those who maintain that nothing more than the actual wording is signified make no inquiry whatever into some matters, such as the goat-stag, the griffin and the vulture, while on others they babble copiously, bringing forward life-less traditions, as for instance when they say, in reference to the sabbath, that each man's 'place' is two thousand cubits.[51] Others, however, among whom is Dositheus the Samaritan, condemn such an interpretation, and believe that in whatever position a man is found on the Sabbath day he should remain there until evening.

Further, the command 'not to carry a burden on the sabbath day'[52] is impossible; and on this account the teachers of the Jews have indulged in endless chatter, asserting that one kind of shoe is a burden, but another is not, and that a sandal with nails is a burden, but one without nails is not, and that what is carried on one shoulder is a burden, but not what is carried on both.

3 If now we approach the gospel in search of similar instances, what can be more irrational than the command: 'Salute no man by the way',[53] which simple people believe that the Saviour enjoined upon the apostles? Again, to speak of the right cheek being struck[54] is most incredible, for every striker, unless he suffers from some unnatural defect, strikes the left cheek with his right hand. And it is impossible to accept the precept from the gospel about the 'right eye that offends'; for granting the possibility of a person being 'offended' through his sense of sight, how can the blame be attributed to the right eye, when there are two eyes that see? And what man, even supposing he accuses himself of 'looking on a woman to lust after her' and attributes the blame to his

right eye alone, would act rationally if he were to cast this eye away?[55]

Further, the apostle lays down this precept: 'Was any called being circumcised? Let him not become uncircumcised'.[56] Now in the first place anyone who wishes can see that these words have no relation to the subject in hand; and how can we help thinking that they have been inserted at random, when we remember that the apostle is here laying down precepts about marriage and purity? In the second place who will maintain that it is wrong for a man to put himself into a condition of uncircumcision, if that were possible, in view of the disgrace which is felt by most people to attach to circumcision?

4 We have mentioned all these instances with the object of showing that the aim of the divine power which bestowed on us the holy scriptures is not that we should accept only what is found in the letter; for occasionally the records taken in a literal sense are not true, but actually absurd and impossible, and even with the history that actually happened and the legislation that is in its literal sense useful there are other matters interwoven.

But someone may suppose that the former statement refers to all the scriptures, and may suspect us of saying that because some of the history did not happen, therefore none of it happened; and because a certain law is irrational or impossible when taken literally, therefore no laws ought to be kept to the letter; or that the records of the Saviour's life are not true in a physical sense; or that no law or commandment of his ought to be obeyed. We must assert, therefore, that in regard to some things we are clearly aware that the historical fact is true; as that Abraham was buried in the double cave at Hebron, together with Isaac and Jacob and one wife of each of them;[57] and that Shechem was given as a portion to Joseph;[58] and

---

51 See Numbers 35:5.
52 See Jer 17:21.
53 See Luke 10:4.
54 See Matt 5:39.

55 See Matt 5:28, 29; 18:9.
56 1 Cor 7:18.
57 See Gen 23:2, 9, 19; 25:9, 10; 49:29–32; 50:13.
58 See Gen 48:22, Josh 24:32.

that Jerusalem is the chief city of Judaea, in which a temple of God was built by Solomon; and thousands of other facts.

For the passages which are historically true are far more numerous than those which are composed with purely spiritual meanings.

And again, who would deny that the command which says: 'Honour thy father and thy mother, that it may be well with thee',[59] is useful quite apart from any spiritual interpretation, and that it ought certainly to be observed, especially when we remember that the apostle Paul has quoted it in the self-same words?[60] And what are we to say of the following: 'Thou shalt not kill; thou shalt not commit adultery; thou shalt not steal; thou shalt not bear false witness'?[61]

Once again, in the gospel there are commandments written which need no inquiry whether they are to be kept literally or not, as that which says, 'I say unto you, whosoever is angry with his brother',[62] and what follows; and, 'I say unto you, swear not at all'.[63] Here, too, is an injunction of the apostle of which the literal meaning must be retained: 'Admonish the disorderly, encourage the faint-hearted, support the weak, be longsuffering toward all;'[64] though in the case of the more earnest readers it is possible to preserve each of the meanings, that is, while not setting aside the commandment in its literal sense, to preserve the 'depths of the wisdom of God.'[65]

5 Nevertheless the exact reader will hesitate in regard to some passages, finding himself unable to decide without considerable investigation whether a particular incident, believed to be history, actually happened or not, and whether the literal meaning of a particular law is to be observed or

not. Accordingly he who reads in an exact manner must, in obedience to the Saviour's precept which says, 'Search the scriptures',[66] carefully investigate how far the literal meaning is true and how far it is impossible, and to the utmost of his power must trace out from the use of similar expressions the meaning scattered everywhere through the scriptures of that which when taken literally is impossible.

When, therefore, as will be clear to those who read, the passage as a connected whole is literally impossible, whereas the outstanding part of it is not impossible but even true, the reader must endeavour to grasp the entire meaning, connecting by an intellectual process the account of what is literally impossible with the parts that are not impossible but are historically true, these being interpreted allegorically in common with the parts which, so far as the letter goes, did not happen at all. For our contention with regard to the whole of divine scripture is, that it all has a spiritual meaning, but not all a bodily meaning; for the bodily meaning is often proved to be an impossibility. Consequently the man who reads the divine books reverently, believing them to be divine writings, must exercise great care. And the method of understanding them appears to us to be as follows.

6 The accounts tell us that God chose out a certain nation on the earth, and they call this nation by many names. For the nation as a whole is called Israel, and it is also spoken of as Jacob. But when it was divided in the days of Jeroboam the son of Nebat,[67] the ten tribes said to have been subject to him were named Israel, and the other two together with the tribe of Levi, which were ruled over by men of the seed of David, were called Judah. The entire country which was inhabited by men of this race and which had been given them by God, is called Judaea, the metropolis of which is Jerusalem, this being the mother city of a number of others whose names lie scattered about

---

59 Exod 20:12.

60 See Eph 6:2, 3.

61 Exod 20:13–16.

62 Matt 5:22 (omitted in Rufinus' text).

63 Matt 5:34.

64 1 Thess 5:14.

65 See Rom 11:33; 1 Cor 2:10.

---

66 John 5:39.

67 See 1 Kings 12:2 ff.

in many different places of scripture but are gathered together into one list in the book of Joshua the son of Nun.[68]

This being so, the apostle, raising our spiritual apprehension to a high level, says somewhere: 'Behold Israel after the flesh',[69] inferring that there is an Israel after the spirit. He says also in another place: 'For it is not the children of the flesh that are children of God',[70] nor are 'all they Israel, who are of Israel'.[71]

And again: 'Neither is he a Jew, who is one outwardly, nor is that circumcision, which is outward in the flesh; but he is a Jew, who is one inwardly, and circumcision is of the heart, in the spirit, not in the letter'.[72] For if we take the phrase 'a Jew inwardly' as a test, we shall realise that as there is a race of bodily Jews, so, too, there is a race of those who are 'Jews inwardly', the soul having acquired this nobility of race in virtue of certain unspeakable words. Moreover there are many prophecies spoken of Israel and Judah, which relate what is going to happen to them. And when we think of the extraordinary promises recorded about these people, promises that so far as literary style goes are poor and distinguished by no elevation or character that is worthy of a promise of God, is it not clear that they demand a mystical interpretation? Well, then, if the promises are of a spiritual kind though announced through material imagery, the people to whom the promises belong are not the bodily Israelites.

7 But we must not spend time discussing who is a 'Jew inwardly' and who an Israelite 'in the inner man', since the above remarks are sufficient for all who are not dull-witted. We will return to the subject before us and say that Jacob was the father of the twelve patriarchs, and they of the rulers of the people, and they in their turn of the Israelites who

came after.[73] Is it not the case, then, that the bodily Israelites carry back their descent to the rulers of the people, the rulers of the people to the patriarchs, and the patriarchs to Jacob and those still more ancient; whereas are not the spiritual Israelites, of whom the bodily ones were a type, descended from the clans, and the clans from the tribes, and the tribes from one whose birth was not bodily, like that of the others, but of a higher kind;[74] and was not he born of Isaac, and Isaac descended from Abraham, while all go back to Adam, who the apostle says is Christ?[75] For the origin of all families that are in touch with the God of the whole world began lower down with Christ, who comes next after the God and Father of the whole world[76] and is thus the father of every soul, as Adam is the father of all men. And if Eve is interpreted by Paul as referring to the Church,[77] it is not surprising (seeing that Cain was born of Eve and all that come after him carry back their descent to Eve) that these two should be figures of the Church; for in the higher sense all men take their beginning from the Church.

8 Now if what we have stated about Israel, its tribes and its clans, is convincing, then when the Saviour says, 'I was not sent but unto the lost sheep of the house of Israel', we do not take these words in the same sense as the poor-minded Ebionites do (men whose very name comes from the poverty of their mind, for in Hebrew ebion is the word for poor), so as to suppose that Christ came especially to the Israelites after the flesh. For 'it is not the children of the flesh that are children of God'.[78]

Again, the apostle gives us the following instances of teaching about Jerusalem: 'The Jerusalem which is above is free, which is our mother';[79]

---

68 See Josh 13–21.

69 1 Cor 10:18.

70 Rom 9:8.

71 Rom 9:6.

72 Rom 2:28, 29.

73 I.e. as in Gen 25:21–23.

74 See 1 Cor 15:45.

75 See Luke 3:38.

76 See Eph 5:31–32.

77 Matt 15:24.

78 Rom 9:8 (omitted from Rufinus)

79 Gal 4:26.

and in another epistle: 'But ye are come to Mount Sion and to the city of the living God, the heavenly Jerusalem, and to an innumerable company of angels, to the general assembly and church of the firstborn who are written in heaven'.[80]

If therefore Israel consists of a race of souls, and Jerusalem is a city in heaven, it follows that the cities of Israel have for their mother city the Jerusalem in the heavens; and so consequently does Judaea as a whole.

In all prophecies concerning Jerusalem, therefore, and in all statements made about it, we must understand, if we listen to Paul's words[81] as the words of God and the utterances of wisdom, that the scriptures are telling us about the heavenly city and the whole region which contains the cities of the holy land. Perhaps it is to these cities that the Saviour lifts our attention when he gives to those who have deserved praise for the good use of their talents authority over ten or over five cities.[82]

9 If therefore the prophecies relating to Judaea, to Jerusalem, and to Israel, Judah and Jacob suggest to us, because we do not interpret them in a fleshly sense, mysteries such as these, it will follow also that the prophecies which relate to Egypt and the Egyptians, to Babylon and the Babylonians, to Tyre and the Tyrians, to Sidon and the Sidonians, or to any of the other nations, are not spoken solely of the bodily Egyptians, Babylonians, Tyrians and Sidonians.[83] If the Israelites are spiritual, it follows that the Egyptians and Babylonians are also spiritual. For the statements made in Ezekiel about Pharaoh king of Egypt entirely fail to apply to any particular man who was or will be ruler of Egypt, as will be clear to those who study the passage carefully.[84]

Similarly the statements concerning the ruler of Tyre cannot be understood of any particular man who is to rule over Tyre.[85] And as for the numerous statements made about Nebuchadnezzar,[86] especially in Isaiah, how it is possible to interpret them of that particular man? For the man Nebuchadnezzar neither 'fell from heaven', nor was he the 'morning star', nor did he 'rise in the morning' over the earth.[87]

Nor indeed will any man of intelligence interpret the statements made in Ezekiel concerning Egypt, that it shall be 'laid waste forty years' so that 'no foot of man' shall be found there, and that it shall one day be so overwhelmed with war, that throughout the whole land there shall be blood up to the knees, as referring to the Egypt which lies next to the Ethiopians whose bodies are blackened by the sun.[88]

10 And perhaps, just as people on earth, when they die the common death of all, are in consequence of the deeds done here so distributed as to obtain different positions according to the proportion of their sins, if they are judged to be worthy of the place called Hades; so the people there, when they die, if I may so speak, descend into this Hades, and are judged worthy of different habitations, better or worse, in the whole of this region of earth . . . . and of being born of such or such parents, so that an Israelite will occasionally fall among Scythians and an Egyptian descend into Judaea. Nevertheless the Saviour came to gather together the 'lost sheep of the house of Israel',[89] and since many from Israel have not submitted to his teaching, those from the Gentiles are also called. . . .

11 But these truths, as we think, have been concealed in the narratives. For 'the kingdom of

---

80 Heb 12:22, 23.

81 See Luke 19:17–19.

82 See 2 Cor 13:3.

83 See Ezek 29: ff.

84 See Ezek 29:1–9.

85 See Ezek 28.

86 See Isa 14:3–23.

87 See Isa 14:12.

88 See Ezekiel 29:11–12; 30:7, 10–12; 32:5–6, 12–13, 15.

89 See Matt 15:24.

heaven is like unto a treasure hid in a field, which when a man findeth he hideth it, and for joy thereof goeth and selleth all that he hath, and buyeth that field.'[90] Now let us consider whether the outward aspect of scripture and its obvious and surface meaning does not correspond to the field as a whole, full of all kinds of plants, whereas the truths that are stored away in it and not seen by all, but lie as if buried beneath the visible plants, are the hidden 'treasures of wisdom and knowledge'.[91] which the Spirit speaking through Isaiah calls 'dark and unseen and concealed'.[92]

These treasures require for their discovery the help of God, who alone is able to 'break in pieces the gates of brass[93] that conceal them and to burst the iron bars that are upon the gates, and so to make known all the truths taught in Genesis concerning the various legitimate races and as it were seeds of souls, whether closely akin to Israel or far apart from him, and the descent of the 'seventy souls' into Egypt, in order that they may there become 'as the stars of the heaven in multitude'.[94] But since not all who are sprung from these are a 'light of the world',[95] for 'they are not all Israel, who are of Israel'[96] there come from the seventy a people 'even as the sand which is by the sea shore innumerable.'[97]

---

90 Matt 13:44.

91 See Col 2:3.

92 See Isa 45:3.

93 See Isa 45:2.

94 For the whole passage see Gen chs. 10, 11, 25, 36, 46; and for the quotations Deut 10:22 (Gen 46: 27, Exod 1:5, Gen 22:17).

95 See Matt 5:14.

96 Rom 9:6.

97 Heb 11:12 (Gen 32:12).

11

The Proclamation of the Word
Homilies in Early Christianity

One of the central components of early Christian worship (see Chapter 13) was the oral exposition of Scripture. Early Christian homilies tended to be didactic (telling Christians what they ought to know), hortatory (urging them how they ought to behave), and theological (indicating what they ought to believe). Usually they were based on specific texts of Scripture—originally the Jewish Bible but also, as soon as the late first century, the writings ascribed to Jesus' apostles. It appears likely that the practice of having a leader within the community interpret Scripture for the gathered faithful was taken over from Judaism; in the New Testament, Jesus and Paul are themselves said to have delivered sermons in Jewish synagogues (see, for example, Luke 4:16–30; Acts 13:15–43).

Examples of Christian sermons are scattered throughout the book of Acts (many of these are actually evangelistic sermons to outsiders); it is commonly thought among scholars that these addresses were composed by Luke himself, the author of the book. The earliest surviving homily that was actually delivered (possibly in writing) from a Christian leader to a Christian congregation is the anonymous book of Hebrews, also preserved in the New Testament. Despite the popularity of this mode of communication, we do not have an abundant number of surviving sermons prior to the fourth century when their publication came to be widespread. The one exception involves the numerous homilies of Origen of Alexandria, the most prolific early Christian author.

Already in the second century, Christian homilies were based on rhetorical models of oral discourse taught and analyzed in Greek institutions of higher learning (i.e., rhetorical schools). With the passing of time, the use of Greek rhetoric in Christian sermons became increasingly pronounced. Among other things, this shows that Christian preachers were among the most highly educated and sophisticated members of the church. The views they express, therefore, and the ways they express them, may not be completely representative of Christendom at large.

We have already seen one example of a Christian sermon in the Passover Homily of Melito of Sardis (Chapter 5) and, possibly, another in the Gnostic-Christian Gospel of Truth (Chapter 6). The following texts of the second and third centuries may also be taken as broadly representative of the genre.

For Further Reading

Black, Clifton C. "The Rhetorical Form of the Hellenistic Jewish and Christian Sermon," *Harvard Theological Review* 81 (1988) 1–18.

Cunningham, Mary B. and Pauline Allen, eds. *Preacher and Audience: Studies in Early Christian and Byzantine Homiletics.* Leiden: E. J. Brill, 1998.

Donfried, Karl. *The Setting of Second Clement in Early Christianity.* Leiden: E. J. Brill, 1974.

Harrison, Carol. *The Art of Listening in the Early Church.* Oxford: Oxford University Press, 2012.

Hunter, David G. *Preaching in the Patristic Age: Studies in Honor of Walter J. Burghardt, S.J.* New York: Paulist Press, 1989.

Kennedy, G. *Classical Rhetoric and Its Christian and Secular Tradition from Ancient to Modern Times.* Chapel Hill: University of North Carolina Press, 1980.

Wills, L. "The Form of the Sermon in Hellenistic Judaism and Early Christianity," *Harvard Theological Review* 77 (1984) 277–299.

THE TEXTS

(See also Melito of Sardis, "On the Passover", in Chapter 5 and the Gospel of Truth in Chapter 6)

68. Second Clement

The earliest surviving Christian homily outside of the New Testament appears to be the book commonly called "The Second Epistle of Clement." In parts of early Christianity, until at least the fifth century, the book was regarded as Scripture. All the same, the traditional title is probably wrong: the book is not a letter but a sermon (see 19:1), and it was not produced by the author of 1 Clement (as is evident on stylistic grounds).

The audience, and probably the author, were former pagans who had converted to Christianity (see 2:6). The sermon is not based entirely on one particular text of Scripture but consists of exhortations backed up by sayings of Jesus, along with the writings of the Old Testament and the apostles. Interestingly, one of the author's sources appears to have been a noncanonical Gospel, possibly the Gospel of Thomas (12:2). He uses these sacred texts to urge his audience to repent and return to upright moral behavior in light of the coming day of judgment. In the course of his exhortation, he stresses the reality of the future resurrection of the flesh and attacks those (presumably Gnostics) who deny it (8:1).

It is difficult to say when, exactly, this sermon was written, but scholars usually date it to the mid- or late second century, and locate its anonymous author possibly in Corinth or Alexandria.

Second Letter of Clement to The Corinthians

1 Brothers, we must think about Jesus Christ as we think about God, as about the judge of the living and the dead.[1] And we must not give little thought to our salvation.

2 For when we think little about him, we also hope to receive but little. And we who listen as if these were little things sin, not realizing where we have been called from, by whom, and to what place, nor how many sufferings Jesus Christ endured for us.

3 What then shall we give to him in exchange? How can we produce anything comparable to what he has given us? And how many holy deeds do we owe him?

4 For he graciously bestowed light upon us. Like a father, he called us children; while we were perishing, he saved us.

---

1 Acts 10:42; 1 Pet 4:5.

---

2 Clement, reproduced from *The Apostolic Fathers*, ed. Bart D. Ehrman; Loeb Classical Library, vol. 1. Cambridge, MA: Harvard University, 2003. Used with permission of Harvard University Press.

5 What praise, then, shall we give him, or what can we pay in exchange for what we have received?

6 We were maimed in our understanding, worshiping stones and pieces of wood and gold and silver and copper—all of them made by humans. And our entire life was nothing other than death. Then when we were beset by darkening gloom, our vision blurred by such mist, we regained our sight through his will by setting aside the cloud that enveloped us.

7 For he showed mercy on us and through his compassion saved us. For he saw that a great error and destruction was in us, and that we had not the slightest hope of being saved, unless it came through him.

8 For he called us while we did not exist, and he wished us to come into being from nonbeing.

2 "Be jubilant, you who are infertile and who do not bear children! Let your voice burst forth and cry out, you who experience no pains of labor! For the one who has been deserted has more children than the one who has a husband."[2] Now when it says, "Be jubilant, you who are infertile and who do not bear children," it is referring to us. For our church was infertile before children were given to it.

2 And when it says, "Cry out, you who experience no pains of labor," it means this: we should raise our prayers up to God sincerely and not grow weary like women in labor.

3 And when it says, "For the one who has been deserted has more children than the one who has a husband," it is because our people appeared to be deserted by God, but now that we believe we have become more numerous than those who appear to have God.

4 And also another Scripture says, "I did not come to call the upright, but sinners."[3]

5 This means that he was to save those who were perishing.

6 For it is a great and astonishing feat to fix in place something that is toppling over, not something that is standing.

7 Thus also Christ wished to save what was perishing. And he did save many; for he came and called us while we were on the brink of destruction.

3 He has shown us such mercy since, to begin with, we who are living do not sacrifice to dead gods or worship them; instead, through him we know the Father of truth. What then is the knowledge that is directed toward to him? Is it not refusing to deny the one through whom we have come to know him?

2 For even he himself says, "I will acknowledge before my Father the one who acknowledges me before others."[4]

3 This then is our reward, if we acknowledge the one through whom we were saved.

4 But how do we acknowledge him? By doing the things he says, not disobeying his commandments, and not honoring him only with our lips but from our whole heart and our whole understanding.[5]

5 For he also says in Isaiah, "This people honors me with their lips, but their heart is far removed from me."[6]

4 For this reason we should not merely call him Lord; for this will not save us.

2 For he says, "Not everyone who says to me, 'Lord, Lord' will be saved, but only the one who practices righteousness."[7]

3 So then, brothers, we should acknowledge him by what we do, by loving one another, by not committing adultery or slandering one another or showing envy. We should be restrained, charitable, and good. We should be sympathetic with one another and not be attached to money. By doing

---

2 Isa 54:1; cf. Gal 4:27.

3 Matt 9:13; Mark 2:17; Luke 5:32.

---

4 Matt 10:32; Luke 12:8.

5 Mark 12:30.

6 Isa 29:13; cf. Matt 15:8; Mark 7:6; 1 Clem 15:2.

7 Matt 7:21.

such deeds we acknowledge him, not by doing their opposites.

4 And we must not fear people, but God.

5 For this reason, when you do these things, the Lord has said, "Even if you were nestled close to my breast but did not do what I have commanded, I would cast you away and say to you, 'Leave me! I do not know where you are from, you who do what is lawless.'"[8]

5 Therefore, brothers, having abandoned our temporary residence in this world, we should do the will of the one who called us and not fear departing from this world.

2 For the Lord said, "You will be like sheep in the midst of wolves."[9]

3 But Peter replied to him, "What if the wolves rip apart the sheep?"

4 Jesus said to Peter, "After they are dead, the sheep should fear the wolves no longer. So too you: do not fear those who kill you and then can do nothing more to you; but fear the one who, after you die, has the power to cast your body and soul into the hell of fire."[10]

5 You should realize, brothers, that our visit in this realm of the flesh is brief and short-lived, but the promise of Christ is great and astounding—namely, a rest in the coming kingdom and eternal life.

6 What then must we do to obtain these things, except conduct ourselves in a holy and upright way and consider these worldly affairs foreign to us, and not yearn after them?

7 For when we yearn to obtain these things we fall away from the right path.

6 But the Lord says, "No household servant can serve as the slave of two masters."[11] If we wish to serve as slaves of both God and wealth, it is of no gain to us.

2 "For what is the advantage of acquiring the whole world while forfeiting your life?"[12]

3 But this age and the age to come are two enemies.

4 This one preaches adultery, depravity, avarice, and deceit, but that one renounces these things.

5 We cannot, therefore, be friends of both. We must renounce this world to obtain that one.

6 We think it better to despise the things that are here, since they are brief, short-lived, and perishable, and to love those other things, which are good and imperishable.

7 For by doing the will of Christ we will find a place of rest; on the other hand, nothing will deliver us from eternal punishment if we disobey his commandments.

8 And the Scripture also says in Ezekiel, "Even if Noah, Job, and Daniel should arise, they will not deliver their children from captivity."[13]

9 But if even such upright men as these cannot deliver their children through acts of righteousness, with what confidence can we enter into the kingdom of God if we do not keep our baptism pure and undefiled? Or who will serve as our advocate, if we are not found doing what is holy and upright?

7 So then, my brothers, we should compete in the games, knowing that the competition is at hand. Many set sail for earthly competitions but not all receive the crown—only those who labor hard and compete well.

2 We should therefore compete that we all may be crowned.

3 And so we should run the straight course, the eternal competition. Many of us should sail to it and compete, that we may receive the crown. And if all of us cannot receive the crown, we should at least come close to it.

4 We must realize that if someone is caught cheating while competing in an earthly contest, he is flogged and thrown out of the stadium.

---

8 Source unknown.

9 Cf. Matt 10:16; Luke 10:3.

10 Source unknown. Cf. Matt 10:28; Luke 12:4–5.

11 Luke 16:13: Matt 6:24.

12 Matt 16:26; Mark 8:36; Luke 9:25.

13 Ezek 14:14 ff.

5 What do you suppose? What will happen to the one who cheats in the eternal competition?

6 As for those who do not keep the seal of their baptism, he says: "Their worm will not die nor their fire be extinguished; and they will be a spectacle for all to see."[14]

8 And so we should repent while we are still on earth.

2 For we are clay in the hand of the artisan. As in the case of a potter: if he is making a vessel that becomes misshapened or crushed in his hands, he then remolds it; but if he has already put it in the kiln, he can no longer fix it. So too with us. While we are still in the world, we should repent from our whole heart of the evil we have done in the flesh, so the Lord will save us—while there is still time for repentance.

3 For after we leave the world we will no longer be able to make confession or repent in that place.

4 So then, brothers, if we do the will of the Father and keep our flesh pure and guard the commandments of the Lord we will receive eternal life.

5 For the Lord says in the Gospel, "If you do not keep what is small, who will give you what is great? For I say to you that the one who is faithful in very little is faithful also in much."[15]

6 This then is what he means: you should keep the flesh pure and the seal of baptism stainless, so that we may receive eternal life.

9 And none of you should say that this flesh is neither judged nor raised.

2 Think about it! In what state were you saved? In what state did you regain your sight? Was it not while you were in this flesh?

3 And so we must guard the flesh like the temple of God.

4 For just as you were called in the flesh, so also you will come in the flesh.

5 Since Jesus Christ—the Lord who saved us—was first a spirit and then became flesh, and in this way called us, so also we will receive the reward in this flesh.

6 And so we should love one another, that we may all enter the Kingdom of God.

7 While we have time to be healed, let us give ourselves over to the God who brings healing, paying him what is due.

8 And what is that? Repentance from a sincere heart.

9 For he knows all things in advance and recognizes what is in our hearts.

10 And so we should give him praise, not from our mouth alone but also from our heart, that he may welcome us as children.

11 For the Lord also said, "My brothers are these who do the will of my Father."[16]

10 So my brothers, let us do the will of the Father who called us, that we may live; even more, let us pursue virtue. But we should abandon evil as a forerunner of our sins; and we should flee from impiety, lest evil overtake us.

2 For if we are eager to do good, peace will pursue us.

3 For this reason no one can find peace when they bring forward human fears and prefer the pleasure of the present to the promise that is yet to come.

4 For they do not realize the kind of torment brought by present pleasure or the kind of delight coming with the future promise.

5 It would be tolerable if they alone were doing these things; but now they persist in teaching such evil notions to innocent people, not knowing that they will bear a double penalty—both they and those who listen to them.

11 For this reason we should be enslaved to God with a pure heart, and then we will be upright. But if we choose not to be enslaved to God, not believing in his promise, we will be miserable.

2 For the prophetic word also says, "How miserable are those of two minds, who doubt in their hearts, who say, 'We heard these things long ago, in

---

14 Isa 66:24, cf. Mark 9:44, 46, 48.

15 Luke 16:10–12.

16 Matt 12:50; Mark 3:35; Luke 8:21.

the time of our parents, but though we have waited day after day, we have seen none of them.'

3 Fools! Compare yourselves to a tree. Take a vine: first it sheds its leaves, then a bud appears, and after these things an unripe grape, and then an entire bunch fully grown.

4 So too my people is now disorderly and afflicted; but then it will receive what is good."[17]

5 So my brothers, we should not be of two minds but should remain hopeful, that we may receive the reward.

6 For the one who has promised to reward each according to his deeds is faithful.[18]

7 If, therefore, we do what is righteous before God, we will enter into his kingdom and receive his promises, which no ear has heard nor eye seen, nor has it entered into the human heart.[19]

12 For this reason, we should await the kingdom of God with love and righteousness every hour, since we do not know the day when God will appear.

2 For when the Lord himself was asked by someone when his kingdom would come, he said, "When the two are one, and the outside like the inside, and the male with the female is neither male nor female."[20]

3 Now "the two are one" when we speak truth to one another and when one soul exists in two bodies with no posturing [Or: with no hypocrisy].

4 And "the outside like the inside" means this: the "inside" refers to the soul and the "outside" to the body. Just as your body is visible, so too your soul should be clearly seen in your good deeds.

5 And the words "the male with the female is neither male nor female" mean this, that a brother who sees a sister should think nothing about her

being female and she [Or: he] should think nothing about his being male.

6 When you do these things, he says, "the kingdom of my Father will come."

13 And so brothers, now at last we should repent and be alert for the good. For we are filled with great foolishness and evil. We should wipe our former sins away from ourselves; and if we repent from deep within we will be saved. We should not be crowd-pleasers nor wish to please only ourselves, but through our righteous activity we should be pleasing as well to those outside the fold, that the name not be blasphemed because of us.

2 For the Lord says, "My name is constantly blasphemed among all the outsiders [Literally: Gentiles, or nations]."[21] And again he says, "Woe to the one who causes my name to be blasphemed."[22] How is it blasphemed? When you fail to do what I wish.

3 For when outsiders hear the sayings of God from our mouths, they are astonished at their beauty and greatness. Then when they discover that our actions do not match our words, they turn from astonishment to blasphemy, saying that our faith is some kind of myth and error.

4 For, on the one hand, they hear from us that God has said, "It is no great accomplishment for you to love those who love you; it is great if you love your enemies and those who hate you."[23] And when they hear these things, they are astonished by their extraordinary goodness. But then when they see that we fail to love not only those who hate us, but even those who love us, they ridicule us and the name is blasphemed.

14 So then, brothers, if we do the will of God our Father we will belong to the first church, the spiritual church, the church that was created before the sun and moon. But if we do not do what the Lord wants, we will belong to the Scripture

---

17 Source unknown. Cf. 1 Clem 23:3–4.

18 Heb 10:23.

19 1 Cor 2:9.

20 Cf. *Gosp Thom* 22; also quoted in Clement of Alexandria, *Stremateis* 3:13, where it is attributed to the otherwise lost *Gospel of the Egyptians*.

---

21 Isa 52:5.

22 Source unknown.

23 Luke 6:32, 35.

that says, "My house has become a cave of thieves."[24] So then, let us choose to belong to the church of life, that we may be saved.

2 But I cannot imagine that you do not realize that the living church is the body of Christ. For the Scripture says, "God made the human male and female."[25] The male is Christ, the female the church. And, as you know, the Bible *[Or: the books]* and the apostles indicate that the church has not come into being just now, but has existed from the beginning. For it existed spiritually, as did our Jesus; but he *[Or: it]* became manifest here in the final days so that he *[Or: it]* might save us.

3 And even though the church was spiritual, it became manifest in Christ's flesh, showing us that any of us who protects the church in the flesh, without corrupting it, will receive it in the Holy Spirit. For this flesh is the mirror image of the Spirit. No one, therefore, who corrupts the mirror image will receive the reality that it represents. And so, brothers, he says this: "Protect the flesh that you may receive the Spirit."[26]

4 But if we say that the flesh is the church and the Spirit is Christ, then the one who abuses the flesh abuses the church. Such a person, therefore, will not receive the Spirit, which is Christ.

5 This flesh is able to receive such a great and incorruptible life when the Holy Spirit clings to it; nor can anyone proclaim or speak about the things that the Lord has prepared for those he has chosen.

15 I do not think that I have given trivial advice about self-restraint. And whoever takes my advice will have no regrets, but will instead save both himself and me, the one who has given the advice. There is no small reward for the one who converts a person who is going astray toward destruction, that he may be saved.

2 For this is what we can offer back to the God who created us—so long as the one who speaks and hears does so with faith and love.

3 For this reason we should continue as upright and holy in the things we have believed, that we may make our requests known to God with bold confidence. For he says, "While you are still speaking I will say, 'See, here I am.'"[27]

4 For this word is a token of a great promise; for the Lord says that he is more ready to give than we are to ask.

5 And so, since we have received such generosity, we should not begrudge one another when we receive such good things. For the pleasure these words bring to those who do them is matched by the condemnation they bring to those who disobey.

16 So then, brothers, since we have received no trivial opportunity to repent, we should turn back to the God who called us, while there is still time—while, that is, we still have one who accepts us.

2 For if we bid farewell to these sweet pleasures and conquer our soul through not doing its evil desires, we will receive mercy from Jesus.

3 But you know that the day of judgment is already coming like a blazing furnace,[28] and some of the heavens and all of the earth will melt like lead in the fire;[29] and then the hidden and secret works that people have done will be made visible.

4 Giving to charity, therefore, is good as a repentance from sin *[Or: is good; so too is repentance from sin]*. Fasting is better than prayer, but giving to charity is better than both. Love covers a multitude of sins,[30] and prayer from a good conscience will rescue a person from death. How fortunate is everyone found to be full of these things. For giving to charity lightens the load of sin.

17 And so we should repent from our whole heart, lest any of us perish. For since we have his commandment and drag people from idols, giving them instruction, how much more must we

24 Jer 7:11; cf. Matt 21:13: Mark 11:17; Luke 19:46.
25 Gen 1:27.
26 Source unknown.
27 Isa 58:9.
28 Malachi 4:1.
29 Cf. Isa 34:4.
30 1 Pet 4:8; cf. Prov 10:12.

keep a person from destruction when he has already come to know God?

2 For this reason we should help one another and bring those who are weak back to what is good, so that we may all be saved and turn one another around and admonish one another.

3 And not only should we appear to believe and pay attention now, while being admonished by the presbyters, but also when we return home we should remember the commandments of the Lord and not be dragged away by worldly desires. But by coming together for worship more frequently we should try to progress in the Lord's commandments, so that all of us, being unified in what we think, may be gathered together to inherit life.

4 For the Lord said, "I am coming to gather all the nations, tribes, and tongues."[31] And this is what he calls the "day of his appearance," when he comes to redeem each of us, according to our deeds.

5 And the unbelievers will see his glory and power and be shocked when they see that the rulership of this world has been given to Jesus. And they will say, "Woe to us! You were here, and we did not know or believe; and we were not persuaded by the presbyters who announced your salvation to us." And their worm will not die nor their fire be extinguished, and they will be a spectacle for all to see.[32]

6 He calls that the day of judgment, when others see those who have acted with impiety among us and distorted the commandments of Jesus Christ.

7 But those who are upright, who have acted well, endured torments, and hated the sweet pleasures of the soul, when they observe those who have deviated from the right path and denied Jesus through their words or deeds are punished with terrible torments in a fire that cannot be extinguished, they, the upright, will give glory to their God, saying "there will be hope for the one who has served as God's slave from his whole heart."

18 For this reason we should be among those who give thanks, who serve as the slaves of God, not among the impious who are condemned.

2 For even I myself am completely sinful and have not yet fled temptation and am still surrounded by the instruments of the Devil; nonetheless I am eager to pursue righteousness, that I may be made strong enough to approach it, for fear of the coming judgment.

19 So then, brothers and sisters, now that we have heard this word from the God of Truth *[Literally: after the God of Truth]*, I am reading you a request to pay attention to what has been written, so that you may save yourselves and the one who is your reader. As a reward I ask that you repent from your whole heart, giving yourselves salvation and life. For when we do this we set a goal for those who are younger, who wish to devote themselves to the piety and generosity that come from God.

2 We who are foolish should not be displeased and indignant when someone admonishes us and turns us away from injustice to righteousness. For sometimes, because we are of two minds and disbelieving in our hearts, we do not realize that we are doing evil; and we are darkened in our understanding[33] through vain desires.

3 And so we should practice righteousness, that we may be saved in the end. How fortunate are those who obey these commandments! Even if they suffer evil for a brief time in this world, they will reap the imperishable fruit of the resurrection.

4 And so the one who is pious should not be despondent over miseries suffered at present. A more fortunate time awaits him! When he is restored to life with our ancestors he will be jubilant, in an age removed from sorrow.

20 But neither should this thought disturb you, that we see the unjust becoming rich while the slaves of God suffer in dire straights.

2 We need to have faith, brothers and sisters! We are competing in the contest of the living God,

---

31 Isa 66:18.

32 Isa 66:18, 24; cf. Mark 9:48.

33 Cf. Eph 4:18.

training in the present life that we may be crowned in the one to come.

3 No one who is upright receives the fruit of his labor quickly; he instead waits for it.

4 For if God were to reward the upright immediately, we would straightaway be engaged in commerce rather than devotion to God. For we would appear to be upright not for the sake of piety but for a profit. And for this reason, a divine judgment harms the spirit that is not upright and burdens it with chains.

5 To the only invisible God,[34] the Father of truth, who sent us the savior and founder of incorruptibility, through whom he also revealed to us the truth and the heavenly life—to him be the glory forever and ever. Amen.

The Second Epistle of Clement to the Corinthians

---

34 Cf. 1 Tim 1:17.

69. Origen: Homilies on Luke

No Christian author of the second and third centuries published more homilies than Origen (see Chapter 4)—more than 300 according to ancient sources. Nearly two-thirds that number still survive, although principally only in Latin translation. These represent actual sermons that Origen delivered during worship services, either on weekday mornings (services were held daily), on Wednesday or Friday mid-afternoon services (when devoted Christians would break their fast with the eucharistic meal), or at the Sunday morning eucharist. Normally, the services included the reading of Scripture followed by an exposition of its meaning (see Chapter 13).

As public interpretations of Scripture for the common Christian (in contrast with Origen's biblical commentaries, written for serious students of the Bible), these homilies were meant to instruct the congregation in the meaning of the text for their beliefs and ethics. Throughout them one can see Origen's distinctive view of the Bible, a view that played a significant role in the development of later Christian theology (see Chapter 16).

In many instances, Origen can be seen to expound and embrace the literal meaning of the scriptural text. But he often found that the literal meaning leads to a contradiction or an absurdity. In such cases, he maintained, one must dig deeper into the text to find its less obvious, hidden, spiritual meaning (see selection 67 in Chapter 10). To do this, Origen used the Bible as its own interpreter, typically appealing to one passage of Scripture to assist in the interpretation and exploration of another. This approach was rooted in Origen's understanding of the Bible as God's word in its fullness. Any word, phrase, or verse could therefore lead him to consider related words, phrases, and verses

---

Origen: Homilies on Luke, from *Origen: Homilies on Luke; Fragments on Luke,* ed. Joseph T. Lienhard. Fathers of the Church, 94; Washington, DC: Catholic University Press of America, 1996. Used with permission.

in other passages. The Bible, then, provided a kind of closed system of meaning, any part of which could be used as an entrée into issues of profound theological and practical importance.

Thirty-nine of Origen's homilies on Luke have survived. The following are four rather short expositions taken from the story of the birth of John the Baptist in Luke 1. The homilies are normally thought to have been written around 240 CE in Caesarea.

Homily 3

Luke 1:11

On the passage, "The angel of the Lord appeared to him, standing at the right side of the altar of incense."

OF THEMSELVES, beings that are corporeal and lack sensation do nothing to be seen by another. The observer's eye is simply directed toward them. Whenever the observer directs his gaze and his regard at them, he sees them, whether the objects will it or not. What can a person or any other object that is enclosed in a solid body do to avoid being seen, when they are in fact there? In contrast, things that are from above and divine are not seen, even when they are there, unless they themselves will it. It lies within their will to be seen or not. It was by an act of his grace that God appeared to Abraham and the other prophets. The eye of Abraham's heart was not the only cause that allowed him to see God; God offered his grace to the sight of a just man to let him see.

2 You should understand this not only of God the Father, but also of our Lord and Savior and of the Holy Spirit and—to come to lesser beings—of cherubim and seraphim. Perhaps an angel is helping us as we are speaking now, but we cannot see him because we do not deserve to. Even though the eye of our body or our soul makes an effort to see, the person who wants to see will not, unless the angel willingly appears and offers himself to sight. Thus, wherever Scripture says, "God appeared" to someone—just as here, for example, "The angel of the Lord appeared to him,

standing at the right side of the altar of incense"—understand it as I explained. Whether it is God or an angel, and whether he appears to Abraham or to Zechariah, he will be seen or not, depending on whether he wishes it or not.

3 And we say this not only of the present age but also of the age to come. When we depart from the world, God or the angels do not appear to everyone, as if anyone who departs from the body immediately deserves to see the angels, the Holy Spirit, the Lord and Savior, and God the Father himself. Only one who has a pure heart and shows himself worthy of the vision of God will see them. One will be pure of heart; another will still be stained with some filth. Although they will be in the same place, the place itself will not be able to help or hinder them. Whoever has a pure heart will see God. Whoever does not will not see what the other beholds. I think we should understand something similar of Christ, too, when he was seen in the body. Not everyone who laid eyes on him was able to see him.

4 They saw his body, but, insofar as he was Christ, they could not see him. But his disciples saw him and beheld the greatness of his divinity. I think this is why, when Philip entreated the Savior and said, "Show us the Father and it is enough for us," the Savior answered him, "Have I been with you for so long a time, and you do not know me? Philip, he who sees me sees the Father also."[1] Pilate, who saw Jesus, did not gaze upon the Father.

---

1 John 14:8–9.

Neither did Judas the traitor. Neither Pilate nor Judas saw Christ as Christ. Nor did the crowd, which pressed around him. Only those whom Jesus judged worthy of beholding him really saw him. Let us, too, therefore, work so that God might appear to us at this moment. The holy word of Scripture has promised, "He is found by those who do not test him, and he appears to those who do not doubt him."[2] In the age to come may he not be hidden from us; may we see him face to face. May we have the assurance of a good life and enjoy the vision of Almighty God in Christ Jesus and in the Holy Spirit, to whom is glory and power for ages of ages. Amen.

Homily 4

Luke 1.13–17

On the passage from, "Do not be afraid, Zechariah," up to the point where it is said of John, "He will go before him in the spirit and power of Elijah."

WHEN ZECHARIAH SAW the angel, he was terrified. If the human gaze beholds a strange form, the mind is agitated and the soul is unsettled. The angel understands that human nature reacts in this way, so he first settles Zechariah's agitation and says, "Do not be afraid, Zechariah." He revives the trembling man and gladdens him by announcing his news. He says, "Your prayer has been heard. Your wife Elizabeth will bear a son. You shall name him John. He will bring you joy and elation."[3] When a just person is born into the world and enters the course of this life, those responsible for his birth rejoice, and their hearts soar upward. But, when someone who is destined for an evil life is born, one who is virtually banished to a prison as a punishment, the one responsible for his birth is thrown into confusion and loses heart.

2 Do you want an example of a holy man, all of whose deeds are praiseworthy? Consider Jacob. He fathered twelve male offspring. All of them became patriarchs, princes of God's people and of Jacob's heritage. Jacob, their father, rejoiced in all of them. The Gospel proclaims joy for all people because of John's birth. Once a man engages in the task of begetting children to benefit others and willingly devotes himself to this service, he should pray to God and ask that any son of his who comes into the world might be like John, one whose birth would bring him joy. Scripture says of John, "He will be great in the Lord's sight."[4] This phrase, "He will be great in the Lord's sight," shows the greatness of John's soul. God's eyes beheld this greatness. There is also a "smallness" of soul, which properly looks to the soul's virtue.

3 This is how I understand the passage in the Gospel that says, "Do not despise one of these least ones in the Church."[5] "Least one" is to be understood in contrast with someone greater. The Gospel does not command me not to despise a great one; a great one cannot be despised. But it tells me, "Do not despise one of these least ones." You should realize that the words "least" and "little" are not used haphazardly. Scripture says, for the reason we just mentioned, "whoever scandalizes one of these least ones."[6] A "least one" can be scandalized; a great one cannot.

4 Then the Gospel says of John, "He will be filled with the Holy Spirit even from his mother's womb."[7] John's birth is filled with miracles. An archangel announced the coming of our Lord and Savior; an archangel also announces John's birth: "He will be filled with the Holy Spirit even from his mother's womb." The Jewish

2 Wis 1:2.
3 Luke 1:13–14.
4 Luke 1:15.
5 Matt 18:10.
6 Matt 18:6.
7 Luke 1:15.

people did not recognize our Lord when he performed signs and wonders and cured their illnesses. But, when John is still in his mother's womb, he rejoices and cannot be restrained. When Jesus' mother arrives, he tries to burst out of the womb. Elizabeth says, "For behold, when your greeting sounded in my ears, the infant leapt for joy in my womb."[8] John was still in his mother's womb when he received the Holy Spirit, but the Spirit was not the principle of his being or nature.

5 Then Scripture says, "He will convert many of the children of Israel to the Lord their God."[9] John converts many; the Lord converts not many but all. This is the Lord's work, to convert all to God the Father. "He will go before Christ in the spirit and power of Elijah."[10] Luke does not say, "in the soul of Elijah," but, "in the spirit and power of Elijah." Power and spirit dwelt in Elijah as in all the prophets and, with regard to his humanity, in the Lord and Savior as well. A little later in the Gospel the angel says to Mary, "The Holy Spirit will come upon you, and the power of the Most High will overshadow you."[11] So the spirit that had been in Elijah came upon John as well, and the power that Elijah had also appeared in John. Elijah was carried off to heaven. John was the Lord's precursor and died before so that he could go down to the underworld and proclaim his coming.

6 I believe that the mystery of John is still being achieved in the world today. If anyone is going to believe in Christ Jesus, John's spirit and power first come to his soul and "prepare a perfect people for the Lord."[12] It makes the roads in the heart's rough places level and straightens out its paths. Not only at that time were the roads made ready

---

8 Luke 1:44.

9 Luke 1:16.

10 Luke 1:17.

11 Luke 1:35.

12 Luke 1:17.

and the paths straight; even today John's spirit and power precede the coming of our Lord and Savior. How great are the Lord's mysteries and his plan! Angels go before Jesus, and today angels go up or down for the salvation of people in Christ Jesus, to whom is glory and power for ages of ages. Amen.

Homily 5

Luke 1.22

On the fact that Zechariah fell mute.

WHEN THE PRIEST Zechariah offers incense in the temple, he is condemned to silence and cannot speak. Or better, he speaks only with gestures. He remains mute until the birth of his son John. What does this mean? Zechariah's silence is the silence of prophets in the people of Israel. God no longer speaks to them. His "Word, which was with the Father from the beginning, and was God,"[13] has passed over to us. For us Christ is not silent; for the Jews he is silent even to this day. Therefore, Zechariah the prophet was also silent. His words make it quite clear that he was both a prophet and a priest. But what does the phrase that follows mean, namely, "He kept nodding to them"[14]—that is, he compensated for the loss of his voice with signs? I think that there are deeds that are no different from empty signs because they lack words and reason. But, when words and reason come first and the deed follows, the deeds are not mere signs; they are endowed with rationality.

2 Consider the Jewish practices. They lack words and reason. The Jews cannot give a reason for their practices. Realize that what happened in the past in Zechariah is a type of what is fulfilled in the Jews even to this day. Their circumcision is like an empty sign. Unless the meaning of circumcision is provided, it remains

---

13 John 1:1–2.

14 Luke 1:22.

an empty sign, a mute deed. Passover and other feasts are empty signs rather than the truth. To this very day the people of Israel are mute and dumb. The people who rejected the Word from their midst could not be anything but mute and dumb.

3 Moses himself once said, "I am *alogos*[15] (word-less)." After he said this, he received reason and speech, which he admitted that he did not have before. When the people of Israel were in Egypt, before they had received the Law, they too were without words and reason and thus, in a sense, mute. Then they received the Word; Moses was the image of it. So these people do not admit now what Moses had once admitted—that they are mute and wordless—but show by signs and silence that they have neither words nor reason. Do you not realize that the Jews are confessing their folly when none of them can give a reasonable explanation of the precepts of their Law and of the predictions of their prophets?

4 Christ ceased to be in them. The Word deserted them. What Isaiah wrote was fulfilled, "The daughter of Zion will be deserted like a tent in the vineyard or like a hut in the cucumber patch; she is as desolate as a plundered city."[16] The Jews were left behind and salvation passed to the Gentiles. God meant to spur on the Jews with envy. We contemplate God's mysterious plan, how for our salvation he rejected Israel. We ought to be careful. The Jews were rejected for our sake; on our account they were abandoned. We would deserve even greater punishment if we did nothing worthy of our adoption by God and of his mercy. In his mercy God adopted us and made us his sons in Christ Jesus, to whom is glory and power for ages of ages. Amen.

Homily 6
Luke 1.24–32

On the passage from, "But, when Elizabeth conceived, she kept herself hidden" up to the point where it says, "He will be great."

WHEN ELIZABETH CONCEIVED, "she kept herself hidden for five months. She said, 'The Lord did this for me when he showed concern for me and took away the reason people reproach me.'"[17] I ask why she avoided public notice after she realized that she was pregnant. Unless I am mistaken, the reason is this. Even those who are joined in marriage do not consider every season free for intercourse. At times they abstain from the use of marriage. If the husband and wife are both aged, it is a disgraceful for them to yield to lust and turn to mating. The decline of the body, old age itself, and God's will all inhibit this act. But Elizabeth had relations with her husband once again, because of the angel's word and God's dispensation. She was embarrassed because she was an old and feeble woman, and had gone back to what young people do.

2 Hence "she kept herself hidden for five months"—not until the ninth month, when childbirth was impending, but until Mary also conceived. When Mary conceived and came to Elizabeth, and "her greeting resounded in [her] ears, the child in [Elizabeth's] womb leapt for joy."[18] Elizabeth prophesied. She was filled with the Holy Spirit. She spoke the words recorded in the Gospel account and "these words spread through the entire hill country."[19] A rumor spread among the people that Elizabeth bore a prophet in her womb, and that what she was carrying was greater than a human. Then she does not hide her condition. In full freedom she appears in public

---

15 Exod 4:10.

16 Isa 1:8.

---

17 Luke 1:24–25.

18 Luke 1:44.

19 Luke 1:65.

and rejoices, because she is bearing the precursor of the Savior in her womb.

3 Scripture then relates that, six months after Elizabeth conceived, "the angel Gabriel was sent by God to a town of Galilee named Nazareth, to a virgin betrothed to a man named Joseph of the house of David, and the virgin's name was Mary."[20] Again I turn the matter over in my mind and ask why, when God had decided that the Savior should be born of a virgin, he chose not a girl who was not betrothed, but precisely one that was already betrothed. Unless I am mistaken, this is the reason. The Savior ought to have been born of a virgin who was not only betrothed, but as Matthew writes, had already been given to her husband, although he had not yet had relations with her. Otherwise, if the virgin were seen growing big with child, the state of virginity itself would be a cause of disgrace.

4 I found an elegant statement in the letter of a martyr—I mean Ignatius, the second bishop of Antioch after Peter. During a persecution, he fought against wild animals at Rome. He stated, "Mary's virginity escaped the notice of the ruler of this age."[21] It escaped his notice because of Joseph, and because of their wedding, and because Mary was thought to have a husband. If she had not been betrothed or not had (as people thought) a husband, her virginity could never have been concealed from the ruler of this age. Immediately, a silent thought would have occurred to the devil: "How can this woman, who has not slept with a man, be pregnant? This conception must be divine. It must be something more sublime than human nature." But the Savior had so arranged his plan that the devil did not know that he had taken on a body. When he was conceived, he escaped the devil's notice. Later he commanded his disciples "not to make him known."[22]

5 When the Savior was tempted by the devil himself, he never admitted that he was the Son of God. He merely said, "It is not right for me to adore you or to turn these stones into loaves of bread or to throw myself down from a high place."[23] He said that, but never said he was the Son of God. Look in other books of Scripture, too. You will find that it was Christ's will that the devil should be ignorant of the coming of God's Son. For, the apostle maintains that the opposing powers were ignorant of his passion. He writes, "We speak wisdom among the perfect, but not the wisdom of this age or the wisdom of the rulers of this age. They are being destroyed. We speak God's wisdom, hidden in a mystery. None of the rulers of this age knows it. If they had known it, they would never have crucified the Lord of glory."[24] Thus the mystery of the Savior was hidden from the rulers of this age.

6 An objection to this explanation can be raised, and I think I should resolve it before someone else raises it. The problem is why something that was hidden from the rulers of this age was not hidden from the demon who said in the Gospel, "Have you come here to torture us before the assigned time? We know who you are—the Son of God."[25] Bear this in mind. The demon, who is less evil, knew the Savior, But the devil's wickedness is greater; he is fickle and depraved. The fact that his wickedness is greater prevents him from knowing the Son of God. We ourselves can advance to virtue more easily if we are less sinful. But, if we are more sinful, then we need sweat and hard labor to be freed from our greater evil. This is my explanation of why Mary was betrothed.

7 The angel greeted Mary with a new address, which I could not find anywhere else in Scripture. I ought to explain this expression briefly. The angel says, "Hail, full of grace."[26] The Greek word

---

20 Luke 1:26–27.

21 Ign Eph 19:1.

22 Matt 12:16.

23 Cf. Matt 4:3–10; Luke 4:3–13.

24 1 Cor 2:6–8.

25 Matt 8:29.

26 Luke 1:28.

is *kecharitōmenē*. I do not remember having read this word elsewhere in Scripture. An expression of this kind, "Hail, full of grace," is not addressed to a male. This greeting was reserved for Mary alone. Mary knew the Law; she was holy, and had learned the writings of the prophets by meditating on them daily. If Mary had known that someone else had been greeted by words like these, she would never have been frightened by this strange greeting. Hence the angel says to her, "Do not be afraid, Mary! You have found grace in God's eyes. Behold, you will conceive in your womb. You will bear a son, and you will name him 'Jesus.' He will be great, and will be called 'Son of the Most High.'"[27]

8 Scripture also says of John, "He will be great,"[28] and the angel Gabriel attests to this. But, when Jesus (who is truly great and truly exalted) comes, then John (who earlier had been "great") becomes less. Jesus said, "He was a lamp, burning and shining, and at that hour you wished to rejoice in his light."[29] The greatness of our Savior was not manifested when he was born. It has shone forth only afterward, when his enemies seemed to have extinguished it.

9 Behold the Lord's greatness. "The sound of his teaching has gone out into every land, and his words to the ends of the earth."[30] Our Lord Jesus has been spread out to the whole world, because he is God's power. And now he is with us, according to the apostle's words: "You are gathered together in my spirit also, with the power of the Lord Jesus."[31] The power of the Lord and Savior is with those who are in Britain, separated from our world, and with those who are in Mauretania, and with everyone under the sun who has believed in his name. Behold the Savior's greatness. It extends to all the world. And still I have not expounded his true greatness.

10 Go up to the heavens. See how he fills the celestial regions: "He appeared to the angels."[32] Go down in your mind to the nether world. See that he went down there, too, "He went down, the one who also went up, to fulfill everything,"[33] "so that at Jesus' name every knee might bend—those of heavenly beings, and earthly beings, and beings in the nether world."[34] Ponder the Lord's power, how it has filled the world—that is, the heavens, the earth, and the nether regions. He passed through heaven itself and rose to the regions above. We have read that the Son of God "passed through the heavens."[35]

If you understand this, you will also realize that Scripture does not say, "He will be great," carelessly, but the word has been fulfilled in deed. Jesus our Lord is great, both present and absent. He has endowed this assembly and gathering of ours with a share of his fortitude. That each of us may deserve to receive it, we pray the Lord Jesus, to whom it glory and power for all ages. Amen.

---

27 Luke 1:30–32.

28 Luke 1:15.

29 John 5:35.

30 Ps 19:4; Rom 10:18.

31 1 Cor 5:14.

32 1 Tim 3:16.

33 Eph 4:10.

34 Phil 2:10.

35 Heb 4:14.

70. Origen: Homilies on Genesis

For Origen, the Old Testament was very much a Christian book, part of the entire revelation of God that conveys its full meaning only in relation to the salvation brought by Christ, as set forth in the writings of the New Testament. Origen is able therefore to interpret the Old Testament, even the creation account of the book of Genesis, in light of his knowledge of Christ. This becomes particularly clear in his Homilies on Genesis, written about 240 CE and delivered, probably, to the Christian congregation in Caesarea in Palestine.

The following excerpt comprises the first part of Homily 1, based on the story of creation found in the first chapter of Genesis.

Homily 1

"In the beginning God made heaven and earth."[1] What is the beginning of all things except our Lord and Savior of all, Jesus Christ "the firstborn of every creature"?[2] In this beginning, therefore, that is, in his Word, "God made heaven and earth," as the evangelist John also says in the beginning of his Gospel: "In the beginning was the Word, and the Word was with God, and the Word was God. The same was in the beginning with God. All things were made by him and without him nothing was made."[3] Scripture is not speaking here of any temporal beginning, but it says that the heaven and the earth and all things which were made were made "in the beginning," that is, in the Savior.

"And the earth was invisible and disordered and darkness was upon the abyss, and the spirit of God moved over the waters."[4] "The earth was invisible and disordered" before God said: "Let there be light," and before he divided the light from the darkness, as the order of the account shows.[5] But since in the words which follow he orders the firmament to come into existence and calls this heaven, when we come to that place the reason for the difference between heaven and the firmament will be explained there and also why the firmament was called heaven. But now the text says: "Darkness was upon the abyss."[6] What is "the abyss"? That place, of course, where the devil and his angels will be. This indeed is most clearly designated also in the Gospel when it is said of the Savior: "And the demons which he was casting out were asking him that he not command them to go into the abyss."[7]

For this reason, therefore, God dissolved the darkness as the Scripture says: "And God said, 'Let there be light,' and there was light. And God

---

1 Gen 1:1.

2 Col 1:15.

3 John 1:1–3.

4 Gen 1:2.

5 Gen 1:3.

6 Gen 1:2.

7 Luke 8:31.

Origen: Homilies on Genesis, from *Origen: Homilies on Genesis and Exodus,* ed. Ronald Heine. Fathers of the Church, 71; Washington, DC: Catholic University Press of America, 1996. Used with permission.

saw that the light was good; and God divided between the light and the darkness. And God called the light day and he called the darkness night. And there was evening and there was morning, one day."[8]

According to the letter God calls both the light day and the darkness night. But let us see according to the spiritual meaning why it is that when God, in that beginning which we discussed above, "made heaven and earth," and said, "let there be light" and "divided between the light and the darkness and called the light day and the darkness night," and the text said that "there was evening and there was morning," it did not say: "the first day," but said, "one day." It is because there was not yet time before the world existed. But time begins to exist with the following days. For the second day and the third and the fourth and all the rest begin to designate time.

2 "And God said: 'Let there be a firmament in the midst of the water and let it divide water from water.' And it was so done. And God made the firmament."[9]

Although God had already previously made heaven, now he makes the firmament. For he made heaven first, about which he says, "heaven is my throne."[10] But after that he makes the firmament, that is, the corporeal heaven. For every corporeal object is, without doubt, firm and solid; and it is this which "divides the water which is above heaven from the water which is below heaven."[11]

For since everything which God was to make would consist of spirit and body, for that reason heaven, that is, all spiritual substance upon which God rests as on a kind of throne or seat, is said to be made "in the beginning" and before everything. But this heaven, that is, the firmament, is

corporeal. And, therefore, that first heaven indeed, which we said is spiritual, is our mind, which is also itself spirit, that is, our spiritual person which sees and perceives God. But that corporeal heaven, which is called the firmament, is our outer person which looks at things in a corporeal way.

As therefore, heaven is called the firmament because it divides between those waters which are above it and those which are below it, so also a human, who has been placed in a body, will also himself be called heaven, that is, heavenly person, in the opinion of the apostle Paul who says: "But our citizenship is in heaven."[12] if he can divide and discern what the waters are which are higher, "above the firmament," and what those are which are below the firmament.

The very words of Scripture, therefore, contain it thus: "And God made the firmament, and divided the water which is under the firmament from the water which is above the firmament. And God called the firmament heaven. And God saw that it was good; and there was evening and there was morning, the second day."[13] Let each of you, therefore, be zealous to become a divider of that water which is above and that which is below. The purpose, of course, is that, attaining an understanding and participation in that spiritual water which is above the firmament one may draw forth "from within himself rivers of living water springing up into life eternal,"[14] removed without doubt and separated from that water which is below, that is, the water of the abyss in which darkness is said to be, in which the prince of this world and the adversary, the dragon and his angels dwell, as was indicated above.

Therefore, by participation in that celestial water which is said to be above the heavens, each of the faithful becomes heavenly, that is, when he applies his mind to lofty and exalted things, thinking

---

8 Gen 1:3–5.

9 Gen 1:6–7.

10 Isa 66:1.

11 Gen 1:7.

---

12 Phil 3:20.

13 Gen 1:7–8.

14 John 7:38; 4:14.

nothing about the earth but totally about heavenly things. "seeking the things which are above, where Christ is at the right hand of the Father."[15] For then he also will be considered worthy of that praise from God which is written here when the text says: "And God saw that it was good."[16]

And then also those things which are described in the following statements about the third day signify this same meaning. For the text says: "And God said, 'Let the water which is under heaven be gathered into one gathering, and let the dry land appear.' And it was so done."[17]

Let us labor, therefore, to gather the water which is under heaven and cast it from us that the dry land, which it our deeds done in the flesh, might appear when this has been done so that, of course, "people seeing our good works may glorify our Father who is in heaven."[18] For if we have not separated from us those waters which are under heaven, that is, the sins and vices of our body, our dry land will not be able to appear nor have the courage to advance to the light. "For everyone who does evil hates the light and does not come to the light [lest his works be reproved. But he that does truth comes to the light that] his works may be made manifest" and appear, if "they are done in God."[19] This courage certainly will not be given unless like the waters, we cast off from us and remove the vices of the body which are the materials of sins. Once this has been done our dry land will not remain "dry land" as is shown from what follows.

For the text says: "And the water which is under heaven was gathered into its gatherings and the dry land appeared. And God called the dry land earth, and the gathering together of the waters he called seas."[20] As, therefore, this dry land, after the water was removed from it, as we

said above, did not continue further as "dry land," but is now named "earth," in this manner also our bodies, if this separation from them takes place, will no longer remain "dry land." They will, on the contrary, be called "earth" because they can now bear fruit for God.

Whereas indeed "in the beginning God made heaven and earth," but later made "the firmament" and the "the dry land"; and "the firmament" indeed "he called heaven" giving it the name of that heaven which he had created earlier, but he called "the dry land" "earth" because he bestowed on it the capability of bearing fruits. If, therefore, anyone by his failure still remains dry and offers no fruit but thorns and thistles, producing, as it were, fuel for the fire, in accordance with those things which he brought forth from himself, he also himself becomes fuel for the fire. But if, after the waters of the abyss, which are the thoughts of demons, have been separated from himself, he has shown himself fruitful earth by his zeal and diligence, he ought to expect similar things because he also is led by God into a land flowing with milk and honey.

3 But let us see from the following words what those fruits are which God orders the earth, on which he himself bestowed this name, to produce. "And God saw," the text says, "that it was good, and God said: 'Let the earth bring forth vegetation producing seed according to its kind and likeness, and the fruit tree bearing fruit whose seed is within it according to its likeness on the earth.' And it was so done."[21]

According to the letter, the fruits are clearly those which "the earth," not "the dry land" produces. But again let us also relate the meaning to ourselves. If we have already been made "earth," if we are no longer "dry land," let us offer copious and diverse fruits to God, that we also may be blessed by the Father who says: "Behold the smell of my son is as the smell of a plentiful field which the Lord has blessed,"[22] and that that which the

15 Col 3:1.
16 Gen 1:8.
17 Gen 1:9.
18 Matt 5:16.
19 John 3:20–21.
20 Gen 1:9.

21 Gen 1:10–11.
22 Gen 27:27.

apostle said might be fulfilled in us: "For the earth that receives the rain which comes frequently upon it and brings forth vegetation fit for those by whom it is cultivated will receive blessings from God. But that which brings forth thorns and briars is reprobate and very near a curse, whose end is to be burned."[23]

4 "And the earth brought forth green vegetation producing seed according to its kind and likeness and the fruit tree bearing fruit containing seed producing fruit according to its kind on the earth. And God saw that it was good. And there was evening and there was morning, the third day."[24]

Not only does God order the earth to bring forth "green vegetation," but also to bring forth "seed" that it can always bear fruit. And not only does God order that there be "the fruit tree," but also that it "produce fruit containing seed according to its kind" that is, that it can always bear fruit from these seeds which it contains.

And we, therefore, ought thus both to bear fruit and to have seeds within ourselves, that is, to contain in our heart the seeds of all good works and virtues, that, having these fixed in our minds, from them now we might justly perform all the acts which occur to us. For those are the fruits of that seed, namely our acts, which are brought forth from the good treasure of our heart.

But if, on the one hand, we hear "the word" and from the hearing "immediately" our earth produces vegetation, and this vegetation "wither" before it should come to maturity or fruit, our earth will be called "rocky." But if those things which are said should press forward in our hearts with deeper roots so that they both "bear fruit" of works and contain the seeds of future works, then truly the earth of each of us will bear fruit in accordance with its potential, some "a hundred fold," some "sixty," other "thirty." But also we have considered it necessary to admonish that our fruit

have no "darnel," that is, no tares, that it not be "beside the way," but be sown in the way itself, in that way which says, "I am the way,"[25] that the birds of heaven may not eat our fruits nor our vine. If, however, any of us should deserve to be a vine, let him beware lest he bear thorns for grapes, and for this reason "will no longer be pruned or digged" nor will "the clouds" be ordered "to rain upon it," but on the contrary it will be left "deserted" that "thorns" may overgrow it.[26]

5 But now, after this, the firmament deserves also to be adorned with lights. For God says: "Let there be lights in the firmament of heaven, that they may give light on the earth and divide between day and night."[27]

As in that firmament which had already been called heaven God orders lights to come into existence that "they might divide between day and night," so it also can happen in us if only we also are zealous to be called and made heaven. We shall have lights in us which illuminate us, namely, Christ and his church. For he himself is "the light of the world"[28] who also illuminates the church by his light. For just as the moon is said to receive light from the sun so that the night likewise can be illuminated by it, so also the church, when the light of Christ has been received, illuminates all those who live in the night of ignorance.

But if someone progresses in this so that he is already made a "child of the day," so that "he walks honestly in the day," as "a child of the day and a child of light,"[29] this person is illuminated by Christ himself just as the day is illuminated by the sun.

6 "'And let them be for signs and seasons, and for days and years; and let them be for illumination

---

23 Heb 6:7–8.
24 Gen 1:12–13.
25 John 14:6.
26 Isa 5:2, 6.
27 Gen 1:14.
28 John 8:12.
29 1 Thes 5:5; Rom 13:13.

in the firmament of heaven, to give light on the earth.' And it was so done."[30]

As those lights of heaven which we see have been set "for signs and seasons and days and years," that they might give light from the firmament of heaven for those who are on the earth, so also Christ, illuminating his church, gives signs by his precepts, that one might know how, when the sign has been received, to escape the wrath to come, lest that day overtake him like a thief, but that rather he can reach the acceptable year of the Lord.

Christ, therefore, is "the true light which enlightens every man coming into this world."[31] From his light the church itself also having been enlightened is made "the light of the world" enlightening those "who are in darkness," as also Christ himself testifies to his disciples saying: "You are the light of the world."[32] From this it is shown that Christ indeed is the light of the apostles, but the apostles are "the light of the world." For they, "not having spot or wrinkle or anything of this kind," are the true Church, as also the Apostle says: "That he might present it to himself a glorious Church not having spot or wrinkle or any such thing."[33]

7 "And God made two great lights, a greater light to rule the day and a lesser light to rule the night, and the stars. And God set them in the firmament of heaven to shine upon the earth and to have authority over the day and the night and to divide between the light and the darkness. And God saw that it was good. And there was evening and there was morning, the fourth day."[34]

Just as the sun and the moon are said to be the great lights in the firmament of heaven, so also are Christ and the church in us. But since God also placed stars in the firmament, let us see what are also stars in us, that is, in the heaven of our heart.

Moses is a star in us, which shines and enlightens us by his acts. And Abraham, Isaac, Jacob, Isaiah, Jeremiah, Ezechiel, David, Daniel, and all to whom the Holy Scriptures testify that they pleased God. For just as "star differs from star in glory,"[35] so also each of the saints, according to his own greatness, sheds his light upon us.

Moreover, just as the sun and the moon enlighten our bodies so also our minds are enlightened by Christ and the church. We are enlightened in this way, however, if we are not blind in our minds. For although the sun and moon shine on those who are blind in their bodily eyes, they, nevertheless, cannot receive the light. In the same way also Christ offers his light to our minds, but it will so enlighten us only if blindness of mind impede in no way. But even if this happen, those who are blind must follow Christ saying and crying out: "Have mercy on us, son of David,"[36] that also receiving sight from him they can then also be radiant in the splendor of his light.

But all who see are not equally enlightened by Christ, but individuals are enlightened according to the measure in which they are able to receive the power of the light. And just as the eyes of our body are not equally enlightened by the sun, but to the extent that one shall have ascended to higher places and contemplated its risings with a gaze form a higher vantage point, to such an extent will he perceive more of both its splendor and its heat. So also to the extent that our mind shall have approached Christ in a more exalted and lofty manner and shall have presented itself nearer the splendor of his light, to such an extent will it be made to shine more magnificently and clearly in his light as also he himself says through the prophet: "Draw near to me and I shall draw near to you, says the Lord,"[37]

---

30 Gen 1:14–15.

31 John 1:9.

32 Matt 5:14.

33 Eph 5:27.

34 Gen 1:16–19.

35 1 Cor 15:41.

36 Matt 9:27.

37 Zech 1:3; James 4:8.

And again he says: "I am a God who draws near, and not a God afar off."[38]

We do not, however, all come to him in the same way, but each one according to his own proper ability. For either we come to him with the crowds and he refreshes us by parables to this end only, lest we faint in the way from many fasts, or, of course, we sit always and incessantly at his feet, being free for this alone, that we might hear his word, not at all disturbed about "much serving," but choosing "the best part which shall not be taken away" from us.[39] And certainly those who thus approach him obtain much more of his light. But if, as the apostles, we should be moved from him in no way at all, but should always remain with him in all his tribulations, then he expounds and solves for us in secret those things which he has spoken to the crowds and enlightens us much more clearly. But if in addition someone should be such as can also ascend the mountain with him, as Peter, James, and John, he will be enlightened not only by the light of Christ, but also by the voice of the Father himself.

8 "And God said: 'Let the waters bring forth creeping creatures having life and birds flying over the earth in the firmament of heaven.' And it was so done."[40]

According to the letter, "creeping creatures" and "birds" are brought forth by the waters at the command of God and we recognize by whom these things which we see have been made. But let us see how also these same things come to be in our firmament of heaven, that is, in the firmness of our mind or heart.

I think that if our mind has been enlightened by Christ, our sun, it is ordered afterwards to bring forth from these waters which are in it "creeping creatures" and "birds which fly," that is, to bring out into the open good or evil thoughts that there might be a distinction of the good thoughts from

the evil, which certainly both proceed from the heart. For both good and evil thoughts are brought forth from our heart as from the waters. But by the word and precept of God let us offer both to God's view and judgment that, with his enlightenment we may be able to distinguish what is evil from the good, that is, that we may separate from ourselves those things which creep upon the earth and bear earthly cares.

But let us permit those things which are better, that is, the "birds," to fly not only "above the earth," but also "in the region of the firmament of heaven," that is, let us explore in ourselves the meaning and plan of heavenly things as well as earthly, that we can also understand which of the creeping creatures in us may be harmful. If we should see "a woman to lust after her,"[41] that is a poisonous reptile in us. But if we have the disposition of continence, even if an Egyptian mistress love us deeply, we become birds and, leaving the Egyptian garments in her hands, will fly away from the indecent snare. If we should have in inclination inciting us to steal, that is a most evil reptile. But if we have an inclination that even if we should have "two mites" we would offer these very mites out of mercy as a "gift of God,"[42] that inclination is a bird thinking nothing about earthly things, but striving for the firmament of heaven in its flights. If an inclination should come to us persuading us that we ought not bear the tortures of martyrdom, that will be a poisonous reptile. But if an inclination and thought such as this should spring up in us, that we struggle for the truth even to death, this will be a bird straining from earthly things to the things above. In the same manner also we should perceive and distinguish concerning other forms of either sins or virtues, which are "creeping creatures" and which are "birds" which our waters are commanded to bring forth for separation before God.

9 "And God made the great whales, and every creeping creature having life which the waters

38 Jer 23:23.
39 Luke 10:39–42.
40 Gen 1:20.
41 Matt 5:28.
42 Luke 21:2.

brought forth according to their kind, and every winged bird according to its kind."[43]

And we should observe concerning these words in the same way as those which we discussed above, that we too ought to bring forth "great whales" and "creeping creatures having life

according to their kind." I think impious thoughts and abominable understandings which are against God are indicated in those great whales. All of these, nevertheless, are to be brought forth in the sight of God and placed before him that we may divide and separate the good from the evil, that the Lord might allot to each its place, as is shown from these words which follow. . . .

43 Gen 1:21.

12

The Structure of Early Christianity
The Development of Church Offices

Early Christian communities had none of the formal structures that characterized the church throughout the Middle Ages—with a Pope in Rome, powerful regional bishops, ordained priests, and sundry other church officers with positions of influence. Our earliest sources do not attest even a basic division between priests and laity.

The first Christian churches we know about were those associated with the apostle Paul, the earliest Christian writer whose works have survived. Rather than being organized around highly qualified and well-trained professional ministers, these gatherings of Christians were charismatic communities, groups of believers who were all understood to have been provided with a spiritual gift (Greek: *charisma*) to enable them to minister to the spiritual and physical needs of the entire congregation—gifts like wisdom, teaching, and healing (see 1 Corinthians 12–14). These gifts were endowments from the Spirit, given, evidently, at baptism. They were for the mutual upbuilding and edification of the church, in the interim period between the resurrection of Jesus (the "beginning of the end") and his return from heaven (its consummation). Paul and his congregations apparently believed that this interim would be very brief, that Christ would return within their own generation (see, for example, 1 Thessalonians 4:13–5:11). No surprise, then, that they made scant efforts to organize the church for the long haul.

As a result, these communities did not have "officially" appointed leaders. They did not even meet in public buildings constructed for the purpose. The first church building known to have existed (from literary sources) dates to 201 CE; the first one actually discovered by archaeologists was built (out of a private home) nearly half a century after that. Christians of the first two centuries met in the homes of their wealthier members, who had places large enough to accommodate the congregation. There were several, possibly many, such house-churches in the large urban areas around the Mediterranean. The earliest leaders of these communities were evidently the persons who owned the homes—the wealthiest and, probably, most highly educated members of the church— who provided not only a place to meet but possibly other resources for the church as well. They may also have taken the responsibility of running the meetings.

Women may have enjoyed a significant representation among these unofficial early church leaders. Although women in that world were for the most part denied access to public avenues of power, since men tended to assert their dominance in the public arena, they were by and large granted authority in the home. As a result, women in house-churches appear to have played a much more prominent role than they did in the community at large (see Chapter 14).

In any event, in the small house-churches of earliest Christianity there were no ordained officers in charge of the spiritual lives of the congregation. Everyone had an endowment of the spirit and so was responsible for a set task. As a result, problems that arose were sometimes hard to deal with, as can be seen just from Paul's letters themselves. When severe ethical and doctrinal difficulties arose in Corinth, for example, Paul wrote a letter to the entire congregation trying to urge them to act and believe in appropriate ways. Why did he not write the pastor of the church to urge him to set his congregation in order? There was no pastor.

It is not difficult to imagine the long-term problems that might set in with churches organized under a charismatic model. As more people flocked into the church, decisions had to be made concerning the direction the church was to take. If everyone had an equal endowment of the Spirit and felt that the Spirit was speaking directly to them, how was one to decide which course of action to take when different people felt led differently? How was one to deal with different theological opinions, some of them completely at odds with one another, and with different senses of how the congregation's worship services were to be run or of how its alms were to be distributed, and so on?

Largely as a result of the chaos that could (and did) develop without a more rigorous structure, these charismatic communities eventually transformed themselves into more structured social groups, with leaders of set qualification and specified function. Already by the end of the first century, the churches Paul had founded some decades earlier were organized around "bishops" (literally: overseers), who were ultimately in charge of the community, and "deacons" (literally: ministers or servers). The churches, rapidly becoming public institutions, were principally run by men; women were increasingly demoted from positions of active involvement.

These developments can be seen already in the Pastoral Epistles of the New Testament (1 and 2 Timothy and Titus), which most scholars see as pseudonymous, written in Paul's name by a member of one of his churches near the end of the first century. By the mid–second century, much of the church structure that would later develop into the hierarchy of the Roman Catholic Church was already in place, in nucleus at least, in proto-orthodox communities (the ones about which we are best informed) throughout the Mediterranean. Procedures were developed for determining which persons were to serve as bishops; moreover, these bishops were understood as standing in a spiritual line of descent from the apostles of Jesus themselves (the "apostolic succession," see Chapter 7). Under the bishop served a board of "elders" (literally: presbyters), who assisted him in his administration and instruction of the congregation. Below them was a group of "deacons," who assisted during the worship services and in the collection and distribution of alms. Other offices are in evidence as well, including "widows," single women appointed specifically to engage in prayer and acts of charity for the poor and sick.

There are various theories of how these offices developed. Generally it is agreed that Christians followed models of organization already known to them from other kinds of social groups with which they were intimately familiar, such as the household (which tended to be organized hierarchically, with the *paterfamilias* as the undisputed head), the synagogue (which also had boards of "elders"), and the voluntary associations that were ubiquitous throughout the empire (for example, various trade organizations in which members of the same profession gathered periodically for meals and other social events, including the worship of the patron deity). It is likely that churches in different localities were organized and structured differently, depending on local conditions (such as whether most members came from the synagogue or out of pagan cults), especially in the early part of our period when the diversity of the Christian movement is particularly evident.

Already by the early second century, we find proto-orthodox Christians urging that the bishop is to have supreme control over the congregation and to be respected like God himself, and that the presbyters who serve with him are to be accorded all the respect of Jesus' own apostles. Authoritative tractates specify the qualifications for these offices, the specific duties they comprise, and instructions for carrying them out. Bishops of certain localities are widely recognized authorities in matters pertaining to the church throughout the entire world, not just in their own locality; the authority of the bishop of Rome is becoming widely recognized throughout the church. Moreover, women are by and large being excluded from leadership roles, at least within the proto-orthodox communities (not so elsewhere, especially among some groups of Gnostics).

And so, well before the end of our period, the hierarchical structures that were to become such a key feature of later medieval Christianity were already essentially in place, as can be seen in the following selection of texts.

For Further Reading

Burtchaell, James T. *From Synagogue to Church: Public Services and Offices in the Earliest Christian Communities.* Cambridge: Cambridge University Press, 1992.

Campenhausen, Hans von. *Ecclesiastical Authority and Spiritual Power in the Early Church.* Peabody: Hendrickson, 1997 (reprint of 1969).

Eisen, Ute. *Women Officeholders in Early Christianity: Epigraphical and Literary Studies.* Collegeville: The Liturgical Press, 2000.

Kaufman, Peter I. *Church, Book, and Bishop: Conflict and Authority in Early Latin Christianity.* Boulder: Westview Press, 1996.

Maier, Harry O. *The Social Setting of the Ministry as Reflected in the Writings of Hermas, Clement, and Ignatius.* Waterloo, Ont: Wilfrid Laurier University, 1991.

Stewart-Sykes, Alistair. *The Didascalia Apostolorum.* Turnhout: Brepols, 2009.

Torjesen, Karen Jo. *When Women Were Priests: Women's Leadership in the Early Church and the Scandal of the Subordination in the Rise of Christianity.* San Francisco: HarperSanFrancisco, 1993.

White, L. Michael, "Christianity: Early Social Life and Organization," *Anchor Bible Dictionary,* ed. David Noel Freedman. New York: Doubleday, 1992; 1. 927–935.

THE TEXTS

71. First Clement

Sent from "the church of God in Rome" to "the church of God in Corinth" (1:1), this letter has been traditionally ascribed to Clement, the fourth bishop of Rome. The letter itself, however, never names its actual author or mentions Clement. The purpose of the writing, in any event, is perfectly clear. There has been a division in the church in Corinth in which the elders have been ousted from their positions (3:2–4). For the Roman Christians, this is an altogether unacceptable situation, exceedingly shameful (47:6), which should be rectified at once. The new leaders are to relinquish their authority to the old.

At the core of the letter's argument is one of the earliest expressions of the notion of "apostolic succession." The leaders of the Christian churches were appointed by the successors of the apostles, who had been chosen by Christ, who was sent by God: anyone who opposes those in authority, therefore, is in rebellion against God himself (chapters 42–44). Much of the argument revolves around the history of the people of God as known from the Jewish Scriptures, where envy and strife were always promoted by sinners opposed to the righteous. The new leaders of the Corinthian congregation stand within this nefarious line.

Because of several hints within the letter itself—such as the personal references to Peter and Paul in chapter 5 and the designation of the Corinthian church as "ancient" in chapter 47—most scholars date it near the end of the first century, possibly around 95 CE during the reign of Domitian.

First Letter of Clement to the Corinthians

The church of God that temporarily resides in Rome, to the church of God that temporarily resides in Corinth, to those who have been called and made holy by the will of God through our Lord Jesus Christ. May grace and peace be increased among you, from the all-powerful God, through Jesus Christ.

1 Because of the sudden and repeated misfortunes and set-backs we have experienced, we realize that we have been slow to turn our attention to the matters causing disputes among you, loved ones, involving that vile and profane faction that is alien and foreign to God's chosen people—a faction stoked by a few reckless and headstrong persons to such a pitch of madness that your venerable and renowned reputation, worthy of everyone's love, has been greatly slandered.

2 For who has ever visited you and not approved your highly virtuous and stable faith? And not been astonished by your temperate and gentle piety in Christ? And not proclaimed the

---

1 Clement reproduced from *The Apostolic Fathers*, ed. Bart D. Ehrman; Loeb Classical Library, vol. 1. Cambridge, MA: Harvard University, 2003. Used with permission of Harvard University Press.

magnificent character of your hospitality? And not uttered a blessing for your perfect and unwavering knowledge?

3 For you used to act impartially in all that you did, and you walked according to the ordinances of God, submitting yourselves to your leaders and rendering all due honor to those who were older *[Or: presbyters]* among you. You instructed your young people to think moderate and respectful thoughts. You directed women to accomplish all things with a blameless, respectful, and pure conscience, dutifully loving their husbands. And you taught them to run their households respectfully, living under the rule of submission, practicing discretion in every way.

2 And all of you used to be humble in mind, not arrogant in the least, being submissive rather than forcing submission, giving more gladly than receiving,[1] being satisfied with the provisions supplied by Christ. You heeded his words, carefully storing them up in your inner selves. And his sufferings were present before your eyes.

2 For this reason a deep and rich peace was given to all, along with an insatiable desire for doing good; and a full outpouring of the Holy Spirit came upon everyone.

3 And being filled with his holy will, you used to stretch out your hands to the all-powerful God, zealous for the good, with pious confidence, begging him to be gracious if you inadvertently committed any sin.

4 Day and night you struggled on behalf of the entire brotherhood, that the total number of his chosen ones might be saved, with mortal fear and self-awareness *[Or: conscientiously]*.

5 You were sincere and innocent and bore no grudges against one another.

6 Every faction and schism was loathsome to you. You used to grieve over the unlawful acts of your neighbors and considered their shortcomings your own.

7 You had no regrets when doing good; you were prepared for every good deed.[2]

8 You were adorned with a highly virtuous and honorable way of life, and you accomplished all things in reverential awe of him. The commandments and righteous demands of the Lord were inscribed upon the tablets of your heart.[3]

3 All glory and enlargement was given to you, and that which was written was fulfilled: "My loved one ate and drank and became large and grew fat and kicked out with his heels."[4]

2 From this came jealousy and envy, strife and faction, persecution and disorderliness, war and captivity.

3 And so the dishonorable rose up against the honorable, the disreputable against the reputable, the senseless against the sensible, the young against the old *[Or: the presbyters]*.[5]

4 For this reason, righteousness and peace are far removed,[6] since each has abandoned the reverential awe of God and become dim-sighted in faith, failing to proceed in the ordinances of his commandments and not living according to what is appropriate in Christ. Instead, each one walks according to the desires of his evil heart, which have aroused unrighteous and impious jealousy—through which also death entered the world.[7]

42 The apostles were given the gospel for us by the Lord Jesus Christ, and Jesus Christ was sent forth from God.

2 Thus Christ came from God and the apostles from Christ. Both things happened, then, in an orderly way according to the will of God.

3 When, therefore, the apostles received his commands and were fully convinced through the

---

1 Acts 20:35.

2 Titus 3:1.

3 Prov 7:3.

4 Deut 32:15.

5 Isa 3:5.

6 Isa 59:14.

7 Wis 2:24.

resurrection of our Lord Jesus Christ and persuaded by the word of God, they went forth proclaiming the good news that the Kingdom of God was about to come, brimming with confidence through the Holy Spirit.

4 And as they preached throughout the countryside and in the cities, they appointed the first fruits of their ministries as bishops and deacons of those who were about to believe, testing them by the Spirit.

5 And this was no recent development. For indeed, bishops and deacons had been mentioned in writings long before. For thus the Scripture says in one place, "I will appoint their bishops in righteousness and their deacons in faith."[8]

44 So too our apostles knew through our Lord Jesus Christ that strife would arise over the office of the bishop.

2 For this reason, since they understood perfectly well in advance what would happen, they appointed those we have already mentioned; and afterwards they added a codicil, to the effect that if these should die, other approved men should succeed them in their ministry.

3 Thus we do not think it right to remove from the ministry those who were appointed by them or, afterwards, by other reputable men, with the entire church giving its approval. For they have ministered over the flock of Christ blamelessly and with humility, gently and unselfishly, receiving a good witness by all, many times over.

4 Indeed we commit no little sin if we remove from the bishop's office those who offer the gifts in a blameless and holy way.

5 How fortunate are the presbyters who passed on before, who enjoyed a fruitful and perfect departure from this life. For they have no fear that someone will remove them from the place established for them.

6 But we see that you have deposed some from the ministry held blamelessly in honor among them, even though they had been conducting themselves well.

45 You should strive hard, brothers, and be zealous *[Or: You are contentious, brothers, and envious]* in matters that pertain to salvation!

2 You have gazed into the holy and true Scriptures that were given through the Holy Spirit.

3 You realize that there is nothing unjust or counterfeit written in them. There you will not find the upright cast out by men who were holy.

4 The upright were persecuted, but by the lawless. They were imprisoned, but by the unholy. They were stoned by those who transgressed the law and killed by those who embraced vile and unjust envy.

5 And they bore up gloriously while suffering these things.

6 For what shall we say, brothers? Was Daniel cast into the lions' den by those who feared God?[9]

7 Or were Ananias, Azarias, and Misael shut up in the fiery furnace by those who participated in the magnificent and glorious worship of the Most High?[10] This could never be! Who then did these things? Those who were hateful and full of every evil were roused to such a pitch of anger that they tortured those who served God with holy and blameless resolve. But they did not know that the Most High is the champion and protector of those who minister to his all-virtuous name with a pure conscience. To him be the glory forever and ever. Amen.

8 But those who endured in confidence inherited glory and honor; and they were exalted and inscribed by God in their own memorial forever and ever. Amen.

46 And so, we too must cling to these examples, brothers.

2 For it is written, "Cling to those who are holy; for those who cling to them will themselves be made holy."[11]

---

8 Isa 60:17 (LXX).

9 Dan 6:16.

10 Dan 3:19 ff.

11 Source unknown.

3 And again in another place it says, "With an innocent man, you too will be innocent and with one who is chosen, you will be chosen. But with one who is corrupt, you will cause corruption."[12]

4 Therefore we should cling to those who are innocent and upright, for these are God's chosen.

5 Why are there conflicts, fits of anger, dissensions, factions, and war among you?

6 Do we not have one God, and one Christ, and one gracious Spirit that has been poured out upon us, and one calling in Christ?[13]

7 Why do we mangle and mutilate the members of Christ and create factions in our own body? Why do we come to such a pitch of madness as to forget that we are members of one another? Remember the words of our Lord Jesus,

8 for he said, "Woe to that person! It would have been good for him not to be born, rather than cause one of my chosen to stumble. Better for him to have a millstone cast about his neck and be drowned in the sea than to have corrupted one of my chosen."[14]

9 Your schism has corrupted many and cast many into despondency, many into doubt, and all of us into grief. And your faction persists even now!

47 Take up the epistle of that blessed apostle, Paul.

2 What did he write to you at first, at the beginning of his proclamation of the gospel?

3 To be sure, he sent you a letter in the Spirit concerning himself and Cephas and Apollos, since you were even then engaged in partisanship.[15]

4 But that partisanship involved you in a relatively minor sin, for you were partisan towards reputable apostles and a man approved by them.

5 But now consider who has corrupted you and diminished the respect you had because of your esteemed love of others.

6 It is shameful, loved ones, exceedingly shameful and unworthy of your conduct in Christ, that the most secure and ancient church of the Corinthians is reported to have created a faction against its presbyters, at the instigation of one or two persons.

7 And this report has reached not only us but even those who stand opposed to us, so that blasphemies have been uttered against the Lord's name because of your foolishness; and you are exposing yourselves to danger.

48 And so let us dispose of this problem quickly and fall down before the Master and weep, begging him to be merciful and to be reconciled to us, and to restore us to our respected and holy conduct, seen in our love of others.

2 For this is a gate of righteousness that opens up onto life, just as it is written, "Open up for me gates of righteousness; when I enter through them I will give praises to the Lord.

3 This is the gate of the Lord, and the upright will enter through it."[16]

4 Although many gates open, this is the one that leads to righteousness—the one that is in Christ. All those who enter it are most fortunate; they make their path straight in holiness and righteousness, accomplishing all things without disorder.

5 Let a person be faithful, let him be able to speak forth knowledge, let him be wise in his discernment of words, let him be pure in deeds.

6 For the more he appears to be great, the more he should be humble, striving for the good of all, not just of himself.

---

12 Ps 18:25–26.

13 Eph 4:4–6.

14 Matt 26:24; Luke 17:2.

15 1 Cor 1:12.

16 Ps 118:19–20.

72. The Didache

Discovered in 1873 in a monastery library in Constantinople (Istanbul), the Didache (literally, "The Teaching") of the Twelve Apostles, has made a significant impact on our understanding of the social life and ritual practices of the early church. It is, in fact, the first "church manual" to have survived from early Christianity.

The bulk of the book gives instructions for the ritual observances and social interactions of the Christian community (for further excerpts, see Chapters 13 and 15). But near the end, the author addresses the problem of wandering "apostles," "teachers," and "prophets" of dubious moral character; evidently, some Christians had become itinerant preachers simply for financial gain. The communities are to test the sincerity of these wandering ministers and to limit the length of their stay at the community's expense; moreover, the communities are to appoint leaders of their own to direct their affairs.

Because the book represents an early attempt to deal with such itinerant Christian leaders—a well-attested feature of earliest Christianity (cf. Mark 6:7–13 and the book of Acts)—and does not evidence the rigid form of church hierarchy that developed later in the second century (even though it speaks of bishops and deacons), most scholars think it was composed sometime around 100 CE.

11 And so, welcome anyone who comes and teaches you everything mentioned above.

2 But if the teacher should himself turn away and teach something different, undermining these things, do not listen to him. But if his teaching brings righteousness and the knowledge of the Lord, then welcome him as the Lord.

3 But act towards the apostles and prophets as the gospel decrees.

4 Let every apostle who comes to you be welcomed as the Lord.

5 But he should not remain more than a day. If he must, he may stay one more. But if he stays three days, he is a false prophet.

[...] ould take noth-[...] at his night's [...] a false prophet. [...] phet speaking [...] forgiven, but

8 Not everyone who speaks in the Spirit is a prophet, but only one who conducts himself like the Lord. Thus the false prophet and the prophet will both be known by their conduct.

9 No prophet who orders a meal in the Spirit eats of it; if he does, he is a false prophet.

10 Every prophet who teaches the truth but does not do what he himself teaches is a false prophet.

11 You are not to condemn any prophet who has been approved and is true, and who acts on behalf of the earthly mystery of the church, even if he does not teach others to do what he himself does, since he has his judgment with God. For even the ancient prophets behaved in this way.

12 Do not listen to anyone who says in the Spirit, "Give me money" (or something else). But if he tells you to give to others who are in need, let no one judge him.

Apostolic Fathers, ed. Bart D. Ehrman; Loeb Classical Library, vol. 1. Cambridge, MA: Harvard University Press, 2003. Used with permission of Harvard University Press.

12 Everyone who comes in the name of the Lord should be welcomed. Then, when you exercise your critical judgment, you will know him; for you understand what is true and what is false.

2 If the one who comes is simply passing through, help him as much as you can. He should not stay with you more than two or three days, if need be.

3 If he wants to remain with you, and is a tradesman, let him work and eat.

4 If he does not have a trade, use your foresight to determine how he as a Christian may live among you without being idle [*Or: through your understanding you should know in advance that no idle Christian is to live among you*].

5 If he does not want to behave like this, he is a Christmonger. Avoid such people.

13 Every true prophet who wants to settle down with you deserves his food.

2 So too a true teacher, like the worker, deserves his food.[1]

3 Therefore you shall take every first portion of the produce from the wine vat and the threshing floor, and the first portion of both cattle and sheep, and give it to the prophets. For they are your high priests.

4 If you do not have a prophet, then give it to the poor.

5 If you make bread, take the first portion and give it according to the commandment.

6 So too if you open a jar of wine or oil, take the first portion of it and give it to the prophets.

7 And take the first portion of your money, clothing, and everything you own, as it seems good to you, and give it according to the commandment.

15 And so, elect for yourselves bishops and deacons who are worthy of the Lord, gentle men who are not fond of money, who are true and approved. For these also conduct the ministry of the prophets and teachers among you.

2 And so, do not disregard them. For these are the ones who have found honor among you, along with the prophets and teachers.

3 Do not reprimand one another in anger, but in peace, as you have learned from the gospel. Let no one speak with a person who has committed a sin against his neighbor, nor let him hear anything from you, until he repents.

4 But say your prayers, give to charity, and engage in all your activities as you have learned in the gospel of our Lord.

---

1 Matt 10:10.

73. The Letters of Ignatius to the Ephesians, Magnesians, and Smyrneans

We have already seen Ignatius of Antioch as an important figure in early proto-orthodox Christianity (see Chapter 3). The letters that Ignatius wrote on his path to martyrdom are principally concerned with two issues in the churches of Asia Minor: heresy and division. For both problems, Ignatius has a single, overarching

---

"The Letters of Ignatius" reproduced from *The Apostolic Fathers*, ed. Bart D. Ehrman; Loeb Classical Library, vol. 1. Cambridge, MA: Harvard University Press, 2003. Used with permission of Harvard University Press.

solution: each church must adhere closely to the authority of its bishop, along with his ruling board of elders (the "presbytery") and the group of ministering deacons. The bishop has the authority of God himself; the elders are to be obeyed like the apostles. Nothing is to be done in the church without the bishop's sanction. Those who fail to follow the bishop's lead are outside the church, which is the only possible sphere of salvation.

Ignatius's notion of the "monarchial episcopate," of the sole authority of the ruling bishop, became standard fare within proto-orthodox Christian circles of the later second and third centuries as they wrestled with the problems of heresy and schism. These particular letters were written around 110 CE.

To The Ephesians

Ignatius, who is also called God-bearer, to the church that is blessed with greatness by the fullness of God the Father, a church foreordained from eternity past to obtain a constant glory which is enduring and unchanging, a church that has been unified and chosen in true suffering *[Or: a glory which is enduring, unchanging, unified, and chosen through true suffering]* by the will of the Father and of Jesus Christ, our God; to the church in Ephesus of Asia, which is worthy of all good fortune. Warmest greetings in Jesus Christ and in blameless joy!

1 Now that I have received in God your greatly loved name, which you have obtained because of your upright nature, according to the faith and love that is in Christ Jesus our Savior—for you are imitators of God and have rekindled, through the blood of God, the work we share as members of the same family, and brought it to perfect completion.

2 For you were eager to see me, since you heard that I was being brought in chains from Syria because of the name and hope we share, and that I was hoping, through your prayer, to be allowed to fight the beasts in Rome, that by doing so I might be able to be a disciple.

3 Since, then, I have received your entire congregation in the name of God through Onesimus, who abides in a love that defies description and serves as your bishop in the flesh—and I ask by Jesus Christ that you love him, and that all of you

be like him. For blessed is the one who have graciously granted you, who are worthy, to obtain such a bishop.

2 But as to my fellow slave Burrhus, your godly deacon who is blessed in all things. I ask that he stay here for the honor of both you and the bishop. And Crocus as well—who is worthy of God and of you, whom I received as an embodiment of your love—has revived me in every way. So may the Father of Jesus Christ refresh him, along with Onesimus, Burrhus, Euplus, and Fronto, those through whom I lovingly saw all of you.

2 I hope to enjoy you at all times, if indeed I am worthy. For it is fitting for you in every way to give glory to Jesus Christ, the one who glorified you, so that you may be holy in all respects, being made complete through a single subjection, being subject to the bishop and the presbytery.

3 I am not giving you orders as if I were someone. For even though I have been bound in the name, I have not yet been perfected in Jesus Christ. For now I have merely begun to be a disciple and am speaking to you as my fellow learners. For I have needed you to prepare me for the struggle in faith, admonishment, endurance, and patience.

2 But since love does not allow me to be silent concerning you, I decided to encourage you, that you may run together in harmony with the mind of God. For also Jesus Christ, who cannot be distinguished from our life, is the Father's mind, just as also the bishops who have

been appointed throughout the world share the mind of Jesus Christ.

4 For this reason it is fitting for you to run together in harmony with the mind of the bishop, which is exactly what you are doing. For your presbytery, which is both worthy of the name and worthy of God, is attuned to the bishop as strings to the lyre. Therefore Jesus Christ is sung in your harmony and symphonic love.

2 And each of you should join the chorus, that by being symphonic in your harmony, taking up God's pitch in unison, you may sing in one voice through Jesus Christ to the Father, that he may both hear and recognize you through the things you do well, since you are members of his Son. Therefore it is useful for you to be in flawless unison, that you may partake of God at all times as well.

5 For since I was able to establish such an intimacy with your bishop so quickly (an intimacy that was not human but spiritual), how much more do I consider you fortunate, you who are mingled together with him as the church is mingled with Jesus Christ and Jesus Christ with the Father, so that all things may be symphonic in unison.

2 Let no one be deceived. Anyone who is not inside the sanctuary lacks the bread of God. For if the prayer of one or two persons has such power, how much more will that of the bishop and the entire church?

3 Therefore the one who does not join the entire congregation is already haughty and passes judgment on himself. For it is written, "God opposes the haughty."[1] And so we should be eager not to oppose the bishop, that we may be subject to God.

6 The more one notices that the bishop is silent, the more he should stand in awe of him. For we must receive everyone that the master of the house sends to take care of his affairs as if he were

---

1 Prov 3.34; cf. Jas 4:6; 1 Pet 5.5.

the sender himself. And so we are clearly obliged to look upon the bishop as the Lord himself.

2 Thus Onesimus himself praises you highly for being so well ordered in God, because all of you live according to the truth and no heresy resides among you. On the contrary, you no longer listen to anyone, except one who speaks truthfully about Jesus Christ.

To the Magnesians

Ignatius, who is also called God-bearer, to the one that has been blessed by the gracious gift of God the Father in Christ Jesus our Savior, in whom I greet the church that is in Magnesia on the Meander and extend warmest greetings in God the Father and in Jesus Christ.

1 Knowing the great orderliness of your godly love, I have joyfully decided to speak with you in the faith of Jesus Christ.

2 For since I have been made worthy of a most godly name, by the bonds that I bear I sing the praises of the churches, praying that they may experience the unity of the flesh and spirit of Jesus Christ—our constant life—and of faith and love, to which nothing is preferred, and (more important still) of Jesus and the Father. If we endure in him all the abusive treatment of the ruler of this age and escape, we will attain to God.

2 Since, then, I have been found worthy to see you through Damas, your bishop who is worthy of God, through your worthy presbyters Bassus and Apollonius, and through my fellow slave, the deacon Zotion—whom I hope to enjoy, for he is subject to the bishop as to the grace of God, and to the presbytery as to the law of Jesus Christ.

3 But it is not right for you to take advantage of your bishop because of his age. You should render him all due respect according to the power of God the Father, just as I have learned that even your holy presbyters have not exploited his

seemingly youthful appearance *[Or: rank; or: po-sition]*; but they have deferred to him as one who is wise in God—and not to him, but to the Father of Jesus Christ, the bishop of all.

2 And so it is fitting for us to be obedient apart from all hypocrisy, for the honor of the one who has desired us. For it is not that a person deceives this bishop who is seen, but he deals falsely with the one who is invisible. In such a case, an account must be rendered not to human flesh, but to God, who knows the things that are hidden.

4 And so it is fitting not only to be called Christians, but also to be Christians, just as there are some who call a person the bishop but do everything without him. Such persons do not seem to me to be acting in good conscience, because they do not hold valid meetings in accordance with the commandment.

5 Since, then, these matters have an end, and the two things are set together, death and life, and each person is about to depart to his own place—

2 for just as there are two kinds of coin, one from God and the other from the world, and each of them has its own stamp set upon it: the unbelievers the stamp of this world and the believers the stamp of God the Father, in love, through Jesus Christ. If we do not choose to die voluntarily in his suffering, his life is not in us.

6 Since, then, I have observed, by the eyes of faith, your entire congregation through those I have already mentioned, and loved it, I urge you to hasten to do all things in the harmony of God, with the bishop presiding in the place of God and the presbyters in the place of the council of the apostles, and the deacons, who are especially dear to me, entrusted with the ministry of Jesus Christ, who was with the Father before the ages and has been manifest at the end.

2 You should assume the character of God and all respect one another. No one should consider his neighbor in a fleshly way, but you should love one another in Jesus Christ at all times. Let there be nothing among you that can divide you, but be unified with the bishop and with those who preside according to the model and teaching of incorruptibility.

7 And so, just as the Lord did nothing apart from the Father—being united with him—neither on his own nor through the apostles, so too you should do nothing apart from the bishop and the presbyters. Do not try to maintain that it is reasonable for you to do something among yourselves in private; instead, for the common purpose, let there be one prayer, one petition, one mind, one hope in love and in blameless joy, which is Jesus Christ. Nothing is superior to him.

2 You should all run together, as into one temple of God, as upon one altar, upon one Jesus Christ, who came forth from one Father and was with the one *[Or: and was one with him]* and returned to the one.[2]

To the Smyrneans

Ignatius, who is also called God-bearer, to the church of God the Father and the beloved Jesus Christ which is in Smyrna of Asia, which has been shown mercy in every gracious gift, filled with faith and love, and lacking no gracious gift, a church that is most worthy of God and bears what is holy. Warmest greetings in a blameless spirit and the word of God. . . .

6 Let no one be deceived. Judgment is prepared even for the heavenly beings, for the glory of the angels, and for the rulers both visible and invisible, if they do not believe in the blood of Christ. Let the one who can receive this receive it.[3] Let no one become haughty because of his position. For faith and love are everything; nothing is preferable to them.

---

2 Cf. John 16:28.

3 Matt 19:12.

2 But take note of those who spout false opinions about the gracious gift of Jesus Christ that has come to us, and see how they are opposed to the mind of God. They have no interest in love, in the widow, the orphan, the oppressed, the one who is in chains or the one set free, the one who is hungry or the one who thirsts.

7 They abstain from the eucharist and prayer, since they do not confess that the eucharist is the flesh of our savior Jesus Christ, which suffered on behalf of our sins and which the Father raised in his kindness. And so, those who dispute the gift of God perish while still arguing the point. It would be better for them to engage in acts of love, that they might also rise up.

2 And so it is fitting to avoid such people and not even to speak about them, either privately or in public, but instead to pay attention to the prophets, and especially to the gospel, in which the passion is clearly shown to us and the resurrection is perfected. But flee divisions as the beginning of evils.

8 All of you should follow the bishop as Jesus Christ follows the Father; and follow the presbytery as you would the apostles. Respect the deacons as the commandment of God. Let no one do anything involving the church without the bishop. Let that eucharist be considered valid that occurs under the bishop or the one to whom he entrusts it.

2 Let the congregation be wherever the bishop is; just as wherever Jesus Christ is, there also is the universal church. It is not permitted either to baptize or to hold a love feast without the bishop. But whatever he approves is acceptable to God, so that everything you do should be secure and valid.

9 Finally, it is reasonable for us to return to sobriety, while we still have time to repent to God. It is good to know both God and the bishop. The one who honors the bishop is honored by God; the one who does anything behind the bishop's back serves the devil.

2 Let all things abound to you in grace, for you are worthy. You have refreshed me in every way and Jesus Christ has refreshed you. You have loved me when absent as well as when present. God is your recompense; if you endure all things for his sake, you will attain to him.

74. Hippolytus: The Apostolic Tradition

This treatise has traditionally been ascribed to Hippolytus of Rome (160–235 CE), although scholars debate whether it comes from his pen or not. Hippolytus was one of the intriguing figures of early Christianity about whom we would like to know far more than we do. A prominent presbyter in the church of Rome near the end of the second century and beginning of the third, his most important literary work was a ten-volume catalogue and refutation of heresies. His struggle against false teaching became particularly acute when he charged the bishop of Rome with embracing a heretical Christology. A schism erupted around 217 CE, with the followers of Hippolytus appointing him as a kind of rival pope.

Hippolytus: The Apostolic Tradition, reproduced from Alistair Stewart-Sykes, tr. *On the Apostolic Tradition.* New York: St. Vladimir's Seminary Press, 2001. Used with permission of St. Vladimir's Seminary Press.

If Hippolytus wrote the "Apostolic Tradition," then it provides us a glimpse into the church of Rome in the early third century. Whether or not he wrote it, the treatise gives instructions for conducting the affairs of the church. In particular, the treatise clearly advances a particular form of church structure. Firm instructions are given for ordaining bishops, presbyters, and deacons, and for appointing other officials: church widows, readers, virgins, and subdeacons. Moreover, some of the official duties of these positions are discussed. For further excerpts dealing with the closely related issues of Christian liturgy, see Chapter 13.

2 Let the bishop be ordained as we appointed above, having been elected by all the people.

2 When he has been named and found pleasing to all, let the people come together with the presbyters, and any bishops who are present, on the Lord's day.

3 When all give their consent they lay hands on him, and the presbytery stands in silence.

4 And all shall keep silence, praying in their heart for the descent of the Holy Spirit.

5 After this, at the request of all, one of the bishops who is present, laying a hand on him who is being ordained bishop, shall pray thus: . . . .

7 When a presbyter is ordained the bishop will lay a hand upon his head, the presbyters likewise touching him, and he shall speak as we said above, as we said before concerning the bishop, praying and saying:

2 God and Father of our Lord Jesus Christ, look upon this your servant and impart the Spirit of grace and counsel of presbyterate so that he might assist and guide your people with a pure heart,

3 as you looked upon the people of your choice and directed Moses to choose presbyters whom you filled with your spirit which you gave to your servant.

4 And now Lord, grant that the Spirit of your grace may be preserved unceasingly in us, filling us and making us worthy to minister to you in simplicity of heart, praising you

5 through your child Jesus Christ, through whom be glory and might to you, with the Holy Spirit in the holy church both now, and to the ages of the ages. Amen.

8 And when a deacon is installed let him be chosen in accordance with those things which were said above, in the same way the bishop alone laying hands. Just so we prescribe that at the ordination of a deacon the bishop alone lays hands,

2 for the reason that he is not ordained to priesthood, but to serve the bishop, that he might do those things which are commanded by him.

3 For he is not a participant in the council of the clergy but looks after and indicates to the bishop what is necessary,

4 not receiving the spirit of the presbytery which the presbyters share, but that which is entrusted him under the power of the bishop.

5 For which reason the bishop alone shall ordain a deacon;

6 on a presbyter however the presbyters also lay their hands because of the common and like spirit of their order.

7 For the presbyter has authority in this matter only, that he may receive; he does not, however, have the authority to give.

8 Therefore he does not appoint clergy; at the ordination of a presbyter he seals, as the bishop lays hands.

9 Now if a confessor is in chains for the sake of the name of the Lord, a hand is not laid on him for the diaconate or for presbyterate. For he has the honor of the presbyterate on account of his confession. If he is to be installed as bishop, then is the hand to be laid upon him.

2 If a confessor has not been taken to trial, or has not been punished with chains, or has not been shut up in prison or has not been condemned

with any penalty but by chance has been merely abused on account of the name of our Lord and has been punished with domestic punishment, although he bore witness, let the hand be laid on him for whatever orders of which he is deserving.

3 When the Bishop gives thanks in accordance with what was said above it is not absolutely incumbent on him that he recite the identical words which we stated above as though performing a set declamatory exercise! In giving thanks to God let each pray according to his ability. If he has the ability to pray easily in a sophisticated manner then that is good. If someone, when he prays, offers a mean prayer do not seek to prevent him, only he must pray in an orthodox manner.

10 When a widow is appointed she does not receive laying on of hands but is chosen by the name.

2 If her husband has been dead a long time let her be appointed.

3 If her husband is recently dead do not believe her. Even if she is elderly she should be tested for a time, for often the passions grow old in one who finds a place for them in himself.

4 Let the widow be installed with the word only and let her join the rest. But a hand shall not be laid on her because she does not lift up the sacrifice nor does she have a proper liturgy.

5 For the laying on of hands is with the clergy on account of the liturgy, whereas the widow is installed on account of prayer, which is for everybody.

11 A reader is installed as the bishop hands him a book. He has no laying on of hands.

12 A hand is not laid on a virgin but her choice alone makes her a virgin.

13 A hand is not laid on the subdeacon; rather he is named so that he might go after the deacon.

14 If somebody appears to have received the gift of healing or revelation a hand is not

laid on him for the facts of the matter will reveal whether he has spoken the truth.

23 Widows and virgins should fast often and pray for the church. Presbyters, should they wish, and laypersons may likewise fast. A bishop cannot fast except when all the people are fasting. It may be that somebody wishes to make an offering, and he cannot be refused. When he breaks he should always taste.

26 [When he eats in the company of other believers,]

2 they shall take from the hand of the bishop a single fragment of bread, before anyone breaks the bread which is in front of him. For that is a blessing and not the eucharist, as is the body of the Lord.

3 (Sahidic version) It is proper that all, before they drink, should take a cup and give thanks over it and in this manner to drink and to eat with purity. Exorcized bread and a cup should be given to catechumens.

27 A catechumen shall not sit at the Lord's Supper.

2 But throughout every meal the one who eats should be mindful of the one who invited him; for this reason he was asked to come under the other's roof.

28 When you eat and drink, do so with integrity and do not get drunk so that you become ridiculous and cause grief to the one who invites you through your unruliness, but rather let him give thanks that he is worthy that the saints should come to him. For he said "You are the salt of the earth."

2 And if a portion is offered to all in common, take from it.

3 And if you are invited to eat, eat so that you have <just> had enough, and so that there is food left over, so that the one who invited you might send it out to all who want it as left by the saints, and he may confidently rejoice.

4 Let those who are invited to eat do so in silence, and not wrangle with words. But when the bishop has exhorted then, if anyone asks anything, he should be answered. And when the bishop is speaking, listen in silence until he is asked again.

5 And if the faithful are present at supper in the absence of a bishop but a presbyter or deacon is present, let them act in a similarly proper manner. And let everyone be glad to accept a blessed portion from the hand of the presbyter or the deacon. In the same way let a catechumen receive the same, though exorcized. If the laity are present together let them act with understanding. For a layperson cannot give the blessing.

29 Let everyone eat in the name of the Lord. We should compete among the heathen in being like-minded and sober, for this is what pleases God.

30 If anyone wishes that widows, who should have attained seniority in age, should have a supper, he should send them home before evening. If, however, he is unable because of the lot which has fallen to him, he should give them food and wine and send them away so that they can partake of the gifts at home when it suits them.

31 Let all hasten to offer the new fruits of the harvest to the bishop as first-fruits.

2 And as he offers them, he shall bless them and name the one who offered saying:

3 We give thanks to you, O God, and we offer you the firstlings of the fruits you have granted us to receive; through your Word you nourished them, ordering the earth to bring forth all fruits for the enjoyment and nourishment of people and for all animals.

4 We praise you, O God, for all these things and in all the things in which you have assisted us, for us adorning the whole creation with various fruits;

5 through your child Jesus Christ Our Lord, through whom be glory to you for the ages of ages.

32 Fruits are indeed blessed, that is, grapes, figs, pomegranates, olives, pears, apples, mulberries, peaches, cherries, almonds, plums; but not leeks, pumpkins, melons, cucumbers, onions, garlic, or any other vegetable.

2 But sometimes flowers are also offered. So let the rose and the lily be offered, but no other.

3 And in all things which are eaten they shall give thanks to the holy God, eating to his glory.

33 At the Pascha, nobody may eat before the offering is made. For if anyone acts thus it is not reckoned to him as fasting.

2 If anyone is pregnant or sick, and cannot fast for two days, they should fast on the Saturday on account of their necessity, confining themselves to bread and water.

3 But if anyone was on a boat or, through the circumstance of some other necessity, did not know the day, when he has learned it should keep the fast after the Pentecost.

4 For the Pascha which we keep is not the type, for the type has passed away, for which reason it ended in the second month. And we should keep the fast when we have learnt the truth.

34 Each deacon should wait upon the bishop with the subdeacons. It should be told him if any is sick so that, if it please the bishop, he may visit them. For a sick person is encouraged indeed when the chief of the priests remembers him.

39 The deacons and the presbyters should gather daily at the place which the bishop appoints for them. Let the deacons not fail to assemble at all times, unless illness prevents them.

2 When all have gathered together, they should teach those who are in the church, and in this way, when they have prayed, each should go to the task which falls to him.

40 No man may be heavily charged for burying a man in the cemeteries, for it is the property of all the poor. Except the fee of the workman should be paid to him who digs and the price of the tiles be given.

2 The bishop should provide for those who are in that place from that which is offered to the church and look after it, so that there may be no heavy charge for those who come to those places.

41 Every faithful man and woman, when they have risen from sleep in the morning, before they touch any work at all, should wash their hands and pray to God, and so go to their work.

2 But if instruction in the word of God takes place, each one should choose to go to that place, reckoning in his heart that it is God whom he hears in the one who instructs. For he who prays in the church will be able to pass by the wickedness of the day. He who is God-fearing should think it a great loss if he does not go to the place where instruction is given, and especially if he can read, or if a teacher comes.

3 Let none of you be late in the church, the place where teaching is given. Then it shall be given to the speaker to say things profitable to all, and you will hear things of which you would not think, and profit from things which the Holy Spirit will give you through the one who instructs. In this way your faith will be strengthened in regard to matters about which you heard. What you ought to do in your house will also be told in that place. Therefore let everyone hurry in coming to the assembly, the place where the Holy Spirit abounds.

4 And if there is a day on which there is no instruction, and each one is in the house, he should take a holy book and read in it as much as seems profitable.

5 And if indeed you are in the house, pray at the third hour and praise God. But if you are elsewhere and the occasion comes about, pray in your heart to God.

6 For at that hour Christ was displayed nailed to the tree. For this reason also in the Old ‹Testament›, the Law prescribed that the shewbread should be offered at every hour as a type of the Body and Blood of Christ; and the slaughter of the speechless lamb is this, a type of the perfect lamb. For the shepherd is Christ, and also the bread which came down from heaven.

7 Pray likewise at the time of the sixth hour. For as Christ was fixed on the wood of the cross that day was divided, and a great darkness descended. Therefore they should pray a powerful prayer at that hour, imitating the voice of him who prayed and darkened the whole creation on account of the unbelieving Jews.

8 And they should pray at the ninth hour also a great prayer and give great praise, following the manner in which the soul of the righteous praises the Lord, the God of truth, who remembered his saints and sent them his Son, that is his Word, to enlighten them.

9 For at that hour Christ, pierced in the side, poured forth water and blood and lit up the rest of that day and brought it so to the evening. Hence, in beginning to sleep, he made it the beginning of another day which fulfilled the image of resurrection.

10 Pray also before your body rests on the bed.

11 Rising around midnight wash your hands with water, and pray.

12 And if you have a wife, pray both together; if she is not yet among the faithful, take yourself into another room and pray, and go back to bed again. Do not be dilatory about praying.

13 [He who is bound in the marriage bond is not defiled. Those who have washed have no need of washing again for they are clean.

14 Through signing yourself with moist breath, caught as spittle in your hand, your body is purified all the way to your feet. For when (prayer) is offered with a believing heart, the gift of the Spirit and the pouring of baptism sanctify the one who believes, as though from the font.]

15 For this reason it is necessary to pray at this hour, for those elders who handed on the tradition taught us to do so because at that hour all creation is still for a moment to praise the Lord. Stars and trees and waters stop for an instant, and all the host of the angels which ministers to him praises God at this hour with the souls of the just.

16 This is why believers should take good care to pray at this hour. Bearing witness to this matter also the Lord says thus: "Behold, a shout went up around the middle of the night, of people saying: 'Look, the bridegroom is coming: get up to meet him.'" And he goes on saying: "Therefore be watchful, for you do not know at what hour he comes."

17 And likewise pray, getting up around cock-crow. For at the hour when the cock crew the sons of Israel denied Christ, whom we have known by faith, looking each day in hope for the appearing of eternal light at the resurrection of the dead.

18 Therefore if you faithful act thus and keep them in your memory and teach them in turn and encourage the catechumens, you shall not undergo temptation, nor will you perish, for you shall have Christ always in mind.

42B If you are tempted, reverently sign yourself on the forehead. For this sign of the passion is shown and is proven against the Devil if you make it in faith, and not so that you may show it to people, but present it through knowledge like a shield.

2 For when the Adversary sees the power which comes from the heart, and when he sees that the inner man, who is rational, outwardly displays the likeness of the Word which is impressed on him internally, he is put to flight, not by your spitting but by your breathing with your mouth.

3 This Moses showed in the paschal sheep which was slaughtered. He sprinkled the blood on the threshold and anointed the doorposts, and showed forth that faith in the perfect sheep which is now in us.

4 By signing forehead and eyes with the hand we shall escape the one who is seeking our destruction.

43B And so if these things are received with thankfulness and true faith, they provide upbuilding in the church and eternal life for those who believe.

2 I advise that these things should be guarded by all those who are truly wise. For if all of you hear the apostolic tradition and follow it and keep it, no heretic or anyone at all can deceive you.

3 For in this way many heresies have grown up, because the pre-eminent ones were unwilling to learn the purpose of the apostles but, following their own desires, did as they wished and not what was fitting.

4 If we have passed over anything, beloved, God will reveal it to those who are worthy, since he steers the church, which is holy, until it reaches the peaceable haven.

75. The Didascalia

The Didascalia (literally: "Teaching") of the Apostles is a church manual pseudonymously written in the name of the twelve apostles, along with the apostle Paul and James the brother of Jesus. Originally produced in the early third century, only fragments of the book survive in the original Greek. It was translated early on, however, especially into Syriac (on which modern editions are largely based), and later authors sometimes incorporated portions of it wholesale into their own manuals.

The Didascalia, from *The Didascalia Apostolorum Corpus Scriptorum Christianorum Orientalium*, ed. Arthur Vööbus. Louvain: Peeters, 1979. Used with permission.

As the following excerpts show, the book provides a full account of the qualifications, duties, and conduct of persons holding various offices in the church—especially the bishop, but also presbyters, deacons, widows, and readers. In addition, the book instructs Christians regarding how they should relate to their leaders. Other portions of the Didascalia deal more directly with aspects of Christian liturgy, as will be seen in Chapter 13.

3 But concerning the bishop, hear likewise. The shepherd who is appointed bishop and head among the presbyterate in the church in every congregation—"It is required of him that he shall be blameless, in nothing reproachable,"[1] one remote from all evil, a man not less than fifty years of age, who is now removed from the conduct of youth and from the lusts of the adversary, and from the slander and blasphemy of false brethren, which they bring against many because they understand not that word which is said in the Gospel: "Everyone that shall say an idle word shall give an answer regarding it to the Lord in the day of judgment; for from your words shall you be justified, and from your words shall you be convicted."[2] But if it is possible, let him be instructed and able to teach; but if he does not know letters, he shall be capable and skilful in the word; and let him be advanced in years.

However, if the congregation is a small one, and there is not found a man advanced in years of whom they testify that he is wise and suitable to stand in the episcopacy, but there shall be found a brother who is young, of whom these who are with him testify that he deserves to stand in the episcopacy, and who even if he is young through humility and quietness of conduct demonstrates maturity—he shall be tried whether everyone testifies concerning him, and so let him sit in peace. Because Solomon also at the age of twelve years ruled over Israel. And Josiah at the age of eight years ruled in righteousness, and again, Joash also ruled when seven years old.

On this account, even if he is young, yet let him be humble and fearful and quiet; for the Lord God said in Isaiah: "On whom shall I look and be at rest, but on the quiet and humble, that tremble at my sayings?"[3] In the Gospel also he says thus: "Blessed are the humble, for they shall inherit the earth."[4] And let him be merciful—for he said again in the Gospel thus: "Blessed are the merciful, for mercy shall be upon them."[5] And again let him be a peacemaker—for he said: "Blessed are the peacemakers, for they shall be called the sons of God."[6] And let him be pure of all evil and injustice and inequity—for he said again: "Blessed are those who are pure in heart, for they shall see God."[7]

And let him be vigilant and chaste and stable and orderly; and let him not be violent, and let him not be one who exceeds in wine; and let him not be malicious; but let him be quiet and not be contentious; and let him not be money-loving. And let him not be youthful in mind, lest he be lifted up and fall into the judgment of Satan, for everyone that exalts himself is humbled.

But it is required that the bishop shall be "a man that has taken one wife, and who has managed his house well."[8] And thus let him be proved when he receives the imposition of hands to sit in the position of the episcopacy: whether he is chaste, and whether his wife also is a believer and

---

1 1 Tim 3:2; Tit 1:7.
2 Matt 12:36–37.
3 Isa 66:2.
4 Matt 5:5.
5 Matt 5:7.
6 Matt 5:9.
7 Matt 5:8.
8 1 Tim 3:2, 4.

chaste; and whether he has brought up his children in the fear of God, and admonished and taught them; and whether his household fear and reverence him and all of them obey him. For if his household in the flesh stands against him and does not obey him, how shall they who are without his house become his, and be subject to him? . . .

And let him be very diligent in his teaching, and constant in reading the divine Scripture diligently in order that he may interpret and expound the Scriptures thoroughly. And let him compare the Law and the prophets with the Gospel in order that the sayings of the Law and the prophets may agree with the Gospel. But before all let him be a good discerner between the Law and the second legislation in order that he may distinguish and demonstrate what is the Law of the faithful, and what are the bonds of them who do not believe, lest anyone of those under your dominion may hold the bonds for the Law, and may put upon himself heavy burdens, and become a child of perdition. Be diligent therefore and take care of the Word, bishop, in order that, if you can, you explain every saying so that with much instruction you may richly nourish and give drink to your people—for it is written in Wisdom: "Be careful of the herb of the field, that you may sheer your flock: and gather the grass of summer, that you may have sheep for your garments; take care and take pains of your pasture, in order that you may have lambs."[9]

Thus let not the bishop be "a lover of defiled lucre,"[10] especially from the heathen. Let him be cheated and not (himself) cheat (others). And let him not love riches. And let him not think (ill) of any one nor bear false witness. And let him not be angry, nor loving strife. And let him not love the governorship. And let him not be double-minded or double-tongued, nor one who loves to incline his ear to words of slander and disparagement. And let him have no favoritism for persons. And let him not love the festivals of the heathen, nor

occupy himself with vain error. And let him not be lustful nor money-loving because all these things are of the activity of demons.

All these things, however, let the bishop command and admonish all the people. And let him be wise and ascetic. And let him be admonishing and teaching in the instruction and discipline of God. And let his mind be fair, and remote from all the evil crafts of this world, and from all the evil lust of the heathen. And let his mind be sharp to estimate, in order that he may know beforehand those who are evil and to keep you from them. But let him be the friend of all, being an upright judge.

And whatever of good there is and is found in people, let those be in the bishop. For as the shepherd is remote from all evil, so shall he be able to constrain also his disciples and encourage them through his good manners to be imitators of his good works—as the Lord has said in the Twelve Prophets: "The people shall be as the priest."[11] For it is required of you to be an example to the people, because you also have Christ for an example. Be you then also a good example to your people, for the Lord said in Ezekiel: "And the utterance of the Lord was upon me, saying: Son of Man, speak to the sons of your people, and say unto them: When I bring the sword upon a land, the people of that land shall take one man from among them and make him their watchman: and he shall see the sword that comes upon the land, and shall blow the horn and warn the people: and everyone who hears the sound of the horn shall obey; and if he shall not take heed, and the sword shall come and taken him away, his blood shall be upon his head. Because he heard the sound of the horn, and took not heed, his blood shall be upon his head. But he that took heed has saved himself. But if the watchman shall see the sword coming, and shall not blow the horn, and the people shall not be warned, and the sword shall come and take away a soul from them: he has been taken away in his sins, and I shall demand his blood from the hands

---

9 Prov 27:25–27.

10 1 Tim 3:8.

11 Hos 4:9.

of the watchman."[12] Now the sword is the judgment, and the horn is the Gospel, but the watchman is the bishop who is set over the church. . . .

5 . . . But if also the bishop (himself) is not of a clean conscience, and shall accept persons for the sake of defiled gains, or for the sake of the presents he receives, and shall spare one who iniquitously sins, and shall allow him to stay in the church—a bishop who is such has defiled his congregation with God. Again also people, and with many of the partakers who are young in their minds, or with the hearers; and again he destroys youth and maidens beside with him. For because of the wantonness of a wicked person, when they have seen such a one among them, they too will doubt in themselves, and will imitate him, and they also will stumble and be seized by the same passion, and will perish with him.

But if he who sins shall see that the bishop and the deacons are free from rebuke and the entire flock pure, first of all he will not dare to enter the congregation, because he will be reproved by his conscience. But if, however, it should happen that he is bold, and shall come to the church in his obstinancy, and shall be reproved and convicted by the bishop, and shall look upon all and shall find no offense in any of them, neither in the bishop nor in those who are with him, he will then be confused and in great shame will go out quietly, weeping and in remorse of soul. And so shall the flock remain pure. Moreover, when he is gone out, he will repent of his sin and weep and groan before God and there shall be hope for him. But again the entire flock itself also, when it sees the weeping and tears of that one, will fear, knowing and understanding that everyone who sins perishes.

On this account, bishop, take pains now to be pure in your works. And know your place, (namely) that you are set in the likeness of God Almighty, and do hold the place of God Almighty. And so sit in the church and teach as having authority to judge those who sin—instead of God Almighty. For to you bishops it is said in the Gospel: "Something that you shall bind on earth, it shall be bound in heaven. . . ."[13]

6 . . . It is required of you therefore, O bishops, to judge according to the Scripture those who sin, with kindness and with mercy. For he who is walking on the brink of the river and is (ready) to slip—if you leave him, you have thrust (and) cast him into the river, and you have committed murder. But if a person were to slip on the brink of a river and be near to perish, stretch out quickly a hand to him and drag him out, so that he will not perish altogether. Thus, therefore do (all) that your people may learn and also act wisely, and (that) on the other hand he who sins may not utterly perish.

But when you have seen one who has sinned, be angry at him, and command that they cast him out. And when he is cast out, let them be angry at him, and contend with him and keep him outside of the church. And then let them come in and plead for him. For even our Savior was pleading with His father for those who sinned, as it is written in the Gospel: "My brethren, they know not what they do, nor what they speak; but if it be possible forgive them."[14] And then, O bishop, command him to come in, and ask him whether he repents. And if he is worthy to be received into the church, appoint him days of fasting according to his transgression, two weeks, or three, or five, or seven. And so dismiss him that he may go, saying to him all that is right for admonition and instruction. And rebuke him and say to him that he should be by himself in humiliation, and that he should pray and beseech in the days of his fast to be found worthy of the forgiveness of sins—as it is written in Genesis: "Have you sinned? Be silent: your repentance shall be with you, and you shall have power over it."[15] To Miriam the sister of

---

12 Ezek 33:1–6.

13 Matt 18:18.

14 Luke 23:34; Matt 26:39.

15 Gen 4:7.

Moses also, when she had spoken against Moses and afterwards repented and was esteemed worthy of forgiveness, it was said by the Lord: "If her father had but spit in her face, it were right for her to be ashamed, and to be separated seven days without the camp, and then to come in."[16] Likewise it also is required of you to do: to put out of the church those who promise to repent of their sins as is right for their transgressions—and afterwards receive them as merciful fathers. . . .

8 You shall not be lovers of wine, nor drunken, and you shall not be much puffed up nor luxurious, nor incurring expense that is not right, as not your own you should make use of the gifts of God, in as much as you are appointed good stewards of God who is ready to require at your hands an account of the management of the stewardship with which you are entrusted. Let then that suffice you which is enough for you, food and clothing and whatever else is necessary. And you shall not make use of these (things) that come in (as gifts) beyond what is right, as from alien (funds), but in moderation. And you shall not enjoy yourselves and be luxurious from these things that come into the church—for to a laborer his clothing and his food are sufficient.

As good stewards of God, therefore, do well in dispensing those things that are given and come into the church according to the commandment to orphans and widows and those who are afflicted and to strangers, like people who know that you have God who will require an account at your hands, who committed his stewardship to you. Thus distribute and give to all who are in want.

But be you also nourished and live from these things which come in to the church. And do not consume them by yourselves alone, but let those who are in want be sharers with you, and you shall be without offense with God. For God accuses those bishops who in greed and for themselves make use of these things which come in to the church, and do not make the poor to be sharers

with them, saying thus: "You eat the milk, and with the wool you clothe yourselves." For it is required of you, the bishops, that you shall be nourished from these things which come into the church, but not to devour them; for it is written: "You shall not muzzle the ox that grinds."[17] As then the ox which works in the threshing floor without a muzzle, eats, indeed, but does not consume it all, so also you, who work in the threshing floor which is the church of God, be nourished from the church, in the manner of the Levites who served in the tabernacle of witness, which in everything was a type of the church. Indeed, even by its name, it tells (us this), for the tabernacle "of witness" manifested the church beforehand. Thus, the Levites who ministered therein were nourished unhindered from those things which were given to the offerings of God by all the people: gifts, and oblations, and first fruits, and tithes, and sacrifices, and offerings, and whole burnt offerings, they and their wives and their sons and their daughters, because their work was the ministry of the tabernacle alone. And therefore they received no inheritance of land among the children of Israel, because the inheritance of Levi and his tribe was the produce of the people.

9 Hear these things now, you lay people also, the elect church of God. For the former people also were called a church; you, however, are the catholic Church, the holy and perfect, a royal priesthood, a holy assembly, a people for inheritance, the great Church, the bride adorned for the Lord God. Those things then which were said before, hear also now. Set apart oblations and tithes and firstfruits to Christ, the true High Priest, and to his servants, tithes of salvation (to him) the beginning of whose name is the Decade. Hear, you catholic Church of God, that were rescued from the ten plagues and did receive the ten sayings, and did learn the Law, and hold the faith and believe in the Yod in the beginning of the Name, and are fixed in the perfection of his

---

16 Num 12:14.

17 Deut 25:4; 1 Cor 9:9; 1 Tim 5:18.

glory: instead of the sacrifices of that time, offer now prayers and supplications and thanksgivings. At that time there were firstfruits and tithes and oblations and gifts, but today the offerings which are presented through the bishops to the Lord God, for they are your high priests. But the priests and Levites now are the presbyters and deacons, and the orphans and widows—but the Levite and high priest is the bishop. He is a servant of the word and mediator, but to you a teacher, and your father after God, who has begotten you through the water. This is your chief and your leader and he is a mighty king to you. He guides in the place of the Almighty. But let him be honored by you as God (is), because the bishop sits for you in the place of God Almighty. But the deacon stands in the place of Christ, and you should love him. The deaconess, however, shall be honored by you in the place of the Holy Spirit. But the presbyters shall be to you in the likeness of the apostles, and the orphans and the widows shall be reckoned by you in the likeness of the altar. For as it was not lawful for a stranger, that is for one who was not a Levite, to approach the altar or to offer anything apart from the high priest, so you also shall do nothing apart from the bishop. But if any one should do something apart from the bishop, he does it in vain, for it shall not be accounted to him for a work, for it is not right that any one should do something apart from the high priest.

Present therefore your offerings to the bishop, either you yourselves, or through the deacons. And from that which what he has received he distributes justly. For the bishop is well acquainted with those who are afflicted and dispenses and gives to each one as it is right for him, so that one may not receive several times in the same day or in the same week, whereas another would not receive even a little. For whomever the priest and steward of God knows to be much afflicted, to him he does good as it is required of him.

And to those who invite widows to the agapes, let him frequently send her whom he knows to be afflicted in particular. And again, if anyone gives gifts to widows, let him send in particular her who is in want.

But let the portion of the shepherd be separated and be divided for him according to rule at the agapes or the gifts, even though he be not present, in honor of Almighty God. But however much is given to one of the widows, let the double be given to each of the deacons in honor of Christ, (but) twice double to the leader for the glory of the Almighty.

But if anyone wished to honor the presbyters also, let him give him a double, as to the deacons, for it is required for them that they should be honored as the apostles, and as the counsellors of the bishop, and as the crown of the church, for they are the fashioners and counsellors of the church.

But if there be also a lector, let him also receive with the presbyters. To every position, therefore, let each of the laity pay the honor which is right to him, by gifts and honors and with earthly reverence.

But let them have great boldness with the deacons, and let them not be troubling the leader at all hours; but rather (let them) make known whatever they require through the servants, that is through the deacons. For not even to the Lord God Almighty can one approach except through Christ. Everything therefore that they desire to do, let them make known to the bishop through the deacons, and (only) then do them. . . .

On this account, for the honor of the bishop, make known to him everything that you do. And let them be completed through him. And if you know that one is much afflicted, but the bishop does not know of him, inform him.

But apart from him do not do anything, to his dishonor, that you bring no shame upon him as a despiser of the poor.

For he who puts forth an evil report against the bishop, whether by word or by deed, offends God Almighty. And again, if any one shall speak evil against a deacon, whether by word or by deed, he stumbles against Christ. Wherefore also in the Law it is written: "You shall not revile your gods, and you shall not speak evil of the chiefs of your people."[18] Now let no one think that (here) the Lord speaks of idols of stone, but he calls "gods" those who stand as representing you. Moses also says again in the Book of Numbers, when the people had murmured against him and against Aaron: "You do not murmur against us, but against the Lord God".[19] Also our Savior said: "Everyone that wrongs you, wrongs me, and him that sent me."[20]

What hope, indeed, is there, even a little, for him who speaks evil against the bishop, or against a deacon? For if one called a layperson "fool or raca, he is liable to the assembly,"[21] as one of those who rise up against Christ—because that he calls "empty" his brother, him, in whom Christ dwells, who is not empty but fulfilled; or a "fool" him in whom the Holy Spirit of God dwells, fulfilled with all wisdom—as though he should become a fool from the Spirit that dwells in him! If then one who should say one of these things to a layperson is found to fall into all this condemnation, how much more if he should dare to say anything against the deacon, or against the bishop, through whom the Lord gave you the Holy Spirit, and through whom you have learned the word and have known God, and through whom you have been known of God, and through whom you were sealed, and through whom you became children of the light, and through whom the Lord in baptism, by the laying on of the hand of the bishop, bore witness to each one of you and caused his holy voice to be heard that said: "You are my son: this day have I begotten you."[22]

On this account, know your bishops, those through whom you were made a child of God, and the right hand, your mother. And love him

who is become, after God, your father and your mother—for "whosoever shall revile his father or his mother, shall die the death."[23] But honor the bishops, those who have loosed you from sins, those who by the water have begotten you anew, those who filled you with the Holy Spirit, those who brought you up with the word as with milk, those who established you with doctrine, those who confirmed you with admonition, and made you to partake of the holy eucharist of God, and made you partakers and joint heirs of the promise of God. Indeed, reverence these, and honor them with all honor for they have received from God the authority of life and death, not as judging those who sin and condemning them to death in fire everlasting, but excommunicating and expelling those who are judged—God forbid and may this never happen!—but that they may receive and revive those who return and repent.

14 Appoint as a widow one who is not less than fifty years of age, who in some way, by reason of her years, is remote from the reflection of having a second husband. But if you appoint one who is young to the office of a widow, and she does not endure widowhood because of her youth, and she become (a wife) to a man, she will bring a shame upon the glory of widowhood, (for which) she shall have to given an account to God. First, because she has become (a wife) for two husbands; and again, because she promised to be a widow unto God, and was receiving (alms) as a widow, but did not abide in widowhood.

But if there be one who is young, who has been a short time with her husband and her husband die, or for some other cause there be a separation, and she remains by herself alone, being in the honor of widowhood—she shall be blessed by God. For she resembles the widow of Sarepta of Sidon with whom the holy angel, the prophet of

18 Exod 22:28.

19 Exod 16:8; cf. Num 14:2.

20 Luke 10:16.

21 Matt 5:22.

22 Ps 2:7; Luke 3:22.

23 Exod 21:16.

God, rested.[24] Or again, she shall be like Annah,[25] who praised the coming of Christ and there was a (good) testimony to her; and she shall be honored because of her gift, honor (being given) her by people, and praise from God in heaven.

But let not widows, those who are young, be appointed to the office of widows, yet let them be taken care of and helped in order that by cause of their being in need they may not desire to become (a wife) to a man for a second time, which would be an act of damage. This, indeed, you know—she who has had one husband may lawfully become (wife) for a second (but) beyond this she is (to be accounted) a harlot. On this account, support those who are young that they may continue in chastity unto God. And thus take care of them, O bishop.

And remember also the poor, hold them by the hand and nourish them even though there be among them those who are not widowers or widows, yet are in need of help because of poverty or because of sickness or because of the rearing of children, and are afflicted. . . .

15 . . . A widow should care for nothing else except this, to pray for those who give, and for the whole church. And when she is asked regarding an affair by anyone, let her not too quickly give an answer, except only about righteousness and about faith in God.

But let her send those who desire to be instructed to the leader. And to those who ask them let them (namely the widows) give answer only about the destruction of idols and about this, that there is only one God. It is not right for the widows to teach nor for a layperson. About punishment and about the rest, and about the kingdom of the name of Christ, and about his dispensation, neither a widow nor a layperson ought to speak. Indeed, when they speak without the knowledge of doctrine, they bring blasphemy against the word.

For our Lord likened the word of his Gospel to mustard.[26] But mustard if it is not prepared with skill, is bitter and sharp to those who use it. On this account our Lord said in the Gospel, to widows and to all the laity: "Do not throw your pearls before swine, lest they trample upon them and turn against you and rend you.[27] Indeed, when the Gentiles, those who are being instructed, hear the word of God spoken not firmly, as it ought to be, unto edification of life everlasting— and especially because it is spoken to them by a woman—about how our Lord clothed himself in the body, and about the passion of Christ, they will deride and mock, instead of praising the word of doctrine. And she shall be guilty of a hard judgment for sin.

Therefore, it is not required nor necessary that women should be teachers, and especially about the name of Christ and about the redemption of his passion. Indeed, you have not been appointed to this, O women, and especially widows, that you should teach, but that you should pray and entreat the Lord God. For he, the Lord God, Jesus Christ our teacher, sent us the Twelve to instruct the people and the nations. And there were with us women disciples, Mary Magdalene and Mary the daughter of James, and the other Mary, and he did not send (them) to instruct the people with us. If it were required, indeed, that women should teach, our teacher himself would have commanded these to give instruction with us.

But let a widow know that she is the altar of God. And let her constantly sit at home, and let her not wander or run about among the houses of the faithful to receive. The altar of God, indeed, never wanders or runs about anywhere, but is fixed in one place.

A widow must not therefore wander or run about among the houses. For those who are roving and who have no shame cannot stay quiet even in their houses. For they are not widows, but blind,

---

24 1 Kings 17:8–24.
25 Luke 2:36–38.

26 Mark 4:31.
27 Matt 7:6.

and they care for nothing else but making themselves ready to receive. And because they are talkative and chatterers and murmurers, they incite strifes, and they are bold and they have no shame. They that are such, indeed, are unworthy of him who called them. For neither in the fellowship of

the assembly of rest on the Sunday, once they have come, are such women or men watchful, but they either fall asleep or whisper about something else, so that through them others also are taken captive by the enemy Satan, who does not allow them, those who are such, to be watchful unto the Lord. . . .

76. Cyprian: On the Unity of the Church

A wealthy and prominent rhetorician prior to his conversion in 246 CE, Cyprian was to become one of the most significant church leaders of the mid–third century. Just two years after joining the church he was elected its bishop, a position he was to hold until his martyrdom in 258.

It was early in his bishopric that the empire-wide persecution under Decius broke out (see Chapter 3). Cyprian fled Carthage to rule his church in exile. Upon returning in 251, he found his Christian community split over what to do with those who had "lapsed" during the persecution—those who, under pressure from the persecuting authorities, had sacrificed to the pagan deities or bribed their way into securing a certificate to indicate they had done so. In Cyprian's absence, and against his own better judgment, some of his presbyters were urging that such people were to be allowed back into the good graces of the church without a long period of public penance. Moreover, it soon became known that a schism had occurred in Rome over just this issue, as a popular leader named Novatian insisted, in opposition to the Roman bishop Cornelius, that the lapsed undergo a long and rigorous course of repentance. Novatian's followers soon elected him to be a rival pope.

Cyprian wrote his treatise, "On the Unity of the Church," to address such problems of schism, urging the bishops of the various churches to become unified amongst themselves for the sake of the body of Christ. Because some of his readers understood him to embrace the rightly elected bishop of Rome as the sole and ultimate authority over the church universal (as the "pope")—a meaning that Cyprian evidently did not intend—he later revised his treatise. Both versions are given in the excerpt that follows.

> The Lord says to Peter: "I say to you, that you are Peter
> and upon this rock I will build my Church, and the gates
> of hell shall not overcome it. I will give to you the keys

"Cyprian: The Unity of the Catholic Church" from *St. Cyprian: The Lapsed: The Unity of the Catholic Church*, ed. Maurice Bévenot. Mahwah: Paulist Press, 1956. Used by permission of Paulist Press.

of the kingdom of heaven. And what you shall bind upon earth shall be bound also in heaven, and whatsoever you shall loose on earth shall be loosed also in heaven."[1]

[1st edition]

And he says to him again after the resurrection: "Feed my sheep."[2] It is on him that he builds the Church, and to him that he entrusts the sheep to feed. And although he assigns a like power to all the apostles, yet he founded a single Chair, thus establishing by his own authority the source and hallmark of the [church's] oneness. No doubt the others were all that Peter was, but a primacy is given to Peter, and it is [thus] made clear that there is but one church and one chair. So too, even if they are all shepherds, we are shown but one flock which is to be fed by all the apostles in common accord. If a person does not hold fast to this oneness of Peter, does he imagine that he still holds the faith? If he deserts the chair of Peter upon whom the church was built, has he still confidence that he is in the church?

[2nd edition]

It is on one person that he builds the Church, and although he assigns a like power to all the apostles after his resurrection, saying: "As the Father sent me, I also send you. . . . Receive the Holy Spirit: if you forgive any one his sins, they shall be forgiven him; if you retain any one's, they shall be retained,"[3] yet, in order that the oneness might be unmistakable, he established by his own authority a source for that oneness having its origin in one man alone. No doubt the other apostles were all that Peter was, endowed with equal dignity and power, but the start comes from him alone, in order to show that the church of Christ is unique. Indeed this oneness of the church is figured in the Canticle of Canticles when the Holy Spirit,

speaking in our Lord's name, says: "One is my dove, my perfect one: to her mother she is the only one, the darling of her womb."[4] If a person does not hold fast to this oneness of the church, does he imagine that he still holds the faith? If he resists and withstands the church, has he still confidence that he is in the church, when the blessed apostle Paul gives us this very teaching and points to the mystery of oneness saying: "One body and one Spirit, one hope of your calling, one Lord, one Faith, one Baptism, one God"?[5]

Now this oneness we must hold to firmly and insist on—especially we who are bishops and exercise authority in the church—so as to demonstrate that the episcopal power is one and undivided too. Let none mislead the brethren with a lie, let none corrupt the true content of the faith by a faithless perversion of the truth.

The authority of the bishops forms a unity, of which each holds his part in its totality. And the church forms a unity, however far she spreads and multiples by the progeny of her fecundity; just as the sun's rays are many, yet the light is one, and a tree's branches are many, yet the strength deriving from its sturdy root is one. So too, though many streams flow from a single spring, though its multiplicity seems scattered abroad by the copiousness of its welling waters, yet their oneness abides by reason of their starting point. Cut off one of the sun's rays—the unity of that body permits no [such] division of its light; break off a branch from the tree, it can bud no more; dam off a stream from its source, it dries up below the cut. So too our Lord's church is radiant with light and pours her rays over the whole world; but it is one and the same light which is spread everywhere, and the unity of her body suffers no division. She spreads

---

1 Matt 16:18–19.

2 John 21:17.

3 John 20:21–23.

---

4 Song of Sol 6:8.

5 Eph 4:4–6.

her branches in generous growth over all the earth, she extends her abundant streams ever further; yet one is the head-spring, one the source, one the mother who is prolific in her offspring, generation after generation: of her womb are we born, of her milk are we fed, of her Spirit our souls draw their life breath.

The spouse of Christ cannot be defiled, she is inviolate and chaste; she knows one home alone, in all modesty she keeps faithfully to one only couch. It is she who rescues us for God, she who seals for the kingdom the children whom she has borne. Whoever breaks with the church and enters on an adulterous union, cuts himself off from the promises made to the church; and he who has turned his back on the church of Christ shall not come to the rewards of Christ: he is an alien, a worldling, an enemy. You cannot have God for your Father if you have not the church for your mother. If there was escape for anyone who was outside the ark of Noah, there is escape too for one who is found to be outside the church. Our Lord warns us when he says: "He that is not with me is against me, and he that gathers not with me, scatters."[6] Whoever breaks the peace and harmony of Christ acts against Christ; whoever gathers elsewhere than in the church, scatters the church of Christ. Our Lord says: "I and the Father are One"[7]; and again, of Father, Son, and Holy Spirit it is written: "And the three are One."[8] Does anyone think then that this oneness, which derives from the stability of God and is welded together after the celestial pattern, can be sundered in the church and divided by the clash of discordant wills? If a person does not keep this unity, he is not keeping the law of God; he has lost his faith about Father and Son, he has lost his life and his soul.

---

6   Matt 12:30.

7   John 10:30.

8   1 John 5:8.

13

The Development of the Liturgy
Ritual Practices in Early Christianity

Early Christians understood themselves to be the "body" of Christ, a distinct social group that stood over against the rest of the world, united together and different from everyone else. The distinctiveness of those within the group came especially in their unique relationship with the one true God. To that extent, Christians understood themselves to be a worshipping community.

The earliest Christian forms of worship were taken over principally from the Jewish synagogue, the place of worship for Jesus himself and his original followers, rather than from pagan cultic practices (although the celebration of the Lord's Supper does share numerous similarities with cultic meals celebrated widely in pagan associations). Thus, unlike pagan cults, Christians had no sacred statues, no temples (other than the Jewish Temple in Jerusalem), and no rituals of sacrifice. Instead, Christian worship, much like Jewish worship, stressed the reading and exposition of Scripture (originally the Jewish Bible; see Chapter 9), prayer, confession, exhortation, the singing of psalms and hymns, and the collection of alms. Christians were distinguished from Jews, however, in having their own places of worship in worshipping on a different day (the day of the resurrection, Sunday, rather than the Sabbath, Saturday), in accepting a different locus of authority (a new set of Scriptures and a new way of understanding the Old in light of Christ), and, perhaps most obviously, in having a different focus of worship (in seeing Christ as Lord of all, whose death was the ultimate sacrifice for sins). Eventually, ritualistic practices that were shared with Jews, like fasting, came to be differentiated from them as some Christians insisted, for example, on fasting on Wednesdays and Fridays instead of Mondays and Thursdays as in the Jewish tradition.

In order to secure and maintain their unique status over against the rest of the world, Christians had clear boundary markers to show who was "in" the group and who was not. In particular, from the earliest of times these boundary markers included a one-time initiatory rite, baptism, and a periodic ritual meal, the eucharist (i.e., the Lord's supper), reserved for those who belonged to the group. Both ritual practices were believed to have been inaugurated by Jesus himself in his Great Commission after his resurrection (Matthew 28:19–20) and in his own Last Supper (for example, Matthew 26:26–30). As might be expected, the practice and understanding of both rituals changed over time, probably in different ways in different Christian communities.

Our earliest sources indicate that baptism was initially practiced immediately upon conversion for those who came to believe in Christ, as well as for their entire households, which would include their extended families, slaves, and possibly, for wealthier people, their clients and other dependents (see, for example, 1 Corinthians 1:16; Acts 16:15). The earliest known interpretation of the act comes in the writings of Paul, who saw baptism as a ritualistic, mystical unification with Christ in his death, which enabled the baptized Christian to experience his or her own death to the powers of sin that dominated the rest of humankind (Romans 6:1–6). Later the rite came to be understood as an official step to joining the church, to be preceded by a lengthy period of catechetical instruction, prayer, confession, fasting, and exorcism. Only later did Christian theologians begin to reflect on the efficacy of the act for the removal of original sin.

The eucharist evidently began as a weekly meal for the worshipping community, a celebration in which people would share food and drink with one another in commemoration of Jesus' last meal (and the sacrifice it presaged) and in anticipation of his imminent return (1 Corinthians 11:23–25). It soon took on other overtones, however, particularly as it symbolized both the unity of the Christian community implicit in the act of sharing (1 Corinthians 11:17–34) and the union of this community with God through the death of Christ. It was not long before the mystical significance of the meal itself, evident to some extent already in our earliest sources (for example, 1 Corinthians 11:28–32), became increasingly pronounced. Thus, in the early second century, when the weekly celebration may have already become less of an actual meal then a ritualistic service of remembrance of Christ's salvation, Ignatius speaks of the eucharist as the "bread which is a medicine that brings immortality, an antidote that allows us not to die" (Ignatius Ephesians. 20:2). The salvific effect of this spiritual food, of course, could come only to those who were within the church, those who had been baptized and allowed to participate in the Christian services of worship.

The significance of these rituals for Christians appears to have been known outside of the Christian communities, although the nature of the actual practices was not, since they were done in private. Their secretive character, however, led to widespread apprehensions among suspicious non-Christians, who had heard rumors about Christians coming together at night or early in the morning, calling one another brother and sister, greeting each other with a kiss, and eating the body of the Son and drinking his blood. Rumors began to circulate that Christians engaged in incestuous nocturnal orgies—brothers and sisters kissing at will—that involved murder and cannibalism (see Chapter 4). In part to ward off such charges, starting in the middle of the second century Christian apologists such as Justin and Tertullian began to explain openly what Christians did in their private meetings and rituals. These public explanations, along with the in-house discussions that were passed along among the Christians themselves for purposes of instruction and correction, provide us with our best information concerning how the liturgical practices of the early Christians were conducted over the course of the first three centuries.

We are less informed about other Christian rituals, known as far back as the New Testament period but referred to only briefly in our later sources, such as the "kiss" given during the services of worship (see Romans 16:16; 1 Corinthians 16:20), the "anointing with oil" practiced for healing (for example James 5:14; Mark 6:13), and the "laying on of hands" for healing or consecrating an individual (Acts 3:7; 1 Timothy 4:14).

For Further Reading

Aune, David. "Worship: Early Christian," *Anchor Bible Dictionary*, ed. David Noel Freedman. New York: Doubleday, 1992; VI. 973–989.

Bradshaw, Paul F. *Early Christian Worship: A Basic Introduction to Ideas and Practice*. Collegeville: Liturgical Press, 2010.

Bradshaw, Paul F. *The Origins of Feasts, Fasts, and Seasons in Early Christianity*. Collegeville: Liturgical Press, 2011.

Bradshaw, Paul F. *The Search for the Origins of Christian Worship*. Oxford: Oxford University Press, 1992.

Dix, Gregory. *The Shape of the Liturgy*. London: Dacre, 1945.

Ferguson, Everett. *Baptism in the Early Church: History, Theology, and Liturgy in the First Five Centuries*. Grand Rapids: Eerdmans, 2009 (a collection of classic essays).

Ferguson, Everett, ed. *Worship in Early Christianity*. New York: Garland, 1993 (a collection of classic essays).

Jungmann, Josef A. *The Early Liturgy, To the Time of Gregory the Great*, trans. Francis A. Brunner. Notre Dame: University of Notre Dame, 1959.

McGowan, Andrew. *Ascetic Eucharists: Food and Drink in Early Christian Ritual Meals*. Oxford: Clarendon Press, 1999.

Penn, Michael. *Kissing Christians: Ritual and Community in the Late Ancient Church*. Philadelphia: University of Pennsylvania Press, 2005.

THE TEXTS

77. The Didache

Outside of the New Testament, the first explicit discussion of early Christian ritual is found in the Didache (see Chapter 12). After an introductory section that provides ethical instruction for his readers (see Chapter 15), the unknown author gives directions for how Christians are to perform baptisms (preferably in cold, running water), when they are to fast (every Wednesday and Friday), what they are to pray (the Lord's Prayer, three times a day), and how they are to celebrate the eucharist (first giving thanks for the cup, then for the bread, an order reversed from other early accounts; see 1 Corinthians 11:22–24; Mark 14:22–24). Some scholars believe that the words of thanksgiving that the author cites in the context of the eucharist may represent the prayers actually said in his own community. Unfortunately, the text gives no clear indications as to where that community was located.

7 But with respect to baptism, baptize as follows. Having said all these things in advance, baptize in the name of the Father and of the Son and of the Holy Spirit,[1] in running water.

2 But if you do not have running water, baptize in some other water. And if you cannot baptize in cold water, use warm.

3 But if you have neither, pour water on the head three times in the name of Father and Son and Holy Spirit.

4 But both the one baptizing and the one being baptized should fast before the baptism, along with some others if they can. But command the one being baptized to fast one or two days in advance.

8 And do not keep your fasts with the hypocrites.[2] For they fast on Monday and Thursday; but you should fast on Wednesday and Friday.

2 Nor should you pray like the hypocrites,[3] but as the Lord commanded in his gospel, you should pray as follows: "Our Father in heaven, may your name be kept holy, may your kingdom come, may your will be done on earth as in heaven. Give us today our daily bread *[Or: the bread that we need; or: our bread for tomorrow]*. And forgive us our debt, as we forgive our debtors. And do not bring us into temptation but deliver us from the evil one *[Or: from evil]*. For the power and the glory are yours forever."[4]

3 Pray like this three times a day.

9 And with respect to the thanksgiving meal *[Literally: eucharist]*, you shall give thanks as follows.

---

1 Matt 28:19.

2 Cf. Matt 6:16.

3 Cf. Matt 6:5.

4 Matt 6:9–13.

The Didache, reproduced from *The Apostolic Fathers*, ed. Bart D. Ehrman; Loeb Classical Library, vol. 1. Cambridge, MA: Harvard University Press, 2003. Used with permission of Harvard University Press.

2 First, with respect to the cup: "We give you thanks, our Father, for the holy vine of David, your child, which you made known to us through Jesus your child. To you be the glory forever."

3 And with respect to the fragment of bread: "We give you thanks, our Father, for the life and knowledge that you made known to us through Jesus your child. To you be the glory forever.

4 As this fragment of bread was scattered upon the mountains and was gathered to become one, so may your church be gathered together from the ends of the earth into your kingdom. For the glory and the power are yours through Jesus Christ forever."

5 But let no one eat or drink from your thanksgiving meal unless they have been baptized in the name of the Lord. For also the Lord has said about this, "Do not give what is holy to the dogs."[5]

10 And when you have had enough to eat, you should give thanks as follows:

2 "We give you thanks, holy Father, for your holy name which you have made reside in our hearts, and for the knowledge, faith, and immortality that you made known to us through Jesus your child. To you be the glory forever.

3 You, O Master Almighty, created all things for the sake of your name, and gave both food and drink to humans for their refreshment, that they might give you thanks. And you graciously provided us with spiritual food and drink, and eternal life through your child.

4 Above all we thank you because you are powerful. To you be the glory forever.

5 Remember your church, O Lord; save it from all evil, and perfect it in your love. And gather it from the four winds into your kingdom, which you prepared for it. For yours is the power and the glory forever.

6 May grace come and this world pass away. Hosanna to the God of David. If anyone is holy, let him come; if any one is not, let him repent. Maranatha![6] Amen."

7 But permit the prophets to give thanks *[Or: hold the eucharist]* as often as they wish.[7]

---

5 Matt 7:6.

6 Cf. 1 Cor 16:22.

7 Two important witnesses add a verse (with variations). "But concerning the matter of the ointment, give thanks, saying, 'We give you thanks, O Father, for the ointment you have made known to us through Jesus your child. To you be the glory forever, Amen.'"

78. Justin: The First Apology

One of clearest accounts of early Christian ritual comes in the First Apology of Justin Martyr, written, possibly, in 155 CE (see Chapters 2 and 4). In order to defend Christians against charges of nefarious activities during their secret rites, Justin describes what actually took place during baptism, the eucharist, and the weekly services of worship. The account is interspersed with scriptural justifications for these practices and theological explanations of several important features. Moreover, it

---

Justin: First Apology, from *St. Justin Martyr: The First and Second Apologies,* ed. Leslie William Barnard. Mahwah: Paulist Press, 1997. Used by permission of Paulist Press.

is interlaced with apologetic concerns (see esp. Chapter 4), as Justin stresses that Jesus is the fulfillment of prophecy, that Christians are upright, law-abiding citizens, that their secret rituals are completely innocuous, and that these rituals have been imitated by the evil demons in pagan cults.

The description of the Sunday worship service, with its readings, exhortations, prayers, eucharist, and collection, is the earliest to survive. The entire account is usually thought to reflect the actual practices of the Roman church in the mid–second century.

61 I will also explain the manner in which we dedicated ourselves to God when we were made new through Christ, since if we left this out in our exposition we would seem to falsify something. As many as are persuaded and believe that the things we teach and say are true, and undertake to live accordingly, are instructed to pray and ask God with fasting for the remission of their past sins, while we pray and fast with them. Then they are brought by us where there is water, and are born again in the same manner of rebirth by which we ourselves were born again, for they then receive washing in water in the name of God the Father and Master of all, and of our Savior, Jesus Christ, and of the Holy Spirit. For Christ also said, "Except you are born again, you will not enter into the Kingdom of heaven."[1] Now it is clear to all that it is impossible for those who have once come into being to enter into their mothers' wombs. And it is said through Isaiah the prophet, as we wrote before, in what manner those who have sinned and repent shall escape from their sins. He thus spoke: "Wash, become clean, put away evil doings from our souls, learn to do good, judge the orphan and plead for the widow, and come and let us reason together, says the Lord. And though your sins be as scarlet, I will make them white as wool, and though they be as crimson, I will make them white as snow. But if you will not listen to me, a sword will devour you; for the mouth of the Lord has spoken these things."[2] And we have learned from

the apostles this reason for this [rite]. Since at our first birth we were born of necessity without our knowledge, from moist seed by the intercourse of our parents with each other, and were brought up in bad habits and wicked behavior; in order that we should not remain children of necessity and ignorance, but of free choice and knowledge, and obtain remission of the sins formerly committed, there is named at the water over him who has chosen to be born again, and has repented of his sinful acts, the name of God the Father and Master of all; they who lead to the washing the one who is to be washed call on this [name] alone. For no one can give a name to the ineffable God; and if anyone should dare say there is one, he raves with a hopeless insanity. And this washing is called illumination, as those who learn these things are illuminated in the mind. And he who is illuminated is washed in the name of Jesus Christ, who was crucified under Pontius Pilate, and in the name of the Holy Spirit, who through the prophets foretold all the things about Jesus. . . .

65 But we, after thus washing the one who has been convinced and has assented [to our instruction], lead him to those who are called brethren, where they are assembled; and we offer prayers in common for ourselves and for the one who has been illuminated and for all others everywhere, that we may be accounted worthy, having learned the truth, by our deeds also to be found good citizens and guardians of what is commanded, so that we may be saved with eternal salvation. Having ended the prayers we greet one

---

1 John 3:3.

2 Isa 1:16–20.

another with a kiss. Then there is brought to the Ruler of the Brethren bread and a cup of water and [a cup] of wine mixed with water, and he taking them sends up praise and glory to the Father of the universe through the name of the Son and of the Holy Spirit, and offers thanksgiving at some length for our being accounted worthy to receive these things from him. When he has concluded the prayers and the thanksgiving, all the people present assent by saying, "Amen." Amen in the Hebrew language signifies "so be it." And when the Ruler has given thanks and all the people have assented, those who are called by us deacons give to each of those present a portion of the eucharistized bread and wine and water, and they carry it away to those who are absent.

66 And this food is called among us eucharist, of which no one is allowed to partake except one who believes that the things which we teach are true, and has received the washing that is for the remission of sins and for rebirth, and who so lives as Christ handed down. For we do not receive these things as common bread nor common drink; but in like manner as Jesus Christ our Savior having been incarnate by God's logos took both flesh and blood for our salvation, so also we have been taught that the food eucharistized through the word of prayer that is from him, from which our blood and flesh are nourished by transformation, is the flesh and blood of that Jesus who became incarnate. For the apostles in the memoirs composed by them, which are called Gospels, thus handed down what was commanded them: that Jesus took bread and having given thanks said: "Do this for my memorial, this is my body"; and likewise he took the chalice and having given thanks said: "This is my blood"; and gave it to them alone.[3] Which also the wicked demons have imitated in

the mysteries of Mithra and handed down to be done; for that bread and a cup of water are placed with certain words said over them in the secret rites of initiation, you either know or can learn.

67 And afterward we constantly remind each other of these things. And the wealthy come to the aid of the poor, and we are always together. Over all that we receive we bless the Maker of all through his Son Jesus Christ and through the Holy Spirit. And on the day called Sunday all who live in cities or in the country gather together in one place, and the memoirs of the apostles or the writings of the prophets are read, as long as time permits. Then when the reader has finished, the Ruler in a discourse instructs and exhorts to the imitation of these good things. Then we all stand up together and offer prayers; and, as we said before, when we have finished the prayer, bread is brought and wine and water, and the Ruler likewise offers up prayers and thanksgivings to the best of his ability, and the people assent, saying the Amen; and the distribution and the partaking of the eucharistized elements is to each, and to those who are absent a portion is sent by the deacons. And those who prosper, and so wish, contribute what each thinks fit; and what is collected is deposited with the Ruler, who takes care of the orphans and widows, and those who, on account of sickness or any other cause, are in want, and those who are in bonds, and the strangers who are sojourners among us, and in a word [he] is the guardian of all those in need. But we all hold this common gathering on Sunday, since it is the first day, on which God transforming darkness and matter made the universe, and Jesus Christ our Savior on the same day rose from the dead. For they crucified him on the day before Saturday, and on the day after Saturday, he appeared to his apostles and disciples and taught them these things which we have passed on to you also for your consideration.

---

3 Matt 26:26–27; Mark 14:22–24.

79. Tertullian: Apology

Some forty years after Justin, and in a different city (Carthage, in North Africa), Tertullian provided another discussion of the Christian services of worship (see Chapter 4). Like Justin, Tertullian sought to explain the Christians' practices to his pagan critics in order to defend the church against charges leveled against it. In particular, he describes the so-called "agape meal" (i.e., the "love feast," a term that raised eyebrows outside the community), to show that it was in no way scandalous but involved a simple meal that benefited the poor, along with a hymn, reading of scripture, and prayer. Throughout the description, Tertullian emphasizes the community benefits reaped by the love of Christians both for one another and for those in need, and lays particular stress on the high morality embodied by members of the Christian family, where "all things are held in common among us, except our wives."

Chapter 39

1 Now I myself will explain the practices of the Christian Church, that is, after having refuted the charges that they are evil, I myself will also point out that they are good. We form one body because of our religious convictions, and because of the divine origin of our way of life and the bond of common hope.

2 We come together for a meeting and a congregation, in order to besiege God with prayers, like an army in battle formation. Such violence is pleasing to God. We pray, also, for the emperors, for their ministers and those in power, that their reign may continue, that the state may be at peace, and that the end of the world may be postponed.

3 We assemble for the consideration of the holy Scriptures, [to see] if the circumstances of the present times demand that we look ahead or reflect. Certainly, we nourish our faith with holy conversation, we uplift our hope, we strengthen our trust, intensifying our discipline at the same time by the inculcation of moral precepts.

4 At the same occasion, there are words of encouragement, of correction, and holy censure. Then, too, judgment is passed which is very impressive, as it is before people who are certain of the presence of God, and it is a deeply affecting foretaste of the future judgment, if anyone has so sinned that he is dismissed from sharing in common prayer, assembly, and all holy intercourse.

5 Certain approved elders preside, men who have obtained this honor not by money, but by the evidence of good character. For, nothing that pertains to God is to be had for money.

Even if there is some kind of treasury, it is not accumulated from a high initiation fee as if the religion were something bought and paid for. Each person deposits a small amount on a certain day of the month or whenever he wishes, and only on condition that he is willing and able to do so. No one is forced; each makes his contribution voluntarily.

6 These are, so to speak, the deposits of piety. The money therefrom is spent not for banquets or drinking parties or good-for-nothing eating houses,

---

Tertullian: Apology, from *Tertullian: Apologetical Works and Minucius Felix: Octavius,* ed. Rudolph Arbesmann. Fathers of the Church, 10; 2nd ed. Washington, DC: Catholic University Press of America, 1977. Used with permission.

but for the support and burial of the poor, for children who are without their parents and means of subsistence, for aged men who are confined to the house; likewise, for shipwrecked sailors, and for any in the mines, on islands or in prisons. Provided only it be for the sake of fellowship with God, they become entitled to loving and protective care for their confession.

7 The practice of such a special love brands us in the eyes of some. "See," they say, "how they love one another"; (for *they* hate one another), "and how ready they are to die for each other." (They themselves would be more ready to kill each other.)

8 Over the fact that we call ourselves brothers, they fall into a rage—for no other reason, I suppose, than because among them every term of kinship is only a hypocritical pretense of affection. But, we are your brothers, too, according to the law of nature, our common mother, although you are hardly men since you are evil brothers.

9 But, with how much more right are they called brothers and considered such who have acknowledged one father, God, who have drunk one spirit of holiness, who in fear and wonder have come forth from the one womb of their common ignorance to the one light of truth!

10 Perhaps this is why we are considered less legitimate brothers, because no tragic drama has our brotherhood as its theme, or because we are brothers who use the same family substance which, among you, as a rule, destroys brotherhood.

11 So, we who are united in mind and soul have no hesitation about sharing what we have. Everything is in common among us—except our wives.

12 In this matter—which is the only matter in which the rest of humankind practise partnership—we dissolve partnership. They not only usurp the marriage rights of their friends, but they even hand over their own rights to their friends with the greatest equanimity. This results, I suppose, from the teaching they have learned from those who were older and wiser, the Greek Socrates and the Roman Cato, who shared with their friends the wives whom they had married, so that they could bear children in other families, too.

13 As a matter of fact, perhaps the wives were not exactly unwilling. For, why should they care about a chastity which their husbands had so readily given away? Oh, what an example of Attic wisdom and Roman dignity! The philosopher a pander, and the censor, too!

14 Why wonder, then, if such dear friends take their meals together? You attack our modest repasts—apart from saying that they are disgraced by crimes—as being extravagant. It was, of course, to us that Diogenes's remark referred: "The people of Megara purchase supplies as if they were to die tomorrow, but put up buildings as though they were never to die."

15 However, anyone sees the bit of straw in another's eye more easily than a mote in his own. With so many tribes, courts, and sub-courts belching, the air becomes foul: if the Salii are going to dine, someone will have to give a loan; the city clerks will have to count up the cost of the tithes and extravagant banquets in honor of Hercules; for the festival of the Apaturia, for the Dionysiac revels, for the mysteries of Attica, they proclaim a draft of cooks; at the smoke of a feast of Serapis the firemen will become alarmed. But, only about the repast of the Christians is any objection brought forth.

16 Our repast, by its very name, indicates its purpose. It is called by a name which to the Greeks means "love." Whatever it costs, it is gain to incur expense in the name of piety, since by this refreshment we comfort the needy, not as, among you, parasites contend for the glory of reducing their liberty to slavery for the price of filling their belly amidst insults, but as, before God, greater consideration is given to those of lower station.

17 If the motive of our repast is honorable, then on the basis of that motive appraise the entire procedure of our discipline. What concerns the duty of religion tolerates no vulgarity, no immorality. No one sits down to table without first partaking of a prayer to God. They eat as much as those who are hungry take; they drink as much as temperate people need.

18 They satisfy themselves as people who remember that they must worship God even throughout the night; they converse as people who know that the Lord is listening. After this, the hands are washed and lamps are lit, and each one, according to his ability to do so, reads the Holy Scriptures or is invited into the center to sing a hymn to God. This is the test of how much he has drunk. Similarly, prayer puts an end to the meal.

19 From here they depart, not to unite in bands for murder, or to run around in gangs, or for stealthy attacks of lewdness, but to observe the same regard for modesty and chastity as people do who have partaken not only of a repast but of a rule of life.

20 Such is the gathering of Christians. There is no question about it—it deserves to be called illegal, provided it is like those which are illegal; it deserves to be condemned, if any complaint is lodged against it on the same ground that complaints are made about other secret societies.

21 But, for whose destruction have we ever held a meeting? We are the same when assembled as when separate; we are collectively the same as we are individually, doing no one any injury, causing no one any harm. When people who are upright and good assemble, when the pious and virtuous gather together, the meeting should be called not a secret society but a senate.

80. Tertullian: On the Crown

In his treatise, "On the Crown," written around 205 CE, Tertullian addresses the issue of whether it was right for a Christian to serve in the Roman army, since, among other things, doing so meant paying homage to the Roman emperor by wearing a ceremonial crown associated with pagan worship. In reply to those who pointed out that the practice is not forbidden in Scripture, Tertullian argues that some Christian practices are prescribed or forbidden not by Scripture but by venerable Christian tradition. As a case in point, he discusses traditions associated with the liturgy, thereby providing a rare glimpse into some of the specific customs involved in the practices of baptism (for example, the renunciation of the devil beforehand, a three-fold immersion, the drink of milk and honey afterwards, and the refusal to bathe for the week that follows), eucharist (taken before daybreak), and worship (for example, the refusal to kneel on Sundays and the use of the sign of the cross). These particular practices appear to reflect the traditions of Tertullian's own church in early third-century Carthage.

How can anything come into use, if it has not first been handed down? Even in pleading tradition, written authority, you say, must be demanded. Let us inquire, therefore, whether tradition, unless it be written, should not be admitted. Certainly we shall say that it ought not to be admitted, if no cases of other practices which, without any written instrument, we maintain on the ground of

Tertullian: On the Crown, from "Chaplet," *The Ante-Nicene Fathers*, vol. 3, *Latin Christianity: Its Founder, Tertullian,* ed. A. Cleveland Coxe. Reprint; 2nd ed. Grand Rapids: Eerdmans, 1989.

tradition alone, and the countenance thereafter of custom, affords us any precedent. To deal with this matter briefly, I shall begin with baptism. When we are going to enter the water, but a little before, in the presence of the congregation and under the hand of the president, we solemnly profess that we disown the devil, and his pomp, and his angels. Hereupon we are thrice immersed, making a somewhat ampler pledge than the Lord has appointed in the Gospel. Then, when we are taken up (as new-born children), we taste first of all a mixture of milk and honey, and from that day we refrain from the daily bath for a whole week. We take also, in congregations before daybreak, and from the hand of none but the presidents, the sacrament of the Eucharist, which the Lord both commanded to be eaten at meal-times, and enjoined to be taken by all alike.

As often as the anniversary comes round, we make offerings for the dead as birthday honors. We count fasting or kneeling in worship on the Lord's day to be unlawful. We rejoice in the same privilege also from Easter to Whitsunday. We feel pained should any wine or bread, even though our own, be cast upon the ground. At every forward step and movement, at every going in and out, when we put on our clothes and shoes, when we bathe, when we sit at table, when we light the lamps, on couch, on seat, in all the ordinary actions of daily life, we trace upon the forehead the sign.

If, for these and other such rules, you insist upon having positive Scripture injunction, you will find none. Tradition will be held forth to you as the originator of them, custom as their strengthener, and faith as their observer.

81. Hippolytus: The Apostolic Tradition

The "Apostolic Tradition," possibly by Hippolytus of Rome (see Chapter 12), describes not only the ordination and duties of church leaders but also Christian liturgical practices. The following excerpt details the entire baptism ritual, including the examination of recent converts to Christianity (in which anyone found to be engaged in an "unchristian" occupation was required to find a different job), the instruction of catechumens anticipating baptism (for three years), the detailed preparations for the baptism itself, and a full description of the actual ritual, including the creed that was recited, the prayer that was said, and the eucharist that was then celebrated.

15 Those who come to hear the word for the first time should first be brought to the teachers in the house, before the people come in.

2 And they should enquire concerning the reason why they have turned to the faith. And

those who brought them shall bear witness whether they have the ability to hear the word.

3 They might be questioned about their state of life, whether he has a wife, or whether he is a slave.

Hippolytus: The Apostolic Tradition, reproduced from Alistair Stewart-Sykes, tr. *On the Apostolic Tradition.* New York: St. Vladimir's Seminary Press, 2001. Used with permission of St. Vladimir's Seminary Press.

4 If he is the slave of a believer and his master encourages him, let him hear the word. If his master does not bear witness to him, that he is good, he should be rejected.

5 If his master is a pagan, teach him to please his master, that there should be no scandal.

6 If there is somebody who has a wife, or if a woman has a husband, so should they be taught that the man be contented with his wife and the wife with her husband.

7 If there is somebody who does not live with a wife he should be taught not to fornicate but that he should either take a wife in accordance with the law or should remain <as he is> in accordance with the law.

8 But if there is one who has a demon, let him not hear the word of teaching until he be purified.

16 ···

2 If any is a pimp or ~~~~tutes he should ~~~~

3 If ~~~~ould be instruc~~~~ ~~~~esist or he sho~~~~

4 If ~~~~tions in the the~~~~ ~~~~uld be rejected~~~~

5 If s~~~~ ~~~~that he desist; if~~~~ ~~other trade let him be allowed.

6 Likewise a charioteer who competes, or anyone who goes to the races, should desist or be rejected. If any is a gladiator, or trains gladiators in fighting, or one who fights with beasts in the games, or a public official engaged in gladiatorial business should desist, or he should be rejected.

7 If any is a priest of idols, or a guardian of idols, he should desist, or he should be rejected.

8 A soldier in command must be told not to kill people; if he is ordered so to do, he shall not carry it out. Nor should he take the oath. If he will not agree, he should be rejected.

9 Anyone who has the power of the sword, or who is a civil magistrate wearing the purple, should desist, or should be rejected.

10 If a catechumen or a believer wishes to become a soldier they should be rejected, for they have despised God.

11 A prostitute or a wastrel or any who has been castrated, or any who has performed any other unspeakable deed, should be rejected, for they are impure.

12 A magician should not be brought for a decision. A maker of spells or an astrologer or a soothsayer or an interpreter of dreams or a rabble-rouser or somebody who cuts fringes on clothes (that is to say scissor-users) or any who makes amulets, should desist, or they should be rejected.

13 Somebody's concubine, if she is his slave, if she has raised his children and holds to him alone, should hear; otherwise she should be rejected.

14 A man who has a concubine should desist, and take a wife in accordance with the law. If he does not wish to do so he should be rejected.

14b If a believing woman consort with a slave she should desist, or she should be rejected.

15 If we have omitted any other matter the works will instruct your eyes. For we all have the spirit of God.

17 Catechumens should hear the word for three years.

2 But if a man is keen and perseveres well in the matter, the length of time should not be considered but his manner alone should be considered.

18 Whenever the teacher ceases to give instruction the catechumens should pray by themselves, separated from the faithful,

2 and the women should stand and pray by themselves in another place in the church, both women faithful and women catechumens.

3 When they have prayed they shall not give the kiss of peace for their kiss is not yet holy.

4 The faithful should greet one another, the men with each other and the women with each other. No man should greet a woman.

5 All the women should cover their head with a veil, but not with just a piece of linen, for that is no covering.

19 When the teacher lays his hand on the catechumens after their prayer he should pray and dismiss them. Whether he be ecclesiastic or a layman he should do so.

2 If a catechumen should be arrested for the sake of the name of the Lord he should not be double-minded in respect of his witness. For if violence is brought against him and he is killed before receiving baptism for the remission of his sins he will be justified. For he has received baptism in his own blood.

20 When those who are to receive baptism are chosen their lives should be examined; whether they lived uprightly as catechumens, whether they honored the widows, whether they visited the sick, whether they were thorough in performing good works;

2 and if those who brought them bear witness that they have acted thus, so they should hear the Gospel.

3 From the time they are set apart a hand is laid on them daily whilst they are exorcized. When the day of their baptism draws near the bishop should exorcise each of them so that he may be sure that they are pure.

4 If there is one of them who is not good or is not pure he should be put to one side, because he has not heard the word in faith. For it is impossible that the alien spirit should remain with him.

5 Those who have been set apart for baptism should be instructed to bathe themselves and wash on the fifth day of the week.

6 And if a woman is in the manner of women she should be put aside and should receive baptism another day.

7 Those who are to be baptized should fast on the day of preparation for the Sabbath. On the Sabbath those who are to be baptized are gathered at the will of the bishop in one place. They shall be instructed to pray and to bend the knee.

8 And when he lays his hand on them he shall exorcize them of every foreign spirit and they shall flee away from them and shall not return to them. And when he has finished exorcizing them

he should blow on their faces; and when he has sealed their forehead, their ears and their noses he should make them stand up.

9 They should spend the entire night in vigil, hearing readings and receiving instruction.

10 Those who are to be baptized should not bring anything with them, except what they bring for the eucharist. For it is fitting that those who are made worthy should bring an offering on that occasion.

21 Now at the time when the cock crows they shall first pray over the water.

2 The water should be flowing into the tank or be poured down into it. It should be so if there is no necessity, but if there is continuous and sudden necessity use any water you can find.

3 And they should take off their clothes.

4 You are to baptize the little ones first. All those who are able to speak for themselves should speak. With regard to those who cannot speak for themselves their parents, or somebody who belongs to their family, should speak.

5 Then baptize the grown men and finally the women, after they have let down their hair and laid down the gold and silver ornaments which they have on them. Nobody should take any alien object down into the water.

6 And at the time determined for baptism the bishop shall give thanks over the oil and put it into a vessel and call it the oil of thanksgiving.

7 And he shall take other oil and perform the exorcism over it and call it the oil of exorcism.

8 And a deacon brings the oil of exorcism and places himself on the left hand of the presbyter, and another deacon takes the oil of thanksgiving and stands on the right hand of the presbyter.

9 And when the presbyter takes hold of each of those who are to be baptized he should bid him renounce saying: "I renounce you Satan, and all your service and all your works."

10 And when he has renounced all this he should anoint him with the oil of exorcism saying to him: "Let all evil spirits depart far from you."

11 Then he should hand him over to the bishop or the presbyter who stands at the water to baptize;

and they should stand in the water naked. And a deacon likewise should go down with him into the water.

12 When the one being baptized goes down into the waters the one who baptizes, placing a hand on him, should say thus: "Do you believe in God the Father Almighty?"

13 And he who is being baptized should reply: "I believe."

14 Let him baptize him once immediately, having his hand placed upon his head.

15 And after this he should say: "Do you believe in Christ Jesus, the son of God, who was born of the Holy Spirit and Mary the virgin and was crucified under Pontius Pilate and was dead [and buried] and rose on the third day alive from the dead and ascended in the heavens and sits at the right hand of the Father and will come to judge the living and the dead?"

16 And when he has said, "I believe," he is baptized again.

17 And again he should say: "Do you believe in the Holy Spirit and the holy church and the resurrection of the flesh?"

18 And he who is being baptized should say: "I believe." And so he should be baptized a third time.

19 And afterwards, when he has come up from the water, he is anointed by the presbyter with that sanctified oil, saying: "I anoint you with holy oil in the name of Jesus Christ."

20 And afterwards, each drying himself, they shall dress themselves, and afterwards let them go into the church.

21 And the bishop, laying his hand on them invokes, saying:

"Lord God, you have made them worthy to deserve the remission of sins through the laver of regeneration: make them worthy to be filled with the Holy Spirit, send your grace upon them that they may serve you in accordance with your will; for to you is glory, to the Father and the Son with the Holy Spirit in the holy church both now and to the ages of the ages. Amen."

22 After this, pouring the sanctified oil from his hand and putting it on his head he shall say: "I anoint you with holy oil in God the Father Almighty and Christ Jesus and the Holy Spirit."

23 And signing him on the forehead he shall give him the kiss and say: "The Lord be with you." And he who has been signed shall say: "And with your spirit."

24 And thus he shall do to each.

25 And thenceforth they shall pray with all the people; they shall not pray with the people until they have performed all these things.

26 And after they have prayed they should give the kiss of peace.

27 And then let the oblation be brought at once by the deacons to the bishop, and let him give thanks over the bread as the antitype of the body of Christ; and the cup mixed with wine on account of the likeness of the blood which was shed for all who have put their faith in him.

28 At the same time milk and honey mixed in fulfillment of the promise which was to the fathers, which stated "a land flowing with milk and honey," which Christ gave as his flesh, through which those who believe are nourished just like little children, the serenity of his word making sweet the bitterness of the heart.

29 And water is offered as a sign of the washing, so that the inner person, which is made up of the soul, should receive the same as the body.

30 And the bishop should give an address concerning all these things to those who receive.

31 Breaking the bread, and handing fragments to each he shall say: "Heavenly bread in Christ Jesus."

32 And the one who receives shall reply: "Amen."

33 The presbyters, and if there are not enough the deacons also, shall hold the cups; they should stand in good order [and with reverence]. First the one who holds the water, second the one with milk, third the one with the wine.

34 And they who partake shall taste of each cup three times, as he who gives says: "In God the Father Almighty."

And the one who receives shall say: "Amen."

35 "And in the Lord Jesus Christ."

And he shall say: "Amen."

36 "And in the Holy Spirit and the holy church." And he shall say: "Amen."

37 And thus let it be done to each.

38 And when these things are done, let each hurry to do good works, to please God and to live properly, being devoted to the church, putting into action what he has learnt and progressing in piety.

39 We have handed over to you in brief these things about holy baptism and the holy offering, since you have already been instructed about the resurrection of the flesh and the other things according to the Scriptures.

40 But if anything else should be said, the bishop shall say it privately to those who have received. Unbelievers must not get to know it, unless they first receive. This is the white stone of which John said: "A new name is written on it, which nobody knows except him who receives."

82. The Didascalia

Among the interesting features of the church manual known as the "Didascalia" (see Chapter 12) are its detailed guidelines for certain church practices. As will be seen from the following excerpts, this kind of church manual was becoming increasingly detailed in its prescriptions of what was and what was not to be done in the context of the church's worship and ministry. Covered are such matters as the practice of excommunication—including instructions for how those who were excommunicated could return to the church's good graces and how they could be involved with the church in the meantime—the seating arrangements of the congregation during the worship services, and the subsidiary role of women in ministry, particularly in teaching and baptizing.

10 "... As a heathen," thus, "and as a publican let him be accounted by you"[1] who has been convicted of evil deeds and of falsehood. And afterwards, if he promise to repent as in the case when the heathen desire and promise to repent, and say "we believe," we receive them into the congregation that they may hear the word. But we do not communicate with them until they receive the seal and become perfected. Thus also do we not communicate with these until they show the fruits of repentance. But let them certainly come in, if they wish to hear the word, that they may not completely perish. But let them not communicate in prayer, but go outside. For they also, when they have seen that they do not communicate with the church, will subdue themselves, and repent of their former deeds, and strive to be received into the church for prayer. And again they likewise who see and hear them go forth like the heathen and publicans, will fear and

---

1 Matt 18:17.

The Didascalia, from *The Didascalia Apostolorum Corpus Scriptorum Christianorum Orientalium*, ed. Arthur Vööbus. Louvain: Peeters, 1979. Used with permission.

take warning to take heed to themselves not to sin, lest it happens thus to them also, and being convicted of sin or falsehood they go out from the church.

But you shall by no means hinder them to enter the church and to hear the word, O bishop. For even our Lord and Savior did not completely put away and cast out publicans and sinners, but did even eat with them. On this account the Pharisees murmured against him and said: "He eats with publicans and sinners."[2] Then our Savior answered and said against their thoughts and their murmuring, and said: "The whole ones have no need of a physician, but they that are sick."[3] Therefore, deal with those who have been convicted of sins and are sick, and associate them with yourselves, and take care of their fate, and speak to them and console them, and keep hold of them, and make them to return. And afterwards, as each one of them repents and shows the fruits of repentance, then receive him for prayer in the same way as a heathen. And so as you baptize a heathen and receive him, so also lay the hand upon this person while everyone is praying for him, and then bring him in and let him communicate with the church. Indeed, the laying on of the hand shall be to him instead of baptism—indeed, whether by the laying on of the hand, or by baptism, that they receive the fellowship of the Holy Spirit.

On this account, as a compassionate physician, heal all those who sin. And distribute with all skill, and offer healing for the remedy of their lives. And you shall not be ready to cut off the members of the church, but use the word of bandages and the admonitions of fomentations and the compresses of intercession. But if the ulcer goes deep and decreases his flesh, nourish it and counter-act it with healing medicine. And if there be filth in it, cleanse it with sharp medicine, that is with a word of reproof. But if the flesh be over-swollen, reduce it and counter-act it with a strong

medicine, that is with the threat of judgment. But if gangrene should be in it, cauterize it with branding irons, that is, with incisions of much fasting cut away and clear out the foulness of the ulcer. But again if the gangrene should gain strength and prevail even over the burnings, give judgment. And then, whichever member it be that is decayed, then with advice and much consultation with other physicians, cut off that decayed member, that it may not corrupt the whole body. Yet be not ready to amputate hastily, and do not hasten very quickly and run to the saw of many teeth, but use first the scalpel and cut the ulcer, that it may be known what is the cause of the pain that is hidden inside, so that the whole body may be kept uninjured. But if you see that a person will not repent, but has completely cut off hope for himself, then with grief and mourning cut him off and cast him out of the church. . . .

12 But in your congregations in the holy churches hold your assemblies in (accordance with) all good manners, and fashion the places for the brethren carefully in sobriety. And for the presbyters let there be separated a place on the eastern side of the house, and let the bishop's chair be among them and let the presbyters sit with him.

And again, let the laymen sit in another eastern part of the house. For thus is it required that the presbyters shall sit in the eastern part of the house with the bishops, and afterwards the laymen, and then the women; so that when you stand up to pray, the leaders may stand first, and after them the laymen, and then also the women.

Indeed, it is required that you pray toward the east, as knowing that which is written: "Give glory to God, who rides upon the heaven of heavens toward the east."

As for the deacons, let one continue and stand by the oblations of the eucharist, but let another stand outside the door and observe those who come in. And afterwards, when you offer, let them serve together in the church. And if anyone be found sitting in a place which is not his, let the

2 Matt 9:11.
3 Matt 9:12.

deacon who is within reprove him and make him rise up and sit in the place that is proper for him.

Indeed, our Lord likened the church to a lodge: for, as we see, the dumb animals, we mean oxen and sheep and goats, lie down and rise up according to their families, and feed and mate, none of them separating itself from its race. And again the wild beasts also go severally upon the mountains with those who are like them. So it is likewise required in the church that those who are young shall sit by themselves, if there be room, and if not, let them stand up; and those who are advanced in years shall sit by themselves. However, let the children stand on one side, or let their fathers and mothers take them to themselves; and let them stand up. And again let those who are girls also sit by themselves; but if there be no room, let them stand up behind the women. And let those who are married and young and have children stand by themselves, and let the aged women and widows sit by themselves. And let the deacons see that as each of them enters, he goes to his place, so that no one may sit in a place that is not his. And again let the deacon also observe that no one whispers or sleeps or laughs or makes signs. For thus it is required that with good manners and (great) care they watch in the church, and with their ears open to the word of the Lord.

But if there comes a person from another congregation, a brother or a sister, let the deacon ask and learn whether she is a wife of a man, or again whether she is a widow, a believer; and whether she is a daughter of the church, or whether she is of one of the heresies; and then let him conduct her and set her in a place that is right for her. But if a presbyter should come from another congregation, you the presbyters receive him with fellowship into your place.

And if it be a bishop, let him sit with the bishop, and let him be esteemed worthy of the honor of his rank, even as himself. And you, O bishop, tell him that he preach to your people. Indeed, the intercession and admonition of strangers is very helpful, especially because it is written: "There is no prophet that is acceptable in his country."[4] And when you offer the oblation, let him speak. But if he is wise and gives the honor to you, and does not wish to offer, yet let him speak over the cup.

But if, as you are sitting, another person should come, whether a man or a woman, who has honor in the world, either of the same locus or of another congregation—you, O bishop, if you are speaking the word of God, or hearing, or reading, shall not respect persons and leave off the service of your word and set them a place. But remain still as you are and do not interrupt your work, and let the brethren themselves receive them. And if there be no place, let one of the brethren who is full of charity and loves his brethren, who is (prone) to honor, rise and give them place, but let himself stand up.

If, however, these who are younger men or women sit, (and) an older man or woman should rise and give up their place, you, O deacon, look at those who are sitting and see which man or woman of them is younger than his companions, and make them stand up, and cause him to sit who had risen and given up his place. And him whom you have caused to stand up, lead him away and make him stand behind his companions—that others also may be educated and learn to give place to others who are more honorable than themselves.

But if a poor man or woman should come, whether from the members of your congregation or from another congregation, and especially if they are advanced in years, and there be no place for those as such, do you, O bishop, with all your heart appoint a place for them—and even if you have to sit upon the ground, that you be not as one who respects the persons of others, but that your ministry be acceptable with God. . . .

15 Everyone who shall pray or communicate with one who is expelled from the church must rightly be reckoned with him. Indeed, these things lead to the dissolution and destruction of souls. For if one communicate and pray with him

---

4 Luke 4:24.

who is expelled from the church, and obey not the bishop, he does not obey God, and he is defiled with him (who is expelled). And moreover he does not allow him to repent. For if no one communicate with him, he will repent and weep, and will ask and beseech to be received, and he will repent of what he has done, and he will be saved.

About this, however, that a woman should baptize, or that one should be baptized by a woman, we do not counsel, for it is a transgression of the commandment and a great peril to her who baptizes and to him who is baptized. Indeed, if it were lawful to be baptized by a woman, our Lord and teacher himself would have been baptized by Mary his Mother. Now he was baptized by John, like other also of the people. Therefore do not bring danger upon yourselves, brethren and sisters, by acting beyond the law of the Gospel.

16 Therefore, O bishop, appoint yourself workers of righteousness, helpers who cooperate with you unto life. Those that please you out of all the people, you shall choose and appoint as deacons: on the one hand, a man for the administration of many things that are required, on the other hand a woman for the ministry of women.

For there are houses where you cannot send a deacon to the women, on account of the pagans, but (where) you may send a deaconess; also, because in many other matters the office of a deaconess is required. In the first place, when women go down into the water, it is required that those who go down into the water shall be anointed by deaconesses with the oil of anointing. And where there is no woman present, and especially no deaconess, it is necessary for him who baptizes to anoint her who is being baptized. But where there is a woman, and especially a deaconess, it is not right that women should be seen by men, but with the laying on of hand anoint the head only. As of old time the priests and kings in Israel were anointed, so in like manner, anoint the head of those who receive baptism, whether of men or of women. And afterwards, whether you yourself baptize or you command the deacons or presbyters to baptize—let a woman deacon, as we have said before, anoint the women. But let a man recite over them the invocation of the divine names in the water.

And when she who is being baptized has come up from the water, let the deaconess receive her, and teach and educate her in order that the unbreakable seal of baptism shall be (kept) in chastity and holiness. On this account, we say that the ministry of a woman deacon is especially required and urgent. For our Lord and Savior also was ministered unto by deaconesses who were Mary Magdalene, and Mary the daughter of James and mother of Jose, and the mother of the sons of Zebedee, with other women as well. Also for you the ministry of a deaconess is necessary for many things. Indeed, a deaconess is required for the houses of the pagans where there are believing women, that they enter and visit those who are sick, and to minister to them in something which is required for them, and to wash those who have begun to recover from sickness.

And let the deacons imitate the bishops in their conversation. However, let them labor even more than he. And let them not love polluted lucre, but let them be diligent in the ministry.

And in accordance with the number of the congregation of the people of the church, so let there be the deacons, that they may be able to distinguish (each) severally and give rest to everyone, so that for the aged women, those who have no strength, and for brethren and sisters, those who are in sickness—for everyone of them—they may provide the ministry which is proper for him. But let a woman especially be diligent in the service of women, and a man, a deacon to the service of men. And let him be ready to obey and submit himself to the command of the bishop.

14

Women and Gender

Christianity in a Patriarchal World

Women played significant roles in the early Christian movement, starting with ministry of Jesus himself. In Gospel traditions both early and late, Jesus is said to have had women among his followers in his travels (Mark 15:40–41; Luke 8:1–3; Gospel of Thomas 114). He was evidently supported in his itinerant preaching activities by the financial support of women, who functioned as his patrons (Mark 15:40–51; Luke 8:1–3). He is said to have engaged in public dialogue and debate with women who were not among his immediate followers (Mark 7:24–30; John 4:1–42). And he is said to have had physical contact with women during his ministry (Mark 14:3–9; John 12:1–8). In all four of the canonical Gospels, women are said to have accompanied Jesus from Galilee to Jerusalem during the last week of his life, and (unlike his male disciples) to have been present at his crucifixion (Matt 27:55; Mark 15:40–41; Luke 23:49; John 9:25). From these Gospels and the relatively early Gospel of Peter we are told that it was women followers who first came to believe that Jesus' body was no longer in the tomb (Matt.28:1–10; Mark 16:1–8; Luke 23:55–24:10; John 20:1–2; Gospel of Peter 50–57). Thus women evidently were the first to proclaim that Jesus had been raised. In that very real sense, it can be said that women started Christianity.

Women continued to be important in the Christian movement, as is evident in the letters of Paul. In the extensive greetings Paul sends in chapter 16 of his letter to the Romans, for example, he does indeed mention more men; but there are a significant number of women as well, and they were obviously playing a significant role in the church. These include Phoebe, a "deacon" of the church of Cenchrea, and Paul's own patron, who has been entrusted by Paul with the task of carrying this letter to Rome; Prisca, who with her husband Aquila is said to be largely responsible for the gentile mission and who supports a congregation in her home; Mary, Paul's colleague who works with the Romans; Tryphaena, Tryphosa, and Persis, women Paul calls his "co-workers" for the gospel; Julia, and the mother of Rufus, and the sister of Nereous, all of whom appear to have a high profile in the community; and most impressive of all, Junia, a woman whom Paul says is "foremost among the apostles."

Whatever roles women played in his churches, Paul's attitudes toward and views of women have been matters of great dispute over the years, in no small measure because of the ambiguities of the evidence. On one hand, Paul makes pronouncements that sound remarkably liberated for the patriarchal world he inhabited, especially Galatians 3:28, that "in Christ there is no male and female." On the other hand, when it comes to social—as opposed to hypothetical or eschatological—realities Paul appears to bow to the pressures of his environment. In his letter to the Corinthians he is quite insistent that women wear head coverings in church, in no small measure in order to show that they are subservient to their husbands, who are their "heads" (a complicated passage, 1 Corinthians 11:2–15).

Both the traditionally conservative and the progressively liberated Paul were influential on later branches of the Christian church. The conservative Paul was transformed into a radical opponent of women and their role in the churches by such texts as the Pastoral epistles (1 Timothy 2:11–15; and the interpolator of 1 Corinthians 14:33–36, a passage that Paul himself almost certainly did not write). Such views lived on into the second and third centuries in such authors as Tertullian (see selection 88), who argued that women are inherently inferior to men and need to be subservient to them. The occasionally enlightened Paul was taken up by such texts as the Acts of Thecla (see selection 83), a legendary female convert of Paul who is liberated from the constraints of a patriarchal marriage by embracing Paul's teaching of rigid asceticism, and who is ultimately commissioned by Paul to carry forth the Christian mission of proclaiming the gospel without male oversight. Such freedom from patriarchal constraints may be seen in other texts as well, throughout this collection, as in the Martyrdom of Perpetua (selection 9 in Chapter 3).

These glimmers of hope, starting with Jesus and Paul, that Christianity would decisively break with its patriarchal milieu never came to fruition in our period—or ever, one might say. The traditional forces proved too strong, as women eventually came for the most part to be silenced and subordinated to the men of their world. As just intimated, however, the rise of an ascetic form of Christianity, already in the second century (or arguably even in the first) and heightening until it reached its zenith sometime after our period, did provide one avenue of deliverance for women wishing to escape the patriarchal constraints of their society. Christian women who chose both not to marry and to have the church itself as their primary social locus (rather than their families, with father or husband as *paterfamilias*), were no longer subjected to male domination. This has often been read as a liberating feature of the early Christian movement, as well it should be.

But it was liberation with a price. By following an ascetic option, women were limited in what they could do precisely as women—for example, if they spurned childbearing and raising a family—not because that was their life decision but because such a choice was forced upon them if they wanted, even more desperately, to escape the constricted possibilities of life in a patriarchal world. So even the option of asceticism appears ambivalent at best—a bypassing of some of the patriarchal restrictions inherent in the woman's world only on terms that could be seen, by some at least, to have been set again by the patriarchy that was then dominant, forcing women to escape male domination only by compromising other conditions of their humanity.

We see all of these tensions in a range of texts from the second and third century, as the following selection attests.

For Further Reading

Clark, Elizabeth. *Women in the Early Church*. Collegeville: Liturgical Press, 1983.

Cooper, Kate. *Band of Angels: The Forgotten World of Early Christian Women*. London: Atlantic Books, 2013.

Davis, Stephen. *The Cult of Saint Thecla: A Tradition of Women's Piety in Late Antiquity*. Oxford: Oxford University Press, 2001.

Kraemer, Ross. *Her Share of the Blessings: Women's Religions among Pagans, Jews, and Christians in the Greco-Roman World*. New York: Oxford University Press, 1992.

Kraemer, Ross and Mary Rose D'Angelo, eds. *Women and Christian Origins*. New York: Oxford University Press, 1999.

Madigan, Kevin and Carolyn Osiek. *Ordained Women in the Early Church: A Documentary History*. Baltimore: Johns Hopkins University Press, 2005.

Osiek, Carolyn and M. MacDonald. *A Woman's Place: House Churches in Earliest Christianity*. Minneapolis: Fortress, 2006.

Torjesen, Karen Jo. *When Women Were Priests: Women's Leadership in the Early Church and the Scandal of Their Subordination in the Rise of Christianity*. San Francisco: HarperSanFrancisco, 1993.

Trevett, Christine. *Montanism: Gender, Authority and the New Prophecy*. Cambridge: Cambridge University Press, 1996.

Trevett, Christine. *Christian Women and the Time of the Apostolic Fathers (AD 80–160)*. Cardiff: University of Wales Press, 2006.

THE TEXTS

83. The Acts of Thecla

The Acts of Thecla is a legendary account of the adventures of Thecla, a woman converted to the Christian faith through the preaching of the apostle Paul. Paul himself appears on the fringes of the story, as a socially disruptive evangelist who converts women to a life of strict asceticism and sexual renunciation, much to the chagrin of their husbands and fiancés.

Upon hearing Paul's message, Thecla abandons her fiancé to join the apostle on his journeys, liberated from the concerns of marriage and the potential domination by a future husband. Seeking revenge, however, Thecla's fiancé brings her up before the authorities on charges of being a Christian. But in a remarkable series of episodes (in which, among other things, Thecla baptizes herself in a pool of flesh-eating seals), God intervenes on Thecla's behalf, preserving her from death and reuniting her with her beloved apostle, who authorizes her to share fully in his ministry of teaching the word.

The Acts of Thecla was evidently in circulation near the end of the second century, along with other narratives found in the "Acts of Paul" (see selections 50 and 53). Soon thereafter, and for centuries following, Thecla became a much-revered a model for Christian women as her stories circulated and expanded.

1 As Paul was going to Iconium after his flight from Antioch, his fellow-travellers were Demas and Hermogenes, the copper-smith, who were full of hypocrisy and flattered Paul as if they loved him. Paul, looking only to the goodness of Christ, did them no harm but loved them exceedingly so that he made sweet to them all the words of the Lord and the interpretation of the gospel concerning the birth and resurrection of the Beloved; and he gave them an account, word for word, of the great deeds of Christ as they were revealed to him.

2 And a certain man, by name Onesiphorus, hearing that Paul was to come to Iconium, went out to meet him with his children Simmias and Zeno and his wife Lectra, in order that he might entertain him. Titus had informed him what Paul looked like, for he had not seen him in the flesh, but only in the spirit.

3 And he went along the royal road to Lystra and kept looking at the passers-by according to the description of Titus. And he saw Paul coming, a man small in size, bald-headed, bandylegged, of noble mien, with eyebrows meeting, rather hook-nosed, full of grace. Sometimes he seemed like a man, and sometimes he had the face of an angel.

4 And Paul, seeing Onesiphorus, smiled; and Onesiphorus said, "Hail, O servant of the blessed God." And he said, "Grace be with you

and your house." And Demas and Hermogenes were jealous and showed greater hypocrisy, so that Demas said, "Are we not of the blessed God that you have not thus saluted us?" And Onesiphorus said, "I do not see in you the fruit of righteousness, but if such you be, come also into my house and refresh yourselves."

5 And after Paul had gone into the house of Onesiphorus there was great joy and bowing of knees and breaking of bread and the word of God about abstinence and the resurrection. Paul said, "Blessed are the pure in heart, for they shall see God, blessed are those who have kept the flesh chaste, for they shall become a temple of God; blessed are the continent, for God shall speak with them; blessed are those who have kept aloof from this world, for they shall be pleasing to God; blessed are those who have wives as not having them, for they experience God; blessed are those who have fear of God, for they shall become angels of God.

6 "Blessed are those who respect the word of God, for they shall be comforted; blessed are those who have received the wisdom of Jesus Christ, for they shall be called the sons of the Most High; blessed are those who have kept the baptism, for they shall be refreshed by the Father and the Son; blessed are those who have come to a knowledge of Jesus Christ, for they shall be in the light; blessed are those who through love of God no longer conform to the world, for they shall judge angels, and shall be blessed at the right hand of the Father; blessed are the merciful, for they shall obtain mercy and shall not see the bitter day of judgment; blessed are the bodies of the virgins, for they shall be well pleasing to God and shall not lose the reward of their chastity. For the word of the Father shall become to them a work of salvation in the day of the Son, and they shall have rest for ever and ever."

7 And while Paul was speaking in the midst of the church in the house of Onesiphorus a certain virgin named Thecla, the daughter of Theoclia, betrothed to a man named Thamyris, was sitting at the window close by and listened day and night to the discourse of virginity, as proclaimed by Paul. And she did not look away from the window, but was led on by faith, rejoicing exceedingly. And when she saw many women and virgins going in to Paul she also had an eager desire to be deemed worthy to stand in Paul's presence and hear the word of Christ. For she had not yet seen Paul in person, but only heard his word.

8 As she did not move from the window her mother sent to Thamyris. And he came gladly as if already receiving her in marriage. And Thamyris said to Theoclia, "Where, then, is my Thecla [that I may see her]?" And Theoclia answered, "I have a strange story to tell you, Thamyris. For three days and three nights Thecla does not rise from the window either to eat or to drink; but looking earnestly as if upon some pleasant sight she is devoted to a foreigner teaching deceitful and artful discourses, so that I wonder how a virgin of her great modesty exposes herself to such extreme discomfort.

9 "Thamyris, this man will overturn the city of the Iconians and your Thecla too; for all the women and the young men go in to him to be taught by him. He says one must fear only one God and live in chastity. Moreover, my daughter, clinging to the window like a spider, lays hold of what is said by him with a strange eagerness and fearful emotion. For the virgin looks eagerly at what is said by him and has been captivated. But go near and speak to her, for she is betrothed to you."

10 And Thamyris greeted her with a kiss, but at the same time being afraid of her overpowering emotion said, "Thecla, my betrothed, why do you sit thus? And what sort of feeling holds you distracted? Come back to your Thamyris and be ashamed." Moreover, her mother said the same, "Why do you sit thus looking down, my child, and answering nothing, like a sick woman?" And those who were in the house wept bitterly,

Thamyris for the loss of a wife, Theoclia for that of a child, and the maidservants for that of a mistress. And there was a great outpouring of lamentation in the house. And while these things were going on Thecla did not turn away but kept attending to the word of Paul.

11 And Thamyris, jumping up, went into the street, and watched all who went in to Paul and came out. And he saw two men bitterly quarrelling with each other and he said to them, "Men, who are you and tell me who is this man among you, leading astray the souls of young men and deceiving virgins so that they should not marry but remain as they are? I promise you money enough if you tell me about him, for I am the chief man of this city."

12 And Demas and Hermogenes said to him, "Who he is we do not know. But he deprives the husbands of wives and maidens of husbands, saying, 'There is for you no resurrection unless you remain chaste and do not pollute the flesh.'"

13 And Thamyris said to them, "Come into my house and refresh yourselves." And they went to a sumptuous supper and much wine and great wealth and a splendid table. And Thamyris made them drink, for he loved Thecla and wished to take her as wife. And during the supper Thamyris said, "Men, tell me what is his teaching that I also may know it, for I am greatly distressed about Thecla, because she so loves the stranger and I am prevented from marrying."

14 And Demas and Hermogenes said, "Bring him before the Governor Castellius because he persuades the multitude to embrace the new teaching of the Christians, and he will destroy him and you shall have Thecla as your wife. And we shall teach you about the resurrection which he says is to come, that it is has already taken place in the children[1] and that we rise again, after having come to the knowledge of the true God."

15 And when Thamyris heard these things he rose up early in the morning and, filled with jealousy and anger, went into the house of Onesiphorus with rulers and officers and a great crowd with batons and said to Paul, "You have deceived the city of the Iconians and especially my betrothed bride so that she will not have let me! Let us go to the governor Castellius!" And the whole crowd cried, "Away with the sorcerer for he has misled all our wives!" And the multitude was also incited.

16 And Thamyris standing before the tribunal said with a great shout, "O proconsul, this man—we do not know where he comes from—makes virgins averse to marriage. Let him say before you why he teaches thus." But Demas and Hermogenes said to Thamyris, "Say that he is a Christian and he will die at once." But the governor kept his resolve and called Paul, saying, "Who are you and what do you teach? For they bring no small accusation against you."

17 And Paul, lifting up his voice, said, "If I today must tell any of my teachings then listen, O proconsul. The living God, the God of vengeance, the jealous God, the God who has need of nothing, who seeks the salvation of people, has sent me that I may rescue them from corruption and uncleanness and from all pleasure, and from death, that they may sin no more. On this account God sent his Son whose gospel I preach and teach, that in him people have hope, who alone has had compassion upon a world led astray, that people may be no longer under judgment but may have faith and fear of God and knowledge of honesty and love of truth. If then I teach the things revealed to me by God what harm do I do, O proconsul?" When the governor heard this he ordered Paul to be bound and sent to prison until he had time to hear him more attentively.

18 And Thecla, by night, took off her bracelets and gave them to the gatekeeper; and when the door was opened to her she went into the

---

1 2 Tim 2:18.

prison. To the jailer she gave a silver mirror and was thus enabled to go in to Paul and, sitting at his feet, she heard the great deeds of God. And Paul was afraid of nothing, but trusted in God. And her faith also increased and she kissed his bonds.

19 And when Thecla was sought for by her family and Thamyris they were hunting through the streets as if she had been lost. One of the gatekeeper's fellow slaves informed them that she had gone out by night. And they examined the gatekeeper who said to them, "She has gone to the foreigner in the prison." And they went and found her, so to say, chained to him by affection. And having gone out from there they incited the people and informed the governor what had happened.

20 And he ordered Paul to be brought before the tribunal, but Thecla was riveted to the place where Paul had sat while in prison. And the governor ordered her also to be brought to the tribunal, and she came with an exceedingly great joy. And when Paul had been led forth the crowd vehemently cried out, "He is a sorcerer. Away with him!" But the governor gladly heard Paul speak about the holy works of Christ. And having taken counsel, he summoned Thecla and said, "Why do you not marry Thamyris, according to the law of the Iconians?" But she stood looking earnestly at Paul. And when she gave no answer Theoclia, her mother, cried out saying, "Burn the wicked one; burn her who will not marry in the midst of the theater, that all the women who have been taught by this man may be afraid."

21 And the governor was greatly moved, and after scourging Paul he cast him out of the city. But Thecla he condemned to be burned. And immediately the governor arose and went away to the theater. And the whole multitude went out to witness the spectacle. But as a lamb in the wilderness looks around for the shepherd, so Thecla kept searching for Paul. And having looked into the crowd she saw the Lord sitting in the likeness of

Paul and said, "As if I were unable to endure, Paul has come to look after me." And she gazed upon him with great earnestness, but he went up into heaven.

22 And the boys and girls brought wood and straw in order that Thecla might be burned. And when she came in naked the governor wept and admired the power that was in her. And the executioners arranged the wood and told her to go up on the pile. And having made the sign of the cross she went up on the pile. And they lighted the fire. And though a great fire was blazing it did not touch her. For God, having compassion upon her, made an underground rumbling, and a cloud full of water and hail overshadowed the theater from above, and all its contents were poured out so that many were in danger of death. And the fire was put out and Thecla saved.

23 And Paul was fasting with Onesiphorus and his wife and his children in a new tomb on the way which led from Iconium to Daphne. And after many days had been spent in fasting the children said to Paul, "We are hungry." And they had nothing with which to buy bread, for Onesiphorus had left the things of this world and followed Paul with all his house. And Paul, having taken off his cloak, said, "Go, my child, sell this and buy some loaves and bring them." And when the child was buying them he saw Thecla their neighbor and was astonished and said, "Thecla, where are you going?" And she said, "I have been saved from the fire and am following Paul." And the child said, "Come, I shall take you to him; for he has been mourning for you and praying and fasting six days already."

24 And when she had come to the tomb Paul was kneeling and praying, "Father of Christ, let not the fire touch Thecla but stand by her, for she is yours'; she, standing behind him, cried out, "O Father who made the heaven and the earth, the Father of your beloved Son Jesus Christ, I praise you that you have saved me from the fire that I may see Paul again." And Paul, rising up, saw her and said, "O God, who knows the heart, Father of our Lord Jesus Christ, I praise you because you have speedily heard my prayer."

25 And there was great love in the tomb as Paul and Onesiphorus and the others all rejoiced. And they had five loaves and vegetables and water, and they rejoiced in the holy works of Christ. And Thecla said to Paul, "I will cut my hair off and I shall follow you wherever you go." But he said, "Times are evil and you are beautiful. I am afraid lest another temptation come upon you worse than the first and that you do not withstand it but become mad after men." And Thecla said, "Only give me the seal in Christ, and no temptation shall touch me." And Paul said, "Thecla, be patient; you shall receive the water."

26 And Paul sent away Onesiphorus and all his family to Iconium and went into Antioch, taking Thecla with him. And as soon as they had arrived a certain Syrian, Alexander by name, an influential citizen of Antioch, seeing Thecla, became enamored of her and tried to bribe Paul with gifts and presents. But Paul said, "I know not the woman of whom you speak, nor is she mine." But he, being of great power, embraced her in the street. But she would not endure it and looked about for Paul. And she cried out bitterly, saying, "Do not force the stranger; do not force the servant of God. I am one of the chief persons of the Iconians and because I would not marry Thamyris I have been cast out of the city." And taking hold of Alexander, she tore his cloak and pulled off his crown and made him a laughing-stock.

27 And he, although loving her, nevertheless felt ashamed of what had happened and led her before the governor; and as she confessed that she had done these things he condemned her to the wild beasts. The women of the city cried out before the tribunal, "Evil judgment! Impious judgment!" And Thecla asked the governor that she

might remain pure until she was to fight with the wild beasts. And a rich woman named Queen Tryphaena, whose daughter was dead, took her under her protection and had her for a consolation.

28 And when the beasts were exhibited they bound her to a fierce lioness, and Queen Tryphaena followed her. And the lioness, with Thecla sitting upon her, licked her feet; and all the multitude was astonished. And the charge on her inscription was "Sacrilegious." And the women and children cried out again and again, "O God, outrageous things take place in this city." And after the exhibition Tryphaena received her again. For her dead daughter Falconilla had said to her in a dream, "Mother, receive this stranger, the forsaken Thecla, in my place, that she may pray for me and I may come to the place of the just."

29 And when, after the exhibition, Tryphaena had received her she was grieved because Thecla had to fight on the following day with the wild beasts, but on the other hand she loved her dearly like a daughter Falconilla and said, "Thecla, my second child, come, pray for my child that she may live in eternity, for this I saw in my sleep." And without hesitation she lifted up her voice and said, "My God, Son of the Most High, who are in heaven, grant her wish that her daughter Falconilla may live in eternity." And when Thecla had spoken Tryphaena grieved very much, considering that such beauty was to be thrown to the wild beasts.

30 And when it was dawn Alexander came to her, for it was he who arranged the exhibition of wild beasts, and said, "The governor has taken his seat and the crowd is clamoring for us; get ready, I will take her to fight with the wild beasts." And Tryphaena put him to flight with a loud cry, saying, "A second mourning for my Falconilla has come upon my house, and there is no one to help, neither the child for she is dead, nor kinsman for I am a widow. God of Thecla, my child, help Thecla."

31 And the governor sent soldiers to bring Thecla. Tryphaena did not leave her but took her by the hand and led her away saying, "My daughter Falconilla I took away to the tomb, but you, Thecla, I take to fight the wild beasts." And Thecla wept bitterly and sighed to the Lord, "O Lord God, in whom I trust, to whom I have fled for refuge, who did deliver me from the fire, reward Tryphaena who has had compassion on your servant and because she kept me pure."

32 And there arose a tumult: the wild beasts roared, the people and the women sitting together were crying, some saying, "Away with the sacrilegious person!", others saying, "O that the city would be destroyed on account of this iniquity! Kill us all, proconsul; miserable spectacle, evil judgment!"

33 And Thecla, having been taken from the hands of Tryphaena, was stripped and received a girdle and was thrown into the arena. And lions and bears were let loose upon her. And a fierce lioness ran up and lay down at her feet. And the multitude of the women cried aloud. And a bear ran upon her, but the lioness went to meet it and tore the bear to pieces. And again a lion that had been trained to fight against men, which belonged to Alexander, ran upon her. And the lioness, encountering the lion, was killed along with it. And the women cried the more since the lioness, her protector, was dead.

34 Then they sent in many beasts as she was standing and stretching forth her hands and praying. And when she had finished her prayer she turned around and saw a large pit full of water and said, "Now it is time to wash myself." And she threw herself in saying, "In the name of Jesus Christ I baptize myself on my last day." When the woman and the multitude saw it they wept and said, "Do not throw yourself into the water!"; even the governor shed tears because the seals were to devour such beauty. She then threw herself into the water in the name of Jesus Christ,

but the seals, having seen a flash of lightning, floated dead on the surface. And there was round her a cloud of fire so that the beasts could neither touch her nor could she be seen naked.

35 But the women lamented when other and fiercer animals were let loose; some threw petals, others nard, others cassia, others amomum, so that there was an abundance of perfumes. And all the wild beasts were hypnotized and did not touch her. And Alexander said to the governor, "I have some terrible bulls to which we will bind her." And the governor consented grudgingly, "Do what you will." And they bound her by the feet between the bulls and put red-hot irons under their genitals so that they, being rendered more furious, might kill her. They rushed forward but the burning flame around her consumed the ropes, and she was as if she had not been bound.

36 And Tryphaena fainted standing beside the arena, so that the servants said, "Queen Tryphaena is dead." And the governor put a stop to the games and the whole city was in dismay. And Alexander fell down at the feet of the governor and cried, "Have mercy upon me and upon the city and set the woman free, lest the city also be destroyed. For if Caesar hear of these things he will possibly destroy the city along with us because his kinswoman, Queen Tryphaena, has died at the theater gate."

37 And the governor summoned Thecla out of the midst of the beasts and said to her, "Who are you? And what is there about you that not one of the wild beasts touched you?" She answered, "I am a servant of the living God and, as to what there is about me, I have believed in the Son of God in whom he is well pleased; that is why not one of the beasts touched me. For he alone is the goal of salvation and the basis of immortal life. For he is a refuge to the tempest tossed, a solace to the afflicted, a shelter to the despairing; in brief, whoever does not believe in him shall not live but be dead forever."

38 When the governor heard these things he ordered garments to be brought and to be put on her. And she said, "He who clothed me when I was naked among the beasts will in the day of judgment clothe me with salvation." And taking the garments she put them on.

And the governor immediately issued an edict saying, "I release to you the pious Thecla, the servant of God." And the women shouted aloud and with one voice praised God, "One is the God, who saved Thecla," so that the whole city was shaken by their voices.

39 And Tryphaena, having received the good news, went with the multitude to meet Thecla. After embracing her she said, "Now I believe that the dead are raised! Now I believe that my child lives. Come inside and all that is mine I shall assign to you." And Thecla went in with her and rested eight days, instructing her in the word of God, so that many of the maidservants believed. And there was great joy in the house.

40 And Thecla longed for Paul and sought him, looking in every direction. And she was told that he was in Myra. And wearing a mantle that she had altered so as to make a man's cloak, she came with a band of young men and maidens to Myra, where she found Paul speaking the word of God and went to him. And he was astonished at seeing her and her companions, thinking that some new temptation was coming upon her. And perceiving this, she said to him, "I have received baptism, O Paul; for he who worked with you for the gospel has worked with me also for baptism."

41 And Paul, taking her, led her to the house of Hermias and heard everything from her, so that he greatly wondered and those who heard were strengthened and prayed for Tryphaena. And Thecla rose up and said to Paul, "I am going to Iconium." Paul answered, "Go, and teach the word of God." And Tryphaena sent her much clothing and gold so that she could leave many things to Paul for the service of the poor.

42 And coming to Iconium she went into the house of Onesiphorus and fell upon the place where Paul had sat and taught the word of God, and she cried and said, "My God and God of this house where the light shone upon me, Jesus Christ, Son of God, my help in prison, my help before the governors, my help in the fire, my help among the wild beasts, you alone are God and to you be glory for ever. Amen."

43 And she found Thamyris dead but her mother alive. And calling her mother she said, "Theoclia, my mother, can you believe that the Lord lives in heaven? For if you desire wealth the Lord will give it to you through me; or if you desire your child, behold, I am standing beside you."

And having thus testified, she went to Seleucia and enlightened many by the word of God; then she rested in a glorious sleep.

84. The Acts of Peter

We have already seen excerpts from the Acts of Peter (Chapter 8). The excerpts that follow are from two different accounts of Peter's life after Jesus' death and resurrection. The first is sometimes called the "Act of Peter" (it comes from a different manuscript from the other). It presents the strange story of Peter's refusal to heal his paralyzed daughter because doing so would make her an able-bodied tempter to the men in her life. Given ancient views of women, it is no accident that the woman, Peter's daughter, is the one disabled for life rather than the man, her abductor and would-be rapist, for the foul deed that he committed.

The other two excerpts are from the Acts of Peter already discussed. One shows how women could be highly beneficial to the spread of the Christian mission through their divinely ordained munificence (chapter 30). The other shows how Christianity provided an alternative possibility for women who were living under the rule of their husbands in a patriarchal society (chapters 33–35). By promoting the possibility of asceticism—urging women (as well as men) not to concede their conjugal rights to their spouses—the Christian gospel offered the option of self-determination for women, much to the consternation of the men they had spurned.

The Act of Peter

But on the first day of the week, which is the Lord's Day, a multitude gathered together, and they brought many sick people to Peter for him to cure them. And one of the multitude was bold enough to say to Peter, "Peter, behold, before our eyes you made many blind see and deaf hear and the lame walk, and you have helped the weak and given them strength; why have you not helped your virgin daughter, who has grown up beautiful and believed in the name of God? For behold, one of her sides is completely paralysed, and there she is helpless in the corner. We can see those whom you have cured, but you have neglected your own daughter."

But Peter smiled and said to him, "My son, God alone knows why her body is sick. Know that God is not unable or powerless to give his gift to my daughter. But in order that your soul may be convinced and those present believe the more"—he looked at his daughter and said to her, "Arise from your place with the help of none except Jesus, and walk naturally before those present and come to me." And she arose and came to him. The multitude rejoiced at what had taken place. And Peter said to them, "Behold, your hearts are convinced that God is not powerless concerning the things which we ask of him." They rejoiced the more and glorified God. Then Peter said to his daughter, "Return to your place, sit down there and be helpless again, for it is good for me and you." And the girl went back, lay down in her place and became as before. The whole multitude wept and besought Peter to make her well.

Peter said to them, "As the Lord lives, this is good for her and for me. For on the day on which she was born to me I saw a vision and the Lord said to me, 'Peter, this day has been born for you a great affliction, for this daughter will harm many

The Acts of Peter, reproduced from J. K. Elliott, *Apocryphal New Testament*. Oxford: Clarendon Press, 1993. Used with permission of Oxford University Press.

souls, if her body remains well!' I, however, thought that the vision mocked me.

"When the girl was ten years old she became a stumbling-block to many. And a very rich man, Ptolemy by name, when he saw the girl bathing with her mother, sent for her to take her for his wife, but her mother did not consent. He often sent for her, for he could not wait . . .

"Ptolemy brought the girl, and leaving her before the door of the house went away.

"When I saw this, I and her mother went downstairs and found the girl with one side of her body paralysed from head to foot and dried up. We carried her away, praising the Lord that he had kept his servant from defilement and violation and . . . This is the reason why the girl remains thus to this day. But now you shall hear what happened to Ptolemy. He repented and lamented night and day over that which had happened to him, and because of the many tears which he shed he became blind. Having decided to hang himself, behold, about the ninth hour of that day, whilst alone in his bedroom, he saw a great light which illuminated the whole house, and he heard a voice saying to him, 'Ptolemy, God has not given the vessels for corruption and shame; it is not right for you, as a believer in me, to violate my virgin, whom you are to know as your sister, as if I had become one spirit to both of you—but arise, and speedily go to the house of the apostle Peter and you shall see my glory. He will explain the matter to you.' And Ptolemy did not delay, but ordered his servants to show him the way and bring him to me. When he had come to me, he told all that had happened to him in the power of Jesus Christ, our Lord. And he saw with the eyes of his flesh and with the eyes of his soul, and many people set their hope on Christ; he did good to them and gave them the gift of God.

"After this Ptolemy died; he departed and went to his Lord. When he made his will, he left a piece of land in the name of my daughter because through her he became a believer in God and was made whole. I, however, who was appointed trustee, have acted carefully. I sold the acre, and God alone knows that neither I nor my daughter have kept anything from the money of the acre, but I sent the whole sum to the poor. Know, therefore, O servant of Christ Jesus, that God cares for his people and prepares for each what is good—even when we think that God has forgotten us. Now then, brethren, let us mourn, be watchful, and pray, and God's goodness will look upon us, and we hope for it."

And Peter delivered other speeches before them, and glorifying the name of the Lord Christ he gave of the bread to all of them, and after distributing it he rose and went into the house.

The Acts of Peter

30(1). And on Sunday Peter spoke to the brethren and encouraged them in the faith of Christ. And many senators and knights and wealthy women and matrons were present, and they were strengthened in the faith. There was also present a very rich woman, named Chryse, because all her vessels were of gold—since her birth she had never used a vessel of silver or of glass, but only of gold. She said to Peter, "Peter, servant of God, in a dream the one whom you call God came and said to me, 'Chryse, bring ten thousand pieces of gold to my servant Peter; you owe them to him.' So I have brought them, fearing that some evil may come from him whom I saw and who has gone to heaven." And having said this she laid down the money and went away. And Peter seeing this praised God that the poor could now be provided for. Some of those present said to him, "Peter, is it not wrong to have accepted this money from her? All Rome knows of her fornication, and it is reported that she is not satisfied with one husband; she uses even her own slaves. Therefore have nothing to do with the Chryse's table, but let everything be sent back to her that came from her." When Peter heard this he laughed and said to the brethren, "As to her conduct, I know nothing of it; since I have received this money I received it not without reason; she brought it to me as a debtor to Christ and gives it to the servants of Christ. For he himself has provided for them". . . .

33(4). Now Peter remained in Rome and rejoiced with the brethren in the Lord, returning thanks day and night for the multitude who were daily added to the holy name by the grace of the Lord. And the four concubines of the prefect Agrippa also came to Peter, Agrippina, Nicaria, Euphemia, and Doris. And they heard preaching concerning chastity and all the words of the Lord, and repented and agreed among themselves to abstain from cohabitation with Agrippa, but were molested by him. When Agrippa became perplexed and distressed—for he loved them very much—he had them secretly observed where they went, and he found out that they went to Peter. When they came back he said to them, "That Christian has taught you not to consort with me. I tell you that I will destroy you and burn him alive." But they were ready to endure anything by the hand of Agrippa but would no longer allow themselves to satisfy his lust; they had become strong in the power of Jesus.

34(5). And a very beautiful women named Xanthippe, the wife of Albinus, a friend of the emperor, also came to Peter with the other ladies and kept away from Albinus. Being in love with Xanthippe, he became enraged and wondered why she no longer slept with him, and raging like a beast he intended to kill Peter, for he perceived that he was the cause of her leaving his bed. And many other women delighted in the preaching concerning chastity and separated from their husbands, and men too ceased to sleep with their wives, because they wished to serve God in chastity and purity. And there was a great commotion in Rome, and Albinus told Agrippa what had happened to him and said, "Either you avenge me of Peter, who has alienated my wife from me, or I shall do it myself." And Agrippa said, "I suffered the same, for he has alienated my concubines." And Albinus said to him, "Why are you waiting, Agrippa? Let us seize him and kill him as a troublemaker, so that we may get our wives back and avenge those who cannot kill him but whose wives he has also alienated."

35(6). And as they made plans together, Xanthippe heard of the conspiracy which her husband had with Agrippa, and she sent word to Peter and asked him to leave Rome. And the other brethren, together with Marcellus, requested him to leave.

85. The Gospel of the Egyptians

We do not have a complete manuscript that contains the Gospel of the Egyptians; we know of it only from six quotations that have come down to us in the writings of Clement of Alexandria at the end of the second century or beginning of the third (see selection 87). In these six passages, Clement quotes a conversation between Jesus and a woman named Salome, who appears as one of Jesus' followers in other early Christian writings (for example, Mark 15:40; 16:1; Gospel of Thomas 61). In each case Clement quotes the Gospel before giving his own interpretation of it; in every instance, his interpretation appears to run counter to the literal meaning of the text. A more straightforward reading of these passages suggests that the Gospel was written, in part at least, to support an ascetic lifestyle that rejected the pleasures of sex and denied the

The Gospel of the Egyptians, reproduced from Bart D. Ehrman and Zlatko Pleše, *The Apocryphal Gospels: Texts and Translations*. New York: Oxford University Press, 2011; used with permission of Oxford University Press.

value of procreation. These views appear to be based on a close reading of the Adam and Eve stories of Genesis 2–3, where, for example, pain in childbirth and death itself result directly from the appearance of sin in the world.

It is difficult to discern whether the anonymous author of this Gospel had a positive or negative evaluation of women. On one hand, by freeing women from the obligation of childbirth the text may be seen as opening up other possibilities for their lives; on the other hand, by denying the distinctively female role of bearing children, it may be denying to women a full means of bodily expression and existence. In either event it is quite clear that this author was firmly opposed to sexual relations, procreation, and children.

1 When Salome asked, "How long will death prevail?" the Lord replied, "For as long as you women bear children." But he did not say this because life is evil or the creation wicked; instead he was teaching the natural succession of things; for everything degenerates after coming into being. (Clement of Alexandria, *Miscellanies* 3.45.3)

2 Those who oppose God's creation through self-control—which sounds good—also quote the words spoken to Salome, some of which we have already mentioned, found, I think, in the Gospel according to the Egyptians. For they claim that the Savior himself said, "I have come to destroy the works of the female." By "the female" he meant desire and by "works" he meant birth and degeneration. (Clement of Alexandria, *Miscellanies* 3.63.1)

3 Therefore it is probably with regard to the final consummation, as the argument indicates, that Salome says, "How long will people continue to die?" Now Scripture refers to a human being in two senses: that which is visible and the soul, that is, one subject to salvation and one not, And sin is called the death of the soul. For this reason, the Lord also replied shrewdly, "For as long as women bear children"—that is to say, for as long as desires continue to be active. (Clement of Alexandria, *Miscellanies* 3.64.1)

4 Why do those who adhere more to everything other than the true gospel rule not cite the following words spoken to Salome? For when she said, "Then I have done well not to bear children" (supposing that it was not necessary to give birth), the Lord responded, "Eat every herb, but not the one that is bitter." (Clement of Alexandria, *Miscellanies* 3.66.1–2)

5 This is why Cassian says, "When Salome inquired when the things she had asked about would become known, the Lord replied: 'When you (pl.) trample on the garment of shame and when the two become one and the male with the female is neither male nor female.' "[1] The first thing to note, then, is that we do not find this saying in the four Gospels handed down to us, but in the Gospel according to the Egyptians. (Clement of Alexandria, *Miscellanies* 3.92.2–93.1)

6 And when the Savior said to Salome, "Death will last as long as women give birth," he was not denigrating birth—since it is, after all, necessary for the salvation of those who believe. (Clement of Alexandria, *Excerpts from Theodotus* 67.2)

---

1 Cf. Gospel of Thomas 22, 37.

86. Irenaeus: Against the Heresies

We have seen several sections of Irenaeus's five-volume magnum opus, *Against the Heresies* (see selections 35, 60, 64). The selection here is an attack on a Gnostic teacher named Marcus, who allegedly engaged in nefarious religious activities in order to lure women and subject them to his lascivious demands. Although Irenaeus is principally interested in showing how unprincipled, unethical, and generally loathsome Gnostic heretical leaders were, there is a lot that can be learned here about Irenaeus's views of the women who were targeted by this teacher of falsehood.

Marcus's women converts are portrayed as highly gullible, flighty, credulous, undiscerning, and open—to a remarkable extent—to chicanery and seduction. All in all, it is not a highly favorable portrait either of this Gnostic profligate or of his women victims. Whether there is any historical truth in this description is open to considerable doubt; Irenaeus typically pulled out all stops in order to slander his Gnostic opponents and make them look detestable. But in so doing he seems to show his hand as well, in his views of women who were so easily duped and seduced.

Chapter 13

1 A certain member of their company, Marcus by name, who boasts of correcting his teacher, is also very skilled in magical imposture. By this means he deceived many men and not a few women, and converted them to himself as to one most learned and most perfect, possessed of the greatest power from invisible and unnameable regions. In truth, he was the forerunner of the Antichrist. For example, he combines the buffooneries of Anaxilaus with the craftiness of so-called magicians. As a result those who have no sense and have lost their mind think he is working wonders.

2 As he feigns to give thanks over the cup mixed with wine, and draws out at great length the prayer of invocation, he makes the cup appear to be purple or red so that it seems that Grace, who is from the regions which are above all things, dropped her own blood into that cup because of his invocation, and that those who are present greatly desire to taste of that drink, so that Grace, who was invoked by this magician, might rain upon them too. Moreover, having handed mixed cups to the women, he commands them to give thanks over them in his presence. And when this has been done, he himself brings forward another cup much larger than that over which the duped woman gave thanks, and pours from the smaller cup, over which thanks had been given by the woman, into the one which he himself brought forward. At the same time he says over it these words: "May Grace who is before all things, unthinkable and unspeakable, fill your inner self and increase in you her own knowledge, by planting the mustard seed in good ground." By saying some such words and driving the wretched woman to madness, he appears to have worked wonders, namely, that the large cup was filled from the

Irenaeus: Against the Heresies, Book 1, from *St. Irenaeus of Lyons Against the Heresies,* ed. Dominic Unger. Mahwah: Paulist Press, 1992. Used by permission of Paulist Press.

small one, even to overflowing. Still other acts similar to these he performed and deceived many and drew them after himself.

3 It is probable that he possesses even some demon as a familiar, through whom he himself seems to prophesy, and through whom whatever woman he considers worthy to partake of his Grace he makes prophesy. Especially about women he is concerned, and that, about those who are well-dressed and clothed in purple and who are very rich, whom he often attempts to seduce. Flatteringly he says to them: "I want you to partake of my Grace, because the Father of all always sees your Angel in his presence. But the dwelling place of your Greatness [angel] is within us. It behooves us to be united. First receive Grace from me and through me. Adorn yourself as a bride awaiting her bridegroom that you may be what I am, and I may be what you are. Put the 'seed' of light in your bridal chamber. Take from me the bridegroom. Receive him [in yourself] and be received in him. Look, Grace is descending upon you. Open your mouth and prophesy." Now, if the woman should answer: "I have never prophesied and do not know how to prophesy," he will again utter some invocations to the amazement of the duped woman. He says to her: "Open your mouth and say anything whatsoever and prophesy." Thereupon she becomes puffed up and elated by those words, her soul becomes aroused at the prospect of prophesying, her heart beats faster than usual. She dares idly and boldly to say nonsensical things and whatever happens to come to mind, since she has been heated by an empty wind. (This is what one superior to us said about such people, "A soul that is heated by empty air is bold and impudent.") From now on she considers herself a prophetess and thanks Marcus for having given her of his Grace. She tries to reward him not only by the gift of her possessions—in that manner he has amassed a fortune—but by sharing her body, desiring to unite herself with him in every way so that she may become one with him.

4 But some of the most faithful women, who have the fear of God and could not be deceived—whom he tried to beguile like the rest by commanding them to prophesy—rejected and condemned him, and withdrew from such company. They knew very well that the gift of prophecy does not enter a person through Marcus, the magician. On the contrary, upon whomever God sends his grace from above, they are the ones who possess the God-given prophetic power and then speak where and when God wills, but not when Marcus commands. For whoever commands is greater and of higher authority than the one who is commanded, since the one rules, but the other has been made subject. If, then, Marcus commands, or someone else—since they all have the custom of drawing lots at the banquets and of commanding one another to prophesy, and, in keeping with their own desires, of prophesying for their own benefit—the one who commands, though he is a human, will be greater and of higher authority than the prophetic spirit. This, of course, is impossible. On the contrary, such spirits that are commanded by these people and speak whatever the people wish are perishable and weak, bold and impudent, sent by Satan to deceive and destroy those who have not kept that vigorous faith, which they had received through the Church in the beginning.

5 Furthermore, often these women returned to the Church of God and confessed that this Marcus concocts love potions and charms for some of them, though not for all, in order to insult even their bodies; and that they were violated in body by him, and on their part loved him very erotically. So it happened that a certain deacon from among our own people in Asia, who while giving Marcus hospitality in his own house fell victim to such a misfortune. His wife, who was very beautiful, was defiled in mind and body by this magician. For a long time she traveled about with him. When, however, with much effort the brothers converted her, she spent the whole time doing penance amid weeping and lamentation over the defilement she had suffered through this magician. . . .

87. Clement of Alexandria: Miscellanies

Although his writings have been among the most studied of early Christianity, there is little known about the life of Clement of Alexandria (150–215 CE). He is often thought to have been born to pagan parents in Athens and then converted to Christianity, possibly as a young adult. Ancient legend indicates that he was Origen's predecessor as the head of the famous Alexandrian catechetical school, a kind of institution for Christian higher learning designed for converts to the faith. When a persecution arose in 202 CE, Clement fled Alexandria never to return.

Among Clement's best known writings is a book called *Miscellanies* (sometimes called "Stromateis"). This is a collection—at times randomly organized—of reflections on theological, philosophical, and ethical issues. In the present selection, Clement deals with issues involving women, sexual relations, and marriage. This is clearly a set of instructions given by a man principally to other men about women. But it is interesting for the light it can throw on this proto-orthodox author's understanding of women in relation to his own overarching masculine concerns.

It is also interesting because in it, Clement mentions the views on sexuality and marriage taken by some of his Gnostic opponents. To some extent Clement's own views on such matters represent an attempt to strike a balance between two positions that he sees as heretical extremes: wild sexual profligacy on one hand and rigorous asceticism, with its rejection of marriage altogether, on the other.

1 The Valentinians, who hold that the union of man and woman is derived from the divine emanation in heaven above, approve of marriage. The followers of Basilides, on the other hand, say that when the apostles asked whether it was not better not to marry, the Lord replied: "Not all can receive this saying; there are some eunuchs who are so from their birth, others are so of necessity."[1] And their explanation of this saying is roughly as follows: Some men, from their birth, have a natural sense of repulsion from a woman; and those who are naturally so constituted do well not to marry. Those who are eunuchs of necessity are those theatrical ascetics who only control themselves because they have a passion for the limelight. [And those who have suffered accidental castration have become eunuchs of necessity.] Those, then, who are eunuchs of necessity have no sound reason for their abstinence from marriage. But those who for the sake of the eternal kingdom have made themselves eunuchs derive this idea, they say, from a wish to avoid the distractions involved in marriage, because they are afraid of having to waste time in providing for the necessities of life.

1 Matt 19:11 f.

Clement Miscellanies, reproduced from Andrew Oulton and Henry Chadwick, *Alexandrian Christianity*. Westminster John Knox / SCM Press, 1954. Used with permission of Westminster John Knox and SCM Press.

2 And they say that by the words "it is better to marry than to burn"[2] the apostle means this: "Do not cast your soul into the fire, so that you have to endure night and day and go in fear lest you should fall from continence. For a soul which has to concentrate upon endurance has lost hope." In his *Ethics* Isidore says in these very words: "Abstain, then, from a quarrelsome woman[3] lest you are distracted from the grace of God. But when you have rejected the fire of the seed, then pray with an undisturbed conscience. And when your prayer of thanksgiving," he says, "descends to a prayer of request, and your request is not that in future you may do right, but that you may do no wrong, then marry." But perhaps a man is too young or poor or suffers from weak health, and has not the will to marry as the apostle's saying suggests. Such a man should not separate himself from his brother Christian. He should say, I have come into the sanctuary, I can suffer nothing. And if he has a presentiment that he may fall, he may say, Brother, lay your hand on me lest I sin, and he will receive help both spiritually and physically. Let him only wish to accomplish what is right and he will achieve his object.

3 "Sometimes, however, we say with our mouth 'I wish not to sin' while our mind is really inclined towards sin. Such a man does not do what he wishes for fear lest any punishment should be in store for him. Human nature has some wants which are necessary and natural, and others which are only natural. To be clothed is necessary and natural; sexual intercourse is natural but not necessary."

I have quoted these remarks to prove in error those Basilidians who do not live purely, supposing either that they have the power even to commit sin because of their perfection, or indeed that they will be saved by nature even if they sin in this life because they possess an innate election. For the original teachers of their doctrines do not allow one to do the same as they are now doing. They

ought not, therefore, to take as a covering cloak the name of Christ and, by living lewder lives than the most uncontrolled heathen, bring blasphemy upon his name. "For such people are false apostles, deceitful workers" as far as the words "whose end shall be like their works."[4]

4 Continence is an ignoring of the body in accordance with the confession of faith in God. For continence is not merely a matter of sexual abstinence, but applies also to the other things for which the soul has an evil desire because it is not satisfied with the necessities of life. There is also a continence of the tongue, of money, of use, and of desire. It does not only teach us to exercise self-control; it is rather that self-control is granted to us, since it is a divine power and grace. Accordingly I must declare what is the opinion of our people about this subject. Our view is that we welcome as blessed the state of abstinence from marriage in those to whom this has been granted by God. We admire monogamy and the high standing of single marriage, holding that we ought to share suffering with another and "bear one another's burdens,"[5] lest anyone who thinks he stands securely should himself fall.[6] It is of second marriage that the apostle says, If you burn, marry.[7]

27 There are some who call Aphrodite *Pandemos* [i.e., physical love] a mystical communion. This is an insult to the name of communion. To do something wrong is called an action, just as also to do right is likewise called an action. Similarly communion is good when the word refers to sharing of money and food and clothing. But they have impiously called by the name of communion any common sexual intercourse. The story goes that one of them came to a virgin of our church who had a lovely face and said to her: "Scripture

2 1 Cor 7:9.
3 Cf. Prov 21:19.
4 2 Cor 11:13, 15.
5 Gal 6:2.
6 1 Cor 10:12.
7 1 Cor 7:9.

says, 'Give to every one that asks you.' "[8] She, however, not understanding the lascivious intention of the man gave the dignified reply: "On the subject of marriage, talk to my mother." What godlessness! Even the words of the Lord are perverted by these immoral fellows, the brethren of lust, a shame not only to philosophy but to all human life, who corrupt the truth, or rather destroy it, as far as they can. These thrice wretched men treat carnal and sexual intercourse as a sacred religious mystery, and think that it will bring them to the kingdom of God.

28 It is to the brothels that this "communion" leads. They can have pigs and goats as their associates. Those who have most to hope from them are the public harlots who shamelessly receive all who want to come to them. "But you have not so learned Christ, if you have heard him and have been taught by him as the truth is in Christ Jesus; put off with the ways of your former life your old man which is corrupted by the deceitful lusts. Be renewed in the spirit of your mind and put on the new man which after God is created in righteousness and true holiness," so as to be made like unto God. "Be therefore imitators of God, as dear children, and walk in love as Christ also loved us and gave himself for us as an offering and sacrifice to God for a sweet smelling savour. But fornication and all impurity and covetousness and shamefulness and foolish talk, let them not be mentioned among you as is fitting for saints."[9] Moreover, the apostle teaches us to be chaste in speech when he writes, "Know this well that no fornicator . . ." and so on as far as the words "but rather expose them."[10]

29 They derived their doctrines from an apocryphal work. I will quote the text which is the mother of their licentiousness. And whether they themselves, I mean the authors of the book,

are responsible (see their madness, for by their licence they do grievous wrong to God) or whether they derived their ideas from some others whom they fell in with, they have taken a sound doctrine and perversely misapplied it. The passage reads as follows: "All things were one; but as it seemed good to its unity not to be alone, an idea came forth from it, and it had intercourse with it and made the beloved. In consequence of this there came forth from him an idea with which he had intercourse and made powers which cannot be seen or heard . . ." down to the words "each by her own name."

If these people spoke of acts of spiritual union like the Valentinians, perhaps one could accept their view. But to suppose that the holy prophets spoke of carnal and wanton intercourse is the way of a man who has renounced salvation.

45 To those, on the other hand, who under a pious cloak blaspheme by their continence both the creation and the holy Creator, the almighty, only God, and teach that one must reject marriage and begetting of children, and should not bring others in their place to live in this wretched world, nor give any sustenance to death, our reply is as follows. We may first quote the word of the apostle John: "And now are many antichrists come, whence we know that it is the last hour. They went out from us, but they were not of us. For if they had been of us, they would have remained with us."[11] Next we may destroy their case on the ground that they pervert the sense of the books they quote, as follows. When Salome asked the Lord: "How long shall death hold sway?" he answered: "As long as you women bear children." Her words do not imply that this life is evil and the creation bad, and his reply only teaches the ordinary course of nature. For birth is invariably followed by death.

46 The task of the law is to deliver us from a dissolute life and all disorderly ways. Its purpose is to lead us from unrighteousness to

---

8 Luke 6:30; Matt 5:42.

9 Eph 4:20–24.

10 Eph 5:1–4, 5–11.

11 1 John 2:18 f.

righteousness, so that it would have us self-controlled in marriage, in begetting children, and in general behaviour. The Lord is not "come to destroy the law but to fulfil it."[12] "To fulfil" does not imply that it was defective, but that by his coming the prophecies of the law are accomplished, since before the law the demand for right conduct was proclaimed by the Logos to those also who lived good lives. The multitude who know nothing of continence live for the body, not for the spirit. But the body without spirit is "earth and ashes."[13] Now the Lord judges adultery which is only committed in thought.[14] What then? Is it not possible to remain continent even in the married state and not to seek to "put asunder what God has joined together"?[15] For such is the teaching of those who divide the yoke of marriage, by reason of whom the Christian name is blasphemed. If it is the view of these people who themselves owe their existence to sexual relations that such relations are impure, must not they be impure? But I hold that even the seed of the sanctified is holy.

47 In us it is not only the spirit which ought to be sanctified, but also our behaviour, manner of life, and our body. What does the apostle Paul mean when he says that the wife is sanctified by the husband and the husband by the wife?[16] And what is the meaning of the Lord's words to those who asked concerning divorce whether it is lawful to put away one's wife as Moses commanded? "Because of the hardness of your hearts," he says, "Moses wrote this; but have you not read that God said to the first man, You two shall be one flesh? Therefore he who divorces his wife except for fornication makes her an adulteress."[17] But "after the resurrection," he says, "they neither

marry nor are given in marriage."[18] Moreover, concerning the belly and its food it is written: "Food is for the belly and the belly for food; but God shall destroy both the one and the other."[19] In this saying he attacks those who think they can live like wild pigs and goats, lest they should indulge their physical appetites without restraint.

48 If, as they say, they have already attained the state of resurrection,[20] and on this account reject marriage let them neither eat nor drink. For the apostle says that in the resurrection the belly and food shall be destroyed. Why then do they hunger and thirst and suffer the weaknesses of the flesh and all the other needs which will not affect the man who through Christ has attained to the hoped for resurrection? Furthermore those who worship idols abstain both from food and from sexual intercourse. "But the kingdom of God does not consist in eating and drinking,"[21] he says. And indeed the Magi make a point of abstaining from wine and the meat of animals and from sexual intercourse while they are worshipping angels and daemons. But just as humility consists in meekness and not in treating one's body roughly, so also continence is a virtue of the soul which is not manifest to others, but is in secret.

49 There are some who say outright that marriage is fornication and teach that it was introduced by the devil. They proudly say that they are imitating the Lord who neither married nor had any possession in this world, boasting that they understand the gospel better than anyone else. The Scripture says to them: "God resists the proud but gives grace to the humble."[22] Further, they do not know the reason why the Lord did not marry. In the first place he had his

---

12 Matt 5:17.

13 Gen 18:27.

14 Matt 5:28.

15 Matt 19:6.

16 1 Cor 7:14.

17 Matt 19:3–9.

---

18 Matt 22:30.

19 1 Cor 6:13.

20 Cf. Introduction, p. 34.

21 Rom 14:17.

22 James 4:6; 1 Peter 5:5.

own bride, the Church; and in the next place he was no ordinary man that he should also be in need of some helpmeet[23] after the flesh. Nor was it necessary for him to beget children since he abides eternally and was born the only Son of God. It is the Lord himself who says: "That which God has joined together, let no man put asunder."[24] And again: "As it was in the days of Noah, they were marrying, and giving in marriage, building and planting, and as it was in the days of Lot, so shall be the coming of the Son of man."[25] And to show that he is not referring to the heathen he adds: "When the Son of man is come, shall he find faith on the earth?"[26] And again: "Woe to those who are with child and are giving suck in those days,"[27] a saying, I admit, to be understood allegorically. The reason why he did not determine "the times which the Father has appointed by his own power"[28] was that the world might continue from generation to generation.

50 Concerning the words, "Not all can receive this saying. There are some eunuchs who were born so, and some who were made eunuchs by men, and some who have made themselves eunuchs for the sake of the kingdom of heaven; let him receive it who can receive it,"[29] they do not realize the context. After his word about divorce some asked him whether, if that is the position in relation to woman, it is better not to marry; and it was then that the Lord said: "Not all can receive this saying, but those to whom it is granted." What the questioners wanted to know was whether, when a man's wife has been condemned for fornication, it is allowable for him to marry another.

It is said, however, that several athletes abstained from sexual intercourse, exercising continence to keep their bodies in training, as Astylos of Croton and Crison of Himera. Even the cithara-player, Amoebeus, though newly married, kept away from his bride. And Aristotle of Cyrene was the only man to disdain the love of Lais when she fell for him.

51 As he had sworn to the courtesan that he would take her to his home country if she rendered him some assistance against his antagonists, when she had rendered it, he kept his oath in an amusing manner by painting the closest possible likeness of her and setting it up in Cyrene. The story is told by Istros in his book on *The Peculiarity of Athletic Contests.* Therefore there is nothing meritorious about abstinence from marriage unless it arises from love to God. At any rate the blessed Paul says of those who revile marriage: "In the last times some shall depart from the faith, turning to spirits of error and doctrines inspired by daemons, forbidding to marry and commanding abstinence from food."[30] And again he says: "Let no one disqualify you by demanding self-imposed ascetic practices and severe treatment of the body."[31] And the same writer has this also: "Are you bound to a wife? Do not seek to be separated from her? Are you free from any wife? Do not seek to find one." And again: "Let every man have his own wife lest Satan tempt you."[32]

52 How then? Did not the righteous in ancient times partake of what God made with thanksgiving? Some begat children and lived chastely in the married state, To Elijah the ravens brought bread and meat for food.[33] And Samuel the prophet brought as food for Saul the remnant

---

23 Gen 2:18.

24 Matt 19:6.

25 Matt 24:37–39.

26 Luke 18:8.

27 Matt 24:19.

28 Acts 1:7.

29 Matt 19:11 f.

30 1 Tim 4:1, 3.

31 Col 2:18, 23.

32 1 Cor 7:27, 2, 5.

33 1 Kings 17:6.

of the thigh, of which he had already eaten.[34] But whereas they say that they are superior to them in behaviour and conduct, they cannot even be compared with them in their deeds. "He who does not eat," then, "let him not despise him who eats; and he who eats let him not judge him who does not eat; for God has accepted him."[35] Moreover, the Lord says of himself: "John came neither eating nor drinking, and they say, He has a devil. The Son of man came eating and drinking and they say, Behold a gluttonous man and a winebibber, a friend of publicans and a sinner."[36]

Or do they also scorn the apostles? Peter and Philip had children, and Philip gave his daughters in marriage.

---

34 1 Sam 9:24.

35 Rom 14:3.

36 Matt 11:18 f.

53 Even Paul did not hesitate in one letter to address his consort. The only reason why he did not take her about with him was that it would have been an inconvenience for his ministry. Accordingly he says in a letter: "Have we not a right to take about with us a wife that is a sister like the other apostles?"[37] But the latter, in accordance with their particular ministry, devoted themselves to preaching without any distraction, and took their wives with them not as women with whom they had marriage relations, but as sisters, that they might be their fellow-ministers in dealing with housewives. It was through them that the Lord's teaching penetrated also the women's quarters without any scandal being aroused. We also know the directions about women deacons which are given by the noble Paul in his second letter to Timothy.[38]

---

37 1 Cor 9:5.

38 1 Tim 5:9 f.

88. Tertullian: On the Dress of Women

We have seen selections from Tertullian a number of times so far, especially in his work as an apologist for Christianity and in his attempts to root out heresy from the church. What we have not seen is his rather infamous views of women (see further: selection 92 in Chapter 15). Tertullian is often portrayed as one of the most notorious misogynists of antiquity. The selection given here will help show why.

This is a clear instance of a man who has power that has been given to him by his high education, his standing in the church, his rhetorical abilities, and, of course, the fact that he was a male in a highly patriarchal society. Tertullian uses that power to tell women how they are to behave. Or in this instance, how they are to dress. Tertullian applies rigorous logic, irrefutable (for him) interpretations of Scripture, rapier wit, and brute force in order to make his point. Along the way, at the outset, it becomes clear why he thinks (or knows) that he has the right to make these pronouncements: women are all descended from that first woman, Eve, who brought sin into the world.

Tertullian On the Apparel of Women, reproduced from *The Ante-Nicene Fathers*, vol. 3, *Latin Christianity: Its Founder, Tertullian*, ed. A. Cleveland Coxe. Reprint; 2nd ed. Grand Rapids: Eerdmans 1989.

As members of the same sex, women not only are heirs of Eve's tradition, they also are bearers of her guilt, so that "the sentence of God on this sex of yours lives in this age." They, like Eve, are "the devil's gateway," the ones through whom the arch-enemy of God works his will in this world. And so they need to be brought under control in every way, including how they dress.

IF there dwelt upon earth a faith as great as is the reward of faith which is expected in the heavens, no one of you at all, best beloved sisters, from the time that she had first "known the Lord," and learned (the truth) concerning her own (that is, woman's) condition, would have desired too gladsome (not to say too ostentatious) a style of dress; so as not rather to go about in humble garb, and rather to affect meanness of appearance, walking about as Eve mourning and repentant, in order that by every garb of penitence she might the more fully expiate that which she derives from Eve,—the ignominy, I mean, of the first sin, and the odium (attaching to her as the cause) of human perdition. "In pains and in anxieties dost thou bear (children), woman; and toward thine husband (is) thy inclination, and he lords it over thee." And do you not know that you are (each) an Eve? The sentence of God on this sex of yours lives in this age: the guilt must of necessity live too. You are the devil's gateway: you are the unsealer of that (forbidden) tree: you are the first deserter of the divine law: you are she who persuaded him whom the devil was not valiant enough to attack. You destroyed so easily God's image, man. On account of your desert—that is, death—even the Son of God had to die. And do you think about adorning yourself over and above your tunics of skins? Come, now; if from the beginning of the world the Milesians sheared sheep, and the Serians spun trees, and the Tyrians dyed, and the Phrygians embroidered with the needle, and the Babylonians with the loom, and pearls gleamed, and onyx-stones flashed; if gold itself also had already issued, with the cupidity (which accompanies it), from the ground; if the mirror, too, already had licence to lie so largely, Eve, expelled from

paradise, (Eve) already dead, would also have coveted these things, I imagine! No more, then, ought she now to crave, or be acquainted with (if she desires to live again), what, when she was living, she had neither had nor known. Accordingly these things are all the baggage of woman in her condemned and dead state, instituted as if to swell the pomp of her funeral.

For they, withal, who instituted them are assigned, under condemnation, to the penalty of death,—those angels, to wit, who rushed from heaven on the daughters of men; so that this ignominy also attaches to woman. For when to an age much more ignorant (than ours) they had disclosed certain well-concealed material substances, and several not well-revealed scientific arts—if it is true that they had laid bare the operations of metallurgy, and had divulged the natural properties of herbs, and had promulgated the powers of enchantments, and had traced out every curious art, even to the interpretation of the stars—they conferred properly and as it were peculiarly upon women that instrumental mean of womanly ostentation, the radiances of jewels wherewith necklaces are variegated, and the circlets of gold wherewith the arms are compressed, and the medicaments of orchil with which wools are coloured, and that black powder itself wherewith the eyelids and eyelashes are made prominent. What is the quality of these things may be declared meantime, even at this point, from the quality and condition of their teachers; in that sinners could never have either shown or supplied anything conducive to integrity, unlawful lovers anything conducive to chastity, renegade spirits anything conducive to the fear of God. If (these things) are to be called teachings, ill masters must of necessity have taught ill; if as wages of lust, there is nothing base of which the wages are honourable. But why was it of so much importance to show these things as well as to confer them? Was it that women, without material causes of splendour, and without ingenious contrivances of grace, could not please men, who, while still un-adorned, and uncouth, and—so to say—crude and rude, had moved (the mind of) angels? or was it that the lovers would appear sordid and—through gratuitous use—contumelious, if they had con-ferred no (compensating) gift on the women who had been enticed into connubial connection with them? But these questions admit of no calculation. Women who possessed angels (as husbands) could desire nothing more; they had, forsooth, made a grand match! Assuredly they who, of course, did sometimes think whence they had fallen, and, after the heated impulses of their lusts, looked up toward heaven, thus requited that very excellence of women, natural beauty, as (having proved) a cause of evil, in order that their good fortune might profit them nothing; but that, being turned from simplicity and sincerity, they, together with (the angels) themselves, might become offensive to God. Sure they were that all ostentation, and ambition, and love of pleasing by carnal means, was displeasing to God. And these are the angels whom we are destined to judge: these are the angels whom in baptism we renounce: these, of course, are the reasons why they have deserved to be judged by man. What business, then, have their things with their judges? What commerce have they who are to condemn with them who are to be con-demned? The same, I take it, as Christ has with Belial. With what consistency do we mount that (future) judgment-seat to pronounce sentence against those whose gifts we (now) seek after? For you too, (women as you are,) have the self-same an-gelic nature promised as your reward, the self-same sex as men: the self-same advancement to the dig-nity of judging, does (the Lord) promise you. Unless, then, we begin even here to pre-judge, by pre-condemning their things, which we are here-after to condemn in themselves, they will rather judge and condemn us.

Female habit carries with it a twofold idea—dress and ornament. By "dress" we mean what they call "womanly gracing;" by "ornament," what it is suitable should be called "womanly disgracing." The former is accounted (to consist) in gold, and silver, and gems, and garments; the latter in care of the hair, and of the skin, and of those parts of the body which attract the eye. Against the one we lay the charge of ambition, against the other of prosti-tution; so that even from this early stage (of our discussion) you may look forward and see what, out of (all) these, is suitable, handmaid of God, to your discipline, inasmuch as you are assessed on different principles (from other women),—those, namely, of humility and chastity.

Book 2

Handmaids of the living God, my fellow-servants and sisters, the right which I enjoy with you—I, the most meanest in that right of fellow-servantship and brotherhood—emboldens me to address to you a discourse, not, of course, of affection, but paving the way for affection in the cause of your salvation. That salvation—and not (the salvation) of women only, but likewise of men—consists in the exhibition principally of modesty. For since, by the introduction into an appropriation (in) us of the Holy Spirit, we are all "the temple of God,"[1] Modesty is the sacristan and priestess of that temple, who is to suffer nothing unclean or pro-fane to be introduced (into it), for fear that the God who inhabits it should be offended, and quite forsake the polluted abode. But on the present oc-casion we (are to speak) not about modesty, for the enjoining and exacting of which the divine pre-cepts which press (upon us) on every side are suf-ficient; but about the matters which pertain to it, that is, the manner in which it behoves you to walk. For most women (which very thing I trust God may permit me, with a view, of course, to my own personal censure, to censure in all), either

---

1 See 1 Cor 11:10, 17; 6:19, 20.

from simple ignorance or else from dissimulation, have the hardihood so to walk as if modesty consisted only in the (bare) integrity of the flesh, and in turning away from (actual) fornication; and there were no need for anything extrinsic to boot—in the matter (I mean) of the arrangement of dress and ornament, the studied graces of form and brilliance:—wearing in their gait the self-same appearance as the women of the nations, from whom the sense of true modesty is absent, because in those who know not God, the Guardian and Master of truth, there is nothing true. For if any modesty can be believed (to exist) in Gentiles, it is plain that it must be imperfect and undisciplined to such a degree that, although it be actively tenacious of itself in the mind up to a certain point, it yet allows itself to relax into licentious extravagances of attire; just in accordance with Gentile perversity, in craving after that of which it carefully shuns the effect. How many a one, in short, is there who does not earnestly desire even to look pleasing to strangers? who does not on that very account take care to have herself painted out, and denies that she has (ever) been an object of (carnal) appetite? And yet, granting that even this is a practice familiar to Gentile modesty—(namely,) not actually to commit the sin, but still to be willing to do so; or even not to be willing, yet still not quite to refuse—what wonder? for all things which are not God's are perverse. Let those women therefore look to it, who, by not holding fast the whole good, easily mingle with evil even what they do hold fast. Necessary it is that you turn aside from them, as in all other things, so also in your gait; since you ought to be "perfect, as (is) your Father who is in the heavens."

You must know that in the eye of perfect, that is, Christian, modesty, (carnal) desire of one's self (on the part of others) is not only not to be desired, but even execrated, by you: first, because the study of making personal grace (which we know to be naturally the inviter of lust) a mean of pleasing does not spring from a sound conscience: why therefore excite toward yourself that evil

(passion)? why invite (that) to which you profess yourself a stranger? secondly, because we ought not to open a way to temptations, which, by their instancy, sometimes achieve (a wickedness) which God expels from them who are His; (or,) at all events, put the spirit into a thorough tumult by (presenting) a stumbling-block (to it). We ought indeed to walk so holily, and with so entire substantiality of faith, as to be confident and secure in regard of our own conscience, desiring that that (gift) may abide in us to the end, yet not presuming (that it will). For he who presumes feels less apprehension; he who feels less apprehension takes less precaution; he who takes less precaution runs more risk. Fear is the foundation of salvation; presumption is an impediment to fear. More useful, then, is it to apprehend that we may possibly fail, than to presume that we cannot; for apprehending will lead us to fear, fearing to caution, and caution to salvation. On the other hand, if we presume, there will be neither fear nor caution to save us. He who acts securely, and not at the same time warily, possesses no safe and firm security; whereas he who is wary will be truly able to be secure. For His own servants, may the Lord by His mercy take care that to them it may be lawful even to presume on His goodness! But why are we a (source of) danger to our neighbour? why do we import concupiscence into our neighbour? which concupiscence, if God, in "amplifying the law," do not dissociate in (the way of) penalty from the actual commission of fornication, I know not whether He allows impunity to him who has been the cause of perdition to some other. For that other, as soon as he has felt concupiscence after your beauty, and has mentally already committed (the deed) which his concupiscence pointed to, perishes; and you have been made the sword which destroys him: so that, albeit you be free from the (actual) crime, you are not free from the odium (attaching to it); as, when a robbery has been committed on some man's estate, the (actual) crime indeed will not be laid to the owner's charge, while yet the domain is branded with ignominy, (and) the owner himself aspersed with the infamy.

Are we to paint ourselves out that our neighbours may perish? Where, then, is (the command), "Thou shalt love thy neighbour as thyself?" "Care not merely about your own (things), but (about your) neighbour's?" No enunciation of the Holy Spirit ought to be (confined) to the subject immediately in hand merely, and not applied and carried out with a view to every occasion to which its application is useful. Since, therefore, both our own interest and that of others is implicated in the studious pursuit of most perilous (outward) comeliness, it is time for you to know that not merely must the pageantry of fictitious and elaborate beauty be rejected by you; but that of even natural grace must be obliterated by concealment and negligence, as equally dangerous to the glances of (the beholder's) eyes. For, albeit comeliness is not to be censured, as being a bodily happiness, as being an additional outlay of the divine plastic art, as being a kind of goodly garment of the soul; yet it is to be feared, just on account of the injuriousness and violence of suitors: which (injuriousness and violence) even the father of the faith, Abraham, greatly feared in regard of his own wife's grace; and Isaac, by falsely representing Rebecca as his sister, purchased safety by insult!

Let it now be granted that excellence of form be not to be feared, as neither troublesome to its possessors, nor destructive to its desirers, nor perilous to its compartners; let it be thought (to be) not exposed to temptations, not surrounded by stumbling-blocks: it is enough that to angels of God it is not necessary. For, where modesty is, there beauty is idle; because properly the use and fruit of beauty is voluptuousness, unless any one thinks that there is some other harvest for bodily grace to reap. Are women who think that, in furnishing to their neighbour that which is demanded of beauty, they are furnishing it to themselves also, to augment that (beauty) when (naturally) given them, and to strive after it when not (thus) given? Some one will say, "Why, then, if voluptuousness be shut out and chastity let in, may (we) not enjoy the praise of beauty alone, and glory in a bodily good?" Let whoever finds

pleasure in "glorying in the flesh" see to that. To us, in the first place, there is no studious pursuit of "glory," because "glory" is the essence of exaltation. Now exaltation is incongruous for professors of humility according to God's precepts. Secondly, if all "glory" is "vain" and insensate, how much more (glory) in the flesh, especially to us? For even if "glorying" is (allowable), we ought to wish our sphere of pleasing to lie in the graces of the Spirit, not in the flesh; because we are "suitors" of things spiritual. In those things wherein our sphere of labour lies, let our joy lie. From the sources whence we hope for salvation, let us cull our "glory." Plainly, a Christian will "glory" even in the flesh; but (it will be) when it has endured laceration for Christ's sake, in order that the spirit may be crowned in it, not in order that it may draw the eyes and sighs of youths after it. Thus (a thing) which, from whatever point you look at it, is in your case superfluous, you may justly disdain if you have it not, and neglect if you have. Let a holy woman, if naturally beautiful, give none so great occasion (for carnal appetite). Certainly, if even she be so, she ought not to set off (her beauty), but even to obscure it.

These suggestions are not made to you, of course, to be developed into an entire crudity and wildness of appearance; nor are we seeking to persuade you of the good of squalor and slovenliness; but of the limit and norm and just measure of cultivation of the person. There must be no overstepping of that line to which simple and sufficient refinements limit their desires—that line which is pleasing to God. For they who rub their skin with medicaments, stain their cheeks with rouge, make their eyes prominent with antimony, sin against HIM. To them, I suppose, the plastic skill of God is displeasing! In their own persons, I suppose, they convict, they censure, the Artificer of all things! For censure they do when they amend, when they add to, (His work;) taking these their additions, of course, from the adversary artificer. That adversary artificer is the devil. For who would show the way to change the body, but he who by wickedness transfigured man's spirit? He it is, undoubtedly, who adapted ingenious devices of this kind; that in your persons it may be apparent that you, in a certain sense, do violence to God. Whatever is born is the work of God. Whatever, then, is plastered on (that), is the devil's work. To superinduce on a divine work Satan's ingenuities, how criminal is it! Our servants borrow nothing from our personal enemies: soldiers eagerly desire nothing from the foes of their own general; for, to demand for (your own) use anything from the adversary of Him in whose hand you are, is a transgression. Shall a Christian be assisted in anything by that evil one? (If he do,) I know not whether this name (of "Christian") will continue (to belong) to him; for he will be his in whose lore he eagerly desires to be instructed. But how alien from your schoolings and professions are (these things)! How unworthy the Christian name, to wear a fictitious face, (you,) on whom simplicity in every form is enjoined!—to lie in your appearance, (you,) to whom (lying) with the tongue is not lawful!—to seek after what is another's, (you,) to whom is delivered (the precept of) abstinence from what is another's!—to practise adultery in your mien, (you,) who make modesty your study! Think, blessed (sisters), how will you keep God's precepts if you shall not keep in your own persons His lineaments?

I see some (women) turn (the colour of) their hair with saffron. They are ashamed even of their own nation, (ashamed) that their procreation did not assign them to Germany and to Gaul: thus, as it is, they transfer their hair (thither)! Ill, ay, most ill, do they augur for themselves with their flame-coloured head, and think that graceful which (in fact) they are polluting! Nay, moreover, the force of the cosmetics burns ruin into the hair; and the constant application of even any undrugged moisture, lays up a store of harm for the head; while the sun's warmth, too, so desirable for imparting to the hair at once growth and dryness, is hurtful. What "grace" is compatible with "injury?" What "beauty" with "impurities?" Shall a Christian woman heap saffron on her head, as upon an altar? For, whatever is wont to be burned to the honour of the unclean spirit, that—unless it is

applied for honest, and necessary, and salutary uses, for which God's creature was provided—may seem to be a sacrifice. But, however, God saith, "Which of you can make a white hair black, or out of a black a white?" And so they refute the Lord! "Behold!" say they, "instead of white or black, we make it yellow,—more winning in grace." And yet such as repent of having lived to old age do attempt to change it even from white to black! O temerity! The age which is the object of our wishes and prayers blushes (for itself)! a theft is effected! youth, wherein we have sinned, is sighed after! the opportunity of sobriety is spoiled! Far from Wisdom's daughters be folly so great! The more old age tries to conceal itself, the more will it be detected. Here is a veritable eternity, in the (perennial) youth of your head! Here we have an "incorruptibility" to "put on," with a view to the new house of the Lord which the divine monarchy promises! Well do you speed toward the Lord; well do you hasten to be quit of this most iniquitous world, to whom it is unsightly to approach (your own) end!

What service, again, does all the labour spent in arranging the hair render to salvation? Why is no rest allowed to your hair, which must now be bound, now loosed, now cultivated, now thinned out? Some are anxious to force their hair into curls, some to let it hang loose and flying; not with good simplicity: beside which, you affix I know not what enormities of subtle and textile perukes; now, after the manner of a helmet of undressed hide, as it were a sheath for the head and a covering for the crown; now, a mass (drawn) backward toward the neck. The wonder is, that there is no (open) contending against the Lord's prescripts! It has been pronounced that no one can add to his own stature. You, however, do add to your weight some kind of rolls, or shield-bosses, to be piled upon your necks! If you feel no shame at the enormity, feel some at the pollution; for fear you may be fitting on a holy and Christian head the slough of some one else's head, unclean perchance, guilty perchance and destined to hell. Nay, rather banish quite away from your "free" head all this slavery of ornamentation. In vain do you labour to seem adorned: in vain do you call in the aid of all the most skilful manufacturers of false hair. God bids you "be veiled." I believe (He does so) for fear the heads of some should be seen! And oh that in "that day" of Christian exultation, I, most miserable (as I am), may elevate my head, even though below (the level of) your heels! I shall (then) see whether you will rise with (your) ceruse and rouge and saffron, and in all that parade of headgear: whether it will be women thus tricked out whom the angels carry up to meet Christ in the air. If these (decorations) are now good, and of God, they will then also present themselves to the rising bodies, and will recognise their several places. But nothing can rise except flesh and spirit sole and pure. Whatever, therefore, does not rise in (the form of) spirit and flesh is condemned, because it is not of God. From things which are condemned abstain, even at the present day. At the present day let God see you such as He will see you then.

Moreover, what causes have you for appearing in public in excessive grandeur, removed as you are from the occasions which call for such exhibitions? For you neither make the circuit of the temples, nor demand (to be present at) public shows, nor have any acquaintance with the holy days of the Gentiles. Now it is for the sake of all these public gatherings, and of much seeing and being seen, that all pomps (of dress) are exhibited before the public eye; either for the purpose of transacting the trade of voluptuousness, or else of inflating "glory."

You, however, have no cause of appearing in public, except such as is serious. Either some brother who is sick is visited, or else the sacrifice is offered, or else the word of God is dispensed. Whichever of these you like to name is a business of sobriety and sanctity, requiring no extraordinary attire, with (studious) arrangement and (wanton) negligence. And if the requirements of Gentile friendships and of kindly offices call you, why not go forth clad in your own armour; (and) all the more, in that (you have to go) to such as are strangers to the faith? so that between the handmaids of God and of the devil there may be a difference; so that you may be an example to them, and they may be edified in you; so that (as the apostle says) "God may be magnified in your body." But magnified He is in the body through modesty: of course, too, through attire suitable to modesty. Well, but it is urged by some, "Let not the Name be blasphemed in us, if we make any derogatory change from our old style and dress." Let us, then, not abolish our old vices! let us maintain the same character, if we must maintain the same appearance (as before); and then truly the nations will not blaspheme! A grand blasphemy is that by which it is said, "Ever since she became a Christian, she walks in poorer garb!" Will you fear to appear poorer, from the time that you have been made more wealthy; and fouler, from the time when you have been made more clean? Is it according to the decree of Gentiles, or according to the decree of God, that it becomes Christians to walk?

89. Women Montanist Prophets

We have seen that virtually all of our early Christian texts were written by men, and even when they claim to represent women's voices they are women's voices as spoken by the voice of men. As a result, in the Christian writings about and for women, often what we find are not women's perspectives but men's views of what women's perspectives either are or ought to be.

As for hearing women's voices themselves, from the first three Christian centuries it may be that the Martyrdom of Perpetua incorporates a diary actually written by the Roman matron herself (see selection 9); that would make the work quite exceptional. One other place where we may find traces of women's voices are in the oracles preserved from the women Montanist prophets.

Montanism was a movement near the end of the second century that stressed the need for rigorous ethical standards—for both men and women—in view of the fact that the end of the age was soon to appear, as taught to the leaders of the movement by the Holy Spirit itself. The main figure for the movement was a man named Montanus, but along with him were two women prophets, Priscilla and Maximilla. We do not have any extensive writings from any of these figures, but we do have quotations of what they proclaimed as cited by later church fathers. Even though we would love to have extensive quotations, all we have are tiny fragments. But at the least these fragments provide us with words that almost certainly issued from the mouths of real, Christian women.

Oracles Attributed to Montanus

1 Epiphanius, *Panarion* 48.11.
But in addition, this same Montanus adds the following words: "I am the Lord God, the Almighty dwelling in man."

2 Ibid.
Then again this miserable little man Montanus says: "Neither angel nor envoy, but I the Lord God the Father have come" (cf. Isa 63:9).

3 Ibid. 48.4.
For Montanus says, for instance: "Behold, man is like a lyre, and I flit about like a plectron; man sleeps, and I awaken him; behold, it is the Lord who changes the hearts of men and gives men a heart."

4 Ibid. 48.10.
For [Montanus] says in his so-called prophecy: "Why do you call the more excellent man saved? For the just, he says, will shine a hundred times brighter than the sun, and the little ones among

"Women Montanist Prophets" reproduced from Ronald Heine, *The Montanist Oracles and Testimonia*. Macon, GA: Mercer Press, 1989. Used with permission of Mercer Press.

you who are saved will shine a hundred times brighter than the moon."

Oracles Attributed to Maximilla

5 Eusebius, *Ecclesiastical History* 5.16.17.
And let not the spirit which speaks through Maximilla say, in the same book according to Asterius Orbanus: "I am pursued like a wolf from the sheep. I am not a wolf (cf. Matt 7:15). I am word, and spirit, and power" (cf. 1 Cor 2:4).

6 Epiphanius, *Panarion* 48.2.4.
For the one they call Maximilla, the prophetess, declares: "After me there will no longer be a prophet, but the end."

7 Ibid. 48.12.4.
For hear, O children of Christ, what this Maximilla who belongs to such as are thus called Cataphrygians says in a straightforward manner: "Hear not me, but hear Christ."

8 Ibid. 48.13.1.
And again the same Maximilla, who claims to be the gnosis of persuasion and doctrine, to speak derisively, declares: "The Lord has sent me as partisan, revealer, and interpreter of this suffering, covenant, and promise. I am compelled to come to understand the knowledge of God whether I want to or not."
Cf. ibid. 48.13.7.

For indeed even Maximilla said she compelled those who were willing and those who were not. . . .

Oracles Attributed to Priscilla/Prisca

9 Tertullian, *On the Resurrection of the Flesh* 11.2.
The Paraclete has also said well of them through the prophetess Prisca:
"They are flesh, and they hate the flesh."

10 Tertullian, *Exhortation to Chastity* 10.5.
Likewise the holy prophetess Prisca preaches that the holy minister should know how to administer purity of life. "For purification produces harmony," she says, "and they see visions, and when they turn their faces downward they also hear salutary voices, as clear as they are secret."

An Oracle Attributed to Quintilla (or Priscilla)

11 Epiphanius, *Panarion* 49.1.
For these Quintillians, or Priscillians, say that in Pepuza either Quintilla or Priscilla, I cannot say precisely, but one of them, as I said before, had been asleep in Pepuza and the Christ came to her and slept with her in the following manner, as that deluded woman described it. "Having assumed the form of a woman," she says, "Christ came to me in a bright robe and put wisdom in me, and revealed to me that this place is holy, and that it is here that Jerusalem will descend from heaven."

15

Leading the Upright Life
The Role of Ethics in Early Christianity

High ethical standards appear to have played an important role in the Christian religion from the very beginning. This helped set Christianity off from other religions in the Greco-Roman world. It is not that non-Christians tended to be immoral; quite the contrary, ethical behavior was as important to people in antiquity as it is today. But for the most part, ethics had little to do with established religion: pagan cults were principally concerned with performing sacrificial acts that were accepted as pleasing to the gods. How one behaved in one's daily life—for example, how one acted towards one's friends, family, and neighbors—was generally left outside of the cult as a matter of social norm and, for the more highly educated, of philosophy.

Judaism, of course, was an exception, in that Jews had an ancient law that specified not only how one was to worship God, but also how one was to treat one's family and neighbors. Christians took over the ethical norms of Judaism, since, starting with Jesus and the apostles themselves, they subscribed to the Law of Moses. In fact, many early Christians maintained that believers in Christ were to follow the ethical prescriptions of the Mosaic Law even better than did the religious leaders of the Jews (see Matthew 5:17–20). Even when gentiles were not required to follow the ceremonial aspects of the Law, which provided social boundary markers for those who considered themselves Jews (for example, circumcision and kosher food laws), they were expected to follow the laws that pertained to social relations, such as the law to "love your neighbor as yourself" (Leviticus 19:18; see Matthew 22:39; Galatians 5:14).

At the outset, Christians understood that proper moral behavior involved following not only the laws of the Old Testament, but also the teachings of Jesus, which were understood to unpack the true meaning of the Jewish Law. These teachings were seen to apply to believers' everyday lives in all their relations—with their families, fellow believers, governing officials, and so forth. In some situations, the upright lives of Christians proved important for their relationship with those outside the faith, for example, when attracting converts by their high ethical standards (see Chapter 2) or when defending themselves against charges of rampant and flagrant immorality (see Chapter 4). This emphasis on strong ethical behavior led Christian leaders to go far beyond the teachings of Jesus himself to become increasingly specific concerning what Christians were and were not allowed to do, what was required, what was permitted, and what was forbidden.

In particular, a number of early Christian groups developed a strong ascetic bent, as believers in Christ insisted that the body's desires were not to be indulged but that, in one way or another, the body was to be denied, trained, or punished. This ascetic impulse may have originally been rooted, at least in part, in Christianity's apocalyptic message. Christians like the apostle Paul, who believed that the end of the age was imminent, saw little sense in accommodating bodily passions and desires. This world, along with all its pleasures, great and small, was soon to be destroyed. Christians should prepare for the coming judgment and not be overly attached to that which was soon to pass away (see, for example, 1 Corinthians 7:26–31).

Eventually this ascetic strain experienced a range of permutations. We have already seen the writings of Christian Gnostics, for example, who believed that the material world was inherently evil and inimical to the true God; for such Christians, the body participated in evil materiality and was therefore itself an enemy to be overcome and punished (see Chapter 6). And there were early Christian women, both Gnostic and proto-orthodox, who saw sexual renunciation as a way of liberation from the constraints and domination of the patriarchal institutions of marriage and family (see Chapter 14).

The goal of Christian distinctiveness and the earnestness of some of the early Christian writers become especially evident in the moral treatises that have been preserved from the first three centuries of the church. Examples of moral guidelines can be found in numerous texts scattered throughout this volume. The following excerpts, however, are particularly germane, as they give some idea of the range of ethical issues that challenged Christians (at least in the eyes of their leaders) and the firm guidelines they were expected to follow when confronting them.

For Further Reading

Brown, Peter R. L. *The Body and Society: Men, Women and Sexual Renunciation in Early Christianity*. New York: Columbia University, 1988.

Meeks, Wayne. *The Origins of Christian Morality: The First Two Centuries*. New Haven: Yale University, 1993.

Murphy, Francis Xavier. *The Christian Way of Life*. Wilmington: M. Glazier, 1986.

Osborn, Eric F. *Ethical Patterns in Early Christian Thought*. Cambridge: Cambridge University Press, 1976.

van Henten, Jan Willem and Joseph Verheyden, eds. *Early Christian Ethics in Interaction with Jewish and Greco-Roman Contexts*. Leiden: Brill, 2013.

Wogaman, J. Philip. *Christian Ethics: A Historical Introduction*. Louisville, KY: Westminster John Knox, 1993; chapters 1–2.

Womer, Jan. *Morality and Ethics in Early Christianity*. Philadelphia: Fortress, 1987.

THE TEXTS

90. The Didache

The opening section of the Didache (see Chapter 12) contains a number of ethical injunctions portrayed as the "Two Ways of Life and Death" (cf. Matthew 7:13–14). The Way that leads to Life (chapters 1–4) is paved with upright behavior: those who choose it are to love one another, avoid evil desires, jealousy, and anger, give alms to the poor, obey God's commandments, and generally lead morally respectable lives. Many of these instructions reflect the teachings of Jesus from the Sermon on the Mount in Matthew 5–7 (for example, praying for one's enemies, turning the other cheek, and going the extra mile). As might be expected, the Way that leads to Death (chapter 5) involves the opposite sorts of behavior: "murders, adulteries, lusts, fornications, thefts," and sundry other transgressive activities.

A similar doctrine of the Two Ways is found near the end of the epistle of Barnabas (see Chapter 5), leading most scholars to think that it was drawn from an earlier source, possibly Jewish, that was more widely available.

The Didache

The teaching of the Lord through the twelve apostles to the Gentiles [Or: nations].

1 There are two paths, one of life and one of death, and the difference between the two paths is great.

2 This then is the path of life. First, love the God who made you, and second, your neighbor as yourself.[1] And whatever you do not want to happen to you, do not do to another.[2]

3 This is the teaching relating to these matters: Bless those who curse you, pray for your enemies, and fast for those who persecute you. For why is it so great to love those who love you? Do the Gentiles not do this as well? But you should love those who hate you[3]—then you will have no enemy.

4 Abstain from fleshly passions.[4] If anyone slaps your right cheek, turn the other to him as well,[5] and you will be perfect.[6] If anyone compels you to go one mile, go with him two. If anyone takes your cloak, give him your shirt as well. If anyone seizes what is yours, do not ask for it back,[7] for you will not be able to get it.

---

1 Matt 22:37–39; Mark 12:30–31; Luke 10:27; Deut 6:5; Lev 19:18.

2 Cf. Matt 7:12; Luke 6:31.

3 Cf. Matt 5:44, 46–47; Luke 6:28, 32–33, 35.

4 1 Pet 2:11.

5 Matt 5:39.

6 Matt 5:48.

7 Matt 4:41, 40; Luke 6:29–30.

The Didache, reproduced from *The Apostolic Fathers*, ed. Bart D. Ehrman; Loeb Classical Library, vol. 1. Cambridge, MA: Harvard University Press, 2003. Used with permission of Harvard University Press.

5 Give to everyone who asks, and do not ask for anything back.[8] For the Father wants everyone to be given something from the gracious gifts he himself provides. How fortunate is the one who gives according to the commandment, for he is without fault. Woe to the one who receives. For if anyone receives because he is in need, he is without fault. But the one who receives without a need will have to testify why he received what he did, and for what purpose. And he will be thrown in prison and interrogated about what he did; and he will not get out until he pays back every last cent.[9]

6 For it has also been said concerning this: "Let your gift to charity sweat in your hands until you know to whom to give it."[10]

2 And now the second commandment of the teaching.

2 Do not murder, do not commit adultery,[11] do not engage in pederasty, do not engage in sexual immorality. Do not steal, do not practice magic, do not use enchanted potions, do not abort a fetus or kill a child that is born.

3 Do not desire what belongs to your neighbor, do not commit perjury, do not give false testimony, do not speak insults, do not bear grudges.

4 Do not be of two minds or speak from both sides of your mouth, for speaking from both sides of your mouth is a deadly trap.

5 Your word must not be empty or false.

6 Do not be greedy, rapacious, hypocritical, spiteful, or haughty. Do not entertain a wicked plot against your neighbor.

7 Do not hate anyone—but reprove some, pray for others, and love still others more than yourself.

3 My child, flee from all evil and everything like it.

2 Do not be prone to anger, for anger leads to murder; nor be zealous, contentious, or irascible. For from all these are born acts of murder.

3 My child, do not be filled with passion, for passion leads to sexual immorality; nor be foul-mouthed or lecherous. For from all these are born acts of adultery.

4 My child, do not practice divination[12] since this leads to idolatry; nor use incantations or astrology or rites of purification, nor even wish to see or hear these things. For from all these is born idolatry.

5 My child, do not be a liar, since lying leads to robbery; nor be fond of money or vain. For from all these are born acts of robbery.

6 My child, do not be a complainer, since this leads to blasphemy; nor be insolent or evil-minded. For from all these are born blasphemies.

7 But be meek, since the meek will inherit the earth.[13]

8 Be patient, merciful, innocent, gentle, and good, trembling at the words you have heard.

9 Do not exalt yourself or become impertinent. You should not join forces with the high and mighty, but should associate with the upright and humble.

10 Welcome whatever happens to you as good, knowing that nothing occurs apart from God.

4 My child, night and day remember the one who speaks the word of God to you; honor him as the Lord. For where his lordship is discussed, there the Lord himself is.

2 Every day seek out the company of the saints, that you may find comfort in their words.

3 Do not create a schism, but bring peace to those who are at odds. Give a fair judgment; do not show favoritism when you reproach others for their unlawful acts.

4 Do not be of two minds, whether this should happen or not.

5 Do not be one who reaches out your hands to receive but draws them back from giving.

---

8 Luke 6:30.

9 Cf. Matt 5:26; Luke 12:59.

10 Source unknown.

11 The following passage elaborates Exod 20:13–17; cf. Matt 19:18; 5:33.

12 I.e., through the flight of birds.

13 Matt 5:5; Ps 37:11.

6 If you acquire something with your hands, give it as a ransom for your sins.

7 Do not doubt whether to give, nor grumble while giving. For you should recognize the good paymaster of the reward.

8 Do not shun a person in need, but share all things with your brother and do not say that anything is your own.[14] For if you are partners in what is immortal, how much more in what is mortal?

9 Do not remove your hand from *[Or: Do not refrain from disciplining; or: Do not shirk your responsibility towards]* your son or daughter, but from their youth teach them the reverential fear of God.

10 Do not give orders to your male slave or female servant—who hope in the same God—out of bitterness, lest they stop fearing the God who is over you both. For he does not come to call those of high status, but those whom the Spirit has prepared.

11 And you who are slaves must be subject to your masters as to a replica of God, with respect and referential fear.

12 Hate all hypocrisy and everything that is not pleasing to the Lord.

13 Do not abandon the commandments of the Lord, but guard what you have received, neither adding to them nor taking away.[15]

14 Confess your unlawful acts in church, and do not come to your prayer with an evil conscience. This is the path of life.

5 And the path of death is this. First of all it is evil and filled with a curse: murders, adulteries, passions, sexual immoralities, robberies, idolatries, feats of magic, sorceries, rapacious acts, false testimonies, hypocrisies, split affection, deceit, arrogance, malice, insolence, greed, obscenity, jealousy, impertinence, pride, haughtiness, irreverence.

2 It is filled with persecutors of the good, haters of the truth, lovers of the lie, who do not know the reward of righteousness, nor cling to the good nor to a fair judgment, who are alert not to do good but to do evil; from whom meekness and patience are far removed. For they love what is vain and pursue a reward, showing no mercy to the poor nor toiling for the oppressed nor knowing the one who made them; murderers of children and corruptors of what God has fashioned, who turn their backs on the needy, oppress the afflicted, and support the wealthy. They are lawless judges of the impoverished, altogether sinful. Be delivered, children, from all such people.

---

14 Acts 4:32.

15 Deut 4:2; 12:32.

91. Clement of Alexandria: "The Educator"

In addition to Clement's *Stromateis* (see Chapter 14), others of his writings deal with important ethical issues, such as his sermon, "What Rich Person Will Be Saved?" Of particular importance is his three-volume treatise called the *Paedagogas*, literally "The Educator." Here Clement portrays Christ as the teacher who molds the character of his followers by revealing how they ought to live.

Clement of Alexandria: "The Educator," from *Clement of Alexandria: Christ the Educator*, ed. Simon P. Wood. Fathers of the Church, 23; Washington, DC: Catholic University Press of America, 1954. Used with permission.

The following selection is important for showing how already, by the beginning of the third century, church leaders were concerned with every aspect of a Christian's public and private life, including such matters as personal eating and drinking habits, sleep and exercise, use of humor, public manners, sexual activities (even within marriage), and the use of public baths.

Book 2

1 In keeping with the purpose we have in mind, we must now select passages from the Scriptures that bear on education in the practical needs of life, and describe the sort of life he who is called a Christian should live throughout his life. We should begin with ourselves, and with the way we should regulate [our actions]. . . .

Other people, indeed, live that they may eat, just like unreasoning beasts; for them life is only their belly. But as for us, our Educator has given the command that we eat only to live. Eating is not our main occupation, nor is pleasure our chief ambition. Food is permitted us simply because of our stay in this world, which the Word is shaping for immortality by his education. Our food should be plain and ungarnished, in keeping with the truth, suitable to children who are plain and unpretentious, adapted to maintaining life, not self-indulgence. . . .

We must shun gluttony and partake of only a few things that are necessary. And if some unbeliever invites us to a banquet and we decide to accept—although it is well not to associate with the disorderly—[the apostle] bids us eat what is set before us, "asking no question for conscience' sake."[1] We do not need to abstain from rich foods completely, but we should not be anxious for them. We must partake of what is set before us, as becomes a Christian, out of respect for him who has invited us and not to lessen or destroy the sociability of the gathering. We should consider the rich variety of dishes that are served as a matter of indifference, and despise delicacies as things that

after a while will cease to be. "Let not him who eats despise him who does not eat, and let not him who does not eat judge him who eats."[2] A little later [the apostle] explains the reason for his command: "He who eats," he says, "eats for the Lord and he gives thanks to God. And he who does not eat, abstains for the Lord and gives thanks to God."[3] We conclude, then, that the true food is thanksgiving. At any rate, he who always offers up thanks will not indulge excessively in pleasure. . . .

Only a fool will hold his breath and gape at what is set before him at a public banquet, expressing his delight in words. But it is only a greater fool who will let his eyes become enslaved to these exotic delicacies, and allow self-control to be swept away, as it were, with the various dishes. Is it not utterly inane to keep leaning forward from one's couch, all but falling on one's nose into the dishes, as though, according to the common saying, one were leaning out from the nest of the couch to catch the escaping vapors with the nostrils? Is it not completely contrary to reason to keep dipping one's hands into these pastries or to be forever stretching them out for some dish, gorging oneself intemperately and boorishly, not like a person tasting a food, but like one taking it by storm? It is easy to consider such people swine or dogs rather than humans, because of their voraciousness. They are in such a hurry to stuff themselves that both cheeks are puffed out at the same time, all the hollows of their face are filled out, and sweat even rolls down

1 1 Cor 10:27.

2 Rom 14:3.
3 Rom 14:6.

as they exert themselves to satisfy their insatiable appetite, wheezing from their intemperance, and cramming food into their stomachs with incredible energy, as though they were gathering a crop for storage rather than nourishment.

Lack of moderation, an evil wherever it is found, is particularly blameworthy in the matter of food. Gourmandising, at least, is nothing more than immoderate use of delicacies; gluttony is a mania for glutting the appetite, and belly-madness, as the name itself suggests, is lack of self-control with regard to food. The apostle, in speaking of those who offend at a banquet, exclaims: "For at the meal, each one takes first his own supper, and one is hungry, and another drinks overmuch. Have you not houses for your eating and drinking? Or do you despise the church of God and put to shame the needy?"[4] If a person is wealthy, yet eats without restraint and shows himself insatiable, he disgraces himself in a special way and does wrong on two scores: first, he adds to the burden of those who do not have, and lays bare, before those who do have, his own lack of temperance. Little wonder, then, that the apostle, after having taken to task those who were shamelessly lavish with their meals, and those who were voracious, never getting their fill, cried out a second time with an angry voice: "Wherefore, my brethren, when you come together to eat, wait for one another. If anyone is hungry, let him eat at home, lest you come together unto judgment."[5]

Therefore, we must keep ourselves free of any suspicion of boorishness or of intemperance, by partaking of what is set before us politely, keeping our hands, as well as our chin and our couch, clean, and by preserving proper decorum of conduct, without twisting about or acting unmannerly while we are swallowing our food. Rather, we should put our hand out only in turn, from time to time; keep from speaking while eating, for speech is inarticulate and ill-mannered when the mouth is full, and the tongue, impeded by the food, cannot function properly but utters only indistinct sounds. It is not polite to eat and drink at the same time, either, because it indicates extreme intemperance to try to do two things together that need to be done separately. . . .

Lavishness is not capable of being enjoyed alone; it must be bestowed upon others. That is why we should shy away from foods that arouse the appetite and lead us to eat when we are not hungry. Even in moderate frugality, is there not a rich and wholesome variety? Roots, olives, all sorts of green vegetables, milk, cheese, fruits, and cooked vegetables of all sorts, but without the sauces. And should there be need for meat, boiled, or dressed, let it be given. "Have you anything here to eat?" the Lord asked his apostles after his resurrection. "And they offered him a piece of broiled fish," because he had taught them to practise frugality. "And when he had finished eating, he said to them," and Luke goes on to record all that he said.[6] We should not overlook the fact, either, that they who dine according to reason, or, rather, according to the Word, are not required to leave sweetmeats and honey out of their fare. Surely, of all the foods available, the most convenient are those which can be used immediately without being cooked. Inexpensive foods come next in order, since these are so accessible, as we have already said.

As long as those other fellows stay hunched over their groaning tables, catering to their lusts, the devil of gluttony leads them by the nose. I, for one, would not hesitate to call that devil the devil of the belly, the most wicked and deadly of them all. He is very much like the so-called *engastrimythos,* because he speaks, as it were, through his belly. It is far better to possess happiness than to have any daemon as a companion; happiness is the practise of the virtues.

Matthew the apostle used to make his meal on seeds and nuts and herbs, without flesh meat; John,

---

4 1 Cor 11:21.

5 1 Cor 11:23.

6 Luke 24:41–44.

maintaining extreme self-restraint, ate locusts and wild-honey, and Peter abstained from pork. But, "he fell into an ecstasy," it is written in the Acts of the Apostles, "and saw heaven standing open and a certain vessel let down by the four corners to the earth; and in it were all the four-footed beasts and creeping things of the earth and birds of the air. And there came a voice to him: Arise and kill and eat. But Peter said: Far be it from me, Lord, for never did I eat anything common or unclean. And there came a voice a second time to him: What God has cleansed, do not thou call common."[7] The use of these foods is a matter of indifference for us, too, "for not that which goes into the mouth defiles a person."[8] but the barren pursuit of wantonness. When God formed man, He said: "All these things will be food for you."[9]

"Herbs with love rather than a fatted calf with deceit."[10] This is reminiscent of what we said before, that herbs are not the agapê, but that meals should be taken with charity. A middle course is good in all things, and no less so in serving a banquet. Extremes, in fact, are dangerous, but the mean is good, and all that avoids dire need is a mean. Natural desires have a limit set to them by self-sufficiency. . . .

2 "Use a little wine," the apostle cautions the water-drinking Timothy, "use a little wine for your stomach's sake."[11] Shrewdly, he recommends a stimulating remedy for a body become ill-disposed and requiring medical attention, but he adds "a little," lest the remedy, taken too freely, itself come to need a cure.

Now, the natural and pure drink demanded by ordinary thirst is water. This it was that the Lord supplied for the Hebrews, causing it to gush from the split rock, as their only drink, a drink of

---

7 Acts 10:10–15.

8 Matt 15:11.

9 Gen 1:29.

10 Prov 15:17.

11 1 Tim 5:23.

sobriety; it was particularly necessary that they who were still wandering should keep far from wine. . . .

I have, then, only admiration for those who profess an austere life, limiting their desires to water, nourishment of sobriety, and avoiding wine as completely as they can, as they would the least threat of fire. It is conceded that boys and girls should, as a general rule, be kept from this sort of drink. It is not well for flaming youth to be filled with the most inflammable of all liquids, wine, for that would be like pouring fire upon fire. When they are under its influence, wild impulses, festering lusts, and hot-bloodedness are aroused; youths already on fire within are so much on the verge of satisfying their passions that the injury inflicted on them becomes evident by anticipation in their bodies, that is, the organs of lust mature before they should. I mean that, as the wine takes effect, the youths begin to grow heated from passion, without inhibition, and the breasts and sexual organs swell as a harbinger and an image of the act of fornication. The wound in their soul compels the body to manifest all the signs of passion, and the unrestrained throbbings aroused by temptation drive on into sin the curiosity of him who before had been sinless. At that point, the freshness of youth has exceeded the bounds of modesty. Therefore, it is imperative to attempt to extinguish the beginnings of passion in the young, as far as possible: first, by excluding them from all that will inflame them—Bacchus and his threat—and second, by pouring on the antidote that will restrain the smouldering soul, contain the aroused sexual movements, and calm the agitation of the storm-tossed desires.

As for adults, when they take their midday lunch, if that is their practise, let them take only a little bread and no liquids at all, so that the excessive moisture in their bodies may be assimilated and absorbed by the dry food. It is an indication, in fact, of disorder in the body caused by an excessive accumulation of liquids flowing through it, if we need to blow our noses constantly and experience a persistent urge to urinate. If they should become thirsty, let them relieve their thirst with water, but not too much of it. It is not good to drink water too freely, lest the food be simply washed away; the meal should be masticated to prepare it for digestion, only a little of it finally passing off as waste.

Minds that bear something of the divine should not be overcome with wine for another reason, too. "Strong wine," in the words of the comic poet, "keeps a man from thinking many thoughts"[12]—or, in fact, from being wise at all. But toward evening, near the time for supper, we may use wine, since we are no longer engaged in the public lectures which demand the absence of wine. At that time of day, the temperature has turned cooler than it was at midday, so that we need to stimulate the failing natural heat of the body with a little artificial warmth. But, even then, we must use only a little wine; certainly, we should not go so far as to demand whole bowls of it, because that would be sheer extravagance.

Again, those who have already passed the prime of life may be permitted more readily to enjoy their cup. They are but harmlessly making use of the medicine of wine to stimulate new warmth for the growing chill of old age as its heat dies down with the years. The passions of the aged are, for the most part, no longer storm-tossed with the threat of shipwreck from intemperance. Securely moored by the anchors of reason and of maturity, they easily bear the violent storm of passion aroused by drink, and they can even indulge in the merriment of feasts with composure. But, even for them, there is a limit: the point where they can still keep their minds clear, their memories active, and their bodies steady and under control, despite the wine. Those who know about these things call this the last drop before too much. It is well to stop short before this point, for fear of disaster.

A certain Artorius, I recall, in a book on longevity, is of the opinion that we should drink only so much as is needed to moisten our food, if we would live a long life. It is certainly a good idea to use wine, as some do, only for the sake of health, as a tonic, or for relaxation and enjoyment, as others do. Wine makes the person who drinks more mellow toward himself, better disposed toward his servants, and more genial with his friends. But, when he is overcome by wine, then he returns every offense of a drunken neighbor.

Wine is warm and gives out a sweet smell; therefore, in the proper mixture it thaws out the constipation of the intestines and with its sweetness dilutes every pungent or offensive odor. A quotation from Scripture will express it aptly: "Wine drunken with moderation was created from the beginning as the joy of the soul and of the heart."[13] But it is wise to dilute the wine with as much water as possible (and to avoid depending upon it as we do water), as well as to restrain our appetite for drinking bouts and to keep from drinking wine like water simply from intemperance. Both are creatures of God, and so the mixture of both, water and wine, contributes to our health. Life is made up of what is necessary, together with what is merely useful. The merely useful should be combined with a very large part of what is necessary, that is, with water.

When wine is indulged in too freely, the tongue becomes thick, the jaw sags, the eyes begin to roll, for all the world as if they were swimming in pools of moisture, and the vision, forced to deceive, conceives everything as going round in a circle, and is not sure whether things are single or double. "Indeed, I think I see two suns," the old Theban in his cups complained.[14] Truly, the sense of sight is deranged by the heat of wine and imagines it sees many times over what is only one. But there is no difference between deranging the sense of sight and distorting the object that is seen: in either case, the vision is affected the same way in its derangement and cannot accurately perceive the object. Similarly, the gait takes on the appearance of being swept along in a stream, and then there arises, as maids-in-waiting, hiccoughing,

---

12 Menander *Fragment* 779.

13 Sirach 31:27–28.

14 Euripidus, *Bacch* 918.

retching, and silliness. For, "every man overcome by wine," says the tragedian, "becomes subject to his passions and empty of mind, pours out idle chatter and is forced to hear against his will things he had said so willingly."[15] Even before these words were written, Wisdom had warned: "Wine drunken with excess raises quarrels and many ruins."[16] . . .

5 . . . As for laughter itself, it, too, should be kept under restraint. Of course, when it rings out as it should, it proves the presence of discipline, but if it gets out of hand, it is a sure index of lack of self-control. We need not take away from a person any of the things that are natural to him, but only set a limit and due proportion to them. It is true that a human is an animal who can laugh; but it is not true that he therefore should laugh at everything. The horse is an animal that neighs, yet it does not neigh at everything. As rational animals, we must ever maintain proper balance, gently relaxing the rigor of seriousness and intensity without dissipating it out of all bounds.

Now, the proper relaxation of the features within due limits—as though the face were a musical instrument—is called a smile (that is the way joy is reflected on the face); it is the good humor of the self-contained. But the sudden loss of control over one's composure, in the case of women, is called a giggle, the laugh of harlots, and in the case of men, a guffaw, the laughter of idle suitors, offensive to the ear. "A fool lifts up his voice in laughter," Scripture says, "but a cunning person will scarce laugh low to himself."[17] The one called cunning here is really the prudent person, just the opposite of a fool. On the other hand, we should not become gloomy, either; only serious-minded. I certainly welcome the smiling fellow who showed up with a smile on his grim face, for then his laughter would be less disdainful.

It is well that even the smile be kept under the influence of the Educator. If it is a question of indecencies, we should make it plain that we are blushing in shame, rather than smiling, lest we be thought to give consent and agreement. If it is some misfortune, we should not manifest a light-hearted appearance, but look sorrowfully sober. That indicates human tact; the other would be cruelty. But, we should not be always laughing—that would be lack of judgment—nor should we laugh in the presence of older persons or of those who deserve respect, unless, perhaps, they themselves make some witticism to put us at our ease. Nor should we give way to laughter with every chance companion, nor in every place, nor at everything, nor with everyone. Laughter can easily give rise to misunderstandings, particularly among boys and women. . . .

7 . . . If we meet at banquets for charity's sake, and if the purpose of such feasts is the good-fellowship created among the guests, with the food and drink merely accessories of charity, then should we not maintain a behavior that bespeaks the control of reason? (Incidentally, we need not impoverish ourselves to practise charity.) And if we gather with the intention of showing good-will toward one another, then why do we stir up ill-will by railing at others? It is better to keep silent than to engage in bickering, adding the fault of deed to that of boorishness. Surely, "blessed is the one that has not slipped by a word out of his mouth, and is not pricked with the remorse of sin."[18] or at least has repented of the sins committed in speech, or has conversed without inflicting pain on anyone. . . .

Let young men and women be kept from banquets of this sort, as a general rule, so that they may not fall into any improper misconduct. There can be no doubt that the indecent things heard, and the unbecoming things seen, unsettle their faith, set their imagination afire, and add fuel to the natural fickleness of their youth to make them

---

15 Sophocles *Frag* 843.

16 Sirach 31:29.

17 Sirach 21:20.

18 Sirach 14:1.

ready victims of their passions. At times, too, they are to blame for the fall of others, proving how dangerous an occasion such a banquet can be. It is a good command that Wisdom gives: "Sit not at all with another man's wife, nor repose upon a couch with her," that is, do not dine or eat with her too often. Then it adds: "Do not have a meal with her in wine, lest perhaps your heart decline toward her, and by your blood, you fall into destruction."[19] Drinking unrestrainedly is dangerous because it can so easily degenerate into licentiousness. Scripture speaks of "another man's wife," because there is a greater danger in such a case of destroying the wedding bond.

But, if there arise any need for women to be present, let them be amply clothed: exteriorly with a cloak, interiorly with modesty. The worst accusation that can be brought against any woman not subject to a husband is that she was present at a party for men, and, at that, for men in their cups. And as for young men, let them keep their eyes fixed on their own couch, lean on their elbow without too much fidgeting, and be present only with their ears. If they should be sitting down, let them not put their feet one on top of the other, nor cross their legs, nor rest their chin on their hands. It is lack of good breeding to fail to support oneself, yet a fault common in the young. To be forever restlessly shifting one's position argues for levity of character. . . .

Then, too, whistling and hissing and snapping the fingers—all sounds made to summon servants—should not be used by people who have the ability to speak, since these are wordless signals. At banquets, we should not be forever spitting or violently coughing or blowing our nose. We must consider the feelings of our companions at table, and avoid disgusting or nauseating them by our crude conduct, testifying to our own lack of self-control. Not even cattle or asses relieve nature at their feeding troughs, yet many people blow their nose and keep spitting while engaged at table. Again, if a sneeze take us by surprise, or,

even more so, a belch, we need not deafen our neighbor with the noise and in so doing exhibit our lack of manners. A belch should be released silently, as we exhale, with our mouths shut, not wide open and gaping like the masks of the tragedy. The irritation that causes a sneeze may be relieved by quietly holding the breath; therefore, we should suppress the accumulated force of the breath politely by controlling our exhaling, so as to try to pass unnoticed if some of the excessive air, under pressure, escapes.

It is a sign of boorishness and of lack of discipline to want to add to the noises, rather than lessen them. And those who scrape their teeth so much that they draw blood from their gums, besides injuring themselves, also annoy their companions. And beyond a doubt, scratching the ear and irritations to prompt sneezing are gestures proper to swine, suggestive of the search for immoral pleasures. Unbecoming glances and indecent conversations about such things must be renounced. Let the gaze be composed, and the movement of the head and the gestures be steady, as well as the motion of the hands in conversation. In general, the Christian is, by nature, a person of gentleness and quiet, of serenity and peace. . . .

9 Now we must discuss the way we are to sleep, still mindful of the precepts of temperance. After our dinner, once we have given thanks to God for having granted us such pleasures and for the completion of the day, then we should dispose our minds for sleep. We must forbid ourselves the use of expensive bedding, gold-sprinkled rugs and plain carpets embroidered in gold, rich purple bed robes or precious thick cloaks, purple blankets of elaborate art, with fleecy cloaks thrown over them, and beds too soft to be slept in. The habit of sleeping in soft down is injurious, apart from the danger of pampering the body, because those who sleep in it sink deep into the softness of the bed; it is not healthy for the sleeper who cannot move about in it because of the high elevation on either side of his body. Sleep is the time for digesting food, but such a bed causes the food simply to

---

19 Sirach 9:9.

bum up and be destroyed, while those who can toss about on their beds, level as though a natural place of exercise during sleep, digest their food more easily and prepare themselves the better to face any contingencies. . . .

Following the dictates of reason, then, we should make use of a bed that is level and unadorned, yet affording some minimum of convenience: of protection, if it be summer; of warmth, if it be winter. Let the couch, too, be unadorned and its posts plain, for ornamented and molded wood readily and frequently becomes an easy path for creeping animals, providing them sure footing in the grooves carved by the craftsmen. But we must specially keep the softness of the bed within limits, for sleep is meant to relax the body, not to debilitate it. For that reason, I say that sleep should be taken not as self-indulgence, but as rest from activity. . . .

10 It remains for us now to consider the restriction of sexual intercourse to those who are joined in wedlock. Begetting children is the goal of those who wed, and the fulfillment of that goal is a large family, just as hope of a crop drives the farmer to sow his seed, while the fulfillment of his hope is the actual harvesting of the crop. But he who sow in a living soil is far superior, for the one tills the land to provide food only for a season, the other to secure the preservation of the whole human race; the one tends his crop for himself, the other, for God. We have received the command: "Be fruitful,"[20] and we must obey. In this role man becomes like God, because he cooperates, in his human way, in the birth of another person.

Now, not every land is suited to the reception of seed, and, even if it were, not at the hands of the same farmer. Seed should not be sown on rocky ground nor scattered everywhere, for it is the primary substance of generation and contains imbedded in itself the principle of nature. It is undeniably godless, then, to dishonor principles of nature by

wasting them on unnatural resting places. In fact, you recall how Moses, in his wisdom, once denounced seed that bears no fruit, saying symbolically: "Do not eat the hare nor the hyena."[21] He does not want a person to be contaminated by their traits nor even to taste of their wantonness, for these animals have an insatiable appetite for coition. As regards the hare, legend claims that it needs to void excrement only once a year, and possesses as many anuses as the years it has lived. Therefore, the prohibition against eating the hare is nothing else than a condemnation of pederasty. And with regard to the hyena, it is said that the male changes every year successively into a female, so that Moses means that he who abstains from the hyena is commanded not to lust after adultery.[22]

While I agree that the all-wise Moses means, by this prohibition just mentioned, that we should not become like these beasts, I do not entirely agree with the explanation given these symbolic prohibitions. A nature can never be made to change; what has been once formed in it cannot be reformed by any sort of change. Change does not involve the nature itself; it necessarily modifies, but does not transform the structure. For instance, although many birds are said to change their color and their voice according to the season (like the blackbird which changes its black feathers to yellow, and its melodious voice to a harsh one, or the nightingale which changes its plumage and song at the same time), even so, their nature itself is not so affected that a male becomes female. Rather, a new growth of feathers, like a new garment, is bright with one color, but a little later, as winter threatens, it fades away, like a flower when its color goes. In the same way, the voice, affected unfavorably by the cold, loses its vibrancy: the surface of the whole body contracts with the climate, and the bronchial tubes, narrowly constricted in the throat, restrict the breath to the point that it is made quite muffled and capable of producing only harsh sounds. Later on,

20 Gen 1:28.

21 Deut 14:7.

22 *Barn* 10:6–7.

in the spring, responding to the weather and relaxing, the breath is once again freed of all constraint and is carried through passages that were tightly closed but are now wide open. No longer does the voice croak in dying tones, but bursts forth clear, pouring out in full-throated voice, and now in springtime there arises melodious song from the throats of the birds.

Therefore, we should not believe at all that the hyena changes its sex. Neither does it possess both the male and the female sexual organs at the same time, as some claim, conjuring up some freakish hermaphrodite and creating this female-male, a third new category halfway in between the male and the female. Erroneously they misconstrue the strategy of nature, mother of all and author of all existence. Because the hyena is of all animals the most sensual, there is a knob of flesh underneath its tail, in front of the anus, closely resembling the female sex organ in shape. It is not a passage, I mean it serves no useful purpose, opening neither into the womb nor into the intestines. It has only a good-sized opening to permit an ineffective sexual act when the vagina is preparing for childbirth and is impenetrable. This is characteristic of both male and female hyena, because of hyperactive abnormal sexuality; the male lies with the male so that it rarely approaches the female. For that reason, births are infrequent among hyenas, because they so freely sow their seed contrary to nature.

This is the reason, I believe, that Plato, in excoriating pederasty in *Phaedrus,* terms it bestiality and says that these libertines who have so surrendered to pleasure, "taking the bit in their own mouths, like brutish beasts rush on to enjoy and beget."[23] Such godless people "God has given over," the apostle says, "to shameful lusts. For the women change their natural use to that which is against nature, and in like manner the men, also, having abandoned the natural use of the women, have burned in their lusts one towards another, men with men doing shameful things, and receiving in themselves the fitting recompense of their

perversity."[24] Yet, nature has not allowed even the most sensual of beasts to sexually misuse the passage made for excrement. Urine she gathers into the bladder; undigested food in the intestines; tears in the eyes; blood in the veins; wax in the ear, and mucous in the nose; so, too, there is a passage connected to the end of the intestines by means of which excrement is passed off. In the case of hyenas, nature, in her diversity, has added this additional organ to accomodate their excessive sexual activity. Therefore, it is large enough for the service of the lusting organs, but its opening is obstructed within. In short, it is not made to serve any purpose in generation. The clear conclusion that we must draw, then, is that we must condemn sodomy, all fruitless sowing of seed, any unnatural methods of holding intercourse and the reversal of the sexual role in intercourse. We must rather follow the guidance of nature, which obviously disapproves of such practises from the very way she has fashioned the male organ, adapted not for receiving the seed, but for implanting it. When Jeremiah, or, rather, the Spirit through him, said: "The cave of the hyena is my home,"[25] he was resorting to an expressive figure to excoriate idolatry and to manifest his scorn for the nourishment provided for dead bodies. The house of the living God surely ought to be free of idols.

Again, Moses issued a prohibition against eating the hare. The hare is forever mounting the female, leaping upon her crouching form from behind. In fact, this manner of having intercourse is a characteristic of the hare. The female conceives every month, and, even before the first offspring is born, she become pregnant again. She conceives and begets, and as soon as she gives birth is fertilized again by the first hare she meets. Not satisfied with one mate, she conceives again, although she is still nursing. The explanation is that the female hare has a double womb, and therefore her desire for intercourse is stimulated not only by the emptiness of the womb, in that

---

23 *Phaedr* 254, 250E.

24 Rom 1:26–27.

25 Jer 12:9.

every empty space seeks to be filled, but also, when she is with young, her other womb begins to feel lustful desires. That is why hares have one birth after the other. So the mysterious prohibition [of Moses] in reality is but counsel to restrain violent sexual impulses, and intercourse is too frequent succession, relations with a pregnant woman, pederasty, adultery, and lewdness. . . .

We should consider boys as our sons, and the wives of other men as our daughters. We must keep a firm control over the pleasures of the stomach, and an absolutely uncompromising control over the organs beneath the stomach. If, as the Stoics teach, we should not move even a finger on mere impulse, how much more necessary is it that they who seek wisdom control the organ of intercourse? I feel that the reason this organ is also called the private part is that we are to treat it with privacy and modesty more than we do any other member. In lawful wedlock, as with eating, nature permits whatever is comfortable to nature and helpful and decent; it allows us to desire the act of procreation. However, whoever is guilty of excess sins against nature and, by violating the laws regulating intercourse, harms himself. First of all, it is decidedly wrong ever to touch youths in any sexual way as though they were girls. The philosopher who learned from Moses taught; "Do not sow seeds on rocks and stones, on which they will never take root."[26] The Word, too, commands emphatically, through Moses: "You shall not lie with mankind as with womankind, for it is an abomination."[27] Again, further on, noble Plato advises: "Abstain from every female field of increase,"[28] because it does not belong to you. (He had read this in the holy Scripture and from it had taken the law: "You shall not give the coition of your seed to your neighbor's wife, to be defiled because of her."[29]) Then he goes on to say: "Do not sow the

unconsecrated and bastard seed with concubines, where you would not want what is sown to grow."[30] In fact, he says: "Do not touch anyone, except your wedded wife,"[31] because she is the only one with whom it is lawful to enjoy the pleasures of the flesh for the purpose of begetting lawful heirs. This is a share in God's own work of creation, and in such a work the seed ought not be wasted nor scattered thoughtlessly nor sown in a way it cannot grow. As an illustration of this last restriction, the same Moses forbade the Jews to approach even their own wives if they happened to be in the period of menstruation.[32] The reason is that it is wrong to contaminate fertile seed, destined to become a human being, with corrupt matter of the body, or to allow it be diverted from the furrow of the womb and swept away in a fetid flow of matter and excrement.

He discouraged the ancient Jews, also, from having relations with a wife already with child. Pleasure sought for its own sake, even within the marriage bonds, is a sin and contrary both to law and to reason. Moses cautioned them, then, to keep away from their pregnant wives until they be delivered. In fact, the womb, situated just below the bladder and above the part of the intestine known as the rectum, extends its neck in between the edges of the bladder, and the outlet of this neck, by which the sperm enters, closes tight when the womb is full, opening again only when delivered of the fetus. It is only when it has become empty of its fruit that it can receive the sperm again. (It is not wrong for us to name the organs of generation, when God is not ashamed of their function.) The womb welcomes the seed when it yearns for procreation, but it refuses the seed when intercourse is contrary to nature; that is, once impregnated, it makes immoral relations impossible by drawing its neck tight together. All its instincts, up to now aroused by loving intercourse,

---

26 Plato, *Laws* 328E.

27 Lev 18:22.

28 *Laws* 828E.

29 Lev 18:20.

---

30 *Laws* 839A.

31 *Laws* 841D.

32 Lev 15:19.

begin to be directed differently, absorbed in the development of the child within, co-operating with the Creator. It is wrong, indeed, to interfere with the workings of nature by indulging in the extravagances of wantonness. . . .

In my treatise on continence, I have discussed in a general way the question whether we should marry or not (and this is the point of our investigation). Now, if we have to consider whether we may marry at all, then how can we possibly permit ourselves to indulge in intercourse each time without restraint, as we would food, as if it were a necessity? Certainly, we can see at a glance that the nerves are strained by it as on a loom and, in the intense feeling aroused by intercourse, are stretched to the breaking point. It spreads a mist over the senses and tires the muscles. This is obvious in irrational animals and in men in training. Of these last, those who practise abstinence while engaging in contests get the best of their opponents; while animals are easily captured if they are caught at and all but torn from coition, because then they are entirely emptied of strength and energy.

The sophist of Abdera called intercourse "a minor epilepsy," and considered it an incurable disease. Indeed, does not lassitude succeed intercourse because of the quantity of seed lost? "For a man is formed and torn out of a man."[33] See how much harm is done. A whole man is torn out when the seed is lost in intercourse. "This is bone of my bone, and flesh of my flesh,"[34] Scripture says. Man is emptied of as much seed as is needed for a body that can be seen. After all, that which is separated from him is the beginning of a new birth. Besides that, the very agitation of matter upsets and disturbs the harmony of his whole body. Wise indeed was he who replied to someone asking him his attitude toward the pleasures of sex: "O man, quiet! I have been supremely happy in avoiding them as a fierce and wild tyrant."[35]

Yet marriage in itself merits esteem and the highest approval, for the Lord wished people to "be fruitful and multiply."[36] He did not tell them, however, to act like libertines, nor did he intend them to surrender themselves to pleasure as though born only to indulge in sexual relations. Let the Educator put us to shame with the word of Ezechiel: "Put away your fornications."[37] Why, even unreasoning beasts know enough not to mate at certain times. To indulge in intercourse without intending children is to outrage nature, whom we should take as our instructor. Her wise directions concerning the periods of life are meant to be obeyed; I mean that she allows us to marry at any time but after the advent of old age and during childhood (for she does not permit the one to marry yet, the other, any more). The attempt to procreate children is marriage, but the promiscuous scattering of seed contrary to law and to reason definitely is not. If we should but control our lusts at the start and if we would not kill off the human race born and developing according to the divine plan, then our whole lives would be lived according to nature. But women who resort to some sort of deadly abortion drug kill not only the embryo but, along with it, all human kindness.

Those whom nature has joined in wedlock need the Educator that they might learn not to celebrate the mystic rites of nature during the day, nor like the rooster copulate at dawn, or after they have come from church, or even from the market, when they should be praying or reading or performing the good works that are best done by day. In the evening, after dinner, it is proper to retire after giving thanks for the good things that have been received. Sometimes, nature denies them the opportunity to accomplish the marriage act so that it may be all the more desirable because it is delayed. Yet, they must not forget modesty at night time under the pretext of the cover of darkness; like the light of reason, modesty must ever

---

33 Democritus *Frag* 86?

34 Gen 2:23.

35 Sophocles? Cf. Plato *Republic* 329 B.C.

---

36 Gen 1:28.

37 Ezek 43:9.

dwell in their souls. If we weave the ideals of chastity by day and then unravel them in the marriage bed at night, we do not better than Penelope at her loom. Certainly, if we are required to practise self-control—as we are—we ought to manifest it even more with our wives, in the way we avoid every indecency in intimate embraces. Let the reliability and trustworthiness of the husband's purity in his dealings with his neighbor be present also in his home. He cannot possibly enjoy a reputation for self-control with his wife if she can see no signs of self-control in such intense acts of pleasure. Love, which tends toward sexual relations by its very nature, is in full bloom only for a time, then grows old with the body; but sometimes, if immoral pleasure mars the chastity of the marriage bed, desire becomes insipid and love ages before the body does. The hearts of lovers have wings; affection can be quenched by a change of heart, and love can turn into hate if there creep in too many grounds for loss of respect. . . .

Book 3

9 There are four reasons prompting us to frequent the baths (it was at this point that I digressed a while back in my discussion): either for cleanliness, for warmth, for health, or for the satisfaction of pleasure. We must not think of bathing for pleasure, because we must ruthlessly expel all unworthy pleasure. Women may make use of the bath for the sake of cleanliness and of health; men, only for the sake of their health. The motive of seeking warmth is scarcely urgent, since we can find relief from cold in other ways.

The continued use of baths undermines a man's strength, weakening the muscles of his body and often inducing lassitude and even fainting spells. Bodies drink up water in a definite way in the baths, like trees, not only by mouth, but also, as they say, through the pores of the whole body. A proof of this is that, often, when a man has been thirsty, his thirst is quenched on entering the water. Therefore, if the bath has no real benefit to offer, it should be completely avoided.

The ancients called it a fulling shop for men, since it wrinkles the body before time, and forces the body to become old early; in much the way that iron is tempered by heat, the flesh is made soft by heat. We need to be hardened, as it were, by being doused in cold.

We ought not bathe on every occasion, either, but if at times we are too hungry, or too full, we should omit it. As a matter of fact, [it should be adjusted] to the age of the individual, and to the season of the year. It is not useful at all times, nor to everyone at all times, as those versed in these things agree. Due proportion is sufficient guide for us; we call upon it for help in every part of our life. Again, we should not linger in the bath so long that we will need someone to lead us out by the hand, nor should we loiter long or frequently in it, as we might in the public square. Finally, to have a score of servants pouring water over one is grievously to offend a neighbor; it is a sign of one far advanced in self-indulgence and unwilling to understand that the bath should be common, on an equal footing to all who bathe there.

It is our souls, above all, that we should wash in the purifying Word; only now and then, our bodies, to get rid of the dirt that adheres to them, and, sometimes, to refresh ourselves after hard labor. "Woe to you, Scribes and Pharisees," the Lord says, "hypocrites! For you are like whitened tombs; outwardly the tomb appears beautiful, but within it is full of dead men's bones and of all uncleanness."[38] And again he said to them: "Woe to you, because you clean the outside of the cup and of the plate, but within are full of uncleanness. Cleanse first the inside of the cup that the outside may also become clean."[39]

The most excellent cleansing is that which removes the filth of the soul, and is a spiritual bath; the inspired word says about such a cleansing: "The Lord shall wash away the filth of the sons and daughters of Israel and shall wash away the blood

---

38 Matt 23:27.
39 Matt 23:25.

from their midst,"[40] that is, the blood of immorality, as well as the slaughtering of the prophets; that is the purification he meant, because he adds: "by the spirit of judgment and by the spirit of burning." But the washing of the body is something material and is accomplished only by water; in fact, it can be done even in fields away from the baths.

10 The gymnasium is sufficient for the needs of young boys, even if there is a bath at hand. This is all the more true when even men may legitimately make use of it in preference to the bath. It offers considerable benefit to the health of the young, and besides, instils in them a desire and ambition to develop not only a healthy constitution, but also a wholesome character. If physical exercise is engaged in without distracting them from more worthwhile deeds, it is entertaining and not without profit.

For that reason, even women should be allowed some sort of physical exercise, not on the wrestling-mat or the racecourse, but in spinning and weaving and supervising the cooking, if need arise. Again, the women should themselves bring whatever we need from the storeroom, and it is no disgrace for them to take their place at the mill. Then, too, for her to busy herself about the meals that they may be pleasing to her husband is a deed one who is housewife, spouse, and helpmate will not be reproached for performing. If she should also make the beds herself, and bring her husband drink when he is thirsty, and prepare the food, she would be exercising herself in a very becoming way, and maintaining her health by self-restraint. The Educator approves of such a woman who "stretches forth her hands to useful things, and who applies her fingers vigorously to the spindle, who opens her hands to the needy and stretches forth fruit to the poor,"[41] and who, in imitation of Sarah, is not ashamed to serve wayfarers generously. Abraham said to Sarah: "Quick, three

measures of fine flour! Knead it, and make loaves."[42] Again, Scripture says: "Rachel, daughter of Jacob, arrived with her father's sheep," and, as if this was not enough, it adds, to give a convincing lesson of lowliness: "for it was her custom to tend them."[43] There are innumerable examples given in the Scriptures both of frugality and of self-service, as well as of physical exercise.

As for the men, let some of them engage in wrestling stripped; let others play the game called *phaenind* with a small ball, particularly out in the sun. A walk will be sufficient for others, either strolling out into the country or into town. If, besides all this, they lay hold of the mattock, such a money-saving way of taking exercise will not be beneath their dignity. But I am almost forgetting to mention Pittacus, king of the Mitylenians, who wandered about taking energetic exercise.[44] It is well if a person draws his own water for his needs, and himself cuts the wood that he uses. Jacob pastured the sheep that Laban had given him with a rod of storax (which is a sign of royalty), and he took care to influence their nature for the better with such a rod.[45] Sometimes, reading out loud will be a good exercise for many.

But let them especially engage in wrestling, which we approve of, not for vain competition's sake, which serves no end, but to get rid of manly sweat. They should not cultivate the tricks meant only for display, but only the art of wrestling erect, keeping the neck and hands and sides free. Such movements are much more orderly and manly, are performed with controlled strength, and are clearly undertaken to benefit one's health—a very desirable thing. The other exercises of the gymnasium demand the practise of postures beneath our dignity. We must aim for moderation in all things. For, just as it is better for labor to precede meals, so, too, to labor beyond measure is both harmful

---

40 Isa 4:4.

41 Cf. Prov 31:19–20.

42 Gen 18:6.

43 Gen 29:9.

44 Diog Laertius 1:81.

45 Cf. Gen 30:37–43.

and tiring, and leads to sickness. We should not be idle, yet we should not become completely exhausted by our labor, either. We were just discussing the proper conduct to be observed in taking food; similarly, in every thing and every place we should not live for pleasure nor for immorality; neither should we go to the other extreme. We should, instead, choose a course of life in between, well-balanced, temperate, and free from either evil: extravagance or parsimony.

As we have already said, self-service is an exercise without any trace of pride: for example, to put on one's own sandals, wash one's own feet, and also to rub off the oil that has been put on. To rub down someone who has done the same for us is both a physical exercise and an act of communal justice, as is also sleeping by a sick friend, waiting on someone who cannot wait on himself, and providing for someone in need. "And Abraham set before the three men a lunch under the tree and he stood by while they ate."[46] So is fishing, as it was for Peter, if we have leisure left over from the instruction we need in the word. But the best catch is the one the Lord entrusted to his disciples, when he taught them to catch people, as though fish from a sea.

---

46 Gen 18:8.

92. Tertullian: To His Wife

The proto-orthodox writer Tertullian has turned up a number of times already in this collection (Chapters 4, 5, 7, 13, 14). In an effort to promote more rigorous standards among his fellow Christians, Tertullian devoted a good deal of his time to writing about ethical issues, urging stringent behavior and condemning those who refused to adopt it. Among his surviving ethical treatises are discussions of monogamy, chastity, women's head coverings and make-up, and other issues relevant for his views of gender relations. The following example shows the fervor with which Tertullian could set forth his views, and is particularly interesting because it deals with a personal matter. As a kind of "open letter" to his wife, the treatise instructs her about what do if he precedes her in death. In short, Tertullian marshals arguments from far and wide to convince her not to remarry, a stance perhaps not surprising to those already familiar with his character.

I thought it would be well, my dearest companion in the service of the Lord, to give some consideration, even at this early date, to the manner of life that ought to be yours after my departure from this world, should I be called before you. I trust your own loyalty to follow the suggestions I shall offer. For if we pursue our purposes with such diligence when worldly issues are at stake, even drawing up legal instruments in our anxiety to secure each other's interests, ought we not to be all

---

Tertullian: To His Wife, from *Tertullian: Treatises on Marriage and Remarriage,* ed. William P. Le Saint. Mahwah: Paulist Press, 1951. Used by permission of Paulist Press.

the more solicitous in providing for the welfare of those we leave behind us when there is question of securing their best advantage in matters concerning God and heaven? Ought we not, acting as it were before the event, bequeath them legacies of loving-counsel, and make clear our will respecting goods which constitute the eternal portion of their heavenly inheritance? God grant that you may be disposed to receive in its entirety the loving-counsel I now commit in trust to your fidelity. To him be honor, glory, splendor, grandeur, and power, now and forever.

This charge, then, I lay on you—that, exercising all the self-control of which you are capable, you renounce marriage after I have passed away. You will not, on that account, confer any benefit on me, apart from the good you do yourself. I would not want you to think that I now advise you to remain a widow because I fear to suffer hardship if you fail to preserve your person inviolate for myself alone. No, when the future time arrives, we shall not resume the gratification of unseemly passion. It is not such worthless, filthy things that God promises to those who are his own. Moreover, there is no promise given Christians who have departed this life that on the day of their resurrection they will be restored once more to the married state. They will, it is clear, be changed to the state of holy angels.[1] For this reason they will remain undisturbed by feelings of carnal jealousy. Even that woman who was said to have married seven brothers in succession, will give no offense to a single one of all her husbands when she rises from the dead; nor does a single one of them await her there to put her in the blush. The teaching of our Lord has settled this quibble of the Sadducees. Yet it is still permitted us to consider whether the course of action I recommend is of advantage to you personally or, for that matter, to the advantage of any other woman who belongs to God.

2 Of course, we do not reject the union of man and woman in marriage. It is an institution blessed by God for the reproduction of the human race. It was planned by him for the purpose of populating the earth and to make provision for the propagation of mankind. Hence, it was permitted; but only once may it be contracted. For Adam was the only husband that Eve had and Eve was his only wife; one rib, one woman.

Now, everybody knows that it was allowed our forefathers, even the Patriarchs themselves, not only to marry but actually to multiply marriages. They even kept concubines. But, although figurative language is used in speaking of both church and synagogue, yet we may explain this difficult matter simply by saying that it was necessary in former times that there be practices which afterwards had to be abrogated or modified. For the Law had first to intervene; too, at a later date, the Word of God was to replace the law and introduce spiritual circumcision. Therefore, the licentiousness and promiscuity of earlier days—and there must needs have been abuses which called for the institution of a law—were responsible for that subsequent corrective legislation by which the Lord through his gospel, and the apostle in these latter days did away with excesses or controlled irregularities.

3 But I would not have you suppose that I have premised these remarks on the liberty which was allowed in former times and the severity of later legislation, because I wish to lay the foundation of an argument proving that Christ has come into the world for the purpose of separating those who are joined in wedlock and forbidding the conjugal relationship, as though from now on all marriages were to be outlawed. This is a charge they must be prepared to answer who, among other perversions of doctrine, teach their followers to divide those who are two in one flesh, opposing the will of him who first subtracted woman from man and then, in the mathematics of marriage, added two together again who had originally been substantially one. Finally, we do not read anywhere at all that marriage is forbidden; and this for the obvious reason that marriage is actually a good.

---

1 Matt 22:23–30.

The apostle, however, teaches us what is better than this "good," when he says that he permits marriage, but prefers celibacy[2]—the former because of the snares of the flesh, the latter because the times are straitened. Hence, if we consider the reasons which he gives for each of these views, we shall have no difficulty in seeing that marriage is conceded to us on the principle that marry we may because marry we must. But what necessity proffers necessity cheapens. Scripture says that it is better to marry than to burn;[3] but what sort of good, I ask you, can that be which is such only when it is compared to what is bad? Marriage, forsooth, is better because burning is worse! How much better it is neither to marry nor to burn!

In time of persecution it is better to flee from place to place, as we are permitted, than to be arrested and to deny the faith under torture. Yet, far happier are they who find courage to bear witness and to undergo martyrdom for the faith. It can be said that what is merely tolerated is never really good. Suppose I am doomed to die. If I quail at this, then it is good to flee. If, however, I hesitate to use the permission given, this itself shows that there is something suspect about the very reasons for which the permission is granted. Nobody merely *permits* that which is better, since this is something of which there can be no doubt; it is a thing which recommends itself by its own transparent goodness.

Nothing is to be sought after for the sole reason that it is not forbidden. When we come to think of it, even such things are, in a sense, forbidden because other things are preferred to them. To prefer the lofty is to exclude the low. Nothing is good just because it is not bad, nor is it, therefore, not bad simply for the reason that it does you no hurt. A thing that is good in the full sense of the word is to be preferred because it helps us, not merely because it does not harm us. You ought to choose things that are good for you rather than things which are merely not bad for you.

Every contest is a straining for the first prize. When a person comes out second, he has consolation, but he does not have victory. If we listen to the apostle, then, "forgetting the things that are behind, let us stretch forth to those that are before,"[4] and be "zealous for the better gifts."[5] Thus, although the apostle does not cast a snare upon us, he does show us where our advantage lies when he writes: "The unmarried woman . . . thinks on the things of the Lord, that she may be holy both in body and in spirit. But she that is married is solicitous . . . how she may please her husband."[6] In other places, also, the apostle is nowhere so tolerant of marriage that he fails to point out his own preference, and this is that we strive to follow his example. Blessed is he who is like Paul!

4 But we read that the flesh is weak; and this serves us as an excuse for pampering ourselves in a number of ways. We also read, however, that the spirit is strong. Both statements are made in the same sentence.[7] The flesh is of the earth, the spirit is of heaven. Now, why is it that, habitually seeking excuses for ourselves, we plead the weakness of our nature and disregard its strength? Should not the things of earth yield to the things of heaven? If the spirit, being nobler in origin, is stronger than the flesh, then we have no one to blame but ourselves when we yield to the weaker force.

There are two weaknesses in human nature which appear to make it necessary that those who have lost a spouse should marry again. First, there is the concupiscence of the flesh, and this has the strongest pull; second, there is the concupiscence of the world. We servants of God ought to scorn both weaknesses, since we renounce both lust and ambition.

Concupiscence of the flesh urges in its defense the right to exercise the functions of maturity; it

2 1 Cor 7:1–2.
3 1 Cor 7:9.
4 Phil 3:13.
5 1 Cor 12:31.
6 1 Cor 7:34–35.
7 Matt 26:41.

seeks to pluck the fruits of beauty; it glories in its shame; it declares that woman's sex requires a husband to be her strength and comfort, or to protect her good name from ugly gossip.

But as for you, do you oppose against such specious arguments the example of those sisters of ours—their names are known to the Lord—who, having seen their husbands go to God, prefer chastity to the opportunities of marriage afforded them by their youth and beauty. They choose to be wedded to God. They are God's fair ones, God's beloved. With him they live, with him they converse, with him they treat on intimate terms day and night. Prayers are the dowry they bring the Lord and for them they receive his favors as marriage gifts in return. Thus they have made their own a blessing for eternity, given them by the Lord; and, remaining unmarried, they are reckoned, even while still on earth, as belonging to the household of the angels. Train yourself to imitate the example of continence furnished by such women as these and, in your love for things of the spirit, you will bury concupiscence of the flesh. You will root out the fleeting, vagrant desires which come of beauty and youth, and make compensation for their loss with the blessings of heaven, which last forever.

The concupiscence of the world which I mentioned has its roots in pride, avarice, ambition, and the plea that one is unable to get along alone. Arguments drawn from sources such as these it uses to urge the necessity of marriage; and, of course, it promises heavenly rewards in return: to queen it over another man's household; to gloat over another man's wealth; to wheedle the price of a wardrobe out of another man's pocket; to be extravagant at no cost to yourself!

Far be it from Christians to desire such things as these! We are not solicitous about how we are to be supplied with the necessities of life—unless we have no confidence in the promises of God. He it is who clothes the lilies of the field in such great beauty; who feeds the birds of the air, though they labor not; who bids us not to be concerned about the morrow, what we shall eat or what we shall put on. He assures us that he knows what is necessary for each of his servants. And this, certainly, is not a mass of jeweled pendants, nor a surfeit of clothing, nor mules brought from Gaul, nor porters from Germany. Such things do lend lustre to a wedding, but what is necessary for us is, rather, a sufficiency which is consistent with sobriety and modesty. You may take it for granted that you will have need of nothing, if you but serve the Lord; indeed, all things are yours if you possess the Lord of all. Meditate on the things of heaven and you will despise the things of earth. The widow whose life is stamped with the seal of God's approval has need of nothing—except perseverance!

5 In addition to the reasons already advanced, some say that they wish to contract marriage because they desire to live on in their posterity and because they seek the bitter sweet which comes of having children. To us this is sheer nonsense. For, why should we be so anxious to propagate children since, when we do, it is our hope—in view, that is, of the straitened times which are at hand—that they will go to God before us. We ourselves desire, as did the Apostle, to be delivered from this wicked world and received into the arms of our Lord.

Of course, to the servant of God posterity is a great necessity! We are so sure of our own salvation that we have time for children! We must hunt up burdens for ourselves with which, for the most part, even pagans refuse to be encumbered—burdens which are forced upon people by law, but of which they rid themselves by resorting to murder of their own flesh and blood; burdens, in fine, which are especially troublesome to us because they constitute a danger to the faith. Why did our Lord prophesy, "Woe to them that are with child and that give suck,"[8] if he did not mean that on the day of our great exodus children will be a handicap to those who bear them? This is what comes of marriage. There will be no problem here for widows, however. At the first sound of the angel's trumpet they will leap forth lightly, easily able to

---

8 Matt 24:19.

endure any distress or persecution, with none of the heaving baggage of marriage in their wombs or at their breasts.

Accordingly, whether marriage be for the flesh or for the world or for the sake of posterity, the servant of God is above all such supposed necessities. I should think it quite enough to have succumbed once to any one of them and to have satisfied all such wants as these in a single marriage.

Are we to have weddings every day and, in the midst of nuptials, to be overtaken by the day of dread, even as were Sodom and Gomorrha? For in those places they were not just getting married and transacting business! When our Lord says that they were marrying and they were buying, he wishes to stigmatize those gross vices of the flesh and the world which most withdraw people from the things of God—the one by the sweet seduction of lust, the other by greed for gain.[9] And yet, these people were afflicted by blindness of this kind at a time when the end of the world was still far off. How shall we fare, if the vices God then found detestable keep up back from divine things now? "The time is short," Scripture says; "it remains that they who have wives, act as if they had none."[10]

6 But now, if those who actually have wives are to put them out of their minds, how much more are those who have none prohibited from seeking a second time what they no longer have! Accordingly, she whose husband has departed this life ought to refrain from marrying and have done with sex forever. This is what many a pagan woman does in order to honor the memory of a beloved spouse.

When something seems difficult to us, let us think of those who put up with difficulties greater than our own. For example, how many are there who vow virginity from the very moment of their baptism! How many, too, who in wedlock abstain, by mutual consent, from the use of marriage! They have "made themselves eunuchs because of their desire for the kingdom of Heaven."[11] If they are able to practice continence while remaining married, how much easier is it to do so when marriage has been dissolved! For I rather imagine it is more difficult to sacrifice something we actually have than it is to be indifferent about something we no longer possess.

A hard thing it is, forsooth, and arduous, that a Christian woman, out of love for God, should practice continence after her husband's death, when pagans use the priestly offices of virgins and widows in the service of their own Satan! At Rome, for example, those women are called "virgins" who guard a flame which typifies the unquenchable fire, watching over that which is an omen of the punishment which awaits them together with the Dragon himself. At the town of Aegium a virgin is selected for the cult of the Achaean Juno; and the women who rave at Delphi do not marry. Further, we know that "widows" minister to the African Ceres, women whom a most harsh insensibility has withdrawn from married life. For, while their husbands are still living, they not only separate from them but even introduce new wives to take their place—no doubt with the cheerful acquiescence of the husbands themselves! Such "widows" deprive themselves of all contact with men, even to the exclusion of kissing their own sons. Yet they become used to this discipline and persevere in a widowhood which rejects even those consolations which are found in the sacred bonds of natural affection. This is what the devil teaches his disciples. And they obey! As though on equal terms, the chastity of his followers challenges that of the servants of God. The very priests of hell are continent. For Satan has discovered how to turn the cultivation of virtue itself to a man's destruction, and it makes no difference to him whether he ruins souls by lust or chastity.

7 We have been taught by the Lord and God of salvation that continence is a means of attaining eternal life, a proof of the faith that is in us, a

---

9 Luke 17:28–30.

10 1 Cor 7:29.

11 Matt 19:12.

pledge of the glory of that body which will be ours when we put on the garb of immortality, and, finally, an obligation imposed upon us by the will of God. Regarding this last statement, I suggest that you reflect seriously on the following: if it is a fact that not a leaf falls to the ground unless God wills it, then it is equally true that no one departs this life unless God wills it. For it is necessary that he who brought us into the world should also usher us forth from it. Therefore, when God wills that a woman lose her husband in death, he also wills that she should be done with marriage itself. Why attempt to restore what God has put asunder? Why spurn the liberty which is offered you by enslaving yourself once more in the bonds of matrimony? "Are you bound in marriage?" Scripture says, "seek not to be loosed. Are you loosed from marriage? seek not to be bound."[12] For, though you sin not in remarrying, yet, according to Scripture, "tribulation of the flesh will follow"[13] if you do.

Hence, as far as such a sentiment is possible, let us be grateful for the opportunity offered us of practicing continence and let us embrace it immediately, once it is offered. Thus, what we were unable to do in marriage we will be able to do in bereavement. We ought to make the most of a situation which removes what necessity imposed.

The law of the church and the precept of the apostle show clearly how prejudicial second marriages are to the faith and how great an obstacle to holiness. For men who have been married twice are not allowed to preside in the church[14] nor is it permissible that a widow be chosen unless she was the wife of but one man.[15] The altar of God must be an altar of manifest purity and all the glory which surrounds the Church is the glory of sanctity.

The pagans have a priesthood of widows and celibates—though, of course, this is part of Satan's malevolence; and the ruler of this world, their Pontifex Maximus, is not permitted to marry a second time. How greatly purity must please God, since even the Enemy affects it! He does this, not because he has any real affinity with virtue but because it is his purpose to make a mockery of what is pleasing to the Lord God.

8 There is a brief saying, revealed through the mouth of the prophet, which shows how greatly God honors widowhood: "Deal justly with the widow and the orphan and then come and let us reason together, saith the Lord."[16] The two groups mentioned here have no human means of support whatever; they are dependent on God's mercy, and the Father of all takes it upon himself to be their protector. See how familiarly the widow's benefactor is treated by God! In what esteem, then, is the widow herself held when he who is her advocate will reason with the Lord! Not even to virgins themselves, I fancy, is so much given.

Although virgins, because of their perfect integrity and inviolate purity, will look upon the face of God most closely, yet the life a widow leads is the more difficult, since it is easy not to desire that of which you are ignorant and easy to turn your back upon what you have never desired. Chastity is most praiseworthy when it is sensible of the right it has sacrificed and knows what it has experienced. The condition of the virgin may be regarded as one of greater felicity, but that of the widow is one of greater difficulty; the former has always possessed the good, the latter has had to find it on her own. In the former it is grace which is crowned, in the latter, virtue. For some things there are which come to us from the divine bounty, and others we have of our own efforts. Those which are bestowed upon us by the Lord are governed by his generosity; those which are achieved by humans are won at the cost of personal endeavor.

Therefore, cultivate the virtue of self-restraint, which ministers to chastity; cultivate industry, which prevents idleness; temperance, which spurns the world. Keep company and converse worthy of

12 1 Cor 7:27.

13 1 Cor 7:28.

14 1 Tim 3:2; Tit 1:6.

15 1 Tim 5:9.

16 Isa 1:17–18.

God, remembering the quotation sanctified by the apostle: "Evil associations corrupt good manners."[17] Chattering, idle, winebibbing, scandal-mongering women do the greatest possible harm to a widow's high resolve. Their loquaciousness leads to the use of words offensive to modesty; their slothfulness engenders disloyalty to the austere life; their tippling issues in every sort of evil and their prurient gossip is responsible for inciting others to engage in the lustful conduct which such talk exemplifies. No woman of this kind can have anything good to say about monogamy. "Their god is their belly,"[18] as the apostle says; and so also is that which lies adjacent to it.

Here, then, my dearest fellow servant, is the counsel which even now I leave with you. And, really, although my words are superfluous after what the apostle has written on the subject, yet for you they will be words of consolation as often as, in thinking on them, you think of me.

---

17 1 Cor 15:33.

18 Phil 3:19.

16

The Emergence of Orthodoxy
Theological Writings of Proto-orthodox Christians

Throughout this volume we have seen that two distinctive features of early Christianity were its exclusivity and its focus on doctrine. Christians maintained that they alone worshipped the true God and that this worship involved believing the right things about him. In tandem, these features made Christianity a confessional religion, unlike any other in the Greco-Roman world.

The Christian emphasis on theological affirmation brought with it a cluster of problems unparalleled in ancient religion. As people poured into the church from a wide range of backgrounds and with a host of perspectives, divergent viewpoints were propounded as true and apostolic. Given the importance of right belief, these differences quickly led to harsh and vitriolic debates over "orthodoxy" and "heresy" (see Chapters 6 and 7). The views that eventually became dominant were developed over a long period of time and largely in opposition to views set forth by opposing parties. Just within the realm of Christology, for example, when "docetists" argued that Jesus was divine but not human, proto-orthodox Christians insisted that he was actually human; when "adoptionists" argued that he was actually human but not divine, proto-orthodox Christians maintained that he was fully divine as well; when Gnostics concluded that he was divine and human because he was two separate beings, the proto-orthodox claimed that he was one solitary and unitary being, both divine and human. This "orthodox" view eventually came to be embodied in the Christian confessions of faith, such as the Apostles' Creed and the Nicene Creed, formulations that were devised in the fourth century and have come down to us today.

Before the creeds were formalized, proto-orthodox Christians subscribed to a set of beliefs that they labeled the "Rule of Faith" (Latin: *regula fidei*). This "rule" strongly insisted on such anti-heretical views as the belief in one God, the creator of the entire material world, and in Christ his son, who was both God and human. Such basic beliefs, though, still left a huge arena of interpretation even within proto-orthodox circles. In part, the complexities were created by the paradoxes found within the proto-orthodox doctrines themselves, paradoxes that were created precisely because these doctrines were established in opposition to the unpalatable views of others. How was it possible, for example, to reconcile two of the most basic proto-orthodox beliefs, (a) that there was only one true God (over against, for example, Marcion and the Gnostics) and (b) that Christ himself was fully divine? If God is God and Christ is God, are there not two Gods? And what about the Spirit, who was also thought to be God? Are there not three Gods?

No, proto-orthodox Christians insisted that there was only one God. But how can there be one if there are three? Is it possible, for example, that Christ was actually God himself on earth, and that there was no other God than he, that in fact the Father became the Son to die for the sins of the world? That was the view of one group of Christians near the end of the first century, a group labeled by their opponents "patri-passianists" (literally: "father sufferers") because they were forced by the logic of their position to maintain that the Father himself had suffered and died on the cross, a view unpalatable to other proto-orthodox Christians (see Chapter 7). But if the patripassian-ists were wrong—that is, if Jesus was not himself the Father, but at the same time he really was God—how could one avoid being called a ditheist (i.e., one who believes in two gods) or, if the Spirit were included in the mix, a tritheist?

The debates over how to resolve these issues were long and hard, and became in-creasingly complicated and nuanced with the passing of time. Near the end of the second century and throughout the third Christians began to speak of the "Trinity" as a way of resolving the problem; but there were various ways proto-orthodox thinkers worked out the details until a view emerged, which eventually became widely accepted as orthodox: to put the matter simply, the relationship of the three—Father, Son, and Spirit—was a mystery (i.e., above and beyond reason) that involved three distinct "persons" all sharing one "substance."

The philosophical sophistication required to work through these problems was far beyond the ability of average Christians, of course, most of whom were not even literate let alone philosophically trained. Many of our surviving literary texts from the period, however, are heavily invested in precisely such questions, as they come from the pens of the Christian literary elite. As a rule, these authors attempt to solve the problems of right doctrine by applying philosophically sophisticated arguments to the text of Scrip-ture, understood by them to be the ultimate revelation of divine truth. One of the reasons for their wide-ranging disagreements is that the authors of Scripture them-selves did not deal with these kinds of theological problems or anything like them, so that proto-orthodox theologians were set on systematizing the doctrinal innuendos of authors who were addressing entirely different issues and concerns.

In this early period of Christian theology, some of the prominent spokespersons for proto-orthodox views developed their ideas in ways later deemed, by those with the benefit of hindsight, to be completely wrongheaded and dangerous. At the time, how-ever, such views were seen as both acceptable and attractive. The clearest instance comes in the writings of Origen, the greatest intellect and most prolific Christian author of the second and third centuries, known and respected as a leading voice among the proto-orthodox. Origen's views provided the foundation upon which much subse-quent theology came to be built; yet he himself came to be condemned as a heretic some three centuries after his death.

The following selections, including an important portion of Origen's theological writing "On First Principles" (see also Chapter 10), represent some of the more inter-esting attempts by second- and third-century Christians to make sense of the doctrines that they understood to be central to the faith.

For Further Reading

Behr, John. *The Way to Nicaea*. Crestwood: St. Vladimir's Seminary Press, 2001.

Edwards, Mark J. *Catholicity and Heresy in the Early Church*. Burlington: Ashgate, 2009.

Ehrman, Bart D. *How Jesus Became God: The Exaltation of a Preacher from Galilee*. San Francisco: HarperOne, 2014.

Harnack, Adolf von. *History of Dogma*, trans. Neil Buchanan. New York: Dover, 1961.

Lyman, Rebecca. *Christology and Cosmology: Models of Divine Activity in Origen, Eusebius, and Athanasius*. Oxford: Clarendon, 1993.

Norris, Richard. *The Christological Controversy*. Philadelphia: Fortress, 1980.

Pelikan, Jeroslav. *The Christian Tradition*, vol. 1. Chicago: University of Chicago, 1971.

Rusch, William G. *The Trinitarian Controversy*. Philadelphia: Fortress, 1980.

Trigg, Joseph. *Origen: The Bible and Philosophy in the Third Century Church*. Rev. ed. London: SCM Press, 2012.

THE TEXTS

93. Tertullian: Against Praxeas

In the early part of the third century, Tertullian (see Chapter 4) wrote a vitriolic treatise against a man called Praxeas, who maintained that Christ was God the Father himself become flesh, so that there was no distinction between the Father and Son (for another selection, see Chapter 7). Some scholars have suspected that "Praxeas" is actually a cipher for someone else in the Roman church. He is not mentioned by other ancient sources, yet Tertullian assigns an inordinate significance to him: Praxeas is said not only to have infected the church with his patripassianist views but also to have driven out the Montanists, a rigorist Christian sect that Tertullian himself eventually joined, who stressed the ongoing work of the Spirit (see Chapter 14).

Tertullian bars no holds in his attack, maintaining that Praxeas's notions have been inspired directly by the Devil. In support of his counter-position, Tertullian provides a detailed exposition of the *regula fidei* allegedly confessed by all Christians, giving a creative and influential elaboration of the relation of the Father and the Son and developing in his own way, then, the doctrine of the Trinity: there is one God who exists in three persons, "three not in condition but in degree; not in substance but in form . . . of one substance and of one condition, and of one power, inasmuch as he is one God . . . susceptible of number without division" (Against Praxeas, ch. 2; see Chapter 7 above).

Particularly notable are Tertullian's closely argued logic and, especially, his detailed appeals to the very words of inspired Scripture.

4 . . . We have been already able to show that the Father and the Son are two separate Persons, not only by the mention of their separate names as Father and the Son, but also by the fact that he who delivered up the kingdom, and he to whom it is delivered up—and in like manner, he who subjected (all things), and he to whom they were subjected—must necessarily be two different beings.

5 But since they [the followers of Praxeas] will have the two to be but one, so that the Father shall be deemed to be the same as the Son, it is only right that the whole question respecting the Son should be examined, as to whether he exists, and who he is and the mode of his existence. Thus shall the truth itself secure its own sanction from the Scriptures, and the interpretations which guard them. There are some who allege that even Genesis opens thus in Hebrew: "In the beginning God made for himself a Son." As there is no ground for this, I am led to other arguments derived from God's own dispensation, in which he existed before the creation of the world, up to the

Tertullian: Against Praxeas, from *The Ante-Nicene Fathers*; vol. 3, *Latin Christianity: Its Founder, Tertullian*, ed. A. Cleveland Coxe. Reprint, 2nd ed. Grand Rapids: Eerdmans, 1989.

generation of the Son. For before all things God was alone—being in himself and for himself universe, and space, and all things. Moreover, he was alone, because there was nothing external to him but himself. Yet even not then was he alone; for he had with him that which he possessed in himself, that is to say, his own Reason. For God is rational, and Reason was first in him; and so all things were from himself. This reason is his own Thought (or Consciousness) which the Greeks call *logos* by which term we also designate Word or Discourse and therefore it is now usual with our people, owing to the mere simple interpretation of the term, to say that the Word was in the beginning with God; although it would be more suitable to regard Reason as the more ancient; because God had not Word from the beginning, but he had Reason even before the beginning; because also Word itself consists of Reason, which it thus proves to have been the prior existence as being its own substance. Not that this distinction is of any practical moment. For although God had not yet sent out his word, he still had him within himself, both in company with and included within his very Reason, as he silently planned and arranged within himself everything which he was afterwards about to utter through his Word. Now, while he was thus planning and arranging with his own Reason, he was actually causing that to become Word which he was dealing with in the way of Word or Discourse. And that you may the more readily understand this, consider first of all, from your own self, who are made in the image and likeness of God, for what purpose it is that you also possess reason in yourself, who are a rational creature, as being not only made by a rational artificer, but actually animated out of his substance. Observe, then, that when you are silently conversing with yourself, this very process is carried on within you by your reason, which meets you with a word at every movement of your thought, at every impulse of your conception. Whatever you think, there is a word; whatever you conceive, there is reason. You must speak it in your mind; and while you are speaking, you admit speech as an interlocutor with you, involved in which there is this very reason, whereby, while in thought you are holding converse with your word, you are (by reciprocal action) producing thought by means of that converse with your word. Thus, in a certain sense, the word is a second person within you, through which in thinking you utter speech, and through which also, (by reciprocity of process,) in uttering speech you generate thought. The word is itself a different thing from yourself. Now how much more fully is all this transacted in God, whose image and likeness even you are regarded as being, inasmuch as he has reason within himself even while he is silent, and involved in that Reason his word! I may therefore without rashness first lay this down (as a fixed principle) that even then before the creation of the universe God was not alone, since he had within himself both Reason, and, inherent in Reason, his Word, which he made second to himself by agitating it within himself. . . .

9 Bear always in mind that this is the rule of faith which I profess; by it I testify that the Father, and the Son, and the Spirit are inseparable from each other, and so will you know in what sense this is said. Now, observe, my assertion is that the Father is one, and the Son one, and the Spirit one, and that they are distinct from each other. This statement is taken in a wrong sense by every uneducated as well as every perversely disposed person, as if it predicated a diversity, in such a sense as to imply a separation among the Father, and the Son, and the Spirit. I am, moreover, obliged to say this, when (extolling the Monarchy at the expense of the Economy) they contend for the identity of the Father and Son and Spirit, that it is not by way of diversity that the Son differs from the Father, but by distribution: it is not by division that he is different, but by distinction; because the Father is not the same as the Son, since they differ one from the other in the mode of their being. For the Father is the entire substance, but the Son is a derivation and portion of the whole, as he himself acknowledges: "My Father is greater

than I."[1] In the Psalm his inferiority is described as being "a little lower than the angels."[2] Thus the Father is distinct from the Son, being greater than the Son, inasmuch as he who begets is one, and he who is begotten is another; he, too, who sends is one, and he who is sent is another, and he, again, who makes is one, and he through whom the thing is made is another. Happily the Lord himself employs this expression of the person of the Paraclete, so as to signify not a division or severance, but a disposition (of mutual relations in the Godhead); for he says, "I will pray the Father, and he shall send you another Comforter. . . . even the Spirit of truth,"[3] thus making the Paraclete distinct from himself, even as we say that the Son is also distinct from the Father; so that he showed a third degree in the Paraclete, as we believe the second degree is in the Son, by reason of the order observed in the Economy. Besides, does not the very fact that they have the distinct names of Father and Son amount to a declaration that they are distinct in personality? For, of course, all things will be what their names represent them to be; and what they are and ever will be, that will they be called; and the distinction indicated by the names does not at all admit of any confusion, because there is none in the things which they designate. "Yes is yes, and no is no; for what is more than these; come of evil."[4]

10 So it is either the Father or the Son, and the day is not the same as the night; nor is the Father the same as the Son, in such a way that both of them should be one, and one or the other should be both,—an opinion which the most conceited "Monarchians" maintain. He himself, they say, made himself a Son to himself. Now a Father makes a Son, and a Son makes a Father; and they who thus become reciprocally related out of each other to each other cannot in any way

by themselves simply become so related to themselves, that the Father can make himself a Son to himself, and the Son render himself a Father to himself. And the relations which God establishes, them does he also guard. A father must have a son, in order to be a father; so likewise a son, to be a son, must have a father. It is, however, one thing to have, and another thing to be. For instance, in order to be a husband, I must have a wife; I can never myself be my own wife. In like manner, in order to be a father, I have a son, for I never can be a son to myself; and in order to be a son, I have a father, it being impossible for me ever to be my own father. And it is these relations which make me (what I am), when I come to possess them: I shall then be a father. when I have a son; and a son, when I have a father. Now, if I am to be to myself any one of these relations, I no longer have what I am myself to be: neither a father, because I am to be my own father; nor a son, because I shall be my own son. Moreover, inasmuch as I ought to have one of these relations in order to be the other; so, if I am to be both together, I shall fail to be one while I possess not the other. For if I must be myself my son, who am also a father, I now cease to have a son, since I am my own son. But by reason of not having a son, since I am my own son, how can I be a father? For I ought to have a son, in order to be a father. Therefore I am not a son, because I have not a father, who makes a son. . . .

11 It will be your duty, however, to adduce your proofs out of the Scriptures as plainly as we do, when we prove that he made his Word a Son to himself. For if he calls him Son, and if the Son is none other than he who has proceeded from the Father himself, and if the Word has proceeded from the Father himself, he will then be the Son, and not himself from whom he proceeded. For the Father himself did not proceed from himself. Now, you who say that the Father is the same as the Son, do really make the same Person both to have sent forth from himself (and at the same time to have gone out from himself as)

---

1 John 14:28.

2 Ps 8:5.

3 John 14:16.

4 Matt 5:37.

that Being which is God. If it was possible for him to have done this, he at all events did not do it. You must bring forth the proof which I require of you—one like my own; that is, (you must prove to me) that the Scriptures show the Son and the Father to be the same, just as on our side the Father and the Son are demonstrated to be distinct; I say distinct, but not separate: for as on my part I produce the words of God Himself, "My heart has emitted my most excellent Word,"[5] so you in like manner ought to adduce in opposition to me some text where God has said, "My heart has emitted myself as my own most excellent Word," in such a sense that he is himself both the emitter and the emitted, both he who sent forth and he who was sent forth, since he is both the Word and God. I bid you also observe, that on my side I advance the passage where the Father said to the Son, "You are my Son, this day have I begotten."[6] If you want me to believe him to be both the Father and the Son, show me some other passage where it is declared, "The Lord said to himself, I am my own Son, today have I begotten myself"; or again, "Before the morning did I beget myself"[7]; and likewise, "I the Lord possessed myself the beginning of my ways for my own works; before all the hills, too, did I beget myself"[8]; and whatever other passages are to the same effect. . . .

12 If the number of the trinity also offends you, as if it were not connected in the simple unity, I ask you how it is possible for a being who is merely and absolutely one and singular, to speak in plural phrase, saying, "Let us make man in our own image, and after our own likeness";[9] whereas he ought to have said, "Let me make man in my own image, and after my own

likeness," as being a unique and singular being? In the following passage, however, "Behold the man is become as one of us,"[10] he is either deceiving or amusing us in speaking plurally, if he is one only and singular. Or was it to the angels that he spoke, as the Jews interpret the passage, because these also acknowledge not the Son? Or was it because he was at once the Father, the Son, and the Spirit, that he spoke to himself in plural terms, making himself plural on that very account? Nay, it was because he had already his Son close at his side, as a second person, his own Word, and a third person also, the Spirit in the Word, that he purposely adopted the plural phrase, "Let us make"; and, "in our image"; and, "become as one of us." For with whom did he make man? and to whom did he make him like? (The answer must be), the Son on the one hand, who was one day to put on human nature; and the Spirit on the other, who was to sanctify humans. With these did he then speak, in the unity of the trinity, as with his ministers and witnesses. In the following text also he distinguishes among the persons: "So God created man in his own image; in the image of God created he him."[11] Why say "image of God"? Why not "his own image" merely, if he was only one who was the Maker, and if there was not also one in whose image he made man? But there was one in whose image God was making man, that is to say, Christ's image, who, being one day about to become man (more surely and more truly so), had already caused the man to be called his image, who was then going to be formed of clay—the image and similitude of the true and perfect man. But in respect of the previous works of the world what says the Scripture? Its first statement indeed is made, when the Son has not yet appeared: "And God said, Let there be light, and there was light."[12] Immediately there appears the Word, "that true light, which light humans on his coming

---

5 Ps 45:1.

6 Ps 2:7.

7 Cf. Ps 110:3.

8 Cf. Prov 8:22.

9 Gen 1:26.

---

10 Gen 3:22.

11 Gen 1:27.

12 Gen 1:3.

into the worlds,"[13] and through him also came light upon the world. From that moment God willed creation to be effected in the Word, Christ being present and ministering to him: and so God created. And God said, "Let there be a firmament, . . . and God made the firmament";[14] and God also said, "Let there be lights (in the firmament); and so God made a greater and a lesser light."[15] But all the rest of the created things did he in like manner make, who made the former ones—I mean the Word of God, "through whom all things were made, and without whom nothing was made."[16]

Now if he too is God, according to John, (who says,) "The Word was God,"[17] then you have two beings—one that commands that the things be made, and the other that executes the order and creates. In what sense, however, you ought to understand him to be another, I have already explained, on the ground of personality, not of substance—in the way of distinction, not of division. But although I must everywhere hold one only substance in three coherent and inseparable (persons), yet I am bound to acknowledge, from the necessity of the case, that he who issues a command is different from him who executes it. For, indeed, he would not be issuing a command if he were all the while doing the work himself, while ordering it to be done by the second. But still he did issue the command, although he would not have intended to command himself if he were only one; or else he must have worked without any command, because he would not have waited to command himself. . . .

27 . . . Now what Divine Person was born in [the flesh]? The Word, and the Spirit which became incarnate with the Word by the will of the Father. The Word, therefore, is incarnate; and this

must be the point of our inquiry: How the Word became flesh—whether it was by having been transfigured, as it were, in the flesh, or by having really clothed himself in flesh. Certainly it was a real clothing of himself in flesh. For the rest, we must believe God to be unchangeable, and incapable of form, as being eternal. But transfiguration is the destruction of that which previously existed. For whatsoever is transfigured into some other thing ceases to be that which it had been, and begins to be that which it previously was not. God, however, neither ceases to be what he was, nor can he be any other thing than what he is. The Word is God, and the Word of the Lord remains for ever—even by holding on unchangeably in his own proper form. Now, if he admits not of being transfigured, it must follow that he be understood in this sense to have become flesh, when he comes to be in the flesh, and is manifested, and is seen, and is handled by means of the flesh; since all the other points likewise require to be thus understood. For if the Word became flesh by a transfiguration and change of substance, it follows at once that Jesus must be a substance compounded of two substances—of flesh and spirit—a kind of mixture, like *electrum,* composed of gold and silver; and it begins to be neither gold (that is to say, spirit) nor silver (that is to say, flesh), the one being changed by the other, and a third substance produced. Jesus, therefore, cannot at this rate be God, for he has ceased to be the Word, which was made flesh; nor can he be man incarnate, for he is not properly flesh, and it was flesh which the Word became. Being compounded, therefore, of both, he actually is neither; he is rather some third substance, very different from either. But the truth is, we find that he is expressly set forth as both God and man; the very psalm which we have quoted intimating (of the flesh), that "God became man in the midst of it, he therefore established it by the will of the Father"[18]—certainly in all respects as the Son of God and the Son of Man, being God and man, differing no doubt according

13 John 1:9.
14 Gen 1:6, 7.
15 Gen 1:14, 16.
16 John 1:3.
17 John 1:1.

18 Ps 87:5.

to each substance in its own especial property, inasmuch as the Word is nothing else but God, and the flesh nothing else but man. Thus does the apostle also teach respecting his two substances, saying, "who was made of the seed of David"[19]; in which words he will be man and Son of Man. "Who was declared to be the Son of God, according to the Spirit";[20] in which words he will be God, and the Word—the Son of God. We see plainly the twofold state, which is not confounded, but conjoined in one person—Jesus, God and man. Concerning Christ, indeed, I defer what I have to say. (I remark here), that the property of each nature is so wholly preserved, that the Spirit on the one hand did all things in Jesus suitable to itself, such as miracles and mighty deeds and wonders; and the flesh, on the other hand, exhibited the affections which belong to it. It was hungry under the devil's temptation, thirsty with the Samaritan woman, wept over Lazarus, was troubled even unto death, and at last actually died. If, however, it was only a *tertium quid*, some composite essence formed out of the two substances, like the *electrum* (which we have mentioned), there would be no distinct proofs apparent of either nature. But by a transfer of functions, the Spirit would have done things to be done by the flesh, and the flesh such as are effected by the Spirit: or else such things as are suited neither to the flesh nor to the Spirit, but confusedly of some third character. Nay more, on this supposition, either

the Word underwent death, or the flesh did not die, if so be the Word was converted into flesh; because either the flesh was immortal, or the Word was mortal. Forasmuch, however, as the two substances acted distinctly, each in its own character, there necessarily accrued to them severally their own operations, and their own issues. Learn then, together with Nicodemus, that "that which is born in the flesh is flesh, and that which is born of the Spirit is Spirit."[21] Neither the flesh becomes Spirit, nor the Spirit flesh. In one Person they no doubt are well able to be co-existent. Of them Jesus consists—man, of the flesh; of the Spirit, God—and the angel designated him as "the Son of God,"[22] in respect of that nature, in which he was Spirit, reserving for the flesh the appellation "Son of Man." In like manner, again, the apostle calls him "the mediator between God and humans,"[23] and so affirmed his participation of both substances. Now, to end the matter, will you, who interpret the Son of God to be flesh, be so good as to show us what the Son of Man is? Will he then, I want to know, be the Spirit? But you insist upon it that the Father himself is the Spirit, on the ground that "God is a Spirit,"[24] just as if we did not read also that there is "the Spirit of God"; in the same manner as we find that as "the Word was God," so also there is "the Word of God."

---

19 Rom 1:3.

20 Rom 1:4.

21 John 3:6.

22 Lk 1:35.

23 1 Tim 2:5.

24 John 4:24.

94. Origen: On First Principles

Of the nearly two thousand writings that Origen of Alexandria reputedly produced during his prolific career, none proved more significant for the development of Christian doctrine than his four-volume work, "On First Principles." This represents the first major attempt by a Christian intellectual to produce a systematic theology. It was a brilliant achievement that provided much of the conceptual framework for subsequent theological reflection (See Chapter 10).

As did his proto-orthodox predecessors, Origen begins by affirming the *regula fidei*; but he notes that this "rule of faith" leaves many points completely ambiguous. His treatise then takes up some of these critical issues, including such fundamental matters as the nature of God; the relationship of the divine and human natures within Christ; the (subordinate) relationship of Christ to God, from eternity past; the role of the Holy Spirit; the nature of the human soul and its preexistence, including the pre-existent soul of Jesus; the inspiration of Scripture as the word of God; and, correspondingly, the proper way that it is to be interpreted.

Despite its brilliance, this venture into largely uncharted waters proved hazardous for Origen, or at least for his posthumous reputation. Although he was considered a bastion of orthodoxy in his own day, later, when Christian intellectuals began developing theological systems with increasing nuance, many of Origen's views came to be seen as implausible and, eventually, heretical—especially his notions that human souls pre-existed their births and "fell" into human bodies, and that, at the end of all things, God would redeem his entire creation, including the Devil himself. Some three centuries later these views, along with Origen himself, came to be condemned at the Second Council of Constantinople (553 CE).

The following Selection from "On First Principles" includes many of its central theological points, revealing something of the workings of the mind of this great Christian intellect. (NB: a translation of the original Greek text is given whenever it is available; otherwise the excerpts are of the Latin translation)

Book I

Preface

1 All who believe and are convinced that grace and truth came by Jesus Christ and that Christ is the truth (in accordance with his own saying, "I am the truth"[1]) derive the knowledge which calls people to lead a good and blessed life from no other source but the very words and teaching of Christ. By the words of Christ we do not mean only those which formed his teaching when he was made man and dwelt in the flesh, since even before that Christ the Word of God was in Moses and the prophets. For without the Word of God how could they have prophesied about Christ? In proof of which we should not find it difficult to show

---

1 John 14:6.

Origen: On First Principles, from *Origen: On First Principles*, ed. G. W. Butterworth. London: SPCK, 1973. Used with permission.

from the divine scriptures how that Moses or the prophets were filled with the spirit of Christ in all their words and deeds, were we not anxious to confine the present work within the briefest possible limits. I count it sufficient, therefore, to quote this one testimony of Paul, taken from the epistle which he writes to the Hebrews, where he speaks as follows: "By faith Moses, when he was grown up, refused to be called the son of Pharaoh's daughter, choosing rather to suffer affliction with the people of God than to enjoy the pleasures of sin for a season, accounting the reproach of Christ greater riches than the treasures of Egypt."[2]

2 Many of those, however, who profess to believe in Christ, hold conflicting opinions not only on small and trivial questions but also on some that are great and important; on the nature, for instance, of God or of the Lord Jesus Christ or of the Holy Spirit, and in addition on the natures of those created beings, the dominions and the holy powers. In view of this it seems necessary first to lay down a definite line and unmistakable rule in regard to each of these, and to postpone the inquiry into other matters until afterwards. For just as there are many among Greeks and barbarians alike who promise us the truth, and yet we gave up seeking for it from all who claimed it for false opinions after we had come to believe that Christ was the Son of God and had become convinced that we must learn the truth from him; in the same way when we find many who think they hold the doctrine of Christ, some of them differing in their beliefs from the Christians of earlier times, and yet the teaching of the church, handed down in unbroken succession from the apostles, is still preserved and continues to exist in the churches up to the present day, we maintain that that only is to be believed as the truth which in no way conflicts with the tradition of the church and the apostles.

3 But the following fact should be understood. The holy apostles, when preaching the faith of Christ, took certain doctrines, those namely which they believed to be necessary ones, and delivered

them in the plainest terms to all believers, even to such as appeared to be somewhat dull in the investigation of divine knowledge. The grounds of their statements they left to be investigated by such as should merit the higher gifts of the Spirit and in particular by such as should afterwards receive through the Holy Spirit himself the graces of language, wisdom, and knowledge. There were other doctrines, however, about which the apostles simply said that things were so, keeping silence as to the how or why; their intention undoubtedly being to supply the more diligent of those who came after them, such as should prove to be lovers of wisdom, with an exercise on which to display the fruit of their ability. The people I refer to are those who train themselves to become worthy and capable of receiving wisdom.

4 The kind of doctrines which are believed in plain terms through the apostolic teaching are the following:—

First, that God is one, who created and set in order all things, and who, when nothing existed, caused the universe to be. He is God from the first creation and foundation of the world, the God of all righteous men, of Adam, Abel, Seth, Enos, Enoch, Noah, Shem, Abraham, Isaac, Jacob, of the twelve patriarchs, of Moses and the prophets. This God, in these last days, according to the previous announcements made through his prophets, sent the Lord Jesus Christ, first for the purpose of calling Israel, and secondly, after the unbelief of the people of Israel, of calling the Gentiles also. This just and good God, the Father of our Lord Jesus Christ, himself gave the law, the prophets and the gospels, and he is God both of the apostles and also of the Old and New Testaments.

Then again: Christ Jesus, he who came to earth, was begotten of the Father before every created thing.[3] And after he had ministered to the Father in the foundation of all things, for "all things were made through him,"[3] in these last times he emptied himself and was made man, was made flesh, although he was God, and being made

---

man, he still remained what he was, namely, God. He took to himself a body like our body, differing in this alone, that it was born of a virgin and of the Holy Spirit. And this Jesus Christ was born and suffered in truth and not merely in appearance, and truly died our common death. Moreover he truly rose from the dead, and after the resurrection companied with his disciples and was then taken up into heaven.

Then again, the apostles, delivered this doctrine, that the Holy Spirit is united in honor and dignity with the Father and the Son. In regard to him it is not yet clearly known whether he is to be thought of as begotten or unbegotten, or as being himself also a Son of God or not; but these are matters which we must investigate to the best of our power from holy scripture, inquiring with wisdom and diligence. It is, however, certainly taught with the utmost clearness in the church, that this Spirit inspired each one of the saints, both the prophets and the apostles, and that there was not one Spirit in the people of old and another in those who were inspired at the coming of Christ.

5 Next after this the apostles taught that the soul, having a substance and life of its own, will be rewarded according to its deserts after its departure from this world; for it will either obtain an inheritance of eternal life and blessedness, if its deeds shall warrant this, or it must be given over to eternal fire and torments, if the guilt of its crimes shall so determine. Further, there will be a time for the resurrection of the dead, when this body, which is now "sown in corruption," shall "rise in incorruption," and that which is "sown in dishonor" shall "rise in glory."[4]

This also is laid down in the church's teaching, that every rational soul is possessed of free will and choice; and also, that it is engaged in a struggle against the devil and his angels and the opposing powers; for these strive to weigh the soul down with sins, whereas we, if we lead a wise and upright life, endeavor to free ourselves from such a burden. There follows from this the conviction

that we are not subject to necessity, so as to be compelled by every means, even against our will, to do either good or evil. For if we are possessed of free will, some spiritual powers may very likely be able to urge us on to sin and others to assist us to salvation; we are not, however, compelled by necessity to act either rightly or wrongly, as is thought to be the case by those who say that human events are due to the course and motion of the stars, not only those events which fall outside the sphere of our freedom of will but even those that lie within our own power.

In regard to the soul, whether it takes its rise from the transference of the seed, in such a way that the principle or substance of the soul may be regarded as inherent in the seminal particles of the body itself; or whether it has some other beginning, and whether this beginning is begotten or unbegotten, or at any rate whether it is imparted to the body from without or no; all this is not very clearly defined in the teaching.

6 Further, in regard to the devil and his angels and the opposing spiritual powers, the church teaching lays it down that these beings exist, but what they are or how they exist it has not explained very clearly. Among most Christians, however, the following opinion is held, that this devil was formerly an angel, but became an apostate and persuaded as many angels as he could to fall away with him; and these are even now called his angels.

7 The church teaching also includes the doctrine that this world was made and began to exist at a definite time and that by reason of its corruptible nature it must suffer dissolution. But what existed before this world, or what will exist after it, has not yet been made known openly to the many, for no clear statement on the point is set forth in the church teaching.

8 Then there is the doctrine that the scriptures were composed through the Spirit of God and that they have not only that meaning which is obvious, but also another which is hidden from the majority of readers. For the contents of scripture are the outward forms of certain mysteries and the images of divine things. On this point the entire

---

4 1 Cor 15:42–43.

church is unanimous, that while the whole law is spiritual, the inspired meaning is not recognized by all, but only by those who are gifted with the grace of the Holy Spirit in the word of wisdom and knowledge. . . .

Everyone therefore who is desirous of constructing out of the foregoing a connected body of doctrine must use points like these as elementary and foundation principles, in accordance with the commandment which says, "Enlighten yourselves with the light of knowledge."[5] Thus by clear and cogent arguments he will discover the truth about each particular point and so will produce, as we have said, a single body of doctrine, with the aid of such illustrations and declarations as he shall find in the holy scriptures and of such conclusions as he shall ascertain to follow logically from them when rigidly understood. . . .

Chapter 1

1 . . . God must not be thought to be any kind of body, nor to exist in a body, but to be a simple intellectual existence, admitting in himself of no addition whatever, so that he cannot be believed to have in himself a more or a less, but is Unity, or if I may so say, Oneness throughout, and the mind and fount from which originates all intellectual existence or mind. Now mind does not need physical space in which to move and operate, nor does it need a magnitude discernible by the senses, nor bodily shape or color, nor anything else whatever like these, which are suitable to bodies and matter. Accordingly that simply and wholly mental existence can admit no delay or hesitation in any of its movements or operations; for if it did so, the simplicity of its divine nature would appear to be in some degree limited and impeded by such an addition, and that which is the first principle of all things would be found to be composite and diverse, and would be many and not one; since only the species of deity, if I may so call it, has the privilege of existing apart from all material intermixture.

That mind needs no space in which to move according to its own nature is certain even from the evidence of our own mind. For if this abides in its own proper sphere and nothing occurs from any cause to enfeeble it, it will never be at all retarded by reason of differences of place from acting in conformity with its own movements; nor on the other hand will it gain any increase or accession of speed from the peculiar nature of any place. And if it be objected, for example, that when people are travelling by sea and tossed by the waves, their mind is somewhat less vigorous than it is wont to be on land, we must believe this experience to be due not to the difference of place but to the movement and disturbance of the body with which the mind is joined or intermingled. For it seems almost against nature for the human body to live on the sea, and on this account the body, as if unequal to its task, appears to sustain the mind's movements in irregular and disordered manner, giving feebler assistance to its keen flashes, precisely as happens even with people on land when they are in the grip of a fever; in whose case it is certain that, if the mind fulfils its functions less effectively through the strength of the fever, the cause is to be found not in any defect of locality but in the disease of the body, which renders it disturbed and confused and altogether unable to bestow its customary services on the mind under the well-known and natural conditions. For we people are animals, formed by a union of body and soul, and thus alone did it become possible for us to live on the earth. But God, who is the beginning of all things, must not be regarded as a composite being, lest perchance we find that the elements, out of which everything that is called composite has been composed, are prior to the first principle himself. . . .

Chapter 2

1 First [with respect to Christ] we must know this, that in Christ there is one nature, his deity, because he is the only-begotten Son of the Father, and another human nature, which in very recent

---

5 Hos 10:12.

times he took upon him to fulfil the divine purpose. Our first task therefore is to see what the only-begotten Son of God is, seeing he is called by many different names according to the circumstances and beliefs of the different writers. He is called Wisdom, as Solomon said, speaking in the person of Wisdom: "The Lord created me the beginning of his ways for his works. Before he made anything, before the ages he established me. In the beginning before he made the earth, before the springs of waters came forth, before the mountains were settled, before all the hills he begets me."[6] He is also called Firstborn, as the apostle Paul says: "who is the firstborn of all creation."[7] The Firstborn is not, however, by nature a different being from Wisdom, but is one and the same. Finally, the apostle Paul says, "Christ, the power of God and the wisdom of God."[8]

2 Let no one think, however, that when we give him the name "wisdom of God" we mean anything without hypostatic existence, that is, to take an illustration, that we understand him to be not as it were some wise living being, but a certain thing which makes people wise by revealing and imparting itself to the minds of such as are able to receive its influence and intelligence. If then it is once rightly accepted that the only-begotten Son of God is God's wisdom hypostatically existing, I do not think that our mind ought to stray beyond this to the suspicion that this hypostatis or substance could possibly possess bodily characteristics, since everything that is corporeal is distinguished by shape or color or size. And who in his sober senses ever looked for shape or color or measurable size in wisdom, considered solely as wisdom? And can anyone who has learned to regard God with feelings of reverence suppose or believe that God the Father ever existed, even for a single moment, without begetting this wisdom? For he would either say that God could not have

begotten wisdom before he did beget her, so that he brought wisdom into being when she had not existed before, or else that he could have begotten her and—what it is profanity even to say about God—that he was unwilling to do so; each of which alternatives, as everyone can see, is absurd and impious, that is, either that God should advance from being unable to being able, or that, while being able, he should act as if he were not and should delay to beget wisdom.

Wherefore we recognise that God was always the Father of his only-begotten Son, who was born indeed of him and draws his being from him, but is yet without any beginning, not only of that kind which can be distinguished by periods of time, but even of that other kind which the mind alone is wont to contemplate in itself and to perceive, if I may so say, with the bare intellect and reason. Wisdom, therefore, must be believed to have been begotten beyond the limits of any beginning that we can speak of or understand. And because in this very subsistence of wisdom there was implicit every capacity and form of the creation that was to be, both of those things that exist in a primary sense and of those which happen in consequence of them, the whole being fashioned and arranged before-hand by the power of foreknowledge, wisdom, speaking through Solomon in regard to these very created things that had been as it were outlined and prefigured in herself, says that she was created as a "beginning of the ways" of God, which means that she contains within herself both the beginnings and causes and species of the whole creation.

3 Now just as we have learned in what sense wisdom is the "beginning of the ways" of God and is said to have been created, in the sense, namely, that she fashions beforehand and contains within herself the species and causes of the entire creation, in the same manner also must wisdom be understood to be the Word of God. For wisdom opens to all other beings, that is, to the whole creation, the meaning of the mysteries and secrets which are contained within the wisdom of God, and so she is called the Word, because she is as it

---

6 Prov 8:22–25.

7 Col 1:15.

8 1 Cor 1:24.

were an interpreter of the mind's secrets. Hence I consider that to be a true saying which is written in the Acts of Paul, "He is the Word, a living being." John, however, uses yet more exalted and wonderful language in the beginning of his gospel, when by an appropriate declaration he defines the Word to be God; "And the Word was God, and he was in the beginning with God."[9] Let him who assigns a beginning to the Word of God or the wisdom of God beware lest he utters impiety against the unbegotten Father himself, in denying that he was always a Father and that he begat the Word and possessed wisdom in all previous times or ages or whatever else they may be called.

4 . . . Whatever then we have said of the wisdom of God will also fitly apply to and be understood of him in his other titles as the Son of God, the life, the word, the truth, the way, and the resurrection. For all these titles are derived from his works and powers, and in none of them is there the least reason to understand anything corporeal, which might seem to denote either size or shape or color. But whereas the offspring of humans or of the other animals whom we see around us correspond to the seed of those by whom they were begotten, or of the mothers in whose womb they are formed and nourished, drawing from these parents whatever it is that they take and bring into the light of day when they are born, it is impious and shocking to regard God the Father in the begetting of his only-begotten Son and in the Son's subsistence as being similar to any human being or other animal in the act of begetting; but there must be some exceptional process, worthy of God, to which we can find no comparison whatever, not merely in things, but even in thought and imagination, such that by its aid human thought could apprehend how the unbegotten God becomes Father of the only-begotten Son. This is an eternal and everlasting begetting, as brightness is begotten from light. For he does not become Son in an external way through the adoption of the Spirit, but is Son by nature. . . .

---

9 John 1:1–2.

10 Let us now look into the saying that wisdom is "an effluence," that is, an emanation, "of the clear glory of the Almighty," and if we first consider what "the glory of the Almighty" is, we shall then understand what its "effluence" is. Now as one cannot be a father apart from having a son, nor a lord apart from holding a possession or a slave, so we cannot even call God almighty if there are none over whom he can exercise his power. Accordingly, to prove that God is almighty we must assume the existence of the universe. For if anyone would have it that certain ages, or periods of time, or whatever he cares to call them, elapsed during which the present creation did not exist, he would undoubtedly prove that in those ages or periods God was not almighty, but that he afterwards became almighty from the time when he began to have creatures over whom he could exercise power. Thus God will apparently have experienced a kind of progress, for there can be no doubt that it is better for him to be almighty than not to be so.

Now how is it anything but absurd that God should at first not possess something that is appropriate to him and then should come to possess it? But if there was no time when he was not almighty, there must always have existed the things in virtue of which he is almighty; and there must always have existed things under his sway, which own him as their ruler.

Chapter 3

We come, therefore, to the investigation in as brief a manner as possible, of the subject of the Holy Spirit. . . .

3 It is proved by many declarations throughout the whole of scripture that the universe was created by God and that there is no substance which has not received its existence from him; which refutes and dismisses the doctrines falsely taught by some, that there is a matter which is coeternal with God, or that there are unbegotten souls, in whom they would have it that God implanted not so much the principle of existence as the quality and rank of their life. Moreover in that little book composed by Hermas, called "The Shepherd, or the Angel of Repentance," it is thus written: "First of all, believe that God is one, who created and set in order all things; who, when nothing existed before, caused all things to be; who contains all things, but himself is contained by none."[10] Similar statements are also made in the book of Enoch. But up to the present we have been able to find no passage in the holy scriptures which would warrant us in saying that the Holy Spirit was a being made or created, not even in that manner in which we have shown above that Solomon speaks of wisdom, nor in the manner in which the expressions we have dealt with, such as life, or word, or other titles of the Son of God, are to be understood. The "Spirit of God," therefore, who "moved upon the waters,"[11] as it is written, in the beginning of the creation of the world, I reckon to be none other than the Holy Spirit, so far as I can understand; which indeed I have demonstrated in my exposition of these passages, not, however, according to their literal but according to their spiritual meaning.

4 . . . And my Hebrew master used to say that the two six-winged seraphim in Isaiah who cry one to another and say, Holy, holy, holy is the Lord of hosts,[12] were the only-begotten Son of God and the Holy Spirit. And we ourselves think that the expression in the song of Habakkuk, "In the midst of the two living creatures you shall be known."[13] is spoken of Christ and the Holy Spirit.

For all knowledge of the Father, when the Son reveals him, is made known to us through the Holy Spirit. So that both of these, who in the words of the prophet are called "animals" or "living beings," are the cause of our knowledge of God the Father. For as it is said of the Son that "no one knows the Father but the Son, and he to whom the Son wills to reveal him,"[14] so in the

same way does the apostle speak of the Holy Spirit; "God has revealed them to us by his Spirit: for the Spirit searches all things, even the deep things of God."[15]

15 . . . The God and Father, who holds the universe together, is superior to every being that exists, for he imparts to each one from his own existence that which each one is; the Son, being less than the Father, is superior to rational creatures alone (for he is second to the Father); the Holy Spirit is still less, and dwells within the saints alone. So that in this way the power of the Father is greater than that of the Son and of the Holy Spirit, and that of the Son is more than that of the Holy Spirit, and in turn the power of the Holy Spirit exceeds that of every other holy being.

Chapter 8

1 . . . . God did not begin to create minds; before the ages minds were all pure, both daemons and souls and angels, offering service to God and keeping his commandments. But the devil, who was one of them, since he possessed free-will, desired to resist God, and God drove him away. With him revolted all the other powers. Some sinned deeply and became daemons, others less and became angels; others still less and became archangels; and thus each in turn received the reward for his individual sin. But there remained some souls who had not sinned so greatly as to become daemons, nor on the other hand so very lightly as to become angels. God therefore made the present world and bound the soul to the body as a punishment. For God is no respecter of persons, that among all these beings who are of one nature (for all the immortal beings are rational) he should make some daemons, some souls and some angels; rather is it clear that God made one a daemon, one a soul and one an angel as a means of punishing each in proportion to its sin. For if this were not so, and souls had no pre-existence, why do we find some new-born babes to be blind, when

---

10 Herm *Vis* 5.8.

11 Gen 1:2.

12 Isa 6:2–3.

13 Heb 3:2.

14 Matt 11:27.

15 1 Cor 2:10.

they have committed no sin, while others are born with no defect at all? But it is clear that certain sins existed before the souls, and as a result of these sins each soul receives a recompense in proportion to its deserts. They are sent forth from God as a punishment, that they must undergo on earth a first judgment. That is why the body is called a frame, because the soul is enclosed within it.

But when they had revolted from their former blessedness they were endowed with bodies in consequence of the fall from their first estate which had taken place in them, and allotted to various ranks. So from being "minds" they have become angels, archangels. . . .

Just as the daemons, sitting by the altars of the Gentiles, used to feed on the steam of the sacrifices, so also the angels, allured by the blood of victims which Israel offered as symbols of spiritual things, and by the smoke of the incense, used to dwell near the altars and to be nourished on food of this sort.

But when they fell away, as the New Testament says, from their unity with God, they were given the rule and lordship over those who had fallen lower still and were also "sent forth to minister to those who are to inherit salvation,"[16] though they themselves had fallen from this salvation and were in need of one to lead them back. . . .

9 . . . . Whole nations of souls are stored away somewhere in a realm of their own, with an existence comparable to our bodily life, but in consequence of the fineness and mobility of their nature they are carried round with the whirl of the universe. There the representations of evil and of virtue are set before them; and so long as a soul continues to abide in the good it has no experience of union with a body. But by some inclination towards evil these souls lose their wings and come into bodies, first of humans; then through their association with the irrational passions, after the allotted span of human life they are changed into beasts; from which they sink to the level of insensate nature. Thus that which is by nature fine and

mobile, namely the soul, first becomes heavy and weighed down, and because of its wickedness comes to dwell in a human body; after that, when the faculty of reason is extinguished, it lives the life of an irrational animal; and finally even the gracious gift of sensation is withdrawn and it changes into the insensate life of a plant. From this condition it rises again through the same stages and is restored to its heavenly place. On earth by means of virtue souls grow wings and soar aloft, but when in heaven their wings fall off through evil and they sink down and become earthbound and are mingled with the gross nature of matter.

Book II

Chapter 6

1 Now that these points have been discussed, it is time to resume our inquiry into the incarnation of our Lord and Saviour, how he became man and dwelt among people. . . .

2 . . . . Of all the marvellous and splendid things about him there is one that utterly transcends the limits of human wonder and is beyond the capacity of our weak mortal intelligence to think of or understand, namely, how this mighty power of the divine majesty, the very word of the Father, and the very wisdom of God, in which were created "all things visible and invisible," can be believed to have existed within the compass of that man who appeared in Judaea; yes, and how the wisdom of God can have entered into a woman's womb and been born as a little child and uttered noises like those of crying children. . . .

When, therefore, we see in him some things so human that they appear in no way to differ from the common frailty of mortals, and some things so divine that they are appropriate to nothing else but the primal and ineffable nature of deity, the human understanding with its narrow limits is baffled, and struck with amazement at so mighty a wonder knows not which way to turn, what to hold to, or whither to betake itself. If it thinks of God, it sees a human; if it thinks of a human, it beholds one returning from the dead

---

16 Heb 1:14.

with spoils after vanquishing the kingdom of death. For this reason we must pursue our contemplation with all fear and reverence, as we seek to prove how the reality of each nature exists in one and the same person, in such a way that nothing unworthy or unfitting may be thought to reside in that divine and ineffable existence, nor on the other hand may the events of his life be supposed to be the illusions caused by deceptive fantasies. . . .

3 The only-begotten Son of God, therefore, through whom, as the course of our discussion in the previous chapters has shown, all things visible and invisible were made, according to the teaching of scripture both made all things and "loves what he made."[17] For since he is the invisible "image" of the "invisible God,"[18] he granted invisibly to all rational creatures whatsoever a participation in himself, in such a way that each obtained a degree of participation proportionate to the loving affection with which he had clung to him. But whereas, by reason of the faculty of free-will, variety and diversity had taken hold of individual souls, so that one was attached to its author with a warmer and another with a feebler and weaker love, that soul of which Jesus said, "No man takes from me my soul,"[19] clinging to God from the beginning of the creation and ever after in a union inseparable and indissoluble, as being the soul of the wisdom and word of God and of the truth and the true light, and receiving him wholly, and itself entering into his light and splendor, was made with him in a preeminent degree one spirit, just as the apostle promises to them whose duty it is to initiate Jesus, that "the one who is joined to the Lord is one spirit."[20] This soul, then, acting as a medium between God and the flesh (for it was not possible for the nature of God to mingle with a body apart from some medium), there is born, as we said, the God-man, the medium being that

existence to whose nature it was not contrary to assume a body. Yet neither, on the other hand, was it contrary to nature for that soul, being as it was a rational existence, to receive God, into whom, as we said above, it had already completely entered by entering into the word and wisdom and truth.

It is therefore right that this soul, either because it was wholly in the Son of God, or because it received the Son of God wholly into itself, should itself be called, along with that flesh which it has taken, the Son of God and the power of God, Christ and the wisdom of God; and on the other hand that the Son of God, "through whom all things were created," should be termed Jesus and the Son of man. Moreover the Son of God is said to have died, in virtue of that nature which could certainly admit of death, while he of whom it is proclaimed that "he shall come in the glory of God the Father with the holy angels" is called the Son of man.[21] And for this reason, throughout the whole of scripture, while the divine nature is spoken of in human terms, the human nature is in its turn adorned with marks that belong to the divine prerogative. For to this more than to anything else can the passage of Scripture be applied, "They shall both be in one flesh, and they are no longer two, but one flesh."[22] For the Word of God is to be thought of as being more "in one flesh" with his soul than a man is with his wife. Moreover what could more appropriately be "one spirit" with God than this soul, which joined itself so firmly in love to God as to be worthy of being called "one spirit" with him?

It was on this account also that the man became Christ, for he obtained this lot by reason of his goodness, as the prophet bears witness when he says, "You have loved righteousness and hated iniquity; wherefore God has anointed you, your God with the oil of gladness above your fellows."[23] It was appropriate that he who had never

---

17 Wisd 11:24.

18 Col 1:15.

19 John 10:18.

20 1 Cor 6:17.

21 Matt 16:27; Mark 8:28; Luke 9:26.

22 Matt 19:5–6; Gen 2:24.

23 Ps 45:7.

been separated from the Only-begotten should be called by the name of the Only-begotten and glorified together with him.

As a reward for its love, therefore, it is anointed with the "oil of gladness," that is the soul with the word of God is made Christ; for to be anointed with the oil of gladness means nothing else but to be filled with the Holy Spirit. . . .

5 But if the above argument, that there exists in Christ a rational soul, should seem to anyone to constitute a difficulty, on the ground that in the course of our discussion we have often shown that souls are by their nature capable of good and evil, we shall resolve the difficulty in the following manner. It cannot be doubted that the nature of his soul was the same as that of all souls; otherwise it could not be called a soul, if it were not truly one. But since the ability to choose good or evil is within the immediate reach of all, this soul which belongs to Christ so chose to love righteousness as to cling to it unchangeably and inseparably in accordance with the immensity of its love; the result being that by firmness of purpose, immensity of affection, and an inextinguishable warmth of love all susceptibility to change or alteration was destroyed, and what formerly depended upon the will was by the influence of long custom changed into nature. Thus we must believe that there did exist in Christ a human and rational soul, and yet not suppose that it had any susceptibility to or possibility of sin.

6 To explain the matter more fully it will not appear absurd if we use an illustration, although on so high and difficult a subject there is but a small supply of suitable examples. However, if we may use this one without offence, the metal iron is susceptible of both cold and heat. Suppose then a lump of iron be placed for some time in a fire. It receives the fire in all its pores and all its veins, and becomes completely changed into fire, provided the fire is never removed from it and itself is not separated from the fire. Are we then to say that this, which is by nature a lump of iron, when placed in the fire and ceaselessly burning can ever admit cold? Certainly not; it is far truer to say of it, what indeed we often detect happening in furnaces, that it has been completely changed into fire, because we can discern nothing else in it except fire. Further, if anyone were to try to touch or handle it, he would feel the power of the fire, not of the iron. In this manner, then, that soul which, like a piece of iron in the fire, was for ever placed in the word, for ever in the wisdom, for ever in God, is God in all its acts and feelings and thoughts; and therefore it cannot be called changeable or alterable, since by being ceaselessly kindled it came to possess unchangeability through its unity with the word of God. And while, indeed, some warmth of the Word of God must be thought to have reached all the saints, in this soul we must believe that the divine fire itself essentially rested, and that it is from this that some warmth has come to all others. . . .

95. Novatian: On the Trinity

Novatian was a leading member of the Roman church in the mid–third century. After the persecution of the emperor Decius (251 CE), in which many members of the church had compromised their Christian convictions, Novatian opposed the Bishop of Rome, Cornelius, by insisting on a rigorist position: the "lapsed" should be required to undergo a long and public period of penance before being admitted back into the church's good graces (see the Introduction to Cyprian in Chapter 12). A schism erupted as Novatian and his party were excommunicated from the church only to start their own, with Novatian himself elected as a rival pope. He was martyred several years later during the persecution under the emperor Valerian (258 CE).

That the Novatian controversy was not over doctrine but church policy becomes clear upon reading Novatian's own treatise "On the Trinity," a work that embodies a completely orthodox theology, as can be seen in the following excerpt dealing with the nature of God.

Chapter 1

The rule of truth requires that we believe, first in God the Father and almighty Lord, the most perfect Creator of all things. He suspended the heavens above in their lofty height, made firm the earth with the heavy mass under it, poured forth the free flowing water of the seas; and he arranged all these, in full abundance and order, with appropriate and suitable appurtenances. In the firmament of heaven he summoned forth the light of the rising sun. He filled the candescent sphere of the moon with its monthly waxings to relieve the darkness. He also illuminated the rays of the stars with varying flashes of twinkling light. He willed that all these things in their lawfully regulated orbits encircle the entire earth's surface to form days, months, years, seasons, signs, and other things useful for humankind. On earth he lifted up the highest mountains to a peak, threw down the valleys into the lowlands, leveled the plains, and created the different kinds of animals for the various needs of humans. He also hardened the sturdy trees of the forests to serve people's needs, brought forth the fruits of the earth for food, opened the mouths of springs, and poured them into the flowing rivers. After these things, lest he should have failed to provide our eyes with beautiful objects, he clothed all things with the various colors of flowers to delight all those who look upon them. Although the sea was wonderful both in its extent and for its usefulness, yet in it also he fashioned many kinds of living creatures, both small and large, which show the intelligence of the Creator by the variety of his creation. Not content with all this, lest the rushing and the flowing of the waters occupy territory not its own with loss to its human possessor, he enclosed its limits with shores, so that when the roaring waves and the foaming surge would come forth from the sea's bosom, they would return into themselves and would not pass beyond the limits allowed them. They would obey their prescribed laws, in order that people would more readily keep

Novatian: On the Trinity, from *Novatian,* ed. Russell J. DeSimone. Fathers of the Church, 67; Washington, DC: Catholic University Press of America, 1974. Used with permission.

God's laws, seeing that even the elements themselves obey them.

After all these things had been accomplished, he placed man at the head of the world—man made to the image of God, endowed with intelligence, discernment, and prudence so that he could imitate God. Although the primordial elements of his body were earthly, nevertheless the substance was infused by a heavenly and divine breath. When God gave him all these things for his service, he willed that man alone should be free. Nevertheless, lest man's unrestrained freedom prove dangerous, God imposed a command in which he stated that indeed evil was not in the fruit of the tree, but warned that evil would follow if, in the use of his free will, man disregarded the command laid down. On the one hand, man ought to be free lest the image of God serve in unbecoming manner. On the other hand, a law had to be imposed that unrestrained liberty might not break forth even to contempt for its Giver. Hence, man might receive either merited rewards or due punishments as the result of his actions, recognizing these actions as his own doings, because it was in his power to act, through the movement of his mind in the one or the other direction. Whence, indeed, hated mortality comes back upon him. He could have avoided mortality by obedience, but he subjected himself to it by his headlong and perverse determination to be God. Nevertheless, God mercifully mitigated his punishment by cursing not so much man as his labors on earth. The fact that God searches for him does not proceed from any ignorance on the part of God but it manifests man's hope of a future discovery and salvation in Christ. Furthermore, that man was prevented from touching the wood of the tree of life did not spring from the malicious ill-will of envy but from a fear that man, living forever, would always bear about with him for his punishment an abiding guilt, had not Christ previously pardoned his sins.

In the higher regions—those above the very firmament itself, which at present are beyond our sight—he previously called the angels into being, arranged the spiritual powers, set over them the Thrones and Powers, created many other measureless spaces of heavens and mysterious works without limit. Therefore, even this measureless universe seems to be the latest of God's material creations rather than his only work. Even the regions that lie beneath the earth are not without their ruling powers duly appointed and set out. For there is a place to which are taken the souls of the just and the unjust, already aware of the sentence awaiting them at the future judgment. We see, therefore, that the vast works of God, exuberant on all sides, are not shut up within the confines of this world spacious to the utmost as we have said: but we can also contemplate them beneath both the depths and the heights of the world itself. Thus, after having considered the greatness of his works, we can fittingly admire the Maker of such a mighty mass.

Chapter 2

Over all these things is God himself, who contains all things and who leaves nothing devoid of himself; he has left no room for a superior god as some think. Since he himself has enclosed all things in the bosom of his perfect greatness and power, he is always intent on his own work and pervades all things, moves all things, gives life to all things, and observes all things. He binds together the discordant materials of all the elements into such harmony that out of these dissimilar elements, there exists a unique world so compacted by this consolidated harmony that no force can dissolve it, save when he alone who created it orders it to be dissolved in order to grant us greater blessings. We read that he contains all things; therefore nothing could have existed outside of him. For indeed he who has no beginning whatsoever, must necessarily experience no end, unless—far be the thought from us—he began to exist at a certain time and is therefore not above all things. But if he began to exist after something else, he would be inferior to that previously existing thing; hence he would be found to be of lesser power, since designated as subsequent even in time itself. For this reason, therefore, he is always infinite because there is nothing greater than he, ever eternal, because nothing is more ancient than he. In fact, that which is without a beginning can be preceded by nothing, because it lacks time. Therefore he is immortal, for he does not pass away to a consummate end. And since whatever is without a beginning is without a law, he excludes the restriction of time because he feels himself a debtor to no one.

Concerning him, therefore, and concerning those things which are of him and in him, the mind of humans cannot fittingly conceive what they are, how great they are, and of what their nature; nor has human eloquence the power to express his greatness. For all eloquence is certainly dumb and every mind is inadequate to conceive and to utter his greatness. In fact, he is greater than the mind itself, so that his greatness is inconceivable; for if he could be conceived, he would be less than the human mind which could conceive him. He is also greater than all speech, so that he cannot be expressed; for if he could be expressed, he would be less than human speech, which through expressing Him would then comprehend and contain him. Whatever can be thought about him is less than he; whatever can be uttered about him will be less than he when compared with him. When we are silent we can experience him to some extent, but we cannot express him in words as he really is. If, for instance, you should speak of him as light, you would be speaking of a created thing of his, not of him, you would not express what he is. If you should speak of him as power, you would be speaking of and bringing out his might rather than himself. If you should speak of him as majesty, you would be describing his honor rather than him. But why am I making a protracted affair of this matter by running through his attributes one by one? Once and for all I will sum up everything: whatever you might affirm about him would be expressing some possession or power of his rather than God himself. For what can you fittingly say or think about

him who is above all speech and thought? There is only one thing that can fittingly be said or thought about him who is above all speech and thought: namely, that—within our power, our grasp, our understanding—there is only one way in which we may mentally conceive what God is—viz., by realizing that he is that Being of whose nature and greatness there is no possible understanding, nor even any possibility of thinking. If the keen sight of our eyes grows dim by looking at the sun so that their gaze, overpowered by the bright rays that meet it, cannot look at the orb itself, our mental vision undergoes this very same thing in its every thought of God. The more it endeavors to contemplate God, the more is it blinded by the light of its own thought. In fact, what (to repeat once more) can you worthily say about him, who is more sublime than all sublimity, loftier than all loftiness, more profound than all profundity, brighter than all light, more brilliant than all brilliance, more splendid than all splendor, mightier than all might, more powerful than all power, more beautiful than all beauty, truer than all truth, stronger than all strength, greater than all majesty, more potent than all potency, richer than all riches, and more prudent than all prudence, and kinder than all kindness, better than all goodness, more just than all justice, more clement than all clemency? Every kind of virtue must of necessity be less than he who is the God and Author of them all, so that it can really be said that God is that which is of such a nature that nothing can be compared to him. For he is above everything that can be said of him. he is, so to speak, an intelligent Being who without any beginning or ending in time engenders and fills all things and governs, for the good of all, with supreme and perfect reason, the causes of things naturally linked together.

Chapter 3

We acknowledge, therefore, and know that he is God, the Creator of all things; their Lord, because of his power; their Author, because of creation.

"He," I say, "spoke and all things were made; he commanded, and all things came forth."[1] Of him it is written: "You have made all things in wisdom."[2] Moses says of him: "God is in heaven above and on earth below,"[3] and according to Isaiah, "He has measured the heavens with a span, the earth with the width of the fist, who looks upon the earth and makes it tremble, who holds the orb of the earth and those who live on it as if they were locusts; who weighed the mountains on scales and the groves on a balance, by the exact precision of the divine plan. And he laid out this weight of the earth's mass with precise equipoise, lest the huge ill-balanced mass should easily fall to ruin, if it were not balanced with proportionate weights."[4] It is he who says through the prophet: "I am God, and there is none beside me."[5] He says by means of the same prophet: "I will not give my majesty to another,"[6] so that he might exclude all heathens and heretics with their images, proving that he is not God who is made by the hand of an artificer; nor is he God whom heretical ingenuity, has devised. For he is not God whose existence requires an artificer. Again, he says through the prophet: "Heaven is my throne, earth the footstool under my feet: what sort of home will you build for me, or what is the place of my rest?"[7]—this to make it clear that since the world cannot contain him, much less can a temple enclose him. God says these things for our instruction, not to boast of himself. Nor does he seek from us glory for his own greatness; rather, as a Father, he desires to bestow on us God-fearing wisdom. He desires, moreover, to attract our minds, so cruel, so proud, and so obstinate in their rude ferocity, to gentleness; hence he says: "And upon whom shall my spirit rest but upon him who is humble and peaceful, and trembles at my words?"[8] Thus a person may know, to some extent, how great God is, while he learns to fear him through the spirit given to him. Ever desiring to become more completely known to us and to incite our minds to his worship, he said: "I am the Lord who made the light and created the darkness,"[9] that we may not think that a certain "nature"—I know not what—was the artificer of those alternations whereby the nights and days are regulated; but rather, and with greater truth, we may acknowledge God as their Creator. Since we cannot see him with the sight of our eyes, we learn to know him from the greatness, the power, and the majesty of his works. "For since the creation of the world," says the apostle, "his invisible attributes are clearly seen—his everlasting power also and divinity—being understood through the things that are made."[10] Thus the human mind, learning to know the hidden things from those which are manifest, may consider in spirit the greatness of the Maker from the greatness of his works which it sees with the eyes of the mind. The same apostle says of him: "To the King of the ages, who is immortal, invisible, the one only God, be honor and glory."[11] He who has surpassed the greatness of thought has passed beyond the contemplation of our eyes; for, he says, "from him and through him and in him are all things."[12] All things exist by his command, so that they are "from him"; they are set in order by his word and therefore "through him." Finally, all these things have recourse to his judgment so that, while they long for freedom "in him," after corruption has been done away with, they appear to be recalled "to him."

---

1 Ps 148:5.

2 Ps 104:24.

3 Deut 4:39.

4 Isa 40:12, 22; Ps 104:5, 32.

5 Isa 45:21–22.

6 Isa 42:8; 48:11.

7 Isa 66:1.

8 Isa 66:2.

9 Isa 45:6–7.

10 Rom 1:20.

11 1 Tim 1:17.

12 Rom 11:36.

Chapter 4

The Lord rightly declares that God alone is good, of whose goodness the whole world is witness. He would have not have created it if he were not good. For if "all things were very good,"[13] it logically follows that not only do those things which were created good prove the Creator is good, but they also prove that those things which owe their origin to a good creator cannot be other than good themselves. All evil, therefore, is a departure from God. It is impossible that he who claims for himself the title of perfect Father and Judge would be the instigator or author of any form of evil, precisely because he is the Judge and the Avenger of every evil deed. A person encounters evil only by his departure from the good God. This very departure is blameworthy in a human, not because it was necessary but because the person himself willed it. Hence it was made clear to us not only what evil was but also from whom evil had taken its origin, lest there should seem to be envy in God.

He is always, therefore, equal to himself; he never changes or transforms himself into other forms, lest through change he should appear to be also mortal. For the modification implied in change from one thing to another involves a share in death of some sort. Therefore there is never any addition of parts or of glory in him, lest anything should seem to have ever been wanting to the perfect one. Nor can there be any question of diminution in him, for that would imply that some degree of mortality is in him. On the contrary, what he is, he always is; who he is he always is; such as he is, he always is. For increase in growth indicates a beginning; whereas any wasting away evidences death and destruction. And therefore he says: "I am God, and have not changed."[14] He always retains his manner of being, because what is not born is not subject to change. For—whatever that being may be that is God—this must always be true of him, that he always is God, preserving himself by his own powers. And therefore he says: "I am who am."[15] That which is has this name because it always preserves its same manner of being. Change takes away the name, "That which is"; for whatever changes at all is shown to be mortal by the very fact that it changes. It ceases to be what it was and consequently begins to be what it was not. Of necessity, then, God always retains his manner of being, because he is always like unto himself, always equal to himself without any loss arising from change. For that which is not born cannot change, since only those things undergo change which are made or which are begotten; whereas things which at one time were not, experience existence by coming into being, and by coming into being they undergo change. On the contrary, things which have neither birth nor maker are exempt from change because they have not a beginning, the cause of change.

And so God is said to be also unique since he has no equal. For God (whatever that Being may be that is God) must necessarily be supreme. Now whatever is supreme must be supreme in such wise that an equal is excluded. Therefore he must be the one and only being with whom nothing can be compared, because he has no equal. As the very nature of things demands, there cannot be two infinities. That alone is infinite which has absolutely neither beginning nor end; for whatever occupies the whole excludes the beginning of another. If the infinite does not contain all that exists (whatever it be), then it will find itself within that which contains it and therefore it will be less than the containing element. Hence it will cease to be God, since it has been brought under the dominion of another whose magnitude will include it because it is the smaller. As a result what contained it would itself claim to be God.

It results from this that God's own name is ineffable because it cannot be conceived. The name of a thing connotes whatever comes under the demands of its nature. For a name is significant of

---

13 Gen 1:31.

14 Mal 3:6.

15 Exod 3:14.

the reality which could be grasped from the name. However, when it is a question of something of such a nature that not even the intellectual powers themselves can form a proper concept, then how will it be expressed fittingly by a single word of designation, for it so exceeds the intellect that it is necessarily beyond the comprehension of any name? When God takes for himself a name or manifests it for certain reasons and on certain occasions, we know that it is not so much the real nature of the name that has been made known to us as a vague symbol appointed for our use, to which people may have recourse and find that they can appeal to God's mercy through it.

God is, therefore, immortal and incorruptible, experiencing neither diminution nor end of any sort. Because he is incorruptible, he is also immortal, and because he is immortal, he is therefore also incorruptible. Both attributes are reciprocally linked together between and in themselves by a mutual relationship. Thus are they brought by the ensuing union to the condition of eternity: immortality proceeding from incorruptibility and incorruptibility coming from immortality.

Chapter 5

If in Scripture we consider instances of his legitimate wrath and descriptions of his anger and learn of the instances recorded of his hatred, we are not to regard these things asserted of him as examples of human vices. Although all these things can corrupt humans, they cannot vitiate the divine power in any way. Passions such as these are rightly said to exist in humans but would wrongly be declared to exist in God. Humans can be corrupted by them because they are capable of corruption; God cannot be corrupted by them because he is not capable of corruption. Therefore they have a power of their own which they can exercise only where they find passible matter, not where they find an impassible substance. The fact also that God is angry does not arise from any vice in him; rather he acts thus for our benefit. He is merciful even when he threatens, because by these threats people are recalled to the right path. Fear is necessary for those who lack an incentive to good living, so that they who have rejected reason may at least be moved by terror. And so all these instances of anger, hatred, and the like, on God's part, are revealed, as the truth of the matter shows, for our healing and arise from deliberate purpose, neither from vice nor from weakness. Therefore they do not have the power to corrupt God. The different elements of which we are made are wont to arouse in us the discord of anger which corrupts us; but this diversity of elements cannot exist in God either by nature or from vice, because he cannot conceivably be made up of a union of corporeal parts. He is simple, without any corporeal admixture—whatever be the total of the being that only he himself knows—since he is called spirit.[16] Thus those things which are faulty and the cause of corruption in humans, inasmuch as they arise from the corruptibility of his body and matter itself, cannot exercise their power of corruptibility in God. As we have already said, they did indeed spring not from any vice in him but from reason. . . .

---

16 John 4:24.

96. Dionysius of Rome: Letter to Dionysius of Alexandria

As an example of the way orthodox theological opinions, when pursued rigorously, could lead to views that themselves were deemed heretical, consider the following letter written by Dionysius of Rome to his namesake, Dionysius of Alexandria (ca. 260 CE). The latter had taken a strong stand against patripassianism (supported by a Christian named "Sabellius"), which maintained that Christ, the Son of God, was actually God the Father himself become human. But in voicing his opposition, Dionysius of Alexandria had gone too far in the other direction, in the opinion of his colleague in Rome. This letter warns that Dionysius should not differentiate too firmly between the Father and the Son, since to do so could lead one (a) to maintain that the Son was not eternal but had been created at some point in time, like other creatures, and/or (b) to think that there were three different Gods (Father, Son, and Spirit) instead of one God, as affirmed by orthodox Christians from time immemorial.

Evidently this letter had its effect, as Dionysius of Alexandria later convinced his counterpart in Rome that he was not in fact propounding a view of tritheism.

In this connexion I may naturally proceed to attack those who divide and cut up and destroy that most revered doctrine of the church of God, the Monarchy, reducing it to three powers and separated substances and three deities. For I learn that there are some of you, among the catechists and teachers of the Divine Word, who inculcate this opinion, who are, one might say, diametrically opposed to the views of Sabellius; he blasphemously says that the Son is the Father and the Father the Son, while they in a manner preach three Gods, dividing the sacred Monad into three substances foreign to each other and utterly separate. For the Divine Word must of necessity be united to the God of the Universe, and the Holy Spirit must have his habitation and abode in God; thus it is absolutely necessary that the Divine Triad be summed up and gathered into a unity, brought as it were to an apex, and by that Unity I mean the all sovereign God of the Universe. . . . Equally to be censured are they who hold that the Son is a work, and think that the Lord came into being, whereas the Divine Oracles testify to a generation fitting and becoming to him, but not to any fashioning or making. . . . For if he came to be a Son, there was when he was not; but he was always, if, that is, he is in the Father, as he himself says, and if the Christ is Word and Wisdom and Power, as, you know, the Divine Scriptures say he is, and if these are attributes of God. For if the Son came into being there was when these attributes were not; therefore there was a time when

God was without them; which is most absurd. . . . Neither then must we divide into three deities the wonderful and divine Monad: nor hinder the dignity and exceeding majesty of the Lord by describing him as a "work." But we must believe in God the Father all sovereign, and in Jesus Christ his Son and in the Holy Spirit, and hold that the Word is united to the God of the universe. For "I," says he, "and the Father are one,"[1] and "I in the Father and the Father in me."[2] For thus both the Holy Triad and the holy preaching of the Monarchy will be preserved.

---

1 John 10:30.

2 John 14:10.